PRAISE FOR

George Washington

"Stewart has written an outstanding biography that both avoids hagiography and acknowledges the greatness of Washington's character, all while playing close attention to his rarely voiced but no less fierce political ambitions. . . . Mr. Stewart's writing is clear, often superlative, his judgments are nuanced, and the whole has a narrative drive such a life deserves."

—*The Wall Street Journal*

"David O. Stewart brings his characteristic grace and skill to this portrait of the political George Washington, liberating the most elusive of our Founders from the mists of myth to discover a shrewd and approachable human being. At a time when politics seems beyond redemption, Stewart's book is a welcome reminder of the possibilities, however imperfect, of the public arena."

—Jon Meacham, Pulitzer Prize–winning author of *His Truth Is Marching On*

"By focusing on the political genius of George Washington, David O. Stewart has produced an important new portrait of our first president. As Stewart demonstrates time and time again, with vivid prose and a wonderful sense of pacing, great leaders are also great learners. In this time of division and turmoil, this is the book we need."

—Nathaniel Philbrick, National Book Award–winning author of *In the Hurricane's Eye: The Genius of George Washington and the Victory at Yorktown*

"David O. Stewart's innovative and important study of George Washington's political career succeeds because it places his successes as president of the United States within the context of his whole life and times. The most fascinating thing about Washington is not how he was great, but how he became great over the course of a dramatic career, compellingly chronicled in this book."

—Edward G. Lengel, author of *General George Washington: A Military Life*

"In this lively and admirable study, Stewart offers a balanced and thoughtfully well-written appreciation of George Washington's life and leadership. A must for fans of biographies."

—*Library Journal* (starred review)

"Engaging . . . Devotees of the Founding Fathers will not want to miss the volume about the master politician, and American history buffs will be amazed by Stewart's ability to hold your attention in this lengthy tome."

—*The Virginia Gazette*

"Examines in detail and with excellent analysis how Washington developed the political skills that would serve him in both war and peace . . . a truly fresh look at one of the most chronicled figures in American history."

—*New York Journal of Books*

"Under Stewart's energetic hand, the cold-marble hero warms into a flawed yet remarkable person: ambitious, evenhanded, tender, callous, impetuous in his youth, wiser with age."

—Washington Independent Review of Books

"One of the most insightful books about George Washington. [Stewart's] explanation of Washington as a masterful politician is important and convincing."

—*Virginia Magazine of History & Biography*

"Stewart addresses the political aptitude of the father of the nation . . . [in this] readable and revealing contemporary look at Washington."

—*Booklist* (starred review)

GEORGE WASHINGTON

The POLITICAL RISE of
AMERICA'S FOUNDING FATHER

DAVID O. STEWART

DUTTON

DUTTON

An imprint of Penguin Random House LLC
penguinrandomhouse.com

Previously published as a Dutton hardcover in February 2021

First Dutton trade paperback printing: February 2022

The Library of Congress has cataloged the hardcover of this book as follows:

Names: Stewart, David O., author.
Title: George Washington : the political rise of America's founding
father / David O. Stewart.
Description: New York : Dutton, Penguin Random House LLC, 2021. | Includes
bibliographical references and index. |
Identifiers: LCCN 2020036458 (print) | LCCN 2020036459 (ebook) |
ISBN 9780451488985 (hardcover) | ISBN 9780451488992 (ebook)
Subjects: LCSH: Washington, George, 1732–1799. | Washington, George,
1732–1799—Influence. | Generals—United States—Biography. | Presidents—United
States—Biography. | United States—Politics and government—1775–1783. | United
States—Politics and government—1783–1809. | United States—History—
Revolution, 1775–1783—Influence.
Classification: LCC E312 .S85 2021 (print) | LCC E312 (ebook) |
DDC 973.4/1092 [B]—dc23
LC record available at https://lccn.loc.gov/2020036458
LC ebook record available at https://lccn.loc.gov/2020036459

Dutton trade paperback ISBN: 9780451489005

Printed in the United States of America
1st Printing

To Matthew, Colin, and Rebecca

Contents

PART II

PART III

Dramatis Personae

Abigail Adams—Often separated from her husband, John Adams of Massachusetts, Adams sustained their wise and fascinating correspondence of several decades, offering insightful observations on events and personalities. Unlike her husband, she was an unabashed admirer of Washington.

John Adams—A brilliant lawyer from Massachusetts, Adams was a leading figure in the two Continental Congresses. He pressed for Washington's appointment as commander in chief of the Continental Army and then for the Declaration of Independence. As a diplomat, Adams helped negotiate the peace treaty of 1783 and served as minister to Britain. He was Washington's vice president for two terms and succeeded him in the presidency. Longtime political allies, Washington and Adams shared a mutual respect, but not much warmth.

Samuel Adams—Leader of the Massachusetts resistance to British policies before the Revolutionary War, Adams served as president of the Continental Congress and governor of his home state.

William Alexander, "Lord Stirling"—A wealthy New Jerseyan who unsuccessfully claimed a Scottish peerage, Alexander was a regimental and divisional commander in the Continental Army. He helped thwart the "Conway Cabal," which aimed to supplant Washington as commander in chief. Alexander also served as major general at the Battle of Monmouth Court House and presided over the subsequent court-martial of Major General Charles Lee.

Anna Maria Dandridge Bassett—Younger and favorite sister of Martha Dandridge Washington. Her home with Burwell Bassett, Eltham Plantation, was a favorite stop for George and Martha Washington when they traveled between Mount Vernon and the Virginia colonial capital in Williamsburg.

Burwell Bassett—Husband of Anna Maria Dandridge, Bassett was a planter in New Kent County, Virginia, and enjoyed an easy friendship with Washington and his family. After the Battle of Yorktown, Martha's son, John Parke Custis, died of camp fever at Bassett's Eltham Plantation.

John Carlyle—A Scottish merchant who settled in Alexandria, Virginia, Carlyle married a daughter of Colonel William Fairfax, served as commissary for the Virginia Regiment at the beginning of the French and Indian War, and was a justice of the Fairfax County Court with Washington.

General Thomas Conway—Though the "Conway Cabal" is named for him, this Irishman and veteran of French military service was a junior partner of that effort to supersede Washington as commander in chief in 1777–78. An able battlefield commander, Conway made enemies because of his arrogance and ambition. He returned to Europe in summer 1778, after being shot in the mouth in a duel.

Dr. James Craik—A Scot trained in medicine at the University of Edinburgh, Craik emigrated to Virginia and settled in Winchester, where he served as surgeon for the Virginia Regiment during the French and Indian War. In 1770 and again in 1784, Craik traveled with Washington through western Virginia and other frontier lands. He also served as a surgeon in the Continental Army. A lifelong friend of Washington's, Craik moved to Alexandria after the war and led the physicians who cared for Washington in his final illness in 1799.

John (Jacky) Parke Custis—Martha Washington's son by her first marriage to Daniel Parke Custis, Jacky Custis inherited great wealth at a young age, though his indifference to education frustrated Washington. Custis was eighteen when he married Eleanor Calvert of Maryland, and served in Virginia's assembly during the Revolutionary War. He died of camp fever in 1783 at age twenty-six, shortly after the Battle of Yorktown, where he had joined Washington's staff. He left four children, two of whom were raised by George and Martha Washington.

Robert Dinwiddie—Scottish merchant and British official who was colonial governor of Virginia from 1751–58. Dinwiddie sent Washington on his first public mission to French forts on the Pennsylvania frontier in 1753–54, and appointed Washington to lead the Virginia Regiment during the French and Indian War. Relations between the two men soured before Dinwiddie returned to England.

Bryan Fairfax—Son of Colonel William Fairfax, Bryan was a neighbor of Washington's who often joined him on fox hunts before the Revolutionary

War. Bryan served with Washington as a justice of the Fairfax County Court. After the war, he became an Episcopal priest and was recognized as the eighth Lord Fairfax for a short time before his death in 1802.

Ferdinando Fairfax—The youngest son of Bryan Fairfax, in 1790 Ferdinando published a proposal for liberating slaves and colonizing them in Africa.

George William Fairfax—Son of Colonel William Fairfax and Washington's close friend, George William inherited the Belvoir estate adjacent to Mount Vernon, served on the governor's council of colonial Virginia, and joined Washington on the Fairfax County Court and the Truro Parish vestry. When he moved to England in 1772, George William left his American affairs in Washington's hands. An opponent of the British policies that led to the Revolutionary War, George William never returned to America.

Sarah (Sally) Cary Fairfax—Married to George William Fairfax in her late teens, Sally and her husband were intimate friends with their neighbors, George and Martha Washington. Based on two letters Washington sent to her in 1758, some speculate that he had romantic feelings for her.

Thomas, Lord Fairfax—The sixth Lord Fairfax, he was the proprietor of the huge royal land grant comprising the Northern Neck of Virginia, an area equivalent to the state of New Hampshire. Lord Fairfax lived in England until the late 1740s, holding royal sinecures and reputedly mixing with playwright Joseph Addison and other society wits. Nearly fifty when he arrived in Virginia, he settled in Winchester and devoted himself to managing his lands.

Colonel William Fairfax—A British colonial official in the Caribbean and Massachusetts, Colonel Fairfax in 1732 was appointed land agent for the vast Northern Neck land holdings of his cousin, Lord Fairfax. In Virginia, Colonel Fairfax built his estate at Belvoir on the Potomac River, next to Mount Vernon. He served in the colony's House of Burgesses and then on the governor's council. He was mentor for both Lawrence and George Washington.

Jean Antoine Joseph Fauchet—French minister to the United States from 1794 to 1796, appointed to succeed (and arrest) Edmond-Charles Genêt ("Citizen Genêt"). His reports of conversations with Secretary of State Edmund Randolph prompted Randolph's resignation in 1795.

General Horatio Gates—British officer who served with Washington during the French and Indian War and later emigrated to Virginia. Gates became a major general in the Continental Army, winning the pivotal Battle of Saratoga in autumn 1777. The Conway Cabal, which included Gates, aimed to elevate him above Washington, but failed. Gates remained in the army until the peace treaty of 1783.

Edmond-Charles Genêt—French minister to the United States in 1793, "Citizen Genêt" commissioned privateers to raid British shipping from American ports, recruited Americans to invade British and Spanish colonies, and pressed for American assistance to France. After Genêt threatened to appeal to the American people over Washington's head, the president asked the French government to recall Genêt, and blamed the Frenchman for inciting opposition to his administration.

Christopher Gist—A frontiersman and explorer who undertook expeditions for the Ohio Company when it was led by Lawrence Washington, Gist accompanied Washington on his first public engagement, carrying a message from Virginia colonial governor Dinwiddie to the French military in western Pennsylvania in 1753–54. Gist was at the Battle of Fort Necessity in 1754 and on Braddock's expedition the following year.

General Nathanael Greene—A Rhode Island ironmaker who forsook Quakerism to fight the British, Greene was Washington's most trusted commander, often assigned the most difficult duties. Rising to major general and command of the southern theater of the war in 1780–81, Greene died in 1786, when only forty-six years old.

Alexander Hamilton—A native of the West Indies who came to America as a teenager, the brilliant Hamilton impressed Washington as a young artillery officer, then served as an aide for several years. As secretary of the treasury for the first five years of Washington's presidency, Hamilton helped establish the new government's financial footing. He championed the Constitution in *The Federalist* essays, and his newspaper advocacy provided critical support for the Washington administration.

Patrick Henry—A brilliant orator and savvy politician, Henry served with Washington in the Virginia House of Burgesses and also in the Continental Congress. Though they parted ways over ratification of the Constitution, they remained friendly until Henry's death in 1799.

Thomas Jefferson—Jefferson and Washington, colleagues in the House of Burgesses and the Continental Congress, shared an enthusiasm for developing western lands from the Appalachians to the Mississippi River. Washington recruited Jefferson as his first secretary of state, enduring an eight-month wait for his fellow Virginian to return from his diplomatic post in Paris and a visit to his home at Monticello. They worked effectively in Washington's first administration, but Jefferson resigned after becoming disenchanted with the president's preference for a strong national government and by clashes with Treasury Secretary Hamilton. Jefferson became the leader of the opposition to Washington, was elected vice president in 1796, and thereafter became the third president.

Thomas Johnson—A Maryland political figure and ally of Washington's, Johnson was the first governor of his state. Working with Washington on opening the Potomac to navigation, he served on the board of the Potomac Company, and also was one of the original commissioners of the District of Columbia. Johnson served for a short time on the U.S. Supreme Court.

Henry Knox—A bookseller from Boston with no military experience, Knox became chief of the Continental Army's artillery service and Washington's trusted adviser. Knox also was the nation's first secretary of war.

Gilbert du Motier, Marquis de Lafayette—Often considered Washington's surrogate son, Lafayette came to America to fight the British in 1777 and was commissioned as a major general before his twentieth birthday. Lafayette stood by Washington through the Conway Cabal and led American troops in several engagements, including the Battle of Yorktown. After the war, he returned to France, where he was an early leader of that nation's 1789 revolution. Lafayette urged Washington to free his slaves.

Henry Laurens—A merchant and slave trader in South Carolina, Laurens represented that state in the Continental Congress and served as its president in 1777–78. Laurens provided essential political support for Washington during the Conway Cabal and the Valley Forge encampment.

John Laurens—Son of Henry Laurens and staff officer for Washington in the Continental Army, the South Carolinian opposed slavery and sought unsuccessfully to establish a regiment of Southern slaves who could win their freedom through military service.

Tobias Lear—A New Hampshire native and Harvard graduate who served as Washington's personal secretary from 1784 to 1799, Lear married Martha Washington's niece, Fanny Bassett Washington. He wrote a moving eyewitness account of Washington's final illness.

Charles Lee—A member of the large Lee clan of Westmoreland County, Charles Lee performed legal work for Washington in the 1790s and served as attorney general for the last fifteen months of Washington's presidency.

General Charles Lee—An officer in the British Army during the French and Indian War, who later served in the armies of Poland and Portugal, the eccentric Lee—usually accompanied by multiple dogs—moved to America and was a major general in the Continental Army. After his erratic performance at the Battle of Monmouth Court House in 1778, he demanded a court-martial to review his conduct, which suspended Lee from the army for a year. He never returned to the army.

Henry ("Light Horse Harry") Lee—A cavalry commander in the Continental Army and brother to Attorney General Charles Lee, Henry became governor of Virginia and Washington's political ally. One of his sons, Robert

E. Lee, married a daughter of Martha Washington's grandson, George Washington Parke Custis.

Richard Bland Lee—Younger brother of Henry and Charles Lee, he represented Washington's district in the House of Representatives for the first six years of the Washington administration and was a key swing vote in the 1790 compromise that brought the seat of government to the Potomac region and the adoption of the financial system proposed by Washington and Hamilton.

Richard Henry Lee—A contemporary of Washington, he was a leader in the House of Burgesses and the Continental Congresses, signing the Declaration of Independence. Lee opposed ratification of the Constitution but then served as a senator from Virginia.

Betty Washington Lewis—Washington's next-younger sibling, she married Fielding Lewis, a Fredericksburg merchant, and had eight children who survived to adulthood. Washington employed several of her sons as secretary or farm manager. When her mother, Mary Ball Washington, gave up control of Ferry Farm at the age of sixty-two, Mary moved close to Betty, who cared for her.

Fielding Lewis—Husband of Betty Washington, Lewis was a Fredericksburg merchant and served as commissary general of munitions for the Continental Army. Washington often stopped with the Lewis family on trips between Mount Vernon and Williamsburg.

James Madison—Washington's closest political confidant during the crucial years leading up to the Constitutional Convention of 1787 and during the first year of the new government, Madison steered the ten amendments of the Bill of Rights through Congress and sponsored essential early legislation. Troubled by the powers exercised by Washington as president, Madison joined with Jefferson to found the "Republican interest," which became the Republican Party, which became the Democratic Party. He served as Jefferson's secretary of state and then as the fourth president.

George Mason—A neighbor of Mount Vernon, Mason provided much of the intellectual and rhetorical ammunition for Washington's opposition to British policies from 1769 to 1774, including the Fairfax Resolves. Chronically ill, Mason often declined public service. He was a delegate to the Constitutional Convention of 1787, but his refusal to sign the final document opened a rift between him and Washington.

James McHenry—Born in Ireland and trained as a surgeon in America, McHenry settled in Maryland and served as a secretary to Washington during the war. He was secretary of war for the final year of Washington's presidency, and then under President Adams.

Timothy Pickering—Adjutant general and quartermaster general of the Continental Army, Pickering of Massachusetts served in the Washington administration as postmaster general, secretary of war, and then secretary of state (after four others declined the position). He continued as secretary of state in the Adams administration.

Edmund Randolph—After briefly serving as an aide to Washington in the Continental Army, Randolph rose through Virginia politics to become governor and a delegate to the Constitutional Convention of 1787, where he presented the Virginia Plan at the beginning of the deliberations. Randolph refused to sign the Constitution, then switched to support ratification. He served as attorney general in Washington's administration and then as secretary of state until his resignation under a cloud in the summer of 1795.

Adam Stephen—A Scot trained in medicine, Stephen settled in western Virginia. He joined the Virginia forces in the French and Indian War, becoming Washington's second-in-command in the Virginia Regiment. He unsuccessfully opposed Washington in the 1761 election for the House of Burgesses in Frederick County. His actions as senior officer of the Virginia Regiment were criticized by the House of Burgesses. In the Revolutionary War, Stephen rose to major general, but a court-martial dismissed him from the army after the Battle of Germantown in 1777.

David Stuart—A physician in Alexandria, in 1783 Stuart married the widow of Washington's stepson, John Parke Custis, and became a confidant of Washington's. He served in the Virginia House of Delegates and the Virginia Convention that ratified the Constitution in 1788. Stuart was a leader in the campaign to bring the seat of government to the Potomac region.

Anne Fairfax Washington—Daughter of Colonel William Fairfax, Anne married Washington's beloved half-brother, Lawrence, and inherited Mount Vernon from him. When she remarried, she leased the property to Washington, who inherited the property after the deaths of Anne and the daughter she had with Lawrence.

Augustine (Gus) Washington—Washington's father moved his young family from Popes Creek in Westmoreland County to the Little Hunting Creek property on the Potomac, which became Mount Vernon. Gus devoted much of his energy to an ironworks. He died at forty-nine, when Washington was eleven years old.

Augustine (Austin) Washington Jr.—Half-brother to Washington, he inherited the family's Popes Creek property in Westmoreland County and served in the House of Burgesses for four years. Called Austin within the family, he died at age forty-two.

Bushrod Washington—Bushrod was the eldest son of Washington's cherished younger brother John Augustine ("Jack"). As a private attorney, Bushrod served in Virginia's House of Delegates and that state's constitutional ratifying convention. John Adams appointed him to the U.S. Supreme Court. He served as lead executor of Washington's will and inherited Mount Vernon.

Charles Washington—Washington's youngest brother, Charles settled in western Virginia in 1780 and laid out Charles Town, named for him, which now is in West Virginia.

Frances (Fanny) Bassett Washington [Lear]—Daughter of Burwell and Anna Maria Bassett, Fanny moved to Mount Vernon after her mother's death in 1778. She married Washington's nephew, George Augustine, and after her husband's early death, married Washington's secretary, Tobias Lear.

George Augustine Washington—Son of Washington's brother Charles, George Augustine served as a major in the Continental Army. After the war, he traveled to the Caribbean seeking a cure for his tuberculosis. Upon his return, he worked as manager of Mount Vernon and married Fanny Bassett, but died in his early thirties.

John (Jack) Augustine Washington—The fourth child of Mary and Gus Washington, Jack was Washington's favorite among his younger brothers. Jack served as a member of Westmoreland County's Committee of Safety during the Revolutionary War and managed their mother's business affairs for some years.

Lawrence Washington—Fourteen years older than his half-brother George and educated in England, Lawrence rose swiftly in Virginia society. He led a military unit in a British expedition to the Caribbean, married a daughter of Colonel William Fairfax of Belvoir, served in the House of Burgesses and on the Truro Parish vestry, and was president of the Ohio Company, which aimed to settle western lands. After futilely seeking cures for his tuberculosis, he died at age thirty-four. Lawrence was a surrogate father to Washington after their own father's death, introducing him to the Fairfaxes and other Virginia leaders. Washington described Lawrence as his best friend and kept Lawrence's portrait in his office at Mount Vernon.

Lund Washington—A distant cousin of Washington's from the Chotank region of Virginia, Lund managed Mount Vernon for more than twenty years. At Lund's request, his widow freed his slaves after his death in 1796.

Mary Ball Washington—Washington's mother, Mary Ball was orphaned at age twelve and lived with her elder sister until marrying Gus Washington, by whom she had five children who lived to adulthood. Mary was thirty-six when she became a widow and single mother. She managed Ferry Farm near

Fredericksburg for more than two decades thereafter. Contemporaries thought Washington's strong character and self-discipline derived from Mary. Mother and son shared chronic anxiety about money.

Samuel Washington—The second son born to Mary and Gus Washington, Samuel served in the Virginia militia during the early years of the Revolutionary War. He settled in western Virginia but died at age forty-seven, leaving three minor children whom Washington provided for.

PART I

Nor during his life has [Washington] ever performed a single action that could entitle him to the least share of merit or praise, much less of glory. But as a politician he has certainly distinguished himself; having by his political maneuvers, and his cautious plausible management, raised himself to a degree of eminence in his own country unrivalled.

—John F. D. Smyth,
former British soldier (1784)

CHAPTER 1

Time for a New Plan

In late 1757, a man on horseback rode toward a large house that overlooked the Potomac River, several miles south of Alexandria, Virginia. Draped with a soldier's cloak, the man's figure was martial, tall, and lean. His russet hair was tied at the nape of the neck. His face reflected weeks of grinding illness. His fair complexion, usually ruddy from wind and sun, had paled. Though he was particular about the fit of his garments, now they sagged from his long frame.

Colonel George Washington, the twenty-five-year-old master of Mount Vernon, was home from war on Virginia's western frontier. Though he was taller and stronger than most men, four years in the wilderness had sapped his health. Some days before, he had left his command of the Virginia Regiment in the Shenandoah valley. Charged with stopping bloody Indian raids with a thousand-man regiment, but often having fewer than half that number, Washington had met with little success. Sick and dispirited, he left for home without permission from his British commander or from the colony's royal governor.

Washington's affliction had lingered for nearly three months, then worsened. A frontier doctor had bled him, but it did not help. When the doctor said that Washington might die unless he had an immediate rest, the young officer left for Mount Vernon, assuming that the Indian attacks would subside in the cold months, when even tough Shawnee warriors stayed near their home fires.[1]

Washington had the "bloody flux," a vivid term for dysentery, which haunted military camps. Often fatal, the bloody flux was a grim ordeal under the best of conditions: cramps, diarrhea, intermittent chills and fever, dehydration, and debilitating fatigue. Its eighteenth-century name reflects the stage when the sufferer expels blood. Through the frosty autumn, commanding too few troops against a skilled enemy, Washington might have felt the disease was part of a curse against him.

For four years, Washington had ridden thousands of miles through Virginia and Pennsylvania, back to eastern Virginia, and as far as Boston, but few of those journeys could have been as difficult as his ride home to Mount Vernon that November. The bloody flux compelled frequent stops for undignified squats. Remounting the horse would be another trial.

Washington stopped in Alexandria, not far from Mount Vernon, to see the Reverend Charles Green.[2] Like many pastors, Green ministered to bodies as well as souls. He directed the young commander to eat only jellies and the like, avoiding meat. Green also prescribed gum Arabic (gum from African acacia trees) and sweet wine from the Canary Islands.[3]

No friend or family member greeted Washington at Mount Vernon, though the estate was far from empty. More than a dozen Black slaves, along with white servants and overseers, cared for the house and worked the fields.[4] Jonathan Alton, servant to Washington earlier in the war, likely settled the ailing squire in a warm room.

Finding the cupboards bare of the items prescribed by Reverend Green, Washington sent to Belvoir, the nearby estate of the aristocratic Fairfaxes. His friend George William Fairfax was away in England, so Washington asked Mrs. Fairfax to lend him Canary wine, green tea from China, and a pound of hartshorn shavings to make jellies. "I am quite out," he confessed, "and cannot get a supply anywhere in these parts." He added a bachelor's plea for "such materials to make jellies as you think I may not just at this time have."[5]

For the next six weeks, no correspondence survives from Washington's pen. No evidence shows visitors coming to Mount Vernon—not his mother or sister from Fredericksburg, nor any of his four surviving brothers. Through the shortening days, Washington's disease maintained its grip in a house heated by wood fires. Cramping and sweating and shivering, Washington ate jellies while sipping tea and sweet wine. He had time—nothing but time—to reflect on where he stood in life and what might lie ahead.

The truth, one that likely gnawed at him, was harsh. After a brilliant beginning, he had stumbled from setback to disappointment.

At twenty-two, he was acclaimed a hero, his exploits recounted throughout British North America and in England. As commander of the Virginia Regiment, he gave orders to men decades older. Blessed with athletic ability, stern self-discipline, and polished manners, Washington was good at most things he tried. He expected success.

But his war had taken an ill turn. Washington led his men to an indefensible position and endured a grisly defeat by the French and their Indian allies. His surrender saved lives, but the truce terms proved controversial. Then a British army, with Washington as aide to the commander, marched into the wilderness and was slaughtered, suffering unprecedented casualties. Washington's reputation survived because he had not been in command and showed signal courage, but the episode was an epic failure.

Since that disaster, Washington's Virginia Regiment had flailed ineffectively against raids by France's Indian allies. The raiders killed or kidnapped nearly at will, looting settlements while easily evading Washington's men. Settlers fled east, as did Virginia soldiers who deserted in record numbers. Washington's current situation—eighty miles from his overmatched force, staring into a fire, his world defined by chills and fever and the chamber pot—was far from the soaring trajectory he had imagined for himself.[6]

From his earliest days, Washington hungered for distinction, for high reputation that would validate his worth. He never minced words about it: His goal was renown. Two years before, he wrote that "the chief part of my happiness" was "the esteem and notice the country has been pleased to honor me with." Serving as an unpaid volunteer for part of his military service, he said he wanted only the "regard and esteem" of Virginians.[7] Years later, he wrote that his "only ambition is to do my duty in this world as well as I am capable of performing it and to merit the good opinion of all good men."[8] Yet in late 1757, his military career seemed to promise only failure. For a man who ached for recognition, that prospect would be a horror.

His personal life offered little solace. He had courted women, once proposing marriage before entering military service. That woman's father rejected him, skeptical that George Washington would be an advantageous match. Service on Virginia's frontier had offered few opportunities for finding a life partner of the type Washington needed, one with social standing and financial assets.

Washington's challenge was to remount the ladder of his high aspirations. The challenge was greater because he could no longer turn to the men who had propelled his early ascent. His father, Augustine (called Gus), died when George was eleven. He left George, his third son, a good name and enough slaves and land to stand above the middling classes, but nowhere near enough to enter Virginia's elite.

Two other men played paternal roles for George. Half-brother Lawrence, fourteen years older, hauled his brother up in the world alongside him. And Lawrence presented George to Colonel William Fairfax, who had managed his family's huge lands from the Belvoir mansion where the colonel's son

George William now lived. A power in the colony's government, Colonel Fairfax boosted Washington into high military office while dispensing sound advice. But Lawrence had died some years before, Colonel Fairfax only a few months back.

A fourth sponsor was alive, but no longer a friend. Virginia governor Robert Dinwiddie had advanced Washington at Colonel Fairfax's suggestion. Dinwiddie stuck by the young commander through difficult times, but then disappointment made each man testy and quarrelsome. Now the governor, in poor health himself, was bound for England, embittered by the ingratitude of the young Virginian whose career he had launched.

Washington still possessed advantages that might help him progress from his station as the third son of a Virginia family of the second rank. His military reputation had survived his many reverses. Some influential friends remained, including the eccentric Lord Fairfax, elder cousin of the departed Colonel Fairfax; the officers from his regiment; and some of the leaders of the House of Burgesses, the elected lower house of the colony's General Assembly.

He also occupied a fine home at Mount Vernon, though he did not own it. Built by his father and improved by Lawrence, the house offered a commanding view of the river and the lands beyond. On mild days, Washington could venture out the riverside entrance and draw strength from that prospect.

Washington's greatest advantage was his ambition and drive, which never rested. He knew he was capable of great things. He could feel it when he entered a room to admiring glances, when he swiftly won the trust of others. That special talent—his ability to inspire trust—would carry him to heights not even he imagined.

Washington left no record of his musings at Mount Vernon during that difficult winter of 1757–58, when his society consisted mostly of servants and his enslaved workers. In late December, he felt well enough to send carping letters to merchants in Britain. He protested delivery delays, incomplete and misrouted shipments, poorly selected or damaged items, and high prices.[9]

By the first week of the New Year, Washington plainly felt better. Colonel John Stanwix, his military superior, wrote to congratulate him on his recovery. Washington's neighbor George Mason urged him not to return to duty until the weather warmed.[10]

Dysentery, however, can wax and wane. When Virginia's interim governor, John Blair, asked Washington to attend a council with frontier Indians, Washington declined and consulted another doctor. A few weeks later, he headed to Williamsburg to report on the regiment, but found "my fever and pain increase[d] upon me to a high degree." Doctors again said his life was at risk. Washington retreated to the Mount Vernon fire, once more ailing and solitary, uncertain if he would ever recover.[11]

By early March, self-pity seeped into Washington's letter to Colonel Stanwix. "My constitution," he wrote, "has received great injury, and ... nothing can retrieve it but the greatest care, and most circumspect conduct." Viewing his illness together with his failures on the frontier, Washington added, "I now see no prospect of preferment in military life ... I have some thoughts of quitting my command and retiring from all public business." Someone else, he added, "may perhaps have their endeavors crowned with better success."[12]

Yet a few days after writing those weary, humble words, Washington was restored as a forceful man of action. Over the next several weeks, he twice visited the country home of Martha Dandridge Custis, a pleasingly rich widow about his age. In those two visits, he wooed her and won her.[13] He made it to Williamsburg in mid-March, where he reported to Acting Governor Blair and again wrote stinging letters to his British suppliers. By early April, he had returned to command the regiment at Winchester while ordering cloth for his wedding suit. Martha, in her turn, ordered "genteel" cloth for a new gown, "to be grave but not to be extravagant."[14]

Washington's transformation was complete. With self-deprecating humor, he admitted to a merchant, "You will perhaps think me a crazy fellow to be ordering and counterordering goods almost in a breath."[15] He wrote no more about leaving the army. Rather, he avidly sought preferment in a new offensive. He would "gladly be distinguished," Washington confided to Stanwix, "from the common run of provincial officers; as I understand there will be a motley herd of us."[16]

This reversal in Washington's spirits is not easy to explain. Restored physical vigor may account for much of it. When he reached Williamsburg in March, he consulted a doctor who proclaimed Washington nearly recovered. The encouraging prediction may have helped Washington to reclaim his vitality.[17]

Also, the new British expedition aimed to follow the strategy that Washington had been urging. Early in the war, he concluded that Virginia's frontier posts were too small to resist attack and too widely dispersed to protect settlers. The better strategy, he insisted, was to drive the French from Fort Duquesne (today's Pittsburgh, where the Monongahela and Allegheny Rivers combine to form the Ohio), thereby severing French support for their Indian allies. By mid-March, Williamsburg buzzed with news that the British advance would target Fort Duquesne.[18]

But more was happening by March of 1758 than Washington's return to health, or his engagement to Martha Custis, or even the shift in British war strategy. Through that prolonged period of forced introspection, Washington evidently resolved on a fundamental change of direction, one previewed in his letter to Stanwix. He had spent nearly five years trying to build a military career. Repeatedly, he sought either an officer's commission in King George's army, or the absorption of his Virginia Regiment into the British military. Each plea had withered under British contempt for colonists. Moreover, in 1758 British officers purchased their commissions. A lieutenant colonelcy, one rank below Washington's position with the Virginia Regiment, cost £3,400.[19] Washington could not imagine having so much cash in hand, equivalent to roughly fifty years of a teacher's annual salary in Virginia, or close to $300,000 today. He would never hold a British Army commission.[20]

Nor could Washington expect a career as a soldier for Virginia. For seventy years before the current conflict with France, the colony had maintained no military force. Whenever this fighting ended, Virginia again would rely on citizen militia to defend against Indian raids and slave insurrections.

His military ambitions blocked, Washington charted a new path that began at Mount Vernon. The estate included enough acreage to establish him as gentry. He would remodel the house and improve its farms. A good marriage could bring more farmland.

And he would turn to the west. Like many Virginians, Washington saw frontier lands as the likeliest source of wealth. The war with France had stalled westward migration, but peace would reignite it. From soldiering and surveying, Washington knew the west. By examining new lands early, surveyors could acquire choice parcels to resell at a profit. Thomas Jefferson's father did that, as did Patrick Henry's and John Marshall's. Washington meant to do it too.

And he would turn to politics. Washington's grandfather and great-grandfather had served in the House of Burgesses. So had his brother Lawrence. His surviving older brother, Augustine Jr. (called Austin), had just won a seat from Westmoreland County. With Fairfax support plus his military reputation, Washington would be a strong candidate. Three years earlier, he had been on the ballot in a Frederick County contest, though he did not campaign for the office. In October 1757, struggling with dysentery while commanding the regiment, he brought a court proceeding to confirm that he was qualified to represent Frederick County.[21] Brother Lawrence had been justice of his county court and a member of his parish vestry. Washington could aim at those positions too.

When a revived Washington reached Winchester in April 1758, he knew his remaining time in uniform would be short. He had a fiancée to wed, an estate to improve, an economic fortune to create, and political aspirations to follow. If the expedition against Fort Duquesne succeeded, Washington could resign with a sense of accomplishment. If it failed, the British would mount no other offensive on the Virginia frontier for years. Washington had a plan. It would take him beyond even his high ambitions.

∾

Shortly after his death in 1799, George Washington stopped being a real person for Americans, dissolving into a hazy, godlike figure. His first biographer invented stories about his virtues, and those fictions (chopping down his father's cherry tree, throwing a dollar across a river) became better known than the historical facts. For more than a century, accounts of Washington's life approached idolatry. In a typical example from 1898, the writer gushed that "his was a moral grandeur, joined with practical wisdom, never surpassed amongst the most renowned figures in the world's history."[22]

The conversion of Washington into a marble caricature was nearly complete. His monument in Washington, DC, is a massive stone phallic symbol. His name is everywhere, not only on his country's capital, but on the only state named solely for a person, and at least seven mountains, eight streams, eight parks, four bridges, ten lakes, thirty-three counties, and more than one hundred towns and villages. For more than two centuries, Americans have celebrated his birthday and appropriated his name as a badge of membership in a community of liberty—writer Washington Irving, scientist George Washington Carver, and educator Booker T. Washington.

Washington built barriers to conceal the man behind the myths. In the second half of his life, he crafted his public image as steady, disinterested, and wise. His self-restraint could lapse into aloofness. As the flesh-and-blood person receded from view, Americans were left with the titanic, impeccable Washington, both superhuman and tedious.[23]

Eventually, the clichés about his perfection wore thin. His status as a major slaveholder became uncomfortable. When the hunt for the real Washington began several decades ago, only cold records of his life remained.

There was a real man named George Washington, one who stuffed his sixty-seven years with remarkable achievements. This book examines a principal feature of his greatness that can be overlooked: a mastery of politics that allowed him to dominate the most crucial period of American history. For the twenty years from 1776 to 1796, he was a central force in every important event in the nation; often, he was the determining factor. A former British soldier, far from an admirer, wrote in 1784 that Washington's "political maneuvers, and his cautious plausible management," had raised him "to a degree of eminence in his own country unrivalled."[24] One measure of Washington's political skill was that when he denied having political talent or ambitions, people mostly believed him, and have continued to believe him ever since.

That those denials were disingenuous is beyond dispute. Washington won several major elections in his life: In 1775, the Second Continental Congress selected him as commander in chief of the Continental Army; his colleagues at the Constitutional Convention in 1787 made him presiding officer of that pivotal effort to invent a system of self-government; then the new nation elected him as its first president, and reelected him. As pointed out by others, the fact to linger over is that Washington did not merely win those four critical contests; he won them unanimously.[25] Unanimous election was no more common in the late eighteenth century than it is today.

Washington did not achieve such preeminence due to natural advantages or happy accidents, or because he was tall, rich, brave, and married to a rich woman. Nothing about Washington's success was easy. He had modest inherited wealth, so had to acquire the money that made his career possible. He had a meager education, a temper that terrified those who saw him lose it, a cockiness that could make him reckless, and a deep financial insecurity that could lead him close to greed.

Washington studied his flaws. From a young age, he struggled against his own nature. His early missteps might have crippled the prospects of a person with less dogged commitment to self-improvement. He ruthlessly suppressed qualities that could hinder his advancement and mastered those that could assist it. Washington's story is not one of effortless superiority, but one of excellence achieved with great effort.

That Washington was the paramount political figure of the turbulent founding era may be enough to deem him a master politician. Yet the appellation applies even more firmly because of the restraint and even benevolence with which he exercised the power his contemporaries placed in his hands. Acclaimed at countless public ceremonies through the last quarter century of his life, he never became grandiose or self-important. Often called "affable" by those who knew him, despite a personal reserve he maintained in public, his intense modesty and sense of his own fallibility allowed him to seek the advice of others on difficult decisions without preventing him from following his own judgment. As the embodiment of the republican ideals of his time and place, he defined the expectations that Americans would have of their leaders for many generations.

This book explores Washington's political mastery from two perspectives. First, it examines his first forty-three years, years in which Washington learned hard truths about the world, about leadership, and about himself. The George Washington who arrived at the First Continental Congress in 1774 is almost unrecognizable when compared to the man who led the Virginia Regiment two decades before.

The second part of the book studies five treacherous political minefields that Washington navigated in his mature career:

- Bringing his army through a winter of despair at Valley Forge in 1778, while thwarting a combination to supersede him as commander in chief, then winning a crucial battle at Monmouth Court House.
- Persuading mutinous, unpaid soldiers and officers to lay down their arms and embrace peace in 1783, then playing the crucial role in the effort to resolve the nation's political chaos with a new constitution that created a framework of self-government in 1787.
- Leading the new federal government as it was created from next to nothing, then guiding the bargain for a financial program that restored the nation's credit and ensured its solvency.
- Keeping the nation out of the European war that followed the French Revolution, cooling the passionate American adherents of both France and Britain.
- Struggling, in his final years, with America's original sin, human slavery—his own sin, too—hoping to point his countrymen toward repentance and even redemption.

The book's ultimate goal is to explore how George Washington became the titanic, near-legendary figure of the American Founding. The answers are necessarily as complicated as the man was.

In navigating his life's obstacles, Washington's strategies and tactics were often subtle. Although he presented himself as a straightforward military man, he was capable of maneuvering worthy of a Richelieu or a Borgia. When he acted, he moved with a sure sense of drama and performance. Yet his maneuvers were not ordinarily designed to win personal power or wealth, but rather to bring independence, self-government, and union to Americans. At critical moments, it was Washington who exercised the judgment and the leadership that carried the nation through dark troubles. Washington gave the United States something every nation needs, but few get: a national hero who understands that heroism includes giving up power and trusting your neighbors, that integrity and virtue—old-fashioned concepts even in the eighteenth century—are a greater legacy than personal aggrandizement and national conquest.

The recurring debate over whether the United States was created as a Hamiltonian or Jeffersonian society largely misses the point; we are Washingtonians.

CHAPTER 2

Beginnings

The first Washington in America arrived in 1657. He did not intend to stay, but then his ship sank in the Potomac River. He met that adversity by marrying a rich man's daughter, acquiring land, and winning a seat in the House of Burgesses, as a county court justice and as a parish vestryman.[1]

Virginia welcomed settlers then. Game was abundant and crops grew readily on land that was wet and soft enough that poor men did not shoe their horses. The previous residents of the land—more than thirty Indian groups sometimes called the Powhatan Confederacy—had been decimated by disease and war. One-sided treaties took their land and drove them west.[2] Oceangoing ships plied Chesapeake Bay and the colony's eastward-flowing rivers, docking at the wharves of riverside plantations to carry away crops for distant markets.[3]

The ships brought laborers: at first, poor English and Germans, Scots and Irish who signed indentures to work for a term of years. Then the ships brought Africans in chains to labor for no pay. The gentry lived well enough, while laborers—white and Black—did not. The laboring class knew the rage and despair of those who have masters, but only the Africans were property, expensive assets with fearsome potential for violent revolt.[4]

The grandson of that first Washington, called Gus (for Augustine), was tall and fair. An acquaintance claimed that Gus could lift into a wagon a load that would overmatch two ordinary men. After inheriting a thousand acres, Gus invested in an ironworks and acquired land on Little Hunting Creek that became Mount Vernon.[5]

When his first wife died, Gus took another, twenty-three-year-old Mary Ball. His two sons, Lawrence and Austin, were attending the Appleby School in the north of England, where Gus had been educated. His young daughter stayed with the newlyweds in a modest house where Popes Creek enters the brackish waters of the Potomac in Westmoreland County. On February 22, 1732, a new son arrived. They named him George.

ᴄᴡ

In 1732, British America consisted of twelve colonies, plus part of Nova Scotia and several Caribbean islands where sugar cultivation produced tremendous profits. It was a world of agriculture and trade. Depending on wind and weather, Atlantic crossings could take five weeks or five months. Shipwrecks happened. Travel on land was no faster than a horse could trot or a team could pull a coach. Roads, most of them bad, crossed innumerable rivers and streams. News spread slowly. British immigrants brought with them the old class structure and attitudes. One Virginian of common birth recalled the gentry as "beings of a superior order."[6]

Tobacco was the cash crop, sometimes doubling as a medium of exchange, but it was a hard crop, demanding constant care while wearing out the soil. Pests or too little rain would ruin it. So would too much rain. Some called it "the chopping herb of hell."[7] Many Virginians moved west for new land, but that way was not easy. Native tribes fought back. American forests held European rivals—Frenchmen and Spaniards—who were as violent and unscrupulous as any Virginian.

After the birth of a daughter and another son, Gus Washington built a house at Little Hunting Creek, closer to his ironworks and distant from neighbors. The new home had four rooms on the main floor plus a garret level with two sleeping chambers, a storeroom, and possibly more. It was the first home George would remember.[8]

With his father often away on business—Washington recalled his father as affectionate, but offered no other memories—mother Mary loomed large. For years, Americans exalted her as a Madonna figure, mother of the great Washington, but then the pendulum swung. A leading biographer described her as a money-grubbing termagant. Others have piled on with "harpy" and "harridan," insisting that Washington viewed her with "frigid deference." That there are few written remembrances of her, one biographer wrote, suggests "a conspiracy of silence" to conceal her appalling qualities.[9]

Mary was a strong and independent woman, unusually so for her time. She was orphaned at twelve and never remarried after Gus died. Either she preferred her independence and freedom from pregnancies, or received no offers to wed. She held the household together, managed modest farmlands with some twenty slaves, and raised five children. Most of her children turned out well; one spectacularly so.[10] One of George's cousins remembered her with respect, and a small shudder:

> Of the mother I was ten times more afraid than I ever was of my own parents. She awed me in the midst of her kindness . . . I have often been present with her sons, proper tall fellows too, and we were all as mute as mice; and even now, when time has whitened my locks, . . . I could not behold that remarkable woman without feelings it is impossible to describe. Whoever has seen that awe-inspiring air and manner so characteristic in the Father of his Country will remember the matron as she appeared [as] the presiding genius of her well-ordered household, commanding and being obeyed.[11]

That Mary could be stern was confirmed by the Marquis de Lafayette, a fervent Washington enthusiast. Meeting Mary when she was old, the Frenchman found her "in force of character rather resembling the matrons of Rome or Sparta." He attributed her son's achievements to "above all, her Spartan discipline."[12]

Washington's salient traits through life included a gift for organization and a powerful air of command. Underneath those qualities lurked a fearsome temper, one he struggled to master. He shared those qualities with his mother, as well as a passion for horses and riding. Thomas Jefferson (himself an admired rider) recalled Washington as "the most graceful figure that could be seen on horseback." A key to riding well is a close connection between horse and rider. The rider must be in command, which came naturally for mother and son. But the rider also must feel and respond to the horse, forming a nonverbal connection. Mother and son could do that too.[13]

That Washington might be formal in dealing with his mother is hardly startling for a man with his reserved nature. He was not one to grow maudlin over a mother's love as the punch bowl drained. His mother, too, plainly kept rein over her emotions. Effusions of sentiment would not flow between two such buttoned-up people, yet Washington usually visited her when he was near Fredericksburg, and managed her affairs as she aged.

∾

When George was six, his father's ambitions uprooted the family again. To be closer to his ironworks, Gus bought a house and farm across the Rappahannock River from bustling Fredericksburg.

The move covered only forty miles, but the change was considerable. No longer surrounded by empty acres, the family lived on a main road. A ferry crossed the river at the foot of their land and gave the home its name, Ferry Farm. Wagons rumbled by. Ships ascended the Rappahannock and docked at the town wharf.[14]

The new home, perched on a bluff above the river, had seven rooms for a family with five children below the age of seven. George was the eldest. Next came the only girl, Betty, and Samuel (four), Jack (two), and Charles (eight months). The surrounding lands totaled only three hundred acres. Gus focused on mining, not farming.[15]

At roughly the same time, another powerful figure entered Washington's life. His half-brother Lawrence returned from school in England and occupied the vacated estate at Little Hunting Creek.[16] Fourteen years older than George, Lawrence combined the camaraderie of a brother with nearly adult authority and the polish acquired overseas. George idolized him.

Shortly after arriving, Lawrence became captain of a Virginia company that joined a British attack on Cartagena, in what is now Colombia. Decked out in his uniform, serving king and country, Lawrence took on heroic stature in his younger brother's eyes.[17]

The expedition, however, was a wretched failure. Captain Lawrence Washington and his Virginians never left their ships. He acknowledged in a letter home that the Spanish had killed six hundred of the attacking British, but "the climate killed us in greater number."

Despite the inglorious experience, Lawrence described it in an offhand fashion sure to fire a boy's dreams of glory. "War is horrid in fact," Lawrence wrote, "but much more so in imagination." The Virginians had to learn to "disregard the noise or shot of cannon."[18] Returning home in 1742, Lawrence could tell of broad oceans, Spanish forts, amphibious assaults, and the world beyond Ferry Farm. George's eyes had to widen at the sight of Lawrence's sword, inspired to lead his younger brothers in mock battles along the Rappahannock.

The Cartagena expedition's failure did not dampen Lawrence's military ardor. Though only twenty-four and still without combat experience, he became adjutant of the Virginia militia. The likely force behind that appointment was his neighbor Colonel William Fairfax, who was beginning years of sponsoring Washingtons.[19]

Lawrence was the first Washington to leave behind a portrait, by an unknown artist, which shows a dark young man with an open countenance and modest physical vitality. The face has well-defined eyebrows, a high forehead, a strong jaw, and a chin dimple. Only a certain meatiness to the nose suggests his younger half-brother. The portrait does not reveal the charm and ability that must have fueled Lawrence's success.

In the spring of 1743, Gus fell ill and died. Death was a constant in the eighteenth century. When George was three, his older half-sister died; a baby sister died when he was eight. Neither death could prepare him for the loss of his father, which removed the family's central financial support.

In a will composed on his deathbed, Gus followed Virginia traditions by favoring his two elder sons. Lawrence received roughly 40 percent of the assets, including the iron mine and Little Hunting Creek. Second son Austin acquired the original family home on Popes Creek and surrounding lands, plus other property. George, only eleven, got Ferry Farm, some lots in Fredericksburg, a half share in another parcel, and ten slaves. It was more than many Virginians owned, but placed him at the low end of the gentry.[20] Until he came of age, his mother would manage his property and slaves; he was past forty before he controlled Ferry Farm. Gus left less to his younger children.

Mary got less too. She would have to support her family with what she could earn from Ferry Farm, from five years of income from the Popes Creek property, and from a parcel she owned before marriage.

The family's horizons shrank. No more Washingtons attended school in England. George always would be self-conscious about his limited education. In a later time of financial distress, Washington wrote that he had "never felt the want of money so sensibly since I was a boy of 15 years old." Neither mother nor son would ever be free of financial anxiety.

For the next decade, Lawrence served as George's surrogate father, role model, and companion. Little Hunting Creek, which Lawrence named Mount Vernon after his former commander, became George's second home, a place of refuge from being the eldest son of a hard-pressed single mother. Most conspicuously, Lawrence would set an example for mounting a pell-mell assault on the top echelon of Virginia society.

At age fourteen, George described Lawrence more simply, as his best friend.[21]

CHAPTER 3

The School of Fairfax

Washington was vague about his education, including whether he was
tutored at home or attended school. He offered no fond remembrances of lessons or instructors. At a time when gentlemen knew languages
and the classics, Washington learned neither. His schoolwork shows no exposure to philosophy or political thought, nor to Shakespeare. While his
mother evidently molded his character and imbued in him the Christian
religion, Washington acquired much of his learning from books and from
the world around him—most conspicuously, from the Fairfax family of Belvoir, one estate over from Lawrence's home at Mount Vernon.[1]

Lawrence built the first link to the Fairfaxes by marrying the daughter of
Colonel William Fairfax, master of Belvoir, only three months after Gus
Washington's death in 1743. Anne Fairfax brought 4,000 acres into the marriage, which was a minute portion of her family's Virginia domain, which
equaled New Hampshire in size. The lasting Fairfax legacy, though, would be
George Washington.

∾

Washington's boyhood copybooks, lovingly preserved, reflect math and science that a teacher must have explained. Calculations appear in a fine hand
and without crossing out, the answers derived elsewhere and then transcribed. Geometric figures are drawn crisply. An aesthetic sensibility shows
in decorated title pages.

The lessons prepared him to be an owner of land and slaves. To learn
decimals, Washington calculated interest on loans. He estimated the floor

area of a building or the size of a land parcel. He figured the volume of containers for grain and liquor. He studied legal forms: bills of exchange, land leases, and servant indentures. A few pages record information about distant lands, which always intrigued Washington.

Washington was adept at quantitative and mechanical subjects, but the written word challenged him. His early compositions were woefully tangled, the sentences weighed down with complex clauses and grandiloquent vocabulary. Over many years, Washington would simplify and strengthen his writing, but also would rely on talented wordsmiths like James Madison and Alexander Hamilton.[2]

Ferry Farm was not cluttered with books. Gus Washington was a man of business. Mary's letters show that she, like most women of the time, had little education, though she was a devoted reader of religious works. Washington also became an eager reader, inhaling *The Spectator,* Joseph Addison's London-based newspaper that circulated in bound volumes and was considered the model of graceful composition. On a visit to a home with a library, Washington dove into a history of English kings, getting as far as King John.[3]

He read Defoe's *Tour Thro' the Whole Island of Great Britain.* Military adventure came from Caesar's *Commentaries* and the biography of a German military hero. The stoicism of *Seneca's Morals* was heavier fare, but included prescriptions with Washingtonian resonance. "Hope and fear," Seneca warned, "are the bane of human life." He also advised that "contempt of death makes all the miseries of life easy to us."[4]

One feature of Washington's education has drawn disproportionate attention: his copying of 110 "Rules of Civility and Decent Behavior," a code of conduct drafted by French Jesuits 150 years before. Some construe the "Rules of Civility" as a guide to Washington's future life, rather than as the penmanship exercise it appears to be. Over the next five decades, Washington never mentioned them, even when counseling his numerous younger relatives.

ക

The Fairfax family played an outsized role in Washington's formative years. Colonel Fairfax came to Virginia to manage the family lands on behalf of his cousin Thomas, the sixth Lord Fairfax, who owned most of the land between the Potomac and Rappahannock Rivers, Virginia's Northern Neck. (Virginians called land between rivers a "neck.") While Lord Fairfax was young, he had neglected his American empire, and that neglect had taken a toll. Colonial governors granted some Fairfax land to others. The previous Fairfax agent in Virginia purloined massive tracts for himself and his relatives. After that agent's death, Lord Fairfax filled the position with his reliable cousin, who had held royal offices in Barbados, Bermuda, and Massachusetts.[5]

Colonel Fairfax built the brick mansion at Belvoir, occupying it in 1741 with his wife and seven children, also taking a seat in Virginia's House of Burgesses. The Fairfaxes mixed easily with their neighbor, young Lawrence Washington, who had the polish and refinement of an elite English education. Lawrence often brought along his younger brother George, large for his age and already a skilled horseman.

The people of Mount Vernon and Belvoir socialized at dinners, dances, and fox hunts. The Fairfaxes ate off china, drank from crystal, and exuded the amiable condescension of gentlefolk who kept an eye on the main chance. Colonel Fairfax mixed with the highest colonial officials. He knew the political issues and maneuverings of the day. From the Fairfaxes and Lawrence, Washington could learn how a man of position carried himself, the correct mix of friendliness and reserve, how to put others at ease, when to be lighthearted, and when and how to discuss serious matters. Most intoxicating, these exemplars of gracious gentry life embraced the Washington brothers. Lawrence cemented the tie between the families with his marriage to fifteen-year-old Anne Fairfax in 1743.[6]

George fully understood the importance of the Fairfaxes to his future. He later advised younger brother Jack to cultivate them. "I should be glad to hear," he wrote, "that you live in perfect harmony and good fellowship with the family at Belvoir, as it is in their power to be very serviceable." Washington concluded with the obvious truth: "to that family I am under many obligations, particularly to the old gentleman [Colonel Fairfax]." George doubtless had received similar advice from Lawrence.[7]

Lawrence and the colonel arranged for George to enter the Royal Navy as a fourteen-year-old midshipman, despite mother Mary's apparent opposition. To advance that project, Colonel Fairfax carried to Fredericksburg a letter for George and another for his mother. The colonel instructed the boy to deliver the letter to his mother when the time felt right. Colonel Fairfax also lobbied one of Mary Washington's friends to recommend sending George to sea.[8]

Despite those efforts, Mary withheld her consent. Good reasons for her course came from her half-brother in England. The navy, he warned, will "cut [George] and staple him and use him like a Negro, or rather, like a dog." He warned that a colonial lad could not advance in the navy. Too many well-born naval officers had powerful English sponsors, which George had not.

Ultimately, the midshipman project dissolved, ending George Washington's nascent career in the Royal Navy.[9]

The adults had wrangled over George's future because he seemed so promising. Nearing his full height, he moved with a grace that cannot be taught. His build was slender but strong. Later in life, he would say he never met a man who could match the distance he could throw a stone. When he was forty, Washington came upon young men "pitching the bar," a heavy iron rod. He asked what their longest throw had been. Noting the mark, wrote a contestant, Washington heaved the bar "far, very far beyond our utmost limits." With a grin, Washington said, "When you beat my pitch, young gentlemen, I'll try again."[10]

Washington's physical gifts influenced his personality. His height drew attention, while his athletic prowess bred confidence. Competition holds less anxiety for the physically talented. Success brings praise. The athletic boy can attempt bolder deeds than his fellows.

Though Mary prevailed in the contest over the midshipman position, Lawrence's influence with George grew. Lawrence had inherited the best house and the most slaves. He had style and traveled in the great world. At Ferry Farm, George had to help his mother's daily routines; at Mount Vernon, he could become a gentleman. Mount Vernon's appeal increased in 1747 when Lord Fairfax arrived at Belvoir, the only titled Englishman to make his home in colonial America.

❧

Lord Fairfax was not much to look at: short, plump, and careless about dress. His indifference to convention reflected wealth and entitlement. He was a baron who owned millions of acres. He had been a member of the king's household, attended balls and rode in fox hunts with the empire's most august figures, had frequented London coffeehouses with Addison, and supposedly penned contributions to the *Spectator*. For him, all Americans were hired hands.

The lord's fat times had ended in 1730, with creditors baying at the gates of the family castle. Needing income, he thought of his neglected property in Virginia and began to exert closer control over it. Nearly two decades later, in his mid-fifties, the proprietor of the Northern Neck moved to Virginia with one overriding goal: to sell or lease his lands for profit.

Land was Virginia's economic religion, and surveyors were essential to its rituals. The colony held 45,000 square miles that could not be sold until it was marked off in parcels. Twenty-five new counties sprang into existence between 1720 and 1754; new towns formed every year; all needed defined borders. To convert his land into the funds he craved, Lord Fairfax needed reliable surveys, and plenty of them. Young George Washington saw the opportunity. At fifteen, using his father's hand-me-down equipment, he completed a survey of Lawrence's turnip field. After that effort, Washington began to hire out as a surveyor. Lawrence supported the initiative. A surveyor in the family would be an advantage and knit another connection to the Fairfaxes.[11]

The work suited Washington. It required attention to detail, spatial sensibility, and drawing skill, all of which show in Washington's copybooks. It also required a rugged constitution. The best times for surveying were late autumn and early spring, when leaves were down and visibility best. Washington thrived in rugged country, sleeping outside in freezing temperatures.[12]

When one was surveying empty lands, precision was elusive. The surveyor ordinarily ran a first line from a prominent tree to another tree or a rock outcropping or watercourse, drawing the next line the same way, and so on until he returned to the initial point, turning corners at right angles when possible. Such rough-and-ready methods created profit opportunities for surveyors with easy ethics, who might include "overplus" acreage of as much as 25 percent: happy news for their clients. False surveys were common.[13]

Washington's first taste of frontier surveying came in a Fairfax expedition in March 1748, just after his sixteenth birthday. An experienced surveyor led the party, while Colonel Fairfax's eldest son, George William, represented the proprietor.

Seven years older and schooled in England, George William warmed to Washington, whose size and demeanor led elders to accept him. A contemporary described the impression he made.

> [He was] straight as an Indian, measuring six feet two inches in his stockings and weighing 175 pounds . . . His frame is padded with well-developed muscles, indicating great strength. His bones and joints are large, as are his hands and feet. He is wide shouldered but has not a deep or round chest; is neat waisted, but is broad across the hips and has rather long legs and arms. . . . A large and straight rather than a prominent nose; blue gray penetrating eyes which are widely separated and overhung by a heavy brow. . . . His movements and gestures are graceful, his walk majestic, and he is a splendid horseman.

Washington had imperfections. His skin burned in the sun. Because of bad teeth, a curse through life, he kept his mouth closed. His voice was soft, almost breathy, maybe due to an early respiratory illness. But his poise overcame defects: "In conversation he looks at you full in the face, is deliberate, deferential, and engaging. His demeanor is at all times composed and dignified."[14]

That first wilderness journey was difficult. Washington learned to sleep in his clothes in the open air, avoiding frontier cabins that were infested with lice and fleas. Spring rains and melting snow swelled creeks and rivers, forcing the surveyors to swim their horses across strong currents. Rain and wind lashed their tents and campfires. Washington declared one trail "the worst road that ever was trod by man or beast."[15]

But there were adventures too. Meeting some thirty Indians, the surveyors shared out their liquor. The Indians responded with a "grand speech," Washington wrote, after which "the best dancer jumps up as one awaked out of a sleep and runs and jumps about the ring in a most comical manner." The teenager offered an equally patronizing account of German settlers who followed the party, "showing their antic tricks." He called them "as ignorant a set of people as the Indians," noting disdainfully that they spoke no English.[16]

Washington and George William headed home wiser about frontier life though not yet frontiersmen. Their return took extra days following a wrong turn in the woods.[17]

For the rest of the year, Belvoir and Mount Vernon swirled with activity. In June, Lawrence successfully defended his Fairfax County seat in the House of Burgesses. Washington, fascinated by politics, saved the vote tally sheet. George William Fairfax won a seat from Frederick County on the frontier, where Lord Fairfax soon would settle. Because Virginia allowed a man to run wherever he owned sufficient land, the Fairfaxes could be candidates in multiple counties.[18] Lawrence and the Fairfaxes joined the new Ohio Company's petition to acquire 200,000 acres of land beyond the Blue Ridge.[19]

Lawrence and Anne, who had already lost two babies, had a little girl.[20] In December, George William Fairfax married Sarah Cary, the tall daughter of a wealthy Virginia family. Known as Sally, the bride was eighteen, two years older than Washington. She would become a friend. Amid these happy events, however, Lawrence developed a cough that would not go away. In mid-December, he took a leave from the burgesses' deliberations, pleading ill health. By May of 1749, he was thinking of traveling in search of a cure. "I hope your cough is much mended," Washington wrote to his brother.[21]

It wasn't.

CHAPTER 4

His Brother's Keeper

In 1749, with his mother still controlling Ferry Farm, the seventeen-year-old Washington was so short of money that he declined a trip to Mount Vernon because his horse was underfed.[1] A Virginian unable to keep his horse in feed was no gentleman.

Washington struck out to make his way as a surveyor. When the colony incorporated a new city ten miles upstream from Mount Vernon, he used family and Fairfax connections to become assistant to the surveyor who laid out Alexandria's building lots. When it came time to auction off the lots, the purchasers included two sons of Colonel Fairfax, plus Lawrence and Austin Washington. George, however, lacked the funds to bid.[2]

Fortunately, newly created Culpeper County, west of Fredericksburg, needed a surveyor. Responding to Fairfax influence, the local court appointed Washington, a teenager.[3] He promptly surveyed a four-hundred-acre site and drew other work.

Through the autumn, Washington completed dozens of surveys around the Shenandoah valley, mostly for people acquiring grants from Lord Fairfax. Working with rugged characters in rough surroundings, the young man toughened. "I have not slept above three nights or four in a bed," he wrote, but often lay down before a fire on straw or a bearskin, "with man, wife, and children like a parcel of dogs or cats." In cold weather, he slept in his clothes "like a Negro," and "happy's he that gets the berth nearest the fire." The money was good. Based on his customary survey fee of 2 pounds, 3 shillings, Washington earned more than £100 in less than two months, outstanding income for one so young.[4]

Washington's surveying, built on the Fairfax connection, flourished anew in the spring, when he marked off forty-seven tracts, earning more than £140. He picked up more jobs over the summer, then returned to the Shenandoah for autumn surveys.[5]

With money in hand, Washington accumulated the trappings of a gentleman. He bought a "pole-chair harness," a two-seat, one-horse riding chair: the equivalent of his first car. He bought about one thousand acres in two parcels (one from Lord Fairfax) bordering Bullskin Creek in Frederick County.[6] Washington began his gentleman's wardrobe. He would always be fussy about his appearance, understanding that clothes framed the impression he made. For an early visit to Mount Vernon, he packed seven shirts, six linen waistcoats, seven caps, and four neck cloths. In a memorandum for a tailor, he specified the number of buttonholes in his coat, its length, and the width of the lapels.[7]

A gentleman enjoyed the chase, horse racing, and gambling. Though Washington often called gambling a vice, he nonetheless enjoyed it, especially cards (whist and loo) and billiards. According to his financial accounts, Lawrence could best him at the card table, but Washington had more success with brother Austin and Lawrence's wife Anne.[8]

Washington employed a dancing master for instruction in that essential social grace, for which his athleticism served him well.[9] Writing still did not come easily. One letter began with a single sentence of more than two hundred words. His admission that he was sending a fourth missive to a young lady without receiving any reply suggests that he had missed important cues of her disinterest.[10]

Family events crowded in. Betty, his surviving sister (who bore an uncanny resemblance to her brother George), married a wealthy Fredericksburg merchant, Fielding Lewis. Lawrence and his wife had another baby girl. A tragedy struck among the slaves at Ferry Farm when one murdered another.[11] But Lawrence's lingering illness overshadowed everything. He sailed to England for medical advice, but returned unimproved. He resolved to try the healing qualities of the mineral waters of Berkeley Springs in the Shenandoah country. Because Lawrence's wife was pregnant, George accompanied his brother on the trip, performing surveying jobs as they moved west. Lawrence again found no relief. He had tuberculosis, then called consumption. There would be no cure for two more centuries.[12]

In the spring of 1751, the brothers tried another trip to Berkeley Springs. As they proceeded, Washington completed more surveys while Lawrence saw to land business.[13] Again, the older brother did not improve. The hand of death was upon him. For nearly two years, he had endured consumption's wracking cough, fevers, and night sweats. His breathing sometimes hurt and he tired easily. He had been to English doctors, Virginia doctors, and the waters of Berkeley Springs. Nothing helped.

The British colony of Barbados was said to offer a healing climate for lung disorders, plus renowned physicians. As luck would have it, Colonel Fairfax's wife had a brother there who could present them to Barbados society. The Fairfax connection rarely failed.

With another new baby in her arms, Lawrence's wife could not travel, so Washington undertook the melancholy journey with his brother. He would see a new part of the world. He might make advantageous connections among wealthy sugar planters and British military officers. And perhaps Lawrence would find a miracle.

∾

The brothers sailed from Virginia in late September, the heart of the Caribbean hurricane season. Washington kept a daily log, recording the ship's direction and speed, distance covered, winds, latitude and longitude, plus remarks about the weather and the ships they passed. For a surveyor with a mathematical bent, keeping such records was second nature. On fine days, Washington fished off the deck.[14]

After more than two weeks, heavy storms struck. The sailors, Washington reported, "never had seen such weather before." When the howling winds and churning seas subsided, the crew discovered that much of the ship's food had been eaten by maggots and other pests. Finally tied up at Bridgetown in early November, the Washingtons lodged with friends of Major Gedney Clarke, brother to Colonel Fairfax's wife.[15]

Because of its fabulous sugar wealth, the island, which measured only fourteen miles by twenty-two miles, held 90,000 people. Bridgetown was home to 10,000, more than four times larger than the most populous Virginia town. Blacks outnumbered whites more than four to one.[16]

Washington waxed ecstatic over Barbados, declaring himself "perfectly ravished by the beautiful prospects which on every side presented to our view. The fields of cane, corn, fruit trees, etc. in a delightful green."[17] Hills afforded "a beautiful prospect both of sea and land." The warmth of the climate, according to another visitor, meant that residents were "very thinly clad," while the Negroes "have no more covering on them than what decency requires to cover their nakedness."[18]

A leading doctor pronounced that Lawrence's affliction could be cured. Buoyed by this sunny diagnosis, the brothers rented a hillside house overlooking the harbor's bright blue waters, although Washington thought the rent "extravagantly dear."[19] Clarke, wealthy from trading slaves and smuggling rum, injected the Washingtons into Barbadian society, as Clarke's home regularly filled with navy and army officers and "strangers of every respectable denomination."[20]

A view of Carlisle Bay, Barbados, 1820

Washington watched a fireworks show on Guy Fawkes Day and toured Bridgetown's fort, built to withstand maritime assaults. He attended a production of *The Tragedy of George Barnwell*, a taste of theater that would ripen into a lifelong enthusiasm with a practical benefit for a political actor with a gift for performance. The actor's tools—how to stand and move, how to convey messages with gestures and expression, how to modulate the voice and pace your speech—serve a politician well.[21]

The fun ended after only two weeks, when Washington contracted smallpox. He was bedridden for more weeks. Though the illness left Washington's face with telltale pockmarks, it also gave him lifelong immunity against further attacks.[22]

George's recovery only underscored Lawrence's grim prospects. Despite the cheery initial prognosis, as Lawrence wrote to Colonel Fairfax, he did not improve. Lawrence bemoaned the island's warm, unchanging climate. "By the time the sun is half an hour high," he wrote, "it is as hot as at any time of the day." He craved more variety in the weather.[23]

Those long days of illness in Barbados may help account for Washington's future willingness to ignore risks that would cause other brave men to turn away. Honor would always be more important to him than saving a few days that he might never see anyway. The brothers decided that Washington should return home alone. Lawrence, now on his fourth journey to retrieve his health, was running out of options. If he did not rally soon, he resolved to move on to Bermuda and hope to do better there.

On December 22, just ten days after rising from his sickbed, Washington took ship for home. In his journal, he recorded none of his feelings, noting only, "Took leave of my brother."[24] Instead of introspection, he wrote of the rich Barbadian soil and the economics of sugarcane production, the islanders' hospitality and the agreeable manners of the women, the debts that plagued many planters, and the acquittal of a rich man accused of raping his servant, a verdict which offended Washington's sense of justice.[25]

He thought the island's government fees were arbitrarily high, while Barbadians were "either very rich or very poor." He praised the island's royal governor, who performed his duties well enough, yet by "declining much familiarity is not overzealously beloved." Washington's future public deportment would have some of those characteristics.[26]

Winter sailing proved as difficult as the hurricane season had been. Seasickness struck Washington on the first day afloat, and his journal describes gales, violent storms, hail, snow, and on several days a "mountainous sea."[27] Mid-journey, he discovered that his belongings had been rifled and his money was gone. Another life lesson.

After landing in Virginia, Washington stopped in the colonial capital of Williamsburg to meet the energetic new governor, Robert Dinwiddie.[28] A partner in the Ohio Company venture that Lawrence had joined, Dinwiddie had his eyes firmly fixed on Virginia's western country, which he intended to secure for Britain against French encroachments. The tall young man coming to meet with him was not yet twenty years old, but would become central to that effort.

CHAPTER 5

Turning Point

Little about Williamsburg inspired awe when Washington arrived in late January 1752. The town held barely a thousand residents—a fraction the size of Bridgetown on Barbados. The population swelled four times a year during "court days," when markets, legal proceedings, and social events drew Virginians from their plantations, but late January was quiet. An earlier visitor called Williamsburg "a most wretched, contrived affair." Its capitol had burned five years before; a replacement was under construction. The Governor's Palace was also under repair.[1]

The sixty-year-old Dinwiddie had been governor for only two months, but he knew Virginia and its politics. Born to a merchant family in Scotland, he had traded and held public offices in Bermuda. Appointed tax collector for America's southern colonies, Dinwiddie settled near Williamsburg, taking a seat on Virginia's Executive Council. Powerful Virginians mistrusted Dinwiddie—a Scot who collected taxes had two black marks against him—but he was a vigorous public servant intent on vindicating Britain's claims to western lands.[2]

After Washington presented letters from Barbados, the men talked through dinner. They were an unlikely pair: a tall, lanky teenager and a stout man who might have been his grandfather, linked by their mutual interest in the west and by mutual friends, the Fairfaxes. Dinwiddie surely asked after Lawrence, the colony's senior military official, whose health mattered if the governor's policies provoked a frontier war. Washington combined a gentleman's manner with a toughness earned surveying. Accustomed to responsibility—as a surveyor and while caring for his brother—he had a quiet confidence. Dinwiddie might have uses for him.[3]

Spring brought surveying work; Washington bought more land on Bull-skin Creek.[4] In April, Lawrence wrote from his new perch in Bermuda, reporting that he felt "like a criminal condemned, though not without hopes of reprieve." A local doctor had banned him from consuming meat or liquor, and ordered that he ride around the small island. Lawrence had rallied, then fallen back. "If I grow worse," he concluded, "I shall hurry home to my grave."[5]

∞

Having fought three wars over the previous sixty years, France and Britain now were colliding in North America.

New France stretched in a crescent from Cape Breton Island in the Atlantic, across Canada, down the Mississippi valley to New Orleans, and west to the Rocky Mountains.[6] To connect its far-flung settlements, France needed to control the Ohio River, the best water route between the Atlantic and the Mississippi. From Montreal, travelers could ascend the St. Lawrence River, cross Lake Ontario and Lake Erie, then paddle to a land connection to streams that fed the Ohio. Control of the Ohio would solidify France's settlements.[7]

Though the French lands were massive, the British population in America was twenty times larger. If the French won control of the Ohio, while the Spanish held Florida, British settlers might be unable to spread out as they intended. Four British syndicates, including the Ohio Company, each held grants of at least 100,000 acres in the west, heedless of conflicting claims of Indian tribes or the French.[8]

The contest for the Ohio began in earnest in the 1740s. Offering cheaper, more plentiful goods, the British moved in on the Indian fur trade.[9] A French military mission in 1749 aimed to solidify the Ohio tribes' allegiance to King Louis XV.[10] Three years later, the French employed sterner measures, leading an attack on Miami Indians who traded with the British. The attackers boiled and ate the Miami chief.[11]

The Ohio Company, with Lawrence Washington as president, was in the thick of the struggle. It built a storehouse where Wills Creek entered the Potomac (now Cumberland, Maryland) and sent backwoodsman Christopher Gist on expeditions to confirm the French attacks on British traders and "note every parcel of good land" in the west. Gist invited Indian leaders to a meeting with Dinwiddie at Logstown (near Braden, Pennsylvania), but warned his employers that the Indians feared the British hunger for land.[12]

The tribes held the balance of power between the European empires.

Though reduced by disease and war, the Indians were unparalleled forest fighters, skilled at silent stalking and swift ambush. Indian ways of war—scalping, occasional torture, and rare cannibalism—terrified Europeans. Most tribes wanted neither set of Europeans to prevail, so they changed sides when one grew too strong. Some Indian villages flew the flags of both nations.[13]

Virginia's elite, hoping to cash in on western land, worried about the French initiative. So did Dinwiddie, the Ohio Company partner and agent of empire. He demanded reports of any violence caused by Indians or Frenchmen, so he could petition the French for redress; if his petition were refused, he wrote with a wink, "we may proceed in another manner." The governor proclaimed, "I have the success and prosperity of the Ohio Company much at heart."[14]

Dinwiddie's 1752 meeting with the Indians illustrated the miscommunication that snarled relations between whites and Indians. Tribes tended not to designate a single leader, entrusting functions to individuals based on their talents. The tribe's speaker at a council might not be its war leader, or even its senior elder. Whites puzzled over who made the tribe's decisions. Also, tribal leaders were usually not literate, so formed agreements through council speeches. Unimpressed with the European fetish for written understandings, they often signed papers that differed from what they had agreed to verbally.[15]

At Dinwiddie's Logstown conference, the Virginia commissioners could not decide whether the tribal spokesman, Tanaghrisson, was a Seneca or a Mingo or a Catawba. His authority seemed to derive from the Iroquois in New York. With a shrug, they called him "the Half-King."[16] Tanaghrisson, who disliked the French, agreed that the British could build a single fort on the Ohio, but not the full-scale settlement that the British and the Ohio Company had in mind. The British drafted a written agreement that authorized both. Tanaghrisson signed, but then said the treaty had no effect until the Iroquois council approved.[17]

For Dinwiddie, the signed treaty was enough.

ᴖ

Washington was facing his own troubles. A surveying trip to the Shenandoah in early spring brought on an attack of pleurisy, a lung ailment that likely contributed to his breathy speech as an adult. When recovered, Washington returned to an unsuccessful courtship of sixteen-year-old Elizabeth Fauntleroy of Richmond County. He wrote to her father that he hoped to visit

Miss Fauntleroy and persuade her to reverse "the former, cruel sentence" against him. The requested visit was denied and the cruel sentence against him stood. The Fauntleroys declined to link their daughter's future with the young surveyor who owned only frontier lands.[18]

Worse was coming. Lawrence hurried home from Bermuda, reaching Mount Vernon by the middle of June. He signed over to George three lots in Fredericksburg, then prepared his will. By late July, he was dead.[19]

Though certainly a death foretold, Lawrence's passing had to sear the younger brother. Lawrence had been his guide, his protector, his best friend, the person he likely felt closest to in the world. Washington did not use words to express his feelings for Lawrence, but later made those feelings visible at Mount Vernon. He kept Lawrence's portrait in the office where he worked every day. It hangs there still.

Washington inherited little from his brother. Mount Vernon and its farms went to Lawrence's widow and surviving daughter. Mining interests went to his full brother Austin. George would, however, receive those assets if all three died. Of immediate value, Lawrence's death cleared Washington's path for advancement. His other four brothers lacked the drive that he and Lawrence shared. George became the Washington family's alpha male.[20]

Only weeks before Lawrence died, the twenty-year-old Washington applied to be military adjutant for one of Virginia's four districts. Neither his youth nor his inexperience proved an obstacle, not for a candidate with Fairfax support who had impressed the governor. Perhaps appointing Washington was Dinwiddie's way of honoring Lawrence. Whatever the reason, in December 1752, Washington became a Virginia militia major, commanding the colony's southern district.[21]

Washington's new duties were light, largely because the militia was not a serious military organization. Over peaceful decades, training had become routine, then lax, then almost farcical. Musters became social events featuring liquor and politicking. The militia's most important function was to deter slave insurrections.[22]

Nevertheless, the young surveyor had become a soldier just as Virginia was sliding into war.

∾

In 1753, the French sent nearly 3,000 soldiers to a landing on Lake Erie (now Erie, Pennsylvania). They planned to construct forts along the route between the lake and the pivotal Forks of the Ohio, but drought made their boats useless in dried-up streams; then came sickness and desertion. The French advance ground to a halt. Leaving small garrisons in three forts, the rest returned to Montreal for the winter.[23]

The British roused themselves. London instructed Governor Dinwiddie to "repel force by force" if the French entered the king's lands, but since the two nations disputed which lands belonged to which king, those instructions were murky, at best. The governor resolved to send young George Washington to demand the French justification for trespassing on King George's land. Washington's orders from the Executive Council, drafted by Colonel Fairfax, were complicated.[24]

After meeting the Half-King and other sachems, Washington was to request an escort to the French forts. Indian escorts, the reasoning went, would deter the French from making him a prisoner. Washington should deliver Dinwiddie's demand that the French explain their presence on King George's land. Washington also should gather intelligence: how many Frenchmen were there, their supplies, what fortifications they had built, and their goals.[25]

Despite his youth, Washington had some qualifications for the mission. As a surveyor, he could produce maps and diagrams of French forts. Unlike most frontiersmen, Washington had the polish to represent His Majesty. That he spoke no French was unfortunate, but few frontiersmen did. Plus, Colonel Fairfax sponsored him.

As Washington left Williamsburg, he could take some satisfaction in his position. Only twenty-one, he was on a critical mission for the colony. At a personal level, he now owned more than 4,000 acres, mostly in the west. His home was still Ferry Farm, still in his mother's grip, but he was moving forward.

∾

Washington recruited two aides for his mission, beginning with Christopher Gist, the Ohio Company explorer who was respected by the Indians. Washington praised Gist as tireless and patient. Jacob Van Braam, a Dutchman with military experience, would be translator.[26]

The weather turned severe, bringing what Washington called "excessive rains and vast quantity of snow." Over two weeks in December, rain or snow fell on all but one day.[27] Slogging through the mess, Washington reached the Forks after three weeks. Despite having no military background, he criticized the site selected for the British fort. Moving on to Logstown, where he waited for Tanaghrisson, he found French deserters who told him about settlements as far as New Orleans.

Tanaghrisson arrived in a rage against the French. Through an interpreter, the Half-King recounted a fierce speech he had made to the French, ordering them out of the west. The French commander, Tanaghrisson continued, had dismissed him. "I am not afraid of flies or mosquitoes," the Frenchman had said, "for Indians are such as those . . . It is my land, and I will have it." The Half-King dealt with Washington, forty years his junior, as an equal, but his account of French attitudes did not augur well for Washington's mission.[28]

At a council with Indian leaders, Washington announced his purpose and requested an escort to the French. Tanaghrisson pledged a guard of Mingoes, Shawnees, and Delawares. They could leave as soon as he retrieved wampum belts to return to the French, an act that would end their alliance against the British. Since Washington hoped to coax the tribes away from French influence, he waited. And waited.

Conferring again with Indian leaders, Washington learned that though most French soldiers were again returning to Montreal for the winter, they would come back in springtime; France intended to control the region. When Washington finally left Logstown, his escort numbered but three chiefs and one young man, with no wampum belts to give back to the French. The French officer's threats had cooled Indian support for the British.[29]

After several days trudging through cold, wet forest, Washington's party reached the French post at Venango (now Franklin, Pennsylvania). Three French officers gave Washington dinner and wine, telling him, as he recorded it, "their absolute design to take possession of the Ohio." They disparaged the British as numerous but slow. They tried to entice Tanaghrisson with presents and liquor; when that failed, the French got drunk themselves.[30]

A small French contingent escorted Washington's party onward to Fort Le Boeuf, through four more days of "rains, snows, and bad travelling." To cross one creek, they tied their baggage onto logs, then swam the horses across, hauling the logs behind them. At Le Boeuf, Washington presented Dinwiddie's letter. While the French considered it, Washington examined the fort and its garrison. More than two hundred canoes on the shores announced the scope of French ambitions, while Washington worried that the Half-King might switch sides. Washington was glad to head home with the French reply in hand.[31]

The horses gave out halfway to Virginia, so the men walked. The temperature plunged. Snow heaped and froze on the path. Dismayed by their slow progress, Washington resolved to abandon the trail and set off through the woods, leaving the others to manage the baggage. Failing to dissuade him from this dangerous course, Gist went with him.

A party of French-allied Indians, according to Washington, lay in wait for them. After one of them shot at the Virginians from "not 15 steps [away], but

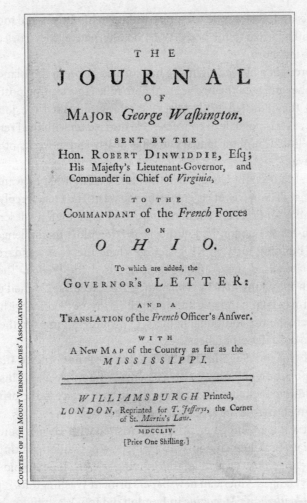

THE

JOURNAL

OF

MAJOR *George Washington,*

SENT BY THE

Hon. ROBERT DINWIDDIE, Efq;
His Majefty's Lieutenant-Governor, and
Commander in Chief of *Virginia,*

TO THE

COMMANDANT of the *French* Forces

ON

OHIO.

To which are added, the

GOVERNOR's LETTER:

AND A

TRANSLATION of the *French* Officer's Anfwer.

WITH

A New MAP of the Country as far as the
MISSISSIPPI.

WILLIAMSBURGH Printed,
LONDON, Reprinted for *T. Jefferys,* the Corner
of St. *Martin's Lane.*
MDCCLIV.
[Price One Shilling.]

COURTESY OF THE MOUNT VERNON LADIES' ASSOCIATION

Title page of Washington's journal of his frontier expedition

fortunately missed," he and Gist detained the shooter until nightfall. Gist reported that Washington refused to kill the man, perhaps because their mission was diplomatic. After setting the shooter free, they walked through the night to get away from him.

They had hoped to walk across a frozen Allegheny River, but the river's ice extended only fifty feet from shore, leaving a torrent in the center with large ice chunks thundering through. Taking turns swinging a small hatchet, they spent a day rigging a raft. Once on the river, the flimsy craft jammed in some ice and threatened to sink. Washington fell into the frigid water, then hauled himself onto the raft with one hand. Drenched and half-frozen, they reached a midriver island. Gist was developing frostbite in his fingers and toes. Washington's clothes froze to his body. With no alternative, they curled up and slept on the icy shore.

Dawn brought a blessed sight: Ice had formed between the island and the far shore. They dragged themselves ten more miles to a trading post. By New Year's Day, they reached Wills Creek. Washington called the journey "as fatiguing . . . as it is possible to conceive." He hurried on with the French reply, reaching Williamsburg on January 16 after nearly eleven weeks of grueling, freezing travel.[32]

Washington brought Governor Dinwiddie exactly what he wanted: confirmation that Britain was at risk of losing the west. The French reply claimed the Ohio valley for France, a claim reinforced by Washington's description of new French forts. London had authorized Dinwiddie to challenge French "hostility"; building forts on King George's land met that standard. Washington also reported that Tanaghrisson opposed the French. Thoroughly pleased with the young man's performance, the Executive Council promptly called for him to command one hundred militia on the frontier, with Captain William Trent to raise additional fighters. Dinwiddie summoned the General Assembly to consider other measures.[33]

To justify his move against the French, the governor ordered that Washington's report be published. With customary humility about his writing skills, Washington apologized for his prose in the preface to the printed edition, claiming he wrote the report in a single day.[34]

His saga was a gripping narrative that bristled with savages of uncertain loyalties, diabolical Frenchmen who swilled wine while insulting British rights, and dangerous travel in an unforgiving season. The intrepid narrator eluded every danger. American newspapers printed Washington's report verbatim. *The Gentleman's Magazine* in London did too. Washington became a hero at barely twenty-two years old.[35]

For the young colonial, it was a brilliant start. He had exercised judgment and tenacity in navigating tricky diplomatic ground among Indians and Frenchmen, also displaying physical stamina, strength, and courage. The world celebrated him. It was a heady experience for one so young, an experience that might breed self-assurance. Even overconfidence.

CHAPTER 6

First Command

Virginia's lack of military tradition had allowed Washington to rise speedily, but it muddled the attempt to send an effective fighting force to the frontier. The colonial government had no system of recruitment or supply, and little money. Leading citizens held the title of colonel of their county militias, but few had led soldiers on campaign. The colony's last armed expedition had been the Cartagena embarrassment that Lawrence Washington joined a decade before. A British officer had scorned those Americans as "all the banditry the colonies could afford."[1]

Nonetheless, Governor Dinwiddie proposed to send Virginians against French professionals, Canadian frontiersmen, and Indian warriors. Because the Forks of the Ohio was so important, he ordered Captain Trent, a trader, to build a fort there and hold it with a hundred "woodsmen" plus sympathetic Indians. The governor issued a parallel commission for Washington to support Trent with fifty militia from each of the two counties nearest the Forks.[2]

Because Virginia militia had no duty to serve beyond the colony's borders, Washington's men never appeared. Many Virginians suspected that the expedition was designed to further the Ohio Company's business. The governor pivoted to a new approach, proposing that the colony raise a volunteer force. As an incentive, he pledged that 200,000 acres of land—half near the Forks, the rest near the Ohio River—would be divided among volunteers when they completed their service.[3]

Dinwiddie also sought funding for war from the colony's General Assembly, which consisted of a twelve-member upper house (the Executive Council), appointed by the governor, and the House of Burgesses, which held two representatives elected from each county.[4] Both houses and the governor had to approve legislation, which then had to be blessed by the king's government in London. Although the lawmaking process could consume a year or more, Virginians had greater political autonomy than most human beings in 1759. Both legislative bodies met in closed session. Only their final actions were announced publicly.

The House of Burgesses, discontented with the governor's spending, approved only £10,000 for the military push, while requiring that a legislative committee approve all expenditures. Dinwiddie thought that condition illegal, but he swallowed it. Money in hand, he announced that the colony would recruit six companies of fifty volunteers each.[5]

Events did not wait for the politicians. Captain Trent's company, with some Indians, reached the Forks in mid-February. In the freezing Appalachian winter, Tanaghrisson showed his British allegiance by laying the fort's first timber, but he complained that the British never intended to stay. Growing nervous over reports that four hundred Frenchmen were approaching, Trent's men urged Washington to hurry with reinforcements.[6]

Even with the offer of free land, few volunteers stepped forward, and those few, Washington reported, were "loose, idle persons" without homes or clothes. Supplies ranged from haphazard to nonexistent. Washington complained that he had neither weapons nor uniforms for the twenty-five men on hand. He feared the men could not survive the winter, while they raised "a pretty general clamor" about not being paid.[7]

Undeterred, the governor pressed on, awarding overall command to Joshua Fry, a former math professor at the College of William & Mary. Fry had negotiated with Indians and served as a militia captain, but had never seen combat. Though Washington acknowledged that his inexperience disqualified him for the top position, he agitated for "a commission above that of a major, and to be ranked among the chief officers of this expedition." Dinwiddie complied, appointing him lieutenant colonel.[8]

On April 2, Washington marched out of Alexandria with 120 untrained men he called "selfwilled, ungovernable." When they reached Winchester a week later, another forty joined them under the command of a Scot, Adam Stephen. Destined to be Washington's colleague and rival, Stephen was a physician nearly a decade older. He had served in the Royal Navy, then began a medical practice in Virginia. Colonel Fairfax recommended him.[9]

Washington scoured the Winchester area for wagons and horses to haul supplies to the Forks two hundred miles away. After a week, he fumed that some of his horses were so broken down that "the soldiers were obliged to assist them up the hills." He claimed twenty-four wagons from surrounding farms, but only ten arrived. Washington's seizures became so high-handed that the county court issued three warrants for *his* arrest. The sheriff returned all three warrants without executing them, noting meekly that Washington "would not be taken he kept me off by force of arms."[10]

Feeding the men was a challenge. In springtime, no crops were ripening, and settlers had consumed their winter stores. On forest paths, horses found little grazing, so wagons had to carry their feed. Livestock grew gaunt. Nonetheless, Washington pressed on, fearing that the French were closing in on Trent's company at the Forks. Dinwiddie relayed encouraging information. London had ordered to Virginia three "independent companies," colonist-soldiers commanded by regular army officers—two from New York and one from South Carolina. Washington rode ahead to Wills Creek, still searching for horses and wagons.[11]

On April 22, a messenger arrived from the Forks with bad news. More than a thousand Frenchmen, with eighteen cannons and four hundred boats, had reached the Forks. The garrison's thirty-odd defenders briskly surrendered and left. Tanaghrisson's message was that without British aid, "we are entirely undone, and imagine we shall never meet again."[12]

It was a deflating failure. Without firing a shot, the French already had taken the principal objective of both sides. The failure was not Washington's. Had he managed to reach the Forks with his ill-prepared company, he would have been overwhelmed too. The French had prepared their advance for two years and executed it methodically. The British had resolved on a military effort three months before and then mostly ran in circles.

To reassure Tanaghrisson, Washington wrote that the British were clearing a road for "a great number of our warriors that are immediately to follow with our great guns, our ammunition, and our provisions." Having substantially overstated the facts, he pledged to continue resisting the French. The young officer's next steps demonstrated more energy than judgment. Following a council with his officers, Washington set off for the junction of Redstone Creek and the Monongahela River, about thirty-five miles upstream (to the south) from the Forks. He proposed to build a base there to support a waterborne advance on the Forks. The move was ill conceived. Washington's company was too small to oppose the French, while his supply situation grew worse every day.[13]

Through the next several weeks, Washington struggled to control his men while fielding alarming reports of French strength. He sent sixty men to improve the road toward Redstone Creek while he tried to determine the best route from there to the Forks, setting out in a canoe to scout alternatives. No reinforcements arrived. The independent company from South Carolina, commanded by Captain James Mackay, was in Virginia by early May but made no move toward the frontier. Colonel Fry lingered at Alexandria.[14]

In the midst of these frustrations, Washington forwarded to the governor his officers' complaints that their pay was too low, a grievance he seconded, describing himself as "slaving dangerously for the shadow of pay." He offered to serve for no reward other "than the satisfaction of serving my country," and concluded with a bracing gust of realism: "Upon the whole, I find so many clogs upon the expedition that I quite despair of success."[15]

Although the officers and soldiers in Washington's service were receiving lower pay than Trent's men (who had been hired as laborers) or those in the independent companies, Dinwiddie's response was tart: Objections to pay, he noted, "should have been made before engaging in the service. The gentlemen very well knew the terms on which they were to serve and were satisfied then with it." The governor told Washington to control the men he commanded.[16]

Dinwiddie's message came from Winchester, where the governor was to confer with Tanaghrisson and other chiefs of the Ohio Indians, hoping to recruit Indian allies to buttress Virginia's too-small numbers against the French. Colonel Fairfax and two other Executive Council members were there too.[17]

Thus, for several months in the late spring and early summer of 1754, Virginia's colonial government largely revolved around Washington and his grumbling soldiers in the western forests. In that heady moment, he was squarely in the unforgiving spotlight of history. From an exposed position, Washington faced a much stronger enemy who might be a short march away. His supply system was dodgy and his soldiers poorly trained. No matter how much he scanned the eastern horizon, it never filled with reinforcements. If he did not withdraw his men in time, they could be at the mercy of the enemy.

CHAPTER 7

Blooded

By May 29, Washington had much to tell Dinwiddie. Stung by the governor's criticism on the pay issue, Washington affirmed he would stay in the service despite its hardships, boasting that he had "a constitution hardy enough to encounter and undergo the most severe trials." He acknowledged the governor's generosity toward him, adding he despised the "black and detestable" sin of ingratitude. After devoting twelve hundred words to other matters, he reached the major news: He had fought the French, and he had won.[1]

Tanaghrisson had warned that the French soon would attack Washington's force, which was hacking slowly through the woods to Redstone Creek. The Virginians camped at Great Meadows, a rare clearing. Washington had his men remove bushes to afford open fields of fire, leaving what he called "a charming field for an encounter" with the enemy. An alarm in the middle of the night proved to be false. It was Virginia deserters running away, not a French attack.[2]

On May 27, Christopher Gist reported that the French were nearby. Tanaghrisson sent word that he was tracking some of the enemy. In a heavy nighttime rain, Washington led forty men out to join the hunt. Blundering through the inky darkness, the Virginians strayed from the path, tripping over roots, rocks, and one another. At sunrise, they found Tanaghrisson a short distance from the French camp. Washington resolved to attack.

The French slept without sentries, sheltered on one side by a tall rock wall. Washington divided his small force. Captain Stephen took soldiers to the top of the rock face, which allowed them to fire directly down on the French.

Washington led others to the high end of the camp. Tanaghrisson and his Indians took the low end.

The skirmish lasted barely fifteen minutes, long enough to start a world war and three centuries of controversy. Washington began by leading his men down on the camp. When enemy soldiers scrambled for weapons, he said, the Virginians opened fire, driving the French before them. Stephen said the Virginians advanced with bayonets because rain had soaked their gunpowder. The French later insisted that they called out that they were a peaceful, diplomatic mission. One claimed they never raised their guns, an assertion refuted by the Virginians' loss of one dead and two wounded. The French suffered ten dead and one wounded; twenty-one others were captured.[3]

The ratio of French killed and wounded—ten to one—signals an irregularity; in combat, the injured ordinarily outnumber the dead by two or three to one. The ratio in this skirmish suggests that Frenchmen tried to surrender, but the youthful Virginia commander could not control his Indian allies, who did most of the killing with tomahawks. An especially grisly encounter involved Tanaghrisson's telling the wounded French commander, "You are not dead yet, my father," splitting his skull, then washing his hands with the Frenchman's brains. Several days later, Washington confirmed the basic sequence of the scrap, relating that his Indian allies "served to knock the poor unhappy wounded in the head and bereaved them of their scalps."[4]

When the killing was done, the survivors protested that they were a diplomatic party, a claim that became a sore point when France insisted that Washington assassinated a peaceable diplomat. The French commander, the Sieur de Jumonville, did carry a demand that the British vacate French lands, but that was not his only mission. He also was instructed to "see what is transacting" in the Ohio valley and report his observations—in short, diplomacy plus intelligence-gathering.[5]

Washington insisted the French were spies, stressing that they came in force (thirty-three men), not as a small diplomatic party like the one he had led months before. Rather than approach Washington directly, Jumonville had lain concealed nearby for two nights, sending off runners to report intelligence about the Virginians. Captain Stephen and Tanaghrisson concurred. The French had "bad hearts," the Indian leader said, "and if we were so foolish as to let them go again, he would never . . . have come to us but in a hostile manner."[6]

Washington denied that the French called out to stop the attack. "I was the first man that approached them," he wrote, and they "immediately . . . ran to their arms and fired briskly till they were defeated."[7]

Washington had ample justification for attacking Jumonville's party. For two years and more, the French had seized British traders. They rejected Dinwiddie's demand to vacate the valley, boasted that they would drive off the English, recruited Indian allies, and seized the Forks by force.[8] Under the circumstances, Jumonville's contingent could hardly be surprised by a British attack. Being caught unprepared was their failure.

The encounter exhilarated Washington. He had seen combat, held steady, and won. He boasted to his brother Jack of "a most signal victory," adding that he escaped injury "though the right wing where I stood was exposed to and received all the enemy's fire." He added that he heard bullets whistle and found "something charming in the sound." When that letter appeared in the *London Magazine*—something an ambitious officer might arrange—King George II commented drily: "He would not say so, if he had been used to hear many."[9]

American newspapers reported Washington's exploits, including the Jumonville incident. The Virginian became a man to watch. In early July, a Philadelphia paper published an excerpt from a letter he supposedly wrote: "If the whole detachment of the French behave with no more resolution than this chosen party did," the letter crowed, "I flatter myself we shall have no great trouble in driving them to . . . Montreal." From a stockade built at Great Meadows, he reported, he could repel five hundred men.[10]

The letter was wrong. The bloodletting was only beginning. The French were stronger than Washington was. They would not leave the Ohio valley anytime soon.

∾

Governor Dinwiddie sent Washington a medal and pushed for other British forces to join him. Colonel Fry had been slowed by an "indisposition." The South Carolina company was creeping up the Potomac. North Carolinians and two independent companies from New York had gone missing. Totaling nine hundred men, those groups might jointly recover the Forks if they arrived before the Virginia commander did something reckless. Dinwiddie warned Washington against a "hazardous attempt against a too numerous adversary."[11]

Just two days after the Jumonville encounter, Colonel Fry died in a fall from a horse. Dinwiddie promoted Washington to full colonel, then named James Innes, commander of the North Carolinians, as commander in chief. Washington expressed gratitude for his promotion, professing to be "happy under the command of an experienced officer and a man of sense."[12]

With Innes still in transit, Washington had his hands full. Impressed with the fighting skills of Indians, he sought tribal allies. Early in June, Tanaghrisson brought some eighty Mingoes to the Great Meadows, including women and children, while another chief displayed French scalps to Indian villages, trying to demonstrate British determination.[13]

A week later, Captain James Mackay arrived in camp with his South Carolinians, but they soon became a disruption. Mackay, who had held a king's commission for fifteen years, denied Washington was his superior. In truth, provincial officers like Washington did not ordinarily command those with a king's commission. Yet Mackay took an extreme position, refusing even to recognize the daily password set by Washington for sentries. His men refused, with Mackay's backing, to join the roadbuilding work. Fearing that the squabble "will be a canker that will grate some officers of this regiment beyond all measure," Washington appealed to Dinwiddie to bring Mackay to heel. After proclaiming Innes in charge, Washington as his second, and Mackay as their subordinate, Dinwiddie urged all three to "lay aside any little punctilios in rank."[14]

The Virginians who had been with Colonel Fry finally reached Washington's camp, straining further its limited food supplies. After the first week of June, Washington had no flour, only parched corn and some meat from lean cattle. By month's end, the soldiers went without meat or bread for six days.[15]

Washington, still hoping to reclaim the Forks, did not withdraw. By mid-May, the French fort there stood chest-high, with a thickness of twelve feet of earth and stone. Scouts estimated the French strength at between 600 and 1,000 men, double or triple Washington's numbers.[16]

Washington's attempt to recruit more Indian fighters failed. He twice dispatched men to clear the road to Redstone Creek and the Monongahela. Mackay's South Carolinians again refused to work, idling at the Great Meadows stockade, renamed Fort Necessity.[17]

That last decision—working toward the Monongahela at the end of June—moved Washington's force in the wrong direction despite Dinwiddie's warning that he should fear a surprise, that "the French act with great secrecy and cunning." Scouts reported that more than a thousand Frenchmen and Indians would soon be on the march. The British work party in the woods, starving, straggled back toward Fort Necessity. Undernourished soldiers had to haul cannon by hand. On July 1, they arrived, too worn to withdraw farther.[18]

Fort Necessity, however, offered little safety. The circular stockade, fifty-three feet in diameter, stood at the center of open ground. It consisted of split oak logs sunk into the ground, roughly seven feet high, with trenches along its sides. At a key point, the woods were less than a musket shot away. A modern military expert has called the site "so poorly sited and so dubiously constructed . . . that only an amateur or a fool would have thought it defensible." Washington's error might be charged to inexperience, though Captain Mackay, a soldier since Washington was seven years old, also did not see the structure as a trap. Tanaghrisson did. On the day after the work party reached the fort's illusory shelter, the Indians left, uninterested in noble defeats. Even Tanaghrisson left, calling the fort "that little thing upon the meadow." When the battle began, not a single Indian stood with the British.[19]

A French force of seven hundred, led by the slain Jumonville's brother, took nearly a week to reach Fort Necessity. After waiting in the woods through the night of July 2, they attacked in a morning rainstorm. Washington's outnumbered men were deepening their trenches when the enemy emerged from the forest. The British colonists drew up in formation as French musket fire began, but then the French retired into the woods. The colonists ducked into their trenches and waited for a frontal assault that never came. The enemy shrewdly chose to shoot from cover in the forest.[20]

As Washington saw the battle, the colonists faced an "enemy sheltered behind the trees, ourselves without shelter, in trenches full of water, in a settled rain, and the enemy galling us on all sides." What Washington had called a "charming field for an encounter" turned out to be a killing field for his men.[21]

British muskets misfired in the rain. That problem was so common in the eighteenth century that a special tool was used to clear from a gun barrel the damp powder, ball, and cartridge. The tool (a "screw" or "worm") was a coil attached to the end of a ramrod. When inserted into the barrel and twisted, the ramrod-plus-screw would hook the jammed material so it could be pulled out. Washington's men, however, had only two screws, which meant that many huddled quietly during the fight, unable to return fire, hoping not to be shot.

The firing kept up until late afternoon, Washington recalled later, "when there fell the most tremendous rain that can be conceived—filled our trenches with water." The defenders' casualties piled up. French bullets sheared splinters from the stockade and propelled them deep into the soldiers' flesh. By the battle's end, one-third of Washington's men would be dead or wounded. After a day of receiving French fire, surrounded by corpses and the groans of the wounded, Washington's men plundered the rum supply. Some got drunk.[22]

Although the French held the upper hand, the weather hampered them too. Their ammunition ran low and their Indian allies announced they would leave in the morning. Reports falsely claimed that British reinforcements were approaching. The French decided that they had avenged Jumonville and did not need to exterminate their foes. At nightfall, under a flag of truce, they offered to accept Washington's surrender.[23]

Washington initially thought it was a trick. Why would the enemy relent when his position was so hopeless? Persuaded that the overture was genuine, he sent two officers to negotiate terms. One was Jacob Van Braam, the Dutchman who spoke French. Washington remained in the stockade to try to maintain order.[24]

Having little leverage for bargaining, the colonial officers returned near midnight with a document prepared by the French—in French, of course—and titled "Capitulation." Washington relied on Van Braam to translate it in the rain, surrounded by a nightmarish collection of corpses, drunks, and wounded. The candlelight faltered and the ink on the agreement ran.[25] In return for withdrawing from the Ohio country for one year, the defenders would be allowed to leave with their wounded and their weapons. That last provision, affording Washington the "honors of war," was critical to the proud Virginian. The agreement also required that Washington deliver two officers as hostages until he had relinquished the prisoners taken when Jumonville was killed.

Washington and Adam Stephen always maintained that Van Braam never mentioned a key provision in the document: the statement in the first article that the French had acted to "revenge the *assassination* of" Jumonville.[26] The term was political dynamite, an admission that the attack on Jumonville was unwarranted. Three years later, France published the treaty as justification for its decision to go to war. A British general called the capitulation document "the most infamous a British subject ever put his hand to." Washington fervently insisted "we were willfully, or ignorantly, deceived by our interpreter in regard to the word *assassination,* I do aver, and will to my dying moment; so will every officer that was present." He was paying a high price for his ignorance of the French language.[27]

In the morning, the colonists departed. Washington and Mackay reported their own losses accurately: thirty dead and seventy wounded. To protect their reputations, they vastly inflated French casualties to three hundred killed and wounded. Few were fooled by the lie. The official French tally was three killed and seventeen wounded.[28]

∾

Washington's loss was a strategic setback, compounded by the diplomatic bungle of the capitulation. The most telling criticism came from Tanaghrisson, who complained that Washington tended to "command the Indians as his slaves." The Indian said that he and his fellows left Fort Necessity "because Colonel Washington would never listen to them, but [was] always driving them on to fight by his directions."[29]

Sir William Johnson of New York, that colony's leading agent with the Iroquois, feared that the defeat would drive tribes into the arms of France. He insisted that Washington "should rather have avoided an engagement until our troops were all assembled." A British observer lamented that provincials like Washington "have no knowledge and experience in our [military] profession; consequently there can be no dependence on them!"[30]

Washington's blunders were plain. He had put weak, underfed men in harm's way, clearing a road to Redstone Creek that was not yet needed, ignoring reports of the enemy's strength. He stayed in an indefensible position rather than withdraw to find reinforcements and replenish his supplies. In a paternal letter, Colonel Fairfax made these points. The legendary Duke of Marlborough, he wrote, had ordered "many wise retreats . . . that were not called flights."[31]

Governor Dinwiddie confided privately that "Washington's conduct was in many steps wrong, and did not conform to his orders from me." The Virginian, he continued, should not have engaged the enemy without reinforcements. But Dinwiddie did not dissent when the House of Burgesses voted its thanks to Washington and his officers "for their late gallant and brave behavior in the defense of their country." Dinwiddie, after all, had placed Washington in command and sent him off with not enough men or support, hoping to stitch together a victory from stray units cobbled together at the last moment. If blame were to be assigned for the defeat at Fort Necessity, the governor would receive a healthy slice.[32]

In any event, the defeat might persuade the assembly and London to provide more funds for Dinwiddie's campaign. He had wanted a war over the Ohio valley. After Fort Necessity, he had one.

The experience converted the elation following the Jumonville skirmish into regret and recrimination. Though Washington avoided public admission of his mistakes, his errors had inflicted terrible losses on his men.[33] He never wrote about his feelings when leading men to their deaths. Military commanders rarely do.

Fort Necessity provided important lessons beyond the poor location and layout of the fort itself. Naturally aggressive, Washington had pushed too hard. Eager to take the Forks, he failed to recognize that he was in the wrong place, outnumbered, and unready. He needed to be more attentive to the risks he and his men faced. He would absorb those lessons eventually, but not right away.

The Fort Necessity campaign delivered another important lesson. Half-starved, largely stranded in difficult country, and surrounded by enemies, the officers and men had followed Washington. They hacked at the wilderness for weeks to build a road of little use. They stood with him at Fort Necessity through a day of bloodshed and misery. And afterward, no officer—not even Captain Mackay—criticized him.[34] The experience confirmed that Washington could command men's loyalty and inspire them to grapple with difficult challenges. He had the precognitive gift of command, a gift rooted in the way he walked and held himself, his gestures, how he spoke and connected with people.

He and Captain Mackay brought their unhappy, hurting soldiers to Winchester, then traveled on to Williamsburg to report to the governor. France and Britain would not declare war against each other for another two years, when the conflict spread across the globe, but Washington, not for the last time in his life, had been at the hinge of history.

CHAPTER 8

Picking Up the Pieces

Following the Fort Necessity defeat, many of Washington's shattered men found desertion an appealing option. "There is scarce a night," he wrote in late summer, "but what some or other are deserting, and often two three or 4 at a time." He offered rewards for the return of deserters, but the regiment still lost two-thirds of its men in three months. The officers grumbled anew about their pay. New troops arrived from North Carolina, then turned around and went home.[1]

The powerful men in Williamsburg ignored these problems. Governor Dinwiddie and his Executive Council ordered Colonel James Innes to drive the French from Fort Duquesne. In a slight bow to reality, they added that if he could not do that, he should build a British fort nearby that would threaten the French. The governor insisted on the attack because he did not think "soldiers in pay should eat the bread of idleness."[2]

Washington knew the order was preposterous, but this time he responded indirectly, sending a thoughtful dissent to Colonel Fairfax, knowing that his letter would be shared with Dinwiddie and the council. (The deftness of the move raises the suspicion that it was Colonel Fairfax's idea.) After describing the proposed offensive as impractical and "morally impossible," Washington wrote that the regiment lacked men, provisions, ammunition, and tools. As to clothing, "scarcely a man has either shoes, stockings or hat." Morale had withered. When the rumor spread that they would return to the frontier, six men deserted in one night. An autumn advance, Washington continued, would involve "snows, want of forage, slipperiness of the roads, high waters." Recalling his journey to the French forts the winter before, Washington added that three of the six men in his party had been "rendered useless by the frost," while the horses had weakened and died. He added that he had no gifts with which to recruit tribal allies, who were asking "if we meant to starve them as well as ourselves."[3]

In early September, the House of Burgesses approved £20,000 for a renewed expedition to the frontier, but attached conditions that the Executive Council rejected. A captain in the regiment dismissed the legislators with a Latin phrase (in translation): "They came furtively, they sat idly, they departed in confusion." Dinwiddie sent the burgesses home for six weeks, hoping they would return in a more generous frame of mind.[4]

Denied funds, the governor invited the governors of North Carolina and Maryland to Williamsburg to discuss the western situation. He pleaded with London for money. He ordered Washington to return to Wills Creek and send forty to fifty men to the frontier to protect settlers. He again asked Lord Fairfax to call out the Frederick County militia. Not a single man had answered his lordship's call in January; the Fort Necessity defeat would only reduce the enthusiasm for militia service.[5]

Yet the governor's efforts bore fruit. North Carolina's governor arrived from Britain carrying £10,000 in coin, plus a promise of credit for a like amount, plus promise of a forthcoming arms shipment. The three governors adopted a plan to attack Fort Duquesne. The burgesses matched the home government, approving a tax to produce another £20,000, dropping the conditions the Executive Council had found odious. They also adopted a law to draft for frontier service any men between twenty-one and fifty "who have no visible way of getting an honest livelihood." And Dinwiddie reorganized the Virginia Regiment into ten companies of one hundred men, each commanded by a captain; that eliminated Washington's position as colonel.[6]

The abolition of Washington's position was no accident. A seasoned bureaucratic operator, Dinwiddie did not jettison senior personnel by mistake. He had lost confidence in the prickly young commander who evidently was carrying more responsibility than he could handle.[7]

Washington resigned. When an aide to the new British commander urged him to continue in the service, the Virginian replied haughtily: "The disparity between the present offer of a company, and my former rank, [is] too great to expect any real satisfaction or enjoyment." When an alternative post was suggested, Washington sniffed, "You must entertain a very contemptible opinion of my weakness." Yet Washington did not abandon his military ambitions. He observed near the end of his letter that, nevertheless, "my inclinations are strongly bent to arms."[8]

∾

Washington returned to private life but did not have to support himself with surveying. He had his back pay and rents from the Bullskin Creek properties, and was the military adjutant for the Northern Neck. He did, however, need somewhere to live, a home suitable for the former commander of the Virginia Regiment. He could hardly move in with his mother and brothers at Ferry Farm. He stayed with the Fairfaxes at Belvoir while arranging to take over Mount Vernon, which was vacant because Lawrence's widow had remarried and moved to her new husband's home. She agreed to lease the property and its slaves to Washington for a modest 15,000 pounds of tobacco per year, the equivalent of £64. Should any slave die during the lease period, the rent would drop.[9]

He signed the open-ended lease in December. So long as Washington paid his rent, he had a lifetime right to Mount Vernon. Anne's only surviving child by Lawrence died before the lease was signed. If Anne died next, Washington would inherit the estate under Lawrence's will. A week before signing the lease, Anne and her husband divided Lawrence's remaining sixty slaves, including sixteen children, with Washington and his brothers.[10]

With his personal fortunes improving, Washington ordered clothes from England and began a lifetime of sprucing up Mount Vernon. He bought slaves, furniture, and livestock. In the early spring, his mother arrived to help her bachelor son establish himself in the home she had managed twenty years before. In August, Washington's remaining elder brother, Austin, won a seat in the House of Burgesses from Westmoreland County.[11]

Washington's time in civilian life proved brief. The British government resolved to avenge Fort Necessity, sending two regiments to Virginia with General Edward Braddock in command. Braddock's advance on Fort Duquesne would be part of a three-pronged attack against the French in America. Ironically, enthusiasm for war was greater in London than among Virginians. When the colony's new conscription law took effect, protests and riots erupted in Petersburg and Fredericksburg.[12]

By early January of 1755, Virginians knew that the frontier war was about to grow hotter. Washington would not sit that out at Mount Vernon.[13]

∾

Britain, however, did not send its best to America. The two new regiments were notorious for fleeing the Battle of Prestonpans a decade before, during a Scottish uprising in favor of the Stuart pretenders to the throne. Their commander, Braddock, had little battlefield experience and an overbearing manner. John Carlyle, an Alexandria merchant, came to regret opening his house to Braddock and his staff, as they "used us like an enemy country & took everything they wanted and paid nothing." When the Virginians complained, "they cursed the country and inhabitants, calling us the spawn of convicts, the sweepings of the jails."[14]

General Edward Braddock

More disturbing than Braddock's manners, though, were his work habits. One contemporary described him as "glad for anyone to take business off his hands." An aide thought Braddock, known for a sulfurous temper, "disqualified for the service he is employed in, in almost every respect." John Carlyle dismissed him as a man "of weak understanding, very indolent, [and] slave to his passions, women and wine."[15]

Even if they were less than the nation's best, the British regulars exuded a professionalism that was new to Virginians. At their camp outside Alexandria, the army drilled in crisp red coats with silk cuffs over white collars and waistcoats, red breeches tucked into white spatterdashes and buttoned above the knees. Their hair was clubbed and tied at the nape of the neck with a black ribbon; on important occasions, flour or rice powder whitened their locks. Officers strutted in wigs, lace stock and cuffs, red sashes, and gleaming black boots. Braddock presided from a wide marquee in a forest of white tents.[16]

For Washington, it was a glittering opportunity. If he could find a position with Braddock, he might escape Governor Dinwiddie's disapproval, as well as the bedraggled Virginia soldiers and their modest appetite for combat. Ever eager to advance, he hoped to "form an acquaintance which may be serviceable hereafter" for a military career.[17]

After an overture on Washington's behalf, which certainly came from the Fairfaxes, Braddock's top aide invited him to join the general's personal staff (his "family"). Washington specified that he would serve as a volunteer, without pay, with the rank of colonel, so officers with royal commissions could not claim precedence over him as a mere colonial.[18]

The situation displayed Washington's complex attitudes toward money and reputation. He insisted to a friend that his "sole motive" in joining the expedition was to win Virginia's "approbation and esteem." But he had to balance his craving for reputation with his anxiety over money. Fearing that Mount Vernon would deteriorate during his absence, he claimed reimbursement for losses during the Fort Necessity campaign (a servant's death, plus lost clothes, surveying equipment, and horses). He had to borrow £40 from Lord Fairfax.[19]

Washington's new position exposed him to British military systems, but left him free of cares about supply, ordnance, and transportation.[20] He met men he would fight with and against in the future. Major Thomas Gage, a friend in these years, would become an opponent. Horatio Gates and Charles Lee would become colleagues and rivals. For the next three decades, he would intersect repeatedly with Pennsylvania politician Benjamin Franklin.[21]

When the westward march began in late April, Washington discovered that, despite Braddock's reputation for ill temper, they got along. The general "requires less ceremony than you can easily conceive," Washington wrote to his brother Jack, who was managing Mount Vernon and the Bullskin lands while Washington was away. Although Braddock quarreled with many, Washington reported that the general treated him "with freedom not inconsistent with respect."[22]

Virginia's soldiery, mostly volunteers attracted by a cash bounty, plus homeless men who were conscripted, made a poor impression. A senior British officer wrote that the Virginians' "sloth and ignorance is not to be described." Another found that their "languid, spiritless, and unsoldierlike appearance considered with the lowness and ignorance of most of their officers gave little hope of their future good behavior." Washington's view was nearly as negative. He complained that it took two days to assemble a militia escort for him, but the men instantly would have fled upon the approach of an enemy.[23]

The general and his aide parted company, however, on the fighting qualities of Indians. Washington knew Indian allies were essential to frontier warfare. Braddock did not. He brushed off Ben Franklin's warning about the risk of ambush, assuring the Pennsylvanian that "these savages may, indeed, be a formidable enemy to your raw American militia, but upon the king's regular and disciplined troops, sir, it is impossible they should make any impression."[24] At a council with Indian leaders, Braddock foolishly declared that "no savage should inherit the land." That was exactly what Indians feared. A key war leader of the Delawares, who had intended to join the British, led his warriors home instead, denouncing Braddock. The Delawares would be implacable British foes for the next three years, while Braddock would be crippled by the lack of Indian allies.[25]

CHAPTER 9

A Worse Catastrophe

Washington expected Braddock's advance to Fort Duquesne to be slow and grinding. The British and Virginia troops had to cross mountain ranges divided by plunging ravines and churning waterways. Much of the land was unknown to whites, who feared Indian ambush at every turn. From high points, the forest stretched before them without end.[1]

For nearly half of the two hundred miles to the fort, Braddock's men had to cut a road through the trees and over the mountains. They needed enough horses and wagons to haul twenty-nine artillery pieces, with shot, shells, gunpowder, and equipment. On good roads, that would require more than two hundred horses, plus many more to carry food and equipment for the soldiers and feed for the horses. But the expedition would never see anything like a good road. To speed the advance, Braddock decided against building resupply bases along the line of march, which meant that everything had to be carried from Fort Cumberland all the way to the army (see map on p. 57), multiplying the need for horses and wagons. Braddock calculated that he needed two hundred fifty wagons and twenty-five hundred horses. As Washington had learned the year before, both were scarce on the frontier.[2] The advance stayed close to schedule only because Ben Franklin met his pledge to deliver one hundred wagons and fifteen hundred horses to Fort Cumberland. Braddock proclaimed the episode "almost the only instance of ability and honesty I have known in these provinces."[3]

Braddock raged over supply failures and much else. In early June, Washington reported to Colonel Fairfax that the general showed "want of that temper and moderation which should be used by a man of sense." Washington, who discovered that Braddock did not resent being challenged, advised the general to hold his temper.

We have frequent dispu[tes] . . . , which are maintained with warmth on both sides especially on his, who is incapable of . . . giving up any point he asserts, let it be ever so incompatible with reason or commonsense.[4]

The roads were a nightmare. A senior British officer called the stretch from Fredericksburg to Winchester "very bad," and the one to Fort Cumberland "the worst road I ever traveled." There the roads ended.[5]

On May 30, six hundred men with axes and shovels set out from Fort Cumberland to chop out a twelve-foot-wide passage that crossed countless streams and rivers. Soldiers on either flank patrolled against ambush, bears, and wolves; nothing could protect against poisonous snakes. They opened only two miles that first day, ruining three wagons and damaging many others. "The ascent and descent were almost perpendicular rock," according to Braddock's senior aide. Washington called the effort "very tedious."[6]

Even though eighteenth-century standards for roadbuilding were low, the wilderness made each step more difficult. American roadbuilders ordinarily followed Indian trails, which tracked land contours over high ground and stable soils. The Braddock expedition mostly followed a path marked three years earlier by Christopher Gist and Nemacolin, a Shawnee. Washington's Virginians had scoured out a rough track as far as Fort Necessity at Great Meadows, but never finished the leg to Redstone Creek.[7]

When a full team was at work, a hundred axmen chopped at once; a hundred more levered rocks and stumps from the path; another hundred threw the limbs and tree trunks aside, a hundred others used shovels to fill in holes and smoothed the roughest patches with rakes or crude scrapers drawn by horses. They skirted large trees and rocks. If they could not swerve around wetlands, they filled in soft spots with tree trunks laid sideways, producing a bouncy "corduroy" effect. Engineers built rough bridges across streams. They labored in a dark, claustrophobic forest. Swaying branches blotted out the sky. The men called one passage the "Shades of Death" because interlaced treetops blocked most light. Clouds of gnats and mosquitoes tortured roadbuilders and flankers as the work parties chewed through the woods like strange horizontal organisms.[8]

The resulting road ranged from unreliable to atrocious. Horses dragged ponderous wagons around holes and over roots and stumps, through mire and muck on wet days and over bare, rain-slick rock. The horses strained at their loads, weakening daily. Some died in harness. A morning could be consumed in traveling a quarter mile. Numerous wagons smashed on descents.[9]

By the second week of June, dismayed by the slow advance, Braddock sent some of the equipment back to Fort Cumberland. On June 15, he assigned

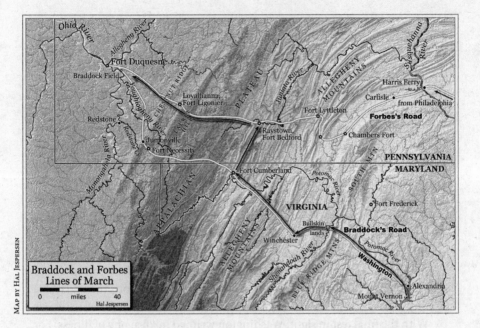

*Braddock's Road and Forbes's Road in white; the black line traces the route of
Washington's Virginians to join Forbes in 1758.*

half the men to push wagons up a difficult slope. So many horses died that the
baggage train lagged. Wagons began to carry half loads to each new campsite, then doubled back for the rest.[10] The army abandoned routes already
built when the horses could not manage them. When wagons and cannons
sank into mudholes to their wheel hubs and beyond, a navy unit pulled them
out with block and tackle.[11]

On the frontier, where no human might be seen for days, Braddock's
army could hardly be concealed from enemy scouts. In addition to using
flankers to guard against ambush, Braddock issued standing orders covering
the pitching of camp at day's end. Half the men were to form a defensive circle
around the campsite, arms at the ready, while the remainder raised their tents.
Then they changed places.[12]

But written orders did not magically translate into action. When the column of men and wagons encountered difficult going, it could stretch out for
four miles, beyond the shelter of flankers. If the column "had been attacked
either in front, center or rear," Washington fretted, it would be "cut off or
totally routed."[13]

Braddock issued no special instructions for repelling an attack, which
meant that the soldiers would respond as they had been trained: Assemble in

formations several lines deep to concentrate musket fire against an enemy in a similar formation. Braddock and his soldiers would soon learn how those tactics worked against Indians in the forest.

In the third week of June, the impatient commander adopted a recommendation from Washington to speed the advance by dividing his force.[14] Braddock moved ahead with his twelve hundred best troops, carrying only light baggage on packhorses, plus three wagonloads of tools. The lead column still had to halt for two days on June 20 to wait for road gangs to finish a mountainside track and fill in swamps. On June 24, the army used rope-and-tackle to lower gun carriages down a steep hill.

Though the progress felt glacial, enemy resistance told the British that they were nearing Fort Duquesne. On June 25, Indian raiders shot and scalped three British soldiers who strayed from camp. The same thing happened on July 6, less than twenty miles from the French fort. Scouts reported that the French were low on supplies. The tension built. The fighting would come soon. If Braddock could train his heavy guns on the fort, the odds were heavily in his favor. The British grew eager.[15]

With the final test in sight, Washington writhed in an agony of illness. For nine days, he was "seized with violent fevers and pains in my head which continued without intermission." The doctor warned that if Washington stayed on duty, he would die. Braddock ordered Washington into confinement, and gave the Virginian his Dr. James's Fever Powder, a favored nostrum.[16]

Washington sputtered with frustration to his brother Jack. "Instead of pushing on with vigor, without regarding a little rough road," he wrote, "they were halting to level every mol[e] hill, and to erect bridges over every brook." Sick as he was, Washington lusted for battle. Braddock promised to summon him to the column's front before reaching Fort Duquesne.[17]

On the night of July 8, Washington rode into the advance camp, less than ten miles from the French.[18] The next day would bring battle.

❧

On that final morning, Washington, weak from sickness, placed cushions on his saddle so he could ride with Braddock. He probably had the bloody flux.[19]

The British chose a route that risked ambush at two crossings of the northward-flowing Monongahela. The second crossing was tricky, the far bank looming almost twelve feet over the water. The advance guard had to regrade the slope so horses, wagons, and cannon could lumber up to the forest level above.[20]

Once it was across, the army's mood lightened. The forest was open;

evidently Indians had cleared the undergrowth to facilitate hunting. "The ground was extraordinary good when compared to the rest of the country," one soldier recalled. "The trees were high very open and little or no underwood." The threat of ambush seemed remote.[21]

Captain Adam Stephen, commanding Virginians in the rear, remembered a jaunty attitude. "The British gentlemen were confident they never would be attacked," he recalled, "until they came before the fort." Some thought the French would demolish the fort rather than yield it. "There never was an army in the world in more spirits than we were," a survivor wrote. That ebullience, according to Stephen, "lull[ed] them into a fatal security."[22]

Thomas Gage commanded the advance guard. Then came an independent company guarding a working party. Two light cannon and their crews were next, then tool wagons and five hundred regulars plus thirty cavalry. Two hundred men flanked either side, alert for ambush. Washerwomen, cattle, packhorses, and wagons came last, with Virginia units. Braddock and Washington rode with the main body.[23]

Six weeks earlier, the high hopes of the British officers would have been rewarded. Then the French were too few to resist a British assault. But reinforcements had swelled the fort's defenders to six hundred, plus several hundred Indians. They decided to attack before British cannons could knock down the fort's walls. A French attack might fail, but it would delay the advance, creating time for the British to make a mistake and also allowing France's Indian allies to win booty and prisoners.[24] Hoping to surprise the British, Captain Daniel Liénard de Beaujeu led more than eight hundred fighters out of Fort Duquesne: About three-quarters were Indians from at least six different tribes.[25]

The two forces collided in the woods. After scattered musket fire, Gage's advance guard snapped into formation and loosed a withering volley. The two forward cannons fired. The French force wavered. Captain de Beaujeu fell dead. The battle might be decided in the next minutes.

With heart-stopping whoops, the Indians filtered through the woods on both sides of the British column, sheltering behind trees, downed logs, and in swales. They began to shoot. Their most effective weapon may have been their screams, which a Frenchman said "echoed through the forest, struck terror into the hearts of the entire enemy." A British officer agreed. "The yell of the Indians is fresh on my ear," he wrote, "and the terrific sound will haunt me till the hour of my dissolution." As Braddock's aide, Washington on horseback carried the commander's orders back and forth along the British column, constantly exposed to enemy bullets.[26]

The crucial British mistake came early. At the sound of shooting, the middle and rear of the column rushed forward. The advance guard pulled back.

The flankers hurried in to support the main body. But the passage was only twelve feet wide, too narrow for hundreds of soldiers crowding into an area perhaps 150 yards long. In "irretrievable disorder," in Washington's words, the British crashed together.[27]

The redcoats stood between twelve and thirty ranks deep. As one officer remembered, "he thought himself securest who was in the center." But there was no safety. The concealed enemy fired into the huddle. Aiming was unnecessary.[28] Gunfire and savage shrieks mingled with the moans and cries of wounded and dying men, the smell of powder, the sight of spattering blood and oozing gore. Indians scalped those who fell.

Facing fire from elevated positions, according to Braddock's senior aide, "the men could never be persuaded to form regularly . . . no order could ever be restored." Washington agreed. As the British dropped, "a general panic took place among the troops from which no exertions of the officers could recover them." Another officer wrote that the men became "stupid and insensible and would not obey their officers."[29]

The mob of British soldiers mounted no serious challenge. If one shot at an attacker, a British officer recalled, the others fired in that direction "though they saw nothing but trees." The French and Indians "kept on their bellies in the bushes, and behind the trees." Survivors swore they never saw more than four of the enemy at a time. Captain Stephen scorned the British, who "were thunderstruck to feel the effects of a heavy fire, [but] see no enemy. They threw away their fire in the most indiscreet manner." The enemy shot the crews of the two cannons at the front. The other cannons never fired.[30]

The attackers concentrated on officers. In one regiment, twenty of twenty-five officers were killed or wounded. Lacking leaders, a survivor wrote, British soldiers "were seized with so strong a panic, that nothing could recover them." Another remembered that after "the greatest part of the officers were either killed or wounded . . . the soldiers [were] deaf to the commands of those few that were left alive."[31]

Withering fire came from a slope on the British right. Braddock called for an assault there, but the effort sputtered. Washington, who commanded no troops, led a second assault. Other Virginians attempted a third. All failed. When British troops on the slope huddled behind trees, their countrymen mistook them for the enemy and shot them down. British survivors agreed that their soldiers often shot one another. Washington estimated that two-thirds of the British losses came from "friendly fire." Another reported after the battle: "It's the general opinion more were killed by our own troops than by the enemy."[32]

A British doctor confirmed those impressions. The attackers' guns fired smaller bullets than the British used. The bullets extracted from the British were mostly of the larger caliber, and "were chiefly on the back parts of the body." The physician concluded that "many more of our men were killed by their own part than by the enemy."[33]

On a day of failure, the Virginians in Adam Stephen's company performed well. Like the attackers, they fought from cover. Stephen reported that half of the twelve Virginia officers were killed. Washington, who saw the entire fight as he galloped to and fro, took pride in the Virginians' performance, writing that they "showed a good deal of bravery, and were near all killed; for I believe out of 3 companies that were there, there is scarce 30 Men left alive." Even an Englishman said of the Virginians, "I believe they did the most execution of any" on the British side.[34]

On that day of slaughter, perhaps the most remarkable feature was how long the British held out. They fought for an hour, ignoring their officers, gradually giving ground. Then they fought for another hour, terrified, killing more of themselves than the enemy. They gave more ground, but they did not run. They were in a peculiar form of panic: frantic enough to fight stupidly, yet not frightened enough to flee.

Braddock's column finally crumbled when the battle reached, or even passed, its third hour. Ammunition was low. Most officers were dead or out of action. The soldiers feared being surrounded. The chaos and butchery had stretched on and on. One soldier thought the British perseverance grew from the Indians' reputation for savagery. "If it was not for their [the Indians'] barbarous usage [with] which we knew they would treat us, we should never have fought them as long as we did, but having only death before us made the men fight almost longer than they was able."[35] The battle's length also reflected how inaccurate the attackers' muskets were.[36]

A retreat began in earnest when Braddock fell. Whatever the general's failings, survivors credited him with bravery, though not the wisdom to break off the one-sided fight.[37] Conspicuous throughout, shouting orders that few followed, Braddock had four horses shot out from under him before he took a ball in the side. With the ball lodged in his chest and the day lost, he ordered a retreat. Fittingly, the retreat was a bungle.

Wagoners unhitched their horses and trotted away, stranding many wounded. Survivors "left the field and crossed the river with great precipitation, abandoning the artillery, ammunition, provision, and baggage to the enemy . . . many of them threw away their arms." Speed seemed essential with Indians pursuing, "butchering as they came." Some "tomahawk[ed] some of our women and wounded people."[38] On the far riverbank, British officers attempted to organize the withdrawal. They failed. The men fled through the forest for forty miles to Colonel Thomas Dunbar's baggage train.[39]

With the senior officers killed or wounded, Washington loaded Braddock on a cart, assembled a guard, and crossed the river. At that point, Braddock ordered the Virginian to ride to Dunbar with orders to cover the retreat.[40]

Though he had been confined to a sickbed for ten days, Washington rode all night through a landscape of terrors worthy of a Hieronymus Bosch painting. He later recalled:

> shocking scenes which presented themselves in this Night's march . . .
> The dead—the dying—the groans—lamentation—and cries along the
> road of the wounded for help . . . were enough to pierce a heart of ada-
> mant. The gloom & horror . . . was not a little increased by the imper-
> vious darkness occasioned by the close shade of thick woods.

On the battlefield, a Frenchman saw "the bodies of slain men in great numbers . . . mingled with the bodies of dead horses along a road for more than half a league."[41]

∾

The blaming started quickly. Washington denounced the British soldiers, writing that they "behaved with more cowardice than it is possible to conceive." He railed against "the dastardly behavior of thos[e] they call regulars," which "exposed all others that were inclined to do their duty to almost certain death; and at last, in despite of all the efforts of the officers to the contrary, they broke, and run as sheep pursued by dogs."[42]

Press accounts echoed the theme, carrying the statement by Braddock's chief aide that the "officers were absolutely sacrificed by their unparalleled good behavior." British accounts added the snide reminder that ten years before, the two regiments at the Monongahela "ran away so shamefully at Preston[p]ans."[43]

Washington defended Braddock, loyal to a general who had been generous toward him. Others did not. One survivor suggested that the soldiers' misconduct was "exaggerated, in order to palliate the blunders made by those in the direction." The British had mounted no effective counterattack, having not trained their soldiers to fight in the forest. As Adam Stephen observed, "His Excellency found to his woeful experience, what had been frequently told him, that formal attacks and platoon firing would never answer against the savages and Canadians." At the very least, the officers let their guard down after crossing the Monongahela, were surprised by an unsurprising attack, were flanked, then crushed.[44]

There were other blunders. When Braddock alienated the tribes, he denied himself the most effective forest fighters. By bringing too much equipment and insisting on a single supply line, he slowed the advance and allowed French reinforcements to arrive.

Though never blaming Braddock for the loss, thirty years later Washington provided a clear-eyed judgment of his former chief.

> He was brave even to a fault. . . . His attachments were warm, his enmities were strong, and having no disguise about him, both appeared in full force. He was generous and disinterested, but plain and blunt in his manner even to rudeness.

One trait Washington omitted was arrogance. On this point, the judgment of another American resonates: The British "were too confident of their own strength, and despised their enemy."[45]

The lesson was clear to Virginians. In Washington's convoluted words: "The folly and consequence of opposing compact bodies to the sparse manner of Indian fighting in the woods . . . was now so clearly verified that from hence forward another mode obtained." Stephen made the point more pungently: "It ought to be laid down as a maxim to attack them first, to fight them in their own way, and go against them light and naked, as they come against us." He added, "You might as well send a cow in pursuit of a hare, as an English soldier loaded in their way, with a coat, jacket, etc., after Canadians in their shirts, who can shoot and run well, or naked Indians accustomed to the woods." The years would test how much the British learned.[46]

Governor Dinwiddie was incredulous at the outcome, writing to his London masters that the defeat "appears to me as a dream." Washington, usually a realist, also struggled to accept the dimensions of the defeat:

> Contrary to all expectation and human probability, and even to the common course of things, we were totally defeated . . . had I not been witness to the fact, on that fatal day, I should scarce have given credit to it even now.[47]

Colonel Dunbar decided to march the broken remains of the army to Philadelphia to enter "winter quarters" in July. His soldiers had no fight in them. As an officer wrote, "Our affairs are as bad here as bad can make them." Most of the continent either sniggered or fumed at the spectacle of nearly 2,000 British soldiers skulking into winter quarters in midsummer.[48]

Washington wrote to Governor Dinwiddie for the first time in months. He described the battle bitterly, insisting that two-thirds of the casualties were caused by "our own cowardly regulars, who gathered themselves into a body contrary to orders 10 or 12 deep, and would then level, fire, and shoot down the men before them." Dunbar's withdrawal, he added, would leave the frontier naked but for "the shattered remains of the Virginia troops." He predicted that frontier families would flee eastward.[49]

His letter carried two messages. The explicit message was that Virginia must protect its frontier. Implicit was Washington's wish to patch things up with the governor.

Dinwiddie angrily implored Dunbar to use the next four months of warm weather "to retrieve the dishonor done to the British arms" against an enemy who was short on supplies and men. Dinwiddie made those points to Washington; then, notably, he asked for Washington's opinion.[50] With Braddock's failure, the two men were reaching to each other to revive the war effort.

Though the battle was catastrophic for Britain and for Virginians on the frontier, it brought renown to Washington. Because he was only a staff aide at the Monongahela, the failure was not his; because he had been brave and stood with Braddock to the end, he was acclaimed a hero, the only one on the British side, an avatar of colonial competence and courage. Press reports detailed the horses shot from under him, the bullet holes in his uniform, and Washington "behaving the whole time with the greatest courage and resolution." He received admiring letters from Colonel Fairfax and others, who recommended that Washington command a new Virginia Regiment.[51]

Better yet, Braddock's failure eclipsed Washington's defeat at Fort Necessity, where at least his men had been outnumbered. Braddock was a professional soldier with double the force of his foe, yet failed miserably. Colonel Dunbar's scamper to winter quarters was a final point in Washington's favor. Though only twenty-three, Washington stood as the colony's leading military figure. He would command again.

Washington felt matters moving his way. Three weeks after the battle, he wrote to his brother Austin, who soon would attend a session of the House of Burgesses. Other burgesses would ask Austin about his brother. In a message aimed at Virginia's powerful men, Washington wrote that he was "so little dispirited at what has happened, that I am always ready, and always willing to do my country any services that I am capable of." Washington's passion for a military career was back.

But this time, he insisted, he must be paid fairly, and he had leverage to make that happen. He reviewed for Austin his previous unsatisfactory compensation. He would not serve again, he wrote, "upon the terms I have done, having suffered much in my private fortune beside impairing one of the best of constitutions." Until summoned back into command, Washington found important duties to perform as military adjutant for the Northern Neck. He scheduled reviews of militia companies in nine counties, where he commanded exercises from horseback, impressive in his trim uniform. He made a stirring impression. He always did.[52]

∾

One myth died on July 9, 1755, and another was born.

The expiring myth was about British military superiority. Two regiments shrank to a terrified mass, then were butchered. Braddock led thirteen hundred men that morning. By the end of the day, two-thirds were dead or wounded. Three days later, Braddock himself was dead. The attackers—mostly men despised by the British as savages—suffered twenty-three dead and fifteen seriously wounded.[53]

Aside from British blunders, the battle's shocking element was the effect of Indian warfare on British regulars, whose discipline vanished at the sight of scalping. Washington wrote brother Austin that the battle was "so scandalous that I hate to have it mentioned." No survivor, certainly not George Washington, would again consider British soldiers invincible.[54] The myth that stirred to life was of the hero Washington, a stranger to fear, blessed by the gods. He had dashed from Braddock's side and back, delivering orders through hours of blistering gunfire, his life in danger every moment. He was the tallest man on the field, on horseback, unmistakable to friend and foe. A horse was killed beneath him and another wounded. Each time he remounted. A bullet pierced his hat. Others went through his clothes. Not one touched his flesh. As each aide to Braddock fell, as each senior officer crumpled, Washington kept on. Was he the child of destiny?

Washington admitted he had benefitted from "the miraculous care of Providence." He wondered whether his survival had any meaning beyond battlefield luck:

I have been protected beyond all human probability and expectation, for I had 4 bullets through my coat and two horses shot under me yet although death was leveling my companions on every side of me, escaped unhurt.[55]

Praising Washington's courage, an American gushed, "I cannot sufficiently speak the merit of Washington."[56]

The myth spread widely, embraced by colonists who were otherwise starved for good news about the struggle on the frontier. A Virginia preacher recounted Washington's heroism at the Monongahela. In a sermon, he applauded "that heroic youth Colonel Washington, who I cannot but hope Providence has hitherto preserved in so signal a manner for some important service to his country."[57] The message, which would be reprinted around the country twenty years later at the beginning of the Revolutionary War, was that a higher force watched over Washington, who was indeed a child of destiny.

The myth took flight in a tale supposedly told by Washington's friend Dr. James Craik, who had been with the army on the Monongahela. Dr. Craik, the tale goes, recounted the following speech by an Indian leader at the battle:

> I called to my young men and said, mark yon tall and daring warrior? He is not of the red-coat tribe—he hath an Indian's wisdom, and his warriors fight as we do—he is alone exposed. . . . Our rifles were leveled, rifles which, but for him, knew not how to miss—'twas all in vain, a power mightier far than we, shielded him from harm. He cannot die in battle. . . . The Great Spirit protects that man, and guides his destinies—he will become the chief of nations, and a people yet unborn, will hail him as the founder of a mighty empire.

Dr. Craik allegedly related this tale at the Battle of Monmouth Court House, concluding: "I have often told you, of the old Indian's prophecy. Yes, I do believe, a Great Spirit protects that man—and that one day or other, honored and beloved, he will be the chief of our nation . . . Never mind the enemy, they cannot kill him, and while he lives, our cause will never die."[58]

Like Achilles dipped in the River Styx, like Alexander slicing the Gordian knot, like King Arthur drawing Excalibur from the stone, Washington seemed fated to be more than others could be. The power of myth is that it is impervious to reason or facts. Though he was very mortal and all too conscious of his own failings, Washington understood that power.

CHAPTER 10

The Naked Frontier

Having thrashed a British army, the Ohio Indians swiftly drove western settlers off the land, seizing anything valuable that was left behind. For two years, Braddock's road became a highway for Indian raiding parties.[1]

Within three weeks of the Monongahela disaster, Indian raids killed thirty-five settlers. A large band attacked a private fort on the Greenbrier River, killing thirteen; another incident nearby exacted a similar toll. For a third time, Lord Fairfax called out the Frederick County militia; again, no one answered his call. When George William Fairfax, as militia colonel, jailed several resisters, their friends pulled down the jail and freed them. By October, at least one hundred Virginians had been killed or taken captive in the Shenandoah valley.[2]

The raiders' atrocities spread terror. In one attack, they delivered a farmer's head to his neighbor. The colonial government could not help. Virginia's forces, Adam Stephen reported, were "obliged to let the enemy pass under our noses without ever putting them in bodily fear," which added "to the contemptible opinion the Indians have of us."[3]

Dinwiddie did not summon other county militias, because he wanted farmers to till their fields while also casting their "watchful eye over our negro slaves." Virginia needed a formal military force. In August, the General Assembly approved £40,000 to pay for a new Virginia Regiment consisting of 1,000 soldiers and 200 mounted rangers.[4]

Expecting to command the new regiment, Washington wrote to his worried mother: "If it is in my power to avoid going to the Ohio again, I shall, but if the command is pressed upon me by the general voice of the country, and offered upon such terms as can't be objected against, it would reflect eternal dishonor upon me to refuse it." Mary surely understood that her firstborn was going back to war.[5]

Washington spelled out his terms in a letter to an Executive Council member. He must have a role in appointing officers and a fund to pay incidental expenses. And his political masters had to understand how difficult frontier warfare was. Service under these terms would preserve "the chief part of my happiness, i.e., the esteem and notice the country has been pleased to honor me with."[6]

He had correctly judged his position. Governor Dinwiddie's ensuing instructions to Washington as "Commander in Chief of the Virginia Regiment" allowed him to appoint his adjutant, quartermaster, aide-de-camp, and secretary, plus "such other inferior officers as you shall find absolutely necessary." Washington would command sixteen companies. The assembly showered him with funds, approving £300 for past expenses, plus a salary of 30 shillings a day, another £100 a year for future expenses, and a 2 percent commission on regimental purchases.[7] Despite having won no significant military victory, he was the only Virginian considered for the position.

A familiar problem arose: enlisting soldiers. "I dread the recruiting," Governor Dinwiddie confessed. Those who lived far from the frontier had little interest in fighting. Those on the frontier preferred to move east or to stay home to protect their families. Expecting such reluctance, the assembly created a complex scheme. For the first ninety days after the law took effect, the regiment would accept volunteers. If too few stepped forward, county magistrates would draft unmarried men from the militia, then deserters and married men who had abandoned their wives and those "who have no visible way of getting an honest livelihood." A draftee could escape service by paying £10.[8]

Consequently, only poor men served. As a clergyman wrote in mid-1756, "no person of any property, family or worth" enlisted in a regiment consisting of "worthless vagrants, servants just out of servitude, and convicts," all "utterly unacquainted with the woods and the use of firearms."[9]

Washington tried to impose standards for his soldiers. He prescribed a minimum height of five-foot-four, except for those who "are well made, strong, and active," but none subject to fits or having "old sores" on their legs. A regimental roster in 1756 listed more than five hundred men. Five had only one eye, one was missing two fingers, several were in their forties and one was sixty, while descriptions ranged from "a fawning, cringing behavior" to "a clownish look." Half were foreign-born. Their average height was five-foot-five, which meant their commander towered nearly a head above most. Only seven were six feet tall.[10]

Few soldiers enjoyed their service, its slow pay and poor supplies. Of more than twelve hundred who served in 1756 and 1757, only seventy-six signed up for a second year. In those years, the regiment never reached its authorized strength of 1,000. Desertions continued. The soldiers feared Indians more than they feared their officers.[11]

For the next two years, Washington's task was the military equivalent of holding back a river with his bare hands. He would fight no battles and have no opportunities for glory. Instead, he bore the drudgery of administration, garrison duty, and keeping together a force that was ill paid, ill supplied, and poorly motivated, facing an enemy with superior skills at the only style of warfare it conducted: hit-and-run raids. Again and again, Washington would know the wisdom of Adam Stephen's remark that sending European-style soldiers after Indians was like sending a cow to catch a hare.

∾

By late August 1755, Washington assumed his command with a blizzard of orders intended to improve the soldiers' skills. He directed that recruits be drilled in the "new platoon way of exercising" with regular target practice. Washington also began a battle over supplies with the "irresolute" commissary.[12]

He modeled his administration on Braddock's system. Creating a military bureaucracy from scratch, managing the logistical challenges of the frontier, was a slow process. He had to oversee the acquisition of everything: "shoes, white-yarn stockings, blankets, kettles, tomahawks, . . . cartridge paper, stationery," plus "a proper assortment of Indian goods" to use as gifts. Until then, as John Carlyle of Alexandria observed, Virginians "really never knew what taxes was, nor the great inconvenience attending war."[13]

Washington's goal was to stop the Indian attacks. The Indians, Adam Stephen reported, "commit their outrages at all hours of the day," bringing "desolation and murder heightened with all barbarous circumstances, and unheard of instances of cruelty. . . . The smoke of burning plantations darken the days and hide the neighboring mountains from our sight."[14]

The Virginians had no viable strategy. Through the autumn, Washington's plan involved searching out the invaders and punishing them in a fight. He ordered his captains "frequently to send out strong parties to scour the woods and mountains." Yet those proved to be fools' errands. The Virginians were no match for Indians in the forest. Repeatedly, the Virginians arrived too late or walked into ambush. Within a year, Washington concluded that the Virginia Assembly's plan for a chain of frontier forts was an expensive irrelevance.[15]

His problems multiplied. As new recruits neared the frontier, Washington wrote to the governor, they deserted "constantly, and yesterday while we were at church 25 of them collected and were going off . . . but were stopped and imprisoned." Supplies were inadequate. Colonial law did not define the discipline he could impose. Fort Cumberland, the only fortified outpost in the region, was in Maryland, so Washington's authority there was doubtful. This ambiguity rubbed Washington raw when a Maryland commander, Captain Thomas Dagworthy, denied that Washington was his superior. "I can never," Washington wrote to the governor, "submit to the command of Captain Dagworthy." Dinwiddie agreed but could issue no order to Dagworthy. The governor asked London to grant king's commissions to Virginia officers, which would place Washington above the Marylander.[16]

Washington scrounged for supplies and began to build quarters for the men. Many settlers had left, terrified by the Indian raids. "Everything," Washington wrote from Winchester in early October, was "in the utmost confusion." The people, he confided, "are really frighted out of their senses." A Virginian reported "mothers with a train of helpless children at their heels straggling through woods & mountains to escape the fury of these merciless savages."[17]

The horrors were nurtured by an enemy willing to mutilate the dead. When eighty Virginia soldiers marched to Fort Cumberland, they found one farm owner "half out of the grave, and eaten by the wolves." After Washington joined the column, they reached a farm where a woman, young man, and boy had been scalped. At a third farm, three people had been scalped and thrown into a fire; their brains stuck to their clothing. After one brutal raid, a survivor wrote, "I'm in so much horror and confusion I scarce know what I am writing."[18]

Preaching calm, Washington published a newspaper exhortation that residents return with "the utmost security; that the five companies of rangers, and an independent company . . . are stationed in the best manner . . . and the men under Colonel Washington, will all be disposed of, so as to answer the same purpose." If the settlers had fought back, he continued, "a small number of them, with a proper spirit, might easily have destroyed" the attackers. In a notice three days later, Washington denounced reports by "timorous persons" that Indians had laid waste to the country. "The Frontiers will be so well guarded," he pledged, "that no mischief can be done, either to [the settlers] or their plantations."[19]

Few believed him, nor should they have. In private, he acknowledged that the populace ignored him. No orders were obeyed "but what a party of soldiers, or my own drawn sword enforces." Forced to commandeer horses and wagons, Washington faced threats to "blow out my brains." Washington never backed down. He ordered the jailing of any civilian who resisted the regiment's seizures.[20]

To restore his manpower, he promised amnesty for deserters who returned. Then he announced that those who did not return by November 30 would be prosecuted as felons. He tried shame, placing deserters' names in the newspaper. Finally, he imposed harsh punishments; five were sentenced to receive a thousand lashes apiece.[21]

Cold weather brought relief, as the raiders returned to their home fires for the winter. Washington took advantage of the respite to order a military manual from England, Humphrey Bland's *A Treatise of Military Discipline*. He recommended that his officers read it too.[22]

∾

Through the bloody autumn of 1755, Washington kept a sharp eye on Virginia politics. The House of Burgesses, called into session in early November, approved an issuance of paper currency that Governor Dinwiddie opposed. Exasperated with "mutinous and unmannerly" lawmakers, he called new elections for December.[23]

Elections interested Colonel Washington. Five months before, marching with Braddock, he wrote on the subject to his brother Jack. John Carlyle, he wrote, had asked "in a bantering way" whether Washington would seek a seat from either Fairfax County, where Mount Vernon stood, or Frederick County on the frontier. (Owning land in both counties, Washington could be a candidate in either.) Washington confided, "I should like to go for either, but more particularly for Fairfax, as I am a resident there." Their brother Lawrence had served in the House and brother Austin did now, as had their grandfather and great-grandfather.[24]

Washington moved cautiously to avoid stepping on Fairfax toes. He asked Jack to find out if George William Fairfax intended to run in the county named for his family. If George William would not be a candidate, Washington wrote, "I should be glad to take a poll, if I thought my chance tolerably good." To gauge his opportunity, Washington asked Jack to snuffle out the views of Carlyle, George Mason, and other local worthies, "without disclosing much of mine." If his prospects appeared favorable, Washington authorized his brother to "declare my intentions and beg their assistance"; if unfavorable, "I would have the affair entirely dropped."

Washington stressed that in order to conceal his ambition unless the path was open, Jack should pursue his inquiries "with an air of indifference and unconcern" until he was satisfied there was support for a Washington candidacy. Ten days later, before Jack could have pursued the inquiry with the prescribed indifference, Washington impatiently pressed for "an answer as soon as possible." If Washington ran in Fairfax, he could refer to the poll sheet he had retained from his brother Lawrence's contest seven years before.[25]

Virginia's elections were decentralized and entirely public. The governor's order for elections went to every county sheriff, who scheduled the polling in their respective counties within the next thirty days. Most sheriffs selected the day when the county court sat, since many citizens came to the county seat then for business and socializing. Ministers announced elections at the end of Sunday services. Eligible voters—free white males who owned or leased one hundred acres of raw land, or twenty-five acres of improved land with a house—assembled at the courthouse. Because many owned or leased land, the body of voters was relatively large.[26]

On Election Day, with the candidates present, the sheriff called each voter by name. The voter announced his preferred candidate. That candidate rose, bowed, and thanked the voter. The polling could become rowdy, particularly in close races, as candidates ordinarily treated voters to food and drink (called "swilling the planters with bumbo," or rum). Though the candidates were expected to behave with dignity, their advocates avidly canvassed voters.[27]

For the December 1755 elections, Washington pursued a confusing course. When George William Fairfax declared for Fairfax County, Washington could not run there. Opposing a Fairfax was unthinkable. Instead, Washington took time from his military duties to assist George William's cause, lingering in Alexandria through November and December. His advocacy for his friend goaded a smaller man into knocking Washington down with a stick. When Washington did not immediately retaliate, the town vibrated with anticipation of a duel. In the morning, however, Washington apologized for provoking the other man. It was a humble action by the colony's leading soldier, known to be fearless in battle. When Adam Stephen heard of the episode, he reported to Washington that "we all were ready and violent to run and tear your enemies to pieces." In any event, George William doubtless appreciated Washington's help, since he won by a mere twelve votes out of several hundred cast.[28]

Washington's presence in Fairfax County meant he missed the Frederick County poll in Winchester, even though he was listed as a candidate there. Indeed, Washington made no visible effort to win votes in Frederick, not even mentioning his candidacy to friends. Adam Stephen expressed frustration at not knowing Washington was on that ballot. As a Frederick County landowner, Stephen could have voted for him. Unsurprisingly, Washington drew only forty votes out of more than five hundred cast, though his friends insisted that he would have won if he had campaigned.²⁹

Washington never explained how his name came to be on the Frederick County ballot, or why he neglected that election. Perhaps it was a case of miscommunication, his name submitted by friends who incorrectly thought Washington would campaign for the seat. Or maybe he thought initially that he could win in Frederick, but then decided that 1755 was not his year. Or the candidacy might have been a trial balloon launched by the deliberate Washington, who realized that he had to serve the Fairfax interests first but also wanted his name to circulate in political circles. Or maybe he had a deal with the Fairfaxes, that he would support George William in 1755 in return for their support for him the next time around. Any of these explanations, or some other, could be true.

After the election, Washington returned to his military drudgery. With discipline still inconsistent, Washington agitated with Dinwiddie for new military statutes with a death penalty for deserters. Then he sighed to Adam Stephen, "You must go on in the old way of whipping them stoutly."³⁰

His dissatisfaction covered his officers as well. In early January 1756, Washington lectured them to discharge their duties conscientiously, insisting that "it is the actions, and not the commission, that make the officer— and that there is more expected from him than the title." Annoyed that one captain's wife "sows sedition among the men, and is chief of every mutiny," he demanded that the captain send her from the camp or "I shall take care to drive her out myself and suspend *you*."³¹

Also annoying was the continuing standoff with Maryland's Captain Dagworthy. Desperate for a solution, Washington argued for Virginia to build its own frontier fort so he would no longer have to deal with the presumptuous Marylander at Fort Cumberland.³²

Washington resolved to carry this grievance to a higher authority, Massachusetts governor William Shirley, the British commander in chief in America. Traveling to Boston would allow the Virginia colonel to cut a figure, militarily and politically, across much of British North America. George Washington—about to celebrate his twenty-fourth birthday—would start to make himself a continental character.

CHAPTER 11

A Wilderness of Difficulties

Washington's journey to Boston was an opportunity to see other colonies and to be seen, but also to meet a high official who had impressed the young Virginian. When Governor Shirley had conferred with General Braddock in Alexandria, Washington wrote of Shirley that "every word and every action discovers the gentleman and great politician." The Dagworthy quarrel provided a pretext for meeting with this paragon.[1]

Washington secured Governor Dinwiddie's permission for the round-trip journey of 1,100 miles. Because the Indians rarely raided in winter, Washington could be spared from the frontier. Always conscious of appearances, he recruited two subordinates to make up his entourage. All wore fresh blue uniforms of Washington's design, set off with scarlet waistcoats and cuffs, and silver lace trim. Two mounted servants sported livery matching the Washington coat of arms, red on a white field.[2]

Newspapers in Philadelphia, New York, and Boston noted Washington's arrivals and departures. He cloaked the purpose of his trip—to vault over the presumptuous Captain Dagworthy—with the tale that he was consulting with Shirley about "measures proper to be taken with several tribes of Indians to the southward, and particularly the Cherokees." A Boston newspaper hailed his arrival with a gently candid review of his career, calling him "a gentleman who has deservedly a high reputation for military skill, integrity, and valor," adding, "though success has not always attended his undertakings."[3]

Washington stopped first in Philadelphia, British America's largest city, which held 3,000 homes, many built of brick, plus lighted streets, a hospital, a gracious government building, and two libraries. Its port bustled with ships arriving and departing.[4] Washington called on fifty-year-old Benjamin Franklin, the leading member of Pennsylvania's assembly and deputy postmaster for all the colonies. Despite their age difference, both men had practical, determined minds and supported vigorous action against the French. Also, each was part of a syndicate to develop western lands.[5]

While Virginia's soldiers shivered on the frontier, Washington gambled and danced in the continent's finest drawing rooms. In New York, his flirtation with Miss Polly Philipse, the sister-in-law of his host, set tongues wagging. Everywhere, he shopped. Accustomed to ordering goods from Britain, then waiting a year for them to arrive, overpriced and sometimes broken or ill fitting, Washington spent freely among Philadelphia's tailors, jewelers, hatters, and saddle-makers. He twice viewed an acclaimed exhibition called *Microcosm of the World in Miniature*, which depicted a Roman temple, muses and mythological figures, stars and clouds, and mechanical human figures, powered by more than twelve hundred wheels and pinions.[6]

Dinwiddie paved Washington's way by writing to Shirley that the Dagworthy face-off "makes such noise here" that he (Dinwiddie) "thought it necessary to send" Washington to request Shirley's intercession. Dinwiddie's letter transformed Washington from a whiny provincial seeking advancement into the emissary of Britain's largest American colony on a matter of policy. And Washington won some relief: Shirley granted him precedence over Dagworthy in the chain of command, though not a king's commission. Shirley thus proved to be the deft politician Washington thought he was, appeasing the Virginians without disturbing the army's policy against colonists as officers.[7]

Washington returned home with broader perspectives. He experienced, firsthand, the tensions between the Quakers and non-Quakers of Pennsylvania, and the commercial focus of New Yorkers and New Englanders. He learned that his military exploits brought him recognition. He was known, the essential foundation of a political career, and the journey made him better known. Later that spring, colonial newspapers reported his movements on the frontier.[8]

The journey home brought the news that Maryland governor Horatio Sharpe would command the king's forces in the southern colonies. Wary of this new superior who had sponsored the despised Dagworthy, Washington considered resigning, but resolved against it. In turn, Sharpe appointed him second-in-command for the southern colonies.[9]

As trees leafed out for spring, Indian raids resumed on the frontier. Although Adam Stephen proclaimed that Virginia's soldiers had learned bushfighting, they were not yet good at it. Washington reported that the enemy had returned "in greater numbers; committed several murders not far from Winchester; and even are so daring as to attack our forts in open day." A raiding party killed a settler, carried off his wife and six children, and burned six farms. Washington buried the dead man.[10]

◦

Washington's respect for his Indian foes only grew. They moved so silently that they could close, undetected, within a few yards of Virginians. They were swift to attack, strong in combat, skilled with weapons. And then they disappeared. "Their cunning and craft are not to be equaled," he wrote to Dinwiddie, adding, "They prowl about like wolves, and like them, do their mischief by stealth." He doubted that Virginians could ever defeat them. Only other Indians were a match, he wrote to the Speaker of the House of Burgesses, "and without these, we shall ever fight on unequal terms."[11]

Washington, with but forty soldiers in Winchester, feared an attack. He begged for fighters from pro-British tribes on the colony's southern boundary, the Catawba and Cherokee. He resisted building more forts, arguing that they would require "an inconceivable number of men" he did not have. Also, he wanted no more castoffs in the regiment, but "active, resolute men—men who are practiced to arms and are marksmen."[12]

Recognizing that Virginia's arms were failing, the burgesses proposed to add another thousand-man regiment. Washington lobbied the governor and the House Speaker to have any additional men placed under his command. Colonel Washington was playing politics.[13]

Word reached him that colonial officials were losing confidence in him. Dinwiddie wrote in early April about reports that in the regiment, "the greatest immoralities and drunkenness have been much countenanced and proper discipline neglected." Colonel Fairfax confirmed that the burgesses were considering an inquiry into officers' misbehavior. House Speaker John Robinson reported that Williamsburg was rife with "terrible reports" about the regiment. Washington understood this was an attack on him; he had appointed most of the officers and supervised all of them.[14]

In a self-righteous letter to the governor, Washington defended himself but not his officers, admitting they had "the seeds of idleness very strongly engrafted in their natures." He insisted that he had "both by threats and persuasive means, endeavored to discountenance gaming, drinking, swearing, and irregularities of every other kind." He blamed Dagworthy for any misconduct at Fort Cumberland, since Washington had not visited that fort for months. He concluded with a wan pledge to "act with a little more rigor in the future."

To Speaker Robinson, he ascribed military setbacks to the pusillanimous residents of Frederick County. Only fifteen had responded to his militia call, and some of those refused to serve. A second letter to Robinson offered some contrition. "My experience may have led me into innumerable errors," he admitted, closing with his fifth threat to resign in seven months.[15]

The men in Williamsburg had reason to be impatient with Washington. Through many winter weeks, while regimental discipline frayed, he had gallivanted through Philadelphia, New York, Newport, and Boston, nominally pressing his dispute with Dagworthy. Garrison duty on the Virginia frontier was harsh and unpleasant in good weather, long periods of boredom punctuated by moments of terror. It was miserable in freezing winters. Washington always tried to avoid it.

On the same day that Washington sent his excuses to the House Speaker, Indian raiders ambushed a forty-man patrol, killing a captain and fifteen soldiers. At a council of war, the regiment's officers decided they had too few soldiers to retaliate. Washington could only order that bushes surrounding Winchester be hacked to the ground to deny cover to attackers.[16]

Washington wrote an impassioned letter to the governor. Though he ordinarily strove for self-control, this letter reveals him perilously near a breaking point over the settlers' plight:

> What can I do? If bleeding, dying! would glut their insatiate revenge—
> I would be a willing offering to savage fury: and die by inches to save
> a people! I see their situation, know their danger, and participate [in]
> their sufferings; without having it in my power to give them further
> relief, . . . I see inevitable destruction in so clear a light, that, unless
> vigorous measures are taken by the Assembly, . . . the poor inhabitants
> that are now in forts, must unavoidably fall; while the remainder of
> the county are flying before the barbarous foe.

Yet Washington also saw the dire situation through the lens of his career. He despaired that he had "distant prospects, if any . . . of gaining honor and reputation in the Service." But for the urgency of the crisis, he continued, he would resign immediately, admitting that "the murder of poor innocent babes, and helpless families, may be laid to my account here!"[17]

Two days later, after raiders murdered three families within twelve miles of Winchester, Washington again wrote frantically to the governor. "Every day we have accounts of such cruelties and barbarities as are shocking to human nature. . . . no road is safe to travel: and here, we know not the hour how soon we may be attacked." There was talk in the regiment, he confessed, of capitulating to the French.[18]

Gone was the self-possessed officer who had traveled triumphantly to Boston. His inability to pacify the frontier tortured him. Having known mostly failure in uniform, he felt the weight of the world on his shoulders.

Senior figures in Williamsburg sent reassuring messages. "Our hopes dear George," wrote Speaker Robinson, "are all fixed on you for bringing our affairs to a happy issue." Colonel Fairfax, who knew Washington's dread of any smudge on his reputation, reported soothingly that "your health and success was toasted at almost all tables at Williamsburg."[19]

Those were mere words. Washington needed Indian warriors, but Virginia had no Indian allies willing to fight. The General Assembly approved expanding the regiment to fifteen hundred men, but it was an empty gesture; recruiting was impossible so long as Virginia paid and provisioned so poorly. Moreover, the assembly required service only until December of the year; that meant, Washington pointed out to Dinwiddie, that "by the time they shall have entered the service, they will claim a discharge."[20]

One thing the governor could do was summon county militias. The part-time soldiers flooded into Winchester from eastern counties, but they lacked supplies and weapons, resisted discipline, then left in large groups. Washington feared that their "spirit of desertion" was infecting the regiment. Indeed, in May of 1756, the regiment's numbers sank to barely three hundred, one-fifth of its authorized strength. A council of war resolved to send home all militia "except what were absolutely necessary."[21]

Stung by criticism of the regiment's discipline, Washington turned to brutality. Courts-martial sentenced three defendants to one thousand lashes each, a punishment that could be fatal, while others were sentenced to four hundred or two hundred fifty lashes. Pressing for the maximum penalty for a sergeant convicted of cowardice and two soldiers who deserted multiple times, Washington pledged, "I shall make it my particular care to see them executed." Adam Stephen, now lieutenant colonel, reported that he had "wheeled" two deserters "till they pissed themselves and the spectators shed tears for them."[22]

The Indian attacks continued. "Desolation and murder still increase," Washington wrote to the governor in late April. Knowing that his soldiers would never track down the raiders, Washington ordered them to "waylay and act by stratagem" rather than plunge through the forest and stumble into ambushes.[23]

The new tactics did not help. In late June, two hundred Shawnees destroyed a fort at the far end of the Shenandoah valley, taking one hundred fifty captives. In July, raiders killed ten settlers at a small fort at the mouth of the Conococheague River, and six more near Fort Cumberland. Through the summer, the regiment suffered at least a hundred casualties in more than twenty actions. The colonial press reported a drumbeat of Indian depredations. One newspaper reported an Indian band taking fifty captives and killing forty in a raid, adding that the Indians "are committing outrages every minute."[24]

Dinwiddie and Washington agreed that the best strategy was to capture Fort Duquesne and cut off French support for the raiders.[25] But Washington's forces were too weak to do it. The remaining option was to build frontier forts, which Washington thought was futile. To block the raiders, the forts had to be spaced at fifteen- or eighteen-mile intervals, with at least eighty soldiers in each. That meant more than twenty forts and more than 2,000 soldiers, a manpower level the regiment could never reach. Having no better option, the governor and council nevertheless dictated that forts be built.

Constructing stockades across roughly two hundred and fifty miles, from the Great Cacapon River to the Mayo River, strained the regiment. When the soldiers resisted the work, Washington issued extra rum rations and pay, which increased expenses. Men building forts could not patrol for raiders. Washington's choice, he wrote, was to "neglect the inhabitants and build the forts, or neglect the forts and mind the inhabitants."[26]

The forts, as Washington predicted, achieved little. Most were rude stockades where settlers huddled and hoped that their attackers were too few to overwhelm them. In the first half of 1756, Delaware warriors attacked nine Virginia forts, destroying five and killing or capturing nearly three hundred settlers. In early August, Adam Stephen called the forts a useless burden.[27]

Amid the carnage and frustration, a moment of unspoken irony arose in August. Washington assembled his troops in Winchester to hear the declaration of war that the British government had recently issued against France. Washington and his men had been fighting the French for two years; now their efforts became part of an official war that would rage for seven more in the global rivalry between competing empires. It had started in that forest glen when a few Virginians and Indians, led by Washington, surprised Jumonville's expedition.[28]

Events in autumn 1756 were no more encouraging. A *Virginia Gazette* article excoriated the regiment's officers for their "vice and debauchery," inexperience, and abuse of common soldiers. Writing from Williamsburg, Austin reassured his sensitive brother that "your character does not in the least suffer here," but Washington never could shrug off criticism. As one

historian has put it, "inhumanly fearless against cannon fire, he could become terrified at the threat of a critical word." Washington issued his sixth
resignation threat in less than a year. Austin briskly replied that if Washington resigned, "you will be blamed by your country more for that than every
other action of your life."[29]

Washington's situation did not improve. The royal government sent a new
military commander for North America, Lord Loudoun. With no previous
experience in America, he created a Royal American Regiment and demanded that Virginia provide a large share of its soldiers, draining resources
from Washington's thankless work on the frontier.[30] Washington undertook
a tour of his forts, with a militia escort he described as "whooping, hallooing
gentlemen soldiers." The garrisons, undermanned and indolent, wasted ammunition by gambling on target-shooting contests. As the cold weather approached and the raiding season waned, Washington made a gloomy
assessment:

> The ruinous state of the frontiers, and the vast extent of land we have
> lost . . . must appear incredible to those who are not eyewitnesses of
> this desolation. Upwards of fifty miles of a rich and (once) thick-
> settled country is now quite deserted & abandoned.

His triumphant trip to Boston the previous winter must have seemed very
long ago.[31]

∽

Through Washington's difficult 1756, the horror-filled events left little room
for the private man. His brother Jack married Hannah Bushrod in mid-April,
but Washington could not attend. Until 1758, Jack would manage Washington's lands, moving among Mount Vernon, Ferry Farm (with mother Mary),
and Bullskin Creek. Through life, Washington always felt closest to Jack, and
placed the greatest reliance on him.[32]

Youngest brother Charles, who was eighteen, wanted to join the regiment,
but their mother blocked him. She had lost George to the military, but would
not see her youngest in uniform. In mid-June, Washington visited her in
Fredericksburg and loaned her money, a coolly businesslike arrangement for
a mother and son.[33]

Washington's military responsibilities did not eclipse entirely his interest
in the opposite sex, as reflected in somewhat ribald letters from fellow officers. Writing from South Carolina a year later, George Mercer reported that

the women there lacked "those enticing heaving throbbing alluring . . . exciting plump breasts common with our Northern Belles." The passage suggests bawdy fireside conversations among frontier soldiers. Yet, except for his February flirtation with Miss Philipse in New York, Washington saw few eligible young ladies. That he was familiar with women in the taverns and paths of scruffy Winchester cannot be ruled out.[34]

Expected to defeat a skilled foe with too few men, who had too little training and not enough supplies, an apparently depressed Washington summed up his quandary in early August. "I am wandering," he wrote, "in a wilderness of difficulties, and am ignorant of the ways to extricate myself."[35]

CHAPTER 12

Biting the Hand

Washington's mood darkened further during the autumn of 1756. Constant strain was dulling his political senses. He sparred with Governor Dinwiddie over Fort Cumberland, which Washington yearned to close, insisting it was vulnerable to attack. Dinwiddie replied that they could not close a "king's fort," but then left the decision to Washington. When the regiment's officers opposed closing the fort, as did Lord Loudoun, Washington backed off. In August, he sent to Speaker Robinson a laundry list of grievances against Dinwiddie, claiming that the governor's directions were consistently ambiguous and uncertain. Robinson gave Washington's gripes to the legislative committee overseeing the regiment, revealing to a wider audience the corrosive rift between governor and commander.[1]

In November, the governor scolded Washington, calling one complaint "unmannerly" and another unexplained. He ordered Washington to march one hundred men to Fort Cumberland, enclosing Executive Council minutes that reaffirmed the need to hold that fort.[2]

Washington's reply included an apology for "unmannerly" expression; no Virginia gentleman could wish to be unmannerly. Yet his tone was petulant. "If my open and disinterested way of writing and speaking has the air of pertness and freedom," he wrote, "I shall redress my error by acting reservedly; and shall take care to obey my orders without offering at more." Washington pounced on Dinwiddie's order to send one hundred men to Cumberland. Since Washington had only eighty-one soldiers fit for duty at Winchester, he pledged to march them all to Cumberland, vowing to leave in Winchester "not a man . . . to secure the works, or defend the King's stores." His sarcasm was surely ill received.[3]

In reply, Dinwiddie admitted to having incorrect information about Winchester's manpower; he afforded the commander discretion to assign appropriate garrisons at any western fort. But the governor also reinforced his emphasis on defending Cumberland by enclosing Loudoun's direction that Washington abandon smaller forts to strengthen the defense of Winchester and Cumberland.[4]

Washington complied resentfully. To Speaker Robinson, he complained again about Dinwiddie:

> My strongest representations of matters relative to the peace of the Frontiers are disregarded as idle and frivolous; my propositions and measures, as partial and selfish; and all my sincerest endeavors for the service of my Country, perverted to the worst purposes. My Orders are dark, doubtful and uncertain; *today approved, tomorrow condemned*: Left to act and proceed at hazard: accountable for the consequence; and blamed, without the benefit of defence!

Washington concluded that his best course, despite his weakening political position, was to appeal over Dinwiddie's head to Lord Loudoun.[5] But grinding frontier violence had diminished his heroic reputation as Virginia's unquestioned military leader, while also seasoning officers like Adam Stephen, who might replace him. Washington had support from the Fairfaxes and Speaker Robinson, but Lord Loudoun seemed indifferent to him. Without Loudoun's backing, Washington feared that he balanced "upon a tottering foundation indeed!"[6]

To shore up that foundation, Washington replayed the gambit he had deployed against Captain Dagworthy of Maryland. He would appeal directly to the British commander in America. This time, however, the playing field was different. He was challenging a royal governor (Dinwiddie), not an army captain, and was appealing to a man he had never met—Lord Loudoun. Washington's escalation of the spat with Dinwiddie was intemperate, and a distraction. Both men agreed on the best strategy for fighting the war: to sever French support for the tribes by seizing Fort Duquesne. Without that bold stroke, the purgatorial status quo would continue on the frontier.

∾

When Loudoun arrived in America in the late spring—before the Washington-Dinwiddie split widened—Dinwiddie endorsed Washington's pursuit of a royal commission. Over the summer, Washington wrote Loudoun a brief note expressing the Virginia Regiment's "singular satisfaction and sanguine hopes" for the new commander. Loudoun ignored both overtures.[7]

The new commander embodied the British tradition of promoting rich men with titles, without regard to military skills. He had lost several battles during the 1745 Scottish rising. A senior minister dismissed him as a "pen and ink man," and attributed Loudoun's failures to his "great corpulency added to his short sight." Indeed, Loudoun's great talent was for inaction. Ben Franklin compared him to "St. George on a tavern sign, always on horseback and never rides on." Loudoun was, however, wonderfully rich. He arrived in America with two secretaries, a surgeon, seventeen servants, a cook, a groom, a coachman, a postilion, a footman, uncounted helpers, two women (only one of whom was his mistress), and nineteen horses to pull lavish coaches.[8]

Washington's impassioned petition to Loudoun stretched for 4,500 words, a mountainous output for a man still uncomfortable with literary effort. It covered all three years of fighting on the Virginia frontier. Through that entire time, the letter explained, Dinwiddie and the General Assembly had stumbled repeatedly, while Colonel Washington had never been wrong.

A good deal of Washington's analysis was accurate. Virginia paid its soldiers poorly, provisioned them worse, and recruited from society's lowest rungs. The militia was slow in responding to emergencies and ineffective when it arrived. Yet Washington misjudged how his complaints might be received. Indeed, a logical response to Washington's cri de coeur would be to speedily disband the evidently hopeless Virginia Regiment. Washington's combination of self-righteousness (professing to be "sickened" to serve in such a ragtag military) with flattery (Loudoun's appointment caused "the dawn of hope [to] arise in my breast") was poorly calculated. The letter was such a transparent exercise in settling scores that a reader might well conclude that its author was a chronic complainer best excused from public office.[9]

Washington had hoped to hand his screed to Loudoun when the new commander visited Virginia, but that visit was canceled, so the Virginian submitted it through one of Loudoun's aides. To press his case, Washington requested leave to travel to Philadelphia, where Loudoun was to meet with colonial governors. Dinwiddie approved the leave but added a dry observation: "I cannot conceive what service you can be of in going there."[10]

Loudoun vindicated his reputation for sloth, arriving in Philadelphia weeks late. While the Virginian waited, a local printer began selling copies of the journal Washington had kept during the Battle of Fort Necessity; the document had fallen into the hands of the French, who had published it. Washington insisted that the French had altered his entries, but fresh reminders of his bitter defeat could only undermine his appeal to Loudoun.[11]

Brooding, Washington drafted another complaint to Dinwiddie, this time on the subordination of the Virginia officers to men who held British military commissions. Washington abandoned the servile tone he used with Loudoun and questioned "why we, who spend our blood and treasure in defense of the country are not entitled to equal preferment." British arrogance was chafing him.[12]

When Loudoun finally arrived in Philadelphia, Washington attended a couple of conference sessions, which rejected making an advance against Fort Duquesne in favor of attacking Canada. Far from supporting Washington in his quarrel with Dinwiddie, Loudoun shrank the Virginia Regiment by ordering four hundred Virginia troops to South Carolina. Having unwisely aired to a wide audience his differences with Dinwiddie, Washington's sole good news was that Maryland troops would take over Fort Cumberland, relieving him of that responsibility.[13]

ॐ

Returning to Winchester, Washington found more vexation. He still had to defend two hundred fifty miles of frontier, but now with only four hundred to seven hundred soldiers. He abandoned all but seven forts. Indian raiders rampaged at will. The House of Burgesses reduced the number of regimental companies to seven, so several captains had to be demoted or discharged. Legislation canceled Washington's 2 percent commission on regimental purchases.[14]

Ironically, Washington finally could call on Indian allies, because Dinwiddie had invited Catawba and Cherokee warriors to support the British on the colony's northwestern frontier. But Washington lacked the gifts the Indians expected to receive before they would fight. "An Indian," he observed with regret, "will never forget a promise made to him." Often cheated in trades with local settlers, the supposed Indian allies turned on the Virginians, stealing horses and much else. The colony was forced to hire "conductors" to hurry the Indians back southward to home while trying to restrain their larcenous impulses.[15]

With warmer weather came false alarms of enemy attacks on Cumberland and Winchester, where Washington began building a fort named for Lord Loudoun. Washington longed to attack Fort Duquesne, but could not without Loudoun's support. Militia remained useless, often abandoning assignments without explanation. Desertion ran as high as 25 percent.[16]

Once more, Washington imposed harsh discipline. On a single day in late July, a court-martial handed out ten death sentences, directed that four men receive fifteen hundred lashes, and ordered one thousand lashes for four others. Finally holding legal authority to execute soldiers, Washington boasted that Winchester had a gallows forty feet high. In August, he hanged two frequent deserters.[17]

Washington did not abandon the struggle with Indian raiders. He ordered his captains to keep scouting parties out and "take great pains to make your soldiers good marksmen." Washington also ordered them to stop "licentious swearing and all other unbecoming irregularities," to preserve the soldiers' clothes, and to "study of your profession." He concluded in ringing terms: "Discipline is the soul of an army. It makes small numbers formidable; procures success to the weak, and esteem to all."[18]

He was shouting into the void. The Indian raids continued. When half of a contingent of draftees deserted upon arrival, Washington could no longer summon anger. "They tire my patience," he wrote, "and almost weary me to death." The few remaining local residents, Washington reported, "are terrified almost beyond expression." Without capturing Fort Duquesne, he predicted, "this country will not be another year in our possession."[19]

The bad news continued. Washington lost a mentor when Colonel Fairfax died in late summer. In October, while attending the colonel's funeral, Washington learned that his quartermaster was embezzling. Soldiers were trading stolen equipment at Winchester's taverns. The bloody flux struck Washington hard, incapacitating him on some days.[20]

In low spirits, Washington sniped at Dinwiddie. "I am convinced it would give pleasure to the Governor," he wrote to Speaker Robinson, "to hear that I was involved in trouble: however undeservedly, such are his dispositions toward me." In July, when Washington asked for leave to attend to brother Lawrence's estate, Dinwiddie turned him down.[21]

Both men were becoming petty and ill tempered. The governor, having his own health troubles, repeatedly asked Washington to list the soldiers arriving on the frontier; Washington grudgingly agreed. When Dinwiddie expressed surprise at a change in the regiment's roster, Washington snidely replied, "If your Honor will take the trouble of looking" at Washington's reports, "it will immediately remove your surprise." Dinwiddie griped that Washington had not forwarded a letter and wondered why the construction of Fort Loudoun was taking so long. For months, they argued over how many servants a regimental officer might have, with Washington insisting on the same number allowed to British officers; Dinwiddie pushed for fewer to save money. Addressing payments for Indian gifts, the governor complained of Washington's "loose method of writing," adding, "it's your duty to be more particular to me."[22]

In a convoluted response, Washington apologized while jabbing back. "It is with pleasure I receive reproof, when reproof is due; because no person can be readier to accuse me, than I am to acknowledge an error, when I am guilty of one." But, Washington added, he faced accusations "in matters where I think I have rather exceeded than fallen short." Dinwiddie, unimpressed, repeated his previous complaint.[23]

The carping between two sick men—Dinwiddie's ailments led him to ask to be replaced as governor—reached another level when Washington learned of a rumor in Williamsburg that he had incited the frontier war in 1754 to advance the land claims of the Ohio Company. He exploded.

"It is evident," he wrote to Dinwiddie, "from the change in your Honor's conduct towards me, that some person . . . has made free with my character," giving the governor "so ill an opinion of my honor and honesty!" Washington could not control himself. "No man," he wrote, "that ever was employed in a public capacity has endeavored to discharge the trust reposed in him with greater honesty, and more zeal for the country's interest, than I have done," yet he found "my character arraigned and my actions condemned without a hearing."[24]

The governor denied hearing the rumor that so inflamed Washington, but added his own offended cry of pain:

> My conduct to you from the beginning was always friendly, but you know I had great reason to suspect you of ingratitude, which I'm convinced your own conscience and reflection must allow I had reason to be angry.

Dinwiddie closed by announcing his departure for England in November: "I wish my successor may show you as much friendship as I've done." Instead of bidding Dinwiddie a gracious farewell, Washington responded with a long harrumph: "If instances of my ungrateful behavior had been particularized, I would have answered to them. But I have long been convinced, that my actions and their motives, have been maliciously aggravated."[25]

The wounds would not heal. Dinwiddie denied Washington leave to come to Williamsburg, noting, "You have frequently been indulged with leave of absence." He directed Washington to finish Fort Loudoun. Washington howled back: "It was not to enjoy a party of pleasure I wanted leave of absence: I have been indulged with few of those, winter or summer!" The two men would spit at each other through the mail until Dinwiddie left Virginia in January 1758.[26]

It was a sad close to a relationship that had propelled Washington's advancement. Without appointments by Dinwiddie, the young Virginian might still have been surveying land for rich speculators. Both men were worn raw by an untenable military situation. Both had made errors large and small. Both had grown testy and given offense. Washington's conduct as the subordinate is more difficult to excuse. It was worse than bad manners; it was a mistake. Dinwiddie was returning to England, where Virginians' fates were still decided and where Washington needed influential friends; Dinwiddie would not be one. A cooler head than Washington's would not have erred so.

Throughout the unpleasant year, Washington's thoughts had returned to Mount Vernon and his plans to improve it. In April, he placed a large order with a London merchant for household items, including a marble chimney piece, wallpaper, two mahogany tables with chairs, and a dozen door locks and hinges. In September, he worried about the tobacco harvest and slave purchases.[27]

As the weather grew colder, the bloody flux tightened its grip on Washington. In November, when the doctor said he was dangerously ill, Washington did not bother to tell Dinwiddie. He rode home to Mount Vernon.

CHAPTER 13

New Paths

Through quiet winter days at Mount Vernon in early 1757, Washington could reflect on his three years of military service. His path had been difficult, with few episodes resembling success.

Between 1754 and 1758, French and Indian raiders would kill nearly 1,500 settlers on the Virginia and Pennsylvania frontier and take another 1,000 as captives, nearly 1 percent of the population of those colonies. More than 3 percent of the frontier population was killed or captured. Thousands fled to settled areas, sleeping in barns and stables. When he could, Washington fed them from his regimental supplies. In the eighteen months since Braddock's failure, roughly a third of his regiment's men were casualties or went missing.[1]

Despite this depressing record, in March 1758 Washington burst out of his emotional and physical trough to change his life in fundamental ways. Instead of chasing a military career, he would climb toward the top of Virginia society by improving his lands and winning a seat in the House of Burgesses. An essential part of that climb was finding a wife who could assist him on that path.

Washington won Martha Custis's wealthy hand in marriage during two visits to her home over a nine-day period in March.[2] Though they would long live in the public spotlight, Martha and George kept their relationship private, destroying almost all correspondence between them, including any account of their whirlwind courtship. In those first days, amid whatever flirting or compliments were in the air, they had much to talk about. Certainly Washington spoke of his recent illness and decision to abandon military life, plus his political ambition. They had to decide where they would live, so she learned of Washington's passion for Mount Vernon. It might have been early for Washington to reveal his feelings about his brother Lawrence, his tribe of siblings, or his flinty mother. He usually avoided talking about battles and war, and likely followed that practice when courting.

We also cannot know the thoughts they had but did not express. Did Martha find his size—roughly fourteen inches taller, with outsized hands—reassuring, intimidating, or exciting? Was he anxious about becoming a stepfather to Martha's small son and daughter? Perhaps he brought gifts for four-year-old Jacky and two-year-old Patsy. He should have condoled with Martha over the loss of her husband the year before. All of it must be imagined.

Washington would not have called on her unless they had socialized before, probably during quarterly "public times" in Williamsburg, when well-heeled Virginians came to shop, do business, and mix. As Mrs. Martha Dandridge Custis, she likely admired the tall, graceful soldier when he stepped on the dance floor; perhaps she took a turn with him. The couple had friends in common, including a Williamsburg lawyer who advised them both.[3]

The speed of the courtship carries the whiff of a transaction: that George traded his charisma, ambition, and warrior glory for the Custis fortune and position. Late in life, advising his step-granddaughter, Washington cautioned against a marriage based on mere emotion. "When the fire is beginning to kindle," he wrote, "and your heart growing warm, propound these questions to it. Who is this invader? Have I a competent knowledge of him? Is he a man of good character; a man of sense?" Washington added:

> For, be assured, a sensible woman can never be happy with a fool. What has been his walk of life? Is he a gambler, a spendthrift, or drunkard? Is his fortune sufficient to maintain me in the manner I have been accustomed to live . . . and is he one to whom my friends can have no reasonable objection?[4]

Colonel Washington and Mrs. Custis surely asked themselves such questions. He sought a mate to help build his fortune and his place. Why did Martha accept so quickly this athletic man with an affable manner? She did not need wealth from a second husband; she had money enough, though appearances required that he have enough to be respectable. She needed a stepfather for her two small children, a prudent manager for her wealth, a person with whom she would be proud to stand before the world. Washington met those standards.[5]

Although only twenty-six, he was used to responsibility, having held in his hands the fates of hundreds of soldiers and thousands of settlers. Those burdens had worn him ragged, but the experience taught him to carry them stoically, which he did most of the time. He had not yet achieved the solid and centered calm that would become such a great political asset. The fires in his heart could still burst out. But the trials of command had tempered his character. He was a man trusted by others. Martha Custis certainly thought she, too, could trust him.

But there was more to Washington. Through his life, he would draw sharp insights into the people around him. He was able to read tone and attitude and body language, the nonverbal cues that tell more than words do. His affability and courtesy masked the close attention he paid to others. Never a great wit, he was a warm and considerate companion, one who would wear well. Martha may not have thought through all of those considerations in the dizzying days of courtship, not in a way she would have articulated. But she certainly felt those qualities in the man before her, qualities that led her to say yes.

There were other dimensions to the bond they formed. Though Martha was a pretty and vivacious woman with bright hazel eyes, there was no mistaking which of them would be the peacock. The colonel—tall, magnetic, graceful—led off the dancing at every ball and cotillion. Indeed, one scholar found no record that Martha ever danced with him in public. She was barely five feet tall, with comfortable dimensions. She once ordered gloves "to fit a small hand and pretty large arm" and disarmingly described herself another time as a "fine, healthy girl."[6]

She understood business and plantation management. During her months of widowhood, she managed extensive estates and a large household, while also directing complex litigation over the Custis legacy, which dwarfed Washington's holdings. She and her children owned land and slaves in six counties, which were valued at £13,000, plus almost as much cash held on account in England.[7]

In choosing Martha, Washington did not follow the adage that a man marries a woman resembling his mother. With her small, round stature and warm nature, Martha was very different from tall, hard-edged Mary Washington. The match, of course, had its pragmatic side. Washington would not marry into a poor family, and Martha knew that he was a prominent figure with fine prospects. Whatever passions and infatuation they felt, whatever reasons and consequences they sorted through, they were adults who made their own decisions, and they apparently remained faithful to and loving with each other for forty years.

Washington moved swiftly toward his other goal, a career as a planter and political figure. When he first returned to Mount Vernon to recuperate from the bloody flux, he knew that any governor who succeeded Dinwiddie would call new elections. Friends expected the man from Mount Vernon to seek a seat from Frederick County.[8]

When Washington arrived in Williamsburg in March 1758, he had already passed through two career stages. He had burst on the scene as the boy wonder of the woods, the strapping teenage protégé of Colonel Fairfax and Lawrence, a hardy surveyor and Governor Dinwiddie's intrepid emissary to the French. Then Washington became, by Dinwiddie's appointment and with Colonel Fairfax's sponsorship, Virginia's leading military figure from the Battle of Fort Necessity through the end of 1757. Now Washington was resolved to stand on his own and chart his own course.

He would stay in uniform for one more campaign. The energetic William Pitt, Britain's new prime minister, was committed to the North American struggle with France. He adopted two measures that Washington welcomed.[9]

First, Pitt replaced the indolent Loudoun with General Jeffery Amherst, and appointed General John Forbes, a career military officer, to capture Fort Duquesne. Forbes, who had served in America for several years, brought strengths to his assignment. Having directed quartermaster functions, he knew supply and logistics, central challenges on the frontier. In addition, Forbes, unlike Braddock, formed alliances easily. One historian portrayed Forbes as "patient and open-minded," where Braddock was "arrogant and ignorant." Forbes knew that the effort would involve much more than crashing through the forest and storming the fort. His talents would serve the British well.[10]

Pitt also encouraged Americans to join the military effort. In letters to colonial governors, he pledged to provide ammunition and supplies for provincial troops. Each colony would be responsible only for recruiting the soldiers, clothing them, and paying them. Also, Pitt directed that a provincial officer's rank would be recognized as the equivalent of his British Army counterparts. Finally, British officers would have to respect Colonel Washington's status.[11]

Most colonists, like Washington, responded warmly to Pitt's initiatives. In March, Virginia's General Assembly resolved to raise a second regiment of 1,000 men, adopting new recruiting methods: Virginia would pay an extra £10 to each man who served until December 1. The bounty worked. By May, Washington's regiment numbered 950 men and the new, second regiment had 900. When Washington sought better pay for his soldiers, the Executive Council agreed.[12]

Forbes's expedition would advance against a weakened enemy. Although

British arms had met few successes in North America, the Royal Navy had cut off most ocean-borne supplies to French Canada, which was facing a food shortage. French support for the western tribes had plunged; predictably, Indian enthusiasm for the French cause also diminished.[13]

Washington, his ambition rekindled, angled for preference. He asked Colonel Stanwix to recommend him to Forbes "not as a person who would depend upon him for further recommendation," but solely to "serve this campaign." He made the same request of Major Thomas Gage, a fellow survivor of Braddock's expedition, again stressing that he had "laid aside all hopes of preferment in the military line." Though Stanwix and Gage likely discounted those disclaimers as disingenuous, Washington meant them.[14]

CHAPTER 14

Back into the Woods

To march against Fort Duquesne across what Indians called the "endless mountains" of western Pennsylvania, General Forbes spurned many of the decisions Braddock had made three years before. Forbes resolved to build depots along the route so his force could be resupplied steadily from nearby locations. "We shall be obliged to march like tortoises, very slowly," his top aide wrote, "and carrying everything on our back." Those depots also would provide rallying points if the army needed to withdraw and regroup.[1]

With becoming modesty, Forbes vowed to "learn the art of war from enemy Indians or anyone else who have seen the country and war carried on in it." His senior commander, Colonel Henry Bouquet, agreed that American conditions left them "groping into an unknown country." Bouquet was a different kind of British soldier: not British but Swiss, and willing to listen. Press reports declared him "the delight of the army."[2]

Forbes and Bouquet agreed with Washington that soldiers should be trained in bushfighting. Bouquet proposed to dress American soldiers in moccasins and blankets, cut off their hair, and paint their skin. He and Forbes applauded when Washington's men wore hunting shirts and breeches, not traditional uniforms.[3]

Forbes assembled a powerful force: 2,000 British regulars, plus 5,000 colonists, mostly from Pennsylvania and Virginia. The colonists lacked training and complained about missed paydays and inadequate food. Focused on his supply services, Forbes called the task of finding wagons "the plague of my life."[4]

To neutralize the greatest French advantage, Forbes courted the tribes. He did not need them to join his advance, only that they not oppose it. Patiently, the general worked through traders and Quakers to convene a conference with the tribes living south of the Great Lakes and east of the Wabash River. His representatives pledged that the British would not settle in the Ohio River valley, a promise most tribes doubted, but they could see that the British forces were numerous and determined. Moreover, the Royal Navy was blocking from Canada the supplies and ammunition the French should be giving to the Indians. Following their principle of never backing the losing side, most tribes assented to Forbes's persuasive plea that they "sit by your fires, with your wives and children, quiet and undisturbed, and smoke your pipes in safety. Let the French fight their own battles." When the British neared Fort Duquesne in late November, the French would lack their best fighters.[5]

Most of the army gathered in Philadelphia; only the Virginians joined during the march (see map on page 57). The column had to reach Fort Duquesne by December 1, when many Virginia enlistments would expire. Washington worried that the march would proceed due west from Philadelphia rather than swerve southwest to pick up Braddock's road through western Virginia. Washington pushed hard for the Braddock Road option. Pennsylvanians argued for driving straight over the Alleghenies. Forbes and Bouquet came to suspect that the competing advocates craved the economic advantage of having the road pass through their territories; the army's supply depots could become anchors for future settlement. If Bouquet and Forbes had known that the Braddock Road passed close by Washington's Bullskin lands, they would have dismissed his arguments as a crude lunge for personal gain.[6]

The army traveled west to Bedford on existing roads. After that, only deer and footpaths crossed the mountains. Forbes resolved to cut a new road due west, never entering Virginia. Braddock's road was only three years old and still relatively passable, but the all-Pennsylvania route was forty miles shorter.[7]

Bouquet, traveling with the army's leading edge, repeatedly found conditions to be different from what he had been told. One hill "which has been made a monster," he sputtered, turned out to be "very easy to cross." Forbes soured on the Americans, complaining to Prime Minister Pitt that the colonial officers were

an extreme bad collection of broken inn-keepers, horse jockeys, and Indian traders and that the men under them are a direct copy of their officers . . . as they are a gathering from the scum of the worst of people, in every country, who have wrought themselves up into a panic at the very name of Indians.[8]

When Washington realized that Bouquet and Forbes were bypassing the Braddock Road, he pressed his case even harder. In a late-July conference with Bouquet, he strenuously urged the Virginia route, echoing a recent letter he had sent denouncing the Pennsylvania option. Bouquet was unconvinced.[9] In a long letter to Bouquet, Washington called the Pennsylvania mountains "monstrous" while the Braddock Road's crossings of the Youghiogheny and Monongahela Rivers were "so trivial, they are hardly worth mentioning." After warning that the Pennsylvania route would take too long, he sent a near-hysterical note to an aide to General Forbes, leaping over the chain of command. If Bouquet persisted in rejecting the Braddock Road, Washington pleaded, "all is lost!—All is lost by heavens—our enterprise ruined."[10]

COURTESY OF THE LIBRARY OF CONGRESS

General John Forbes

That note was another impetuous mistake. Forbes disliked everything about it. "By a very unguarded letter of Colonel Washington that accidentally fell into my hands," he wrote, "I am now at the bottom of their scheme against this new road, a scheme that I think was a shame for any officer to be concerned in." He called Washington's efforts ridiculous. Undaunted, Washington continued to lobby for the Virginia route, earning ever greater resentment from Forbes and Bouquet.[11]

Though Washington had never seen the Pennsylvania country to be crossed, his criticism of that route had some force. The mountains were a formidable barrier.[12] Yet the Pennsylvania route required fewer supply depots and offered better locations for them. It also approached Fort Duquesne from a direction that would be more difficult for the French to defend. Since Forbes was using Pennsylvanians to conduct Indian negotiations, he was in their political debt. Finally, there was the power of inertia. Once resolved on the Pennsylvania route, Forbes would appear fickle if he changed his mind.[13]

Washington's choice to make himself obnoxious on the route question reflected more than a military judgment. As Bouquet and Forbes concluded, Washington was speaking as a Virginian. He made certain that his superiors in Williamsburg knew how strongly he urged the Virginia option. The Pennsylvania route, he assured the new governor, Francis Fauquier, would "forebode our manifest ruin." A month later, he lamented, "What a golden opportunity we have lost!" To Speaker Robinson, he wailed, "All is lost," adding that "nothing but a miracle can bring this campaign to a happy issue." He blamed crafty Pennsylvanians, who "prejudiced the General absolutely against the [Braddock] road."[14]

Washington's choice to oppose his army commanders—having previously made an enemy of Dinwiddie—reflected his plan to leave military service; that left little reason to accede quietly to decisions he thought wrong. For his postmilitary career, it would be more important to have defended Virginia's interests; he would never again seek preferment from the British Army.

Yet Washington's advocacy showed a blindness to Forbes's concerns, which undermined his message. Twenty years hence, a wiser Washington would carefully invite the views of others on key decisions, often asking for them in writing so he could study them at leisure. That later Washington was more often criticized as indecisive than as impulsive.

∾

In early summer, while Forbes and Bouquet organized the Fort Duquesne expedition, Washington took a decisive step toward his political career. In June, Governor Fauquier called for elections to the House of Burgesses. Unlike three years before, when Washington did nothing to press his candidacy, this time he proceeded methodically toward a contest in Frederick County, which involved challenging two incumbents. He did not fit his constituency all that well. With his aspirations to ascend Virginia's planter hierarchy, Washington stood apart from many of the people whose votes he needed. Frederick's voters included many Germans and Irish settled on small farms. Washington had sometimes disparaged county residents, calling them "a parcel of barbarians and an uncouth set of people." He had dismissed Winchester as "a vile hole" and had crusaded against the town's tavernkeepers, denouncing them for selling liquor to soldiers.[15]

Yet running in Frederick involved some shrewd calculation. Though he did not live there, his ties to the area were strong. He had surveyed there, owned the Bullskin properties there plus a few lots in Winchester, where his regimental headquarters was. To settlers who had faced Indian raids for three years, Washington was their protector. He also was boosting their economy by building Fort Loudoun in Winchester. Lord Fairfax still owned much of the county and Washington would lean on the Fairfax connection. Indeed, he joined his candidacy with that of Thomas Bryan Martin, a nephew of Lord Fairfax who helped run the family land business. With Fairfax support came the votes of Fairfax tenants. Washington also enlisted support from the founder of Winchester, from the Shenandoah valley's leading lawyer, and from the commander of Fort Loudoun.[16]

Washington's adversaries argued that his military duties would keep him from legislative work. To counter the claim, Washington's friends urged him to come to Winchester for Election Day. A key supporter insisted that if Washington was in Winchester, "I can then promise success." As the day drew close, the fort commander warned Washington that many "pretended friends, . . . now seem doubtful, and will not promise whether they'll give you a vote or not."[17]

Washington was undecided about leaving the regiment to attend the poll in Winchester. Colonel Bouquet grudgingly granted him leave for the trip, but duty won out over self-interest. Washington stayed with the army, fearing that if an emergency arose while he was absent, he would be criticized.[18]

Nevertheless, the poll went off seamlessly, beginning with the county's leading citizens. Lord Fairfax voted first, for Washington. Then came another supporter, then John Carlyle (the Fairfax son-in-law), then Fielding Lewis, married to Washington's sister. Washington won the votes of "gentlemen," three ministers, and nine voters with military titles. His total was 305 votes; Martin came next with 240. For the voters, the absent Washington paid for 160 gallons of wine, beer, rum punch, and cider, which represented roughly a half gallon of liquor for each vote, at a cost of just over 2 shillings apiece. To a supporter, Washington wrote that his "only fear is that you spent with too sparing a hand." The well-lubricated celebrants carried Washington's campaign chief around town in triumph. When Washington received the poll sheet, he created a second sheet that alphabetized the voters, for future reference. He did not intend this to be his last election.[19]

Until he took his seat in the assembly, Washington would continue with the regiment, serving under two senior officers who now viewed him skeptically. His goal was Fort Duquesne, which he had first targeted four years before. Taking the fort could serve as a capstone to his military career and springboard to a public career. Failing again would be a final embarrassment.

CHAPTER 15

The Push to Fort Duquesne

The 1758 advance on Fort Duquesne, like Braddock's three years before, became an exercise in road construction. Soldiers put aside their muskets for picks and shovels. Wagon hulks and smashed casks littered the roadside while rain turned clay soil into impassable goop. To cut one portion of road required more than 1,400 men. Colonial newspapers chronicled each step of the advance, impatient for success. Reporting to Prime Minister Pitt, Forbes blamed the forest, "an immense uninhabited wilderness overgrown everywhere with trees and underbrush, so that nowhere can anyone see twenty yards."[1]

One difference between the Braddock and Forbes expeditions loomed large: Braddock had neared Fort Duquesne in early July, the heart of the fighting season, while Forbes was still far from the fort when the weather turned cold. With Virginia enlistments expiring on December 1, Forbes was racing the calendar.

The British training in bushfighting skills helped little. In mid-September, a force of nearly 800 British and colonial troops (Virginians, but not Washington's regiment) crashed ahead of the roadbuilders to the threshold of Fort Duquesne, hoping to use surprise to inflict a quick reverse, maybe even carry the fort. Once again, French and Indian defenders fired from cover, driving the attackers into panicky retreat. Once again, the casualty figures were lopsided. The British lost 300 dead, more wounded and missing. Forbes, unaware of the thrust beforehand, denounced the officer in charge, whose "thirst of fame [had] brought on his own perdition, and run a great risk of ours."[2]

By November, the situation was dire. "Our affairs," Washington wrote to the governor, "are drawing to a crisis." The soldiers lacked warm clothes.

Provisions were short. The enlistment clock was ticking. Even if the attackers captured the fort, how would they endure the winter? Washington raised these questions in a letter to Bouquet, adding that whichever course the army took, "not a moment's time is left for hesitation." In the letter, Washington thought like an army commander, not a subordinate pursuing a personal agenda.[3]

Washington attended a council of war on November 11 that reviewed the risks he had identified, plus the army's ignorance of the French defenses, the danger of losing their artillery (as Braddock had), and the recognition that "defeat would be catastrophic." The council decided to abandon the advance.[4]

Before the army could turn around, news arrived of an approaching French force. Forbes sent Captain George Mercer with 500 Virginians to track it down. When he heard gunfire, Forbes dispatched Washington with more Virginians to support Mercer. In the fading light of an early winter sunset, the Virginia units opened fire on each other. Before the blundering ended, fourteen Virginians lay dead and more than thirty were wounded. Thirty years later, Washington claimed he was never in "more imminent danger" than when caught between those contending Virginians.[5]

Yet Washington salvaged something essential from the tragic botch. On that foray, his detachment took three prisoners, two Indians and an Englishman who had deserted from the French. The French at Fort Duquesne, the English prisoner reported, were few, had no tribal allies, and lacked supplies or reinforcements. They were dispirited and desperate.[6]

The news energized the British, who headed back into the woods with shovels and axes. After several days, Forbes ordered 2,500 men—with Washington's regiment in the lead—to push ahead without baggage. Forbes ordered dogs sent to the rear or hanged; no barking would disclose the British approach.[7]

On the night of November 24, a week before the Virginians would go home, an Indian scout reported a smoke plume from the direction of Fort Duquesne. Either the fort had suffered an accidental catastrophe or the French were burning it. Washington and the leading units hurried through the last twelve miles of forest, arriving at the Forks after sunset. The French were gone, floating downriver. The fort's ruins smoldered in the dark. The victory, won with neither battle nor glory, brought no treasure, not even provisions. Outside the fort's ruins lay the corpses of British soldiers who had been taken prisoner. Some were charred and tomahawked. It was a somber anticlimax of a victory, but the triumph was real.

In his report to Governor Fauquier, Washington called winning the fort "a matter of great surprise," caused by French "weakness, want of provisions, and the desertion of their Indians." He gave Forbes full credit.

Suffering terribly from the bloody flux, Forbes was only slightly more up-beat, noting that Britain had seized a "fine rich country" while achieving peace with most Indians.[8] But winter was coming and the army was vulnerable. "The men are greatly reduced," Bouquet admitted, "deficient of every necessary, half naked, without shoes, and without means of getting any." Forbes and most of his troops turned back to Philadelphia, where the general soon died. Virginians would hold the fort—renamed Fort Pitt—through the cold months. Washington, however, left to deliver his report in Williamsburg.[9]

∽

Once the British controlled the Forks of the Ohio, the crisis on Virginia's frontier largely ended. The western tribes accepted peace with Britain and its colonists. A Philadelphia newspaper predicted happy times: "Our back settle-ments, instead of being frightful fields of blood, will once more smile with peace and plenty."[10]

Though Washington had fought for four long years to pacify the frontier, the success was not his. He could claim no battlefield triumph, only the sad memory of the "friendly fire" encounter with Mercer's troops. Forbes, having ignored Washington's advice on which route to follow, had succeeded. Wash-ington had largely alienated those to whom he had reported—Dinwiddie, Forbes, Bouquet, and Loudoun.

He had, however, seen the difficult business through and still stood as Virginia's premier military man. By 1758 the Virginia Regiment had emerged as likely the best colonial military body, an extension of Washington's sense of duty and discipline. He could take satisfaction in the allegiance of his of-ficers, the men who knew him best. As one officer wrote, Washington was "an example of fortitude in either danger or hardships, and by his easy, polite behavior, has gained not only the regard but affection of both officers and soldiers." With Washington's departure from the regiment imminent, the officers expressed dismay at losing "such an excellent commander, such a sincere friend, and so affable a companion." Imploring Washington to con-tinue another year, they paid tribute to his "steady adherence to impartial justice, [his] quick discernment and invariable regard to merit." They called him "the actuating soul of the whole corps." In reply, Washington thanked his officers for "the love and regard you have all along shown me. It is in this, I am rewarded. It is herein I glory." [11]

Washington's experience with the Virginia Regiment would shape the general he became in the Revolutionary War. He learned the importance of logistics, paperwork, and organization. Having observed military professionals at close quarters, he understood how to issue clear orders, how to command, and the importance of controlling his temper. He also strove to be fair. When he took command of the Virginia Regiment in 1756, he promised "to study merit and reward the brave and deserving. . . . Partiality shall never bias my conduct, nor shall prejudice injure any." As his officers attested, he remained true to that pledge of "invariable regard to merit," a contrast with the British practice of selling military offices. During the next war, Washington would promote able officers, not rich ones.[12]

His early military service also revealed weaknesses. His lack of connection with common soldiers showed in his enthusiasm for harsh discipline. He was often too disgusted by the militia to use them well. He acquired little actual combat experience and never commanded a large unit. Perhaps most troubling, he could be impatient, self-promoting, and ready to leapfrog the chain of command. He disparaged Governor Dinwiddie and General Forbes to others. His sensitivity to criticism—perhaps the corollary of his aching need to win the regard of others—too often led to threats to resign.[13]

Washington seems to have learned from his missteps. During the Revolutionary War, his patience and deference to his civilian superiors, as well as his deft political maneuvering, would become hallmarks. Moreover, Washington's experience with the Virginia Regiment provided specific lessons in how to fight an American war. Many of the same challenges recurred in the second conflict: shortages of provisions and arms, balky political masters, short enlistments and widespread desertions, inconsistent pay, and inexperienced recruits. In both contests, a third force (the Indians in the first war, the French in the second) held the balance of power and had to be courted.

Most telling, the Forbes expedition illustrated the difference between strategic success and battlefield laurels. During the 1758 advance, the French and Indians prevailed in every significant encounter, but they lost the key strategic point they were defending. The British aimed to win control of the Forks, and they did. That experience would help Washington endure sometimes grim losses during the Revolutionary War. Battlefield triumphs, he had seen, did not guarantee final victory.[14]

Washington's years with the Virginia Regiment also fostered within him a deep disillusionment with Britain, which had resolutely excluded him from its army. That army's senior officers—save for the disgraced Braddock—had never recognized his worth, unable to see past his identity as a provincial. Yet, almost perversely, they were correct that Washington was not suited to a career in their stratified, class-bound institution. Throughout his life, Washington would be largely blind to the social and financial backgrounds of colleagues. Repeatedly, he advanced subordinates from modest backgrounds, solely on the basis of merit. Such an attitude was rare in the British Army and might well have held him back. His exclusion from that army, combined with the disdain with which British officers treated provincials, changed his path. He would never travel again beyond North America, and would never see the great buildings or glittering courts of Europe.[15]

Similarly, the history of America would have been very different if Washington had found a place in the British military. Perhaps, if his imperial masters had accepted him as an equal, some other person would have stepped forward to lead the American rebellion, to guide the nation to a new form of government, and to establish that government on a stable foundation. Then again, American rebels might have had to face British forces led by George Washington of Virginia, with his understanding of American ways and aspirations. But at the end of 1758, when Washington rode off from Fort Duquesne (now Fort Pitt), he turned away from the empire he had grown up in. He would be an American first, and only an unenthusiastic subject of the king.

From his four years on the frontier, Washington also learned that the British Army could stumble badly. In two major campaigns, he never saw it prevail in battle. His later conduct showed his belief that he was the equal of any British officer. That confidence would be invaluable when the time came to fight against Britain. In that contest, he would promote few officers with experience in the British Army, preferring Americans with talent but less experience. On the frontier, he also learned the value of luck. He had walked away from bloody failures at Fort Necessity and with Braddock. He knew he had been fortunate to survive and to retain his good reputation. While leading the Continental Army nearly two decades later, he admitted "grateful remembrance of the escape we had at the Meadows and on the banks of the Monongahela."[16]

For other Americans, too, the French and Indian War eroded their regard for British might. One Virginian suggested that although Americans had acted in the conflict as "dutiful children" of their "common mother," he now entertained the idea of "the children doing well without the parent." He added, "God only knows . . . what grand revolutions may be ripe for birth."[17]

For the new year of 1759, however, Washington's focus was on his impending marriage and prospects as a gentleman politician. Just as ambition and a thirst for public reputation marked his years as a military man, they would remain central to his next stage of life.

CHAPTER 16

Washington in Love

To prepare for married life, the methodical Washington paid his property taxes, settled some financial accounts, and totted up his land holdings (4,715 acres in Fairfax and Frederick Counties).[1] He and Martha married on January 6, 1759, at or near Martha's home in New Kent County, with a few close relatives present. The Washingtons remained there for several weeks while the Mount Vernon renovations continued, allowing Washington to learn about Martha's property, which Virginia law confided to his control as her husband.[2]

More than three months before the ceremony, while part of the advance on Fort Duquesne, Washington wrote a letter to Sally Fairfax, wife of his best friend, George William Fairfax. That letter has become notorious. Many have concluded that it reveals Washington's passion for Mrs. Fairfax, a conclusion that humanizes Washington by showing him the slave of a love that nearly burst his heart, while also painting him as a cad, cheating on his fiancée by making an unsubtle play for his best friend's wife. The truth of the incident is elusive.

By 1758, Washington had known Sally Fairfax for nearly a decade, during most of which time she was married to George William. George William and Sally lived at Belvoir with Colonel Fairfax. Washington was a frequent visitor.

The paper trail of the friendship between Washington and Sally begins with a letter from the beginning of the Braddock march in 1755. Washington offered social gossip, reported army news, and asked that Sally correspond with him, a request he made three weeks later to the wife of another friend, John Carlyle. Sally Fairfax's one-sentence response in late July—also signed by two of her women friends—thanked heaven for his safe return from the slaughter on the Monongahela and promised to visit him at Mount Vernon. Fourteen months later, he learned that a seamstress was staying at Belvoir, so he sent fabric and a shirt of his, asking that the seamstress make him another shirt. When Washington straggled home in late 1757, miserable with the bloody flux, he sought Sally's assistance in assembling the foods for his recovery. In early 1758, Washington sent to her two short notes with mundane messages. Because one transmits to Sally a letter from George William in London, it suggests an opportunity in that winter for a depressed soldier and a lonely wife to find solace in each other's arms.[3]

After those infrequent and thoroughly unromantic exchanges, Washington's letter of September 12, 1758, from Fort Cumberland, represented a sea change. In elaborate, sometimes clumsy phrases, he expressed joy over renewing their correspondence, a joy he claimed to keep in a silence that "speaks more intelligibly than the sweetest eloquence." He denied that his conflict with General Forbes was due to "anxiety" at "the animating prospect of possessing Mrs. Custis"—so his engagement to Martha was no secret from Sally. Washington then wrote the opaque phrases that have confounded for generations:

> Tis true, I profess myself a votary to love—I acknowledge that a lady
> is in the case—and further I confess, that this lady is known to you . . .
> as well as she is to one who is too sensible of her charms to deny the
> power, whose influence he feels and must ever submit to. I feel the
> force of her amiable beauties in the recollection of a thousand tender
> passages that I could wish to obliterate.

The puzzle begins with an omission. Washington states that he is a "votary to love," but does not name his love object. Indeed, rather than pledging himself to Martha, his betrothed, he implies that his devotion is directed to another "known" to Sally—perhaps Sally herself? He then admits, "Experience alas! sadly reminds me how impossible this is." Putting impossibility aside, he then restates his mysterious confession of a simple fact:

> Misconstrue not my meaning— 'tis obvious—doubt it not, nor expose
> it—the world has no business to know the object of my love, declared
> in this manner to—you when I want to conceal it—One thing, above
> all things in this world I wish to know, and only one person of your
> acquaintance can solve me that, or guess my meaning—but adieu to

this, till happier times, . . . I dare believe that you are as happy as you say—I wish I was happy also.

At this point, likely to the relief of both writer and recipient, Washington turned to matters unrelated to love.

Two weeks later, Washington penned another murky passage to Sally, beginning: "Do we still misunderstand the true meaning of each other's letters. I think it must appear so, though I would fain hope the contrary as I cannot speak plainer without—but I'll say no more, and leave you to guess the rest." He then related war news, but circled back with a literary reference to his desire to act as "the Juba to such a Marcia as you must make." That referred to the play *Cato*, by Joseph Addison, popular in colonial Virginia though rarely performed in the last century. At social gatherings, Virginians staged readings of the work. In the drama, Juba is a Numidian prince whose love for Cato's daughter Marcia must be denied. Washington and Sally may have read those roles at a party.

Several factors limit our understanding of the letters. Most obviously, we do not know what he and Sally had spoken to each other beforehand, nor do we know what Sally wrote to him between his first and second letters. She may have written that she wondered what on earth he meant in his first letter. Also, because Washington and Martha destroyed almost all correspondence between them, we cannot compare what he wrote to Martha at the same time, or even how he customarily wrote to the woman he spent most of his life with.

Two conflicting interpretations of these letters suggest themselves.[4]

The first is that Washington was professing his undying secret love for Sally.[5] The words in the letters, though cloudy, will bear that interpretation. Washington's reference to "a thousand tender passages" suggests a long connection with the object of his love; he had, in fact, known Sally for a decade, and had spent far less time with Martha. The references to being a "votary of love" and to the doomed love of Juba and Marcia in *Cato* reinforce the idea that Washington was confessing deep, taboo feelings. (Juba, an African, crossed racial lines in pursuing the Roman Marcia.) Around this time, Washington had written impetuous and ill-advised letters to Governor Dinwiddie. This note to Sally came from the same volatile young man. Also, Sally retained the letter for the next fifty years, an act of preservation that could reveal its significance.

Yet the context of the letters undermines this interpretation. Washington was writing while cooling his heels at Fort Cumberland, bored and (by his own admission) unhappy, four months before his scheduled marriage to

Martha. He specifically refers to "the animating prospect of possessing Mrs. Custis." The first letter also includes the wish to see Sally's family, which certainly included her husband, George William. Indeed, that summer George William was overseeing the repairs to Mount Vernon. On the same day that Washington wrote the first letter to Sally, he also wrote to George William. Both letters—one to husband and one to wife—were delivered by George Mercer, a mutual friend, not by some confidential messenger. Both Sally and her husband thus knew that the other received a letter from Washington in an era when the arrival of correspondence was an event and letters were routinely shared. Washington would expect the Fairfaxes to show those letters to each other, or at least to talk about them. If Washington had truly been proposing a tryst with Sally—or confirming or ending one—he took a huge risk of discovery by his friend.

All of those contextual factors might be dismissed if Washington was known as a risk-taker in his personal life, or if he was likely indifferent to the judgments of society or to the feelings of George William or Martha Custis. But none of those statements is true.

Washington was punctilious in his private conduct and placed extraordinary importance on his public reputation and on the Fairfax connection. Both Colonel Fairfax and Lord Fairfax had been essential sponsors. His election to the House of Burgesses was a festival of Fairfax support. On polling day, Winchester bristled with Fairfaxes supporting Washington, including Lord Thomas, George William, nephew Bryan Martin, and brother-in-law John Carlyle. Washington had urged his brother Jack to cultivate the Fairfaxes. His brother Lawrence had married George William's sister, and a cousin (Warner Washington) had married another Fairfax sister. The notion that Washington would risk tearing up those connections is difficult to swallow. His love affair, as one historian has shrewdly noted, was with the Fairfax family, not with Sally.[6]

Equally difficult to swallow is the idea that he would imperil his marriage to Martha Custis, whose wealth could elevate him in the Virginia hierarchy. While still a teenager, Washington had seen the pain inflicted by the accusation that Reverend Charles Green had taken advantage of Lawrence's young wife, Anne Fairfax. Such sensational episodes linger long in memories, and Washington could hardly have wished for another sex scandal involving a Fairfax woman and a Washington man.[7]

Indeed, a romantic dalliance with Sally Fairfax would have been contrary to Washington's resolutely prudent approach to life, which involved building and burnishing his public reputation. That contradiction has made the possibility of a dalliance between Sally and Washington even more appealing to historians, happy to detect a juicy transgression by the starchy, sanctimonious Washington. That this possibility is entirely implausible seems to enhance its allure. It remains, however, implausible.

The remaining alternative is that Washington's letters to Sally were a mannered, maladroit bit of play between friends. As noted by one editor of Washington's papers, his socializing with Sally Fairfax and other women at Belvoir often groaned under the weight of a "labored gallantry." The eighteenth century featured awkward banter between the sexes. Other messages to ladies from Washington, and some written by Thomas Jefferson and Benjamin Franklin, can induce cringes from modern readers. Washington, bored and frustrated in his frontier posting, might well have hazarded such banter with a friend who should not (he thought) misunderstand him.[8]

Contemporaries portrayed Washington as a man who enjoyed a joke. His letters included occasional jests, though they generally fell short of nimble badinage or deft satire. Sometimes he polished an attempt at wit by repeating it to multiple recipients. Through his many years in public life, under the gaze of dutiful diarists, diligent correspondents, and simple gossips, he made few remarks so humorous that anyone thought to write them down. Accordingly, it should not be shocking to find that, while relatively young, an attempt at drollery was ill considered, opaque, or awkward.[9]

When Washington first proposed that Sally correspond with him in 1755, he suggested it would "enliven dull hours and make me happier than I am able to express." The better explanation of his letters to her in 1758 is that he was, indeed, enlivening dull hours, though somewhat ineptly. That this explanation is an interpretation of cloudy text ensures that the controversy will continue.[10]

∾

On his twenty-seventh birthday, February 22, 1759, Washington took his seat in the House of Burgesses, listening with his new colleagues to the address of Governor Fauquier. Four days later, the House adopted a resolution thanking Washington for his "faithful services . . . and for his brave and steady behavior" in fighting the French. Notably absent was any recitation of a battlefield victory. He might have winced inwardly that the resolution also applauded the "happy reduction of Fort Duquesne," a victory achieved by ignoring his advice.[11]

Any wince would have passed quickly. He was leaving military life behind, though the reputation for bravery won on the frontier would live on. For now, he was resolved on a new career as husband, stepfather, farmer, and politician. His mother, who never wanted him in the army, cheered the change, writing to her brother in England that "there was no end to my trouble while George was in the army."[12]

The man who stood before the burgesses in late February had been shaped by many forces, including three parents. His father, Gus, gave him an agreeable disposition and great physical gifts. Mother Mary imbued in him discipline and drive. Brother Lawrence cared for him through awkward adolescent years and offered both a model for self-advancement and a leg up on that effort. Washington now had to launch himself, without title or great wealth, into the hierarchical world of colonial Virginia and the British Empire.

In April, when the newlyweds finally moved into Washington's "mansion house" on the Potomac, Halley's Comet was lighting up American skies. For those inclined to read portents in the heavens, it could only seem promising. By September, another symptom of married life emerged in Washington's order to a British merchant. Buried in a long list of items was a request for four ounces of Spanish fly, an aphrodisiac of high reputation.[13] Washington was embracing his new life and his new wife.

PART II

I cannot conceive how [George Washington] could . . . have ever been spoken of as a great man. He is shy, silent, stern, slow and cautious, but has no quickness of parts, extraordinary penetration, nor an elevated style of thinking. . . .

—*Jonathan Boucher,*
tutor to Washington's stepson (1776)[1]

CHAPTER 17

The New Life

In 1759, Washington's life transformed. He put aside his uniform. He unbuckled his sword. No longer would he resemble the hero in a boy's adventure tale, thundering on horseback in pursuit of Indians and treacherous Frenchmen, braving icy rivers and scaling craggy peaks. He exchanged military service for a legislative job and the endless trials of plantation management. Martha and her children brought him an instant family. Once he was installed at Mount Vernon, his ascent through Virginia society would proceed by a new route.

Free from physical dangers, he faced other challenges. Stepparenthood brought frustrations and sorrows. Virginia agriculture was entering a decades-long decline that would limit the fortune that Mount Vernon's thin soil could yield. His dream of a western land empire would collide with British policies, resentful tribes, and falling land prices. Conflicts with Britain would simmer, recede, boil, and finally explode, heaving Washington to the front of a movement toward self-government and liberty that still echoes more than two centuries later.

During the sixteen years until public events again seized him by the collar, Washington would develop the political skills and self-mastery that would inspire his countrymen. In place of the impetuous colonel would arise a patient leader, willing to listen to others while keeping a finger on the public pulse. Years of colonial politics would teach him to measure words and consider actions, while gauging the consequences of both.

Some skim over Washington's relatively obscure years between the Virginia Regiment and the Continental Army.[1] Yet those sixteen years—as a businessman, legislator, judge, and community leader—formed the man he became. Washington was not the only person for whom age brought more seasoned judgment, but his evolution was dramatic. He observed closely the leadership styles of prominent Virginians, drawing lessons to meld with his own talents. His private roles as husband, stepfather, and neighbor deepened his understanding of people, his world, and himself. All of those experiences produced a master politician.

∾

In the winter months of 1759, waiting for the Mount Vernon renovations to be finished, Washington had quiet winter days at the Custis estate on the Pamunkey River to learn about the three people who would share his new life: Martha, four-year-old Jacky, and two-year-old Patsy. Having lost two infant children to illness, Martha could be a fretful mother. When she forced herself to spend a few nights away from Jacky, she assumed every noise was a messenger with terrible news. "I often fancied he was sick," she confessed to her sister, "or some accident had happened to him." Martha's anxieties grew when her daughter, Patsy, developed fits and fevers that proved to be epilepsy.[2]

Those first weeks were likely tentative ones as children and adults explored new roles. Washington was a dutiful stepfather, but deferred to Martha on child-rearing matters. Her indulgent mothering style—some described Jacky as spoiled—contrasted with Mary Washington's stern approach. Washington likely had to suppress his preference for discipline and order, qualities that small children rarely display. Stepparents were common in the eighteenth century, an era when parent mortality rivaled infant mortality, yet the relationship brought the same challenges then as in any era. Washington explained his caution as a stepparent in a letter to Jacky's schoolmaster. "[I] conceive there is much greater circumspection by a guardian than a natural parent," he wrote, because "any faux pas in a guardian however well meant the action, seldom fails to meet with malicious construction." That sentence was written by someone who likely had committed such faux pas and been chastised for it.[3]

As Martha's husband and guardian for Jacky and Patsy (he never adopted them), Washington controlled the Custis plantations, which covered thousands of acres between Williamsburg and Richmond. Washington needed to consult with the longtime steward of the Custis lands, meet the farm overseers, and review enslaved laborers and accounts. The Custis properties concentrated on tobacco, a demanding and fickle crop that Washington intended to grow at Mount Vernon. In addition, Washington directed the defense of a

long-running lawsuit brought by illegitimate Custis descendants. Those responsibilities were a constant reminder that Jacky and Patsy were Daniel
Parke Custis's children, blessed with wealth Washington had not known.[4]

After six weeks, the new family moved on to Williamsburg, where the
House of Burgesses was to convene. Lodging was easy. They stopped on the
way at the home of Martha's favorite sister, Anna Maria, and husband Burwell Bassett; in Williamsburg, they stayed in the "six-chimney house" that
Martha owned.[5]

Williamsburg had changed little in the eight years since Washington arrived
there from Barbados. Several miles from coastal ports, without an important
crossroads, its commerce was small. The modest colonial bureaucracy and
the College of William & Mary were the town's highlights. Well-heeled visitors revived the sleepy town whenever the burgesses met, and also during
quarterly market weeks when the courts convened. At those times, the colony's elite socialized, gambled, and drank in taverns and boardinghouses. In
Virginia, more than half of adult white males could vote, but the gentry—
especially the Carters, Randolphs, Byrds, and Nelsons—filled the colony's
top offices.[6]

The Washington carriage rolled into Williamsburg past scattered resi-
dences and three brick college buildings, then down Duke of Gloucester
Street, a wide passage that bustled during market weeks with liveried ser-
vants and sleek riding horses. It passed the Governor's Palace, which rose
three full stories to a steep roof and a cupola that climbed another thirty feet.
That end of town held the wealthiest residents, some of whom sat on the
Executive Council. Taverns and inns clustered at the other end, near the
Capitol.

During the day, merchants and lawyers and planters traded goods, land,
and slaves in an open space across from the courthouse called the Exchange.
William Hunter's print shop produced the colony's newspaper. The racetrack
east of Waller Street drew spectators to wager on horses that ran as many as
three heats, each heat looping four times around the mile-long track. A new
theater stood on the main street.[7]

Most visitors, coming from isolated plantations, brought holiday attitudes. Decades later, Washington recalled "a successive round of visiting and
dinners" in Williamsburg, which made it "not possible for a man to retire
sober." Indeed, he added, anyone remaining sober was subject to an "imputa-
tion which even a person of philosophic cast did not choose to merit." A

Frenchman described the scene as "at night, carousing and drinking in one chamber and box and dice in another, which continues till morning commonly." The colony's leading citizens, he reported, were all gamesters. For a man with Washington's taste for cards, Williamsburg offered ample opportunities.[8]

Two figures dominated the colony's politics. The lieutenant governor, Francis Fauquier, held executive powers and presided when the General Court heard cases. Formerly a director of the South Sea Company, the wealthy Fauquier had written learned articles on public finance. His smooth manners and talent for conciliation compared favorably with the prickly Dinwiddie. Washington would be sure to make Fauquier's acquaintance.

Washington already knew the other powerful man: John Robinson, the House Speaker who also was the colony's treasurer. The assembly session of February 1759 marked Robinson's twenty-first year in office, and his power rivaled the governor's. To his masters in London, Fauquier called Robinson "the darling of the country, as well he deserves to be for his great integrity, assiduity, and ability in business." An early history of Virginia sang Robinson's praises:

> He stated to the house the contents of every bill, and showed himself to be a perfect master of the subject. When he pronounced the rules of order, he convinced the reluctant. When on the floor of a committee of the whole house, he opened the debate, he submitted resolutions and enforced them with simplicity and might.

Yet great power can corrode integrity. That same account acknowledged that Robinson "was for a long time elevated above the criticism of his faults," having built a network of alliances with "the thousand little flattering attentions which can be scattered from the chair."[9]

Some resented Robinson's power, which included naming committee chairs, setting the legislative agenda, and leading debate. Calling Robinson the "big man," one critic lamented, "What he can't do himself he prompts others to do by his nods, . . . as the division must run to whichsoever side he sits." The London Board of Trade directed Fauquier to replace Robinson in the Treasurer's Office, yet Fauquier never felt strong enough to do it.[10]

As an eager speculator in western lands, Robinson had formed the Loyal Company, a competitor with the Ohio Company led by the Washington and Lee families. That competition never undermined relations between Washington and Robinson. While commanding the Virginia Regiment, Washington leaned on the Speaker for support. During Washington's 1756 journey to Boston, he stayed for a week with Robinson's brother in New York.

The Speaker placed the new delegate from Frederick County on the pivotal Committee on Propositions and Grievances. Though a novice legislator, Washington commanded respect for his knowledge of war, Indians, and the militia. Expertise on those subjects was sparse in a body filled with tobacco planters and their lawyers.[11]

On the morning of February 23, the day after his birthday, Washington entered the Capitol's west wing through its twelve-foot-high door. The chamber bore royal trappings, from the Speaker's mace of authority to the king's coat of arms hanging next to Virginia's. The burgesses sat on benches that faced each other on either side of the chamber, in the style of the House of Commons in London. Washington swore an oath of allegiance to King George II and subscribed to the Test Act, which blocked Catholics from holding office. He was the fifth Washington to join the House, though none of his forebears had risen to prominence in it.[12]

The legislative day began with prayers at eight, followed by committee meetings. The full house convened in late morning and usually continued until midafternoon. Washington's first priority was mastering legislative procedures and jargon. Bills were proposed, shunted to committees, reported back, debated, given first and second readings, amended, sent back to committees, amended again, debated again, and perhaps passed, only to be reviewed thereafter by the council, the governor, and the king's ministers. Many bills involved issues that were new to Washington, like tobacco inspection and issuing currency.

Though all burgesses had one vote, not all were equal. Committee chairmen, those with sharp reasoning skills, and those with a gift for speaking counted for more. Oratory mattered. Every day, more than half the burgesses listened to debate. Great landowners like John Robinson also counted for more. The early days of a session were slow, often devoted to individual claims for runaway slaves or deserting soldiers. Significant legislation came up in hectic final days.[13]

Washington's first session addressed no momentous issues. Anxious about finances, the assembly declined to provide more soldiers for the war, adopting a tone of regret. "How sorry then must we be," read its response to Governor Fauquier, "when the incapacity of the country obliges us to inform your honor that we cannot support a greater number of forces."[14]

Washington, never comfortable with public speaking, held his tongue. The legislative journal records no speech or action by him after the resolution honoring his military service. Reticence in debate became a hallmark. Though Washington voiced opinions in conversation, he rarely spoke on the floor, and then only briefly. In a letter to a nephew almost three decades later, Washington's advice reflected his own conduct:

> Speak seldom, but to important subjects, except such as particularly relate to your constituents, and in the former case make yourself *perfectly* master of the subject. Never exceed a *decent* warmth, and submit your sentiments with diffidence. A dictatorial style, though it may carry conviction, is always accompanied with disgust.[15]

Washington focused on bills with an impact on Frederick County. Winchester merchants sought to force Pennsylvania fur traders to pay Virginia fees when they did business in Virginia, and Lord Fairfax petitioned to extend Winchester's municipal limits to include 173 building lots he hoped to sell. Both bills passed, though more experienced legislators sponsored them. Indeed, Washington did not stay to the end of his first session, securing permission to leave nearly two weeks early. He likely was not missed.[16]

Though he left the faintest of footprints on that first session, Washington had begun his education as a legislator, watching and listening to nearly two hundred hours of the maneuvering, posturing, and horse-trading that produces legislation in a deliberative body. He was part of decisions to defy the British request for soldiers, to issue paper money, and raise taxes on liquor.[17] He saw at close hand how political interests clash, how alliances are formed and opinions shaped, and how legislators can be persuaded. He worked at reading men's intentions, a talent he would master. His conduct matched the advice he would give years later when his stepson, Jacky Custis, entered the Virginia legislature. Junior members, Washington observed, are not usually influential, "But it is in your power to be punctual in your attendance . . . —to hear dispassionately—and determine coolly all great questions."[18]

Few House members in 1759 would have foreseen Washington's emergence as a force in Virginia politics. It would take years for that to happen.

CHAPTER 18

To Mount Vernon

While traveling to Mount Vernon from his first legislative session, Washington worried that his home on the Potomac might not impress his new family, so he sent instructions to his senior servant to clean and air out the rooms. The servants, he continued, should assemble "two of the best bedsteads" for the Custis children, polish the staircase, and put out chairs and tables "very well rubbed and cleaned." He also ordered the acquisition of eggs and chickens for meals.[1]

Mount Vernon was central to Washington's deepest aspirations. A worthy home confirmed a gentleman's wealth, status, and taste. Washington had lived there as a small boy, and in stretches when it was Lawrence's home. Mount Vernon had brought him the Fairfax connection. Now he meant to be a country gentleman there, far from Ferry Farm. Lawrence had expanded the residence, widening its foundation and adding decorative elements. While still serving on the frontier, Washington planned more improvements.[2]

He started with a new entrance so guests would approach from the northwest on a path that framed a view of the mansion. Washington created a new parlor and dining room, also on the landward side. For the exterior he ordered beveled boards to be covered with paint sprinkled with sand, which created the illusion that the house was built of stone. Washington designed a shingle roof, an added cornice at the tip, and enlarged chimneys that required 16,000 bricks. Inside the house, he raised most ceilings and installed new flooring. Workmen, many of them enslaved, built baseboards, window and door trims, and moldings. He planned outbuildings for cooking and laundry, with brick walks connecting to the main house.[3]

A few months later, a visitor celebrated Mount Vernon as "beautifully situated upon a high hill on the banks of the Potomac," with "a noble prospect of water, of cliffs, of woods, and plantations."[4] For the next forty years, Washington would ever long to be there with Martha. For a person with burning ambition, a place that brings calm and a mate who reinforces it are gifts. After a few months at home with his new family, Washington wrote, "I am now, I believe, fixed at this seat with an agreeable consort for life and hope to find more happiness in retirement than I ever experienced amidst a wide and bustling world."[5]

George and Martha showed every sign of suiting each other. Martha's upbringing as the eldest of eight had been comfortable, but not grand. Even after marrying the very rich Daniel Parke Custis, she remained a direct, considerate countrywoman. Abigail Adams, who did not trim her judgments, later praised Martha's sociability and grace. "Mrs. Washington," Adams wrote to her sister, "is one of those unassuming characters which create love and esteem." Martha's soft manners concealed a talent for management honed as the mistress of the Custis plantation house. After that experience, she was a match for Mount Vernon.

Through the years, George and Martha appeared to cherish each other's company. "His worthy lady," a friend wrote, "seems to be in perfect felicity while she is by the side of her Old Man as she calls him." Another thought Martha "excessive fond of the general and he of her. . . . They are happy in each other." The youthful Marquis de Lafayette concluded that Martha loved Washington "madly." In Martha's lone surviving note to Washington, she greeted him tenderly as "My dearest," and signed herself "most affectionate."[6]

Washington intended Mount Vernon to frame a life of gentility and distinction. Because Virginians mostly lived far from towns, social life happened in homes. A visit could last a day, or five, with multiple guests overlapping their stays. Visiting gentlemen slept in shared rooms separate from visiting ladies. Large-scale entertaining showed that the host had both means and style. The grandest homes staged dances featuring minuets, country dances, and reels, often ending with a round of improvised jigs.[7]

∾

At Mount Vernon, the Washingtons' life focused on family and neighbors, the men Washington did business with, and a few soldier friends. Washington remained close to his brother Jack and to his lone sister, Betty, who lived in Fredericksburg near their mother. Washington often stopped with her family and his mother on the way to Williamsburg and back. Brothers Sam and Charles, less frequent visitors, lived in the area until moving west to the upper Shenandoah valley.[8]

Martha's relatives came often, especially the Bassetts. Upon the birth of a Bassett child, Washington cheerfully chided the new father for missing Sunday services necessary for "every good Christian man who has as much to answer for as you have." Without sufficient prayer, Washington warned, Bassett's tobacco crop would be "assailed by every villainous worm that has had an existence since the days of Noah (how unkind it was of Noah . . . to suffer such a brood of vermin to get a berth in the ark)."[9]

The most vexing family connection was his mother. Though Mary visited Mount Vernon before the marriage, she seems never to have returned afterward. As Washington moved into more rarefied circles, with his rich and sweet-natured wife on his arm, there may have seemed no place for the blunt-spoken mother. Or perhaps Martha and Mary struck sparks: Mary was never accused of spoiling *her* children, nor of holding her tongue. Nonetheless, the untraveled path from Fredericksburg to Mount Vernon creates a poignant image of Washington leaving behind the mother who had shaped him.[10]

When it came to socializing with neighbors, George William and Sally Fairfax were at the top of the list. Martha and Sally traded notes; the men shared tools and supplies.[11] In 1767, the two couples vacationed together in the Shenandoah valley. Reciprocal visits were constant. Through the first five months of 1760, they swapped nearly a dozen visits. Over a five-year period, they totaled from twenty-five to forty-nine visits each year. Some included Bryan Fairfax, George William's younger brother, who acquired his own estate and became Washington's frequent hunting companion.[12]

Friendship with another neighbor, George Mason of nearby Gunston Hall, was more restrained on Washington's side. Seven years older than Washington, Mason periodically took to his bed in ill health. He sometimes sent grafts from his fruit trees, but Washington offered fewer courtesies in return. The two men occasionally sparred over boundary lines and other financial matters. Nonetheless, they would form a notable political partnership in the 1770s.[13]

"I keep not copies of epistles to my friends," Washington declared, which makes it difficult to chart his friendships. Some ties are plain. In the regiment, he grew close to Captain Robert Stewart, whose frequent letters to Washington could be effusive. Stewart took "extreme pleasure" at hearing from Washington in one, found that pleasure "inexpressible" in another, and wrote in a third "with a heart that overflows with gratitude." Washington did not preserve his replies to Stewart, but when his friend needed money to buy a British Army commission, Washington borrowed the funds, then loaned them to Stewart without charging interest.[14]

The two men fell out of touch when Stewart pursued positions in England, though Washington repeatedly tried to track down his old friend. When the Revolutionary War ended, Stewart surfaced, his lush rhetorical style intact. Referring to his undiminished feeling toward Washington, Stewart trilled that "The poets and historians of after ages shall vie with each other in endeavoring to represent it in its true brilliancy." Then he asked for a job in the new American government. Courteously, and perhaps with sadness for a friendship gone cold, Washington explained that those who had fought for independence would fill the available jobs.[15]

For Washington, the sturdiest ties came from military service, with its shared sacrifices and fellowship. He wrote with affection to two British officers he knew from the frontier war. Dr. James Craik, an Alexandria surgeon with the Virginia Regiment, became a friend for life. Twice, Craik would join Washington on weeks-long rambles to examine western lands. He attended Washington at his death.[16]

Craik also was one of many physicians consulted about young Patsy's epilepsy, an illness whose inexorable advance shadowed the family. Her fits, with convulsions that dropped her to the floor, were terrifying. Superstition attributed the disturbing symptoms to satanic possession or other supernatural cause. Medicine offered no treatment for it.

Symptoms of Patsy's affliction surfaced as early as 1760, when she was four. The Washingtons went well beyond the routine therapies of the era—purging the digestive system and bleeding. At an early stage, Patsy took mercury pills. Other treatments included Peruvian bark, a brew from valerian, hartshorn, "spirit of ether," "fit drops," and the consumption of "light cooling food" such as barley porridge. A blacksmith forged an iron ring around the girl's finger, an ancient remedy that proved no more effective than the others. Though a local physician watched over her, the family sought other opinions whenever they could, including from a renowned Jewish doctor visiting Virginia from London. Nothing helped. In a three-month period in 1770, Patsy had twenty-six epileptic episodes.[17]

Few experiences are as desolate as the slow decline of a child. The Washingtons attempted to give Patsy a normal childhood. She joined outings to Belvoir and trips to Williamsburg, to balls and to the theater, though a fit might strike at any time. She was tutored with her brother and took dancing and music lessons. Martha indulged her with fine clothes, a parrot, and a music box.[18] Yet there was no cure for her fits, nor for the helplessness of those who loved her. For Washington, who had cared for his brother Lawrence through his decline, the feelings of impotence must have felt achingly familiar.

His other stepchild, Jacky Custis, tried Washington's patience. Martha doted on the boy, who early understood the advantages of his family position. Jacky's indifference to learning combined with a profound lack of ambition. As a boy, he was enthusiastic only about horses and hunting. He seemed destined to become a wastrel Virginia aristocrat, a stock figure satirized at the time in words that might have been applied to young Custis: "There is no matter whether he can read or not.... He has money, land and negroes, that's enough. These things procure him every honor, every favor, every title of respect."[19]

To Washington, a life of languorous opulence was a life wasted. He spent years trying to usher Jacky down the path of self-improvement. He confessed to one of Jacky's teachers an "anxiety to make [Jacky] fit for more useful purposes than as a horse racer." Yet Washington had to tread lightly. More than twenty years later, when dealing with the equally low educational energy of Jacky's son, an aide explained Washington's indulgent attitude. "Mrs. W's happiness is bound up in the boy," the aide wrote, so "he is unwilling to take such measures as might reclaim him, [as] rigidity used toward him might be productive of serious effects on her." One historian neatly captured Washington's conundrum, and its resolution: "In short, Washington preferred spoiled youngsters to an unhappy wife."[20]

After Jacky spent eight years at home with a tutor, his schoolmaster found the boy "far from being a brilliant genius." Following a school holiday, Washington despaired that Jacky's mind was "more than ever turned to dogs, horses, and guns." When the stepson turned eighteen, Washington lamented that Jacky's knowledge of classical languages was "trifling," as was his understanding of arithmetic.[21]

ᔔ

In the summer of 1759, two immediate challenges demanded Washington's attention. First, the expanded Mount Vernon had to be furnished in a way that matched its new dimensions. Every summer, Virginia planters prepared meticulous invoices describing the goods they wished to buy from Britain. The invoices traveled by ship to British merchants, who acquired the requested items—or something like them—for the return trip. If all went well, the correct goods at reasonable prices arrived within a year of being ordered. Matters, however, rarely went well.

When he retrieved his spring shipment, Washington usually fumed over shoddy or broken items. One shipment, he wrote to the merchant, included goods "mean in quality but not in price, for in this they excel." Always eager for objects reflecting current tastes, he complained that "instead of getting things good and fashionable," the articles "could only have been used by our forefathers in days of yore."[22]

Payment for the Washingtons' 1759 orders came from Martha's share of the Custis estate. The shopping list that summer covered three separate invoices.[23] It was a binge. They ordered fire screens, a couch, two large mattresses, and a new marriage bed with matching linens. For the dining table, they ordered dessert glasses, china, carving knives, and forks. One invoice detailed hardware items, exotic foods, wines, and medicines, including laudanum. Washington also ordered six dozen metal plates stamped with the Washington crest, an image he displayed proudly.[24]

Finally, Washington requested "the newest and most approved treatise of agriculture," plus three specific titles on that subject. He pored over those volumes, writing notes in the margins, and would order agriculture texts throughout his life.[25]

His thirst for farming treatises reflected his determination to make Mount Vernon the foundation of a fortune. The Northern Neck was not known for its tobacco. Higher quality leaf came from farther south, where the Custis lands were. But if Washington was to be a Virginia planter, he must raise tobacco. He had little experience with it. Ferry Farm was small, not a major producer of anything, much less of a crop as devilish as tobacco. Because the crop exhausted the soil, and because Washington always craved land, he acquired neighboring farms whenever he could. By the time of the Revolutionary War, he had more than doubled the estate's acreage.[26]

Since leaving Ferry Farm, he had been a surveyor and a soldier, not a farmer. He needed to learn about tobacco, and he needed workers, lots of them. Tobacco was a labor-intensive crop, while the mansion house required a staff of thirteen. To meet these needs, Washington shifted twelve slaves from Custis lands to Mount Vernon, then acquired five more in a delayed bequest from Lawrence. He spent £1,500—a large share of Martha's remaining cash—to buy thirty more slaves over the next three years. With the natural increase in the slave population, the number of enslaved people at Mount Vernon nearly tripled from 1759 to 1765. It doubled again by 1775.[27]

Washington later looked back with regret on this spending. To his friend Stewart, he bemoaned that moving into Mount Vernon had required purchases that "swallowed up . . . all the money I got by marriage, nay more, brought me in debt."[28] To dig out of debt, he had to make the best possible use of his land, which would require two skills: managing a plantation and serving as a slave master.

CHAPTER 19

Man of Business, Master of Slaves

Washington in 1759 was a hardworking man of regular habits, as he would be through life. He rose before dawn, saw to paperwork, then checked on the horses and other livestock. He breakfasted on Indian cakes (cornbread), honey, and tea. One story from the Revolutionary War, possibly apocryphal, recounts a subordinate marveling to his commander "at the vast amount of work that you accomplish." Washington's reported reply was, "Sir, I rise at four o'clock and a great deal of my work is done while others are asleep."[1]

After breakfast, except in nasty weather, he reviewed Mount Vernon's farms on horseback, directing workers, planning with overseers, spending extra time at new projects. Because his fair skin burned easily, he sometimes shaded his face with an umbrella. Dinner came at midafternoon with sweet Madeira wine, followed by more time in his office. He joined the company—overnight guests were frequent—for evening tea. Sometimes he read aloud from the newspaper. Most nights he retired by nine.[2]

During those first years at Mount Vernon, Washington aimed to learn tobacco cultivation, a skill that Virginia planters prized. Plantation owners named strains of the plant after themselves, and won renown if their leaf commanded the best prices.[3]

Most crops alternate busy times of sowing and harvesting with quieter stretches during winter or when the plants are growing. Tobacco left no idle times. Planting began in midwinter, with seedbeds covered against frost. Because so many plants died, planters started ten times as many as they wished to harvest. In spring, the seedlings were transferred to larger fields that had to be weeded through the summer. Then came "topping," so the plants would not flower, and trimming off "suckers," extra leaves that drained vitality. The harvest came before end-of-the-year frost, when leaves reached full growth. After curing in dry barns (but not too dry), workers stripped the leaves, removed stems, and packed hogsheads of about a thousand pounds each. With luck, the process ended before new planting began.

The workers' labor never ended, nor did the planters' anxiety. Too much rain or too little, a new weed or a spell of pests, an early frost, humidity in the drying barns—all could sabotage a year's work. Every day the planter evaluated how soon to move to the next step, how best to give the leaf size and flavor. Because a crop was always in the ground or the barns, tobacco country had no harvest festivals. The plant was a demanding mistress.[4]

Washington farmed only a portion of Mount Vernon's land, reserving the rest for firewood and future expansion. Tenants occupied several parcels, paying rent in the form of tobacco. Washington employed an overseer for each of Mount Vernon's three farms.

But his tobacco proved undistinguished and commanded weak prices, which baffled him. "Certain I am," he wrote in 1761, that "no person in Virginia takes more pains to make their tobacco fine than I do." The following year, Washington changed tobacco strains and packing methods. He began to wonder if tobacco was "an art beyond my skill." A poor harvest followed. Then oversupply drove prices to their lowest levels in thirty years. The plants struggled in Mount Vernon's soil, which sat on hard clay that eroded easily. By 1764, Washington's debt to his British agent stood at £1,800. He absorbed the lesson that the marketplace was teaching. Tobacco was not the answer. He considered other cash crops. When flax and hemp did not flourish on his land, he moved to wheat and Indian corn.[5]

Other Chesapeake Bay farmers were also abandoning tobacco. The standard of success became solvency, not high-quality leaf. Grain mills replaced tobacco sheds at Mount Vernon. An Alexandria firm sold Washington's flour in the West Indies and other American colonies. By the end of the 1760s, Mount Vernon produced 7,000 bushels of wheat a year. Washington started paying down his debts.[6]

The shift to wheat involved integrating plantation activities to support each other. Wheat, unlike tobacco, was planted in plowed fields, so Washington needed horses and oxen to pull plows, and Indian corn to feed the animals, whose manure was returned to the fields. Because wheat required less labor, Washington could experiment with other crops too.[7]

He saw opportunity in the seasonal runs of herring and shad in the Potomac. Initially, his slaves fished by casting nets from the shore. Then he built a schooner to spread the nets farther into the river. In 1770, Washington sold 473,000 herring and 4,600 shad; a year later, the numbers were 679,000 herring and 7,760 shad.[8] To produce another revenue stream, he turned Mount Vernon's fruit into cider and brandy.[9]

Washington measured work obsessively, searching for better ways to organize it. His aphorisms could fill an almanac. "System in all things should be aimed at," he instructed Martha's grandson, "for in execution, it renders everything more easy." An overseer received similar counsel: "To establish good rules, and a regular system, is the life and soul of every kind of business."[10] "Every hour misspent," he advised a nephew, "is lost forever." And to an overseer: "Lost labor can never be regained." He always urged planning—his term was "forethought and arrangement"—to apply labor wisely. To avoid multiple trips, only full cartloads should be dispatched and then only when necessary. Work should not be performed during mild weather that could be equally well performed in foul weather, to ensure that workers would have tasks to address on bad days.[11]

Washington lived by these maxims, constantly reconsidering his farming methods. He calculated the time required to plow different fields under different conditions. He compared how long it took to harvest a field using slaves rather than hired laborers. He gauged the weight of livestock before slaughter against the meat and other products they yielded. He burned tallow candles and candles made from whale oil to see which was more cost-effective. He tested ten different combinations of compost to establish which better nourished the crops.[12]

His analyses were not academic exercises but informed how Washington managed his farms. In early 1760, he grew frustrated that four carpenters hewed only 120 feet of timber in a day. The following day, he observed them; they were much more productive with the boss watching. From those observations, he calculated that two carpenters should hew 250 feet per day while the other two sawed 180 feet of planks. A dedicated empiricist, he acknowledged that those results might vary when the carpenters worked different types of wood. Eight years later, he evaluated the cost of importing linen from Britain compared to the cost of having enslaved women spin and weave the material.[13]

A year after that, Washington examined wheat harvesting, noting that harvesters crossed a field in a single line, forcing the entire line to halt whenever a worker stumbled or his equipment fouled. By dividing the workers into three gangs, a disruption halted only one gang's progress, allowing the other two to advance unimpeded.[14]

Washington's devotion to time-and-motion studies paid off. By one calculation, productivity at Mount Vernon rose from fourteen bushels of wheat per worker to more than fifty, and the revenue generated per worker doubled.[15]

Washington also benefitted from the arrival in 1765 of an experienced farm manager, cousin Lund Washington. Although no one could meet Washington's expectations all the time, Lund performed a broad range of responsibilities: managing the crops and supervising the flour mill, livestock, fishing, and distillery. He also secured tools, provisions, and clothes, while keeping records that satisfied Washington.

Washington trusted Lund for the next twenty years. Occupying a room at the mansion house, Lund sometimes joined Washington on fox hunts and family occasions. A measure of his trustworthiness came when Washington and Martha went to Berkeley Springs for a holiday. Martha left the children in the care of Lund and his wife.[16]

Washington's aggressive farm management highlighted a core contradiction inherent to eighteenth-century Virginia. This devotee of hard work and system, of disciplined planning and cost analysis, directed laborers who had no incentive to work.[17]

∾

African slavery was always part of Washington's life, as familiar as breathing. His family owned slaves as he grew up, as did virtually all Virginians of means. Nearly half the population of Virginia was enslaved. At age eleven, he inherited slaves, though his mother managed them. Slavery was legal in all the British colonies he had visited: Barbados, Maryland, Pennsylvania, New York, Connecticut, Rhode Island, and Massachusetts.

Washington used the euphemistic language that slavery bred. In polite company, slaves were servants, or workers, or "my people." Beatings, the cornerstone of a slave system, were "correction." Until the Revolutionary War, Washington betrayed no discomfort with slavery, either its concept or its reality. Slavery for him, in those years, was not something to like or dislike. It simply was, unquestioned, to be managed as well as possible.[18]

When he moved his new family to Mount Vernon, Washington became more extensively involved with slavery. Not every worker at Mount Vernon was enslaved. Washington contracted with white indentured servants and with convicts transported from Britain. Both arrangements tended to last for three or four years. When he needed a special skill or had a crop to bring in, he hired white workers for wages. But enslaved Africans and their enslaved descendants performed the great majority of Mount Vernon's work, and all of the most grueling, least pleasant tasks. Slaves were critical assets in his drive for prosperity. Washington, no longer a mere slaveowner, became a large-scale slave master.[19]

Washington organized Mount Vernon into separate labor units. The slaves working in the mansion house and its outbuildings, including gardeners, bricklayers, and stable men, lived in a dormitory-like structure not far from the house. Field hands lived in raw cabins next to each farm on the property, along with the overseer for each farm. Coopers lived near their workshop, while millers slept above the mill. Washington wanted each laborer near the worksite to avoid "losing much time in marching and countermarching." To minimize "night walking" visits between farms, he tried to group members of a family at each location. Those two policies often conflicted, so many families were split between locations.[20]

The enslaved people labored six days a week, from sunrise to sunset. More than half the field slaves were women, assigned low-skill chores like gathering and spreading manure, grubbing out tree stumps, cleaning grain, building fences, and cleaning stables. Men did the plowing, harrowing, drovering, sowing, harvesting, and ditching. Sundays could be spent hunting or fishing, working on garden plots or on dwellings, playing "prisoner's base" and other games. Night might bring impromptu dances.[21]

Each year, a slave received two shirts, two skirts or pairs of pants, and a blanket, all from coarse fabric. Their food was more varied than at many plantations, with Indian corn supplemented by fish from the river, vegetables and fruit from garden plots, and game they shot in the woods. Most slept on beds and had implements like teakettles and cups. Washington provided doctors for the sick, a prudent step to protect valuable assets. Upon discovering smallpox at his Bullskin farms, he hired a nurse to care for the afflicted. All recovered.[22]

Holding people in bondage and compelling them to work efficiently was no simple challenge. Hard work had little value for the enslaved. For a slave, a day of light labor was a good day. Escape would be the best day, and some at Mount Vernon tried it.

Each participant in the master-slave relationship had techniques for achieving his purposes. A discontented slave might work slowly or ineptly. A favored ploy was to feign illness. Some female slaves pretended pregnancy. Washington complained that his slaves would "lay up a month, at the end of which no visible change in their countenance, nor the loss of an ounce of flesh, is discoverable," while they ate "as if nothing ailed them." One enslaved woman, he insisted, "has a disposition to be one of the most idle creatures on earth, and is besides one of the most deceitful."[23]

For the slave master, the challenge was to maintain his authority without so abusing it that he further sapped workers' efforts. As Washington instructed one manager, treating slaves "civilly is no more than what all men are entitled to," but he recommended "keep[ing] them at a proper distance; for they will grow upon familiarity, in proportion as you will sink in authority."[24]

The balance was not easy. On one occasion, Washington worried that an employee directing the house staff was "not accustomed to Negroes" who were in "no sort of awe of him—of course they do as they please." After years of military command, conveying authority was natural for him. When Washington addressed his slaves, one visitor recalled, "he spoke as differently as if he had been quite another man, or had been in anger." Washington was equally unhappy, however, with overseers who "seem to consider a Negro much as they do the brute beasts on the farms; and oftentimes treat them inhumanely."[25]

Washington understood that force compelled Mount Vernon's labor, and that only unceasing vigilance would get the work done. "There are few Negroes," he wrote to a nephew, "who will work unless there be a constant eye on them." On another occasion he grumbled about "many workmen and little work." His peers shared this view. One major slaveowner confided to his diary, "I find it is almost impossible to make a negro do his work well. No orders can engage it, no encouragement persuade it, nor no punishment oblige it."[26]

Theft of the master's food and goods was routine, although Washington tried to stop it. Traffic in goods stolen by slaves, according to one historian, was "extensive, relatively well organized, and carried on virtually with impunity." Washington believed that his house staff siphoned off two glasses of wine for every one served to guests. He fulminated over theft on a building project: "I cannot conceive how it is possible that 6,000 twelve penny nails be used . . . but of one thing I have no great doubt and that is, if they can be applied to other uses, or converted into cash, rum, or other things, there will be no scruple in doing it."[27]

If a slave master grew sufficiently exasperated with a slave, the law gave him broad power to punish. For theft, a slave could be branded. Enslaved people found with a weapon could receive thirty-nine lashes. Because white slaveowners feared that slaves would poison their masters' food, any slave who passed out medicine, even to another slave, could be hanged. Hanging also applied to an enslaved person who broke into a store, or to enslaved people assembled in a group of five or more for purposes of rebellion. A Frenchman entering Williamsburg in late May 1765 saw three Blacks hanging from the gallows for committing a robbery, their bodies dangling as a grisly reminder.[28]

The slave master's repertoire of punishments included disfigurement. If a slave gave false testimony, his ear could be nailed to a post for an hour, then cut off; then the other ear received the same treatment. On a complaint by George Mason, that punishment was applied to a slave accused of a second incident of hog-stealing. A prominent slaveowner whipped slaves for not reporting an illness, for wetting the bed, and for laziness. He forced a slave to drink a pint of urine for his offenses.[29]

Washington's overseers, with his knowledge, surely whipped slaves.[30] Washington never shied from physical punishment of miscreants. As commander of the Virginia Regiment, he ordered many floggings and hanged at least two men.

Yet intelligent slave masters recognized that their power to punish could become counterproductive. Punishing a malingering slave, Washington wrote, "often produces evils which are worse than the disease." A slave could turn violently on an overseer, which could result in the slave's execution—both bad outcomes for the owner. Alternatively, the angry slave might run away or recruit allies for a rising. On a large property like Mount Vernon, the enslaved far outnumbered their owners.[31]

Plenty of Washington's enslaved people ran off. By one count, forty-seven fled between 1760 and 1799, or more than one a year. Runaways did not always leave because of mistreatment, and not all sought permanent freedom. Some left to be closer to family at other plantations. Others remained nearby, taking a break from work while living on supplies smuggled from the plantation.[32]

Washington had little patience for runaways, offering rewards for their capture.[33] He deemed one slave named Tom to be so incorrigible that he shipped Tom to the West Indies for sale there, even though the man was a good worker and had been a foreman. Washington advised the ship captain "to keep him handcuffed till you get to sea." He used the same method for disposing of Will Shag, who passed for free in Yorktown before recapture, then escaped twice more, once assaulting an overseer. Washington paid to ship Will to Santo Domingo. He sold off a slave carpenter after four escapes in five years.[34]

Fear of slave rebellions haunted white Virginians. The militia's principal duty was to stop uprisings. Virginia law forbade sending militia beyond the colony's borders to ensure that they would be available to suppress rebellions. On holidays, when slaves had leisure time, militiamen attended church with weapons in hand, alert for any unrest.[35]

Washington's slave management should be understood in the time and place of his life. Most of the labor available to him was enslaved. His goal, as expressed many years later, was "getting work well done and quietly by negroes."[36] To do that, he employed the practices that were available. To later

Americans, his world was built on appalling measures of repression: restraints, violence, and harsh deaths. To Washington, that was daily life.

A person with emotional intelligence, like Washington, could not doubt the humanity of those he owned. They had families, dreams, and feelings, which he observed every day. He extended privileges to some slaves whose work impressed him. In 1768, he purchased two mixed-race brothers, Frank and Billy Lee, who became favorites. Frank served as waiter in the dining room, while Billy became his valet.

Davy Gray, who came to Mount Vernon from a Custis estate, also advanced. By 1778, Davy was an overseer. The master gave Davy money, leather breeches, extra pork, and a house with a brick chimney. Davy, Washington wrote, "carries on his business as well as the white overseers, and with more quietness than any of them." When Washington tried a new method of distributing cornmeal, the enslaved workers complained to Davy that they were hungry. When Davy pressed their case with the master, Washington abandoned the experiment.[37]

But it was not until the Revolutionary War, when he had wider experience of the world, that Washington began to question slavery, to see it as not only inefficient but also immoral. Late in life, but with his characteristic tenacity, he would try to set an example for his countrymen by extricating himself from the slave system.

CHAPTER 20

The Backbencher Advances

During his first seven years in the House of Burgesses, Washington was more engaged with life at Mount Vernon than with his public career, though that would change. He won reelection in 1761 and would do so two more times. His full legislative career spanned twenty-two sessions of the House of Burgesses, during which he attended deliberations for approximately sixty weeks when he was actively addressing public issues and mixing with Virginia's leaders. Even when the House was adjourned, Washington had to keep abreast of events.

The road to leadership in Virginia ran through the House of Burgesses. In Williamsburg's intimate spaces, the burgesses took one another's measure in committee meetings, in debates, over long dinners and through alcohol-soaked nights, at horse races and card games. They assessed who remained steady under stress, who could persuade others, who could distill a complex problem, who was self-interested, who foresaw consequences, who had a gift with words, who was devious, who did the work.

Rising to a leadership position in the House was a challenge for Washington, a man of action with a breathy voice who was neither facile in debate nor confident in his learning. He was no overnight sensation but found his way slowly.

Washington started by watching and listening. Voting on matters large and small, he could see how political opinions form and are led, how multiple views can be accommodated through bargaining and compromise, and the importance of striking at the right moment. He developed his own rhetorical style. He learned the nuts and bolts of writing laws. He served on key legislative committees, then chaired a few.

At afternoon dinners, Washington built connections with high officials. Over one seven-year period, he dined on at least sixteen occasions with Virginia's governor, twenty-six times with the House Speaker, sixteen times with the treasurer, and eleven times with the attorney general. Though he enjoyed card games and conversation, many evenings he remained in his room, working. Having leased out Martha's town house (the one with six chimneys), he usually stayed at Mrs. Campbell's inn on the Capitol's west side, screened from the revelry at the twelve taverns on the other side. One contemporary left a scathing account of burgesses "regaling or gaming till 12 every night," a regimen that left them "very unfit for business." Washington, however, was not in Williamsburg for the nightlife.[1]

The years on the back bench were humbling for a man accustomed to command. When he arrived, dozens of legislators were more eminent than he, more skilled in parliamentary maneuver, but Washington never ceased learning. In a lengthy apprenticeship, his stature grew and he absorbed lessons that would serve him well during more than two decades of national preeminence.[2]

∾

On November 10, 1759, Washington rose to deliver his maiden speech. With his height and natural dignity, he could command the chamber's attention. He never spoke so long as to lose it.

The matter was routine. A disabled soldier sought public assistance to support his wife and children. To review the petition, Speaker Robinson had appointed a committee of Washington and Francis Lightfoot Lee, one of six Lee brothers from Westmoreland County, all familiar to the Washingtons. On behalf of the committee, the new burgess advised his colleagues that the claim was truthful. He recommended a grant of £10, plus £5 in future years. His motion passed.[3]

Four days later, the tall burgess for Frederick County reported on another soldier petition, one claiming back pay for eighteen months spent as a French prisoner. Washington recommended £32. His colleagues agreed. Washington served on another committee that reviewed a claim by a supplier to the Virginia Regiment, and participated in a ceremonial presentation to another soldier who had been imprisoned by the French. These modest legislative steps, reflecting his military experience, marked his beginning.[4]

Washington's next visible role came during a three-week session in October 1760. He carried a petition from former soldiers imprisoned by the French. Rather than continue to address such petitions piecemeal, the burgesses asked

Governor Fauquier to award back pay to "all others who shall hereafter appear in the same circumstances." Washington presented the request to the governor.[5]

When the burgesses assembled in the following March, they knew that King George II's death would prompt new elections. Expecting to face voters soon, many turned to matters of local importance. So did Washington. In the previous House session, Winchester residents had sought a law barring "hogs running at large." Roaming pigs trampled property, broke into food stores, and defecated wherever they wished. When the hog-running petition returned in March 1761, the Committee on Propositions and Grievances, on which Washington sat, recommended rejection. Two weeks later, Washington presented the petition again and won its passage by the House, then carried it to the Executive Council. Alas, the council did not concur.[6]

At that point, a higher power—likely Speaker Robinson—intervened. The bid to control Winchester's swine rose from the ashes, repackaged with a new name and a new focus on public health: "A bill to preserve the water for the use of the inhabitants of the town of Winchester . . . by preventing hogs from running at large therein." The new version of the bill, with its new title, went to a committee consisting of Washington and Edmund Pendleton, an adept lawyer and Robinson ally.

Three days later, the water-quality legislation (formerly the hog-running bill) emerged in Pendleton's capable hands. The House passed it. Washington again presented it to the Executive Council. This time all went well. The council embraced the rechristened measure and its new goal of water purity. The governor signed it on the session's last day.[7]

That was not Washington's only legislative accomplishment for Frederick County that spring. He also won creation of a new town and authorization for a new ferry across the Potomac.[8] He was acting like a man expecting an election challenge. Which he was.

∽

Adam Stephen had been a friend. As a senior officer in the Virginia Regiment, Stephen defended Washington after the Fort Necessity debacle. Washington endorsed the Scot as his second-in-command. After Stephen succeeded Washington as commander, however, the friendship frayed. Questions circulated about Stephen's honesty.[9]

In 1761, Stephen was the senior officer at Fort Loudoun in Winchester, the position Washington had occupied during his 1758 election. Stephen used the political opportunities afforded by that position to campaign for the House of Burgesses. A month before the legislative session began, he was already said to be courting voters "incessantly . . . and with indefatigable pains." Contrary to custom, Stephen made campaign promises, projecting business growth that would "diffuse gold and opulence through Frederick [County]." A Washington agent feared Stephen's candidacy; he urged Washington to come and court the voters.[10]

When the assembly adjourned, Washington headed west. He campaigned for himself and another Virginia Regiment veteran, George Mercer, who sought the seat being vacated by Lord Fairfax's nephew. In early May, Washington canvassed voters at a cockfight and a wedding. He stopped by churches on Sunday mornings; on other days, he visited taverns. He paid for his brothers Jack and Sam to canvass for him, and reimbursed Mercer's expenses too.[11]

Washington betrayed his anxiety in a letter written three days before the election to the sheriff who would manage the poll, Van Swearingen. Washington enclosed a copy of a letter written by Stephen that supposedly disparaged the sheriff. Washington wrote that he had already "made a just and proper use" of the letter, adding, "I have the greatest reason to believe you can be no friend to a person of Colonel Stephen's principles."

Then Washington flouted both Virginia statutes and rules of gentlemanly conduct. He insisted he would never ask the sheriff to favor him at the poll, then made precisely that request, observing that "could Mercer's friends and mine be hurried in at the first of the Poll it might be an advantage." Washington knew whereof he spoke. At the 1758 poll, the first ten men called to vote had been stout Washington loyalists, creating a bandwagon effect that drew later voters to Washington. With deep insincerity, Washington added that "as Sheriff I know you cannot appear in this, nor would I by any means have you do anything that can give so designing a man as Colo. Stevens the least trouble." Washington's meaning was clear.[12]

On Election Day, Washington got what he had denied he was asking for. Of the first fourteen voters called by the sheriff, thirteen shouted their preference for Washington and Mercer. Indeed, the first six voters included Washington's brothers and Mercer's father. In the final tally, Washington led with 505 votes; Mercer followed with 400. Stephen trailed with 294. Washington had honored the first rule of politics: He won.[13]

Stalking voters in Frederick County took a physical toll. For the next several months, Washington suffered with a "violent cold" and spells of fever. Though he was as strong as any man of his time, his illnesses are a reminder of how fragile health was in that pre-antibiotic era. He endured several lengthy afflictions that modern medicines likely would have dispatched easily.[14] Despite a journey to Berkeley Springs for its supposedly healing mineral waters, six months after the poll Washington was still struggling to recover.[15]

Even with his health dodgy, Washington had made important strides. Now a second-term burgess, he was no longer just an ex-soldier dabbling in politics. Within the House of Burgesses, he was not yet prominent; the hogs of Winchester had challenged his legislative skills. But, not yet thirty years old, he was making his way.

∾

Over the next four years, the burgesses conducted eight sessions. Half were perfunctory, but the other four extended for periods ranging from three weeks to two months. Washington's attendance at some sessions was interrupted by illness and plantation duties. He knew the House could proceed well enough without him. He continued to review soldier petitions for his colleagues and won creation of another new town. His brother Austin, only forty-two, died in May 1762, reinforcing the pattern of early death for Washington men—first his father, then Lawrence, now Austin.[16]

Washington understood that he needed to move beyond his legislative apprenticeship. After four years in the House, he was ready to handle more than soldier petitions. His opportunity came after France, Spain, and Britain signed the Treaty of Paris in February 1763. News of the peace triggered jubilation in America. Not only soldiers had suffered in the long war. All colonists had endured inflation, trade restrictions, and higher taxes. With peace, Virginians expected prosperity, new western settlements, and lower taxes. Englishmen also anticipated reduced taxes and times of plenty. On neither side of the Atlantic did many think about where the money would come from to pay the war debts, nor were they concerned about what the Indian tribes were thinking. Thus do troubles begin.[17]

Washington, like most landowning Virginians, owed a lot of money. By 1761, his weak tobacco crops, combined with his splurges on British goods, plunged him nearly £2,000 into debt, which he secured by pledging cash belonging to his stepchildren. When his principal London agent urged him to pay up, Washington portrayed himself as "unlucky." He grudgingly agreed to pay interest on the amount due. Despite his own debts, he still made loans to friends; a gentleman did not deny assistance to another gentleman.[18]

Britain also was deep in the red. War spending had nearly doubled the nation's debt; more than half the annual budget went to interest payments.[19]

The government resolved to reduce spending and increase revenues. The American frontier seemed a good place to scale back, beginning by cutting off gifts to the western tribes. That step quickly alienated tribes that were suffering from famine and epidemics and had grown accustomed to French generosity. Also, the Indians had long mistrusted the British hunger for land. The end of gifts was the final straw for several tribes. Through the summer of 1763, warrior bands again raided. In Frederick County, Washington found settlers once more fleeing east or huddling in the few forts still held by the British.[20]

General Amherst, British commander in America, ordered a brutal response to what was named Pontiac's Rebellion. "Destroy their huts and plantations," read one order, "putting to death everyone of that nation that may fall into your hands." Amherst wrote before another expedition, "I wish to hear of no prisoners." By year's end, the British had regained their forts, but they wanted peace, not more military expenses.[21]

To secure that peace, King George III forbade further settlement west of the Appalachian Mountains. His Proclamation of 1763 infuriated Americans hoping to move west or (like Washington) to profit from frontier lands. Moreover, the ban could not be enforced. The colonial governments rarely knew where frontier settlers were and had no means of restraining them. Governor Fauquier warned that the proclamation would foster violence, not reduce it. The new policy struck directly at Washington and the first Virginia recruits in the war against France. Those veterans expected to divide 200,000 acres that Governor Dinwiddie had promised nine years before, but the king's proclamation threw that promise into doubt.[22]

At the same time, British merchants mounted a campaign to recover colonists' debts. The merchants had long extended credit to Virginians, ordinarily in British pounds sterling. During the war years, when Virginians had little hard money, the colony printed "Virginia pounds" to serve as currency. Inflation had sapped the value of those bills, so British merchants stopped accepting them. The colonial assembly tried to pacify the merchants by authorizing Virginia courts to set a "just" exchange rate between Virginia pounds and pounds sterling.[23]

The merchants, uninterested in transatlantic lawsuits before unfriendly judges, struck back by winning a London ruling that Virginia currency was not "legal tender" valid for paying debts. Governor Fauquier urged the General Assembly to mollify the British merchants. Washington and the other burgesses had to decide Virginia's response. The stakes were high. To a friend, Washington confided his fear that the dispute would "set the whole country in flames."[24]

∾

The leading burgesses, beginning with Speaker Robinson, had faced down British policies before. They were practical politicians who aimed to solve problems, not pursue what a contemporary dismissed as "visionary ideas of perfection."[25] The second man in the House was Peyton Randolph, attorney general and chair of the Committee on Propositions and Grievances. The beefy Randolph had a "sweetness of temper" that fostered consensus. Studious Richard Bland wielded a powerful pen, while Edmund Pendleton—who had rescued Washington's hog-running legislation—commanded Jefferson's respect as "the ablest man in debate." Richard Henry Lee's incisive intellect and crisp speaking style made him a rising figure who stood apart from the Speaker's inner circle.[26]

On the legal-tender issue, the House adopted a defiant resolution that scorned the merchants' demand as unjust. Since courts could set a fair exchange rate, the resolution concluded that the merchants were suffering no harm.[27]

In response, the British took a half-step back, agreeing that colonial currency already in circulation could be used as legal tender, but denying that use for future currency emissions. But Virginia pounds fell out of circulation whenever they were used to pay taxes, so they had to be replaced periodically with new notes. As a result, the British gambit granted only a brief breathing space. Soon enough, Virginians would again have in hand only currency that the merchants could refuse to accept. Within a few months, Governor Fauquier reported widespread hardship: "People are really distressed for money of any kind to satisfy their creditors; and this evil is daily increasing." A French visitor observed that coin was so scarce that most business proceeded by barter.[28]

The currency dispute exacerbated the underlying problem: Both Englishmen and Virginians had too much debt. Tobacco crops remained inconsistent and prices low, while Virginians' appetite for British goods knew no limits.[29] Governor Fauquier could only wonder at the way wealthy Virginians bought more than they could pay for. The problem was plain, he continued, but it was "so disagreeable . . . that they shut their eyes against it." A member of the Executive Council bemoaned the "extravagance which hath been our ruin." Many stayed afloat only because British creditors hated to sue them, a slow process that offended other Virginia customers.[30]

Governor Fauquier thought that debt made Virginia politicians "uneasy, peevish, and ready to murmur at every occasion." Thomas Jefferson expressed

that resentment when he complained that Virginians' debts "had become hereditary from father to son for many generations, so that the planters were a
species of property annexed to certain mercantile houses in London."[31]

Virginians sinking under their debts tried to sell land or slaves, but few
had the cash to buy. In desperation, creditors organized lotteries, selling £5
or £10 tickets for drawings with prizes of slaves, land, livestock, and equipment. Washington helped organize several lotteries for bankrupt friends, but
the raffles often failed, either because the tickets did not sell or were purchased on credit that also turned bad.[32]

With money drying up, Virginia's public spending was bound to become
controversial. Most public spending went to protect white settlers from Indian violence. That confluence of factors would hand Washington, who knew
the frontier conflict firsthand, a chance to step forward as a political figure.

❧

Addressing a new legislative session in January 1764, Fauquier reported continuing Indian raids, along with "daily accounts of murders." He had called
out the militia, but General Amherst wanted five hundred Virginia soldiers
recruited to fight the tribes. The assembly, Fauquier continued, had to approve further spending to cover the additional soldiers. The House, including
Washington, said no. The militia would have to suffice.[33]

But even militia had to be paid something. The burgesses named Washington to lead a commission to determine what militia claims should be paid.
Washington certainly helped draft the law creating the commission, then
became its chair and undertook the heaviest responsibility for its work. He
devoted four weeks to the resolution of all claims except for those of six officers whose appointments had been irregular. Washington recommended
that the House grant pay to all six despite bureaucratic defects in their commissions.[34]

The House granted five of those claims. The sixth concerned corruption
charges against Adam Stephen, which placed Washington in an awkward
position, though possibly one of his choosing.[35] After the contested Frederick
County election three years before, an officer in the regiment reported that
Washington had "resolved to have the conduct of Lt. Colonel Stephen examined by the assembly," including "the many crimes of which [Stephen] is accused."[36] Now that examination was under way. For Washington to lead the
investigation of his former opponent might seem vindictive or self-serving.
So Washington needed to find a way to remain above the fray while others
pressed the inquiry.

Washington managed the situation deftly. His initial report did not mention the accusations against Stephen. Instead, another commission member, Thomas Rutherford, made a separate motion to the House that presented three charges against Stephen. The House referred those charges to a committee on which Washington served.

On the first charge—that Stephen had dissuaded volunteers from joining an expedition—the committee reached a mixed judgment, concluding that Colonel Stephen "has not fully acquitted himself." A second charge alleged that, during a time of Indian attacks, Stephen assigned soldiers to escort a shipment of flour that he was selling to the army. The committee found that was a breach of duty. A third charge was dismissed. The House adopted the committee's views, granting Stephen less pay than he had requested. To salve his feelings, the House proclaimed him a "brave, active, and skillful officer," even if a self-serving one.[37]

For Washington, the outcome was satisfactory. The House had embraced the commission's recommendation and his rival had been chastened, but Washington's fingerprints were not evident. Stephen may well have blamed Washington for his troubles, but others might not. After all, Rutherford had presented the charges. Even if Stephen's setback were blamed on Washington, that might not be so bad; a reputation for effective retaliation against opponents can serve a politician very well. In a sticky situation, the man from Mount Vernon had demonstrated a finesse rarely displayed when commanding the Virginia Regiment. Better yet, the episode allowed him to extend his military expertise to financial issues that lie at the heart of every government. Taxes and spending would frame colonial politics for the next decade, as they frame much of political life, and Washington gained recognition as a man who understood financial issues.

∾

Because Britain still had too much debt, a new development menaced the colonies at the end of 1764: reports that Parliament soon would tax Americans to pay the war debt. The new levies, embodied as the Stamp Act, would not become law until the following March, but Governor Fauquier featured them when he greeted the burgesses for a new session and encouraged them to accept the new levies cheerfully. Americans, however, are never cheerful about tax increases.[38]

For several weeks, leading burgesses drafted appeals for Parliament to reconsider the taxes. One emphasized America's difficult economic times, reciting the cratering tobacco market, the lack of hard money, and restrictions on trade.[39] Notably, the burgesses did not claim that Americans should pay no additional taxes. Since much of the war effort involved protecting the colonists, Americans could hardly refuse to help pay. Moreover, Americans paid lower taxes than did the British, an imbalance that British politicians aimed to rectify.[40]

Instead, the Virginians disputed *who* could impose the taxes. Only Americans, they wrote, understood local conditions well enough to design a fair tax. Virginia would accept new taxes "provided it were left to themselves to raise it, by modes least grievous." Otherwise, one submission insisted, Americans "are the slaves of Britons." This argument, expressed in ever more provocative language, soon would resound on both sides of the ocean.[41]

CHAPTER 21

The Wheel of History:
The Stamp Act and the Robinson Scandal

The thirteen months that began in May 1765 brought dramatic changes to political life in America and in Virginia, fundamentally reshaping Washington's world. Violent opposition to new taxes altered how Americans thought of themselves and the mother country. The death of Virginia Speaker John Robinson in May 1766 revealed rot and corruption at the core of the colony's politics.

∾

When the assembly convened in early May, with Washington present, the leading agenda item was tobacco regulation, but tobacco was of little interest to Frederick County farmers or to Washington, who was abandoning the crop. After only a few days in Williamsburg, he hurried home for the planting of wheat, hemp, and flax. Having produced only 257 bushels of wheat the year before, that crop soon would approach thirty times that level. After three more weeks, many others had left a session that, according to one member, "was supposed to be over—except the concluding ceremonies." Fewer than half the burgesses attended the meeting on May 29.[1]

Those few received the dismaying news that Parliament had adopted the Stamp Act, imposing new taxes on fifty-five items, including legal documents, pamphlets, newspapers, playing cards, and dice. The legislation included elements intended to calm the colonists: Tax rates in America were lower than those in Britain, and revenue raised in America would pay for the soldiers protecting the frontier. The colonists, however, were not appeased. For months, disputes over taxes and anti-smuggling enforcement had triggered a boycott of British goods in the northern colonies. Other colonies took up the Virginia Assembly's recent protest that only Americans should impose taxes on Americans. The Stamp Act taxes showed that Parliament did not agree.[2]

Over the next several months, mobs took to the streets in Boston and Newport, Annapolis and New York. They often targeted tax collectors, many of whom chose to resign. The royal governor of New York hid in a fort while angry residents burned his effigy, his carriages, and his sleighs.[3]

In Williamsburg, the taxes drew an immediate response from a new burgess, a young lawyer named Patrick Henry. On May 29, Henry jotted down seven resolutions challenging the taxes. Little in the resolutions was new: They asserted that British subjects could be taxed only by a body in which they were represented. What was original, though, was Henry's willingness to challenge the leaders of the House, who angrily rebuked the brash upstart.[4]

The argument spilled over to the next day. A French visitor attributed to Henry a daring comparison of the British king to tyrants of old: "[Henry] said that Tarquin and Julius [Caesar] had their Brutus, Charles had his Cromwell, and George III . . ." At this point, the narrative continues, an enraged Speaker Robinson accused Henry of treason! The newcomer deftly insisted that he meant to say only that the king might "profit" by the example of those tyrants; then by one account he provocatively added: "If this be treason, make the most of it." Henry's resolutions carried by a single vote. Peyton Randolph stalked from the chamber muttering, "By God, I would have given five hundred guineas for a single vote."[5]

Next day, the fight resumed "very hot" and "most bloody" as the Speaker and his allies strained to rescind Henry's resolutions. The deed, however, was done, and by a rank beginner. A few weeks later, newspapers in Newport and Boston published Henry's resolutions, fanning the flames of resistance. Dismayed by events, Governor Fauquier dissolved the assembly and convened new elections. He explained to London that Speaker Robinson had opposed Henry, who was supported by "young hot and giddy members."[6]

Although Washington missed Henry's fireworks, he also opposed the Stamp Act, though his objections were based on hardheaded economic realities, not political theory. He explained to British correspondents that it was shortsighted for England to adopt legislation certain to enrage Americans and to trigger a boycott of British goods. Most colonists, he wrote, viewed the taxes as "an unconstitutional attack upon their liberties." Passing over that argument, Washington raised a practical point. Since Americans traded mostly with Britain, any measure that reduced that trade "must be hurtful to [British] manufacturers." Americans could forego British luxury items, while acquiring their necessities from American sources. Moreover, Americans lacked currency for paying the stamp taxes on legal documents, so American courts would close, which would block British creditors from suing on debts. "Where then," he asked, "is the utility of these restrictions?"[7]

Washington's critique reflected his habits of mind. Rather than mount the barricades to defend the timeless rights of Britons, he focused on the taxes' impact on both sides of the Atlantic. He appealed to English self-interest rather than assert his own interests. People, he always insisted, consult first their own interests. He hoped his British correspondents would do so, then press their government to rescind the new taxes.[8]

Eight colonial assemblies adopted resolutions echoing Virginia's opposition to the taxes. In Annapolis and New York, a French traveler encountered prominent men who "were all scheming how to rise manufactures . . . they would not have a farthing's worth of anything from England." Mob violence and threats drove more tax collectors to resign. Richard Henry Lee had sought Virginia's tax-collector position, but now was relieved that he had not secured the post. The man who did, he wrote, was "regarded as an execrable monster, who with parricidal heart and hands, hath concern in the ruin of his native country."[9]

The Stamp Act resistance changed how colonists viewed their world. Before, their identity was defined by the mother country and the colony where they lived. Now they began to see themselves as Americans. For nearly three weeks in October, representatives of nine colonies (not including Virginia) met in New York to chart common actions against the Stamp Act. Delegates from six colonies adopted a Declaration of Rights and Grievances, an address to the king, and submissions to Parliament. Though professing loyalty to George III, they never conceded Parliament's power to tax Americans without American participation.[10]

In late October, New York merchants declared a boycott of goods covered by the stamp taxes. The movement caught fire. From roots in Boston, groups calling themselves Sons of Liberty sprang up. Some of their pronouncements were menacing; a New York group declared that any person using British stamps would be "branded with everlasting infamy," while another in Norfolk, Virginia, declared that someone using stamps was "an enemy to his country" who would be "treated accordingly."

In February 1766, more than one hundred Virginians, including Washington's three younger brothers, signed an "association" agreement, pledging to "exert every faculty to prevent the execution" of the new law. Anyone trading in stamped goods faced hostility. When a merchant defied the Virginia associators by announcing he would use stamped paper to clear his goods for shipment, four hundred associators descended on his town. They formed a double line in the main street. They repeated their demand. The merchant agreed to it.[11]

Few men were willing to collect the taxes, most American courts had to shut down, and no revenues flowed to the king. British merchants decided that the Stamp Act was, as Washington argued, counterproductive. Enraging American customers was poor commercial policy. The merchants agitated for repeal, while rumors spread that unemployed workingmen would march on London. In early 1766, a new prime minister won repeal, though Parliament declared in a companion statute that it held "full power and authority to make laws and statutes" binding Americans "in all cases whatsoever."[12]

As colonists rejoiced, Washington's reaction was characteristically sober. Had Parliament not repealed the law, he cautioned a British merchant, "the consequences . . . would have been more direful than is generally apprehended."[13]

Many Americans drew from the episode the lesson that economic retaliation worked. The *Virginia Gazette* boasted that the American boycotts had inflicted "a total stagnation of all business" in Britain. But the core dispute remained over the power to tax. "This country cannot be long subject to Great Britain," wrote a Frenchman traveling in America. No country, he added, "seems better calculated for independency, and the inhabitants are already entirely disposed thereto and talk of nothing more than it."[14]

For Washington, the episode had a more personal consequence. By dissolving the General Assembly and calling new elections, Governor Fauquier created an opportunity for the burgess for Frederick County to reorient his political career. Washington, eager to advance, would seize that opportunity.

∽

A political life involves both capitalizing on opportunities and sidestepping hazards. When a scandal around Speaker Robinson presented substantial risks for Washington, he smoothly evaded them. The scandal grew from Robinson's great power as both Speaker and treasurer. The treasurer was tasked with burning Virginia paper money received as tax payments, to remove it from circulation. For some time before his death in May 1766, Robinson did not burn the bills. Instead, he gave them to high-toned friends who faced bankruptcy. In most instances, he took no collateral; in many, he acquired no written documentation. The sweetheart deals totaled more than £100,000, or roughly 20 percent of Virginia currency issued during the French and Indian War.

The dubious transactions came to light as early as May 1763, when an audit found a £40,000 discrepancy in the treasurer's records. Robinson blamed it on subordinates, and his word went unchallenged. Two years later, to cover the deficit, Robinson and his allies proposed to create a Public Loan Office that would borrow £240,000 from wealthy Englishmen, which then could be loaned to Robinson's friends, who then could pay off the secret "loans." The proposal was a fantasy. Englishmen would not invest in a colonial government that could neither pay its debts nor reveal its financial condition. Patrick Henry's sarcasm was withering: "Is it proposed then to reclaim the spendthrift from his dissipation and extravagance by filling his pockets with money?"[15]

When Robinson died in spring 1766—according to a newspaper account, he suffered "with the most excruciating torment of the stone"—the ugly truth stumbled into the light.[16] Robinson had passed out public funds to more than one hundred members of the Executive Council, the House of Burgesses, and Virginia's leading families. The crimes of Virginia's ruling class scandalized those who had not thrust their snouts into the public trough. At a time when Virginians denounced corrupt British politicians, they found that their own politics included the same larcenous elements.[17]

Some made excuses for Robinson. Governor Fauquier attributed the late Speaker's actions to "the sensibility of his too benevolent heart." Robinson's benevolence, of course, was reserved for elite men who reinforced his powers while mismanaging their inheritances. Although Robinson was considered the richest Virginian, his assets came nowhere near filling the hole in the colony's finances. His lawyer, Edmund Pendleton, spent fifteen years chasing repayment by the borrowers on behalf of Robinson's estate.[18]

Several who received the largest handouts were ruined. Although Robinson's protégé, Peyton Randolph, became the new Speaker, he was a transitional figure to a new generation of leaders. He expanded the key committees of the House, sharing power with younger burgesses like Patrick Henry, Thomas Jefferson, and George Washington, who brought more radical attitudes to the fraying relationship with Britain.[19]

Washington walked a careful line on the Robinson scandal. No account survives of any comment he made on the matter. His silence is deafening, especially since he dealt repeatedly with the consequences of Robinson's misconduct. Several of those taking handouts from Robinson also owed money to the Custis estate. When Jacky Custis came of age, he purchased a Robinson plantation that was sold to help cover the Speaker's debts.[20]

Although construing silence can be hazardous, Washington's reticence seems to reflect the calculation that he had little to gain by attacking a dead man with many friends. Moreover, Robinson had supported Washington, an obligation that Washington would not repay by disparaging Robinson after his death.[21]

Washington's silence also previewed the caution he was learning, which would characterize his future conduct. He occupied a tricky middle ground in the Robinson scandal: He was part of the emerging generation of Virginia leaders and was uninterested in Robinson-style self-dealing, yet had been an intimate of Robinson's. Washington's career would be filled with similar contradictions. He would be an aristocratic revolutionary, a fierce challenger of the British establishment and mainstay of the American establishment, and a slaveholding devotee of liberty. In negotiating such treacherous terrain, silence can be the wisest course.

The Robinson scandal offered political lessons, beginning with the spectacle of a man's legacy thrown in the mud despite years of service, because of a profound misjudgment. The lesson was a hard one for many Virginia aristocrats, long accustomed to the reciprocal favors they had regularly granted one another. On both sides of the Atlantic, political power had always brought economic benefits. The Robinson scandal signaled, however, that standards were changing.

Though Washington cannily avoided the Robinson troubles, he took his time applying the broader lesson about the risks of seeking advantage from political connections. So long as others applied private influence to seek land grants, he continued to play that game. Yet over the years he would become more cautious and deliberate about seeking public advantages. Moreover, the Robinson scandal demonstrated that friends could damage a politician at least as much as his enemies could. Washington learned to resist his friends' pleadings, an attitude that led some to think of him as chilly and aloof, but one that would protect his reputation. Washington came to believe that his reputation could not survive any whiff of self-dealing in conducting public business. The Robinson scandal proved that.

CHAPTER 22

Pivot to Fairfax County

In the election of 1765, Washington took a large step toward greater political prominence. He could have chosen to coast to a third win in Frederick County. He had finished first in two elections there, and rival Adam Stephen's reputation was blackened by the action of the House of Burgesses in his case. But representing Frederick County was inconvenient. Winchester lay eighty miles of hard travel northwest of Mount Vernon. Moreover, burgesses from Frederick, a thinly settled frontier county, commanded less regard in the House than did Tidewater legislators who represented the wealthy and influential.

Washington coveted a seat from Fairfax County, where he lived. Campaigning there and staying abreast of constituents' concerns would be far easier. And he would gain stature if his constituents numbered the Fairfaxes, George Mason, and other notables, people who could not be dismissed as yahoos in buckskins. In 1765, a seat for Fairfax opened up, and no one named Fairfax entered the race. Washington, already prominent in the county due to his large estate and military record, took the plunge.[1]

The election poll went smoothly. Washington led three candidates, winning 201 votes. John West, an incumbent, won the other seat with 148. Since a recent law banned candidates from providing liquor on polling day, Washington spent less than £10 on cakes for the voters. He called it "an easy and a creditable poll."[2] Now Fairfax County's worthies would look to him when they had problems. He would carry no more bills about the running of hogs in a frontier settlement.

Washington was already involved in Fairfax public events through his service on the vestry board that governed the local Truro church. Virginia's

Anglican churches performed many public functions: confirming land boundaries and posting laws relating to servants, slaves, and morals, plus notices
about stray animals, lost property, and runaway slaves. The vestry also made
support payments to poor residents; during Washington's service, the Truro
vestry paid nearly a dozen residents a year.[3]

Before Sunday services, Virginia's churchyards buzzed with talk. When
the starting time arrived, the gentry marched in together to their front pews,
ahead of the women and the humbler folk. Services ended within forty-five
minutes ("prayers read over in haste," according to a disapproving Englishman), followed by more socializing while gentlemen extended and accepted
dinner invitations. Those churchyard encounters kept Washington abreast of
local attitudes, while his vestry service exposed him to the nuts and bolts
of governing.[4]

Washington took his vestry service seriously, attending three-quarters of
its meetings through more than a decade. For the year beginning October
1763, he and George William Fairfax served as the church wardens, managing all church business, including planning a new building and redrawing
the parish boundary line.[5]

In 1768, Washington enlarged his local standing by joining the Fairfax
County Court as a justice, a position he held for the next six years. Many
county justices, like Washington, had no legal training, but brought practical
experience and their sense of right and wrong. Most acquired legal handbooks to help with technical questions. As a member of the House of Burgesses, which wrote the laws, Washington had learned some colonial law.[6]

The court consisted of up to twelve part-time justices who sat in panels of
at least four judges. A senior justice, usually a lawyer, presided over each
panel. One handbook specified that justices should be men "of the best reputation, good governance, and courage for the truth," who would, as "lovers of
justice, judg[e] the people equally and impartially."[7] In Fairfax County, the
court ordinarily met on the third Monday of the month, and thereafter for as
many days as the docket required. Because the judges had other jobs, they
did not sit on every court day, or even for that many.

The court's duties extended well beyond deciding cases, reaching deep
into everyday life and giving Washington a graduate course on civil administration. The judges oversaw tax collection—the function that Washington
considered the lifeblood of any government—and managed elections. They
determined when residents had to work on local roads and bridges, for how
long, and where. The court enforced Virginia's blizzard of economic regulations, supervising the public tobacco warehouses used by planters until their
crops were loaded onto ships that would carry the leaf to market. Inspectors

judged and graded export tobacco to ensure consistent quality. Similar inspections applied to flour, hemp, tar, and five other products. The court licensed tavernkeepers. If a landowner wished to build a mill, the justices reviewed the plans to ensure that no change in flowing waters would injure neighbors. They regulated lawyers' conduct, fixed the rates for blacksmiths working on militia weapons, implemented (or chose not to implement) tariff laws like the Stamp Act, inspected the books of county surveyors, and paid bounties for wolf carcasses. The justices also nominated the candidates for public jobs like inspectors of export goods and revenue collectors, the county clerk, the sheriff, the coroner, and militia officers below the rank of brigadier general. Although the governor formally made those appointments, he ordinarily followed the recommendations from the county courts.[8]

In the courtroom, Washington presided over less serious criminal cases and civil disputes with no more than 25 shillings or two hundred pounds of tobacco at stake. Litigious neighbors swamped the docket. Some visitors concluded that Virginians did not consider a debt payable until the lender sued. On one day, a panel including Washington entered orders in forty-nine cases. Some were uncontested or settled by the parties, but on that day two different juries decided twelve cases. On another day, Washington's panel resolved seventy-five matters.[9]

Washington was on the bench for twenty-five days over a thirty-nine-month period for which records survive. He tended to sit when other business brought him into Alexandria. He heard a horse-stealing case and appointed tobacco and flour inspectors. He approved innumerable settlements of debts. He empaneled a grand jury and granted peace bonds against people who threatened their neighbors. He supervised jury trials and decided damage claims.

Washington and his colleagues appointed men to lay out and build new roads and others to prepare the county tax rolls. They ordered repairs and improvements to public warehouses as well as the construction of a "necessary" (outhouse) and "stocks and whipping post" at the courthouse itself. They supervised the county's budget and spending. Washington's surveying experience was a perfect fit for the resolution of boundary disputes, when the justices walked the disputed fields alongside a surveyor and quarreling neighbors.[10]

The criminal caseload covered all crimes committed by slaves, which were punished brutally. He and the other justices received numerous grand jury charges against tax cheats. The court enforced morality-based laws, including bans on profane swearing, drunkenness, illegal gambling, adultery, bastardy, and cursing. In 1770, the Fairfax court heard ten cases against women accused of bastardy; it heard a single case of fornication in 1771, two more in 1772, and another in 1773. If a child's unwed mother named the father under oath, he could be jailed until agreeing to support the child. If the mother was a slave, her master had the support obligation, but also owned the child. The court supervised the care of orphans. Those with no resources were placed in apprenticeships; the court appointed guardians for those whose parents left assets for their benefit.[11]

When the colony's morality-based laws were applied to enslaved and indentured workers, the results could be heartless. In one case, the Fairfax court fined an unwed, indentured mother for the crime of having a child; when she could not pay, she received twenty-five lashes. After five years, the woman had two illegitimate children, so the court ordered both infants bound to her master as servants. In a case with Justice Washington on the panel, the court bound as servants the five-year-old and three-year-old children of an unmarried, indentured mother.[12] Crossing race lines brought even more callous rulings. In another Fairfax case with Justice Washington on the bench, a white servant woman was to be sold for having a "base born mulatto child." Her white, twelve-year-old son by a previous liaison was bound out as an apprentice.[13]

Court service involved collegial deliberation with Washington's fellow justices, since all cases were decided collectively by panel. Washington often sat with his fellow burgess John West, and John Carlyle, the Alexandria merchant who had married a Fairfax. Other colleagues were Robert Adam and Hector Ross, who marketed Mount Vernon's flour and fish. On only one occasion did Washington sit with George Mason, the Fairfax County judge who showed up least often.[14]

Washington commented little about his judicial work, nor did he complain about it. It was another step in his transition from the bumptious commander of the Virginia Regiment to the inspiring leader of the Continental Army. Like his vestry duties, the court work immersed him in the world of Virginia's common people, seasoning his judgment and his understanding of how government touches people and changes their lives, for good and for ill.

His court work also bolstered his habits of acting cooperatively with peers, listening to differing views, and reconciling his ideas with those of others. By presenting both sides of a dispute, a court proceeding can lead an open-minded person to question assumptions and appreciate new perspectives. That exercise would benefit Washington's growth as a public figure who aimed to act justly.

Finally, his judicial duties further enhanced his stature. Court days drew litigants and observers. Presiding over case after case, Washington built his reputation as a man worthy of public trust. It may seem insincere to applaud a judge for fairly enforcing laws that now appear unfair, even cruel—laws like Virginia's treatment of the mothers of illegitimate children. Yet Virginia's county court judges, as their handbook instructed, were to apply the laws "equally and impartially"; they had no power to question the wisdom or decency of those laws. Washington met that standard.

By 1770, Washington—as burgess, vestryman, judge, farmer, and businessman—could credibly claim to be the leading figure in Fairfax County. Not yet forty, he had built a solid political base. His ambitions, however, would leap beyond the county's borders.

CHAPTER 23

The Master of Mount Vernon

For seven years after the repeal of the Stamp Act in 1766, Washington happily filled the role he sought when he left the Virginia Regiment: master of Mount Vernon, prosperous and public-spirited, with time for his family and for a gentleman's pastimes.

Mount Vernon supported this era of private contentment. Tenants paid him rent from their tobacco crops, while Washington concentrated on wheat and Indian corn. By 1770, his farms produced 7,000 bushels of wheat a year, or approximately 210 tons. He built a large mill with interchangeable millstones to grind flour of different grades. By 1772, Mount Vernon flour was branded, "G. Washington."[1] Wheat and flour sales, combined with revenue from the fish pulled from the river each spring, produced regular income, a welcome improvement from tobacco-growing days.[2]

Yet Washington had not entirely escaped the British merchants, and purchasing from distant sellers still infuriated him. In June 1768, he ordered an elegant carriage "in the newest taste, handsome, genteel, and light," made from "the best seasoned wood, and by a celebrated workman." He identified the decorations he wanted for every inch of the vehicle, plus every interior feature. The carriage that arrived, Washington wrote, was "made of wood so exceedingly green that the panels slipped out of the moldings before it was two months in use—split from one end to the other." The joints separated so drastically that he scrapped it.

Washington's focus on wheat and corn, which required less effort than tobacco, bestowed the gift of free time, as did having his cousin Lund as farm manager. Washington and Martha rented a house in Berkeley Springs for a four-week vacation in late summer 1767, bringing a cook with them. George

William and Sally Fairfax came along. They could take the waters, fish, ride, and be convivial. Washington, though, was not built for total relaxation; meeting an old military comrade, he questioned him closely about Pennsylvania land policies.[3]

Washington embraced fox hunting, an avocation learned at Belvoir. In 1768, Washington rode after foxes on fifty days, with the frequency higher in the winter when farm cares receded. He hunted on fifteen days in January. The hunt might be a social event with neighbors and guests, but more than a third of his hunting days were solitary: just him, the dogs, and the fox. Plainly, Washington loved to pound over the countryside on horseback, matching wits with shrewd animals with a special talent for evasion. His devotion to the sport thrived despite the regularity with which foxes eluded him, or perhaps because of it.[4]

The ancient Greeks, including Xenophon and Plato, connected hunting skills with military prowess. Hunting develops, wrote one enthusiast, "not only physical fitness and courage, but also an 'eye for the country.'" The hunt, he continued, also offers "the feel of a good horse, knowing what to ask of him and what not to ask, requiring the whole range of cross-country riding skills; and the excitement of galloping and jumping." A Washington aide in the 1780s observed that hunting provided Washington with "activity and boldness."[5]

Fox hunting required not only good horses but also well-bred hounds. Washington charted the mating of his hounds, bestowing names that would be familiar today, including Mopsey, Jupiter, Lady, Duchess, Vulcan, Searcher, and Rover. Some of the female names, such as Truelove and Sweetlips, mingled affection with whimsy. Washington was a demanding breeder. Bryan Fairfax remarked with exasperation that Washington had been given "many super excellent dogs . . . which have not answered your expectation."[6]

Washington's hunting dwindled after 1768, whether by choice or because of competing demands on his time. He rode for foxes only thirty days in the following year, then twenty-six the year after, then seventeen in 1771.

Through the years when his hunting declined, Washington's diary shows an increase in the number of days when he was "home alone." That term requires context. He was never alone at Mount Vernon, not with Martha ordinarily around, as well as two children and their tutors, enslaved servants plus overseers and others who brought business to the mansion house. For Washington, "home alone" meant no social guests, an infrequent condition; it happened on only ten days in 1771. Two years later, however, Washington's "home alone" days had more than tripled, and increased again the following year.

Dirty weather dictated some home-alone days. The increasing number of

Mount Vernon

days without guests, however, also reflected Washington's expanding public responsibilities. Political correspondence increased while paperwork relating to Mount Vernon did not slacken. He received more than twice as many letters in 1773 as he had two years before. Washington also devoted considerable time to reading, an activity not always associated with him.

He built his library on the collection assembled by Martha's first husband, which she brought to Mount Vernon. Washington had a taste for practical writings that could guide his business. Early purchases focused on agricultural handbooks, including a six-volume series with articles on brewing beer, increasing milk production, and dyeing wool. He also ordered a volume with advice on business law, mathematics, and correspondence. By one estimate, nearly half his library consisted of practical books, such as encyclopedias, dictionaries, and volumes on law and legislation.[7]

Because much of the political discourse of the era occurred in pamphlets, Washington possessed many of those. He owned John Dickinson's seminal treatment of British-American relations in *Letters from a Farmer in Pennsylvania*, as well as the pamphlet reproducing Benjamin Franklin's testimony on that subject to the House of Commons; he later acquired Thomas Jefferson's *Summary View of the Rights of British America*. He adored maps and books describing geography and travel. He had little taste for works of imagination, yet owned both Tobias Smollett's *The Adventures of Peregrine Pickle* and Fielding's *Tom Jones*.[8]

Washington's great love was for theater. From the first production he attended as a teenager in Barbados, Washington seized every opportunity to attend performances, often bringing his family. Though Washington's surviving diaries cover only about half the years between 1759 and 1775, he recorded attending forty-five plays in Williamsburg, Annapolis, and Alexandria. In June 1770, he saw five performances in seven days in Williamsburg. The performances skewed toward Restoration comedies like *The Beggar's Opera* by John Gay and George Farquhar's *The Recruiting Officer*. In 1773, he saw his first Shakespeare drama, catching *Hamlet* while in New York with his stepson.[9]

Late in life, he told an actor that he considered the stage a valuable resource to society. It portrayed manners, he said, served as a school for poetry, and honored noble principles.[10] For Washington, shy about his limited education, theater offered lessons. At least part of his enthusiasm for it reflected his intuitive understanding that politics, at its core, is a layered form of performance art.

A natural leader has not only wit and vision but also commands attention through demeanor, voice, timing, and expression. Actors know how to stand, how to move, how to engage an audience through gestures and vocal variations. They study when to pause and for how long, as well as when to look directly at an audience and when to look away. For a politician, such skills are essential, and Washington mastered them. John Adams later wrote that Washington was "the best actor of presidency we have ever had," and cited three key moments in Washington's career as "in a strain of Shakespearean . . . excellence in dramatic exhibitions."[11] Washington honed that talent watching professionals in darkened theaters.

In his world, the most important play was Addison's *Cato*, which celebrated the Roman patriot who remained true to republican virtues by resisting Julius Caesar's power grab. *Cato* appears on the list of volumes in Washington's library. He attended numerous performances of the play, including stagings for his troops during the Revolutionary War. He alluded to the drama or quoted it in multiple letters through his life.[12]

For relaxation, he always enjoyed gambling, especially cards. After a round of fox hunting and a good dinner, cards extended the day's social pleasures. If the weather was harsh and congenial companions were at hand, Washington might play cards all day. Washington's sporting instincts also took him to horse races.

Washington's meticulous records show him roughly breaking even as a gambler. A tally of card playing from 1772 to 1774 recorded a loss of a bit over £6, a modest sum for three years of entertainment.[13]

∾

Family, too, demanded attention. That Martha and George had not conceived a child likely was a surprise to both; during Martha's marriage to Daniel Parke Custis, her pregnancies were regular, and a virile figure like Washington would expect to father children. Family tradition suggested that Martha's last pregnancy left her unable to conceive, but that is undocumented. Whatever the reason, no babies came.

Martha's daughter, Patsy, was a constant source of anxiety. Her epilepsy spurred a continuing search for a cure, or a better physician, or some ameliorating therapy, but eighteenth-century medicine had nothing to offer. When the Washingtons took Patsy to the waters of Berkeley Springs for several weeks in 1769, she did not improve.[14]

Less dire but equally intractable was the challenge of educating Jacky Custis. His schoolmaster led the hand-wringing, describing the young man as "exceedingly indolent [and] surprisingly voluptuous. One would suppose nature had intended him for some Asiatic prince." The schoolmaster concocted a plan to conduct young Custis on a tour of Europe, arguing that exposure to sophisticated Europeans would embarrass Jacky into learning. Washington rejected the proposal because of the expense and because Jacky's educational attainments were too thin for him to gain much advantage from travel.[15]

Washington also had to resettle his mother. In 1761, Washington's brother-in-law, Fielding Lewis, built Mary Washington a small house in Fredericksburg, close to where he and her daughter Betty lived. Mary, however, then declined to leave Ferry Farm.[16]

Ten years later, nearly sixty-three, Mary was ready to give up the farm that Washington had inherited nearly three decades earlier. He performed surveys of the land and a nearby parcel, the Little Falls Quarter, that Mary inherited, and agreed to buy her livestock and also rent her slaves and the Little Falls Quarter. The prices were set by his brother Charles and brother-in-law Lewis, sparing mother and son from having to haggle with each other. He placed a down payment on a Fredericksburg house for Mary.[17]

Taking possession of his boyhood home surely triggered memories of his young years there with his mother, sisters, and brothers. His new survey of Ferry Farm reflected a sentimental connection that he never recorded elsewhere. Exercising the surveyor's discretion to choose any physical characteristic as his stopping place, he ended the survey at the burial site of his little sister, Mildred. She was three when she died; Washington was eight.[18]

By spring 1772, Mary was in her new home, steps away from the Lewis mansion. Washington sold Ferry Farm two years later. Until then, as she always had, his mother took its output to support her, her servants, and her horses.[19]

CHAPTER 24

Never Enough Land

Washington's craving for land marked him, in one contemporary's eyes, as "avaricious." No matter how deep his financial distress of the moment, a possible land deal always intrigued him. Before the Revolutionary War, he pursued multiple strategies for acquiring land. Five of them targeted massive tracts, four of which were in the west. Although land transactions could take years to ripen in that era, Washington rarely walked away from a deal, nor did he shy from employing subterfuge or political connections.[1]

Washington repeatedly advised friends and relatives to acquire land. Many Virginia fortunes had been built, he insisted, by "taking up and purchasing at very low rates the rich back lands which were thought nothing of in those days."[2] That Indian tribes dwelled on tracts he coveted was no deterrent. More than most Americans, Washington appreciated how many Indians there were, how established their cultures were, and what dangerous enemies they were. Yet for many years he sought their lands with little worry over the weight of their claims, or where they might live if he succeeded in acquiring their land. This nearly magical thinking was common among whites who chose to imagine the west without Indians. After all, Indians once occupied the Atlantic coast, but no longer did. Surely this pattern would repeat itself.

Washington's passion for land had a dimension beyond profit. He saw immense resources that could bring prosperity to a brawny nation. A builder at heart, whose improvements to Mount Vernon never ended, he dreamt of expansion and an American empire. He had a taste for large ideas and outsized ambitions, so America's potential fired his imagination.[3]

No land rush, by definition, is orderly. Beginning as early as 1743, land-hungry whites lodged overlapping western claims based on shoddy or fraudulent surveys. Twenty years later, when British officials asked for a listing of Virginia's western land grants, the Executive Council threw up its hands. "Insuperable difficulties," it reported, made such a listing impossible. Four American syndicates secured grants of hundreds of thousands of acres, and enlisted powerful Englishmen to support them. "One-half of England," an American observed, was "land mad and everybody there has their eyes fixed on this country." The confusion rendered the Ohio valley a snake pit where the strongest and craftiest succeeded.[4]

Washington's first major land quest sprang from Governor Dinwiddie's 1754 promise of 200,000 acres to Virginia's first volunteers in the fight against France. Having commanded the regiment, Washington sought a large share of that grant. Fellow officers joined the clamor.[5] Washington also formed the Mississippi Land Company with his brother Jack and four of the Lee brothers of Westmoreland County, to seek 2.5 million acres in the Ohio valley, a proposed barony that would reach to the Mississippi River.[6]

The scramble for land guaranteed conflict with Indians, so in the early 1760s, the British sought to keep the peace by blocking new land grants. King George III's proclamation in October 1763 halted the distribution of western lands, including those pledged by Dinwiddie's proclamation.[7] For the colonists, the king's new Proclamation Line, beyond which new settlement was banned, incinerated a central promise of America: land. The British policy also had the unintended effect of favoring the poor and landless over the rich and well-connected. Speculators needed title to land so they could sell or lease it to others, but squatters cared nothing for such formalities, so speculators watched in frustration as the squatters spread.[8]

With his western plans stalled, Washington leapt at a proposal to drain the Great Dismal Swamp of southeastern Virginia. Drained swampland was prized for its fertility, while the Dismal was close to ports at Norfolk and Hampton. After exploring the region in 1763, Washington joined the Dismal Swamp Company; each of ten founders agreed to provide ten slaves to dig drainage ditches and canals.[9] To secure 148,000 acres, the company had to evade the thousand-acre limit on land grants to any single applicant. The ten founders prepared claims in their own names and in the names of 138 brothers, cousins, neighbors, and servants. The government ignored the fraud. Washington installed Lund Washington's brother as overseer of the drainage work.

In 1767, Washington turned to Pennsylvania lands east of the Proclamation

Line, where settlement was permitted. He authorized William Crawford, a surveyor, to find sites for him. Explaining that the Proclamation Line "must fall, of course, in a few years," Washington urged Crawford to employ deception. He should treat his mission as "a profound secret," proceeding "by silent management" and adopting "the pretense of hunting other game." To evade Pennsylvania's limits on the size of individual claims, Crawford should apply the dummy name device used at the Dismal Swamp. After six years of effort, Washington acquired several thousand Pennsylvania acres through Crawford.[10]

When good land became available close to home, Washington pounced. In late 1767, he acquired nearly 3,000 acres in Fauquier and Loudoun counties, which he later leased to tenants in hundred-acre lots.[11] Washington always aimed to make his home estate larger, more impressive, and more productive, so snapped up adjacent tracts from George Mason, from George William Fairfax, and from another neighbor.[12]

Hunting the big score, Washington rarely abandoned any land scheme, no matter how bleak its prospects. In 1770, he was still pressing for grants to the Mississippi Land Company. The ditching in the Dismal Swamp was not completed until nearly three decades after his death. And he never gave up on the bounty lands promised by Dinwiddie in 1754: 100,000 acres near the Forks of the Ohio and another 100,000 acres on or near the Ohio River.[13]

As Washington predicted, the Proclamation Line evaporated in 1768, inspiring him to revive the soldiers' petition. In 1769, he explained it to the current governor, then submitted his case in writing, portraying the soldiers of 1754 as heroic defenders of Virginia, and the Dinwiddie Proclamation as a firm contract. Because the west was filling up quickly, Washington fretted that "none but barren hills and rugged mountains, will be left to those who have toiled and bled for the country." He did not ask that squatters be ousted, which he called a "work of great difficulty, perhaps of equal cruelty, as most of these people are poor," but urged speedy action before more squatters could arrive.[14]

A week later, the Executive Council awarded Washington's petition for 200,000 acres in the valleys of the Ohio River and the Great Kanawha River. The lands had to be identified within five years in twenty separate surveys, a condition that loomed as a major obstacle. Twenty surveys of contiguous parcels would necessarily include less desirable land, which Washington always disdained. Undeterred, he advertised in the *Virginia Gazette* to receive the claims from soldiers who had enlisted before the Battle of Fort Necessity. Washington also started a new effort to purchase land claims from those who were in uniform when a 1763 royal proclamation awarded western lands to those soldiers. Washington described all his efforts as "a kind of lottery." The difficult question, he added, was "whether the chance of a prize" justified the expense. Usually his answer was yes.[15]

Washington pressed hard against the twenty-survey limit on the 1754 claims while directing Crawford, his agent and surveyor, to perform the surveys as best he could. When selecting land, however, Washington trusted only his own eyes. In the autumn of 1770, he journeyed through the frontier for nine weeks accompanied by Crawford, his friend Dr. Craik, and three servants.[16]

In his diary, Washington described traveling through a world of wondrous abundance. Descending the Ohio River by canoe, he saw "innumerable numbers of turkeys and many deer," huge river catfish, and bison. He was wary of "the unsettled state of this country," fearing that some Indians viewed his party "with an uneasy and jealous eye." Always, he judged the land's features, its water access, and its soil. As they canoed up the Kanawha, his enthusiasm grew. The land was "In many places very rich . . . upon the whole exceeding valuable." He marked trees to indicate the soldiers' claims, which ultimately covered eighty square miles.[17]

When surveyor Crawford produced the first ten surveys, they covered barely 61,000 acres, which meant that twenty surveys of good land could never encompass the promised 200,000 acres. In submissions to the governor and the Executive Council in November 1771, Washington again challenged the twenty-survey ceiling, but to no avail. Retaining the ceiling, the council members authorized grants of 400 acres for each private, and then up the chain of command to 15,000 acres for Washington. To a former colleague in the regiment, Washington despaired of the council's "lukewarmness" and the twenty-survey ceiling.[18]

With a new governor, Washington kept pressing for the final land grants. He feared competition from the well-connected Walpole Company, the Philadelphia-based enterprise that included Ben Franklin, which was angling for "every foot of land to the westward of the Allegheny Mountains" and ultimately sought 20 million acres for a new colony named Vandalia. In late 1772, Washington was still agitating over the twenty-survey ceiling, joining the governor on one day for breakfast, dinner, and supper, then submitting a renewed petition to the Executive Council. The ceiling remained in place, but it barely slowed Washington's accumulation of western land.[19] In 1773, he acquired 5,000 acres under the 1763 proclamation, pressing claims he had purchased from former soldiers.[20] He sent an agent to scout land in far-off West Florida on the Gulf of Mexico. In 1773, Washington won another 100,000 acres for the ex-soldiers claiming under the 1754 proclamation, with 20,000 going to him (his 15,000 acres as commanding officer plus claims purchased from other veterans). A final ruling brought his total award under the Dinwiddie Proclamation to 32,000 acres.[21]

In a decade-long enterprise that no one else had been willing to undertake, Washington had redeemed Dinwiddie's promise and won benefits for fellow veterans and himself.[22] The episode should have stood as an example of hard work rewarded. It would not, however, be so simple.

∽

With land patents in hand, Washington resolved to recruit tenants for his new empire. In a broadside and newspaper advertisements, he touted the lands: "None can exceed them in luxuriancy of soil, or convenience of situation; . . . abounding in fine fish and wild fowl of various kinds, as also in most excellent meadows." But no tenants came forward, especially after a resurgence of Indian violence. Emigrants preferred to own land, not lease it. Smaller parcels were available at very low prices or simply for the taking. Washington considered importing settlers from Germany, Ireland, or Scotland, but those notions fizzled.[23]

The situation continued to sour as conflict spread between the colonies and the mother country. In 1774, the British ministry ruled that only British soldiers could receive lands under the 1763 proclamation. Washington denounced the decision as one of "malice, absurdity, and error." A year later, Virginia's governor revoked every grant under the 1754 proclamation on a technicality: Surveyor Crawford had failed to swear the surveyors' oath. Dunmore's spiteful action did not last. Three years into the Revolutionary War, the Virginia Assembly approved the grants based on Crawford's surveys.[24]

Washington, however, never realized his dreams of riches from western lands. In 1794, forty years after Dinwiddie's proclamation, he still lacked tenants. "From the experience of many years," he admitted, "I have found distant property in land more pregnant of perplexities than profit."[25]

Nevertheless, Washington's quest marked him as a man with an expansive vision of America's potential wealth and power, willing to take on ambitious projects and pursue them relentlessly. For a decade, he tugged and hauled at the levers of government until he finally got what he thought he had been promised, and desperately wanted. In so doing, he won the gratitude of his fellow soldiers and the regard of those who knew how difficult his undertaking had been. Anyone watching his pursuit of land should have appreciated Washington's relentless persistence and ultimate effectiveness, qualities that would serve him well in the coming fight with Britain. Moreover, when the royal government repeatedly broke its promises about western settlement and imposed arbitrary conditions, Washington knew injustice at its hands, an experience that reinforced his skepticism of British intentions and his own commitment as a public official to honor his commitments.

CHAPTER 25

Washington's Association

After dissolving the General Assembly amid the Stamp Act ruckus of May 1765, Governor Fauquier waited more than a year before bringing the legislators back to Williamsburg. After those hated taxes were repealed, he decided that tempers should be cool enough for an assembly session in early November 1766. To fill the vacant Speaker's chair following the death of John Robinson, the House chose corpulent, easygoing Peyton Randolph. The governor appointed a new treasurer as well.[1]

Reconciliation was the message of the day. Greeting the burgesses, the governor advised that with the Stamp Act rescinded, Virginia should repay Britain for its "many acts of kindness." The House dutifully applauded the "best of kings" for the "tender regard shown to the rights and liberties of his British subjects in America." Washington's political footprint expanded when he joined the pivotal committee that heard election disputes, but the business of the session was largely unremarkable.[2]

The next assembly session, convened five months later, finally saw Washington shouldering a major legislative assignment: the colony's crippling currency shortage. Sales of land and slaves froze because no one had currency for purchases. A committee developed a plan for issuing currency that blended two elements: a large issue of paper money secured by taxes on rum and tobacco, combined with a large loan from English investors at 5 percent interest (truly, a repackaged version of late Speaker Robinson's earlier "loan office" proposal). The burgesses approved the program, then appointed six leading members to present the legislation to the Executive Council and seek its concurrence. Washington was one of the six.[3]

Having built his political career gradually, one brick at a time, Washington was winning recognition. For the first time, after eight years as a legislator, he was at the center of a critical, non-military issue. The assignment confirmed that his colleagues viewed him not only as a former soldier, but also as a political figure whose views mattered. When the Executive Council declined to endorse the House plan, the burgesses pressed ahead on their own, sending the proposal to Virginia's London agent to present to the king.[4]

The king was uninterested in Virginia's currency problems. His government faced a mountain of war debt and still intended that Americans pay part of it. By late 1767, Parliament changed course again, adopting another fistful of American taxes—called the Townshend duties after the then-Chancellor of the Exchequer—this time on tea, paper, glass, lead, and paint. To underscore its determination, Parliament suspended the colonial assembly in New York to punish that colony's failure to supply army units there, and instructed that British soldiers be quartered in private homes.[5] The truce in the transatlantic face-off had lasted less than eighteen months.

A Virginia legislative session in early spring of 1768 had the modest purpose of approving action against western squatters, but residents of six counties presented petitions protesting the Townshend duties and the sanctions imposed on New York. The House and the Executive Council promptly approved requests for repeal of the new taxes. The burgesses insisted that "no power on earth has a right to impose taxes [on Virginians] . . . without their consent." Urging sister colonies to join them in opposing the taxes, the Virginians stressed that they did not seek "independency of their parent kingdom."[6]

Washington missed that legislative session, instead meeting for several days at Mount Vernon with Crawford, his western agent, to plan his land acquisitions. He may have expected that the assembly would address no important matters, or his absence may simply have reflected his consuming passion for land deals.[7]

Through the rest of 1768, Washington showed little concern over the Townshend duties. His days were full. The family passed much of May visiting Martha's sister, where Washington hunted and fished and attended the theater in Williamsburg. That was the year he hunted on more than fifty days. Over the summer, he delivered Jacky Custis to a school in Annapolis. In the autumn, Washington accepted his new position on the Fairfax County Court and reviewed the ditching progress at the Great Dismal Swamp. The arrival of the new colonial governor, Lord Botetourt, meant new elections, but they were not a serious concern for the man from Mount Vernon. On polling day in Alexandria, he led a field of three candidates by a wide margin, then spent only £25 on the election-night party.[8]

Though Washington's life seemed largely unruffled, the Townshend duties, with their echoes of the Stamp Act, were reviving agitation in other colonies. In Boston, New York, and Philadelphia, Americans again embraced trade sanctions to challenge British policy. They formed "non-importation associations," pledging to boycott British goods until the new taxes were repealed. The association movement spread south, reaching Dr. David Ross of Bladensburg, Maryland, who sent papers about the boycott across the Potomac to his acquaintance George Washington. That package changed Washington's career.[9]

Despite his public silence about the Townshend duties, Washington had followed the controversy. When he studied the boycott proposal from Dr. Ross, a fire flared in Washington's mind that must have smoldered for months before. He wrote a fierce letter to his neighbor George Mason, enclosing the package from Dr. Ross and voicing bitter anger with the British. In that letter, he endorsed resistance to the Townshend duties—including war, if need be:

At a time when our lordly masters in Great Britain will be satisfied with nothing less than the deprivation of American freedom, it seems highly necessary that something should be done to avert the stroke and maintain the liberty which we have derived from our ancestors. . . .

That no man should scruple, or hesitate a moment to use a—ms [arms] in defense of so valuable a blessing, on which all the good and evil of life depends; is clearly my opinion.

Having proclaimed himself ready for war, Washington drew a breath. His political engagement over the last decade had deepened his understanding of public opinion and sobered his judgment. He knew that Americans would not fly to arms as a first response, but only as a last resort. He had no interest in "addresses to the throne, and remonstrances to parliament." He urged the middle course adopted by the northern colonists. Perhaps the British could be "awakened or alarmed by starving their trade and manufactures."

Washington recognized the limitations of non-importation. Smuggling undermined it, and Americans were adept at smuggling. Nonetheless, he concluded that the colonists would join the effort if leaders "would be at some pains to explain matters . . . and stimulate a cordial agreement to purchase none but certain enumerated articles." Accordingly, "the more I consider a scheme of this sort, the more ardently I wish success to it." He proposed that he and Mason present a non-importation plan to the House of Burgesses.[10]

Washington's approach was astute. By having a plan in hand when he arrived in Williamsburg, Washington—the leading man of Fairfax County—could take control of the burgesses' debate. And the well-regarded Mason would fuel the effort with his intellect and pen. After ten years as a burgess, Washington understood that some men shape arguments more crisply and express them more persuasively. Not believing he had those gifts, he respected those who did. Mason was the first of several talented men whom Washington would recruit to translate his ideas into compelling form.

Mason replied on the same day. Having received the same papers from Dr. Ross, he firmly agreed with Washington, proclaiming, "Our all is at stake." He urged that public opinion be nurtured to press the General Assembly to adopt the boycott. Non-importation, he continued, should apply to "finery of all denominations," while Virginians should consider withholding tobacco exports. Because the leaf was taxed heavily, the British government would feel the pinch if supplies were cut off.[11]

Later in April, the two men met in Alexandria, where Washington was sitting on the county court, then adjourned to Mount Vernon to outline a non-importation association for Virginia. Although Mason complained of various ailments, he produced the outline plus a supporting memorandum.[12]

Mason's draft followed one already adopted by Philadelphia merchants. Complaining of British policies that were "reducing [Americans] from a free and happy people to a wretched and miserable state of slavery," the draft announced that the signers would "encourage industry and frugality and discourage all manner of luxury and extravagance" by importing nothing taxed by Parliament to raise revenue. With a few exemptions, the draft also disdained imports of spirits, beer, wine, fine foodstuffs, and high-end goods like jewelry, silks, carriages, clothing, and leather goods. And slaves.[13]

Because Washington was a burgess and Mason was not, and because Mason preferred to stay home, only Washington carried the plan to Williamsburg, where the Townshend duties dominated conversation. Though he was still careful to maintain his connection with colonial officials—on that trip, Washington dined twice with the governor—he explained his opposition to the taxes and outlined his plan.

The assembly convened on May 8 with a ceremonial greeting of the new governor. In a red coat with gold edging, Governor Botetourt rode in an elegant carriage to the Capitol, where he announced the birth of a royal princess. His bland remarks ignored the political powder keg that soon would detonate in that building.[14]

After routine proceedings, the House sat as a committee of the whole "to consider the present state of the colony." The lawmakers addressed four resolutions, beginning with the assertion that only the burgesses could tax Virginians. Other resolutions insisted on colonists' right to trial by jury, which recent British proposals would restrict. All passed by voice vote. Next day, Lord Botetourt summoned the burgesses. "I have heard of your resolves," he announced, "and augur ill of their effect: you have made it my duty to dissolve you; and you are dissolved accordingly."[15]

No one was surprised. Most of the burgesses walked a few hundred yards to the Raleigh Tavern, where they selected a committee to draft their response to the Townshend duties. Washington sat with that committee until ten that evening, offering his plan for an association for the colony.[16]

The following morning, eighty-eight legislators signed the committee's report, which was based on the Mason/Washington draft. The principal change removed the ban on tobacco exports; that step might have threatened the solvency of many burgesses. Richard Henry Lee captured the mood of the moment: "The flame of liberty burns bright and clear, . . . The Americans . . . appear too wise, too brave, and much too honest, to be either talked, terrified or bribed from the assertion of just, equitable, and long possessed rights."[17]

That afternoon, Washington bought a copy of John Dickinson's pamphlet on the rights of Americans, then stayed an extra day in Williamsburg to attend the governor's ball in honor of the queen's birthday. Because he was still angling to acquire western lands, maintaining cordial relations with the governor only made sense for Washington.[18]

The events at the Raleigh Tavern further confirmed Washington's ascent in Virginia's hierarchy. In that status-conscious colony, signatories ordinarily were listed in descending order of importance, with the House Speaker's name coming first; on the association papers, Washington's name appears seventh of eighty-eight. That was no accident. Mason's work on the non-importation association was critical, but it was Washington who presented the proposal and gained stature as a result. At thirty-seven, willing to challenge the British directly, he had become a man of weight in Virginia's political world. His voice, and his leadership, made a difference now.[19]

∽

Washington was unopposed in the elections of September 1769. The Fairfax County sheriff did not even poll the voters. When Washington traveled to Williamsburg for the next legislative session two months later, Martha and Patsy came with him. With Patsy's affliction worsening, they consulted more physicians who could not help her.

Non-importation associations were in force in Fairfax, Loudoun, and

Prince William Counties, and were spreading to other southern colonies, plus Connecticut and Rhode Island.[20] Lord Botetourt began the legislative meeting with the report that Parliament was reversing itself again and would soon rescind all of the Townshend duties *except* one on tea. He explained the reversal not as a concession that Parliament lacked the power to tax Americans, but as based on "true principles of commerce," a phrase without obvious meaning. The colonists again had forced Britain to back down. At an end-of-session ball honoring the governor, most celebrants showed their support for non-importation by wearing garments of American-made fabric.[21]

When Parliament repealed all but one of the Townshend taxes in April 1770, the non-importation movement lost momentum. Virginians remembered their fondness for British goods. From England, Arthur Lee reported seeing no evidence of the association's impact there, while a brother in Virginia lamented "the shameful neglect of the former association among the merchants here."[22]

With the tea tax still in place, Washington clung to the association, but proposed to soften it to increase public acceptance. At the assembly session in mid-May 1770, he was among twenty burgesses appointed to revise the association agreement. After several contentious meetings, they produced a compromise document that was signed in late June.[23]

The revision shortened the list of banned products, allowing imports of some food items, jewelry, leather, and pewter goods. But unlike the earlier version, it introduced an enforcement mechanism. In each county, the associators were to form a five-man committee to inspect merchants' invoices, then shame violators by publishing their names.[24] Washington thought the new agreement "too much relaxed," while a colleague disparaged it as a compromise "just as if there could be any half way between slavery and freedom." But it was the best they could get. Washington joined the associators at the Raleigh Tavern for seventeen toasts to the revised agreement.[25]

Three months later, Washington was named to the five-man committee of the Fairfax County associators, which proceeded to unearth a grand total of two violations, involving twelve improperly imported men's hats. Virginia's Executive Council president, William Nelson, observed at year's end that the association's spirit was "cooling every day." By mid-1771, the Fairfax committee reduced its oversight to tea, paper, glass, and colored paints. Washington promptly ordered several previously banned items from his London agent, including a bearskin hat.[26]

The confrontation with Britain had brought both sides to a rough accommodation that satisfied neither yet eliminated much of the friction between them. The associators had blunted a second attempt by Parliament to impose taxes on Americans, but the British still did not accept the principle that only Americans could tax Americans. That resolution left both sides feeling disgruntled, as though the dispute were not really settled. Presciently, Mason predicted that the associations would have a long-term impact. "Should the oppressive system of taxing us without our consent be continued," he wrote, "the flame, however smothered now, will break out with redoubled ardor." If there was a new conflagration, Washington would be fanning those flames.[27]

CHAPTER 26

Upheavals at Mount Vernon

In 1772, life for Washington seemed to promise stability, prosperity, and prominence. In the House of Burgesses, Washington served on committees that considered clearing the Potomac for navigation and regulating sales of flour, now Mount Vernon's major revenue-producer. Washington plunged into Williamsburg's cultural offerings, attending six plays, a concert, and a ball. A darker development was his chronic dental trouble. Since the only therapy for mouth pain was extraction of an offending tooth, Washington would run out of teeth far too early.[1]

Back at Mount Vernon in May, he arranged for a portrait of himself by Charles Willson Peale. He predicted that the artist would show the world "what manner of man I am." He seized control of the answer to that question by wearing his old uniform for the sitting, even though thirteen years had passed since he last commanded soldiers. The portrait shows him in his Virginia Regiment regalia, sword on his hip and crescent-shaped gorget of rank around his neck. Appearing younger than his forty years, his expression is contemplative, with a trace of melancholy. Peale also painted miniatures of Martha, Jacky, and Patsy.[2]

When the artist was done, matters at Mount Vernon might have seemed as settled as the big river flowing by. Hard changes, however, were coming.

∾

George William and Sally Fairfax, neighbors and intimate friends, resolved to leave for England to manage an inheritance. Having suffered recent health setbacks, both hoped for better medical care in England.[3]

With no one else did the Washingtons socialize so regularly and so informally. The two men shared memories reaching back twenty-five years—of
frontier surveying, rowdy hunts, glittering balls, and elegant evenings with
brother Lawrence and Colonel Fairfax. Belvoir had been Washington's finishing school, where blessed people knew the secrets of how to behave and
how the world worked, secrets that an ambitious colonial youth absorbed
eagerly. While Washington served in the Virginia Regiment in 1758, it was
George William—not Washington's brothers—who supervised the rebuilding of Mount Vernon. The two friends supported each other in elections,
served as church wardens together, and matured into the twin pillars of Fairfax County. While Washington advanced in the House of Burgesses, George
William served on the Executive Council. The prospect of losing such a close
friend had to leave an empty place in Washington's heart.

Like most people, George William trusted Washington. He asked his
friend to supervise the management of his property while he was gone. "In this
part of the colony," George William wrote on New Year's Day 1773, "I have not
a friend (yourself excepted) in whom I can repose such confidence." At a dinner at Mount Vernon the next day, George William pressed the matter, but
Washington evidently resisted. Weighed down by his Mount Vernon responsibilities, his public duties, other guardianships, and his western land quest,
Washington dreaded another burden. Perhaps, also, his friend's departure
made Washington, the one to be left behind, irritable.

More than two weeks later, in a note on other matters, Washington offered an indirect apology, having recovered both his manners and his feelings toward his oldest friend. He had responded in haste, he wrote. "I might
not perhaps have expressed my meaning so clearly as I wished to have done."
If Washington could be useful by supervising Belvoir's care, "I shall undertake it with cheerfulness." His initial reaction, he explained, grew from the
fear that he could not devote enough attention to Belvoir's needs. Since
George William had retained a manager for the estate, Washington thought
he could supervise the manager "with very little difficulty."[4]

In truth, many cares crowded in on Washington. A ship captain carrying
a cargo of his flour had absconded to Honduras with the goods. On behalf of
his brothers, Washington was contesting ownership of a parcel in Lord Fairfax's domain while also straining to collect rents from his tenants. An effort
to build a mill on land in Pennsylvania was floundering. Washington grew
furious when the church in Alexandria for the new Fairfax Parish proposed
to rescind his purchase of a prominent pew.[5]

In the public sphere, matters also were growing messy. A counterfeiting
ring flooded Virginia with fake bills, forcing an emergency assembly session in

March 1773 to approve new currency. From the north came reports of renewed sparring with the British. When Rhode Islanders burned a British customs ship, the British began sending American prisoners to England for trial, a flat denial of colonists' rights. The House of Burgesses revived Virginia's commit-tee of correspondence to share information with other colonies.[6]

In any list of Washington's troubles, Jacky Custis had his place. His lacka-daisical attitude baffled Washington. Jacky's schoolmaster offered the half-hearted defense that the teenager was "a good man, if not a very learned one," admitting that he was "exceedingly indolent." In the fall of 1772, Jacky was smitten with fifteen-year-old Eleanor Calvert, a schoolmate's sister. Wash-ington and the schoolmaster had been considering sending the young heir to college, hoping that a new setting might improve his habits. In early 1773, their plan ripened for him to attend King's College in New York (now Co-lumbia University), which caused the youth to reveal his engagement to Miss Calvert (called Nelly).[7]

The reactions at Mount Vernon were predictable. Martha was delighted. Washington less so.

The stepfather's concern was not with Nelly, by all accounts both charm-ing and an appropriate match. Her grandfather was the fifth Lord Baltimore, one of the hereditary proprietors of Maryland. Other ancestors included il-legitimate descendants of both King Charles II and King George I. Nelly's branch of the Calverts had modest resources, but Jacky's fortune was ample without a significant bridal dowry.

Washington's worry was with the prospective bridegroom. Washington doubted that eighteen-year-old Jack (as he was now called) was prepared to take his place as scion of a wealthy family. Yet Washington also knew that opposing his wife on anything concerning her son was a hazardous business. Martha's feelings were too strong for direct opposition to succeed. Two years before, when the young man chose to be inoculated against smallpox, Wash-ington had to conceal the procedure from Martha until it was successfully completed, so "she might escape those tortures which suspense would throw her into."[8]

Washington played for time. In a careful letter to Nelly's father, he praised her "amiable qualifications," adding that "an alliance with your family will be pleasing." He then noted Jack's "youth, inexperience, and unripened educa-tion." Young Custis was not, Washington continued in a tortured circumlocu-tion, "capable of bestowing that due attention to the important consequences of a marriage state." He proposed an engagement of at least two years, so Jack could continue his studies and become "more deserving of the lady and useful to society." Should their love cool, that "had better precede, than follow after, marriage." To demonstrate that he proposed only delay, Washington turned to business, recounting Jack's ownership of 15,000 acres and more than two hundred slaves, on top of more than £8,000 in investments. Adding the hope that Mr. Calvert "would also be willing to do something genteel by your daughter," he concluded by inviting the Calverts to Mount Vernon.[9]

Calvert's ready agreement to the delay included one caution. Since he had ten children, he wrote, "no very great fortune can be expected," but Nelly would receive the same share of his estate as the other nine. For the moment, that resolution held. Nelly became a frequent visitor to Mount Vernon, another friend for Patsy. The Calverts, having a large supply of children, sometimes sent one of Nelly's sisters with her.

In May, Washington delivered Jack to college in New York. He used the journey to renew connections in Philadelphia and New York, introducing Jack to society. They dined with three different royal governors, and with Pennsylvania's chief justice. Once installed in college, Jack reveled in the privileges his wealth brought him, noting happily that the faculty singled him out "as much . . . as can be expected," and that he was the only student allowed to eat with the instructors.[10]

Washington hurried home, eager to confirm a trip west with Governor Dunmore that might bring more land grants.[11] Shortly after reaching Mount Vernon, however, tragedy struck. At a family dinner, Patsy Custis died. In a letter to his brother-in-law Burwell Bassett, Washington described the scene:

> [Patsy] rose from dinner about four o'clock, in better health and spirits than she appeared to have been in for some time; soon after which she was seized with one of her usual fits, and expired in it, in less than two minutes, without uttering a word, a groan, or scarce a sigh—this sudden and unexpected blow, I scarce need add, has almost reduced my poor wife to the lowest ebb of misery.[12]

Though the Washingtons had feared always for Patsy, her sudden passing at an everyday moment was a horror. Washington prayed and wept at her side, according to one account. "The distress of this family," Washington wrote to Bassett, "is an easier matter to conceive, than to describe." He added the wish that the tragedy "removed the sweet innocent girl into a more happy, and peaceful abode than any she has met with, in the afflicted path she hitherto has trod."[13]

They buried Patsy the next day, which Washington recorded as "hot, overcast, thundery." The only mourners were the Washingtons, brother Jack and his family, the Fairfaxes from Belvoir, and some of Mount Vernon's slaves.[14]

Martha Dandridge Washington, 1772

Troubled by Martha's grief, Washington invited her mother to make Mount Vernon "her entire and absolute home." He canceled his trip west with Lord Dunmore and sent word of Patsy's death to Jack Custis in New York.[15] Two days after the funeral, the Fairfaxes gave dinner to the people from Mount Vernon, though George and Martha did not go. After a few days, Martha managed a visit to Belvoir.

At Mount Vernon, life drifted from its usual patterns. A central figure in the family—the young girl who played the spinet, took dance lessons, huddled with girlfriends, and suffered with epilepsy—was gone. The loss brought on reflection and sadness, especially for Martha, who had been with Patsy always, often wracked with worry. Patsy had been her constant companion as well as her daughter. It would take time for life to find new rhythms.[16]

Washington changed his routines. He stayed close to home. He did not hunt for the rest of the summer. Nor did he view lands he might purchase. On many days, he did not leave the mansion house. He and Martha went riding sometimes, just the two of them, something they had never done very much. He plainly was concerned for her.[17]

When the next blow fell, cruelly soon, at least it was expected. Just three weeks after Patsy's death, it was time for George William and Sally to leave for England. Every parting, especially for an extended and uncertain period, can feel like a small death. That feeling had to weigh heavily as the Washingtons watched their friends leave. Washington and George William would never meet again.[18]

❦

Washington continued to keep close to Mount Vernon. He rode with Martha. Neighbors visited. Nelly Calvert returned with a sister, and John Carlyle's daughters came by. Martha enjoyed the company of young women, especially that summer.[19]

The somber days began to lighten as autumn neared. In late September, Washington met Jack Custis in Annapolis for that town's annual week of horse racing and celebration. Shaking off the summer's gloom, Washington stayed with Maryland's governor, played cards, bet on the races, and attended the theater. A session with his Williamsburg dentist may have brought mixed results, since he visited another dentist a few months later.[20]

Jack announced that he wished to marry right away. Martha, wanting him back from far-off New York, consented. Washington could only agree, "contrary to my judgment, and much against my wishes." As he explained in a letter to the president of King's College, Washington conceded "to the wishes of his mother . . . as he is the last of the family." At least the college reported favorably on Jack's brief time there.[21]

In February 1774, Jack and Nelly married at the Calverts' home in Maryland. With Martha remaining at Mount Vernon, Washington attended with his cousin Lund. Technically an employee, Lund might seem an odd choice as a companion, but he also was family and had known the bridegroom for nearly ten years. It would have been a lonesome trip for Washington to make on his own.[22]

Despite the sorrow surrounding Patsy's death, her passing conferred financial benefits on her family. By law, Jack and Martha divided Patsy's third of the Custis legacy. Washington used some of the funds to purchase an estate for Jack and Nelly on the Pamunkey River, near where Martha grew up. Martha's share gave Washington a fresh injection of Custis money. Once again—as with the deaths of his brother Lawrence, Lawrence's daughter, and Lawrence's widow—Washington prospered by outliving those close to him.

Patsy's money allowed him to pay off debts, close on some land deals, and embark on an even more ambitious overhaul of the mansion house. He resolved to add a new room, the largest of the house, for entertaining, plus a more private master bedroom. In Annapolis and New York he had seen new architectural styles he hoped to apply.[23]

∾

With Patsy's death and Jack's marriage, the Washingtons' lives were likely to grow quieter. They were approaching their mid-forties, a respectable middle age, with no children in the house. Washington had settled his mother's situation, and even had resolved some (though by no means all) of his western land claims. The public world seemed calm, with far less talk of enslavement by the mother country or the transcendent rights of Americans. Tranquility, however, would not be the fate of George and Martha.[24]

In retrospect, 1773 turned out to be the last quiet year in American political life for the next thirty. Conflicts between Britain and America soon would boil over. In only a few months, Washington's life would turn upside down, with public duties taking precedence. He would meet that change as a far wiser and more politically adept person than he had been when he led the Virginia Regiment two decades before.

CHAPTER 27

Seizing the Moment: The Fairfax Resolves

The Boston Tea Party on the evening of December 16, 1773, triggered a chain of events that would catapult Washington to greater prominence in Virginia and across the American colonies.

Many popular notions about that night's events in Boston Harbor are wrong. The men who dumped three shiploads of tea overboard did not perform their work while Boston slept, nor did they emit war whoops while consigning the offending leaves to the briny waters. The tea tax they challenged was not levied on Americans, but on the British East India Company, which passed it through to consumers. Americans, however, objected to indirect taxes as well as those directly levied. If that tax succeeded, Virginian Arthur Lee muttered, "its success may lead to a thousand other artful ways of enslaving us."[1]

The fifty men who boarded the ships in mock Indian garb, faces darkened by lampblack and grease, spoke little while thousands watched from the shore in rapt silence. Across the water came the sound of axes chopping open chests filled with 90,000 pounds of tea, which was heaved overboard. Because the tide was low, tea mounded above the water's surface. Apprentices waded into the water to stamp the tea into the mud. An onshore spectator, lawyer John Adams, enthused that the act was "so bold, so daring, so firm, intrepid and inflexible [that it] must have important consequences."[2]

The event's raw defiance electrified Americans. Torchlit figures wielding axes personified revolution. Inspired, Americans in other port cities turned back tea shipments. Equally important, the tea party goaded George III's government to send four regiments to Boston under the command of General Thomas Gage to enforce harsh new measures, which became known as the Coercive Acts. Britain closed Boston's port to shipments of anything other than food or fuel. Gage housed troops in private homes. His instructions stressed the need for stern action in a high-risk situation:

> The constitutional authority of this kingdom over its colonies must be vindicated, and its laws obeyed throughout the whole empire. . . . should those ideas of independence . . . once take root, that relation between this kingdom and its colonies . . . will soon cease to exist, and destruction must follow disunion.

Boston's port was to remain closed until the colonists paid the value of the drowned tea. The harsh response enraged many Americans who had favored reconciliation with Britain. Richard Henry Lee described it as spurring "astonishment, indignation, and concern."[3]

After the Washingtons reached Williamsburg for a new assembly session in mid-May, the burgesses privately discussed protest resolutions while House sessions addressed routine matters.[4] A younger group—including Patrick Henry, Richard Henry Lee, and Thomas Jefferson—developed a plan of escalating protest, beginning with a day of fasting and prayer. Their prayer resolution used strong language, noting "the heavy calamity which threatens destruction to our civil rights and the evils of civil war."

Two days later, Lord Dunmore dissolved the assembly, complaining that the resolution for a day of fasting and prayer "reflect(s) highly upon his majesty and the Parliament of Great Britain." He acted quickly to cut off more aggressive resolutions that were planned for the session's final days, which likely would have passed easily. Because Dunmore struck before the legislators had enacted bills that would keep the militia functioning and the courts open, Washington grumbled that they had met "22 days for nothing."[5]

Washington was talking to both sides of the confrontation. He dined with the governor on the day before the assembly was dissolved, then rode to Lord Dunmore's estate the next morning. Their conversation likely focused on the west, where Indians and settlers were fighting again, but the Coercive Acts and the plight of Boston could not have gone unmentioned. According to Washington, Dunmore concealed from him any intention to dissolve the assembly.[6]

On the next morning, the senior burgess for Fairfax joined eighty-nine colleagues in the Raleigh Tavern to sign a document denouncing the Coercive Acts and proclaiming a boycott of the East India Company and its tea. Washington's is the eighth signature, reflecting his continuing high stature. He lingered overnight for an evening ball honoring Lady Dunmore, an

occasion that must have been strained. The assembly's committee of correspondence met the following day to propose that each North American colony send delegates to an annual congress.[7]

On the following Monday, Washington and twenty-four other burgesses
returned to the Raleigh Tavern. With Speaker Randolph presiding, they reviewed a letter from Sam Adams in Boston, the protest leader there, which
enclosed the Coercive Act that shut down Boston's port, along with defiant
public resolutions protesting this "stroke of vengeance." The Boston resolutions demanded a stop to trade with Britain and its Caribbean colonies until
the punitive laws were repealed. Bodies in Philadelphia and Annapolis had
been more cautious, and so were the Virginians, who proposed to address the
situation at a reconvened session on August 1. Until then, the burgesses
agreed to test public sentiment in their home counties. Most expected to
adopt another non-importation agreement, perhaps suspending exports at a
later date.[8]

Washington wrote a fiery letter to George William Fairfax in England,
expecting his friend to share it with prominent Englishmen. The British,
Washington insisted, "may rely on it that Americans will never be taxed
without their own consent." Though he did not approve of the tea party, he
wrote that Boston's cause "is and ever will be considered as the cause of
America." He also despaired that an Indian war seemed likely in the west,
"whilst those from whom we have a right to seek protection are endeavoring
by every piece of art and despotism to fix the shackles of slavery upon us."[9]

∾

After returning to Mount Vernon, Washington learned that Parliament was
considering more repressive legislation. Within Fairfax County, which would
provide his political foundation through the gathering crisis, he canvassed
public opinion at both Truro and Fairfax Parish churches. His implacable
defense of American rights attracted notice. He again drew on the talents of
George Mason, although the older man declined Washington's urging that
he seek a vacant House seat in elections scheduled for mid-July.[10]

Many communities shook with rage over the treatment of Boston and
endorsed a total halt to trade until the Coercive Acts were repealed. A Maryland committee endorsed non-importation and appointed delegates to the
continental congress that Virginia had proposed, which was scheduled for
Philadelphia on September 20. So did committees in Philadelphia, Rhode
Island, Massachusetts, and North Carolina.[11]

Washington viewed the conflict with Britain as a test of will. In an exchange of letters with Bryan Fairfax, George William's younger brother, Washington dismissed the idea of another petition to king or Parliament, or both.

> Have we not tried this already? Have we not addressed the Lords, and remonstrated to the Commons? And to what end? Did they deign to look at our petitions? Does it not appear, as clear as the sun in its meridian brightness, that there is a regular, systematic plan formed to fix the right and practice of taxation upon us?

Washington was fed up. This was the third confrontation in a decade over whether Americans controlled their destinies: first the Stamp Act, then the Townshend duties, and now the Coercive Acts. For Washington, only a firm response would do. The strength of his commitment gave his opinion force in the coming tumult.[12]

Fairfax's public meetings began at the Alexandria courthouse in mid-July. The residents chose a committee, with Washington as chair, to draft resolutions on non-importation, non-export, the proposed congress of the colonies, and American rights. To relieve the suffering of Boston's "industrious poor," the meeting approved a public collection totaling £273, thirty-eight barrels of flour, and 150 bushels of wheat. Washington remained in town to confer with the new committee. They started with an energetic draft prepared by Mason.[13]

On July 14, 1774, Washington returned to Alexandria for his reelection to the House of Burgesses. The poll, an observer reported, was concluded "with great order and regularity" and celebrated with punch. At an evening ball, coffee and hot chocolate were served, but not tea.[14]

Three nights later, Mason came to Mount Vernon to sharpen the twenty-four resolutions Washington would present to an Alexandria meeting the next day. The courthouse filled early for the session, spilling residents into the adjoining square. The attendees approved the resolutions with few changes, then elected Washington chair of a committee of correspondence. The resolutions, called the Fairfax Resolves, appeared in the *Virginia Gazette* and then in newspapers across America. Though principally composed by Mason, the name at the top was George Washington, chair of the Fairfax meeting. As the resolutions drew enthusiastic praise, Washington's star rose further.[15]

Although the Fairfax Resolves offered a ritual pledge of loyalty to the king, they also insisted that colonists were not subject to any law "to which they have not given their consent, by representatives freely chosen by themselves." Only the colonial assembly could legislate for them. British claims of power to impose taxes on America, according to two of the resolutions, would "reduce us from a state of freedom and happiness to slavery and misery" and "establish the most grievous and intolerable species of tyranny and oppression that ever was inflicted upon mankind." The Resolves did not mince words about Parliament's intent, accusing it of a "premeditated design and system" that included "inflicting ministerial vengeance upon the town of Boston" and protecting and encouraging murderers.

The eighth resolution disclaimed the goal of independence, but pledged to resist the Coercive Acts with "every means which heaven hath given us." The twelfth reinforced that threat of violence, calling for a "firm union" of the colonies, who "regard every act of violence or oppression inflicted upon any one of them, as aimed at all." Resolutions fourteen through seventeen called for a boycott of luxury goods and a ban on British imports, including slaves. They also pledged to stop lumber exports to the West Indies, to cease raising tobacco if the crisis lasted until November 1, 1775, and to support a congress of all the colonies.[16]

The power of the resolves flowed not only from Mason's words but also from the determination of the man who presented them. To Bryan Fairfax, Washington denounced Britain's actions as "the most despotic system of tyranny that ever was practiced in a free government." In the face of such outrages, he asked, should Americans "whine and cry for relief"? No, he insisted, they must retaliate: "There is no relief for us but in their [British] distress." He was resolute: "the voice of mankind is with me."[17]

Washington had known a heady few weeks. Most of his political life had transpired in meeting rooms and the House chamber, talking soberly with other wealthy men. But for many days that summer, Washington moved among Virginians of all types in streets and taverns and churchyards. He listened to their fears and anger. He led public meetings and won approval from those who welcomed his leadership. Not since the days of the Virginia Regiment had he carried the community's trust in such an immediate way, nor known the powerful connection between a leader and those joining in a shared cause. In the intoxication of those moments, he had to feel again in his bones how good he was at leading.

∾

Washington brought Jack Custis with him to Williamsburg for the August 1 meeting of the former burgesses, now reconstituted as the Virginia Convention, without any involvement of Governor Dunmore. Washington and his stepson made the usual stops along the way: in Fredericksburg with

Washington's sister and mother, and with Martha's sister and her husband near the capital. This time, though, there was no dinner with the governor.[18]

Washington had never seen such full attendance for a legislative session.[19] The principal question was how the delegates would challenge the Coercive Acts. Many counties had called for non-importation and a congress of the colonies. Most stopped short, however, of non-export, which would hit Virginia pocketbooks hard.

Washington brought with him the Fairfax Resolves, which set the convention's course. If the Coercive Acts were not repealed by November 1, the delegates agreed, Virginians should import no goods or slaves from Britain or its colonies. They totally banned imports of tea, "the detestable instrument . . . of the present sufferings" in Boston. If the Coercive Acts were still in effect on August 1, 1775, Virginians should stop exports to Britain. The county committees should enforce the resolutions through public shaming of violators.[20]

By ballot, the convention chose Washington and six others to attend the Continental Congress in Philadelphia. Washington commanded the third highest vote total, only six behind Speaker Randolph and trailing Richard Henry Lee by two. He easily exceeded the totals of Edmund Pendleton and Richard Bland, as well as Patrick Henry. All were more gifted in debate, better at crafting legislation and public statements. Yet, in that time of passion, Washington's blend of determination and steadiness exerted powerful appeal, as did his military experience.

Washington's rise was stunning. By diligent effort, by building relationships with his colleagues, the awkward backbencher of 1759 stood near the pinnacle of a world that was not his natural habitat. The neophyte who had stumbled with simple legislation had developed into a leader of the first rank in the largest American colony, twice providing the blueprint for responding to the crisis with Britain.[21]

To anticipate the issues he would face in Philadelphia, Washington sought data on Virginia's tax patterns, population, and exports and imports. He read pamphlets about non-importation, along with Jefferson's *Summary View of the Rights of British America*. He also addressed mundane matters, attending a sale of Belvoir's household goods and showing that estate to a potential tenant. He could only mourn the sight of the empty mansion, its contents picked over by bargain hunters, a harbinger of Virginia's uncertain future.[22]

Washington had much to reflect on through those late summer days, as the Virginia heat came and went and came again. He expressed no second thoughts about confronting Britain. "An innate spirit of freedom first told me," he wrote to Bryan Fairfax, that British policies were "repugnant to every principle of natural justice." Submitting to oppression, he insisted, "will make us as tame, and abject slaves, as the blacks we rule over with such arbitrary sway."[23] But with attitudes hardening on both sides, Washington might also have reflected on his ties with the mother country. His father and older brothers had been educated there. His best friend was there now. He had worked with the last four royal governors. For four grim years, he had fought for the king. Would he now help plunge his neighbors into war against Britain?

Parliament adopted more punitive laws in June 1774, this time aiming at Virginia and its westward ambitions. The Quebec Act extended Canada's southern boundary to the Ohio River, calling into question previous grants of western lands. Virginians recoiled at having lands they viewed as part of their domain wrested from their control and lumped together with Roman Catholic, French-speaking Quebec.[24]

On August 30, Edmund Pendleton and Patrick Henry reached Mount Vernon on their way to the Philadelphia congress. Mason joined them for a night of talk. They knew not how the congress would go, whether other colonies would share Virginia's views, or what actions the delegates would consider. Pendleton recalled the visit fondly. "I was much pleased with Mrs. Washington and her spirit," he wrote. "She seemed ready to make any sacrifice and was cheerful though I knew she felt anxious. She talked like a Spartan mother to her son on going to battle." She told Pendleton and Henry, "'I hope you will stand firm—I know George will.'"

After dinner the next day, the three delegates readied themselves in the yard before the mansion house. "'God be with you gentlemen,'" Martha called from the doorway.[25]

CHAPTER 28

A Continental Character

Washington joined the Continental Congress in September 1774, though that body had legal authority over nothing. It could order no action. It commanded neither revenue nor employees. The state and local bodies that selected the fifty-six delegates also had no legal authority. The congress in Philadelphia was a singularly audacious act born of years of frustration and conflict, which is how revolutions begin.

Few delegates were planning for revolution. Each had thrived under British rule, but their assertion of rights as British subjects was being denied. Now they had to redefine themselves, perhaps as something more true to the rights Britain denied to them. Many hoped for reconciliation, but the prospects for harmony were mixed, at best. They faced an ill-tempered adversary while hotheaded Americans filled the streets.

Twelve colonies (not Georgia) sent delegates. Roughly one-third were lawyers, trained to support the status quo. Many were Southern slaveholders, like Washington. Almost all had belonged to colonial assemblies; thirteen had served as Speaker. All were wealthy and prominent. Henry Middleton of South Carolina owned nearly 800 slaves and 50,000 acres. Samuel Ward of Rhode Island was the son of a governor and governor himself; James Duane had been New York's attorney general and Indian commissioner. Only the well-to-do could leave their livelihoods on such an uncertain mission.[1]

A special celebrity surrounded the four Massachusetts delegates, veterans of the front-line struggle against British power. Sam Adams, sometimes called America's first professional politician, led the delegation. John Adams, who left the best account of the congress, joined his second cousin and two others in a carriage bound for Philadelphia.

The Massachusetts men stopped frequently along the way, testing public attitudes toward Boston's plight. They feared being labeled as dangerous radicals, but mostly found support. Church bells rang as they entered New Haven, people crowding the streets and windows to gawk. New Yorkers were more ambivalent. At a farewell ceremony for one New York delegate, a band played "God Save the King," while onlookers waved flags reading "The Congress and Liberty" on one side and "The King" on the other.[2]

A few miles from Philadelphia, delegates from other colonies met the Massachusetts men and escorted them to an elegant dinner at the City Tavern, which would be the social hub of the congress. John Adams, who alternated between self-satisfaction and insecurity, found the welcome reassuring. "The spirit, the firmness, the prudence of our province are vastly applauded," he wrote to his wife Abigail, "and we are universally acknowledged the saviors and defenders of American liberty."[3]

The Virginians also commanded attention. Arriving the day before the congress convened, Washington and his two companions rode a crest of enthusiasm for Virginia's resolutions and its non-importation association. A cheering crowd greeted them at the City Tavern. Two Virginians brought star power. Patrick Henry's reputation as a dazzling orator preceded him, while many eyes strayed to tall George Washington, his reputation built on the last French war and the tough-minded Fairfax Resolves.[4]

Most delegates hoped to agree on unified action against the British. Benjamin Franklin had once predicted that differences in culture, economic interests, and even speech would keep the colonies from uniting.[5] Ward of Rhode Island noted divisions based on "the different forms of government in the several colonies, different educations, books, and company." The Connecticut men reported that their colleagues, with distinct "modes of transacting public business, . . . must take some time to become so acquainted with each one's situations." After several weeks, John Adams described the problem to his wife: "Fifty gentlemen meeting together, all strangers, are not acquainted with each other's language, ideas, views, designs. They are therefore jealous of each other—fearful, timid, skittish."[6]

Bridging differences was more difficult because, as Adams noted, few knew each other. Two Virginia delegates (Henry and Benjamin Harrison) had never ventured beyond that colony's borders. Washington, in contrast, knew the Marylanders well, had traveled five times to Philadelphia, also to Boston and New York, and had fought the French alongside Pennsylvanians and Carolinians. He had entertained Pennsylvania's Joseph Galloway at Mount Vernon. Even if he did not know a particular delegate, they often shared mutual acquaintances.[7]

In the early days, the Massachusetts men held back, fearful that stridency would alienate others. Some delegates, Sam Adams confided, thought "that as we are a hardy and brave people we shall in time over run them all." John Adams agreed that they had to "keep ourselves out of sight, and to feel pulses, and sound the depths—to insinuate our sentiments, designs and desires by means of other persons, sometimes of one province and sometimes of another." The Massachusetts strategy yielded center stage to delegates from Virginia and South Carolina, who seemed unexpectedly radical.[8]

Congress met in a new hall constructed by the carpenters' guild, with the Philadelphia Free Library on its second floor next to a meeting room for committees and smaller groups.[9] Without dissent, the delegates selected Peyton Randolph as convention president and Charles Thomson of Pennsylvania as secretary. "Of an affable, open and majestic deportment," Silas Deane of Connecticut wrote about Randolph, "large in size, though not out of proportion, he commands respect and esteem."[10]

To ensure secrecy, the doors remained shut during debate so British authorities would not know what the delegates were saying. Early on, Patrick Henry demonstrated his ability to startle, proclaiming that because of Parliament's legislation, "all government was dissolved and that we were reduced to a state of nature," with no distinctions between colonies. He added that he "conceived of himself not as a Virginian but an American." Despite the sentiment, he advanced Virginia's parochial interests by insisting that voting power be based on a colony's wealth and population. Unsurprisingly, tiny Rhode Island and other small colonies opposed him, and prevailed. Each delegation would cast a single vote.[11]

The delegates appointed two committees. The more important one would "state the rights of the colonies"; it included both Adamses, along with Pendleton and Richard Henry Lee from Virginia. The second was to assemble colonial statutes relating to trade and manufactures. Washington served on neither.[12]

Being passed over for the committees might seem like a snub, but it played to Washington's strengths. For several days, he had few obligations, allowing him to concentrate on getting to know other delegates and Philadelphia's elite. Through the seven-week session, he attended thirty-six private dinners and one public affair. At those events and at the congress, he displayed the dignified yet relaxed manner mastered at Belvoir, combined with the political deftness acquired through fifteen years in Virginia politics. Not many delegates would leave the city without coming to know Washington.

He made a uniformly positive impression. Referring to Washington's height and "hard" countenance, Deane of Connecticut remembered Washington, who spoke "very modestly, and in cool but determined style and accent," as the savior of Braddock's expedition in 1755.[13] Something about the big Virginian made him a magnet for legends and false tales of heroism. John Adams breathlessly recounted Washington's supposed pledge at the Virginia convention to raise "'1000 men, subsist them at my own expense and march myself at their head for the relief of Boston.'" Washington said no such thing. Deane swallowed the same tale, confiding to his wife that Washington's "fortune is said to be equal to such an undertaking."[14]

John Adams shared many delegates' early euphoria. Congress contained, he wrote his wife, "the greatest men upon this continent in point of abilities, virtues, and fortunes." Deane gushed after encountering Southern delegates that he "scarcely had an idea of meeting with men of such firmness, sensibility, spirit, and thorough knowledge of the interests of America."[15]

The delegates' mood shifted when a report arrived that General Gage was bombarding Boston. Muffled church bells tolled while Silas Deane observed "the most unfeigned marks of sorrow . . . in every countenance." Anger quickly replaced sorrow, he continued, "and every tongue pronounces revenge." According to Ward of Rhode Island, "We proposed turning Congress into a Council of War." John Adams reported that the news made the delegates "completely miserable for two days," while "WAR! WAR! WAR! was the cry."

Such talk must have made Colonel Washington's ears prick up, as other delegates looked with renewed interest at the man with a martial bearing and reputation. When the bombardment report proved to be false, the congress returned to its work, but the socializing continued. Silas Deane had a dinner invitation for every night of Congress's third week, but protested that he was working hard: "We meet at nine and set until three, by which time we are unable to do anything but eat & drink the rest of the day."[16]

John Adams delighted in the groaning boards of Philadelphia. He described one dinner featuring "ducks, hams, chickens, beef, pig, tarts, creams, custards, geles, fools, trifles, floating Islands, beer, porter, punch, wine . . ." Another night brought "a most sinful feast again!" with twenty types of tarts, "Whipped sillabubs, &c. &c." A week later, Adams exulted over "a mighty feast again, . . . the very best of claret, madeira and burgundy," followed by dinner with "flummery, . . . sweetmeats of 20 sorts."[17]

∾

The delegates thought unanimity was essential to their task. Internal fractures would only encourage the British, while unanimity held a special moral power. Unanimous acts project conviction, especially when novel matters are at issue. Washington considered unanimity critical. But unanimity meant satisfying conservatives like James Duane of New York, whose goal was "a firm union between the parent state and her colonies," and radicals like Sam Adams and Patrick Henry, who demanded vindication of American rights and repeal of the Coercive Acts.[18]

With the committee on American rights meeting daily, Sam Adams arranged for a clergyman to offer a ripsnorting prayer over the deliberations. The minister exhorted the Lord to "defeat the malicious designs of our cruel adversaries" and "if they persist in their sanguinary purposes, . . . constrain them to drop the weapons of war from their unnerved hands in the day of battle!" The prayer, John Adams wrote, had "an excellent effect."[19]

Before the delegates could return to work, Paul Revere rode in from Boston on September 16 carrying another shock: the Suffolk Resolves, adopted a week earlier in the county that included Boston. Impoverished by the harbor closing, stripped of their government, overrun with British troops, Bostonians spat defiance, pledging to "arrest the hand which would ransack our pockets . . . [to] disarm the parricide who points the dagger at our bosoms, [and] . . . resist that unparalleled usurpation of unconstitutional power." With their streets "thronged with military executioners" and their colonial charter "mutilated and, in effect annihilated," they proclaimed the British constitution "totally wrecked, annulled, and vacated." Bostonians, one resolution snarled, should "acquaint themselves with the art of war as soon as possible."[20]

Congress endorsed those resolutions, but with less ferocious language. Still aiming at unanimity, the delegates urged Americans to persuade Britain "quickly to introduce better men and wiser measures."[21] A week later, intense deliberations followed the report of the committee on American rights. On September 27, Congress unanimously endorsed Richard Henry Lee's call for a ban on imports from Britain starting December 1. Non-export would be the next subject of debate.[22]

At that point, Joseph Galloway of Pennsylvania mounted the only serious effort to avoid confrontation. Predicting that non-exportation would ruin Americans, the Pennsylvanian proposed blending the governments of America and Britain. A new Grand Council of the American colonies would meet once a year as a subordinate branch of Parliament. Its legislation would not take effect, however, until approved by a royally appointed "president-general" of America and also by Parliament, except in time of war.[23]

Galloway won support from conservatives—whom he described as "all the men of property, and most of the ablest speakers"—but no delegate from

Massachusetts or Virginia. Patrick Henry predicted that British bribes would swiftly corrupt Galloway's Grand Council. The implacable Washington rejected Galloway's scheme, which died quietly.[24]

The non-export issue proved thorny. Non-importation meant foregoing luxuries, but an export ban reduced incomes. Congress ultimately agreed to bar exports to British-controlled ports, but that ban would not take effect for a year, on the next September 10. A committee was appointed to consider allowing exports of favored products of specific colonies—North Carolina's tar and pitch, or New Hampshire's lumber and fish, or rice from South Carolina.[25]

Unanimity took time to achieve. Three weeks into the session, many delegates wished that others would talk less. "Slow as snails," John Adams complained to his wife, observing later, "There is so much wit, sense, learning, acuteness, subtlety, eloquence, &c. among fifty gentlemen, each of whom has been habituated to lead and guide in his own province, that an immensity of time is spent unnecessarily." A delegate from Delaware groaned, "This is tiresome duty."[26]

Yet they knew the work required care. Samuel Ward worried about "the danger of taking a false step in a matter of such vast importance." Even impatient John Adams acknowledged that "We have had as great questions to discuss as ever engaged the attention of men, and an infinite multitude of them."[27]

ლ

Through the tedium and the excitement, Washington listened and watched. As he had done in the House of Burgesses, he evaluated the arguments and the delegates, stating his views in conversation but avoiding floor debate. He was affable and polite. He spent 17 shillings on political pamphlets and won 7 shillings at cards. He described his role in that first congress as that of "an attentive observer and witness." Months later, when Congress convened for its second session, it would become clear that Washington had exercised his gift of winning the trust of others.[28]

His dinner hosts included powerful Pennsylvanians whose paths he would cross in the future, men like Thomas Mifflin and John Dickinson.[29] Washington sampled worship services. He spent a Sunday morning in late September in a Quaker meeting and the afternoon at an Anglican service. Two weeks later, he joined the Presbyterians in the morning and the Roman Catholics in the afternoon. No crisis of the soul prompted his visits; he was interested in different faiths. In addition, of course, an astute political leader seeks to understand all of the people in his community.[30]

On October 6, Paul Revere delivered more shocking news from Boston: General Gage had closed the colony's courts and was building fortifications, converting Boston into a British garrison. The Boston committee of correspondence asked the congress whether residents should abandon the city. After debate, the congress advised remaining in the city and encouraged Americans to compensate Bostonians for their losses.[31]

Washington set out his personal views in a letter to a former Virginia Regiment colleague, Robert McKenzie, who was serving with the British Army in Boston. McKenzie had portrayed Massachusetts patriots as "scandalous and ungenerous," with a "fixed aim at total independence." Washington's response began courteously but turned hard. Britain had oppressed Boston, Washington wrote, with "a systematic assertion of an arbitrary power, deeply planned . . . to violate the most essential and valuable rights of mankind." Washington concluded grimly that if Britain resorted to greater force, "more blood will be spilt . . . than history has ever yet furnished instances of in the annals of North America."[32]

Congress devoted its final weeks to non-export and to creating a new association to implement trade restrictions. Responding to passionate advocacy by the South Carolinians, who stalked out of congress for a spell, it exempted rice from any export ban. Congress urged frugality, a freeze on prices, and no slave imports. A new association agreement tracked the Fairfax Resolves.[33]

The association movement revived, with hundreds of local enforcement committees springing up across the thirteen colonies. Those local committees, which often functioned as local governments, had a profound effect on the estimated 7,000 Americans who served on them in the coming years. That epidemic of self-rule spread both resistance to Britain and served as a laboratory of participatory government.[34]

Congress prepared five public documents, which the delegates "debated by paragraphs": a letter of protest to General Gage in Boston; two memorials to the people of British America; another petition to the king; and a letter inviting Quebec to join the resistance. Though Washington despaired at the prospect of sending more petitions and entreaties to London, he went along; unanimity required compromise on all sides.[35]

Reflecting the delegates' diverse attitudes, and the risk of war they courted, the congress could be inconsistent. The memorials and petitions proclaimed loyalty to the king but denounced his ministers. The delegates aimed to coerce Britain to recognize their rights, yet no one spoke for independence or war. "Their opinions are fixed against hostilities and ruptures," John Adams noted, "because it would make a wound which could never be healed." When the

Pennsylvania General Assembly hosted a dinner at the City Tavern, an anxious toast proposed, "May the sword of the parent never be stained with the blood of her children."[36]

On October 26, forty-seven delegates signed the petition to the king and scheduled a second session for May. They expected that fresh challenges would greet them eight months hence. Of the Virginians, only Washington and Lee were present to sign. Randolph had left to preside over a new session of the House of Burgesses, taking four other Virginians with him.[37]

There was symbolism in that sequence. Washington, too, had responsibilities in Virginia, but his priority was the congress. He sensed that the center of American resistance was shifting away from individual colonies. America's future would be continental. Those who left for home, beginning with Randolph, understood the politics of the present, of the American colonies. Washington, however, was looking toward the untidy path to the future.

For forty-six days, he had gauged the leaders of other colonies. He might have imagined himself as a leader among them. He already was a leading figure from Virginia, the premier colony. He could see that he was taken seriously, that his military experience resonated. At forty-two, he was neither too old nor too young. With his business affairs largely under control, with his family life simplified, he had the freedom to consider greater political engagement.

His final purchases in Philadelphia confirm that Washington was looking to the future. To continue his political education, he bought three more pamphlets. For his mother, he ordered a new riding carriage.[38]

CHAPTER 29

The Storm Breaks

A blizzard of obligations pressed in on Washington when he arrived home from Philadelphia. Building a new mill and adding to the mansion house involved coordinating suppliers, overseeing workers, and adjusting designs. He also had to supervise the sale of Belvoir's furniture and of the estate of a former army colleague. For the project to open the upper Potomac to navigation, he attended trustee meetings and reviewed engineering plans, drafted legislation with Mason, then put fifty slaves to work on the river.[1]

To stave off squatters and realize revenue, Washington also needed to settle people on his western lands. He organized a party of indentured workers to begin a settlement, but sickness felled the man who was to lead them. Washington waged battles over land titles, especially with a well-connected North Carolinian claiming 800,000 acres.[2] Washington's public duties also multiplied. He convened Fairfax freeholders to appoint an enforcement committee for non-importation; he, of course, became its chair. The committee seized goods that violated the ban and sold them for the benefit of Boston's poor.[3]

Following Fairfax County's lead, other Virginia counties aggressively enforced the boycott. They condemned merchants and ship captains who refused to submit to audit, punished merchants who raised prices, and forced recantations from those who opposed the boycott. Some merchants relinquished goods that violated the ban; the committees auctioned off those items, reimbursed the merchants for their costs, and sent any remaining funds to Boston. The auctions included anvils, casks, "plaid goods," Irish linens, men's hose, cheap cloth for slave clothing, snuff, cutlery, barley, and lots of salt.[4]

Military enthusiasm skyrocketed; five Virginia counties asked Washington to command their militia. Washington, his martial ardor reviving after fifteen years in civilian life, drilled them personally, ordered weapons and ammunition, and designed their uniforms.[5]

Fairfax County led on military matters, too, creating a company of sixty-eight men who "must make themselves masters of the military exercise." To pay for arms, the committee requested 3 shillings from each working-age resident. Though the committee had no taxing power, the measure was another step toward replacing the colonial government with something popularly based. Washington and Mason advanced the cost of gunpowder, then simmered when their neighbors proved slow to pay up.[6]

The county's militancy reinforced the prominence of its leader, Washington. Another county announced its agreement "with the gentlemen of Fairfax county" on militia training.[7] Two former British army officers, Charles Lee and Horatio Gates, sought out Washington to confer on strategy if there was war with Britain. With Gates's assistance, Lee was preparing an ambitious revamping of the infantry tactics of the day. Both would become American generals.[8]

The mounting demands on Washington's time took a toll. When John West, his fellow burgess and longtime friend, asked Washington to be his son's guardian upon his death, Washington responded with a wail of complaint:

> For this year or two past, there has been scarce a moment that I can properly call my own; for what with my own business—my present wards, my mother's (which is wholly in my hands), Colonel Covill's, Mrs. Savage's, Colonel Fairfax's, Colonel Mercer's . . . and the little assistance I have undertaken to give in the management of my brother Augustine's affairs (for I have absolutely refused to qualify as an executor) keeps me, together with the share I take in public affairs, constantly engaged in writing letters—settling accounts—and negotiating one piece of business or another, . . . by which means I have really been deprived of every kind of enjoyment.[9]

Washington was paying the price of being the man everyone trusted. In the end, West named him guardian and also executor of his estate.

Washington never complained, however, about his public duties. He exuded enthusiasm for the American cause, though he wrote no essays proclaiming the iron determination he brought to most tasks. A simple declarative sentence to his brother Jack captured his commitment: "It is my full intention," he wrote in early spring 1775, "to devote my life and fortune in the cause we are engaged in."[10]

∾

Across America, martial spirits soared after the congress adjourned in late October 1774. A North Carolina delegate found that "patriotic fervor still kindles in the breasts of the inhabitants." A Marylander insisted on the need for "a military force and arms and ammunition," while Richard Henry Lee declared, "All North America is now most firmly united and as firmly resolved to defend their liberties . . . against any power on earth." From Pennsylvania, John Dickinson wrote presciently that "the first act of violence" by the British "will put the whole continent in arms."[11]

Nowhere was conflict more likely to erupt than in Massachusetts. John Adams reported "a total stagnation of law and commerce" there, noting, "We have no council, no house, no legislature, no executive. Not a court of justice has sat since the month of September." No debts could be recovered, nor criminals punished.

Adams breathed defiance, insisting that New England would easily produce 200,000 soldiers to oppose Britain. "Our people," he wrote, "are everywhere learning the military art—exercising perpetually." With a week's notice, he estimated, Massachusetts could put 15,000 armed men into the field. Richard Henry Lee pronounced that six frontier counties of Virginia would produce 6,000 riflemen, who would be "the most formidable light infantry in the world," due to their "amazing hardihood, . . . the exceeding quickness with which they can march," and their stellar marksmanship.[12]

From across the Atlantic, British leaders poured fuel on the flames. In his speech opening Parliament in late 1774, King George bemoaned the "most daring spirit of resistance and disobedience" in Massachusetts, while other colonies made "unwarrantable attempts . . to obstruct [British] commerce." He vowed "firm and steadfast resolution to withstand every attempt to weaken or impair" Parliament's supreme authority. The king's remarks, Washington observed, "prognosticate nothing favorable to us," and "the minds of men are exceedingly disturbed."[13]

As the king signaled, Britain clamped down harder. In February and March, Parliament declared Massachusetts in a state of rebellion, banned American fishermen from the rich Grand Banks off Newfoundland, and excluded New Englanders from trading with Britain and the British Caribbean. In April, the trade ban extended to all colonists except Georgians.[14] The British ministry's most drastic step came in secret orders General Gage received in mid-April, directing him to arrest patriot leaders in Massachusetts because "blows must decide" the crisis. Strike early, the clandestine instructions directed, before the Americans can organize themselves.[15]

In Virginia, Lord Dunmore responded oddly to the escalating tensions: he led a militia expedition against the Ohio Indians, placing him in the western forests as the crisis sharpened. Perhaps he hoped to win support from the colonists by battling a common foe. If that was his plan, it failed. When Dunmore's militia defeated the Indians, Virginians applauded but continued to oppose British taxes and sanctions against Boston. In a report to London, the governor admitted that the county committees effectively enforced nonimportation with "the greatest rigor." Each committee, he wrote:

> assumes an authority to inspect the books, invoices, and all other secrets of the trade and correspondence of merchants; to watch the conduct of every inhabitant, without distinction, and to send for all . . . ; to interrogate them respecting all matters which, at their pleasure, they think fit objects of their inquiry; and to stigmatize, as they term it, such as they find transgressing what they . . . call the Laws of Congress, which stigmatizing is no other than their inviting the vengeance of an outrageous and lawless mob to be exercised upon the happy victims.

Even worse, he added, Virginians embraced the actions of the Continental Congress "with marks of reverence which they never bestowed upon their legal [royal] government."[16]

In January 1775, Speaker Randolph called for Virginia's counties to choose delegates to a convention in March. He picked Richmond for the meeting because it was centrally located and also lay fifty miles from the governor in Williamsburg.[17] Randolph had no power to order the election or the convention, but his word carried greater force than Dunmore's. Royal governors had few tools for imposing their will. Marching against the Ohio Indians, Dunmore had led militia, not British soldiers; only a handful of the latter served in frontier forts. In Massachusetts, General Gage's force was too small to control one colony, much less the other twelve. To bring more soldiers across the ocean would take months and cost money that Britain was reluctant to spend. The light imperial presence allowed militia companies to drill openly and swear allegiance to the people, to their county committees, or to the Continental Congress. Dunmore could not compel them to serve the king.

At the Richmond convention, Patrick Henry moved that Virginia "be immediately put into a posture of defense" since "a well regulated militia . . . is the natural strength and only security of a free government." Washington,

Lee, and Jefferson agreed. Henry's words were powerful: "Gentlemen may cry, Peace, Peace, but there is no peace. The war is actually begun! . . . Our brethren are already in the field! Why stand we here idle?" His concluding statement echoed through the continent: "I know not what course others may take, but as for me . . . give me liberty or give me death!"[18]

The vote was close, but Henry's resolution carried. To translate that resolution into a plan for defending Virginia, the convention created a committee that included Washington. The committee's plan followed Fairfax County's model, including the collection of funds by county committees. Washington also served on a committee tasked with encouraging "arts and manufactures"—code for weapons and ammunition.[19]

When the convention chose the colony's representatives to the next meeting of the Continental Congress, scheduled for Philadelphia in May, Peyton Randolph again led the balloting. This time Washington stood second, a single vote behind. All but two of 108 delegates voted for him.[20]

∾

Preparing to return to Philadelphia, Washington took pride that Virginia's military preparations had produced "a great number of very good companies." Though preferring a peaceful resolution of the crisis, he stressed that the militia "are now in excellent training, the people being resolved."[21]

Toward late April, Lord Dunmore proved the truth of Patrick Henry's insistence that the war had begun. The governor deployed marines from a Royal Navy ship to seize gunpowder from Williamsburg's public storage. Furious, a crowd threatened to march on Dunmore's palace, but Peyton Randolph and others diverted them. Militia in other counties proposed to march on Williamsburg. Two counties requested that Washington lead them. Dunmore defused the confrontation by paying for the powder.[22]

Then news from Boston again heightened tensions. Acting under his secret orders, General Gage sent troops to seize American arms and powder. Fighting broke out when the redcoats reached Lexington and Concord. As the British marched home, local militias exacted a bloody toll. War had begun.[23]

Events were moving in Washington's direction. If the congress should establish an army, a Virginian wrote to him, "there is not the least doubt but you'll have the command of the whole forces in this colony." Washington surely expected that. He likely wondered if he might be trusted with command of all the colonists' forces.[24]

During his last week at home—his last time at Mount Vernon for six years—Washington reviewed the Fairfax militia company, then greeted several guests. Charles Lee and Horatio Gates planned to travel to Philadelphia with Washington and Richard Henry Lee, both congressional delegates. Also present were Bryan Fairfax and two other prominent Virginians.

On warm days, the men could gather on Mount Vernon's rear gallery, with its lush view of the river and Maryland beyond, to review the threats facing Americans. Their military conversation was as knowledgeable as any in America that week. Washington had served with Gage in the Braddock expedition, while both Charles Lee and Gates had spent years in the British Army. Only Washington, though, had commanded Americans. He knew the challenges posed by their lack of military traditions and their ambivalence toward discipline.

For all Americans, the times were thrilling and awful. The fight was upon them. John Dickinson captured the conflicting feelings when he lamented the "butchery" at Lexington, then celebrated that the British "have been defeated with considerable slaughter." He declared that "the impious war of tyranny against innocence has commenced"; for him, the choice was between freedom or an honorable death.[25]

The four men who were bound for Philadelphia left Mount Vernon on May 4. Washington's baggage contained the blue-and-buff uniforms he had designed for the Fairfax militia. Just in case. Some accounts say he wore the uniform as he traveled.[26]

Joined on the road by other Virginia delegates, their progress through Maryland was almost triumphal. A scarlet-clad militia company, marching with fife and drum, escorted them from the Potomac crossing until other units took over. In Baltimore, three companies provided an escort. Washington reviewed a drill there, then townspeople staged a dinner in their honor. Similar scenes occurred in Chester, Pennsylvania, and in Philadelphia, where the welcoming party included a band, troops of cavalry and infantry, and hundreds of civilians.

A Philadelphia loyalist who ate supper with the delegates that evening remembered Washington as "a fine figure, and of a most easy and agreeable address." He was charmed by Washington's quiet affability and commanding presence, qualities that routinely won the trust of others. In the coming congress, they would be on full display.[27]

CHAPTER 30

General Washington

On May 9, Washington entered a Philadelphia that was changing daily. The peace-loving Quaker town was turning to the business of war. An English visitor recorded the transformation:

> I find the drums beating, colors flying, and detachments of newly raised militia parading the streets; the whole country appears determined to assume a military character, and this city, throwing off her pacific aspect, is forming military companies. . . .

According to two North Carolinians, the city's twenty-eight companies each drilled twice every day. "Nothing," one wrote, "is heard but the sound of drums and fifes."[1] With church bells pealing, Philadelphians gave Benjamin Franklin a hero's welcome home from England, then lavished the same treatment on the Virginia delegates, then on those from Massachusetts, Connecticut, and New York. Military units provided escorts and joined processions, marching "with a slow solemn pace."[2]

Washington carried with him not only his militia uniform but also six copies of the British Army's standard drill manual to help him train raw troops.[3] Washington knew he would soon command Virginia's military, and perhaps more. He was the only delegate with significant fighting experience and the leading soldier from the largest colony. Virginia always commanded attention.

Washington later said he had felt the "utmost diffidence" about commanding American forces, because "the situation required greater abilities and more experience than I possessed to conduct a great military machine."

He knew that machine would be "little more than a mere chaos" confronting Britain's huge resources:

> Her fleets covered the ocean, and . . . her troops had harvested laurels in every quarter of the globe. . . . We had no preparation. Money, the nerve of war, was wanting. The sword of war was to be forged on the anvil of necessity.

To prevail, Washington wrote on another occasion, Americans would rely on "the unconquerable resolution of our citizens, the conscious rectitude of our cause, and a confident trust that we should not be forsaken by heaven." Soldiers, he well knew, generally preferred more tangible advantages.[4]

On May 10, anxious delegates convened in the Pennsylvania State House. Facing war, the delegates were grim, but the crisis welded them together. The fighting near Boston, Richard Henry Lee wrote, "roused such a universal military spirit throughout all the colonies, and excited such universal resentment against this savage ministry and their detestable agents," that "there never appeared more perfect unanimity among any set of men." Events loomed so large, a Connecticut delegate confided to his wife, "I tremble when I think of their vast importance."[5]

Fifty of the delegates had attended the previous congress, but there were new faces: Ben Franklin and James Wilson of Pennsylvania, John Hancock from Massachusetts, and Thomas Jefferson of Virginia. With seven other delegates, Washington made a standing reservation for dinner at the City Tavern, but ate there only eight times. As at the first Congress, he dined often in the homes of wealthy Philadelphians. This time, he spent evenings and early mornings chairing four different committees, always wearing his militia uniform. Even prickly John Adams found that "by his great experience and ability in military matters [Washington] is of much service to us."[6]

The image of Washington in full uniform, striding the streets, socializing, and attending congressional sessions, carries the strong whiff of a man intent on high command. Possibly he wore the uniform to show his commitment to the cause, although the image calls to mind the guest who arrives with a guitar slung over one shoulder, desperately hoping that someone will ask for a song. Yet no delegate seems to have found the uniformed Washington ridiculous. Despite statements about how unworthy he felt for command, he pursued that command avidly.

Washington's first committee responsibility came when New York's provincial congress requested advice on what posts it should fortify before British forces arrived. Four days later, Washington's committee report prompted a discussion of "the state of America." After six days, Congress specified three locations for New York to reinforce against naval attack, and recommended that the colony arm up to 3,000 militia.[7]

The debate over New York's defense might have alarmed an aspiring commander. A legislative body with sixty-five members and little military experience was a poor place to make tactical decisions, but there was little alternative. No other continent-wide authority existed. The delegates' micromanagement was the beginning of their education on how to oversee a war. Most had reviewed budgets and revenues, enacted laws, and drafted addresses to the king or Parliament. They were adept at arguing over tone, commas, and clauses. Now their duties were far more grave. They weighed choices with immediate life-and-death consequences for their neighbors.

John Adams recognized that Congress was learning its job while performing it. "Our unwieldy body moves very slow," he wrote. "Such a vast multitude of objects, civil, political, commercial and military, press and crowd upon us so fast, that we know not what to do first." The session unfolded like a Shakespeare history play, with messengers dashing in with news of offstage conflicts that required immediate attention. One day they learned that patriots had seized Fort Ticonderoga in upstate New York; on another day, that a British agent was arrested in Philadelphia Harbor.[8]

Shortly after the New York resolutions passed, Washington chaired a new committee on the acquisition of ammunition and other supplies. The committee had only five days to dig into the vexing problem, which would dog the American cause for years. It recommended distributing Ticonderoga's arms and supplies and borrowing £6,000 to buy powder. Later, Congress called on northern colonies to send gunpowder to Massachusetts and directed New York and Pennsylvania to manufacture it.[9]

Congress drafted "an humble and dutiful petition" to George III, almost out of habit, but war was the reality. A resolution in late May acknowledged that hostilities had begun and directed that "these colonies be immediately put into a state of defense." Congress was, as a Pennsylvanian put it, "preparing for the worst that can happen, viz., a civil war."[10]

Washington wrote to George William Fairfax that he expected war. Thousands of armed Americans formed an impromptu army that ringed Boston, trapping Gage's troops there. Washington called it "unhappy" that the "plains of America are either to be drenched with blood, or inhabited by slaves." But regret would not stay his hand. "Can a virtuous Man," he asked his friend, "hesitate in his choice?"[11]

More committee service beckoned. Washington chaired a panel to develop an "estimate of the money necessary" for the next twelve months. The task, of course, was impossible. No one knew how long or widespread the conflict would be. And Congress had no power to raise funds anyway.[12]

By mid-June, the Massachusetts convention advised that since the Americans surrounding Boston were from different colonies, Congress should assume control of them. Many feared invasion from Canada. Delegates used the term "continental army" to describe the men ringing Boston. Congress authorized ten companies of riflemen from Pennsylvania, Maryland, and Virginia to reinforce the Boston siege. Someone had to lead this Continental Army, defending nearly two thousand miles of coastline against the world's dominant sea power and opposing the army that recently vanquished the French around the globe. The rebellion's fate rested upon who was the choice of Congress.[13]

Washington had another committee to chair, this one charged with preparing rules and regulations for the army. Was the assignment a step to even greater responsibilities? Some thought so. In a letter, an unidentified Virginia delegate reported that Washington "has been pressed to take the supreme command of the American troops and I believe will accept the appointment."[14]

ல

Writing thirty years later, John Adams took credit for Washington's appointment as commander in chief. According to Adams, within Congress there was a "southern party" that opposed "a New England Army under the command of a New England general." Artemas Ward of Massachusetts commanded the forces before Boston, but some Massachusetts delegates did not support him as overall commander, while John Hancock hungered to replace him.[15] Two leaders of the Massachusetts convention wrote to recommend Washington. Adams decided that only Washington would do.

"I rose in my place," Adams recalled, and moved that Congress adopt the army in Massachusetts and appoint a general. "I had no hesitation," he added, "to declare that I had but one gentleman in my mind for that important command, and that was a gentleman from Virginia who was among us." At that point, according to Adams, Washington "from his usual modesty darted into the library room." The Virginian had no wish to be present during a discussion of his merits and demerits. Some worried that a New England army might resent a leader from the South, and praised General Ward. The vote was postponed for a day.[16]

Although some delegates harbored doubts about placing Washington in command, each of the leading alternatives had disqualifying characteristics. Ward was a local judge and political figure, but his military experience consisted of garrison duty during the French and Indian War. He had never witnessed a battle, much less fought in one.

That could not be said of the other prominent alternative, Charles Lee, the former British officer who was hovering around Congress while drilling three independent companies in Philadelphia. Lee had marched with Braddock in 1754, been wounded at Fort Ticonderoga in that war, and fought in the British expedition that captured Montreal. Inclined to quarrel with his commanding officers, he then served with the Portuguese and Polish armies before returning to America. Fluent in French and literate in other languages, Lee was a gifted pamphleteer and critic of George III and his ministers. "He says the king is a fool," wrote one American, "and his ministers rogues and villains." Lee attracted controversy, and fumed when others advanced ahead of him.

Lee also was endlessly peculiar: painfully thin, slovenly, and described by one biographer as having "a nose so startling and so impressive that it won for him . . . the sobriquet 'Naso.'" His dogs, a pack, followed him everywhere. Even John Adams, who liked Lee, could only shrug at his eccentricities: "You must love his dogs if you love him, and forgive a thousand whims." Lee, neither born nor raised in America, seemed an unsteady character.[17]

With Washington, steadiness was a hallmark. "He seems discreet and virtuous," a Connecticut delegate wrote, "no harum scarum ranting swearing fellow but sober, steady, and calm." Another Connecticut delegate reported that Washington's reputation was of being "as fixed and resolute in having his orders on all occasions executed as he is cool and deliberate in giving them." A Massachusetts man summed Washington up as "a complete gentleman. He is sensible, amiable, virtuous, modest, and brave."[18]

It was not really a contest. The delegates knew Washington. They had served in Congress with him for the last five weeks and for seven weeks the year before. They had watched his committees wrestle with intractable problems. They had talked with him casually and on serious matters. They knew his dignity and self-possession. He spoke no more than necessary. He did not dazzle, but he won trust. Moreover, Washington had a military reputation, even if a mixed one. Lee looked odd and talked too much, and he had those dogs. Congress did not want a military genius inclined to argue with them.

Finally, as Adams sensed, the politics were right. New England was already at war, invaded by foreign troops; if Virginia supported New England, other colonies would too. Giving command to a Virginian recognized that colony's importance. The man in their chamber wearing a militia uniform would be their commander. Like the best-planned battles, this one was over before it began. Only Washington would do.

Washington stayed away from Congress on June 15, unwilling to be present for his selection. An old friend, Thomas Johnson of Maryland, moved the appointment of a commanding general for all American forces, then nominated Washington. Both motions passed unanimously. By making his selection unanimous, the delegates showed their unity. When Washington arrived for dinner at Burns's Tavern that afternoon, other delegates greeted him as general. After dinner, he met with his final committee on army regulations.[19]

Knowing that his words would be remembered, Washington asked Edmund Pendleton to help draft remarks for the formal presentation of his command. In a few words the next day, Washington acknowledged the high honor given him, adding his distress that "my abilities and military experience may not be equal to the extensive and important trust." He pledged to "exert every power I possess . . . for support of the glorious cause." Should his reputation be damaged by "some unlucky event," he asked that the delegates remember that "I do not think myself equal to the command." Congress had approved pay of $500, but Washington declined it. He asked only to be reimbursed for his expenses.[20]

Washington's declaration of his inadequacy might seem insincere. If he so doubted himself, why did he so unmistakably seek command? No one forced him to wear that militia uniform day after day. Yet Washington's message was well matched to the moment, to his audience in Congress and across the colonies. In an age of vainglory, of kings and emperors, he was modest. Americans who resented overbearing British aristocrats would find no arrogance in Washington's statements. He did not curry favor as a politician, nor did he promise triumph. He spoke as an honest man would speak to friends, confessing his fears and hopes. And then, in stark contrast to the corruption and self-dealing of the British imperial system, he refused to be paid.

As to the sincerity of Washington's self-doubts, he would hardly be the last person to find that—after eagerly seeking a position—its demands were intimidating. Failure, as Washington wrote after the war, would "have consigned the neck of the American general . . . to the block." Moreover, Washington had only once commanded more than a few hundred soldiers. The patriot effort would involve immense supply and recruitment problems, was an organizational shambles, and would face the British military. The challenges would have sobered most people.[21]

The complexity of Washington's feelings emerged in a letter to his brother-in-law, Burwell Bassett, with whom he had little motive to dissimulate. Three days after accepting the generalship, Washington wrote that he had "embarked on a tempestuous ocean from whence perhaps no friendly harbor is to be found." Claiming he had hoped to avoid the position, which was not entirely true, he pledged to bring three qualities to his duties: "a firm belief of the justice of our Cause—close attention in the prosecution of it—and the strictest Integrity." Acknowledging that "reputation derives its principal support from success," he added the hope that if matters turned out badly, he would have the solace "of having acted to the best of my judgment."[22]

The day before, Washington had sent word of his appointment to Martha with his "inexpressible concern" that the news would make her unhappy. That he had anticipated becoming general, and had discussed it with her, appears from his enclosure of a will drafted for him by Pendleton. Washington said he had intended to prepare one before leaving Mount Vernon. Soldiers going off to war often prepare wills; delegates departing for legislative sessions rarely do.

Describing his appointment as "a kind of destiny," he protested that he could not refuse it without "reflect[ing] dishonor upon myself," which "could not . . . be pleasing to you, and must have lessened me considerably in my own esteem." He included a tender passage:

I should enjoy more real happiness and felicity in one month with you, at home, than I have the most distant prospect of reaping abroad, if my stay was to be seven times seven years.

Worried that Martha would be lonely with her daughter dead, her son married, and her husband gone, he encouraged her to visit family on the Pamunkey River, or to move to a house they kept in Alexandria. He wrote separately to encourage Jack Custis to care for her, and sent the same message to his brother Jack.[23]

∾

Regional politics, as Adams suggested, figured in Washington's selection. A Connecticut delegate explained that Washington's appointment "more firmly cements the southern to the northern" colonies, and removed Southerners' fear that "an enterprising eastern New England" might presume to dictate to the South.[24]

Regional factors also drove the appointments of Washington's generals, who were either Northerners or former British officers. Congress named Artemas Ward and Charles Lee to be major generals, along with Philip Schuyler of New York and Israel Putnam of Connecticut. Eight brigadier general positions were sprinkled among New Hampshire, Rhode Island, Connecticut (two), New York, and Massachusetts (three). Charles Lee insisted that Congress indemnify him if British troops should injure his property, a condition Washington evidently never thought of.[25]

Washington's commission as commander in chief made clear that Congress intended to control him and his army. After noting its "especial trust and confidence in your patriotism, conduct, and fidelity," the document enjoined him "punctually to observe and follow such orders and directions from time to time as you shall receive from this or a future Congress." His commission would continue until Congress revoked it. He would start, however, with wide discretion over military matters.[26]

Before leaving Philadelphia with his generals, Washington bought five new horses and a carriage so he would not always have to travel on horseback. Also, he ordered a new uniform based on his design for the Fairfax militia: a blue coat with yellow buttons and epaulettes. He always wanted to look good.[27]

CHAPTER 31

"One of the Most Important Characters in the World"

As Washington and his senior generals prepared to leave Philadelphia for Boston, many delegates gathered to see them off. Some continued alongside the general for the first six miles, accompanied by a troop of light horse, militia officers, and a band. In towns on the way to Boston, crowds acclaimed Washington and his generals, but especially Washington. News of his appointment had instantly made him the focus of Americans' hopes and fears. He was, as John Adams said, "one of the most important characters in the world" because "the liberties of America depend upon him." Writing after reaching Boston, Washington laconically observed that his trip was "a good deal retarded" because every town wished to show "respect to the general of your armies."[1]

Tall, graceful, and mounted on a fine horse, Washington made a stirring impression. Equally important, though, was the political sensitivity he had learned as a burgess, judge, and vestryman. When the New York Provincial Congress pointedly announced its expectation that when the war ended, "you will cheerfully resign . . . and reassume the character of our worthiest citizen," Washington's reply was calculated to reassure:

> When we assumed the soldier, we did not lay aside the citizen, and we shall most sincerely rejoice with you in that happy hour, when the establishment of American liberty . . . shall enable us to return to our private stations.[2]

Washington's dignified, sober manner persuaded people that he meant those words. Landon Carter, a politician who usually took a dim view of his colleagues, celebrated Washington's integrity and sincerity. "I never knew but one man who resolved not to forget the citizen in the soldier or ruler," Carter noted, "and that man is G[eorge] W[ashington]."[3]

The glorification of Washington happened at high speed, long before he took the field against the British. Only a day after the Continental Congress appointed him commander in chief, a Connecticut delegate wrote about Washington to his wife: "Let our youth look up to this man as a pattern to form themselves by, who unites the bravery of the soldier, with the most consummate modesty and virtue." From Boston to Richmond, Americans began naming their babies for the Virginian. A New York couple named their twins "George Washington" and "Martha Dandridge." A ship was renamed for him. Before the war ended, his name would adorn a frigate, two galleys, two brigantines, a schooner, five sloops, and four other ships; another was called *Lady Washington*.[4]

Those first exultant weeks blessed Washington with a reservoir of public trust. Americans craved a hero. That blazing first impression would survive through repeated military setbacks and years of political strife, then through centuries after his death. In 1781, after three years in which Washington won no battles, a Frenchman marveled at Americans' devotion to their commander:

> Through all the land he appears like a benevolent god; old men, women, children they all flock eagerly to catch a glimpse of him when he travels and congratulate themselves because they have seen him. People carrying torches follow him through the cities; his arrival is marked by public illuminations.[5]

Of the senior army officers appointed by Congress in 1775, only Washington would last the war with his reputation intact—nay, burnished to a bright shine. Artemas Ward quickly returned to obscurity. Charles Lee would stumble from mishap to blunder to failure. Political backbiters drove Philip Schuyler from military office. Israel Putnam ended his service as a garrison commander. Washington, despite battlefield losses, rose above them all—indeed, above every figure in North America and most in the Atlantic world. His political talents were central to that ascendancy.

His failures and mistakes seemed to fade from popular memory, a phenomenon already evident in 1775. After all, at Fort Necessity his forces lost a battle in which he chose his ground poorly and applied worse tactics. With Braddock, he was on the losing side of a catastrophe. During the Forbes expedition, he led troops into a friendly-fire debacle and was a prideful, contentious subordinate, offending his superiors after alienating his civilian benefactor, Governor Dinwiddie.

That Congress still chose him as commander in chief was partly a tribute to the human ability to forget, and also to how uninspiring the other candidates were. It also demonstrated Washington's extraordinary talent for winning the confidence of others, even when objective evidence might not justify such confidence.

But, even more, the forty-three-year-old commander had observed, learned, and grown since his days in the Virginia Regiment. His time in public office had schooled him in the complexities and crosscurrents of collegial decision-making. His time as husband and stepfather had deepened his empathy. He knew more about the world and about himself. He listened more than he spoke, and tried never to speak, even privately, without being certain what he thought about the subject. He understood how government worked on people, how to influence others, how to sense public opinion and something as ephemeral, yet real, as the spirit of the time. He had sensed that spirit the year before, when the Fairfax Resolves drove his political ascent into a steep climb.

That final propulsion came from the powerful forces within Washington that made him a near-perfect figure to carry America's cause forward. His boyhood dreams of military glory were now essential to America's future, which would be won by fighting, not debating. His mastery of the arts of political leadership and persuasion, which had seemed almost a pastime for a man so dedicated to financial success, would serve as the essential balance wheel of the nation for the next two decades, keeping a revolution from sliding into tyranny or anarchy. Most important, those skills were yoked to his fundamental decency and his high moral purpose of securing liberty.

Washington had ample reason to fear how fortune would treat him in his new role. He had never commanded a large army, and the forces he led might evaporate if the volunteers chose to go home rather than face British grapeshot and bayonets. A significant share of the populace did not support the rebellion. Money would be scarce. Having watched Governor Dinwiddie arm-wrestle Virginia's legislators for war financing, and having served as a burgess, he knew that legislators would be slow to levy taxes, especially for armies that did not win. Worse, the thirteen colonies, with their separate histories and competing interests, might descend into rivalry or disunion.

Against those risks, the certainty was that the war would be brutal. Washington had no illusions about war's horrors. Before him lay months and years of slaughter, heartache, and hardship. He knew what it was like to lead men who were overmatched, who lacked food, arms, and clothing, who would desert as soon as their officers looked away.

But that dangerous moment in history also presented Washington with extraordinary opportunities, which he also understood. It was not merely the opportunity to achieve martial glory, which the British Army had refused to grant him. Far more was at stake.

Washington believed in his cause. Few Americans spoke yet for independence, but all knew that the fight was for control over their lives, for self-government, the core idea wrapped up in the ideal of liberty that dominated patriot writings. That ideal would create an irresistible push toward independence. Americans—white male Americans, that is—demanded the right to govern themselves, and for Washington that was a sacred purpose. He could place himself at the center of his epoch by leading this movement for self-government, liberty, and freedom of conscience.

He had prepared himself for this moment, his body and his mind and his heart. His chance to reach for great achievements, to champion human liberty, came from the acts of irascible Americans who hated to pay taxes, and from his shrewd political judgments and power to inspire trust. To steer this audacious movement past the dangers of mob rule at one extreme and strongman rule at the other would require astonishing luck, unrivaled fortitude and vision, and unusual political acumen that produced steady, measured judgments. Washington's public career would become an excruciating balancing act, translating the passion and idealism of rebellion into a military victory and then into a working government that still respected the Revolution's ideals. Revolutions are combustible things; they rarely lead to the destination proclaimed at their outset. Few people in human history had, or ever would have, the opportunity Washington held in his hands. Fewer still could take advantage of that opportunity with such mastery.

He had done one thing more. He had captured the holy grail for public actors, operating as a politician with extraordinary success while at the same time not seeming to be one at all, with all the negative baggage that the label has always carried. He was seen, and ever would be seen, as a farmer, a soldier, a patriot. After sixteen years as a legislator, six years in appointive office as judge and city trustee, and his sponsorship of key political moves like the Association of 1769 and the Fairfax Resolves, almost no one thought of him as a political operator, nor would they in the future. It was magic.

PART III

[Washington] possesses two of the great requisites of a
statesman, the faculty of concealing his own sentiments,
and of discovering those of other men.

—*Edward Thornton (1792)*[1]

For the last third of Washington's life, he was the most conspicuous figure in North America, under constant scrutiny as he led Americans through the Revolutionary War, then the creation of a democratic republic, and finally the perilous early years of that unprecedented form of government. At each stage, Washington's success grew not from incisive intellectual feats. Indeed, some contemporaries slighted his intelligence and mocked his deliberate habits. Rather, Washington repeatedly was in the seat of greatest power because of his sure judgment of events, canny evaluations of people, great energy and determination, and steady focus on critical strategic goals.

This book will examine five watershed periods in his last quarter century of life that illustrate how he applied to America's greatest challenges the political mastery learned through his first forty-three years.

- WINNING THE WAR: Across eight months of war beginning in December 1777, he remade the army during its bitter winter camp at Valley Forge, thwarted a scheme to wrest control of that army from him, and won the critical battle of Monmouth Court House.
- BUILDING A NATION: Through the unsettled, drifting years between the end of the fighting in 1781 and the ratification of the Constitution in 1788, Washington managed soldier mutinies, disbanded the army, and led the creation and acceptance of an effective yet limited government.
- GOVERNING A REPUBLIC: During his first term as president, he engineered the enactment of the laws that laid the foundation for the new union under the Constitution.

- PRESERVING PEACE: During his second presidential term, his controversial policy of neutrality kept the United States out of a bloody European war, and he also quelled internal rebellion, preserving a nation still crippled from eight years of fighting with Britain.
- VALUING FREEDOM: In his final years, Washington searched for a road away from slavery that did not dissolve the union, a futile search that ended with his long-overdue act of freeing his own slaves: an attempt to point his countrymen down a road he never found.

WAR

CHAPTER 32

The Bloody Path to Valley Forge

For eight years, the Revolutionary War pitted neighbors against each other in savage fighting. Sharpshooters sniped from behind trees, saber-wielding horsemen rode down enemies, infantry charged with bayonets, debilitating diseases decimated battalions of men, and prisoners starved. The war touched everyone. Armies took what they needed from farmers and merchants, only sometimes paying. At different times, foreign soldiers occupied the four largest cities—Philadelphia, Boston, New York, and Charleston. A German mercenary fondly remembered Philadelphia, where "every soldier lived lighthearted, merry, and in abundance," although "no resident was certain of his property among the fifteen thousand men from all classes of society."[1]

The fighting even brought prosperity to a few. The British brought goods and silver across the sea, while the revolutionary governments spent heavily to support the war.[2]

Before the war, Americans enjoyed greater freedom than most people then on Earth; they rebelled not to win their liberty but to defend it. That defense brought profound changes that few foresaw, spreading ideals of liberty and self-government and undermining obedience to a king and a class hierarchy.[3]

The fighting seesawed, both sides meeting successes and failures. Attacking Quebec in a blizzard on New Year's Eve of 1775, the rebels failed miserably. A few months later, Washington watched with satisfaction as the British boarded ships and sailed away from Boston, choosing not to take on the New Englanders who had fought so fiercely at the Battle of Bunker Hill nearly a year before. Americans exulted in Washington's bloodless triumph.

But the autumn of 1776 brought brutal defeats around New York City that nearly annihilated the army. The British took 3,000 prisoners and critical supplies. Washington had too few soldiers and weapons, too many officers he thought were incompetent, and even lacked reliable maps of his own country. His inexperience as commander in chief showed. By December 1776, he confessed to his brother, "I think the game is pretty near up."[4] With a daring surprise attack on Trenton on Christmas morning, however, he dragged the cause back from the brink, then won again at Princeton a week later. That last-minute revival allowed the Continental Army to limp into winter quarters at Morristown, New Jersey.

But Trenton and Princeton could not conceal how desperate the situation was. British naval power controlled New York's many waterways. The Continentals melted away with illness and desertion. At least 5,000 had already died in the cause, as many from starvation and disease as on the battlefield. To make his army seem larger than it was, Washington rotated New Jersey militia through his camp.[5]

The rebellion's glory faded. Prices soared. Enlistments declined. Clinging to the myth of citizen-soldiers called from their hearths and then returning home, many Americans despised a "standing army" as too centralized and dangerous to liberty. Experience punctured the myth, as militias skedaddled when combat began, just as Washington had learned during the previous war. He wanted an army of men trained to be soldiers.

The United States proclaimed itself with the Declaration of Independence in July 1776. For all of that document's high-flown sentiment, the new nation had but two institutions: Congress and the Continental Army. Each measured its life-span in months. The United States had no executive officers, no courts, no power to tax. Congress and the army had to mature, at speed, to stave off Britain's global power.

Washington recognized that Congress embodied the nation's legitimacy and authority, even though it was in many ways not a national legislature, but a diplomatic body of thirteen sovereign states.[6] Each state chose and paid its own delegates. To support the army, Congress asked states to send money. If they did not, Congress printed currency that swiftly lost value.

Washington faced immense obstacles. He commanded mostly raw recruits on short enlistments, which meant that untrained soldiers kept replacing untrained soldiers. Officers also were inexperienced, except for Europeans who sought career-advancing commands. Washington took advantage of the foreigners' expertise in engineering and tactics, but preferred Americans for senior positions. Battlefield setbacks brought grumbling about the general. His erratic second-in-command, Charles Lee, lamented that Washington was "most damnably deficient."[7]

Washington's two favorite subordinates—Nathanael Greene and Henry Knox, head of artillery—were self-educated New Englanders from modest backgrounds. Knox was apprenticed to a bookseller at the age of nine and opened his own shop twelve years later, reading voraciously the whole time. A large, beefy man with gracious manners, Knox gave military advice that bristled with references to precedents like Sweden's King Charles XII's tactics at the Battle of Poltava. Greene abandoned his Quaker faith and his iron business to join Rhode Island's forces. Sturdily built and taller than average, Greene had asthma and a pronounced limp that made him seem so unmilitary that when the Rhode Islanders first elected their officers, they passed over him completely. Washington, however, prized competence, talent, and loyalty over pedigree and surface appearances. He saw the strengths that Greene and Knox could bring, but they all were learning their profession on the fly.[8]

Their opponents were formidable, beginning with the many Americans called Tories or loyalists or "the disaffected." The loyalists knew the country as well as Washington's men did; they fought as well; and because they looked and sounded like the Continentals, they were effective spies.

The enemy's professionals, British and German, had years of experience as cohesive military units. Their battlefield skills exceeded anything the Continentals could muster. Washington's chief engineer, the Frenchman Louis Duportail, insisted that Americans were "incapable . . . of resisting the enemy on equal ground." They could succeed, he preached, only from higher ground or a fortified position, as they had at Bunker Hill. Those suggesting otherwise, he wrote, "do not know what troops are." Rather than slug it out with the enemy, he and others urged the strategy of the Roman general Fabius Maximus, who defeated Hannibal of Carthage by avoiding battle until the frustrated Carthaginian launched reckless attacks on entrenched defenses.[9]

Exhilarated by the triumph at Trenton, Congress affirmed Washington's command in late December 1776, stating its "perfect reliance on the wisdom, vigor, and uprightness of General Washington." For the next campaign, the commander wanted a tighter army organization and soldiers on longer enlistment periods.[10] Perhaps 1777 would be better.

∾

Luckily for the Americans, indecision and geography delayed the British offensives that year. An attack led by General John Burgoyne struggled down from Canada through the Champlain valley, aiming to control the Hudson River and sever New England from her sister states. To stop Burgoyne, Horatio Gates commanded the army's northern wing, plus 12,000 militiamen. Washington reinforced Gates with two more regiments and the rifle brigade of Colonel Daniel Morgan, so Gates outnumbered Burgoyne by 3 to 1.[11]

After weeks of dithering in New York City, General Sir William Howe decided not to help Burgoyne but to sail 15,000 men to the Chesapeake Bay. He aimed to seize the American seat of government, Philadelphia. To meet that thrust, Washington hurried across New Jersey with the balance of his army plus militia, about 15,000 in all. By Duportail's formula, the even numbers meant the Americans were overmatched.[12]

In early September, the armies clashed at Brandywine Creek, west of Philadelphia. Duportail was right. Surprised by Howe's flanking maneuver, the Continentals scrambled into a violent fray, but the better-disciplined enemy prevailed. American casualties were roughly double those of the enemy, though the defeat marked the emergence of a twenty-year-old Frenchman named Gilbert du Motier, the Marquis de Lafayette.[13] With a passionate nature and more wealth than experience, Lafayette had secured an honorary major generalship from Congress. At Brandywine, Washington admired how the young Frenchman fought on despite a wound, beginning a father-son relationship that dissolved Washington's customary aloofness.[14]

The Continentals meant to defend Philadelphia, but Howe wrongfooted them with a feint to the north. Pivoting, the British marched into the city without firing a shot.[15]

Washington, however, was not finished. When the news arrived that Burgoyne's army had been checked at the first Battle of Saratoga, Washington challenged his men not to be outdone. On the foggy morning of October 3, Washington's attack at Germantown north of Philadelphia drove the enemy back for two miles. The advance foundered as gun smoke mingled with fog to ruin visibility. A detachment failed to cover an American flank. The British and Hessians clawed back the ground they had lost. The Continentals retreated again.[16]

Although American losses at Germantown exceeded the enemy's, the Continentals emerged with a surprising confidence. They stressed the opening stages of the battle, not its unhappy conclusion. One claimed the contest had been "eight tenths won," while another reported that "our men are now convinced they can drive the chosen troops of the enemy . . . whenever they attack them with ardor." A visitor reported that the soldiers were "sensible only of a disappointment, not a defeat."[17]

∾

After the British seized two Delaware River forts that controlled maritime access to Philadelphia, the Continentals could not recapture the city before winter set in. Washington assured Congress that the British gained little from "possession of our towns, while we have an army in the field . . . It is our arms, not defenseless towns, they have to subdue."[18]

The Continentals needed to rest and reorganize in winter quarters, while keeping watch on the enemy's movements. Sir William, his supplies arriving by ship, was snuggling into Philadelphia to keep his army—and himself—warm and amused through the cold months.[19] Valley Forge, twenty miles west of the city, offered some advantages to the Americans. The site, a rough triangle with the Schuylkill River and Valley Creek on two sides, had fresh water and forests for wood gathering. Perched atop open country that sloped down to Philadelphia, it would overlook any British advance. An army there also could defend York to the west, where Congress had settled after fleeing Philadelphia, or Lancaster to the north, where Pennsylvania's government had relocated. That Valley Forge was barren and windswept, and ill served by roads, would soon become clear.[20]

The march began with a congressionally decreed day of thanksgiving, which disgusted many soldiers. The army's supply services were in a death spiral. A New Hampshire officer recorded that his men had no bread for three days. All he was thankful for was "that we are alive and not in the grave with many of our friends." A Connecticut soldier noted his ration that day was a dollop of rice and a tablespoon of vinegar, followed by a sermon, topped off with "a leg of nothing and no turnips."[21]

The Continentals were, one soldier reported, "not only starved but naked; the greatest part were not only shirtless and barefoot, but destitute of all other clothing, especially blankets." The feet of 2,000 unshod soldiers left blood on the frozen ground. They arrived, he added, in "truly forlorn condition—no clothing, no provisions, and as disheartened as need be." An army surgeon wrote movingly of the suffering:

> There comes a soldier, his bare feet are seen through his worn-out shoes, his legs nearly naked from the tattered remains of an only pair of stockings, his breeches not sufficient to cover his nakedness, his shirt hanging in strings, his hair disheveled, his face meager, his whole appearance pictures a person forsaken and discouraged.[22]

The supply failures mounted. A few days after the march, a Rhode Island general complained of three days without bread and two without meat. "The men must be supplied," he wrote, "or they cannot be commanded." Washington directed each brigade to send men into the country to collect food, but they found little there. Soldiers took to chanting, "No meat, no meat." When Washington ordered a unit to oppose a British sortie from Philadelphia, the soldiers had no provisions, so they stayed in camp. That led, he wrote, to "a dangerous mutiny . . . which with difficulty was suppressed."[23]

Washington's walking scarecrows had to build their own shelters. His orders specified each hut's size (fourteen feet by sixteen feet), the components (logs for the walls, packed with clay, and roofs of split slabs covered with earth, fireplaces of wood lined with clay), and the locations (each regiment along a "street," with officers' huts behind those of the private soldiers).[24] Though Washington ordered that twelve men build each hut, an acute shortage of tools meant that often only three could labor at a time, sharing a single dull ax. For malnourished men in freezing weather, the effort was excruciating.[25]

The pamphleteer Thomas Paine somehow found the spectacle charming. The soldiers reminded him of "a family of beavers, some carrying logs, others mud and the rest fastening them together." Lafayette more realistically called the huts "little shanties that are scarcely gayer than dungeon cells." To demonstrate solidarity with soldiers sleeping in tents, Washington stayed in his tent for the first weeks at Valley Forge, then made a farmhouse his headquarters.[26]

The suffering was constant. A New Jersey officer led twenty shoeless men on a scouting expedition. They cut up blankets to wrap around their feet, but the fabric quickly wore through "and they could be tracked by the blood." A Massachusetts man wrote, "I have seen the soldiers turned out to do their duty in such poor condition that . . . I could not refrain from tears. It would melt the heart of a savage to see the state we are in."[27]

Unwashed men, poorly fed and wearing rags, contracted dysentery and pneumonia and typhus. Scabies, caused by parasites, infected entire brigades. "I have seen the poor fellows," an officer recorded, "covered over and over with scab."[28]

Makeshift hospitals would "prove a grave for many," Nathanael Greene complained. General Anthony Wayne agreed: "Our men are falling sick in numbers every day, contracting vermin and dying in hospitals." In February, a congressional committee found "sickness and mortality . . . in an astonishing degree," noting that "the sick and dead list has increased one third in the last week . . . which was one third greater than the week preceding."[29] Before the encampment ended, one-fifth of the army would die. "The many deaths," a junior officer wrote, "may serve to prepare us all for a dying hour." Another remembered that "death seemed to stare the poor soldiers in the face."[30]

Many had received no pay for as long as ten months. "Besides feeding and clothing a soldier well," Washington lectured Congress, "nothing is of greater importance than paying him with punctuality." Yet, due to failures of Congress, the states, and the army, the Continentals received neither adequate food, nor sufficient clothing, nor pay.[31]

By early February, Washington warned that the conditions drove the soldiers toward mutiny or desertion. "The spirit of desertion," he wrote, "never before rose to such a threatening height." An officer estimated that three-fourths of the men had attempted it. Washington confessed he was "astonished . . . that more of them have not left us." After cataloguing the soldiers' woes, a New Hampshire general wondered, "If any of them desert how can I punish them?" The army nonetheless hanged four as an object lesson. The desertions continued.[32]

Disillusionment spread into the officer ranks. Escalating prices and low pay caused many to fear poverty for their families back home. Every officer promotion brought an avalanche of complaints from those passed over. "My feelings are every day wounded," Washington reported to Congress, "by the discontent, complaints and jarring of officers, not to add resignations." In a single week, more than fifty officers resigned from Greene's division. Ninety officers resigned from nine Virginia regiments. Washington was so disgusted with the resignations that he stopped accepting them, directing officers to petition Congress for release from their commissions. So many left that he feared "being left alone with the soldiers only."[33]

∾

As Pennsylvania winters go, 1778 was not especially frigid, though there were bone-chilling cold snaps in late December and mid-February, and rain and snow ruined roads for days at a time. Even in good weather, however, the army's supply services were fragile. Their challenge was immense.

After forming outside Boston in the summer of 1775, the army had to create an infrastructure that provided clothing, bedding, tents, muskets, ammunition, and food, plus wagons and teams of draft animals to haul them. No American had attempted an enterprise on the scale of supplying 10,000 men for years of war. Lack of money multiplied the failures.

On the day the army arrived, the Valley Forge camp became the third largest city in America, but it was a city with no food stored for the winter, one that produced no goods and had little income. Somehow Washington had to transform that primitive camp into a place that not only supported the soldiers but built them into a fighting force.

Accustomed to managing every detail at Mount Vernon, Washington shouldered duties far beyond the military. He directed waste removal, privy

construction, and hut design; he prescribed the fabrication of shoes, organized wagon convoys and smallpox inoculations, and a hundred other mundane matters. No issue was beneath his attention. To solve the clothing
shortage, he proposed a new jacket design that used less cloth.[34]

He rode through camp every day, just as he rode the grounds daily at
Mount Vernon. He showed himself, reassured the troops that he cared, and
found problems to solve. Were horse carcasses piling up? Was illicit liquor for
sale? Should hospitals be built offsite? Were soldiers stealing from neighboring farms? Washington insisted the army pay for livestock and crops taken
from farms, even if the payment came in flimsy Continental dollars or dubious scrip signed by the officer conducting the seizure.[35]

Each problem led to another. Hungry men grew sick; sick men could not
go on foraging expeditions; men on foraging expeditions deserted; deserters
spread disaffection and undermined recruiting; and while they foraged, soldiers neither drilled nor patrolled. Often, the British may have seemed the
least of Washington's troubles.

He rose before dawn and planned his day, often down to quarter-hour
segments, so he could work ten hours before midafternoon dinner.[36] Any
dispute or uncertainty that no one else could resolve came to him. He reviewed every court-martial verdict, roughly one every day. For six months,
he never left Valley Forge. Mostly he listened, hearing officers' complaints
and aspirations, absorbing the fears, the far-fetched schemes, the recriminations, and the suffering of the soldiers.

After a dinner that could be meager, taken with aides and a few invited
guests, he turned to the never-ending correspondence with Congress, with
distant American commanders, with state governors who might provide
supplies or soldiers, and with the British over prisoner treatment. He whee-
dled support from or conciliated disputes with every level of government:
local pooh-bahs, state dignitaries, congressional grandees, and militia officer
divas. He kept five aides busy acquiring information or summoning people,
screening petitioners on his doorstep, copying letters, and drafting the less
important ones.[37]

Incoming letters included apologies from quartermasters and commissaries who lacked cash as prices skyrocketed. The supply crisis had to be
solved. For the initial three months at Valley Forge, the starving army consumed 2.25 million pounds of beef, 2.3 million pounds of flour, and more
than 16,000 gallons of rum and whiskey. Someone had to find it, buy it, then
carry it by wagon or drive the cattle across rivers, mountains, and bogs.[38]

The army had three supply offices. The Commissary General's Office acquired and distributed food; the Quartermaster General's Office managed

Courtesy of the Library of Congress

A foraging party from Valley Forge

transport and acquired equipment; the Clothier General's Office provided uniforms and blankets. By Valley Forge days, all three were staggering.

After Congress reorganized the Commissary General in early 1777, the resignation of a competent chief elevated bumbling William Buchanan, who was called "as incapable as a child" by one congressional delegate. Widespread resignations in his office left only the incompetent. Depreciating currency combined with state price ceilings to drive farmers into the arms of the British, who paid with silver money.[39]

The Quartermaster General's Office was in a comparable slough. General Thomas Mifflin, a popular Pennsylvania politician, neglected the office for months through 1777, pleading illness. He resigned in November, as speculation swirled about friction between him and Washington. During Mifflin's long period of inattention, regional quartermasters stopped coordinating with each other and hoarded scarce forage, wagons, and teams. Limits on driver pay further confounded the effort. It mattered little what provisions the commissaries acquired if the quartermasters did not transport them.[40]

The head of the Clothier General's Office, James Mease, was hapless. "The complaints against your department have become so loud and universal," Washington thundered, that he issued "a positive and peremptory injunction [for Mease] immediately to repair to headquarters." Instead, Mease resigned.[41]

In late January, Nathanael Greene predicted that these failings, if not reversed, would prevent the army from fighting in 1778.[42] Washington agreed, writing to the president of Congress that without a "great and capital change" in the supply system, the army must "starve—dissolve—or disperse." Washington repeated that apocalyptic warning for weeks. How, amid the chaos and desperate want of Valley Forge, could he plan a campaign against a well-provisioned and well-led enemy?[43]

Washington had to inspire and reassure others while groping toward improvements. He allowed his self-command to fray in letters to Henry Laurens, the South Carolinian who became president of Congress in November 1777. "No man," Washington complained, "ever had his measures more impeded than I have." The general's scolding tone reflected impatience with second-guessing:

> It is a much easier and less distressing thing, to draw remonstrances
> in a comfortable room by a good fire side, than to occupy a cold, bleak
> hill, and sleep under frost and snow without clothes or blankets: How-
> ever, although they [his critics] seem to have little feeling for the na-
> ked and distressed soldier, I . . . from my soul pity those miseries,
> which it is neither in my power to relieve or prevent.[44]

Through the desperate winter, Washington faced three principal adversaries. The greatest risk, of course, arose from the enemy in Philadelphia. For the first few months, however, General Howe rarely stirred. One German officer remembered Philadelphia as offering "no lack of pleasant winter-time activities":

> Almost daily assemblies were held (get-togethers for pleasure); every
> Monday, comedy, and every Tuesday was a dance and card playing for
> the officers. Every week there were trips in groups to the nearby places,
> such as Germantown and Frankford, where pleasure was to be had in
> shooting and pitching hay.

Officers' pastimes included cockfights, horse races, and cricket matches, plus theatricals at the Southwark Theatre. Gamblers gathered nightly at the faro bank organized by the Hessians.[45]

Sir William contentedly gambled and kept company with Mrs. Elizabeth

Loring, his American mistress, who came from Boston to warm his evenings while her husband enjoyed a profitable military position. When springtime arrived, Henry Laurens observed that "had the British general been a man of enterprise," he might have captured Congress: "Our safety lay in Mrs. [Loring's] lap."[46]

To address the military danger, Washington had to solve his second major adversary: the army's broken supply services. That required delicate political maneuvering, both inside the army and with congressional and state officials.

Before he was fairly started on that task, an unexpected letter allowed him to strike at his third major adversary: a small group seeking to wrest control of the army from him. This was a straightforward political knife fight. Given a weapon to employ against those adversaries, he would strike at them hard. They would learn that they might disparage Washington's military ability, but they were no match for his political skills.

CHAPTER 33

The First Adversary: The Conway Cabal

Ageneral who loses will be criticized, so Washington was. A Pennsylvanian lamented that "Thousands of lives and millions of property are yearly sacrificed to the insufficiency of our commander in chief," adding that Washington had committed "two such blunders as might have disgraced a soldier of three months standing." Massachusetts delegate James Lovell agreed. "The spirit of enterprise," he grumbled, "is a stranger in the main army." After Brandywine and Germantown, a North Carolinian observed that British commander Sir William Howe "out general'd us, as usual." A dozen or more delegates and former delegates expressed doubts about Washington as commander in chief. That autumn, two officers close to Washington, Greene and Timothy Pickering, agreed that their commander was indecisive.[1]

With his triumph at Saratoga, which brought Burgoyne's surrender of his entire army, General Horatio Gates became the darling of the disenchanted, the champion who would bring thumping wins if elevated to overall command. Washington and his allies argued that Gates enjoyed advantages at Saratoga that Washington could only dream of. Gates's forces outnumbered the enemy 3 to 1. Burgoyne's men, after slogging through the Adirondacks from Canada, had been hungry, demoralized, and far from the protection of the Royal Navy. Lafayette dismissed Gates's victory as won "in the middle of the woods, expecting an enemy who could arrive to him by one single road . . . it was almost impossible not to conquer." Gates, Greene concurred, was "but the child of fortune."[2]

Older than Washington by several years, Horatio Gates had modest energy and little flair. His men called him "Granny Gates," testament to his fussiness, thinning gray hair, stooped shoulders, and spectacles sliding down his nose. A stunning victory, however, creates its own mystique. Saratoga won Gates a gold medal from Congress and inflated his self-regard.

Though Washington was his superior, Gates sent notice of the victory directly to Congress, not bothering to dispatch a report to the commander in chief. When Washington asked Gates to release the units sent north to help him, Gates dragged his feet. To expedite that transfer, Washington sent the relentless Colonel Alexander Hamilton, who ruffled the feathers of America's newest hero but recovered only some of the loaned troops.[3]

In early November, surprising news arrived on Washington's desk. In an enclosure to a letter, Major General William Alexander (called Lord Stirling for the Scottish title he claimed) wrote a single sentence that embodied the disparagement of Washington then circulating:

In a letter from General Conway to General Gates he says, "Heaven has been determined to save your country; or a weak general and bad counsellors would have ruined it."

Washington did not hesitate. He held in his hand a link between men he thought were scheming to supersede him. To flush out any plan that was afoot, Washington had the explosive message copied, added the flat statement that he had received it, signed the sheet, and sent it to General Thomas Conway, an Irish veteran of the French Army. Washington did not deign to ask for an explanation.[4]

The young Washington might have responded to Stirling's warning with hot anger, firing off a protest to his superior (in this case, Congress) while demanding that Conway account for his words. The mature political operator, however, applied quiet pressure to Conway and his fellows, steadily driving them into blunders, and held his fire when it came to Congress.

Stirling's enclosure derived from Colonel James Wilkinson, a twenty-year-old aide to Gates, who had been carrying the official Saratoga victory notice to Congress in York. On his way to York, Wilkinson stopped at the home of General Thomas Mifflin, the resigning quartermaster general, and drank through the evening with an aide to Stirling. Wilkinson decried Washington's failings, describing a letter from Conway to Gates that disparaged the commander in chief. Next morning Stirling's aide reported the conversation to Stirling, who reported on to Washington.[5]

Conway replied to Washington with neither apology nor regret. He admitted writing to Gates about the army's faults. He noted that, while at Mifflin's home, he made similar remarks in the presence of Dr. James Craik, Washington's old friend (who would be expected to report them to the commander in chief, and later did). Conway denied writing the passage quoted by Washington and volunteered his permission for Gates to disclose his letter. He called Washington "a brave man, an honest man, a patriot, and a man of great sense," but added that the commander had "often been influenced by men who were not equal to [him]." Conway followed that barbed flattery with a threat: that he would report back to France "the operations which I saw during this campaign."[6]

With a single move, Washington had confirmed the involvement of the three principals in what became known as the Conway Cabal, named for its least powerful and most voluble participant. The evidence was sketchy at first. Two weeks earlier, Washington had learned that Congress would promote Conway to major general, vaulting him over twenty-three more senior men. Smelling something amiss, Washington opposed the elevation. Conway's merit, he warned, "exists more in his own imagination than in reality" and the promotion would rankle the other brigadier generals.[7]

A few days after Conway's response to Washington, Congress took steps that triggered more suspicions. James Wilkinson won a brevet promotion to brigadier general, a position he had done little to deserve. Then Congress accepted Mifflin's resignation as quartermaster general but retained him as major general, appointing him and two others to the Board of War, a largely dormant body that initially had been intended to coordinate the war effort. Henceforth, the Board of War would serve as a platform for trying to wrench control of the army from Washington.[8]

Thomas Mifflin

COURTESY OF THE METROPOLITAN MUSEUM OF ART

Although Gates could be unimpressive and Conway irritated more people than he charmed, the smooth Mifflin was an adversary to reckon with. Rivalry between Mifflin and Nathanael Greene led a Massachusetts delegate to predict that the army would split "into Greenites and Mifflineans." Mifflin had recently clashed with Washington, urging a more aggressive defense of Philadelphia and raising "a prodigious clamor" against reinforcing Gates before Saratoga, then resigning as quartermaster general, claiming illness. Mifflin's estate in Reading became a hub for Washington detractors, who included John and Sam Adams, James Lovell, and even Richard Henry Lee, who played a double game, remaining friendly with Washington while flirting with the cabal. Mifflin declared to Gates that the hero of Saratoga should be in overall command. "This army will be totally lost," he wrote, "unless you come down and collect the virtuous band . . . and with their aid save the southern hemisphere. . . . Congress must send for you."[9]

Like Greene, Mifflin was a Quaker who left that faith to fight the British. Washington and his allies came to see the Pennsylvanian as scheming to use the Board of War to promote Gates. By mid-November, Mifflin sought Gates's appointment as president of the board, which would compel Washington to report to Gates. Mifflin argued that "the military knowledge and authority of Gates [was] necessary to procure the indispensable changes in our army."[10]

Then came a speedy bureaucratic shuffle designed to elevate those who wished to see Washington superseded. Conway submitted his resignation from the army, which Washington referred to Congress, which Congress referred to the Board of War. A few days later, Congress installed Gates as the board's president and appointed two more members. Rather than accept Conway's resignation, the Board of War promoted him to major general—the step Washington had opposed—and made him inspector general reporting to the board, not to Washington. As inspector general, Conway would investigate and report on the army's failings. Promoting Conway looked like a calculated insult to the commander in chief.[11]

Swiftly, the cabal had assumed a commanding bureaucratic position, especially with Mifflin and Gates on the Board of War. By breathing life into that body, they could pursue their own military ideas or obstruct Washington's. They could sap his power or force him out of the army. Conway, as inspector general, could publicize the army's problems and blame Washington.[12] Although the commander in chief looked vulnerable, Washington took no impulsive step. The contest was still in its early stages. He waited. Mifflin alerted Gates in Albany that Washington knew of Conway's letter. Gates realized he must write to the commander in chief, but misjudged entirely what to say.[13]

Gates's letter to Washington ignored the substance of Conway's statements, choosing neither to repudiate those sentiments nor to express support for Washington. Instead, he portrayed himself as the victim in the situation, complaining that his correspondence had been revealed. He pressed for Washington's assistance in exposing the culprit who disclosed the letter and might again betray secret matters. Gates demanded to know how Washington learned of Conway's letter. By fretting over the act of disclosure but remaining silent about the criticisms of Washington, Gates came close to admitting complicity with Conway (and Mifflin). Surely Washington thought so. He delayed his reply to Gates, leaving the nation's new Achilles to stew in his own juices.[14]

Shortly thereafter, Inspector General Conway presented himself at Washington's headquarters in order to begin his new duties. Washington was all frosty civility and noncooperation. He noted that Congress had directed the Board of War to provide instructions for Conway, but the board had not done so. Without instructions, Washington explained, Conway could not begin his work, so Washington denied him access to the army. Conway responded with a fervent letter protesting the "cool reception" and making a sneering comparison between Washington and Frederick the Great of Prussia, then considered the finest soldier in Europe.[15]

The battle for control of the army was joined. Reports of the cabal spread, still mostly whispered but more frequent and more insistent. Lafayette called Conway "an ambitious and dangerous man" scheming against Washington. Dr. Craik, Washington's old friend, singled out Mifflin: "He is plausible, sensible, popular and ambitious, [and] takes great pains to draw over every officer he meets with to his own way of thinking."[16] Others shared Craik's suspicions. Congress President Henry Laurens's son, John, an aide to Washington, wrote to his father about "a certain party, formed against the present commander in chief, at the head of which is General Mifflin." Another aide also targeted Mifflin, charging that he was taking "great pains . . . to swell the character of the Northern hero [Gates] and to depreciate that of our worthy general." Gates, the aide insisted, "is but a puppet." Newspaper articles celebrated Gates's military genius; others published forged letters that purported to show Washington disloyal to the patriot cause.[17]

Washington's counterattack included an objection by nine brigadier generals to Conway's promotion. In a stern statement to Henry Laurens, Washington defended his chilly treatment of Conway: "My feelings will not permit me to make professions of friendship to a man I deem my enemy."[18]

Conway proved an unfortunate ally for Mifflin and Gates. In a contest of subtle maneuvers, his tongue and pen were too sharp, his attitude too haughty, and his friends too few. By one account, he referred to Washington's military talents as "miserable indeed," and he accused the commander of subjecting him to "an odious and tyrannical inquisition." Such personal gibes repelled those who knew Washington. The commander in chief might be portrayed as ineffective, but not as despotic. Henry Laurens determined that the European officers disliked Conway, while Washington's allies denounced the Irishman. "A man of much intrigue and little judgment," sniffed Nathanael Greene, while Hamilton called him "vermin."[19]

In early January, Washington answered Gates, explaining that he had initially assumed that the northern commander had intended to warn him "against a secret enemy," meaning Conway. With mock regret, the commander in chief added, "in this, as in other matters of late, I have found myself mistaken." What could Gates answer? His letter in early December had blithely ignored any injury to Washington from the Conway episode.[20]

On February 10, Washington received his most welcome visitor of the season: Martha arrived with her enslaved servants. Although not even headquarters was comfortable at Valley Forge, Martha likely enjoyed the change of scene. Her favorite sister, Anna Maria Bassett, had died two months before, another hard loss after the wrenching death of daughter Patsy. The headquarters already overflowed with the large general, his five aides, and a stream of visitors and messengers. Washington allotted an upstairs room to Martha, where she could receive the wives of the senior officers. For dinners and evening conversation, Washington had a log dining room built as an annex. There was no dancing, no card playing, "no amusement of any kind, except singing." Visitors were coaxed to offer a song or two.[21]

While Martha settled in, Gates and Mifflin and Conway used their new powers at the Board of War to press two initiatives. The first went swimmingly; they persuaded Congress to adopt a reorganization of the failing quartermaster department that gave the board control of that key function. Called a "power grab" in a recent study, the change left Washington at the board's mercy for transport whenever he wished to move his troops.[22] The second initiative, however, contributed to the board's undoing: a plan to invade Canada. Lafayette, Washington's favorite, would be the nominal leader of the invasion, but Conway was to control it.

∽

The American assault on Quebec in late 1775 had involved a punishing winter march with a high desertion rate and then a failed assault, followed by captivity for survivors. The decision to repeat the exercise two years later was mystifying. Pointing to the first assault on Quebec and General Burgoyne's failure at Saratoga, delegate Francis Dana of Massachusetts asked why anyone would want to mount another "distant expedition[] across an inhospitable wilderness where there is but one road by which to advance or retire? Is not the very season against us?" Nevertheless, Gates, Mifflin, and the Board of War embraced the plan.[23]

From Albany, Lafayette was to lead 3,000 men in sleds across frozen Lake Champlain, then on to Canada! With Lafayette as the expedition's figurehead, French-speaking Canadians were supposed to rally to the American cause. As second-in-command, Conway was to be the real leader. The Canadian conquest would show that only Washington's fatal caution was preventing American arms from sweeping the British into the sea.[24]

Among the plan's flaws was its assumption that Lafayette, who lusted after glory, was easily manipulated. Though young, Lafayette was a titled aristocrat who thought for himself and cherished the commander in chief. Even before the Canada plan surfaced, Lafayette had written angrily to Washington about "stupid men who without knowing a single word about war undertake to judge you . . . they are infatuated with Gates." He smelled the trap at once.[25]

Washington publicly shrugged off the Canadian expedition as a project of the Board of War. To Gates, he wrote that he wished success for the effort, but knew so little about it that "it is not in my power to pass any judgment on the subject." To a friend, he confided that the idea was "the child of folly," but "as it is the first fruit of our new board of war I did not incline to say anything against it."[26]

Lafayette accepted the command, but rejected Conway as his second. If Conway were retained, he threatened, he would return to France to inform "the world at large . . . of the unmerited insult offered the general and commander-in-chief." The Board of War and Congress blinked; they replaced Conway.[27]

When Lafayette arrived in Albany, he discovered such poor preparation that his howls could be heard at the Board of War in York. He had found, Lafayette wrote, a "hell of blunders, madness and deception." He denounced Gates as "the greatest poltroon in the world," who knew less about America's northern forces than Lafayette himself had learned in two days. Promised 2,500 soldiers, Lafayette found fewer than half that number, mostly boys or men past sixty. Of the eight hundred sleds needed, he had fifty. There were, however, "an immense number of debts," combined with "the want of clothing, want of men, want of everything indeed to be wanted." The expedition, Lafayette concluded, was "madness and treachery."[28]

Gates, Mifflin, and Conway looked like fools. Worse, they discovered that while they had been planning the Canada frolic, Washington had been winning congressional support. By early March, Congress killed the Canada expedition; thereafter, Congress reversed itself and stripped the Board of War's control over the quartermaster function.[29]

౿

One step in winning congressional support involved a wound Gates inflicted on himself and his co-schemers. When Gates took over the Board of War in mid-January, he brought with him the item that first brought the cabal to Washington's notice: Conway's letter disparaging Washington. Though Gates had assured Washington that the letter was "perfectly harmless," President of Congress Henry Laurens disagreed. After reviewing the letter, Laurens confirmed that Conway did not write the precise words quoted in Lord Stirling's note to Washington; rather, Laurens reported that the actual letter was "ten times worse in every way." Gates's credibility with Laurens and Congress declined precipitously.[30]

Though Laurens and Washington had spent little time with each other, they shared a mutual respect. The South Carolinian had grown rich trading in guns, rum, rice, indigo, and slaves. John Adams praised him for "a clear head and a firm temper . . . as good a member as any we ever had in Congress." After serving as a delegate for only four months, Laurens was unanimously voted president of Congress. By chance, or perhaps by design, he and Washington shared a connection through John Laurens, Washington's aide. In letters to his father, John deplored Gates, Mifflin, and Conway, and praised the commander in chief.[31]

The elder Laurens needed little persuading about Washington's merits, or the perfidy of those scheming against him. "His virtues are the only present props of our cause," Laurens wrote before Brandywine, and that defeat did not shake his view. In early January, he assured his son that the general's "magnanimity, his patience will save his country and confound his enemies," then scorned Washington's opponents in Congress as "prompters and actors, candle-snuffers, shifters of scenes and mutes." The elder Laurens called Conway a "first rate rascal."[32]

By late January, Gates was backing away from Mifflin and Conway. In a letter to Washington, he protested that he had "hardly the smallest acquaintance" with Conway, though still insisted that Conway's letter was harmless. He never did, however, show the letter to Washington.[33]

The commander's grudging response came two weeks later. By concealing

Conway's letter, he noted, Gates had allowed people "to conjecture the worst." Washington unloaded on Conway, who combined the "malignity of detraction, and all the meanness of intrigue, to gratify the absurd resentment of disappointed vanity, or to answer the purposes of personal aggrandizement, and promote the interests of faction." Most of the army's officers remained steadfast behind Washington. As one wrote in April, "the most distant hint against his excellency is looked upon as treason, and resented by almost every officer." Through February, congressional sentiment turned sharply against Gates and his partners.[34]

Gates's star further dulled when the terms of the British surrender at Saratoga turned out to include unwise and expensive elements. Then came the harebrained Canadian invasion. If that was the best idea the Board of War could offer, it should not command a platoon, much less the entire army. Nathanael Greene gloated in early February that the schemers "begin to be most horribly frighted."[35]

Gates gave up the game in a February 19 letter to Washington. "I solemnly declare," he wrote, "that I am of no faction" and had written nothing "offensive to your excellency." Washington agreed to bury the matter in oblivion, "as far as future events will permit." In other words, Washington would be watching Gates, very closely.[36]

A few days later, Washington allowed himself to enjoy his adversaries' troubles. Gates, he wrote to an aide, was tangled in "the most absurd contradictions," while Mifflin had to explain his actions as quartermaster general ("a scrape he does not know how to get out of"). Conway was in Albany on the Canadian expedition, "which all the world knew . . . was not practicable." In April, Conway submitted his resignation from the army; Congress accepted it on the day it was received. Gates moved from the Board of War to a quiet command in Boston. Challenging Washington had not turned out well for any of them.[37]

Some historians have concluded that however much Mifflin and Conway and Gates maneuvered, they posed little threat to Washington. Some contemporaries thought that the cabal had small influence in Congress.[38]

Washington, however, bitterly resented the schemers. The plan, he wrote, was for Gates to be "exalted, on the ruin of my reputation and influence," while Mifflin "bore the second part in the cabal" and Conway "was a very active, and malignant partisan." An aide reported that the cabal haunted Washington. "I have never seen," he wrote, "any stroke of ill fortune affect the General in the manner that this dirty underhanded dealing has done."[39]

Washington had moved deliberately against the cabal, recognizing that Congress would decide the contest and relying on the influence of President

Laurens and other delegates.[40] One key to Washington's success was his quick response to the early November warning from Lord Stirling, when Washington implicitly called on Conway to explain himself. Gates and Conway never could find an honorable explanation for denigrating the commander in chief. Equally important, Washington never overplayed his hand. Holding his temper and staying at his post, he steadily gained a credibility advantage until his adversaries undid themselves. It was a deft political triumph.

∾

While fending off the cabal, Washington also was contending with his second adversary: the misery of the army. He had to find food and clothes for "our sick naked, our well naked, our unfortunate men in captivity naked!" He worried about rising desertion and weak recruitment. Officers demanded to go home or bickered over promotions. At the same time, he had to prepare the army for the 1778 campaign. He needed a victory to hold the army together and quell his critics. Another defeat might doom the cause.[41]

CHAPTER 34

The Second Adversary: "This Fatal Crisis"

Washington called it "this fatal crisis." It began in the second week of February 1778 when numbing cold moved into Valley Forge, followed by heavy snow, then torrential rains. Roads became swamps. Streams flooded. Nothing moved in or out of camp. The clanking gears of the army's supply system seized up. For days, thousands ate no meat.[1]

When the starving time began, Washington reported that "the murmurs on account of provisions are become universal," and the "spirit of desertion among the soldiery never before rose to such a threatening height." A week later, he struggled for words to capture his desperation. "For some days past," he wrote, "there has been little less than a famine in camp." Officers wondered whether the army would end with a final spasm of desertions, or a bloody mutiny.[2]

The soldiers' needs extended beyond food. Almost 4,000 of them, more than a third of the camp, were unfit for duty due to lack of clothes or shoes. Freezing men stripped clothes from the sick and the dead, heedless of diseases that might come with the garments. Officers paraded in coats fashioned from blankets.[3] Angry men confronted officers. The wonder was that so many men stayed, performed their duties, and hoped for better days. Washington honored them. "Naked and starving as they are," he wrote, "we cannot eno[ugh] admire the incomparable patience and fidelity of the soldiery, that they have not been, ere this, excited by their sufferings, to a general mutiny and dispersion."[4]

When the roads dried out, drastic measures were needed. The countryside had to feed and clothe the army. Washington hated taking from private citizens. It inflicted suffering on the old, women, and children, making them resent the army, while also fostering among soldiers "a disposition to licentiousness." He deplored the contradiction between fighting for the people's liberty and taking their property. But he had no choice.[5]

Washington turned, as he often did, to Nathanael Greene, sending him with 2,000 men to forage through New Jersey. The pickings were slim. "The country has been so gleaned," Greene cautioned, "that there is but little left in it." The Continentals were not the only soldiers scrounging for food. When ice in the Delaware River interrupted shipping, the British, too, needed forage for animals and food for soldiers. Nevertheless, if Greene failed, the war effort might whimper to an end. While his expedition lasted, at least there would be 2,000 fewer mouths to feed in camp.[6]

Greene disliked the assignment. "The inhabitants cry out and beset me from all quarters," he reported, but "like Pharaoh I harden my heart." He scoured forests and swamps for hidden livestock and wagons. His men left receipts for what they took so long as the items had not been concealed; he did not reimburse for anything that had been hidden. After several days, he began sending provisions to camp.[7]

Greene, like Washington, lauded the soldiers' fidelity. After "seven days without meat and several days without bread," he recalled, their "patience and moderation . . . does the highest honor to the magnanimity of the American soldiers." On the seventh day, "they came before their superior officers and told their sufferings in as respectful terms as if they had been humble petitioners for special favors."[8]

With the provisions sent by Greene, with the weather relenting and the roads opening, the Continental Army took a step back from dissolution. By March 1, Washington even inserted a small joke in his daily orders. "Occasional distress for want of provisions and other necessities is a spectacle that frequently occurs in every army," he wrote, then added, "perhaps there never was one which has been in general so plentifully supplied in respect to the former as ours."[9] Neither wry remarks nor expeditions like Greene's were substitutes for reliable supplies of food, clothing, and equipment. Washington had to repair the system.

∽

He needed congressional action, but he could not force the legislative response. Deference to Congress was a hallmark of his leadership. Early in his command, he wrote that "if the Congress will say 'Thus far and no farther you shall go,' I will promise not to offend whilst I continue in their service." After fifteen years as a burgess, he knew the challenges of building consensus among legislators with different experiences and attitudes. He also appreciated that today's opposition might reflect a lack of information rather than inveterate hostility, and that a legislature may distract itself with small matters to avoid difficult ones.[10]

Because his army was always in the field or in camp, Washington used letters and reports to inform Congress and urge measures it should consider. He wrote passionate letters to York, but the situation at Valley Forge was too dire for gradual education. He decided to bring Congress to the army so he could persuade the decisionmakers face-to-face.

On Christmas Day, he asked Delegate Elbridge Gerry of Massachusetts to devote "particular attention" to sending a congressional committee to camp "to consult with me, . . . on the best regulations, arrangements, and plans for the next campaign." The committee's scope, he continued, should be "general and extensive."[11]

This Congress was a shadow of the distinguished assembly Washington had joined three years before. Meeting in York's redbrick courthouse, only two of the current delegates had served in June 1775, when Washington became commander in chief. An observer wrote in February 1778 that "all but a few of the men of superior minds had disappeared." Henry Laurens complained that "we want genius, insight, foresight, fortitude and all the virtuous powers of the human mind." Debates, he lamented, ran "into weeds of unmatured conversations from a want of able members."

Though the delegates did not impress, they worked long days. Committee meetings and conferences began early in the morning. Convened by ten or eleven, Congress sat until one or two p.m. After a dinner break, it sat again until eight or nine p.m., at which point the delegates addressed, according to Laurens, "business out of doors." They slept in spare rooms around town, starved for information in a region with no newspaper.[12]

Laurens despaired at the sparse attendance. Eighteen months before, fifty-six delegates had approved the Declaration of Independence. Now Laurens was lucky to have twenty present; often only fifteen arrived. Important matters "are neglected or slovened over, partly from a want of numbers and partly of abilities." He believed that "thousands and millions have been wasted . . . from a want of proper men and sufficient numbers to attend the affairs of the Treasury." High absenteeism meant, he added, "there are not men enough even for the drudgery of committees."[13]

This last limitation was disabling. As the only organ of national government other than the army, Congress addressed a blizzard of minute matters. In a three-day period in November 1777, it approved individual payments of as little as $40, confirmed officer promotions, transferred soldiers, assigned one officer to a new post, and bought a horse for another. Simultaneously, Congress had to wrestle with complex military, financial, and diplomatic issues that would determine the nation's survival.[14]

To manage its work, Congress shunted many matters to temporary committees consisting of three delegates, or occasionally five. The committees launched and expired at a mad pace. In 1777, Congress created 114 committees; the following year, there were 253. Congress preferred short-term bodies because permanent committees would consolidate their power; with short-term committees, however, delegates developed little expertise.[15] Congressional expertise also suffered from the states' rotation of their delegates; few served for as long as two years. "The members of Congress are so perpetually changing," Richard Henry Lee wrote to his brother, "that it is of little use to give you their names."[16]

Congressional dysfunction slowed completion of the Articles of Confederation, the document that would create a rudimentary government for the new nation. The draft articles lingered for sixteen months until Congress approved them in November 1777 and sent them to the states for approval.[17]

Though Washington hated dealing with the crazy quilt of congressional committees, he had to work through Congress in order to circumvent a Board of War controlled by his adversaries, Mifflin and Gates. In the second week of January, Delegate Gerry advised him that a special committee would address the military situation, as Washington had requested. The committee was to have three members from the Board of War and four congressional delegates.[18]

It was called the "Committee in Camp" because it spent almost six weeks at Valley Forge. In a crucial reversal, Congress removed the members of the Board of War from it—Gates and Mifflin could hardly confer productively with Washington while they were maneuvering to overturn his control of the army—so Congress added two more delegates. The committee's large size emphasized its importance. For regional balance, it had two New Englanders, three delegates from the middle states, and a Southerner. The committee's roster should have encouraged Washington. Two members had served in the military, while three were friends. But Washington did not know the chairman, Francis Dana of Massachusetts, who had been in Congress for only two months.[19]

A slightly built lawyer, the thirty-five-year-old Dana came from a region often skeptical of Washington. His fellow Massachusetts delegate James Lovell hoped the committee would "rap a demigod [Washington] over the knuckles." Dana's friend John Adams had welcomed Gates's success at Saratoga with the observation, "Now we can allow a certain citizen to be wise, virtuous, and good, without thinking him a deity or savior." Washington would spare no effort to win Dana's support.[20]

COURTESY OF THE MOUNT VERNON LADIES' ASSOCIATION

Bust by Jean-Antoine Houdon (1785)

When the committee members reached Valley Forge on January 24, Washington handed them a 13,000-word report detailing necessary reforms. Drafted by Hamilton, the sharpest writer on Washington's staff, the report integrated Washington's ideas with some from senior generals. It also reflected Washington's years of experience in organizing local government services through the Fairfax County Court and managing a large labor force at Mount Vernon. The report began with Washington's hardheaded philosophy of government: "With far the greatest part of mankind, [self]-interest is the governing principle." Patriotism and idealism may motivate people for a time, but "are not of themselves sufficient." The army and its officers had to be paid, and paid fairly.

To improve the lot of private soldiers, the report called for reorganizing the commissary and quartermaster corps and establishing regular paydays. The report also urged a yearly draft of soldiers rather than voluntary enlistments; it called for more cavalry, consolidating undersized regiments, adopting standards for promotions, and promulgating a "uniform system of manual maneuvers." Its most controversial passage insisted that Congress must, as the British did, provide half-pay for officers after the war, plus pensions for widows of officers who died in the service. Without those changes, the report concluded, the nation faced "dissolution of the army . . . [or] its operations must infallibly be feeble, languid and ineffectual."[21]

After digesting the report, the committee members rolled up their sleeves. They reviewed internal documents and financial ledgers. They consulted at length with Washington and other senior officers. They addressed the commissary function, forage for draft animals, recruitment, the quartermaster's wagon management, the paymaster's records, the clothier general's meltdown, regimental organization, and officer promotions.[22]

Most important, the committee saw suffering soldiers every day. Its arrival in camp coincided with the starving time of mid-February. Determined to see conditions for himself, Dana rode through camp, stopping to speak with soldiers. He noted that the lack of clothes made many soldiers "totally unfit for duty," but that was not the worst:

> Upon an average every regiment had been destitute of fish or flesh four days. . . . nor have they assurance of regular supplies in future. We do not see from whence the supplies of meat are to come. The want of it will infallibly bring on a mutiny . . . Sunday morning Colonel Brewer's regiment rose in a body and proceeded to General Patterson's quarters, . . . and threatened to quit the army. . . . The same spirit was rising in other regiments, . . . 'tis probable this army will disperse if the commissary department is so damnably managed.[23]

This confirmation of Washington's reports came not from an officer on his staff, but from a New England lawyer who was praised as "most thorough and active" by James Lovell, a Washington critic. Dana's reports gave crucial weight to Washington's demands.[24]

Because the soldiers' hardships were new to committee members, their accounts were powerful. Gouverneur Morris, a committee member, described "a skeleton of an army . . . in a naked starving condition, out of health, out of spirits." Lacking horses and wagons, the committee wrote, the soldiers "without a murmur patiently yoke themselves to little carriages of their own making, or load their wood and provisions on their backs." Morris raged to New York's governor that "an American army in the bosom of America is about to disband for the want of somewhat to eat," adding that the army had been "upon the point of disbanding three times. One dangerous mutiny quelled with difficulty." One report was so moving that President Laurens broke down while reading it to the delegates. "Your description of the miseries of the Army," Laurens told Dana, "affected me beyond common feeling."[25]

After two weeks, the committee began sending recommendations back to York. It was surprised by its conclusions about the commissary function. "We had presumed that there must have been some mistake or fraud," they reported, but the problem was "real scarcity." Other causes, they noted, were currency depreciation, insufficient funds, a shortage of wagons (the quartermaster's responsibility), and the incompetence of the department head, Buchanan.[26]

By the second week of March, Congress adopted commissary reforms that Gouverneur Morris had prepared, including an increase in long-term purchasing and more authority for the department head. Congress also granted commissaries a commission on purchases, to encourage more energetic acquisition efforts.[27] Finally, the committee recommended replacing the Commissary General. Jeremiah Wadsworth, formerly the deputy, took over in April, when death and desertion had shrunk the army to about 7,000. In late spring, provisions began to flow more predictably.[28]

When Dana's committee turned to the quartermaster, it found that corruption had crept in while Mifflin had neglected the office: "The number of little piddling pilfering plunderers . . . is sufficient almost to form an army." Commissions paid on purchases had reached 5 percent.[29] Dana's committee recommended more centralized control and lower commissions while attacking the structure imposed by Mifflin though the Board of War. But the key change was appointment of a vigorous quartermaster. For that position, the committee nominated Washington's solution to many problems, Nathanael Greene.[30]

Greene accepted the position only because Washington insisted. Greene sought glory, not bureaucratic distinction. "Nobody," he complained, "ever heard of a quartermaster." The job was not only obscure but difficult. "It is a very disagreeable department," he wrote, "rendered still more so by mismanagement, by depreciation of our currency and the resources of the country being inadequate to our immediate wants." Yet Greene transformed the service while Congress enacted the committee's recommendations to free it from supervision by the Board of War.[31]

Washington hoped for two more major reforms from Congress, both of which the committee recommended: replacing voluntary enlistments with an annual draft, and the half-pay benefit for officers after the war, with a pension for officers' widows. Dana returned to York in early March to press those recommendations, but with little success.[32] Congress approved drafts to fill the army, but only state governments could implement them. Many state legislators shrank from imposing compulsory military service. Virginia's draft produced few soldiers while triggering a riot in one county.[33]

For weeks, Congress disputed the half-pay/pension issue in what President Laurens called "long and fervorous arguments." Most delegates wanted to support Washington, but feared the cost. Some thought it would violate republican principles by nurturing a permanent army and favoring officers over rank-and-file soldiers, who received much lower pay. Even Laurens, usually Washington's enthusiastic advocate, balked at the proposal.[34]

Despite Congress's reluctance, Washington was adamant. "The salvation of the cause," he told Laurens, "depends upon it." In mid-May, Congress approved a compromise: half-pay for seven years after the war ended, long enough for former officers to regain their incomes in private life. Washington announced the action in his daily orders to the army, and hoped it would "quiet in a great measure the uneasinesses."[35]

Although Washington did not win every reform, he won enough to stabilize the army. The essential step was bringing the congressional committee to Valley Forge, exposing them to his intense feeling for the soldiers' welfare and the power of his presence and personality. The camp's sights, sounds, and smells confirmed his pleas. With the committee on his side, Washington was able to win reorganization of the army, and also to suffocate the efforts by Mifflin, Gates, and the Board of War to gain control of it. By late spring, Washington had solidified both the army's management and his own position.[36]

CHAPTER 35

The Third Adversary: The British

Vanquishing the Conway Cabal and repairing the army's supply system were necessary steps. To win the war, however, Washington wanted a professional army. Local militias, in his experience, could not endure the brutality of combat.

Warfare required training. Because muskets were not accurate, musket fire had to be concentrated in volleys, a line of soldiers firing at the same moment, so the sheer weight of lead screaming across the field would damage the enemy. The cumbersome act of reloading could take thirty seconds or more, so sequenced firing allowed some soldiers to shoot while others reloaded. If volleys flagged, opposing troops would charge with bayonets. A bayonet fight was sheer butchery, slashing blades and trampled men.

Few American units had mastered battle tactics beyond conducting ambushes or skirmishing from cover. Small-scale engagements could extend the war, but not win it. Unless the Americans had the advantages that Gates enjoyed at Saratoga, or the benefit of surprise they had at Trenton, they could not prevail. They could not move across a battlefield quickly, in formation; or move from column to line and back to column; or move diagonally, then form for volley firing. No American general, certainly not Washington, was a true master of formal drill.

Deep in the misery of February, no one at Valley Forge expected that the starving Continentals would learn those tactics over the next three months. Still less did they expect their instructor to be a stout, middle-aged, gay German with little English and an Italian greyhound who howled balefully at off-key singing. Friedrich Wilhelm von Steuben, son of a Prussian officer, had served with Frederick the Great. After soldiering for other princes, he connected in Paris with American diplomats who were prowling for army officers. Ben Franklin packaged Steuben as a Prussian lieutenant general of noble blood, a charade that held up fairly well.[1]

With bluff charm, Steuben sold himself to Congress. He was shrewd enough not to demand a specific rank or even pay, asking only to be "reimbursed" for income lost by leaving Europe. His apparent modesty distinguished him from other Europeans.

At Valley Forge in late February, the Prussian impressed Washington and everyone else. "Baron Steuben has had the fortune to please uncommonly for a stranger," John Laurens wrote to his father. "All the general officers who have seen him are prepossessed in his favor." He rode through camp, translators by his side, to quiz the soldiers, one of whom recalled him as "a perfect personification of Mars. The trappings of his horse, the enormous holsters of his pistols, his large size, and his strikingly martial aspect." American soldiers impressed Steuben. "No European army," he later wrote, "could have been kept together under such dreadful deprivations."[2]

Washington asked Steuben to create a uniform manual of drill, appointing him acting inspector general, responsible for training; ironically, Thomas Conway still was inspector general in name, but Conway was not in camp and never would be so long as Washington commanded. After nearly three years of war, the Continentals lacked a uniform method for training troops; equally missing was a shared vocabulary of commands. When regiments mixed together during battle, which always happened, officers could not be sure their orders were understood. Steuben reduced how many orders soldiers had to recognize and how many movements they had to learn. Every evening, staff officers translated his French manuscripts into English.[3]

In mid-March, Steuben began drilling a model company, drawn largely from Washington's personal guard. The twice-daily sessions became the best entertainment in camp. Officers and soldiers clustered at the parade ground to watch the red-faced German bellow orders in foreign tongues, followed by English translations. He pantomimed correct positions and movements, using his hands to adjust soldiers' arms, feet, or heads. His favorite English word was "Goddamn," sprinkled liberally among profanities in several languages.[4]

Steuben quickly understood his soldiers. "The genius of this nation," he observed, "is not in the least to be compared with that of the Prussians, Austrians or French." With Europeans, he gave an order and they obeyed. But with Americans, "I am obliged to say: 'This is the reason why you ought to do that': and then he does it."[5]

Steuben began at the beginning, with how to stand at attention and at parade rest, then how to turn left and right or reverse direction. He taught a standard marching pace and a quick-step rate. He marched the men in columns, several abreast; until then, the Continentals' principal method of advance had been single file, which left them more vulnerable to attack. He emphasized navigating across the terrors of a battlefield under discipline, fighting as a unit, not as a mob that might flee, as likely to fire on friends as on foes. He showed how to move from column to line and back, to move obliquely, to wheel left and right. He taught the most efficient way to load, fire, and reload, skirmishing techniques, advancing and retreating by platoons. He insisted on fire discipline, shooting only when ordered, which created the heavy volleys needed to break the enemy. Finally came the bayonet charge, preparing the Continentals to turn this chilling maneuver on their enemies. Steuben's message was that war was a skill that required thought and preparation, not just a brief chapter in the life of a citizen-soldier. Once a unit mastered Steuben's lessons, he moved on to another unit while the newly educated soldiers instructed others, spreading the training through the army.[6]

MAJOR GENERAL BARON STEUBEN.

Pub.ᵈ Mav 15ᵗʰ 1783, by R.Wilkinson Nº 58, Cornhill, London.

COURTESY OF THE LIBRARY OF CONGRESS

Baron Friedrich Wilhelm von Steuben

Steuben taught values as well as skills. Prussian officers conducted drill, but sergeants did the job in the British Army, and that had been true for the Continentals too; drill had been beneath an officer's dignity. But here was a general who had served Frederick the Great, festooned with decorations, who was absorbed in drill, swearing when the men blundered and gleeful as a child when they got it right. There was something winning about the fat man sputtering with frustration, his interpreter struggling to translate a string of curses.[7] His written manual stressed an officer's responsibility for his men. The officer, he wrote, should know each soldier by name and visit those who were sick or wounded. Each junior officer "should endeavor to gain the love of his men, by his attention to everything which may contribute to their health and convenience."[8]

Steuben extended that concern to his subordinates. For one dinner at his quarters, he required that all arrive in torn clothes, an act of solidarity with the camp's privations. The dinner, one recalled, was "tough beef-steaks and potatoes, with hickory nuts for our desserts." Lacking wine, they set coarse liquor aflame and "drank it up, flame and all. Such a ragged, and at the same time merry fellows, were never [before] brought together."[9]

Washington advanced Steuben rapidly. By the end of April, the Prussian was major general. Washington barred other officers from drilling their men, insisting that Steuben install a single system; Washington later ordered that all army units everywhere follow Steuben's manual. Washington had neither the experience nor the time to train the soldiers as Steuben could, but he recognized that the Prussian was teaching essential skills to his army.[10]

The transformation was striking. In early June, a member of the Board of War was "astonished at the progress he has made with the troops." Steuben gave the credit to the soldiers. They had, he wrote to President Laurens, made "a more rapid progress than any other army would have made in so short a time."[11]

With the weather warming, there was no time to waste. General Sir William Howe would not loiter in Philadelphia all summer. Congress directed Washington to convene a war council at Valley Forge before the fighting season arrived. By ordering Mifflin and Gates to attend, Congress made clear that they were Washington's subordinates.[12]

The commander considered moving against the British strongholds of New York and Philadelphia. His chief engineer reminded him that the Continentals should fight "protected by a natural or artificial fortification." Even after Steuben's training, facing off on open ground was not a good idea. Washington wrote up his ideas for the campaign. He asked his senior generals for their thoughts in writing.[13]

Then startling developments on the other side of the Atlantic overturned every expectation.

∾

The news arrived in mid-April. Parliament had enacted two laws. The first abandoned its power to impose any taxes on Americans except to regulate trade. The second appointed peace commissioners for America. Had Parliament taken those steps four years before, the war would not have happened.[14]

For Washington, the new laws were far too little, far too late. "Nothing short of independence," he wrote to a Virginia delegate, "can possibly do." Yet he feared that the British moves would "ensnare the people by specious allurements of peace." Peace without independence, he worried, "would be the source of perpetual feuds and animosities," particularly because of Britain's "love of tyranny and lawless domination." The British inevitably would seek again to "bend our necks to the yoke of slavery, . . . for her pride and ambition are unconquerable."[15]

Days after Washington wrote those words, more electrifying news arrived: France had signed a treaty with the infant United States. This changed everything.

From the war's onset, American leaders had longed for a French alliance. They avidly hoped for war to erupt between Britain and any other nation, but best of all with France. Since the end of the Seven Years' War in 1763, the French had rebuilt their military and navy, aiming to avenge their losses. The American rebellion offered an opening for that counterstroke. Though Washington and others worried that Americans hoped too hard for French deliverance, he had used the prospect of French intervention to cheer his army before the march to Valley Forge, predicting that the time "is not very distant" when France would fight Britain.[16]

News of the treaty, which would certainly be followed by a French declaration of war against Britain, brought jubilation in Congress and at Valley Forge. Congress ratified the treaty forty-eight hours after receiving it. "Joy sparkles in every eye," an officer wrote in camp. The tidings left Washington so lighthearted that he joined some soldiers in a game of wicket (an early form of cricket).[17]

The new alliance fundamentally shifted the strategic balance in favor of the Americans. The French could challenge British sea power, reducing British military options and improving the flow of supplies and trade to America. Moreover, any contest between France and Britain would focus on the Caribbean, where the sugar colonies of each nation offered the richest prizes on the planet; that would siphon British resources from the mainland. Admiral Lord Howe, the fleet commander and brother to General Howe, received an order to that effect, noting "the contest in America [was] a secondary consideration."[18]

The home government ordered two more strategic changes. First, it accepted Sir William Howe's earlier request to return to England, leaving Sir Henry Clinton in command. Howe was a skillful general and popular with his troops, though the suspicion has lingered for centuries that his lack of energy reflected an ambivalence about fighting Americans. Howe's successor, Clinton, was an able soldier but had a quarrelsome disposition; in his memoirs, he described himself as a "shy bitch." Clinton would have fewer successes than Howe had because the British reduced their army on the mainland. London ordered Clinton to abandon Philadelphia and concentrate his forces in New York, while transferring 8,000 men to Florida, the Caribbean, and Canada. By diverting British resources to other parts of the hemisphere, by relegating the American conflict to a secondary priority, France's entrance into the war dramatically improved American prospects.[19]

The news prompted each army to stage a public exercise: The Americans mounted a demonstration at Valley Forge called a "feu de joie," while British officers indulged in an extravaganza in Philadelphia to mark Sir William's departure. Though the two events occurred only twenty miles and a few days apart, they expressed unbridgeable differences between the combatants.

Held on May 5, the American *feu de joie* (which translates as "fire of joy"), celebrated the French alliance and the new competence of American arms. After morning services, the Continentals marched to the parade ground in their best dress.

As described by John Laurens, the men formed a double line "with admirable rapidity and precision." Artillery erupted in three rounds of thirteen shots each, thrice honoring each state. Then the infantry unleashed "running fire" musketry, with each man firing in turn down the army's first line, then back up the second line. That, too, was performed three times, in honor of the king of France, the friendly European powers, and the United States, and concluded in ecstatic huzzahs. Young Laurens exulted in "the order with which the whole was conducted—the beautiful effect of the running fire which was executed to perfection—the martial appearance of the troops." When the officers and the few ladies in camp gathered under awnings for refreshments, "triumph beamed in every countenance." The private soldiers ended their day with an extra ration of rum.[20]

After the winter's agonies, the display announced the Continentals' belief in their cause and in themselves. Even Washington indulged in optimism. "The game," he wrote to a friend, "seems now to be verging fast to a favorable issue, and cannot I think be lost, unless we throw it away." To another he marveled how the army's prospects "have so miraculously brightened." The general attended a soldier production of Addison's *Cato,* his favorite play and a reminder of the price men will pay to resist tyranny. President Laurens, however, kept a tight rein on his hopes. "There is blood much blood in our prospect," he warned Steuben, adding that Britain "will be very angry."[21]

The earnestness of the Continentals' *feu de joie* contrasted sharply with the imperial panache of Sir William's sendoff, called a "Mischianza," drawn from the Italian for "medley" or "mixture." The budget was breathtaking: Twenty-two senior officers each contributed £140, which translated to between a half million and a million dollars in today's money. They spent it all. Beginning at four p.m., four hundred guests on flatboats floated a mile down the Delaware, flags flying and music rising from three bands. Landing at an estate south of the city, they entered an amphitheater through two arches built for the occasion. Seven black-clad "Knights of the Burning Mountain" squared off against the same number of white-clad "Knights of the Blended Rose," for their ladies' honor. With trumpets blaring, they charged each other with lances, then fell to sword and hand-to-hand fighting until reaching the inevitable draw.

Ladies in Turkish costumes led the celebrants through another arch into the estate's garden and mansion, where they drank tea and lemonade while an orchestra played in a ballroom lined with eighty-five mirrors. At ten p.m., fireworks burst overhead, followed by more dancing and gambling.

The doors to the banquet hall opened at midnight. Eighteen chandeliers, each with twenty-four candles, dazzled the eye. African American servants in turbans and robes served at two immense tables that held more than a thousand dishes and fifty pyramids of sweetmeats, jellies, and cakes. The dancing continued until sunrise.[22]

At the *feu de joie,* the Continentals celebrated skills they had mastered. At the Mischianza, the elite flaunted its power and riches. To underscore the contrast, while the Mischianza's revelry prevailed, fifty American prisoners escaped a Philadelphia jail through a tunnel.[23] For the Continentals, the best feature of Sir William's departure was that it delayed the beginning of the campaign: Sir William had no appetite for battle in a war he was leaving. Every day of delay gave the Americans more time to train and organize.

❦

The British peace commissioners, led by Lord Carlisle, moved to open negotiations in early June, but the Americans were not interested.[24]

When the commissioners tried to send an emissary to York, Washington intercepted the man and sent him back. Congress said it would never discuss peace until Britain recognized American independence, or withdrew its fleets and armies. Lord Carlisle found his situation "a mixture of ridicule, nullity, and embarrassments," especially when news arrived (considerably exaggerated) that a French fleet hovered off the coast.[25]

The peace overture angered Washington. "They meant to drive us into what they termed rebellion," he fumed in a letter to Bryan Fairfax, to "strip us of the rights and privileges of Englishmen." With "this country deluged in blood," he asked, "what punishment is there in store for the men who have distressed millions—involved thousands in ruin—and plunged numberless families in inextricable woe?" Washington would never reconcile without independence.[26]

Looking forward to the campaign ahead, he felt the tide of war moving in his direction. His army was improved. The French were coming. And his command of the army was assured—at least until the next battle. By the end of May, more than 10,000 men crowded into camp, with more arriving every day.[27]

Planning to leave Valley Forge, Washington paid tribute to the dedication of the men whom John Laurens called "those dear ragged Continentals," the sight of whom brought "tears of blood." "No history," Washington wrote to a Virginia delegate in Congress, "can furnish an instance of an Army's suffering such uncommon hardships as ours have done, and bearing them with the same patience and fortitude." Now—before any French troops had arrived in America and before the British sent any of its soldiers to other theaters of war—he had to confront and defeat his principal adversary, the British Army.[28]

CHAPTER 36

Victory, He Said

In June 1778, the British commander, Sir Henry Clinton, had nearly as many problems as Washington did. London's order to abandon Philadelphia spread panic among loyalists, who feared retribution when patriots resumed control of the city. Viewing their quandary, a Hessian soldier recalled, "the heart of every honest man bled." Clinton decided to take the loyalists to New York by ship, a goodwill gesture that forced most of his army to march across hostile New Jersey, hauling its baggage. To protect the march, Clinton retained the troops that soon would be transferred to Florida, the Caribbean, and Canada. They could leave from New York.[1]

Of Clinton's nearly 20,000 men, about two-thirds were infantry. He had six elite regiments, beginning with the grenadiers, the tallest and toughest. Light infantry units, including Hessian jaegers, were trained to fight in irregular settings. Support units included cavalry and artillery.[2]

Yet the British had morale problems, starting at the top. With France in the war and the Americans "every day growing stronger in number, confidence and discipline," Clinton expected Britain to fare poorly. Evacuating Philadelphia felt like a defeat. Many soldiers who had found romance there chose to desert. Four hundred never left the city; six hundred more slipped away during the march. The army's column—soldiers plus 1,500 wagons plus 5,000 horses—stretched for twelve miles, vulnerable to desertion and ambush.

Washington's Continentals also totaled 15,000, including four artillery regiments. Tolerably well fed and well shod, newly trained, they still were not the equal of the enemy. Washington wanted to steal a victory to bolster spirits in the army and the nation, but he could win only if he fought a portion of

Clinton's army in a favorable situation. In short, he needed Clinton to make a mistake.[3]

In late spring, Washington regained the services of Major General Charles Lee, who could be a great help or an excruciating migraine. Lee had spent more than a year as a British prisoner following an early-morning capture at a New Jersey inn, while still in his nightclothes.

Treated well by his captors, Lee had flirted with treason, preparing for the enemy a plan for defeating the American rebellion. The British did not follow Lee's blueprint, yet the episode sorely compromised him after he was exchanged for a captured British officer. The enemy could reveal his disloyalty whenever they chose. That sword of Damocles, hanging over Washington's senior general, may have influenced the coming campaign. Indeed, when Lee had to swear anew that he had no allegiance to the British Crown, he specifically exempted the Prince of Wales from his oath. Washington chose to overlook that unsettling reservation.[4]

Lee's conduct required considerable overlooking. Washington mounted a formal dinner to welcome him in early April, giving Lee a chamber in his headquarters. Next morning, a visitor found Lee's chamber occupied by the smuggled-in wife of a British sergeant with whom Lee was intimate. Rejecting Steuben's training methods, Lee proposed to reorganize the army. Accompanied by "his usual train of dogs," he also disparaged the commander in chief, remarking that Washington "was not fit to command a sergeant's guard" and informing President Laurens that Washington "cannot do without me." Washington overlooked it all, awarding Lee command of the army's right wing for the new campaign.[5]

When Clinton's army began to move in mid-June, Washington posed six questions to his generals and requested written replies. It was the sort of deliberate procedure that spawned talk of him being indecisive. Yet having opinions in writing allowed Washington to study the reasoning of different advisers; it also ensured a record of who had recommended what, in the event of post-action finger-pointing.[6]

Most of the generals recommended avoiding a large battle, called a "general action." Knox and Charles Lee called it "criminal" to risk one. Outlier advice came from two of Washington's favorites, Lafayette and Greene, who urged a more aggressive course. After all, Greene wrote, Steuben had improved the army, so Washington should use it. Washington tended to agree. He resolved to shadow Clinton's march, watching for an opening to strike.[7]

For both armies, the advance became a gasping ordeal in heat that was infernal. Soldiers in woolen uniforms carried heavy packs and ten-pound muskets. Drenching thunderstorms turned roads into bogs that sucked at

Sir Henry Clinton

feet and wagon wheels, yet brought no relief. The heat and humidity returned in minutes, with swarms of hungry mosquitoes.

Marches began long before sunrise. By noon, the soldiers tumbled out of line to search for shade. Clinton, dragging what he called an "indispensably enormous provision train [that] necessarily clogged me," took whole days off to rest his men. Washington avoided overtaking the enemy, waiting for a moment that offered him an edge. A militia leader suspected that Clinton's slow pace was designed to invite an attack, that the armies were not playing cat-and-mouse but cat-and-cat.[8]

More than a thousand New Jersey militiamen harried the British, smashing bridges and felling trees across roads. They ambushed small groups and took potshots from behind cover. Each step, a Hessian officer recalled, "cost human blood." Clinton's great enemy, though, was the heat. Dozens collapsed and more deserted. The air, one Continental remembered, was "almost impossible to breathe." Greene compared the conditions to the Arabian desert. British and German soldiers, suffering more than the Americans, vented their frustration by looting and burning the farms and villages they passed.[9]

After a week, Washington convened another council. The enemy was nearing the Atlantic coast, where the Royal Navy would greet it. Time was growing short for a battle.

Most of the generals still favored defense. They recommended that a vanguard of 1,500 hover near the British and "act as occasion may serve." Charles Lee was even less warlike, proclaiming that the Americans should build a "bridge of gold" to hurry the British back to New York. Lee's advice disgusted Alexander Hamilton, who thought it worthy of a "society of midwives, and to them only."[10]

Washington's favorites—Lafayette and Greene, joined by Anthony Wayne—still wanted to fight. Greene again stressed political concerns: "People expect something from us and our strength demands it." Lafayette pressed to increase the advance guard to 2,500 men, adding that a general action "might be advantageous" under certain conditions. Wayne urged a vanguard of 3,000, and also favored a general action in proper circumstances.[11]

This sequence illustrates how Washington used his generals to frame and refine his own thoughts. If time allowed, he sifted all views, giving extra weight to those whose judgment he valued most highly. But Washington made the final decision; only he would answer for it. In the last week of June, he expanded the army's vanguard to 5,000 and sent it ahead to find a favorable opportunity for battle.[12]

Greene was right that the country expected the Continentals to fight, and to fight soon. Once the British reached New York, their navy could help them attack anywhere on the Atlantic coast, leaving Washington to scramble overland to oppose them. By increasing the vanguard to nearly half of his fighting power, Washington invited the enemy to wheel and face it, which Clinton wanted to do.

❧

On June 27, Clinton ordered another rest day. One day's march separated his army from nearly impregnable high ground; one more day would bring it to the ships that would ferry it to New York. The Americans, who also rested, had not yet challenged him. If there was to be an attack, it would come in the next twenty-four hours.[13]

For the two days before, command of the American vanguard had bounced crazily, thanks to Charles Lee. When Washington offered Lee the vanguard command, Lee spurned it as too small for an officer of his distinction.

Washington's second choice, Lafayette, leapt at the opportunity, then exhausted his men by marching too far ahead of the main army. Washington ordered Lafayette and the vanguard to rejoin the army at Englishtown. Then Lee changed his mind. Since the vanguard had grown to nearly 6,000, he decided it was "the most honorable command next to Commander in Chief." Refusing to command it, he admitted, had "an odd appearance"; unless he led the vanguard, he would be disgraced.[14]

Lafayette, chastened by his missteps, yielded graciously, saving Washington the choice between an overaggressive youngster and a seasoned officer with little interest in fighting. Washington did not know, of course, that Lee had previously advised the British on how they could win the war.[15]

During the rest day, Washington met with the vanguard's generals. He ordered Lee to attack unless there were "powerful reasons" not to. The other officers understood that they were to attack. Lee, however, later claimed that he had complete discretion to attack or not. In truth, he had some discretion. In 1778, aides on horseback carried battlefield communications. A messenger might spend an hour or more finding the message recipient, and a like time carrying a reply. Consequently, subordinate officers had to respond to developments that the commander could not know about. The extent of Lee's discretion, and how he exercised it, would become controversial. That afternoon before the battle, Lee chose not to reconnoiter the ground over which he would lead his men in the morning, even though it included uneven morasses and several creeks.[16]

At sunrise on June 28, the vanguard advanced tentatively. Lee soon lost control of it. For nearly seven hours, American detachments moved back and forth across largely open fields, sometimes maneuvering under Lee's orders, sometimes at the direction of subordinates. Sporadic firing broke out at times, notably at Monmouth Court House (since renamed Freehold), but nothing like a battle developed.[17]

By late morning, some commanders in the vanguard, flummoxed by incomplete or nonexistent orders from Lee, started to withdraw. The British rear guard included Clinton's finest troops: grenadiers, light infantry, and Hessian jaegers. Confronting a strong foe, unsure where some of his units were, Lee ordered a general withdrawal. Sweaty, thirsty, and worn, the Continentals neither fled nor retired in good order, but achieved something inbetween.[18]

Through the morning, Washington had advanced the balance of the army at a languid pace. He stopped for breakfast, taking time to write a letter to President Laurens that might have been composed on another day. Perhaps he was trying to save his troops' strength as temperatures soared. No news arrived from Lee. When Washington's messenger found Lee near Monmouth Court House and asked about the attack, Lee confessed that he "really did not know what to say."[19]

Washington confronts
General Charles Lee at Monmouth Court House.

Shortly after noon, the heat blistering, Washington was five miles from Monmouth Court House when he met Continentals retiring toward him. There had been no attack, he learned, and the British were close behind. The prospect loomed that the day would end quietly, charged off as another instance of hesitation by indecisive General Washington. Talk would revive of the wonders that Gates had worked at Saratoga. Washington spurred his horse forward.[20]

Lee met the commander in front of Perrine's Hill. Calling out before Lee could speak, Washington demanded, "What is the meaning of all this?" The Englishman, intimidated, did not answer. Washington—"in a great passion," according to an observer—repeated himself. Lee stammered out complaints about bad intelligence and officers who withdrew without orders, which left him no course but to order a general pullback. Lee unwisely reminded Washington that he had previously opposed an attack. The commander replied angrily that no matter what Lee's opinions were, Washington expected him to follow orders. The confrontation drew onlookers. Some remembered Washington at the edge of fury, but he had no time for temper.[21]

With his plans melting in the blazing sun, Washington had to halt the retreat. His army had to stand and fight. He gathered himself for his best afternoon as a battlefield commander, an inspired improvisation superior to most of his planned battles.

The British were a half mile away. He had fifteen minutes. He scanned the soggy morass behind him, the hill on one side. In front were rolling country, creeks, and more morass. He sent some retreating troops to the rear. They were spent, debilitated by eight hours of tramping through sizzling weather. He directed one of his fighting generals, Anthony Wayne, to take two battalions into woods on the left and attack from the flank when the British swept by.

The enemy was closing, fearsome grenadiers in the lead. Washington placed more troops behind a flimsy hedgerow partway up the rising ground. He turned to Lee, who had so disappointed him. Would Lee, he asked, command at the hedgerow and delay the enemy while Washington organized a defense atop Perrine's Hill? Lee pledged to be among the last to leave the field. Each turned to his task.[22]

To reach the hilltop, the British would have to cross a bridge and a morass, then charge uphill into the mouths of muskets and cannon. Washington placed Lord Stirling's men on his left with a ten-gun artillery battery, and Greene's troops on the right with more cannon. Washington stayed at the center, tall and determined. There was no confusion.

The British, who were accustomed to taking any field the Continentals held, attacked eagerly. Lee's men held the hedgerow for four volleys that inflicted damage, then withdrew. Wayne's force struck from the flank, punishing the grenadiers, who turned on them. In grim hand-to-hand fighting, they pushed the Americans back. The British climbed again, the scalding sun making their legs heavy. From the hilltop, massed volleys and roaring cannon stopped them cold. The British, unbelieving, wavered. Then back downhill they went, their dead and dying sprawled behind them.

Clinton halted his men and advanced his artillery, deciding against another uphill attack. He had only half his army with him. The other half had

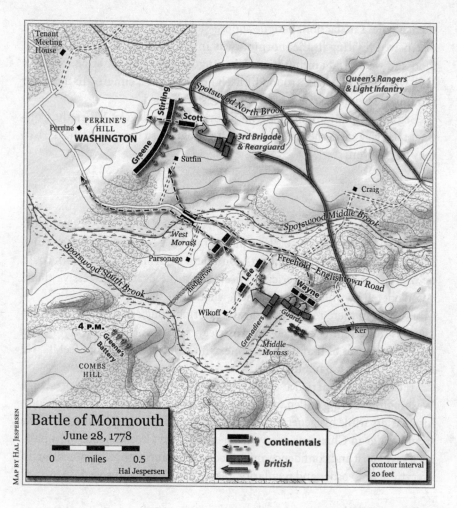

Battle of Monmouth
June 28, 1778

0   miles   0.5
Hal Jespersen

Continentals

British

contour interval
20 feet

MAP BY HAL JESPERSEN

marched off so early that morning that they were far from this fight. For the next two hours, Clinton and Washington waged an artillery duel at a distance of three-quarters of a mile. Washington would not come down. Clinton would not go up. The cannon boomed, over and over. With infantrymen flat on the ground, grateful to be prone, solid shot did little damage.[23]

A New Jersey officer pointed out to Washington some high ground on the right. Washington sent Greene there with four cannons to rake the British flank. By four thirty, Clinton had had enough. He withdrew. Washington sent regiments after the enemy. Wayne led a detachment against the grenadiers, who wheeled with all their pride and skill. Then Greene's hillside battery pivoted to support Wayne's men. The grenadiers yielded.[24]

As the sun set, the Americans held the field, a novel experience that gave them a quiet satisfaction. Fatigue suppressed elation, as did the expectation of renewed fighting in the morning. The improved supply services brought food and water and ammunition. Washington slept that night on Perrine's Hill, wrapping his cloak around himself and Lafayette, clinging to that high ground. He would be ready when the British returned.

Beginning at midnight, though, the British slipped away. When the Continentals awakened, they were alone. After yielding so many battlefields, had they finally won?

∾

Washington ordered no pursuit. His men could not do it. War is a hot business in good weather, as soldiers' pulses race and their body temperatures soar. In oppressive heat like that at Monmouth Court House, the strain could be overpowering. An American officer called the heat "so excessive that I could not tell by which the most died, whether by the heat or the balls."

Every man there recalled the heat. A German officer called it cruel; John Laurens settled for excessive. An American private insisted, "Everyone has heard of the heat of that day, but none can realize it that did not feel it." He called it "almost too hot to live in."[25]

The Americans carried a second powerful memory from the day: of George Washington rallying sullen, worn-out men. At Saratoga, Gates had stayed in his quarters while his generals led the fight. Not so George Washington. "The Commander in Chief was everywhere," Nathanael Greene wrote. "His presence gave spirit and confidence and his command and authority soon brought everything into order and regularity." Another aide was effusive:

> I do not think . . . the general ever in one day displayed more military powers . . . He gave a new turn to the action. He retrieved what had been lost. He was always in danger—examining the enemy's maneuvers—exhorting the troops—and directing the operation of his plans.[26]

The reckoning of dead and wounded was strongly in the Americans' favor. Washington reported fewer than 100 killed and 161 wounded, with 140 missing. (Many of the missing had collapsed from the heat and later recovered.) The British suffered double or triple those losses; sixty Britons died of heat prostration. A British general called Monmouth "a handsome flogging. We had not received such an one in America," while a Hessian commander recorded, "Today the Americans showed much boldness and resolution on all sides."[27]

On the day after, Washington thanked the soldiers and "the supreme disposer of human events." The Continentals took pride in having beaten Britain's best. A Washington aide described the foe as "the very flower of the British army." On the Fourth of July, the Continentals celebrated by bathing in the Raritan River, drinking double rations of rum, and turning out under arms for a thirteen-gun artillery salute and another demonstration of running fire.[28]

Washington quickly announced an American victory, writing to President Laurens on the morning after the battle. Two days later, he wrote a fuller account. Laurens printed it up as a handbill, which appeared verbatim in the *Virginia Gazette*. Washington's tone was factual and objective, his message simple: The Continentals won. Famished for victory, Congress rejoiced. It unanimously approved a resolution thanking Washington personally. Six weeks after the battle, newspapers still ran articles about it.[29]

Charles Lee, however, would not bask in victory's glow. For two days afterward, Washington made no comment on Lee's failure to mount a morning attack. After all, Lee had stood with the troops at the hedgerow. But Lee chose to accuse Washington of inflicting "a cruel injustice" on him. Washington's remarks on the battlefield, Lee wrote, "implied that I was guilty of either want of conduct, or want of courage." Lee requested that Washington charge him in a court-martial so Lee could vindicate himself.[30]

Washington obliged, accusing Lee of disobeying orders to attack, then making "an unnecessary, disorderly, and shameful retreat." Lee fired back on the same day, expressing the hope that Washington's "tinsel dignity" would not obscure "the bright rays of truth."[31]

Lord Stirling swiftly convened the court-martial. In twenty-four days of testimony, the officers closed ranks around Washington. The court convicted Lee and suspended him from the army for a year, though it removed the term "shameful" from the charges against him, and called the retreat disorderly "in a few instances." Washington confirmed the verdict and submitted it to Congress, which upheld it.[32]

Lee's erratic conduct at Monmouth will ever be puzzling. He scorned Washington's leadership, counseled against fighting, declined command of the vanguard and then demanded it. On the morning of battle, he neither planned nor executed an attack despite orders to do so. Then he served ably in the afternoon. When the battle was over, he begged to be court-martialed at a time when no Continental Army officer would rule against Washington's wishes. Determining the motives of long-dead figures is an iffy business. Hindsight allows the speculation that Lee, realizing he had lost Washington's confidence and was compromised by his conduct while a British prisoner, chose career suicide by court-martial. Washington would not miss Charles Lee, who never returned to the army.[33]

&

The Battle of Monmouth Court House did not cripple Clinton's army. After arriving in New York, the British general claimed credit for "this long and difficult retreat in the face of a greatly superior army." Some argue that the battle was a draw. But it marked the Continentals' emergence as a self-assured fighting force, capable of maneuvering on a battlefield and exploiting opportunities. Richard Henry Lee crowed over how the battle had been won, "the best troops of Britain beaten in an open field."[34]

Monmouth solidified Washington's position as commander in chief. He was again the hero, placing his men in position to win, willing them through the fight. Not since Trenton and Princeton had his generalship shown so well. His rivals were rivals no more. Gates was moldering in a quiet command; Mifflin was under investigation; Conway had been shot in the face in a duel and was headed to Europe; Charles Lee was out of the army.[35] Washington's position was unchallenged.

From his experience in the French and Indian War, Washington knew that individual victories did not win a war. In that earlier conflict, Britain lost repeatedly, then prevailed. Washington had lost battles in this war, but still was hopeful. Months before, Greene had explained to his brother why he expected victory. "We cannot conquer the British force at once," Greene admitted, but "they cannot conquer us at all." British power, he insisted, extended no farther than wherever their soldiers stood.[36]

The American cause was having a good summer. The French were entering the war, Philadelphia was recovered, and twelve states had ratified the Articles of Confederation (all but Maryland).[37] More hard times lay ahead. The fighting would shift to the south, and would be vicious. The stalemate around New York would bring winters of deprivation that were colder than Valley Forge. Victory would require crucial interventions by the French Army and Navy.

But in the first half of 1778, Americans completed essential steps toward becoming a nation that could fight its own battles and attract powerful allies. It was a nation that marched behind George Washington, who reinforced his claim on the trust of his soldiers, of Congress, and of ordinary Americans. He would never let it go.

Washington was forty when he posed for this painting by Charles Willson Peale, though he looks younger. He had left military service thirteen years before, yet he donned his old uniform as commander of the Virginia Regiment during the French and Indian War.

George Washington's half-brother Lawrence, fourteen years older, was his surrogate father, essential sponsor, and "best friend." Throughout Washington's life, he kept this portrait on a wall in his private office at Mount Vernon.

Sixteen months younger than Washington, Betty Washington Lewis remained close to her brother throughout their lives. She bore a striking resemblance to him.

Martha Washington at age twenty-six, while still married to Daniel Parke Custis. Two years later, after Custis's death, she married George Washington.

John Parke Custis, Martha Washington's son by her first marriage and heir to a sizable fortune, was a frustration to Washington because of his indifference to learning. Some thought him spoiled.

COURTESY OF THE MOUNT VERNON LADIES' ASSOCIATION

Martha ("Patsy") Parke Custis, Martha Washington's daughter from her first marriage, suffered from epilepsy. The Washingtons consulted numerous physicians in search of a cure and tried many possible therapies.

COURTESY OF THE MOUNT VERNON LADIES' ASSOCIATION

The reconstructed house at Ferry Farm, across the Rappahannock River from Fredericksburg, where Washington lived from the age of six until he leased Mount Vernon from his half-brother Lawrence's widow during the French and Indian War. COURTESY OF THE GEORGE WASHINGTON FOUNDATION

A print version of this painting of the Washington family—George and Martha with Martha's grandchildren, Eleanor Parke Custis and George Washington Parke Custis—gained wide circulation during his presidency. The enslaved servant to the side is Washington's valet, either William Lee or Christopher Sheels. COURTESY OF THE NATIONAL GALLERY OF ART

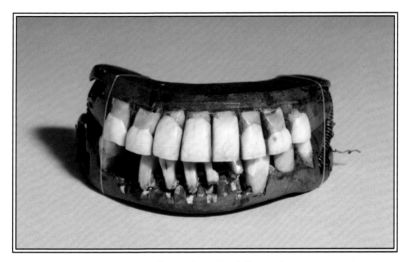

Having lost teeth steadily throughout his life, Washington as president endured the daily agony of inserting this metal-and-ivory contraption into his mouth. His false dentures included material from elephants and walruses, as well as human teeth purchased from the enslaved.

George William Fairfax was Washington's next-door neighbor at Belvoir estate and his intimate friend from youth until Fairfax moved to England shortly before the Revolutionary War. The Fairfax family was critical to Washington's advancement.

CAREER

|||||||||||||||||||||||||||||||||||||||

Lieutenant Governor Robert Dinwiddie of Virginia was an experienced merchant and colonial official. He appointed Washington to several key early posts, though their relationship ultimately became rancorous.

NPG/London

Called "that little thing upon the meadow" by an Indian ally, Washington's Virginians suffered a bloody defeat at Fort Necessity at the hands of a combined force of French and Indians in 1754. Washington signed a controversial capitulation in order to withdraw his surviving troops. Author's collection

In one of the worst failures of British arms in history, General Edward Braddock's column suffered roughly two-thirds casualties at the Battle of the Monongahela in 1755. Washington, in the thick of the hours-long battle, survived without a scratch. COURTESY OF THE WISCONSIN HISTORICAL SOCIETY

From 1759 to 1775, Washington served as a legislator—mostly in the Virginia House of Burgesses in this Williamsburg capitol building. He also served in the Continental Congress and the Second Virginia Convention of 1775. He was a legislator for several years longer than he held military positions.

Washington confided great trust in General Nathanael Greene of Rhode Island, often assigning him to the most difficult tasks facing the Continental Army.

Though portraits sometimes portrayed Washington as almost stout, this image by John Trumbull in 1780 matches more closely contemporary descriptions of him as slender but powerful.

After his great victory at Saratoga, Major General Horatio Gates angled to replace Washington as senior commander of the American forces, but Washington thwarted the effort.

The Battle of Monmouth Court House in late June 1778, on a day of scorching heat, brought Washington's Continentals the battlefield victory that they had prepared for at Valley Forge.

In late December 1783, Washington submitted to Congress his resignation from the Continental Army. By relinquishing his position and power, Washington won the trust of his countrymen and amazed many Europeans.

The Constitutional Convention adopted a charter of government with the key elements Washington sought: a central government that was stronger than the states, had the power to tax, and was led by a true executive department.

James Madison of Virginia, though a generation younger than Washington, was his closest political confidant through the critical period between the Revolutionary War and the adoption of the Constitution, and during the first year of Washington's presidency.

Washington relied on the country's first secretary of state, Thomas Jefferson, for diplomatic and political advice, but his fellow Virginian retired after four years in office, leaving the president with only Federalist advisers.

An impecunious immigrant
from the West Indies,
Alexander Hamilton served
as Washington's army
aide then his secretary
of the treasury. Though
Washington parted from
many political colleagues
throughout his long career,
he and Hamilton were
allies to the end.

Wife of the British
minister to the United
States at the end of the
Washington presidency,
Henrietta Liston
admired Washington
and shrewdly analyzed
his political methods.

GEORGE WASHINGTON PORTRAITS

Portrayed in uniform during the Revolutionary War, Washington's pose was confident and self-assured. Because of his calm demeanor at all times, according to a French officer, "Everyone regards him as his friend and father." Portrait by Charles Willson Peale, 1779–80.

COURTESY OF THE METROPOLITAN MUSEUM OF ART

This 1783 portrait by Robert Edge Pine records the advance of age on Washington's face and captures him in a contemplative moment.

COURTESY OF THE NATIONAL PORTRAIT GALLERY, SMITHSONIAN INSTITUTION

This 1789 miniature keeps President Washington in his military uniform but also shows some of the weariness that made him reluctant to assume the presidency.

Painted by a Swedish artist in 1794, near the end of Washington's presidency, this image emphasizes the president's vitality and intelligence.

Gilbert Stuart painted this iconic image of Washington and profited handsomely from the brisk market for Washington images.

CHAPTER 37

The Long, Bumpy Victory Lap

For three years after Monmouth, Washington warily watched the British Army in New York, but his troops fought only smaller encounters. The Continentals were too weak to mount an assault across waters controlled by the Royal Navy. The British had too few soldiers to attempt anything more than raids. Washington ached to do more. To win.

In an "anguish of soul," he wrote to his brother Jack in the summer of 1780: "I do lament that our fatal and accursed policy should bring the 6th of June upon us and not a single recruit to the army." He condemned the American effort as one of "slumber and sleep when we should be diligent in preparation":

> Pressed by irresistible necessity and when we can delay no longer—then [we] bring ourselves to the brink of destruction by expensive and temporary expedients. In a word, we have no system, and seem determined not to profit by experience. . . . Thus it is, one year rolls over another—and without some change—we are hastening to our ruin.[1]

The British, driven from New England early in the war and now bottled up in New York, launched a new Southern strategy, invading Virginia behind the turncoat Benedict Arnold, while Lord Charles Cornwallis landed troops in South Carolina. When General Gates confronted Cornwallis with a combination of militia and army units, the legend of Saratoga evaporated. The British humiliated his army, while Gates's flight from the battlefield did not end until he was 180 miles away. Through more bloody fighting, patched-together American forces led by Daniel Morgan and Nathanael Greene drained Cornwallis's strength and led the aggressive Englishman deep into North Carolina, then to coastal Virginia in the summer of 1781.

Cornwallis expected to meet his navy at Yorktown, but coordinated moves by Washington's army with French troops and a French fleet left Cornwallis surrounded and hopeless. After a short siege and some sharp fighting, the British surrendered. With the loss of a second army in America—first at Saratoga, now at Yorktown—the British appetite for war dissolved. Peace talks began in early 1782.[2]

Washington's joy over Yorktown was punctured by the death of his stepson, Jack Custis. The twenty-seven-year-old first joined the army at Yorktown, where he contracted fever and died shortly after the surrender, leaving behind four children younger than six. Martha's distress was, Washington wrote, "deep and solemn," and he extended to her and Custis's widow "every comfort in my power to afford them." Washington himself, according to one witness, "was uncommonly affected at [Custis's] death."[3]

For the first time during the war, Washington did not winter with his soldiers. After several weeks at Mount Vernon—his first extended stay there since 1775—he and Martha traveled to Philadelphia, where he marked his fiftieth birthday, an age neither his father nor three of his brothers had reached, and remained through the cold months. He no doubt welcomed the opportunity to escape the rigors of winter camp, but his decision to stay with Martha likely was connected to the death of her son, Jack. As when her daughter Patsy died, Washington made a point of staying close to Martha to help them both through a terrible grief.

Some thought Washington looked older that winter, but he retained the ability to reassure. A French officer praised his calm, adding, "Everyone regards him as his friend and father." Another observed, "He excites another sort of respect, which seems to spring from the sole idea that the safety of each person is attached to his person."[4]

Washington's commitment to fight Britain was undiminished. "My greatest fear," he wrote to Greene, "is that Congress . . . may think our work too nearly closed, and will fall into a state of languor and relaxation." He prepared for an active campaign in 1782, but the fighting was over. The British recalled Clinton, the fifth general felled by the Virginian whom the British Army had refused to accept as an officer.[5]

As peace approached, poorly supplied Continentals idled in camps near New York. Unpaid, their resentment grew. "The insults and neglects which the army have met with from the country," a Connecticut officer wrote, "beggars all description. It must go no farther. [The soldiers] can bear it no longer." Talk of mutiny spread.[6]

In January 1781, troops near Morristown, New Jersey, had erupted when told their enlistments extended until the war's end. Without pay for twelve months and in "a state of nakedness and famine," they seized ammunition and cannons, killing an officer. Setting off for Philadelphia, where they intended to confront Congress, they were intercepted near Princeton and reached a settlement that discharged most of the mutineers from the army.[7]

A second uprising came in the same month among troops in nearby Pompton Lakes. Washington sent five hundred men to restore order. After those mutineers surrendered, two were hanged.[8]

Toward the end of 1782, soldier discontent again neared a crisis. Washington wrote to Congress's secretary of war of the soldiers' "total want of money, or the means of existing from one day to another." He warned against discharging the army, "soured by penury and what they call the ingratitude of the public," having "suffered every thing human nature is capable of enduring this side of death." The soldiers must, Washington insisted, be paid.[9]

The soldiers' plight became entangled with the hope of a few powerful men in Philadelphia to use the threat of army mutiny to secure a congressional tax; revenue from that tax could be used to pay the soldiers and pay down the country's debts. Under the Articles of Confederation, every state had to approve the tax, but such unanimity had never happened. Without tax revenue, Congress had to request funds from states that had limited revenues and their own war expenses to pay. Congress had received 5 percent of the amount it requisitioned from the states in 1781.

Three men at the center of congressional finances aimed to use the soldiers' discontent to secure approval of a tax. Each was a Washington ally: Robert Morris, superintendent of finance; his deputy, Gouverneur Morris; and New York delegate Alexander Hamilton. Peace, they feared, would further reduce the prospects for a national tax, but the threat of an army mutiny might frighten the states into approving one.[10] Their strategy might bring "convulsion," Gouverneur Morris admitted, but it would "terminate in giving to government the power without which government is but a name." It was a high-risk ploy, also a cynical one.[11]

By December 1782, troops stationed in Newburgh, New York, appointed a committee of officers to present their grievances to Congress. Their petition warned that the soldiers' "uneasiness . . . is great and dangerous," that their "hardships are exceedingly disproportionate to those of any other citizens of America," but that "shadows have been offered to us while the substance has been gleaned by others." Washington, having badgered Congress to pay the army, stood apart from the appeal but raised no hand to stop it. If the mission failed, one officer wrote, "I dread the consequences."[12]

In addition to back pay, the officers demanded that Congress allow the "commutation" of the promised pensions—in effect, converting them to lump-sum payments that equaled five years' pay. The officers knew that Congress lacked money to pay either pensions or the commutation amounts, but they hoped to sell to speculators the government promise of a lump-sum payment. Delay in meeting their demands, the soldiers warned, "may have fatal effects."[13]

Congress debated the tax and soldier-pay issues through January, finally punting them to Robert Morris, as superintendent of finance. Morris kicked the issue back to Congress by secretly submitting his resignation, to be effective in future months. His deputy, Gouverneur Morris, warned General Henry Knox in Newburgh that after peace, Congress "will wish to get rid of you and then they will see you starve rather than pay a six penny tax."[14] On February 11, news arrived that King George III had announced preliminary peace terms. Congress greeted the news with "great joy," but noted "the impossibility of discharging the arrears and claims of the army."[15]

The financial men had to act quickly. Hamilton sent an elliptical letter to Washington, noting the dilemma: Peace would destroy any incentive to pay the soldiers; when the army realized it would never be paid, the soldiers might not stay "within the bounds of moderation." In that event, Hamilton observed, Washington could "bring order perhaps even good, out of confusion." Without detailing the scheme, Hamilton had warned Washington that a crisis was coming and that Washington might play a key role in resolving it.[16]

The financial men then revealed Robert Morris's impending resignation, dialing up the pressure on Congress. They also sought support from the army's senior officers. Washington walked a careful line, repelling an overture to join the scheme, yet not obstructing it. The plotters turned to Horatio Gates, now second-in-command at Newburgh despite the Conway Cabal and his debacle in South Carolina. Gates threw in with the financial men, never revealing to Washington that he had.[17]

The opening move came in early March, when an incendiary address circulated among the soldiers in the Newburgh camp. Drafted by a Gates aide, it denounced the nation "that tramples upon your rights, disdains your cries, and insults your distresses." For its crescendo, the address proclaimed that "the army has its alternatives." If peace came, the army could refuse to disband; if war resumed, the army could "retire to some unsettled country, [and] smile in your turn," leaving the country at the mercy of the British. The document summoned a meeting for Tuesday, March 11, to discuss redress of soldier grievances.[18]

Washington immediately canceled the March 11 session, but scheduled another meeting four days later to hear the report of the officers who were negotiating with Congress over pay. He also reported the events to Robert Morris and Hamilton, expressing his suspicion that they were behind this "very mysterious . . . business" and urging them to resolve the situation peacefully.[19]

Before the rescheduled meeting, a second anonymous address circulated at Newburgh. It audaciously claimed that Washington supported those who had called the initial meeting.[20]

Washington was caught between Congress, the financial men, and the soldiers. He detested the mistreatment of his army, yet he could not abide mutiny and had always honored the supremacy of Congress. An army that turns on its own countrymen is no army, but merely armed men. He had to make the officers see that the anonymous addresses would lead them into "a gulf of civil horror."[21]

Gates presided over the meeting in the camp's "Temple of Virtue," built as a chapel and also used as a dancing academy. A lectern stood at one end of its largest room. The officers sat on log benches.[22]

Washington arrived after the meeting came to order. He strode to the lectern, impeccably uniformed yet visibly agitated. After Gates conceded the floor, Washington stood, as one officer wrote later, "single and alone"; he spoke "not at the head of his troops, but as it were in opposition to them; and for a dreadful moment the interests of the army and its general seemed to be in competition."[23]

Reading from a text, Washington first claimed the army's loyalty as "the constant companion and witness of your distresses." He turned to the first anonymous address, which called on the army to remain in uniform if peace prevailed, and to refuse to fight if war resumed. He denounced "this dreadful alternative of either deserting our country in the extremest hour of her distress, or turning our arms against it." Washington raised simple, powerful questions: "What can this writer have in view[?] . . . Can he be a friend to the army? Can he be a friend to this country?" Washington implored the officers to do nothing that would "lessen the dignity and sully the glory" they had earned.[24]

Uncertain whether he had moved his listeners, Washington said he would read from a letter from a congressional delegate. In the emotion of the moment, he stumbled over its opening passage. He reached to his pocket for spectacles he had recently acquired, apologizing that he had "grown gray in their service, and now found himself growing blind."

The remark was "so natural, so unaffected," recalled one officer, that "it forced its way to the heart." Truculent officers melted. "Sensibility moisten[ed] every eye." After he read the letter, Washington left. In his wake, the officer reported, "every doubt was dispelled, and the tide of patriotism rolled again in its wonted course."[25]

The power of that moment had come when Washington's mask of command, earned through eight years of hard service, slipped and revealed the man underneath. In that quiet reference to his own physical decline, he acknowledged the burdens they shared. After all our sacrifices, he told them, after all that our brothers-in-arms have sacrificed, do not throw away your honor. He delivered the message with the impeccable timing of a veteran actor, a man who felt the impact of words and gestures. He reclaimed the officers' hearts.

They affirmed Washington's message not only with their tears but with their prompt adoption of resolutions that rejected the anonymous addresses "with disdain" and "abhorrence." They pledged their confidence that Congress would not send them home unpaid. A situation careening toward mutiny, which could have upended the tottering government in Philadelphia or undermined the peace with Britain, was saved.[26]

Facing down the mutiny was that rarest of political moments: Washington stood before hostile men and changed their minds. Even Patrick Henry, the orator of the age, never did that. Henry inspired his supporters and infuriated his opponents; he did not convert. One analogy might be Mark Antony's funeral oration in Shakespeare's *Julius Caesar*, which persuades the Roman crowd that the slain Caesar was a hero, not a villain. But Shakespeare imagined that scene.

Washington's stature grew. He embodied the Revolution's moral power. Three days after the meeting in the Temple of Virtue, he pleaded with Congress not to abandon the army's officers to "grow old in poverty, wretchedness, and contempt." Should that be permitted, he added, "then shall I have learned what ingratitude is, then shall I have realized a tale which will embitter every moment of my future life."[27]

A few days after receiving his letter, Congress agreed to the commutation of the officers' pensions.[28]

∽

After the risk of mutiny receded, Washington cast no recriminations against Gates or the Morrises or Hamilton. The war was ending. It was no time to reopen wounds. The financial men and Gates had been patriots; the nation would need their talents. Their minds had erred, not their hearts. They made the sort of mistakes that Washington had made when young, but now made rarely. That gift of judgment, steeped in the moral obligations that come with possessing power, allowed him to inspire a nation.[29]

After ratifying the preliminary peace treaty, Congress on April 19 proclaimed the war over; it was the eighth anniversary of Lexington and Concord. The peace, Washington wrote, "has filled my mind with inexpressible satisfaction." Yet uncomfortable duties lay before him.[30]

He had to negotiate the return of prisoners and those slaves who sought freedom with the departing British. Several Mount Vernon slaves were among them. Prisoner exchanges went forward, but the British would not relinquish the former slaves.[31]

Washington despised the prospect of sending soldiers home without pay, which he feared "will drive every man of honor and sensibility to the extremest horrors of despair." He demanded that Congress calculate the pay due for each man's service and pay at least three months of it. Congress did not do it. Washington asked the states to provide funds. They sent little. By late May, unwilling to retain soldiers no longer needed, Congress ordered Washington to send them home, paid or unpaid.[32]

That shabby treatment triggered a final mutiny. Pennsylvania troops in Philadelphia submitted demands to congressional delegates, then were joined by disaffected soldiers from Lancaster. They surrounded the State House as congressional delegates worried how to respond to their intimidating presence. Neither state nor congressional officials could meet their demands. After passing through the jeering mutineers, the delegates relocated to Princeton. The mutiny collapsed when word arrived that Washington had dispatched troops from Newburgh.[33]

The men remaining at Newburgh were just as outraged. "We have punished some severely," one general wrote, which made them "more quiet, but not the less dangerous." He feared "some secret machinations of the soldiery burst[ing] upon us like a clap of thunder."[34]

To provide three months' departure pay, Robert Morris agreed to sign personal notes to be distributed as money. Morris signed his name more than six thousand times on notes called "Bobs," which ranged from five to one hundred dollars. Many soldiers left before the Bobs arrived. Each man also was entitled to a certificate specifying how much the government owed him. Most sold the certificates to speculators to pay for clothes and their journey home. Washington ordered that they could take their muskets with them.[35]

"Starved, ragged and meagre," one veteran recalled, with "not a cent to help themselves with," the soldiers left in twos or threes. The lack of ceremony and paltry compensation tore their feelings. A Connecticut man spoke for all: "When the country had drained the last drop of service it could screw out of the poor soldiers, they were turned adrift like old worn-out horses."[36]

Washington shared his men's sadness. He now, as he had predicted, had "learned what ingratitude is." Some officers tried to mount a farewell dinner, but too many of them, one related, "thought the present period more adapted to sorrow than to mirth" and faced the "wretchedness and distress" of peacetime: "They wished to move from their present situation as quietly as possible."[37]

The commander in chief, however, could not leave until the British evacuated New York City, which took seven more months. With few soldiers to command, Washington turned to personal matters long neglected. To assist with "some teeth which are very troublesome to me," he searched for a French dentist of good reputation. He toured upstate New York with Governor George Clinton. Vacant land for sale still worked on him like catnip. He and Clinton acquired a parcel in Saratoga Springs.[38]

He reflected on the nation's challenges, beginning with Congress's lack of power. "More than half the perplexities of my command," he wrote to Hamilton, "and almost the whole of the difficulties and distresses of the army, have their origin here."[39] Through the war, Washington had issued "circulars to the states," exhorting them to pay their soldiers and send supplies. In a final circular, published as a pamphlet, he called for strengthening the national government, making it superior to the states, and granting it the power to tax. Otherwise, he feared, the union could dissolve. He also outlined a structure for a peacetime army that could control Indian conflicts and protect America's borders with British and Spanish colonies.[40]

Most Americans, struggling in a failing economy, paid little notice. In a private letter, he mused that a convention of the people might be necessary to create a new constitution.[41]

By November, the British were finally ready to leave.

☙

Reclaiming New York, the site of America's worst military defeats and the bastion of British power, carried special meaning. In the early afternoon of November 25, Henry Knox and his artillerymen entered first, followed by Washington and Governor Clinton on horseback, then the infantry and citizenry. Crowds cheered wildly. "Every countenance," one officer wrote, "seemed to express the triumph of republican principles over the military despotism which had so long pervaded this now happy city."[42]

After years amid the spit-and-polish British, a woman thought the Americans "made a forlorn appearance," adding, "but then they were *our* troops." Thinking of "all they had done and suffered for us, my heart and my eyes were full, and I admired and gloried in them." They raised American colors at Fort George on the island's southern tip. Guns fired thirteen times, beginning a week of dinners, music, and tributes to the commander in chief. A fireworks show drew ecstatic newspaper accounts detailing each rocket, "balloon of serpents," "horizontal wheel," "double cone wheel illuminated," and "illuminated pyramid with Archimedian screws." The display, one newspaper insisted, exceeded anything the British had mounted.[43]

Washington's departure for Mount Vernon on December 4 struck a deeper note. At noon, the army's remaining officers waited in an upstairs room at Fraunces Tavern. Most were junior and had not served long. Only three of twenty-nine major generals were present; of the brigadiers, only one. Many barely knew Washington.[44]

He must have thought of absent comrades that morning. Nathanael Greene was still in the South, Lafayette in France. Hamilton stayed away, unsure of his standing after Newburgh. Arnold, the traitor, was in England. Then there were the dead: General Hugh Mercer of Virginia and Washington's aide, John Laurens, both struck down in battle, and Lord Stirling and General Charles Lee, dead from fever.

Washington (1783)

Washington did not keep them waiting. He attempted to eat from the buffet, but could not. He showed an "emotion, too strong to be concealed." He filled his glass and raised it. His toast was simple: "I most devoutly wish that your later days may be as prosperous and happy as your former ones have been glorious and honorable." Noting that he could not come to each officer, he invited them to "come and take me by the hand."

Knox, who had been eight years at Washington's side, stood nearest. When he stepped forward, they grasped hands, then embraced. Washington, "suffused in tears, was incapable of utterance." In silence, each man took his turn, kissed the general, mumbled farewell. "Such a scene of sorrow and weeping," one officer recorded, "I had never before witnessed." They were awed by the general "who had conducted us through a long and bloody war, and under whose conduct the glory and independence of the country had been achieved." They grieved that "we should see his face no more in this world."[45]

The officers followed Washington "in mournful silence" to the barge that would carry him to New Jersey. A large crowd waited. After the barge cast off, he waved his hat in salute. In the two years since Yorktown, Washington had led his men on no campaigns, or on any battlefield, but the inglorious work of holding the army together, then disbanding it peaceably, had been as vital as any battlefield victory.

∾

Washington endured one more farewell. On his way to Mount Vernon, he stopped in Annapolis, where Congress had perched. The commander in chief would report a last time. The occasion did not lack for irony. Gates joined Washington's escort into the city. The president of Congress was Thomas Mifflin. And Congress was in its usual bedraggled condition. Only seven state delegations were present, a mere twenty delegates.

None of it fazed Washington. He had won the power struggles. His army had won the war. And he was going home. At a ball staged by the Maryland governor, he danced every dance. He offered a toast that was near to his heart, if not particularly poetic: "Competent powers to Congress for general purposes!"[46]

At the resignation ceremony on December 23, the delegates held their seats as Washington entered, keeping their hats on to signify that he answered to them. When he rose and bowed to Mifflin, they removed their hats. Dignitaries and locals crowded the chamber. Women watched from the upstairs gallery.

Drawing out a paper, Washington's hand shook violently. He gripped the paper with two hands. The spectators and the delegates wept. Near the end of his statement, Washington's voice wavered. "The whole house," a witness recorded, "felt his agitations." When he mastered himself, Washington concluded:

> Having now finished the work assigned me I retire from the great theatre of action, and bidding an affectionate farewell to this august body under whose orders I have so long acted, I . . . take my leave of all the employments of public life.

The scene, the witness reported, was "inexpressibly solemn and affecting." Mifflin, though, was unmoved. He read a brief response without emotion.[47]

Washington hurried toward the ferry that would take him across the Potomac to home. He arrived on Christmas Eve.

∾

Of all of his achievements, nothing so impressed Washington's contemporaries as this resignation. For a man with a talent for winning trust, it was the ultimate proof of his honor. By ensuring that the army disbanded—even though unpaid—and then going home himself, Washington cemented a tradition of civilian control over the military that is essential in any system of self-government. His resignation completed his identity as the truest American.

Washington's retirement was no savvy career move designed to advance his public standing. He ached to go home. He was worn out. He had no wish for power over his neighbors. His resignation struck a perfect note in a nation that was weary of war and mistrusted powerful men. Victorious generals often take power. Julius Caesar did. So, too, did Oliver Cromwell. Napoleon soon would do it in France, and Simón Bolívar in South America. Washington, however, went home. Englishmen struggled to believe it, according to an American visitor. "'Tis a conduct so novel," he wrote, "so inconceivable to people, who far from giving up powers . . . are willing to convulse the empire to acquire more."[48]

For the rest of Washington's life, that resignation would refute any charge that he acted for self-aggrandizement. Not Washington. Not the man who turned his back on power.

His reputation had reached an almost mythical level, his virtue so immaculate that other mortals could barely aspire to it.[49] Washington surely knew the encomiums were overblown. He felt his limitations. But he also understood his strengths.

As he celebrated Christmas at Mount Vernon that year, he could revel in winning the fight for American independence against long odds. He hoped to glide into a retirement filled with private satisfactions. That would not be so. His country had too many troubles, and it relied on him too much.

THE NATION

CHAPTER 38

Home, Not Retired

Despite icy weather that often left him housebound, Washington reveled in his return to Mount Vernon in early 1784. To Lafayette, he contrasted his new "tranquil enjoyments" with the life of a soldier "ever in pursuit of fame," or a statesman "whose watchful days and sleepless nights are spent in devising schemes to promote the welfare of his own—perhaps the ruin of other countries." Washington resolved to move "gently down the stream of life, until I sleep with my fathers." His relief at escaping the cockpit of events, leaving the nation in the care of others, was genuine.[1]

In late February, he was "just beginning to experience that ease, and freedom from public cares which . . . takes some time to realize." He no longer planned the day's business from the moment he awakened. He felt like a traveler who "after treading many a painful step, with a heavy burden on his shoulders, is eased of the latter," having evaded "the quicksands and mires which lay in his way."[2]

Family came first now, and his had evolved. Small children shouted at Mount Vernon again: Jack Custis's two youngest, four-year-old Eleanor (Nelly), and two-year-old George Washington Parke (Washy). Martha's two older granddaughters lived nearby with their mother and new stepfather, Dr. David Stuart. A nephew, George Augustine Washington (Charles's son), formerly an army major, left for the islands visited by Washington and brother Lawrence thirty years before. Like Lawrence, the young man had tuberculosis.[3]

For Washington's mother, Mary, wartime stress had heightened her chronic money anxieties, which became so well known that Virginia legislators had proposed to support her with public funds. Mortified, Washington blocked the effort, insisting that he provided her with a "commodious house, garden and lots," and that she had regular income.[4]

After the Yorktown surrender, Washington had escorted his mother to a Fredericksburg ball in his honor. He later asked his brother Jack to investigate her complaints about an overseer, cautioning that her "imaginary wants are indefinite, and oftentimes insatiable, because they are boundless and always changing." Shortly after leaving the army, he visited her again.[5]

Mount Vernon had suffered from the war, as had his fortune. By one estimate, the war cost him half his net worth. Not only had farm revenues plunged, but Washington had drawn no salary while inflation sapped the value of investments and loans to friends.[6] Those losses were offset by his incompletely documented claims for $447,000 of wartime expenses. Though Congress had not paid other soldiers, it reimbursed Washington promptly.[7]

He again rose early to work in his office until breakfast, then rode twenty miles through his farms, directing the day's efforts by his enslaved workers. A visitor marveled that his host "has a great turn for mechanics," and oversaw everything, "condescending even to measure the things himself." He fussed over the finishes for the large room being built for entertaining, and the outside gallery with its commanding river view.[8]

After midafternoon dinner, he returned to his office. "It's astonishing the packets of letters that daily come," a visitor reported. Vigilant on money matters, Washington kept "as regular books as any merchant."[9]

If there were no evening guests, he studied the newspapers, reading choice items aloud. Nelly Custis, Martha's granddaughter, recalled him as a "silent, thoughtful man" who never told a war story in her presence. According to a friend, Washington was "uniformly grave, and smiled but seldom, but [was] always agreeable." Martha's good cheer dissolved the spell that Washington could cast over first-time visitors. With those he knew, he passed the wine around freely and grew lively. He avoided talking politics, preferring to discuss farming or improving navigation on the Potomac.[10]

Washington called agriculture "amongst the most favorite amusements of my life," even "delectable." He searched for ways to improve his crops, trying river mud as fertilizer and a new system for harvesting wheat. He experimented with seeds from China, Africa, and Siberia, and with corn strains from around America.[11]

Profits, however, were elusive. Fifteen months after returning home, Washington complained that he survived on a loan secured before he left New York. Nine months later, his message was unchanged: "My wants are pressing—some debts which I am really ashamed to owe are unpaid." And after nine more months: "The fact is, I am *really* in want of money."[12]

Washington tried to capitalize on a gift from King Carlos III of Spain: a jackass for breeding mules. The jackass, called Royal Gift, proved slow to rise to his duties, which amused his owner. The animal, Washington joked, mimicked "his late royal Master, who cannot . . . perform seldomer, or with more majestic solemnity." Washington deployed a female jackass to stir Royal Gift's ardor, then switched in a mare when Royal Gift was ready to couple.[13]

The stream of visitors to Mount Vernon—relatives, neighbors, and passersby—increased the financial strain. Travelers, Robert Morris wrote, "cannot pass . . . without gratifying their wishes by an interview with the first man of the age." They included portrait painters cashing in on Washington's fame, and the French sculptor Houdon, creating a statue of Washington for the Virginia state capitol. When Washington dined alone with Martha in late June 1785, he calculated it was their first dinner without guests for eighteen months.[14]

Washington's recreational pursuits dwindled. He recorded no gambling wins or losses, and confined his fox hunting to a few weeks training hounds sent by Lafayette. He complained about the flood of correspondence and ordered books on history, self-improvement, and geography.[15]

Washington resumed his correspondence with George William Fairfax, long ago moved to England, following a wartime interruption (both men suspected that authorities had intercepted their letters). Washington regretfully reported that fire had destroyed Belvoir, where "the happiest moments of my life had been spent." George William complained good-naturedly of being harassed for letters of introduction to the great Washington.[16]

And Washington continued his quest to ease the pain from bad teeth and worse dentures. He again sought out the dentist who created his false teeth at the end of the war. In 1784, Washington purchased nine teeth from "Negroes," presumably people he owned. Those teeth most likely were used for his new dentures, which also were fashioned from walrus tusks, cows' teeth, and whalebone. Nothing, however, saved his own teeth. By 1789, he would have only one.[17]

Washington still followed public events closely, and was pulled back into them when the Society of the Cincinnati, a fraternal association of former army officers, fell into political controversy. A 1783 pamphlet denounced the society as an aristocratic coup-in-waiting. Critics focused on gauzy references in the society's charter to public affairs (the former officers still hoped to be paid for their army service), and a frankly aristocratic provision that membership passed to the eldest male child. A Massachusetts legislative committee warned that the Cincinnati threatened "the peace, liberty, and safety of the United States." North Carolina considered barring society members from its legislature.[18]

Though not involved in establishing the group, Washington had accepted its presidency, a step he likely came to regret. To calm the storm, he resolved to win reforms of its charter at the society's first general meeting in May 1784 in Philadelphia. To achieve that end, however, he would have to engage in debate, something he usually avoided.[19]

Addressing nearly fifty convention delegates in early May, he proposed eliminating any hereditary element, any political reference in the group's charter, or the appointment of honorary members. When others defended the hereditary feature, Washington repeated himself in "a very long speech," speaking, according to one witness, "with much warmth and agitation." Ultimately, the convention approved his proposals, but the state societies never eliminated hereditary membership.[20]

Washington thought the society's actions were inadequate, but when the controversy faded, he accepted reelection as its president. His identification with the Continentals remained fierce, and he despised "the ungenerous conduct of their country" toward the soldiers. The veterans were his brothers. He would stand with them always.[21]

∾

Washington still saw development of the west as central to America's future, and still hoped for income from his lands there. After leaving the army, he moved to solidify his title to parcels in western Virginia and searched again for new tenants.[22] Jefferson soon channeled Washington's passion for the Potomac as the key that could unlock the frontier. If the upper stretches of the river were cleared of obstacles and connected by road to the Ohio River, it could efficiently carry goods and people back and forth to the interior. Jefferson employed shameless flattery: "What a monument of your retirement would it be!"[23]

Washington required little persuading. Lamenting the "inertitude" of Congress, he thought the project promised "immense advantages." He organized a western trek with his old friend Dr. Craik and his nephew Bushrod, brother Jack's son. He wanted no one else along. "It can be no amusement for others to follow me in a tour of business," he explained, "nor would it suit me to be embarrassed by the plans, movements, or whims of others." He hoped to unleash income from his lands in western Pennsylvania and in what is now West Virginia. His few western tenants paid rent sporadically, and no one was buying his land at his prices.[24]

The trek began on the first of September, the beginning of a rainy spell. Crossing the mountains, which he had done frequently in younger days, now

COURTESY OF THE NATIONAL MUSEUM OF HEALTH AND MEDICINE

Dr. James Craik

was "tedious and fatiguing." Yet he managed rough travel for more than a month. A description from the time portrays him as "about six foot high, perfectly straight and well made, rather inclined to be lusty."[25]

Washington collected rents from some of the tenants on Bullskin Creek lands he'd bought as a teenager, but squatters on other land disputed his title. In Pennsylvania, he found that a mill he had paid to have built was in ruins and that squatters had settled there too. He retained a lawyer to evict illegal tenants and hired an agent to find new ones who would pay.[26]

In those travels, which were cut short by Indian unrest, he gathered information about settlements, trade routes, and connections between streams and rivers. In the journey's third week, he left the baggage with Dr. Craik and searched alone for alternate routes between east and west. Arriving home in early October, he acknowledged that he had not much improved his finances, but was glad to learn "the temper and disposition of the western inhabitants." Washington saw them in limbo, with communication and trade difficult in every direction: east to the Atlantic states, north to British Canada, or south and west to Spanish colonies. That left western loyalties "on a pivot—the touch of a feather would almost incline them any way."

Washington agreed with Jefferson that trade was central to retaining the region's loyalty. Virginians must "make a smooth way for the produce of that country to pass to our markets" lest the British or Spaniards beat them to it. The Potomac, he insisted, was the solution. Rising not far from Ohio River tributaries, it could bind the west to the thirteen states.[27]

∾

Washington had thought about improving the river since his time leading the Virginia Regiment, but advances in canal-building now made the effort more feasible. Perhaps more important, this time the man leading the project knew everyone who mattered, had influence with all of them, and did not discourage easily.[28]

Washington called a November 15 organizational meeting for the river project, barely five weeks after reaching home from the west. Because he had to go to Richmond, the new state capital, to seek authorizing legislation, a friend chaired that meeting. A newspaper report of the Alexandria session described the project as "a work so big that the intellectual faculties cannot take it at a view," and predicted that riches would "pour down on us."[29]

Bell-ringing and a cannon salute marked Washington's entrance to Richmond. At night, the residents illuminated their homes in his honor. Virginia legislators presented a resolution praising Washington's "transcendent services" to the country. Some might be distracted by such adulation, but Washington was all business. He explained the project to young James Madison, providing legislation for a bi-state commission to sponsor the river improvement.[30]

By late November, Washington was in Annapolis to secure parallel legislation from Maryland. Both states adopted his statutes and immediately appointed commissioners. Virginia's three included Washington and Horatio Gates (him again!). With the other two Virginians staying home, Washington remained alone in Annapolis through Christmas to hammer out enabling legislation with four Maryland commissioners. On December 28, after Maryland enacted the new legislation, Washington sent it to Madison for Virginia's concurrence. The measure authorized clearing the river of obstructions, digging canals around waterfalls, and building a road from its headwaters to either the Monongahela or the Cheat Rivers. Washington's cover note, written at midnight, admitted that the effort had left him with "an aching head." Virginia concurred on January 4.[31]

In less than two months, Washington had secured four laws in two states, plus one interstate agreement. That record would be impressive in the Internet era; it was breathtaking in the eighteenth century. Madison marveled at

Washington's energy and effectiveness: "The earnestness with which he espouses the undertaking is hardly to be described."[32]

Without a pause, Washington turned to the project's next stages: recruiting board members, touting the new company's shares, and starting the
work. He collected maps of the river and its lands, fired off letters to solicit
European investors, and imagined Alexandria as a boomtown. By mid-April,
he had raised £43,000 for the project's first stage; by mid-May, the Potomac
Company board convened with Washington as president.[33]

The board adopted Washington's model of "sluice navigation" for five of
the river's seven dangerous stretches. Workers would clear channels (sluices)
into the riverbed that cargo boats could follow. The company would have to
build locks to circumvent Little Falls, where the river dropped thirty-seven
feet, and Great Falls, where the drop exceeded seventy feet.[34]

When the Virginia legislature granted him fifty shares in the company,
Washington fretted that the award would be seen as corrupt self-dealing,
since he expected the project to generate massive profits. Then again, he worried, he might appear ungrateful if he declined the shares. Washington repeatedly asked friends what he should do. After months of indecision, he
pledged the income from the shares to educate the orphans of soldiers.[35]

Washington managed the project for the next four years. By the fall of
1785, two teams of fifty men were cutting the sluice channels. The work was
hard, involving hauling and blasting boulders from the river. Most free and
indentured workers ran off. The company rented slaves from nearby residents, but many owners were reluctant to send their people to perform such
dangerous work.[36]

A relentless cheerleader, Washington minimized troubles. "The difficulties," he announced early on, "rather vanish than increase as we proceed."
Despite his sunny forecasts, the system did not open until 1802, three years
after his death. Featuring five locks around the Great Falls but never connecting to the Ohio River, it operated for more than twenty years without returning much profit.[37]

For Washington, the project meant more than profit. At one point, he
described western settlement as a way to deliver humanity from war, which
could be "banished from the earth" by dispersing people more widely and
opening greater opportunities for their advancement. Even without such uto-
pian rhetoric, Washington saw western settlement as building the nation.[38]

The project also began to pull Washington back into public service. At the
end of 1784, Virginia and Maryland resolved to address issues surrounding their shared waterways, the Potomac and Chesapeake Bay. Each state

appointed commissioners to thrash out tolls, fishing and navigation rights, and lighthouse responsibilities. In late March 1785, the Marylanders arrived in Alexandria, ready to negotiate, but no Virginians met them. Governor Patrick Henry had not informed the Virginia commissioners of their appointments.[39]

The Marylanders contacted George Mason, one of the Virginia appointees. Dismayed by the botched arrangements, Mason consulted Washington and lassoed another Virginia commissioner who lived nearby. To smooth the conference, Washington hosted it at his home, feeding and housing the commissioners for four days. The resulting Mount Vernon Compact defined navigational and fishing rights, tolls, and tariffs. Madison, who was supposed to have been a Virginia commissioner, won legislative approval of it.[40]

At the end of 1785, frustrated anew by Congress's impotence, Madison proposed the Mount Vernon Compact as a model for addressing the nation's problems. For Virginia to call a multi-state conference to address commercial issues, he wrote to Washington, "seems naturally to grow out of" the Mount Vernon agreement. Virginia's legislature agreed, inviting the other states to send delegates to Annapolis in September 1786.[41] The United States, and Washington, were starting down the road to remaking the nation. Navigating that road successfully would require all of Washington's political skills.

CHAPTER 39

Back into Harness

After two years back home, Washington complained that, contrary to popular impression, he had not "retired to ease, and that kind of tranquility which would grow tiresome for want of employment." Rather, he was stranded at Mount Vernon without any secretary while deluged with "a thousand references of old matters with which I ought not to be troubled, but which nevertheless must receive some answer."[1] New matters also crowded into his life. The Potomac work often lacked laborers and struggled with high water, unhappy neighbors, and delinquent investors. Managing Mount Vernon and his western lands was a cycle of tasks and setbacks, drought and floods, hurricanes and pests, mixed with agricultural experiments. Whatever Washington tried, his crops remained disappointing. His finances grew no stronger.

His money woes were hardly unique. Americans in the 1780s endured what was likely the nation's worst economic depression ever. Compared to 1774, real incomes plummeted by 18 to 30 percent, largely due to the war.[2] Eight years of conflict had siphoned off productive labor. About 200,000 men (and a few women) served in the Continental Army or state militias, and about 20,000 women performed army work (cooking, washing uniforms). Soldiers and camp women planted no fields, built no buildings, and wove no linen.

More than 30,000 patriots died in battle, of illness, or in prison; loyalists died too. More suffered severe injuries. Perhaps 20,000 enslaved people left with the British. Civilians suffered illness, want, and soldier atrocities. With a population under 4 million in 1790, the productivity loss was substantial. In addition, raids by both sides destroyed buildings and crops, while the

Royal Navy bombarded seaside towns and patriots put Indian settlements to the torch.[3]

After the war, roughly 60,000 loyalists left, a serious drain of talent and capital. Hamilton predicted that New York City, which lost half its population, would not recover from those departures for a generation.[4]

Exports tumbled during wartime, with British markets closed to Americans and the Royal Navy capturing American cargoes. Shipping tonnage from Philadelphia declined by 90 percent. Even after peace, exports of tobacco, indigo, and rice were barely half of prewar levels, as the British still barred Americans from their West Indies ports. New England shipbuilding plummeted; Massachusetts dropped from building 125 ships per year to 15 or 20. Frontier conflicts disrupted the fur trade with Indians.[5]

Lack of specie (coins or hard money) shriveled every form of economic activity, fostering a barter economy. In the six years after the peace, some Americans splurged on goods unavailable in wartime, more than doubling imports from Britain while exports lagged, which further reduced the specie in the country. States printed currency and foreign money circulated (British pounds, Portuguese johannes, and Spanish dollars), which converted simple transactions into currency negotiations.[6]

Paper money brought punishing inflation. Congress printed $241 million in bills, which by 1780 were worth 1 percent of their face value. States printed another $200 million. By the end of 1781, Virginia's currency was worth 0.1 percent of face value. Maryland food prices skyrocketed 1,900 percent between 1777 and 1800.[7]

Behind the numbers were lives become desperate. In Baltimore, bankruptcies were reported daily. In October 1784, a Philadelphian reported that the streets "swarm with servants and persons seeking menial employment," while others "crowd to the back country," hoping for a fresh start. In two Pennsylvania counties, foreclosure orders outnumbered taxpayers between 1782 and 1789. When emigrants found western land owned by absentee landlords (like Washington), they often settled without worrying about niceties like land titles.[8]

Neither Congress nor most states had a stable fiscal base. Congress's requisitions on the states produced steadily lower returns, reaching 2 percent in August 1786. New Jersey refused to pay requisitions until New York approved the import tax that Congress had been trying to enact for five years. New York, enjoying revenues from its own import tax, did nothing. In early 1786, a congressional committee pronounced the requisition system "dangerous to the welfare and peace of the Union."[9]

The nation's economic troubles, and congressional impotence, had profound consequences. Having promised to vacate nine military posts around the Great Lakes and in northern New York, the British simply stayed, daring Congress to eject them. When Indians and settlers fought, Congress could only wring its hands. When states violated the pledge to allow Britons to sue for prewar debts, Congress shook its head. When the corsairs of North Africa targeted American ships and enslaved American sailors, Congress could not retaliate.[10]

As early as 1784, Americans considered dissolving the seemingly feckless union. "Many people," Nathanael Greene wrote, "secretly wish that every state should be completely independent and . . . that Congress should be no more."[11]

Washington tried to be optimistic about the country's prospects. Shortly after arriving home, he was certain that "the good sense of the people will ultimately get the better of their prejudices." To an anxious friend, Washington soothingly compared America to "a young heir, come a little prematurely to a large inheritance," bound to "run riot until we have brought our reputation to the brink of ruin," then "to do what prudence and common policy" require. He offered a calming aphorism, that "democratical states must always *feel* before they can *see*: It is this that makes their governments slow—but the people will be right at last."[12]

Yet Washington's view darkened steadily. He came to deplore the "half starved, limping government, that appears to be always moving upon crutches, and tottering at every step." For Washington, disunion was the great risk; Congress needed greater power and the states less. "We are either a united people," he fumed to Madison in late 1785, "or we are not. If the former, let us, in all matters of general concern act as a nation, . . . If we are not, let us no longer act a farce by pretending to it." He despaired that the Confederation was "little more than an empty sound, and Congress a nugatory body."[13]

In 1786, dissension flared when Spain limited American trade at its ports and excluded Americans from the lower Mississippi, which blocked western crops from reaching Caribbean markets. John Jay of New York, secretary of foreign affairs for Congress, explored a deal with Spanish Minister Gardoqui to open Spain's ports in return for a twenty-five-year exclusion of Americans from the Mississippi River. When Jay asked Congress for guidance, an angry debate pitted New Englanders desperate for Spanish trade against Southerners demanding Mississippi access. James Monroe, representing Virginia, warned of Northern intrigues to dissolve the nation.[14]

While Congress quarreled in New York (its fourth home since fleeing Philadelphia in 1783), delegates from the states were to gather in Annapolis to address commercial issues. Washington was hopeful about the conference, though he wished its mandate were broader.[15]

The conscientious Madison arrived in Annapolis on time, but after nearly two weeks, only eleven other delegates representing five states had joined him. They were too few to do anything except agree on the need to address *all* of the government's defects, not just commercial problems. Those twelve delegates unanimously called for a second convention to meet on "the second Monday of May next," to devise measures "to render the constitution of the federal government adequate to the exigencies of the union."[16]

Months before the Annapolis meeting, Washington wrote that "something must be done" because the government "certainly is tottering!" Yet he questioned whether the time was right. In any event, he wrote to a fellow Virginian, no convention would happen unless the nation suffered "another convulsion."[17]

As the Annapolis delegates met, that convulsion was coming.

∾

The depression struck hard in western Massachusetts. When farmers and tradesmen could not pay taxes to the state government, foreclosures took their homes, tools, and livestock. Beginning in late summer, protesters blocked judges from holding court. The protesters' logic was admirably linear: If the courts never convened, they could not order foreclosures. When militia were summoned to support the judges, they sometimes joined the protesters. The unrest spread. Armed force suppressed protests in New Hampshire and Connecticut. In Virginia, South Carolina, and Pennsylvania, protesters targeted tax collectors and courthouses.[18]

Through autumn of 1786, Washington's New England friends sounded alarm after alarm over conditions in Massachusetts. A delegate in Congress fretted that insurgents would take control of Springfield's federal arsenal. Henry Knox reported that a majority in his state opposed the government, that insurgents proposed joining Vermont (not yet a state) to become part of Canada. It was, Knox concluded, "a beginning of anarchy."[19]

Concerned, Washington asked a New Hampshire friend about the causes. If the risings were due to "real grievances which admit of redress," he demanded, "why has the remedy been delayed?" If due to "licentiousness" or British influence, the protests should be squelched. From Knox came the answer that "high taxes are the ostensible cause," but the real spurs were class resentment and government weakness. Perhaps 15,000 men, Knox predicted, soon would mount a "formidable rebellion."[20]

Urged to use his influence to calm the insurgents, Washington refused. "Influence is not government," he replied tersely. "Let us have one." He would not wade into a civil upheaval with little idea of what caused it, nor any armed force behind him. Yet Washington feared that the situation showed "that mankind left to themselves are unfit for their own government." He was "mortified beyond expression whenever [he] view[ed] the clouds which have spread over the brightest morn that ever dawned upon any country."[21]

The Massachusetts unrest intensified until several thousand farmers and mechanics marched through a January blizzard toward the Springfield Arsenal, where they confronted a militia force composed of their neighbors. Cannon volleys dispersed the rebels, killing three and wounding many others. In a ten-day period, the nearly hysterical Knox sent to Washington five separate reports about the confrontation.[22]

That rising entered history as the Shays Rebellion, named for a leader about whom little is known. Though they won no military success, the rebels upended Massachusetts politics; the next elections returned a legislature that slashed taxes and adopted other reforms. The rebels terrified men like Washington, who thought the union might crumble. "Without some alteration in our political creed," Washington wrote to Madison, "the superstructure we have been seven years raising at the expense of much blood and treasure, must fall. We are fast verging to anarchy & confusion!" He feared the worst: "Thirteen Sovereignties pulling against each other, and all tugging at the federal head, will soon bring ruin on the whole."[23]

The proposed Philadelphia Convention provided the best opportunity to change the government. Madison reported from Richmond that the Virginia Assembly would endorse the convention, and that Washington must be listed as a delegate to give weight to the gathering.[24]

Washington's sense of duty inclined him to heed Madison's call, but he stumbled over a question of politics and etiquette. The Society of the Cincinnati would meet in Philadelphia at the same time. Washington already had announced that he could not attend that session. To participate in this other convention in the same city at the same time would insult his fellow veterans. In addition, attending the convention would violate his pledge to leave public life.[25]

Left unstated were the risks of participating in the convention. If the meeting produced no better blueprint for government, then Washington would have led the country to failure. Alternatively, if a new government emerged, Washington would surely be called to lead it, exposing him to the accusation that he had sought power all along. Then again, if he ignored the convention, he might be denounced for neglecting his duty.

Convention proponents, beginning with Governor Edmund Randolph of Virginia, took turns urging him to attend. Madison insisted that Washington "could not be spared." When Washington stalled, each man wrote again. At least, Madison pleaded, keep the door open "in case the gathering clouds should become so dark and menacing as to supersede every consideration but that of our national existence."[26]

John Jay and Knox took a different approach. In January 1787, they wrote long letters canvassing the government changes needed, prodding Washington to crystallize his own thoughts. By February, five states had joined Virginia's call for the convention. When Madison persuaded Congress to endorse the Philadelphia meeting, Washington grew concerned that his absence might seem "an implied dereliction of republicanism."[27]

Washington's attention to the national situation had lapsed in early January with the unexpected death of his brother Jack. It came only six months after the passing of Nathanael Greene, which Washington had felt deeply. Washington tried to be stoic about death. He had known so much of it, both within his family and during the war. But this latest death was hard. Of his siblings, Washington had written most often to Jack, and on more personal matters. He relied on Jack to manage their mother. After the war, Jack had visited Mount Vernon annually. Washington sponsored and trusted Jack's eldest son, Bushrod, above his other nephews. (He later named Bushrod executor of his will, and John Adams would appoint Bushrod to the Supreme Court.)[28]

Three months after Jack's death, Washington's grief was still sharp. He lamented to Knox that he had "just bid an eternal farewell to a much loved brother who was the intimate companion of my youth," adding that Jack also was "the most affectionate friend of my ripened age." Jack's death left an emptiness that could not be filled.[29]

Jack's death may have sapped Washington's enthusiasm for traveling to Philadelphia. Also, he may not have looked forward to long days of debate over the principles of government. Washington was a man of deeds, not of theory, and did not eagerly spar with nimble thinkers like Madison and Hamilton. Since he rarely left Mount Vernon, he might have felt ill prepared for the convention. Diligent newspaper reading could not supply all the nuances of a complex situation. His unsatisfactory experience at the convention of the Cincinnati also might have made him reluctant to return to such a setting. As ever, he did not wish to be seen seeking power.

Washington's modesty remained a singular trait. His achievements could easily have bred arrogance or narcissism. He received a dozen obsequious letters a month celebrating his greatness. Public ceremonies honored him. His arrival in a town made church bells clang and cannons roar, triggered fireworks, processions, and balls. Yet he remained affable and unassuming.

He seems never to have forgotten the insecurity of the youth visiting the Fairfaxes of Belvoir, careful not to set a foot wrong and anxious to conceal his anxiety.

Washington came to accept that his participation in the Philadelphia Convention would increase its chance of success, and also the public's willingness to accept any changes it proposed. It might well be, he acknowledged, "the last peaceable mode" for repairing the government. The legacy of the American Revolution, for which he had fought so long, was at risk. In view of who he was, and the country's parlous situation, he agreed to attend.[30]

∾

Once more Washington prepared for a long absence from home, from Martha, and from family, which now included nephew George Augustine Washington, back from the Caribbean and recently married to Martha's niece, Fanny Bassett. Washington installed the new bridegroom as estate manager, adding an experienced English farmer to supervise some of the farms. Washington now required a written farm report every week, which would be sent to Philadelphia during the convention. His French dentist paid two visits to Mount Vernon in the winter of 1787, so his mouth pain had been addressed, however imperfectly.[31]

To prepare for Philadelphia, Washington took notes on the advice sent by Knox, Jay, and Madison.[32] All three proposed adding executive and judicial departments to create a three-branch government. Jay urged a dramatic demotion of the states, with national officers appointing and removing state officials. Knox also endorsed a supreme national government, but Madison suggested a middle way, which Washington called "a due supremacy of the national authority" that did not "exclude the local authorities whenever they can be subordinately useful." Madison also urged that the national government have only specific powers, including the power to tax, plus a veto over state laws.[33]

Washington shared his sentiments with Madison in late March. As was true before the Revolution, he had no interest in half-measures. He wanted the delegates to "probe the defects of the constitution to the bottom, and provide radical cures."[34] By setting that tone, he had a powerful impact on the convention's work.

As Washington prepared to leave, word arrived that his mother and sister Betty were near death. He rushed to Fredericksburg, riding fifty miles in less than eight hours, and found his sister almost recovered, but his mother "exceedingly reduced and much debilitated by age and the disorder." Only two months before, appalled that his mother had sought money from his nephew George Augustine, he sent her what he described as his last 15 guineas. Money anxiety would ever connect mother and son. At that time, Washington had invited her to live at Mount Vernon, but the invitation had been ungracious, emphasizing the inconveniences of a household he called a "well resorted tavern," with constant visitors. She did not accept the lukewarm gesture.[35]

With Martha choosing to remain at Mount Vernon with her grandchildren, Washington left for Philadelphia on May 9, traveling alone in an enclosed carriage. Riding outside through rain, high winds, and muddy roads, were the coachman, Paris, the groom, Giles, and William Lee, the valet who had been by his side through the war. Washington's retirement from public life was over.

CHAPTER 40

America's Rebirth

On a rainy afternoon in mid-May 1787, Philadelphia greeted Washington with the customary commotion. A cavalry escort met him at the Schuylkill River. Cannons fired thirteen rounds. Bells rang. Citizens cheered, a local newspaper wrote, "the coming of this great and good man."[1]

Washington intended to lodge at the boardinghouse where many Virginians stayed, having declined Robert Morris's offer of a room in his home. In the hubbub of arrival, Morris and his wife renewed their offer. This time Washington accepted. The public acclamation underscored the advantages of a private resting place.

The general immediately paid an hour-long call on Ben Franklin, Philadelphia's leading citizen at age eighty-one. The imagery was powerful: America's most celebrated figures joining together to reconsider the nation's government. They knew each other, but not terribly well, having intersected during the French and Indian War, then again in the Second Continental Congress.[2] Three days later, Franklin hosted a dinner for the Pennsylvania and Virginia delegates, the only ones present so far; they would be allies through much of the convention. Wet weather and bad roads delayed the others. The impatient Washington called the delay "highly vexatious to those who are idly, and expensively, spending their time here."[3]

As delegates trickled in, the Virginians went to work. In addition to Washington, the delegation included Madison, Randolph, and Mason, along with three lesser lights (George Wythe, James McClurg, and John Blair). They met in the morning at the boardinghouse where Madison lodged, to work out a government structure. In the afternoons, they walked to the State

House (now called Independence Hall) to greet arriving delegates and calculate how far they were from a quorum.[4]

The preliminary effort produced the "Virginia Plan," nineteen resolutions that would frame the convention's work. It called for three branches of government: a true executive, a two-house legislature, and courts. That government would be superior to the states, as Washington had long advocated. The new constitution would not be submitted to the approval of state legislatures, who would resent any loss of power, but for ratification by special conventions chosen by the people.[5]

Several deserve credit for the Virginia Plan. Madison, who had prepared for months for the convention, surely presented concrete ideas and held the pen that sketched it out, while Mason was wise about government. Randolph unveiled the plan in the convention's opening speech. Yet, at its core, the plan embodied Washington's demand for radical cures. His determination that the government must be remade gave the Virginians the essential political cover to propose scrapping the Articles of Confederation and starting over. His implicit yet unmistakable sponsorship of the Virginia Plan made it the starting point for the convention's work.[6]

On May 25, eleven days late, the convention mustered a quorum in the main chamber of the State House. By prearrangement, Robert Morris nominated Washington as convention president. For the second time—the first had been his 1775 appointment as commander in chief—Washington was unanimously elected by his peers. The first occasion had been a striking vote of confidence; this second, twelve years later, confirmed that the nation's confidence had been well placed.

Washington delivered a few words of acceptance, according to Madison, "in a very emphatic manner." He asked the delegates' forgiveness for "involuntary errors which his inexperience might occasion," though he had as much experience in deliberative bodies as any delegate present, from county court and parish vestry to the House of Burgesses, two Continental Congresses, and numberless councils of war.[7]

Through the next four months of spirited, sometimes angry debate, Washington largely muzzled himself. Even in the opening weeks, when another delegate presided over sessions that the delegates conducted as the "committee of the whole," Washington sat silently. Because he cast votes within the Virginia delegation, however, his preferences became known over the summer.

Washington's near silence reflected his preference to listen rather than speak, as well as the comfort he felt acting as the neutral presiding officer. Moreover, most delegates assumed that Washington would lead any executive branch they created. The Virginian chose not to wrangle over a government he might well manage.

Thus, Washington said nothing when the delegates argued over how to allocate legislative representation, the issue that came closest to blowing up the convention. Delegates from small states insisted that each state have an equal vote; Pennsylvanians and Virginians demanded that their states' greater populations should command larger representation. Nor did Washington take the floor in August, when disputes over the slave trade and trade regulation fostered more sharp disagreements.

Yet Washington's influence was plain. For several years, he had argued for a stronger continental government, first in his 1783 circular to the states, and then in letters that were shown around Congress and shared among influential politicians. The Virginia Plan, which framed the debate, carried Washington's imprimatur. Known to support a stronger government, he could preside benignly over the proceedings, the perfect Washingtonian posture.

The convention met six days a week through the summer heat, taking breaks only for the Fourth of July weekend and for ten days in late July and early August, when a five-man committee created a first draft of the Constitution. A total of fifty-five men represented twelve states over the summer. New Hampshire's representatives did not arrive until late July. Two of the three New Yorkers left after six weeks, unhappy with the movement toward limiting state powers; that left Hamilton as the lone New York delegate, barred by his state's rules from acting alone. Rhode Island, certain that the convention would deny the states the right to issue paper currency (as it did), never sent delegates to Philadelphia.

For three months after the convention stopped meeting as the committee of the whole, Washington presided over every session, able to guide debate subtly. He could choose which speaker to recognize, an angry voice or one inclined to conciliation. His demeanor could be persuasive. On one occasion, Washington indicated approval of a motion presented by Franklin and disapproval of Hamilton's objection. The delegates quickly adopted the motion.[8]

Washington inspired respect, even fear. After only three weeks, the delegates were permitted to make copies of the Virginia Plan so long as they kept them confidential. When delegate Thomas Mifflin (him again!) found a copy abandoned outside the State House, Washington frostily lectured the delegates to be more careful not to make premature disclosures of their proceedings. "I know not whose paper it is," he said, "but there it is." He contemptuously threw it on the table before him. "Let him who owns it, take it." He bowed, took up his hat, and exited "with a dignity so severe that every person seemed alarmed." No one claimed the document.[9]

Washington's procedural rulings could be significant. Early on, he decided that when the states voted 5–4–1 on a matter—each state cast one vote, and a state delegation might deadlock—the motion was approved even though it had not commanded a majority of the ten states voting.[10]

When combined with another procedural decision, that ruling took on significance during the explosive dispute over legislative representation. In the early going, the large states prevailed in their quest for proportional representation. With small-state delegates threatening to leave unless equal state votes were restored, another vote was taken. A Georgia delegate unexpectedly changed sides, deadlocking his delegation so it cast no vote on the measure. The absence of a Maryland delegate, Daniel of St. Thomas Jenifer, allowed the sole remaining Marylander to cast that state's vote (under Maryland's rules) in favor of one-state/one-vote. The result was a 5–5–1 tally, derailing the drive for proportional representation and causing consternation among the delegates.

At that moment, the absent Jenifer of Maryland entered the chamber. Quick-witted Rufus King of Massachusetts realized that if Jenifer could vote on the motion that had just failed, he would deadlock Maryland again and shift the outcome to 5-4-2 in favor of proportional representation. King moved to renew the motion. Washington refused to allow a second vote, which he called "too extraordinary."[11]

Yet the convention rules permitted a motion for reconsideration on the same day if no delegate objected, or after one day's notice if there was an objection.[12] Under that rule, Washington should have granted King's motion, or at least scheduled a second vote on it for the next day. By doing neither, Washington may have been trying to encourage a compromise between large and small states. Indeed, his ruling did help force that compromise, which established proportional representation in the House of Representatives and equal state votes in the Senate. That compromise prevailed by that narrowest of margins, one that Washington had previously recognized as binding: 5–4–1.[13]

Washington shared his fears about the convention in a letter to Hamilton, who had left for New York. Matters, Washington wrote on July 10, "are now, if possible, in a worse train than ever . . . I *almost* despair of seeing a favorable issue to the proceedings of the Convention." Those delegates who opposed "a strong and energetic government," he added, "are in my opinion narrow minded politicians, or are under the influence of local views."[14]

Madison recorded a few of Washington's specific votes, noting that the general favored a single individual as president, and approved multi-term presidencies. He also supported a requirement that revenue legislation arise in the proportionally chosen House of Representatives, which was part of the large-state/small-state compromise.[15]

Washington's presence may have been felt most powerfully on June 1, when the delegates first addressed the new executive branch. Because delegates expected Washington to be the first president, they evidently were reluctant to discuss the office in his presence. After a long silence, Franklin encouraged them to speak, while John Rutledge of South Carolina noted the "shyness of gentlemen." Some thought later that the Constitution's broad grant of executive power unwisely reflected their confidence in Washington. "The first man put at the helm will be a good one," Franklin told the delegates, then added the warning that, "nobody knows what sort may come afterwards."[16]

∽

Washington enjoyed a vibrant social life in Philadelphia. On at least fifty days, he dined with the Morrises, most often with invited guests. He dined out eleven times with other delegates, "club style" (that is, the diners dividing the bill equally among them). Thrice he ate with Franklin, attended six formal dinners with organizations like the St. Patrick Society, and on more than twenty occasions joined private dinner parties outside the Morris residence. Though he had many opportunities to huddle with other delegates, there is no evidence that he discussed the convention's business outside its formal proceedings.

He resumed friendships formed during previous Philadelphia visits, particularly with Samuel and Elizabeth Powel. Samuel shared Washington's passion for farming, while Elizabeth was recognized as a New World *salonnière*. "She has wit and a good memory," a French visitor recorded, "speaks well and talks a great deal."[17]

Washington attended four public performances during the summer: a concert, a reading, and two plays. On one afternoon he reviewed the city troops. On three days he sat for another portrait by Charles Willson Peale, who built a prosperous trade selling a full range of Washington likenesses. Peale would sell prints of this new portrait for $1 without frame and $2 framed. To a correspondent, Washington apologized for failing to write due to "my attendance in convention—morning business, receiving and returning visits" and all those dinners.[18]

Washington escaped the city when he could. On a half dozen days, he dined beyond the city limits with the Springsbury Club, a group of wealthy

Philadelphians, and also rode through the countryside on at least nine other occasions.

The ten-day recess that began in late July was too brief for a visit to Mount Vernon, so Washington took two fishing trips to nearby waters. On both excursions, he questioned local farmers about their methods, and visited sites from the war, riding through the encampment at Valley Forge and the site of his victory at Trenton on Christmas 1776.[19]

The delegates returned from recess to confront the draft Constitution prepared by the five-man Committee of Detail. On August 6, the summer's business assumed a new gravity when the draft was read aloud and distributed. The delegates held in their hands the embryo of a new government.

∾

For the next six weeks, they addressed the draft's twenty-three articles, probing for errors, omissions, unforeseen consequences, and disadvantages for their home states. Gouverneur Morris provoked a battle when he denounced the protections for slavery and the slave trade. Slavery, he thundered, was a "nefarious institution—it was the curse of heaven."

Morris's tirade stirred delegates from northern and middle states. They questioned the draft's perpetual protection for importing slaves, and the requirement that laws regulating commerce receive a two-thirds vote in each house of Congress. A committee cobbled together another compromise, reducing the protection for slave imports to a fixed term of years (ultimately, twenty) and ditching the two-thirds requirement for commercial laws.[20]

The delegates' impatience to go home was at war with the importance of their work. Washington was among the impatient, complaining that the work progressed by "slow, I wish I could add and sure, movements." If the final product had defects, he added, they would not be due "to the hurry with which the business has been conducted."[21]

Washington may have wished to finish quickly because the emerging Constitution already incorporated the features he most wanted: a power to levy taxes, a true executive branch, and congressional authority over commercial matters. The draft stated that the national government's laws and treaties "shall be the supreme law," binding on state courts and overriding state statutes. He might disagree with specific features of the draft charter, but he had what he wanted on the major questions.[22]

That Washington liked the draft Constitution is evident in his focus on the process for ratification. The Articles of Confederation were failing because amendments required a unanimous vote of the states. Unanimity was an impossible standard. Rhode Island had boycotted this convention and New York had left it. Acknowledging that reality, the convention agreed that ratification by nine states would suffice to bring the new government into being. According to James McHenry of Maryland, who sat next to the Virginians in the convention, Washington thought that seven states should be enough to ratify.[23]

Concern for ratification also lay behind a statement Washington made on the convention's final day, his only substantive remarks on the convention floor. Nine days before, the delegates had rejected a motion to reduce the size of congressional districts from 40,000 to 30,000 residents. When that motion was renewed on September 17, Washington endorsed it, explaining that objections to the Constitution should "be made as few as possible." Smaller congressional districts, he said, would provide greater "security for the rights and interests of the people." The motion passed by acclamation without further debate.[24]

The delegates then turned to the formalities. Despite appeals for unanimity, three refused to sign: Elbridge Gerry of Massachusetts, and Randolph and Mason of Virginia. They thought the Senate was too powerful, wished for less congressional power over trade, and wanted a bill of rights. Nevertheless, all eleven state delegations signed, as did Hamilton, though he lacked the authority to act alone on behalf of New York. The punctilious Washington recorded in his diary that the Constitution was signed by "11 states and Colonel Hamilton."[25]

After a farewell dinner at the City Tavern, Washington retired to his room at the Morris home. The convention's secretary brought him the convention's official records for safekeeping. Washington used the evening to "meditate on the momentous work which had been executed," a meditation that likely included the thoughts he shared two months later with an English historian. The delegates had conciliated "various and opposite interests," he wrote, and subdued local prejudices. "In a work of so intricate and difficult a nature," he concluded, the wonder was "that anything could have been produced with such unanimity."[26]

Washington was staking his place in history on that document. As one historian has written recently, "at core this was Washington's Constitution, especially with respect to the presidency." Washington's signature appeared first on it, and also was affixed to the cover letter to Congress. It was the signature that mattered most to Americans, and it told them that Washington recommended they scrap the loose ties created by the Articles of Confederation and embrace this stronger form of government. To secure the power of that signature, Madison, Knox, Jay, Hamilton, and Randolph had pleaded for him to participate in the convention. But still the Constitution had to be ratified by at least nine states. Washington would be central to that effort.[27]

He started preparing for his return to Mount Vernon in mid-August, when he sent home a dog for Martha, a cupola and spire for the house, and a bust of naval hero John Paul Jones (a gift from Jones). He had kept up with the weekly farm reports, while his money anxiety never eased. He complained that he could "see no more than the man in the moon where I am to get money to pay my taxes."[28]

On the journey home, near the Maryland-Delaware border, he mistrusted a bridge that passed over a surging stream. He stepped out of the carriage and sent it across first. One of the horses stumbled and fell fifteen feet from the span; the other horse almost followed him, which would have crashed the carriage into the water. Luckily, the second horse held his footing, the first was cut from his halter and guided across the stream, and the carriage survived. In reporting the mishap, a Philadelphia newspaper recalled the sermon preached after Braddock's defeat in 1755, which had predicted that Washington's life was spared to perform a great national service. Was the same providential hand still at work, the newspaper asked, "for the great and important purpose of establishing, by his name and future influence, a government that will render safe and permanent the liberties of America?"[29]

CHAPTER 41

A Working Politician

Shortly after arriving home, Washington sent the Constitution to three former Virginia governors with similar cover letters. He wished the charter were "more perfect," he wrote, "but I sincerely believe it is the best that could be obtained." Without a new constitution, "anarchy soon would have ensued," and the nation's future was still "suspended by a thread." That thread was ratification by the states.[1]

If ratification failed, disunion seemed likely, civil war and European intervention possible. The Confederation government was disappearing. Congress managed to enact the Northwest Ordinance while the Philadelphia Convention met, but then lost its purpose. "The prospect of a new Constitution," the president of Congress wrote in early 1788, "seems to deaden the activity of the human mind as to other matters."[2]

Washington expected ratification battles and soon was at the center of them. His support for the Constitution was essential, Hamilton wrote, due to his "universal popularity." Newspapers stressed the public trust he earned by retiring after the war. "Is it possible," a Philadelphia newspaper asked in October 1787, "that the deliverer of our country would have recommended an unsafe form of government?" Gouverneur Morris reported that Washington's signature on the document "has been of infinite service." Newspaper essayists repeatedly invoked his approval of the Constitution as a reason to ratify it.[3]

From Mount Vernon, he tracked the contest through correspondence and newspaper reports. "I never saw him so keen for anything in my life," a visitor reported. Through ten months of drama over ratification, he urged that the Constitution be adopted in scores of letters to friends and acquaintances. When a newspaper, without authorization, published a letter of his that endorsed ratification, he regretted only that he had not composed a better letter. Forty-nine other newspapers reprinted it. Everyone but Washington acknowledged he would be president. As Morris wrote, "Your cool steady temper is indispensably necessary." Morris compared the states to thirteen horses. Once they were trained, a child might manage them, but only Washington could train them.[4]

Madison sought congressional approval for the Constitution, but the best he could wheedle from that hesitant body was the simple transmission of the charter to the state conventions. Washington, cheerleader and coach, stressed that although Congress's action was insipid, at least its vote was unanimous. "The multitude," he observed, "often judge from externals, [so] the appearance of unanimity" had value. Madison pronounced the ratification strategy: Win nine state approvals quickly and leave the "tardy remainder" to straggle into the union. Because Rhode Island had boycotted the convention, it certainly would not ratify any time soon; the Constitution would fail if four other states took the same view.[5]

Recognizing that newspaper essays would sway opinion, Washington urged the recruitment of "good pens" to support ratification. Hamilton launched an essay series under the name "Publius," which grew into the landmark *Federalist Papers*. With a major contribution from Madison, and a small one from Jay, eighty-five essays totaling 190,000 words became classics of American political writing. Washington encouraged its distribution in newspapers and in bound volumes.[6]

By early January, five states had ratified by wide margins.[7] But opposition was forming. Opponents urged that a second convention be summoned to correct the errors of the first. Washington thought that proposal was a stall, designed to bleed momentum from the pro-Constitution movement. Leading Virginians—George Mason and Benjamin Harrison, Richard Henry Lee and Patrick Henry—embraced the objections announced by the non-signers in Philadelphia: There was no declaration of rights, the Senate or the judiciary were too strong, or Congress's commercial power could harm the South. To counter them, Washington worked to entice Edmund Randolph to reverse his position and embrace ratification.[8]

With a shrewd sense of how to shape public opinion, Washington urged allies to frame the ratification decision with simple questions:

1. Is the Constitution . . . preferable to the government . . . under which we now live?

2. Is it probable that . . . there would be a better agreement [from a second convention]?

3. Is there not a constitutional door open for alterations and amendments?[9]

In Washington's view, a fair-minded person would agree that the answers to the first and third questions were yes, while the second would bring a resounding no, which demonstrated that ratification was the only sensible course to follow.

In February 1788, the Massachusetts convention took center stage. Former Shays rebels distrusted a stronger government. The state's pro-ratification forces, assuming the name "Federalists," chose to debate the Constitution sentence by sentence, but made little headway. Washington's pro-ratification letter to a Massachusetts friend arrived too late to help. Nonetheless, his voice was heard when nine Massachusetts newspapers published an earlier letter endorsing the Constitution because "there is no alternative between the adoption of it and anarchy." Washington's support for the Constitution was so well known that one of those newspapers proposed that Federalists adopt the name "Washingtonians." Massachusetts Federalists tried a second tactic, having the convention recommend amendments to the Constitution, though the state's ratification would remain effective even if the amendments never were approved. By giving opponents a method for venting their dissatisfactions, that "recommendatory amendment" approach produced a narrow majority for ratification: 187–168.[10]

Washington was totally engaged in the struggle over ratification. "The Constitution and its circumstances," wrote his secretary from Mount Vernon, "have been almost the sole topics of conversation here for some months past." Visitors numbering "the first and best informed" shared their news and analysis with Washington. They left knowing that the general considered the Constitution "the rock of our political salvation."[11]

Unexpectedly, Federalists in New Hampshire adjourned their convention because they feared they were about to lose the ratification vote. Madison, on his way home to stand for election to the Virginia convention in late March, stopped at Mount Vernon to strategize with the chief. They were worried.[12] Washington put his shoulder to the wheel, encouraging friends at the Maryland convention to resist a delay proposed by anti-ratification forces. Flaunting Washington's letter, Maryland Federalists won easily. In late May, South Carolina ratified too.[13]

That made eight states. Federalists needed to win one of the remaining five. New York and Rhode Island were very unlikely to ratify, while North

Carolina was leaning anti. The contest was coming down to New Hampshire and Virginia.

The campaign had been a roller-coaster ride, with prospects shifting from week to week. One day, Virginia was said to be safe because of votes from western delegates (representing the future states of Kentucky and West Virginia), but then the westerners turned out to be as divided as other delegates were. Federalist hopes in Virginia revived when Randolph reversed himself and backed ratification. Washington longed for victory. Ratification, he wrote to Lafayette, "will be so much beyond anything we had a right to imagine or expect eighteen months ago."[14]

The Virginia convention pitted the electrifying Patrick Henry against the cerebral Madison. That confrontation looked like a mismatch, especially when Madison fell ill, but the small man soldiered on, unintimidated by Henry's eloquence. At Mount Vernon, Washington received updates from Madison and nephew Bushrod, also a delegate. To escape the waiting, Washington visited his mother and sister in Fredericksburg. When he returned home, he found Madison's disconcerting report: "The business is in the most ticklish state that can be imagined. The majority will certainly be small on whatever side it may finally lie."[15]

Washington replied fondly to his hardworking champion. To cure Madison's illness, he prescribed relaxation at Mount Vernon with "moderate exercise, and books occasionally, with the mind unbent." He added, "no one will be happier in your company than your sincere and affectionate servant." When rains kept Washington indoors, the waiting was more difficult. "I am," he groused, "in a manner drowned."[16]

When he wrote those words, Washington did not know that New Hampshire had ratified on June 21, creating the new government. The outcome in Virginia still mattered. It was the largest state, and Washington could not be president unless Virginia joined the union. Four days later, Madison reported ratification by a narrow 89–79 vote, plus a pile of recommendatory amendments.[17]

The glorious news reached Alexandria late on June 27. Next morning, a delegation arrived at Mount Vernon to escort Washington to the town's celebration. Since word had also arrived of New Hampshire's ratification, cannon boomed ten times to honor each ratifying state. Food, drink, music, and dancing filled the day. Within a month, New York also ratified.[18]

Washington offered a measured tribute to his fellow citizens. "By folly and misconduct," he wrote, "we may now and then get bewildered, but I hope and trust that there is good sense and virtue enough left to bring us back into the right way before we shall be entirely lost."[19]

Virginia's ratification was Madison's heroic moment, but Washington's influence had been crucial. When Henry had described Jefferson as no friend of the Constitution, Madison had instantly fired back, "Could we not adduce a character equally great on our side?" They certainly could. An Anti-Federalist in Richmond complained that "were it not for one great character in America, so many men would not be for this government." James Monroe stressed Washington's importance. "Be assured," he wrote to Jefferson, "his influence carried this government."[20]

Through the convention and ratification, Washington focused always on the need for a "respectable" government that could tax and govern. Of the more than two hundred recommendatory amendments proposed by various state conventions, he opposed only those that would strengthen the states or limit the power to tax. "I was ready," he wrote to Jefferson, "to have embraced any tolerable compromise that was competent to save us from impending ruin."[21]

Washington decreed the Constitution "a new phenomenon in the political and moral world: and an astonishing victory of enlightened reason over brutal force." His pride shone through his words:

> We exhibit at present the novel and astonishing spectacle of a whole people deliberating calmly on what form of government will be most conducive to their happiness; and deciding with an unexpected degree of unanimity.[22]

ॐ

Knowing he would be leaving Mount Vernon for renewed public service, Washington turned again to his troubled business affairs. His nearly 60,000 acres of western land generated little income. A malfunctioning chimney started a fire at Mount Vernon's mansion house. Summer storms washed out crops, and a late-July hurricane drove the river's tide to new highs. The heavy rains slowed the work to open the Potomac, while the company's money dwindled.[23]

Washington still rode his property daily, focusing on the building of a brick barn. He dug out his old surveying tools to lay out a road from his ferry landing. On New Year's Day 1789, he prepared detailed instructions to his farm managers for the coming year, outlining a six-year planting cycle designed to coax better yields from the reluctant soil.[24]

Effort and ingenuity, however, were making little headway. In April 1788, he reported that "want of money" was causing "more perplexity and . . .

uneasiness than I ever experienced before." Four months later, he moaned that he "never felt the want of money so sensibly since I was a boy of 15 years old."[25]

The "tardy remainder" of states (North Carolina and Rhode Island) were resisting ratification, but creation of the government would not wait for them. Each ratifying state scheduled an election for the House of Representatives, and for its legislature to choose that state's senators. The expiring Congress set three dates: On the first Wednesday in January, voters would choose the electors who would select the president; on the first Wednesday in February, those electors would meet in each state capital to elect the president and vice president; on the first Wednesday in March, the new government would begin.[26]

Demands poured in that Washington serve as president. "Without you," wrote Henry Lee, "the government can have but little chance of success." Washington always replied that he sought no position, professing the wish only "to live and die in peace and retirement on my own farm." He still feared criticism for returning to office after retiring from the army, and thought the Anti-Federalists would oppose him.[27] He also knew that the job would be difficult. Nevertheless, he understood the force of Gouverneur Morris's insistence that "no other man can fill that office. . . . You alone can awe the insolence of opposing factions."[28]

He truly had no choice. His agreement to attend the Philadelphia Convention had included an implied warranty that if a satisfactory constitution emerged, he would make it work. In the nearly two years since, Washington had transformed into a working politician. For what other reason was he closeted with Madison for five days before Christmas 1788, and again two months later? They had elections to follow and government positions to fill, taxes and budget practices to consider. Trade regulations, military arrangements, and foreign policy had to be reviewed. For the previous two years, Washington had done the things politicians do: developed strategies for change; worked to influence public opinion; polished messages and fostered a network of like-minded individuals; nurtured a public image that would help him achieve his goals.[29]

Washington's pleas that he preferred retirement expressed his fear of failure and his wish never to appear hungry for position. He also was feeling his years. That marvelous physique now ached, and he was, he always recalled, "of a short-lived family."[30] But those reasons were not enough to justify declining the presidency.

By late January, as the electors prepared to choose the president, Washington told Lafayette his goals: to establish a vigorous government that won respect from foreign nations, built prosperity, and developed western lands, while fostering manufactures and inland navigation.[31] Behind these specifics was a powerful idealism. In an earlier letter, he had written that America was entering a new era, "a more happy one than hath before appeared on this checkered scene of existence." The prospect of the new government, he added, "affords me more satisfaction than I have ever before derived from any political event."[32]

~

Later generations would wonder at the presidential election of 1789. No political parties organized campaigns. No candidates stumped for votes. No elector was pledged to any candidate. Politics, eighteenth-century-style, was built on personal connections and the written word. Pro-Constitution leaders pushed for Washington. He rarely mentioned the presidency, but urged the election of Federalists to Congress.[33] He also paid little attention to the vice presidency. When John Adams, a Constitution supporter, emerged among Federalists as a consensus choice for the office, Washington wrote a private letter supporting Adams, but did it only five days before electors were to vote, too late to have any impact on the balloting.[34]

The ten states participating in the vote—New York's legislature failed to agree on how to choose electors—designated electors in different ways. Only in Virginia did individual voters choose by districts; several states used some form of statewide voting, while three state legislatures selected electors. In New Jersey, the governor and his appointed privy council made the choice.[35]

Washington rode to Alexandria in early January 1789 to vote for the elector from his congressional district, and a month later to vote for his congressman. The voting by the presidential electors on the first Wednesday of February was supposed to be secret, but leaked tallies confirmed Washington's victory. Expecting to win, he had already ordered cloth from Connecticut for a new homespun suit that would highlight American industry.[36]

Federalists won a commanding share of congressional seats, but the official count of the presidential vote was delayed by the same defect that afflicted the old Congress: no quorum. On Congress's scheduled opening day, only eight of twenty-two senators and thirteen of fifty-nine representatives were present.[37]

At Mount Vernon, Washington inspected the Potomac improvements, made what he thought would be his last visit to his mother in Fredericksburg, and wrote more instructions for managing his farms. His anxiety about the presidency, expressed to Knox, was unfeigned:

My movements to the chair of government will be accompanied with feelings not unlike those of a culprit who is going to the place of his execution: so unwilling am I, in the evening of a life nearly consumed in public cares, to quit a peaceful abode for an ocean of difficulties, without that competency of political skill—abilities & inclination which is necessary to manage the helm.[38]

Martha shared his misgivings, describing herself as "truly sorry" he would be president. "When, or whether he will ever come home again," she added, "God only knows—I think it was much too late for him to go in to public life again." Unable both to pay off an overdue loan and also to cover the expense of moving, Washington took out a new loan at 6 percent interest.[39]

When a quorum of Congress assembled in early April, it unsealed the electors' votes. Each was supposed to cast two votes; the candidate with the highest total would be president; the runner-up would be vice president. Of the seventy-two electors, three voted for no one. The others all gave one vote to Washington. Adams won thirty-four, fewer than half of the second votes, with the rest spread among ten others. Washington, the colossus of American politics, had won unanimously, again.[40]

∾

On April 16, leaving Martha to follow with the two grandchildren, Washington departed for New York. He bade farewell to his neighbors in Alexandria "from an aching heart," then began a journey that resembled a king's progress. People lined the roads and formed escorts, sometimes choreographed, sometimes improvised.[41]

Greeted by a parade at the Pennsylvania border, Washington sent his carriage to the rear and mounted a horse so he would look more impressive. As he crossed the Schuylkill River Bridge, a mechanism dangled a laurel crown above his head at each end. He rode through military displays, ritual gunfire, and ringing church bells. As 20,000 Philadelphians cheered, he bowed continuously until reaching a banquet and its endless toasts.[42]

Leaving the city in morning rain, Washington sent his escort home to stay dry. The press gushed its approval. "Our beloved magistrate delights to show, upon all occasions, that he is a man," simpered one newspaper, "and . . . acts as if he considered himself the father—the friend—and the servant of the people."[43] Trenton trotted out the obligatory cavalry and infantry, though greater notice went to a choir of thirteen girls in white who sang adoring songs while strewing roses at the feet of Washington's horse. Amid the ceremony, Washington's mind filled with memories of a fierce skirmish fought over that same ground years before.[44]

Thirteen white-clad oarsmen rowed him across New York's Lower Bay as two choirs sang from nearby boats. Playful porpoises leapt alongside, expressing the animal kingdom's evident delight. Ships and shore batteries fired salutes until he reached the landing, where Governor Clinton ushered him to a rented residence.[45] The uproar made Washington somber, not elated. To his diary, he confided that the celebrations "filled my mind with sensations as painful . . . as they are pleasing." He dreaded that his time as president might bring on "the reverse of this scene."[46]

Compared to his journey, the inauguration on April 30 was a low-key affair. Representatives and senators, accompanied by horsemen, escorted him to the newly renovated Federal Hall (formerly city hall). Washington wore his brown suit of Connecticut cloth, knee-high stockings, buckle shoes, and a ceremonial sword.

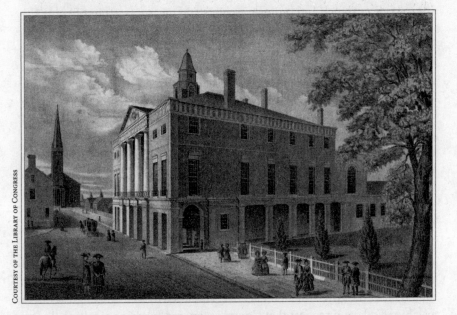

Federal Hall, New York City, 1789

He passed through the Senate chamber to an open second-story balcony, where New York chancellor Robert Livingston administered the constitutional oath before a crowd in the street below. When Livingston proclaimed, "Long live George Washington, President of the United States," a newspaper called the answering roar "the loudest plaudit and acclamation, that love and veneration ever inspired."[47]

As Washington delivered his address, his voice was low and his hands trembled. He had worried over the text for weeks. The first draft, prepared by his usual speechwriter, David Humphreys, had been quite long, covering seventy-three pages and making extensive policy recommendations. Washington turned it over to Madison for his views. His fellow Virginian produced a dramatically shorter speech that conspicuously refrained from proposing specific actions. Washington adopted Madison's draft.[48]

The surviving fragments of the first draft include passages wisely omitted, such as an extended justification of his attendance at the Philadelphia Convention, but they also offer an intriguing window onto Washington's thinking. It denounced the Articles of Confederation and boldly embraced an egalitarian view, predicting that America would reverse "the absurd position that the many were made for the few." It commented on military matters while recommending legislation designed to strengthen the union by creating a single currency and uniform weights and measures, strengthening the postal service, supporting education, and fostering invention with a patent system.[49]

Madison's draft, in contrast, featured inoffensive bromides, expressed in complex, backward-leaning syntax. The address began gloomily with Washington's regret at leaving Mount Vernon in his "declining years," noting the "frequent interruptions in my health [due] to the gradual waste committed on it by time." The mood grew no lighter when he detailed his "inferior endowments from nature" and lamented that he was "unpracticed in the duties of civil administration."

Washington then offered supplication and thanks "to that Almighty Being who rules over the Universe." He applauded Americans for "the important revolution just accomplished in the system of their united government, [and] the tranquil deliberations and voluntary consent of so many distinct communities." He proposed a single action: the adoption of constitutional amendments to calm public "inquietude," though not amendments that would make the government ineffective. He closed by asking Congress not to pay him a salary, a request that Congress ignored (perhaps recalling the extremely high expense reimbursement Washington claimed at the end of the Revolutionary War).[50]

The occasion, the simplicity of the speech, and his awkward delivery moved the emotions of his audience. Many wept. A Massachusetts senator thought Washington appeared as virtue personified, yet "grave, almost to sadness," and weighed down by his years. "Time," the senator wrote, "has made havoc upon his face."

On that day, Washington embodied the transition from monarchical and aristocratic society to self-government. As a republican leader more regal than most kings, he was uniquely suited to mediate that transition. Despite America's ideals of liberty and equality, monarchical styles still framed the expectations of many Americans. "Kingly government," Ben Franklin had said at the Philadelphia Convention, was mankind's natural inclination. A leading delegate had argued for a limited monarchy. Only months before the convention, some Americans invited a Prussian prince to become the American sovereign.[51]

With his martial profile and formal demeanor, Washington brought a regal style. The sword that hung from his belt, like the adulation that marked his travels, drew on the symbolism of kings, their mystical connection to the people and the violent ways they held power. Americans had begun to celebrate his February birthday, as they had always celebrated the birthday of the English king. His convoluted language of modesty echoed disclaimers offered by Virginia's royal governors, who could afford to be self-deprecating because they ruled by the king's hereditary right. Even a fervent foe of aristocracy used a royal comparison to celebrate Washington: "There is not a king in Europe who would not look like a valet de chambre by his side."[52]

Though Washington was urged several times to claim the crown of America, he insisted on the supremacy of the people. His credentials as "a man of the people" were genuine. He had traveled more widely within the country than most Americans. He had led soldiers from every state. His army had included indentured servants, ex-slaves, and many immigrants; he had journeyed with backwoodsmen and represented frontier families in the House of Burgesses. He had parleyed with Indians and fought against them. His life at Mount Vernon was intertwined with African American slaves, some of whom he had promoted to positions of authority.[53]

Moreover, he understood that he and other Americans had rejected the idea of royalty. During the war, he never questioned Congress's power over his army. When mutiny threatened, Washington ensured the army's submission to a people's government that was breaking its promises to that same army. He knew it was the ideal of self-government that brought indigent Americans and wealthy Europeans to fight for independence. At the Philadelphia Convention, he had presided over a national deliberation about how to embody that ideal in a stable, effective government that could survive in a world of kings and tyrants. That ideal, as he pronounced in his inaugural address, inspired him too.

As president, Washington would be the guardian of the union and its system of self-government, while reassuring the people with his authority. He needed to foster a return to prosperity, and to assert American rights on the world stage. The challenges were daunting, but he would not shrink from them.[54] When he had challenged the nation to remake its government, it did so. Now it had placed the new executive branch in his care. He felt the burden was entirely upon him. It mostly was.

GOVERNING

CHAPTER 42

On Untrodden Ground

As the first president under the Constitution, Washington would play a
major role in defining the presidency and constitutional government.
Because, as one scholar recently observed, the Constitution was "deeply in-
determinate," creating a government according to its terms required not only
legal interpretation, but also imagination.[1]

Washington's overarching goal was to strengthen the union of states by
avoiding the paralysis that crippled the Confederation, while also proving that
an effective government need not curtail liberty. There were many ways to fail,
but if he succeeded, the American experiment could be a model for the world.
Fortunately, the new president's most important task was to inspire trust, which
was Washington's greatest gift, one reinforced by his long service during the
Revolutionary War and retirement at the end of it.[2]

Powerful centrifugal forces divided regions: New England, the middle
states, the South, and the raw west. Each had its own economic interests, social
structures, even speech patterns. Against those forces, Washington pledged
that he "would lose the last drop of his blood" to preserve the "experiment on
the practicability of republican government, and with what dose of liberty
man could be trusted."[3]

Washington embodied the government as no later president has. Until
Congress created executive departments at summer's end, he largely was the
executive branch. Two former officers of the Confederation Congress continued to work without formal status: John Jay oversaw foreign affairs from his
law office while Henry Knox managed the nation's few soldiers from rooms
in a tavern. Holdovers from the Confederation sat at the postal service and

the treasury board, with uncertain legitimacy. The president commanded most of America's attention.[4]

A New York newspaper proclaimed Washington at least a demigod, looming "upon a scale of eminence that heaven never before assigned to a mortal." Another observer thought Washington was "the only man which man, woman and child, Whig and Tory, Feds and Antifeds appear to agree on." If a demigod, he was an anxious one, concerned, as he wrote on his fifth day in office, "that more will be expected from me than I shall be able to perform."[5]

The government was lodged in America's second largest city, which then was a grimy seaport rebuilding from fires and neglect during British occupation. The streets, a Virginian grumbled, "are badly paved, very dirty and narrow as well as crooked and . . . full of hogs and mud." A new congressman complained of the smells, which included the contents of chamber pots spilled out from houses. The urban din sometimes drowned out the debates at Federal Hall, the one public structure with pretensions to grandeur. The diverse population included about 2,000 enslaved Blacks, perhaps as many free Blacks.[6]

Washington's first challenge was defining his office. There were many alternative approaches to it, none dictated by the Constitution. The president might choose to be an administrative handmaiden to Congress, a distinguished figurehead mostly trotted out for formal occasions. Or he could attempt to dictate laws for Congress to enact. He might function solely as a constitutional safety net, preserving his authority for moments of crisis. Or perhaps the office should change as situations required.

Washington, a master of public display, struggled with basic questions of how to comport himself. What social interactions should he allow and in what settings? How often should he be available for meetings, with whom, and for how long? These were not mere punctilios of etiquette, but were patterns that would define the new government, which "needs help and props on all sides," a skeptical senator said. "The President's amiable deportment," he added, "smooths and sweetens everything."[7]

Washington sought advice from friends. Most counseled a middle course, neither too casual nor too regal. "Steer clear of extremes," Hamilton wrote, proposing a weekly reception open to the public, plus large entertainments quarterly, and also family dinners with friends. Senator William Maclay of Pennsylvania, whose diary provides an inside view of the new government, recognized that the crowds clamoring to see Washington could distract him from actually doing anything, but also that the president could not withdraw from the public "like an Eastern lama."[8]

Washington published a newspaper announcement that he would receive any person between two and three on Tuesday and Friday afternoons, would return no visits, and would attend no private social events. The Tuesday afternoon receptions evolved into starchy, men-only affairs enjoyed by no one, least of all the president. Martha's arrival in New York converted the Friday events into nonalcoholic evening receptions for both sexes. At the more casual Friday soirees, Washington wore no sword.[9]

Thursday dinners included up to a dozen guests, usually officials and legislators, sometimes with families. The events could lapse into awkward solemnity. A Massachusetts representative compared one to a funeral. The problem often was the host. At one dinner, the president "wore a settled aspect of melancholy." He sometimes absentmindedly tapped the table with his fork or knife, evidently eager for the meal to end. His failing hearing hindered conversation, and so did his adventures with dentures. His current oral device, which must have been a torture to insert against tender gums, contained both human teeth and some fashioned from a hippopotamus tusk.[10]

The exacting scrutiny of Washington's every word and action had to be wearying. Martha chafed at life in a goldfish bowl, describing herself as "more like a state prisoner than anything else." Because of the "bounds set for me which I must not depart from," she often preferred to stay home.[11]

∽

The uncertainty surrounding the president's role in the new government plunged the Senate into three weeks of agonizing over how to address him, a matter on which the Constitution was silent. In the army, Washington had been "Your Excellency," a title that also applied to state governors and the president of the Confederation Congress. Some thought the president's title should be more grand.

The question nonplussed Vice President Adams, who despised the term "president" as mundane, used by such lowly figures as leaders of cricket clubs and fire companies. Something more august, he insisted, would command the respect of foreigners. "Excellency" drew support from some senators, as did "highness," and "elective highness." Senator Maclay—a self-avowed common man—ridiculed the proposals to saddle America with "all the fooleries, fopperies, finches, and pomp of royal etiquette."[12]

Washington was wisely reticent about this unexpected dispute. His majestic silence avoided adopting Adams's position, which was out of step with the entire revolutionary and independence movement, without alienating his own vice president. Goaded by Adams, the Senate settled upon the ludicrous title of "His Highness the President of the United States of America and Protector of the Rights of the Same." The House of Representatives spared the nation, and Washington, when it thumpingly rejected the ponderous title in favor of "President of the United States." The portly Adams was not so fortunate; senators informally christened him "His Rotundity."[13]

However whimsically medieval the debate over titles might seem in retrospect, it appeared to confirm the fears of Anti-Federalists that the government would lean toward the aristocratic. David Stuart, the physician and legislator who became Washington's intimate after marrying Jack Custis's widow, reported from Virginia, "Nothing could equal the ferment and disquietude occasioned by the proposition respecting titles." Stuart added that Virginians applauded Washington for walking the streets like everyone else. "The great herd of mankind form their judgments of characters more from such slight occurrences," he wrote, "and perhaps they are right, as the heart is more immediately consulted" on small matters "and an error of judgement is more easily pardoned than one of the heart." Washington had again sidestepped a controversy.[14]

Through the early days of his presidency, Washington kept a low public profile, much as he had when he entered the House of Burgesses thirty years before. He took time to get the feel of his position, to sniff out political crosscurrents and identify where power lay, who would wield it, and how. He asked Stuart to report the public's opinion "of both men and measures, and of none more than myself," especially his mistakes. Washington had to know the criticisms so he could either reform his conduct or explain himself better.[15]

Everything the government did set a precedent. Madison, the leading figure in Congress, wrote to his father that the legislature was "in a wilderness without a footstep to guide us." Constitutional questions, he noted, were difficult to resolve "and must continue so until its meaning on all great points shall have been settled."[16]

Washington enjoyed several advantages as he ventured into that wilderness. The Philadelphia Convention had been a four-month tutorial on the attitudes and interests of each region, state, and economic group. Nearly a year of debates over ratification reinforced those lessons. Moreover, with only ten representatives and two senators identifying as Anti-Federalist, Washington faced little organized opposition, though North Carolina and Rhode Island still were outside the union and three large states had Anti-Federalist governors (New York, Massachusetts, and Virginia). His alliance with the brainy Madison, whom he consulted constantly, was another advantage. In one request to Madison, the president wrote apologetically, "I am very troublesome, but you must excuse me. Ascribe it to friendship and confidence."[17]

With customary diligence, Washington set about mastering his job. He gathered briefings from Henry Knox on the Indian tribes on the Northwest and Southwest borders. He asked John Jay about foreign negotiations, secured estimates of the nation's crushing debts, and inquired why the postal service was losing money.[18]

∾

Most congressmen were pleasantly surprised by the decorum of their first session. "There is less party spirit," wrote a Massachusetts legislator, "less personality, less intrigue, cabal, management, or cunning than I ever saw in a public assembly."[19]

Their first major task was enacting a tariff that would pay the government's bills, but the effort stretched on as some legislators demanded special treatment for products important back home—molasses for New England, iron and leather goods for Pennsylvania, and so on. A dispute developed over whether the tariff should be lower on ships from countries with which the United States had a commercial treaty (notably, France). Madison urged that distinction, but Congress chose to tax all foreign ships the same, concluding that a tax break for the French would reduce revenue without reducing British commercial domination.[20] Publicly mute on the question, the president wrote in a private letter that Madison had "the purest motives, and most heartfelt conviction," but "the subject was delicate, and perhaps had better not have been stirred." In this situation, Washington exhibited again what John Adams called his "gift of silence."[21]

Washington also said nothing when Congress debated whether the Senate, because it confirmed executive appointments, also should approve dismissals of those officers. Vice President Adams's tie-breaking vote in the Senate ensured the president's power to fire executive officers. Washington's reassuring presence, a South Carolinian worried, caused Congress to trust the executive too much: "Things which alarm and give uneasiness if committed by anyone else are overlooked when done by him."[22]

The president spoke up for the constitutional amendments that would become known as the Bill of Rights. When campaigning for Congress months before, Madison had promised to support some of the amendments recommended by state ratifying conventions. To honor that pledge, he proposed protections for individual rights, omitting any that would limit the government's taxing or commercial power or supremacy over the states. Washington provided a letter calling some of Madison's proposals "importantly necessary," and others "necessary to quiet the fears of some respectable characters and well-meaning men." When Congress adopted many of the proposals, the president sent them to the states for ratification.[23]

After less than two months in New York, however, matters took a dangerous turn: Washington developed a fever from an infection on the back of one thigh, which swelled, a congressman reported, "as large as my two fists." Draining the growth was the only option. Washington bore the brutal procedure without anesthesia, but the attending physician feared for Washington's life. The municipal government blocked traffic in front of the president's residence so street noise would not bother him.[24]

The press reported his illness only in vague generalities. Even fragmentary reports, a Boston newspaper reported, caused public anxiety. Two weeks after the surgery, Washington wrote that "feebleness still hangs upon me, and I am yet much incommoded by the incision," which forced him to lie on one side. His carriage was modified to transport him in a reclining position. For the Fourth of July, he donned his blue-and-buff army uniform and waved at a passing parade from the doorway.[25]

When the wound proved slow to heal, his convalescence stretched out. "I had no conception," he wrote to Dr. Craik, "of being confined to a lying posture on one side [for] six weeks—and that I should feel the remains of it for more than twelve." He blamed the infection on sedentary living and "the cares of office," which would "no doubt hasten my departure for that country from whence no traveler returns."[26]

Before he was fully recovered, the president initiated two confrontations with the Senate that would frame relations between that body and the executive. The first involved the appointment of a revenue collector for the port of Savannah. Though the Senate had confirmed Washington's appointees until then, it declined that one. Annoyed, the president startled senators by barging into their chamber without warning. Vice President Adams yielded his chair. The president asked why the Senate had rejected his nominee.

After a silence, Senator James Gunn of Georgia acknowledged that his opposition likely caused the rejection. The Senate's view, Gunn said, was "that no explanation of their motives or proceedings was ever due or would ever be given to any President of the United States." Because of his respect for this president, Gunn continued, he would explain on this occasion that his opposition grew from a personal dispute unrelated to the nominee's competence. Washington left.[27]

Though the president later expressed "very great regret" over the episode, he accepted the Georgian's position, which was the first exercise of senatorial courtesy, an unwritten practice that still allows a single senator to torpedo an executive appointee who resides in his or her home state. "As the president has a right to nominate without assigning the reasons," Washington wrote at the time, "so has the Senate a right to dissent without giving theirs."[28]

Two weeks later, a second encounter framed the president's power to make treaties "by and with the advice and consent of the Senate." Thinking that the constitutional language directed him to seek the Senate's "advice," Washington decided to confer with the Senate before sending a commission to negotiate with the Creek, Chickasaw, and Cherokee tribes. He and War Secretary Knox were struggling to balance the tribes' rights with the land hunger of whites.[29]

This time, in early August, Washington gave notice that he was coming to the Senate. Forewarning did not, however, produce a more collegial outcome.[30]

Washington again took Adams's chair. He announced that Secretary Knox was present to respond to questions. He handed a paper to Adams that listed seven questions on which he sought the Senate's views. Adams read the paper aloud, but street noise drowned him out. Robert Morris, Washington's close friend, asked Adams to read it again.

Another lengthy silence brought to Washington's face "an aspect of stern displeasure." Senator Maclay objected that the president's questions could not be answered yes or no, but required discussion. As each was posed separately, the senators decided to postpone it. When the Senate had put off several of them, Maclay recorded, Washington "started up in a violent fret" and protested, "'This defeats every purpose of my coming here.'" He agreed to postpone resolution of the matter, then stalked out of the chamber.

Two days later, Washington returned in full command of himself. He sat serenely through the Senate's discussion. Afterward, by one account, he said "he would be damned if he ever went there [the Senate] again." He never did, which set another precedent. Rather than consult the Senate before beginning negotiations, he decided to negotiate treaties first and then present them for approval. The Senate's power to "advise and consent" shrank. The Senate's role would be solely to affirm or reject a completed treaty.[31]

The episode over the Savannah collector cemented the Senate's power over presidential appointees; the treaty episode expanded the president's foreign-affairs power. Future presidents might consult with individual senators on pending treaty talks or appointments, but they would never again attempt to confer with the entire Senate.[32]

By the end of the summer, Congress created the new executive departments, allowing Washington to appoint their heads. He chose younger men of talent: Hamilton as secretary of the treasury, Knox as secretary of war, Jefferson (then serving as minister to France) as secretary of state, and Edmund Randolph as attorney general. Though a generation older than all but Jefferson, Washington knew their abilities. Hamilton and Knox had been officers in the army. Randolph and Hamilton were at the Constitutional Convention. Washington had served with Jefferson in the House of Burgesses and the Continental Congress.

Washington kept them on a short leash. He consulted with them constantly, meeting them by ones and twos, then in 1791 began the practice of meeting with the department heads together, crowding them into the second-floor study in the president's house. Washington's cabinet procedures, described by Jefferson, ensured his control over policy. If a matter came directly to a cabinet officer but required no action, the president was to be informed of the situation. If action was warranted, the president would review the proposed response before it was implemented. Frequently Washington had no comment on proposed responses; sometimes he dictated revisions. Thorny matters required direct consultation between the president and his subordinate. As Jefferson summarized the process, Washington "was always in accurate possession of all facts and proceedings" and took responsibility for "whatever was done."[33]

In short, Washington was in charge. He concealed from the public, and sometimes from history, the hands-on management habits developed in the army and at Mount Vernon. He allowed Hamilton to take the lead on economic policies, Jefferson to sign diplomatic correspondence, and featured Knox on military and Indian issues. Yet Washington's control over executive policy was so tight that some call him the originator of the "hidden hand" presidency. Jefferson followed the same procedures when he became president in 1801.[34]

For the only time in American history, a single person was responsible for appointing every executive official and judicial officer, including every Supreme Court justice. Washington called making appointments "the most irksome" part of his job. He applied three criteria to each appointment: the applicant's fitness for the job, his prior "merits and sufferings" (that is, his war experience), and the geographic distribution of executive jobs. When an appointment had an impact on a congressman's district or a senator's state, he consulted with that legislator.[35]

In August 1789, Washington's mother succumbed to breast cancer at age eighty-one. Unable to reach Virginia in time for the funeral, Washington wrote to his sister that the loss was "awful and affecting," but noted that Mary Washington had reached "an age beyond which few attain, and . . . with the full enjoyment of her mental faculties." As he usually counseled others, he professed "due submission to the decrees of the Creator."[36]

When Congress ended its session, Washington turned to a project for unifying the country: a presidential visit to every state in the union. He hoped to "become acquainted with their principal characters and internal circumstance, . . . [and learn] useful informations and advices on political subjects." In an age when travel was uncomfortable and sometimes risky, it was an ambitious plan for a man in his late fifties who was recovering from severe illness and surgery. Yet he always insisted that activity was the best medicine. It was sitting in rooms, he believed, that compromised his health.[37]

He went to New England first. Soon after leaving on October 15 with two aides and six servants, he recorded in his diary his admiration for the region's prosperity, its agriculture and home construction practices. In Connecticut, he found "a great equality in the people," with "few or no opulent Men and no poor." He visited factories for producing sailcloth, linen, woolens, and glass. Though a man of agriculture, Washington admired the dynamism of commerce and manufacturing. "A people who are possessed of the spirit of commerce," he wrote in 1784, "who see, and who will pursue their advantages, may achieve almost anything."[38]

Local gentry on horseback greeted him as he entered many towns. Sometimes bands played or fireworks soared or cannon boomed. Always, residents strained for a view of the hero while dignitaries jostled to present their proclamations. This was a chance to see Washington in the flesh, not merely his image engraved on a locket or painted on a pitcher. Washington discovered that the crowds preferred him in his old military uniform, so he changed into it whenever he neared a town.[39]

The Boston visit served as the journey's high point, beginning with a parade by all the trades and occupations. From the statehouse balcony, Washington heard the crowd's three cheers, then an ode and a song in his honor, then three more cheers. A banner read, "TO THE MAN WHO UNITES ALL HEARTS." Two days later came an oratorio and a dinner at Faneuil Hall.[40]

Washington often noted the women he encountered. An evening assembly in Boston, he wrote, attracted a hundred "handsome and well dressed ladies." The girls operating machines at a sailcloth factory, he recorded, "are the daughters of decayed families . . . and are girls of character." At another factory, he told a foreman that he employed the prettiest girls in Boston.

Washington also visited Lexington, where the war with Britain began, but did not recount his emotions there.[41]

The travel inevitably involved frustrations. Some roads were disappointing, while Washington sputtered that New Englanders unfailingly gave wrong road directions. Nonetheless, he returned to New York without significant mishap, after less than a month of travel. He attended Martha's reception that evening.[42]

In a letter to British historian Catharine Macaulay Graham, Washington reported that New England was "in a great degree, recovered from the ravages of war—the towns flourishing—and the people delighted with a government instituted by themselves and for their own good." He called his government "the last great experiment for promoting human happiness by reasonable compact in civil Society." He admitted his sense of the importance of his actions and words:

> I walk on untrodden ground. There is scarcely any action, whose motives may not be subject to a double interpretation. There is scarcely any part of my conduct which may not hereafter be drawn into precedent.[43]

As Washington entered his second year in office, his cautious style was working. A French diplomat offered a canny evaluation of Washington's performance as a "happy mixture of authority and modesty."

> While playing the role of the King of England he mingles in the crowd of his fellow citizens and appears to give them advice rather than order, to propose doubts to them rather than principles, to indicate to them the road to public prosperity rather than to want to lead them there himself.[44]

Two great challenges, however, loomed on the horizon: choosing the permanent seat of government and addressing America's war debts. They would test the new government and its president.

CHAPTER 43

The Debt and the Residence

As the new government neared its first anniversary, its credit was in tatters. Public debts exceeded $70 million, or roughly 40 percent of a national economy that had wallowed in depression for a decade. The federal government, and many states, only infrequently paid interest on their debts. Unless those governments made regular debt payments, no one would lend to them in future crises. In his first annual address on January 8, 1790, Washington called the public credit situation "a matter of high importance."[1]

Almost as pressing was the smoldering question of where the government would reside. Though superficially a straightforward geographic choice, the symbolic power of this "residence" question presented a political minefield of local interests and sectional rivalries. The choice would define the nation as urban or rural, steeped in Northern values or Southern customs, westward-looking or leaning toward Europe. The winning region would gain influence over the government and undoubted economic benefits.

To resolve those critical problems, the new president and Congress first had to understand why they had proved so intractable.

～

The residence question had festered longer. Indeed, for thirteen years since declaring independence, Congress had never unpacked its bags, moving from Philadelphia to Baltimore, to York, to Lancaster, back to Philadelphia, to Princeton, to Annapolis, to Trenton, and finally to New York City in 1785. As potential sites for its residence, Congress had considered more than fifty towns between Newburgh, New York, and Norfolk, Virginia, and west to the

Ohio River. When the new Congress gathered in 1789, the residence question was pressing.[2]

The decision loomed large because the United States had so little history, few traditions, and modest shared experience. Symbols of union were vital: the flag, the seal, the Fourth of July, even George Washington. The seat of government could embody the aspirations of the republic dedicated to liberty and justice. Yet the subject inflamed the parochial instincts of legislators. Acquiring the residence would bring a region greater access to government, increased demand for its land and crops and services, higher public spending, transportation improvements, and military protection. Madison estimated the value of the residence at $500,000 per year.[3]

Several criteria had emerged for the decision. The residence should be centrally located, affording all citizens fair access to their government, although centrality could be defined by wealth and population (which would bring the residence toward the north), or by geography (which pointed farther south). If the west were considered, the residence should be on a river that flowed east from the Appalachians, though neither the Mohawk, the Susquehanna, the Potomac, nor the James was navigable for its full length. A coastal location would foster commerce, but would be exposed to enemy warships.[4]

A bias had emerged for founding a new city that would signal America's break with the past. While building a new city, a temporary residence would be needed in an existing city. New York and Philadelphia were the only candidates for that role.[5]

A Virginian offered a pithy distillation of the criteria for the permanent residence: "nearly central, a convenient water communication with the Atlantic Ocean, and an easy access to the Western Territory." Major sites vying for the prize were the falls of the Delaware River (near Trenton, New Jersey); Germantown, Pennsylvania, a Philadelphia suburb; on the Susquehanna River west of Philadelphia; Baltimore; and somewhere on the Potomac River.[6]

Regional blocs sparred over the question. New Englanders and New Yorkers wanted the temporary residence in New York City and thought the Potomac too distant and too southern. Pennsylvanians and middle-state legislators preferred Philadelphia for the temporary residence, but spread their support among the four non-Potomac candidates for the permanent site. Virginians and most Southerners backed the Potomac. Georgians and South Carolinians disliked Philadelphia, which had too many anti-slavery Quakers and a harbor that could freeze in winter. Yet the regional blocs had fractured repeatedly through years of maneuvering.[7]

President Washington's commitment to developing the Potomac placed a heavy thumb on the scale. A congressional committee had toured that region five years before to evaluate it as the seat of government. At roughly the same time, when Congress leaned toward a site near Trenton, Washington wrote to a Virginia delegate that placing "the seat of empire at any spot on the Delaware [River] is . . . demonstrably wrong." Five years later, the Potomac Company was feverishly clearing the river, while its investors included two senators and three representatives from Maryland and Virginia. Promoters of the Potomac as Congress's permanent residence were placing enthusiastic articles in the press.[8]

In late August and September of 1789, the Pennsylvanians—led by Senator Robert Morris—secured New England support for placing both temporary and permanent residences in their state, but the deal fell apart. Madison trolled among the Pennsylvanians for Potomac support, but attention shifted to a site on the Susquehanna seventy miles west of Philadelphia, recently named Columbia, where developers were already raffling off building lots.[9]

Potomac backers responded by securing a requirement that the seat of government be on a navigable river; because Philadelphians would never allow improvement of the Susquehanna to a point where it could compete with Philadelphia's harbor, the Susquehanna option sank. The Germantown option fluttered into prominence when Robert Morris pledged $100,000 to construct buildings there for the government's residence, but last-minute ploys by Madison and New Englanders torpedoed that effort. A Virginia-based lunge on behalf of the Potomac also fell short. The debate took on an antic quality when five senators disputed whether to adjourn so they could view a hot-air balloon exhibition nearby.[10]

In that round of scheming, Washington stood apart from the fray, despite his strong preference for the Potomac. When Robert Morris asked Washington's view of the issue, the president was cautious, but seemed "much dissatisfied."[11] The congressional free-for-all evidently persuaded the president that he should not be a spectator when the question next arose. David Stuart wrote from Virginia that hopes for a Potomac residence "were always centered in you." He urged that Washington veto any other site. Since the president was loath to veto legislation on such a controversial subject—he would veto only two laws in eight years as president—he would need to apply his influence during legislative deliberations, not after they were completed.[12]

The politics of the issue presented a form of multidimensional chess. With two possible outcomes for the temporary residence, five leading candidates for the permanent residence, and as many as nine different voting blocs within Congress on the question, there were at least ninety possible voting configurations—but that calculation does not account for changes of heart, side deals, or political betrayals.

In late November, with Washington only recently back from New England, Madison reported on Robert Morris's latest intrigues. The Pennsylvanian had proposed to pretend to have a deal with Southerners for the Potomac, in order to "alarm" New York and New England into accepting Germantown as the permanent residence.[13]

The Potomac forces were mobilizing too. Merchants and landowners formed a committee to develop what Stuart called "the most flaming accounts" of the Potomac's advantages. They distributed broadsides and pamphlets throughout the nation. Virginia and Maryland nearly doubled Morris's financial offer, promising $192,000 to build the new residence on the Potomac. The battle soon would resume.[14]

∾

To address the nation's troubled finances, the sober Washington turned to his firebrand treasury secretary, Alexander Hamilton. With only three banks in the country, the American economy was unsophisticated. Without a national currency, Americans used some fifty forms of money, including a half dozen state currencies, various pre-Constitution debt instruments, and a grab bag of foreign coinage.[15]

Hamilton, with his high energy and outspoken admiration for British financial and banking practices, made an immediate impact on the new government. Within two days of taking office in September 1789, he arranged two short-term loans and met with the minister from France about payments due to that nation. Treasury, which collected taxes and managed spending, employed people in every state. In Hamilton's hands, it quickly dwarfed other government offices. Soon it would absorb the post office, reaching into every small town.[16]

Congress instructed Hamilton to report on how to restore public credit, which required a system for managing the public debts. Foreign loans to Congress totaled $12 million, plus interest, and domestic debt in several forms totaled another $41 million. "Loan certificates" reflected direct loans that had been made by wealthy citizens; on the open market, they could be bought in 1790 for 20 cents on the dollar. "Final settlement certificates" had been fobbed off on departing soldiers and army suppliers when peace arrived in 1783; they were worth even less. "Indents" had been issued instead of interest payments; they had the least value of all. Hamilton wanted to manage the Revolutionary War debts of the state governments also, which he estimated at more than $20 million. Taken together, public debts exceeded $70 million.[17] As Hamilton settled in, financial markets began to revive. Fortunes could be made if the government's credit recovered. If a note purchased for 10 percent of its face value were later redeemed in full, the profit would be 900 percent. People with money to invest were intensely interested in Hamilton's proposal for the debt, which would come in his January 1790 report to Congress on public credit. Washington reviewed that report in draft and approved it, much as he reviewed and approved every important policy statement of his presidency. The *Report on Public Credit of January 1790* embodied Washington's policy.

Released as a fifty-one-page pamphlet the day after Washington delivered his annual address, the report began with a lecture on paying debts. Nations that pay what they owe, it said, "are respected and trusted, while the reverse is the fate of those who pursue an opposite conduct." Maintaining public credit was the price of liberty.[18]

The report proposed to honor the face value of every debt incurred by the government, but not to pay the promised interest rates. Instead, all debt would command 4 percent interest. Principal would be repaid slowly, only 2 percent of it every year, so the debts would linger for generations; that would keep taxes at moderate levels and encourage wealthy individuals, eager for interest payments, to support the government. Finally, all of those certificates and indents would be replaced with new government debt obligations that could circulate as surrogate currency, greasing the wheels of the economy.

Controversially, the report proposed to pay only the current holder of any debt certificate, who usually was a rich man in a city who had bought it cheap from a struggling former soldier, farmer, or small-scale trader. The original holders would receive nothing. The government's promise to repay, Hamilton argued, had been made to whoever held debt certificates in their hands, not to those who had sold them to others. The government's honor required payment only to the current holder. Others, especially James Madison, disagreed.

Another contentious proposal was for the federal government to assume the Revolutionary War debts of the states. "Assumption" of state obligations would recognize that states incurred those debts for the common purpose of winning independence. Yet a deeper rationale was well explained by a Boston merchant. Assumption would, he wrote to Vice President Adams, unite creditors of the states with creditors of the federal government "in the support of one firm energetic government, and make it in their interest to unite in the regular collection of the revenue." If assumption consolidated all debt at the national level, states would not enact competing taxes, while state creditors would become federal creditors and support federal taxation.[19]

Foreseeing the windfalls that would become available under Hamilton's proposal, some investors dispatched agents to purchase any claims on the government they could find. A Connecticut congressman sent two ships to the South to acquire debt securities at bargain prices. Because Southerners and Westerners were often the targets of those agents, intense regional hostility developed. "Emissaries are still exploring the interior and distant parts of the union," Madison wrote in disgust, "in order to take advantage of the ignorance of holders." From Virginia, Washington's friend Stuart reported that "vermin from the northward" were buying public debt certificates.[20]

Anger flared among those who already mistrusted the new federal government. Assumption, a Virginian emphasized, would further consolidate the central power. Another Virginian predicted that assumption would leave state governments with "little else to do than eat drink and be merry." The wave of speculation prompted Madison to press for partial payments to the original debt holders, but Congress would not do it.[21]

Assumption also threatened to pit states against each other. Since the peace, states like Virginia and Pennsylvania had retired much of their debt. Others had not. Thus, assumption might reward those states that had paid little, since their debts would be repaid by national taxes on all citizens, including those in other states. This prospect bred more resentment.[22]

That problem could be resolved if Congress reimbursed *every* state for its war-related expenses. If the state had already paid its debts, the money from Congress would represent reimbursement; if the state still owed its original creditors, they could be paid with federal dollars. But this "settlements" fix would significantly increase the national government's costs and triggered other questions. Should a state be reimbursed for military costs that Congress never requested? What about Southern states with poor records of their wartime spending?[23]

The Federalist-dominated Congress embraced much of the proposed public-credit program: paying face value plus accrued interest, not paying the original debtholders who had sold their claims, and repaying principal slowly at a lower interest rate. The House of Representatives approved those elements by late March 1790. But it gagged on assumption of state debts, which failed on five separate votes.

Though the assumption fight triggered sectional conflicts, the configurations differed from those on the residence question. When North Carolina's representatives arrived in early April, following that state's recent ratification of the Constitution, they joined Marylanders and Virginians and Georgians in opposing assumption; Massachusetts, South Carolina, and Connecticut demanded it; other state delegations were divided. By May, Congress was stuck. New Englanders vowed to sink the whole credit program rather than approve it without assumption.[24]

Two external shocks worsened the stalemate.

∽

In mid-March, Quakers from the middle states petitioned Congress to end the importation of Africans as slaves. At a meeting with the Quaker leader, Washington was noncommittal on the issue. When Congress turned to the petitions, Georgians and South Carolinians denounced them in language that Madison called "intemperate beyond all example." After more than a week of passionate speechifying, Congress buried the petitions. After all, the Constitution specifically guaranteed slave imports until 1807. But the episode sharpened Southern resentment. Washington's friend Stuart reported that Virginians doubted they could continue in a union with "the Northern phalanx . . . whose interests are so dissimilar."[25]

Although Washington thought the Quaker petitions "an ill-judged bit of business," he dismissed Stuart's complaints. That Northerners pursued their interests, Washington replied, was unremarkable. Southerners should do the same. If New Englanders "move in a solid phalanx to effect their purposes," he asked, while "the Southern are always divided, which of the two is most to be blamed?"[26]

The second shock came when the president fell seriously ill again, the second time in less than a year. The affliction came on slowly. Observers thought Washington looked unwell in April. He, as usual, thought the solution was more activity. His attempts to exercise had made him a familiar sight, striding New York streets with two aides trailing behind, or riding past Manhattan fields. After a four-day outing to Long Island, pneumonia or a virulent flu hit hard on May 9, and carried him to the edge of death.[27]

His aide William Jackson immediately summoned a physician, then more doctors, but they could not relieve Washington's fever and chills. His breathing grew labored as his lungs filled. Six days after the disease struck, Senator Maclay called at the president's residence. Every eye in the house, he recorded, was filled with tears. A physician told him that the president's death was likely. "Too much," wrote Senator Pierce Butler of South Carolina, "hangs on the life of this good man." Abigail Adams reported that when Washington developed hiccups and a rattling in his throat, Martha fled the room, thinking him dying.[28]

Washington's recovery was as dramatic as the affliction's onset had been. At five in the afternoon, a Massachusetts congressman wrote, "the physicians disclosed that they had no hopes of his recovery." Then "about six he began to sweat most profusely, which continued until this morning and we are now told that he is entirely out of danger." As the fever sweated out, Washington coughed up the phlegm that had clogged his breathing.[29]

A week later, Washington described himself as a convalescent with "little inclination to [do] more than what duty to the public required." A month later, he reported still having a cough, chest pain, and shortness of breath. The experience shook him. Observing that he had passed through two severe illnesses in a year, he wrote that another would likely "put me to sleep with my fathers."[30]

According to Abigail Adams, the news of his illness was suppressed to avoid panic. Even news of his recovery was unsettling because it revealed that he had been sick. A New York paper proclaimed that "a life so precious should be watched with the eyes of Argus; health so important should be nurtured with the vigilance of angels." A New Jersey man reported that concern was universal because "he alone has the confidence of the people." A Virginian agreed: "Perhaps the happiness of a country never depended so much upon the life of one man."[31]

After the president's recovery, Congress focused anew on the twin issues it had to resolve: assumption and the residence. Since at least the middle of March, some had wondered if a single grand bargain might resolve both, attracting majorities from the shifting coalitions for each element of the bargain. Largely unseen, the hand of the recovering president would guide that effort. As Maclay wrote in his diary, the order of the day became, "Vote this way for me, and I will vote that way for you."[32]

CHAPTER 44

The Compromise

In his effort to guide the congressional intrigue over the residence and assumption, Washington employed a little-noticed figure. Major William Jackson has been described as Washington's aide, or secretary, or bodyguard. Born in England but raised in America, he served with the Continental Army, traveled as a diplomat, and was assistant secretary of war at the end of the fighting with Britain. Settling in Pennsylvania, he abandoned law studies to sign on as secretary of the Constitutional Convention, which brought him to Washington's presidential staff.[1]

While other aides managed correspondence, Jackson gravitated to active chores. He gathered recommendations for executive jobs, extended invitations for dinners and meetings, and traveled with the president. The thirty-year-old bachelor was nimble in a pinch. When illness struck the president in May 1790, Jackson managed the office during Washington's recuperation because the other senior aide, Tobias Lear, was honeymooning. When a lady's headdress caught fire at a reception, Jackson extinguished the flames with his hands.[2]

In the spring of 1790, Jackson's portfolio expanded to representing the president in the deal-making about the most pressing issues facing Congress.[3]

∾

The bargaining centered on the Pennsylvania delegation, which was large, fractious, and had four horses in the residence race: Philadelphia for the temporary residence, and the Susquehanna, Germantown, and Falls of the Delaware for the permanent. The Pennsylvanians were considering a proposition that they embrace assumption in return for votes for Philadelphia as temporary residence. At the time, the Potomac forces favored a temporary residence in Philadelphia as a stepping-stone to winning the permanent residence. Before Washington fell ill, Jackson conferred several times with the Pennsylvania leader in the House, George Clymer. Jackson then delivered to other Pennsylvanians "a florid harangue on the golden opportunity" presented by the deal.

In his journal, Maclay griped that Jackson's involvement, as Washington's representative, was "far from proper." Five days later, Maclay noted that Jackson and two other Washington aides were outside the Senate when it adjourned, waiting to waylay the members because "the crisis is at hand." Nevertheless, the House narrowly rejected assumption the following Monday, April 12.[4]

Though that vote could not have pleased Washington, the two issues now were linked, and they would stay that way. Some reported that the Pennsylvanians were trying to win the residence by supporting assumption. Others thought Virginians were pursuing the same deal. Many saw that the bargain might be struck, but no one could make it happen.[5]

Some of the blocs in Congress were well defined. Most Pennsylvanians sought the temporary residence for Philadelphia, believing that once the government was in the nation's largest city, it would never leave, certainly not for a new city—what one legislator scornfully called "palaces in the woods."[6] Most New Englanders wanted assumption and proposed to get it by trading their votes for the residence.[7] New Yorkers aligned themselves with New England on assumption, but wanted the temporary residence to stay where it was. Virginians always invoked the president's preference for the Potomac. "No Virginian can talk on any subject," Maclay complained, "but the perfection of General Washington interweaves itself." A South Carolinian summarized the atmosphere in Congress: "Negotiations, cabals, meetings, plots and counterplots."[8]

Several officials who answered to the president—Hamilton, Jackson, and Hamilton's assistants William Duer and Tench Coxe—plunged into the horse trading. Secretary of State Jefferson, fresh from France and Monticello, joined in. Only a few days after the crisis of Washington's illness, Jackson huddled with Robert Morris of Pennsylvania and John Langdon of New Hampshire, senators at the center of the deal-making. "I cannot account for Jackson having meddled in this business," Maclay fumed again.[9]

Jackson, like Jefferson and Hamilton, represented the president. Although Washington respected the independence of Congress, that hardly precluded explaining to lawmakers the true interests of the nation on vital issues.

Madison, the savviest operative in Congress, briefed Washington as the contending forces issued ultimatums and rescinded them, proposed deals and reneged on them. Senators were dragged from sickbeds to cast key votes; one was carried to the Senate floor in his bed wearing his nightcap, with two doctors in tow. In early June, with assumption and the residence unresolved, Rhode Island ratified the Constitution. Its senators rushed to New York, forcing a fresh round of strategizing.[10]

In the second week of June, with the scheming nearing full boil, Washington left with Hamilton and Jefferson for an ocean fishing trip. Though Washington enjoyed fishing, little evidence suggests that the other two did. Moreover, those three did not usually while away casual hours with one another. Nonetheless, they spent three days together, bobbing on the waves off New Jersey.[11]

Newspaper accounts portrayed the president hauling in sea bass and blackfish, more evidence of his return to robust health. Nothing, however, disclosed the shipboard conversations in what resembled an eighteenth-century exercise in executive strategizing. Jefferson shared Washington's enthusiasm for developing the Potomac, while Hamilton and Washington thought assumption essential to restore public credit. It is inconceivable that they did not plan, in detail, how to secure congressional approval for those measures.[12]

Back on land, the deal-making swerved in an unanticipated direction. After the Pennsylvanians won a House vote to adjourn Congress to Philadelphia—a ploy intended to make that city the temporary residence—a countermove by New Yorkers and New Englanders substituted Baltimore as the temporary residence. A day later, on June 11, the House accepted Baltimore by a whopping 53–6, a vote that was more a repudiation of Pennsylvania finagling than an embrace of the city on Chesapeake Bay. Yet Baltimore's star was rising. With a population of 15,000, it offered urban amenities, while its port did not freeze. Southerners liked that Maryland was a slave state. But with the question moving to the Senate, no one was giving up.[13]

Congressmen bemoaned the bargaining. One scorned "this despicable grog shop contest, whether the taverns of New York or Philadelphia shall get the custom of Congress." Another despaired over "such caballing and disgracefully mixing national with local questions that . . . I feel ashamed of the body to which I belong." The scheming, Maclay wrote on June 18, stretched endlessly: "The Very Goddess of Slowness seems to have possessed Congress."[14]

The president's men soon would unstick those jammed congressional gears.

∾

The outlines of the deal had been plain for weeks: Votes for (or against) assumption would be swapped for votes for (or against) a permanent residence and votes for (or against) a temporary residence. Having feverishly tried to pull off this bargain since February, Robert Morris tried again on the evening of June 11. He and two colleagues met with Jackson, Washington's eyes and ears, and also with Hamilton's assistant secretary of the treasury. They agreed that on the following morning, Morris and Hamilton would bump into each other as each innocently strolled along the Battery.

The accidental encounter occurred as planned. Hamilton offered to search for votes to deliver the permanent residence to Pennsylvania if Morris produced votes for assumption. Morris wanted more: the temporary residence in Philadelphia too. Hamilton agreed to Morris's terms, but could not gather the votes to deliver both residences to Pennsylvania, while Morris lacked enough Pennsylvania votes to pass assumption.[15]

When the Hamilton-Morris bargain died, Jefferson approached Morris, announcing that his goals were assumption, placement of the temporary residence in Philadelphia, and placement of the permanent residence on the Potomac. Those, not coincidentally, were the president's goals. Each step showed that a central intelligence was directing Jackson and the cabinet secretaries: President Washington.[16]

On June 14, Jefferson proposed a bargain to Morris and a New Jersey senator: Place the temporary residence in Philadelphia for fifteen years, then the permanent residence on the Potomac. At the same time, Madison, long the president's ally, moved to jump-start assumption, offering pro-assumption votes to New Englanders if they supported a temporary residence in Philadelphia.[17]

The president's men were feverishly trying to fit together the pieces of a maddening puzzle.

∾

Jefferson created the legend that he hosted a dinner where the deal was struck to swap assumption for placing the residence on the Potomac. In three separate documents, he described the conversations that supposedly produced the Compromise of 1790: a contemporaneous letter to James Monroe that mentioned no dinner, and two later memoranda to himself, one composed a few years later and another twenty-five years after that. The first version, to

Monroe, emphasized how dire the situation was: Without the public-credit program, the nation's financial standing would "burst and vanish, and the states [will] separate to take care every one of itself."[18]

The two later versions describe Jefferson encountering Hamilton as he was leaving the president's house, the treasury secretary asking Jefferson to help find votes for assumption, and the benevolent Jefferson presiding over a dinner at which Madison and Hamilton made the deal: Madison agreeing to soften his opposition to assumption and to scrounge up two votes for it from Potomac valley congressmen once legislation was enacted establishing Philadelphia as the temporary residence and the Potomac as the permanent one. Hamilton was to produce New England votes to carry the residence terms of the bargain.[19]

Neither of the other diners ever described that discussion, though the three men may well have discussed the situation over a meal. Jefferson's accounts, however, provide a partial view of the bargaining. Before agreeing to the compromise, Virginia legislators had to be sure their state would be reimbursed for war debts it had already paid but could only incompletely document. By June 20, Madison had spent two days with the federal commissioner appointed to settle those accounts; the Virginian emerged with reimbursement nearly as large as that claimed by any other state.[20]

Moreover, before Jefferson's supposed dinner miracle, it was Madison—not Hamilton—who negotiated with New Englanders to trade the residence and assumption issues. Also, three days before the dinner meeting, Washington himself met for hours with a leading Massachusetts congressman, Theodore Sedgwick, evidently on precisely those matters. Sedgwick, a central player in the final compromise, described his session with the president in a letter to his wife that was both breathless and elliptical:

> I spent two or three hours this afternoon with the President who treated me with a familiarity I have never before experienced, and with a confidence which was highly flattering to me. The substance of the conversation I may hereafter relate to you. The affairs of this country are drawing to a crisis. A very few days will determine what will be the future complexion of the government. I have much stronger hopes than I have for some time entertained of a favorable issue.

Though Sedgwick did not use the terms "assumption" and "residence," no other issues then involved a crisis that could determine the government's future. Washington, having employed Jackson, Jefferson, Hamilton, and Madison to break the congressional logjam, seems to have stepped onto the playing field himself. New England votes for the Potomac residence would be crucial.[21]

The eventual compromise was implemented in a series of votes across several weeks. Massachusetts cemented the deal on June 28 and 29 when its senators broke ranks from other New Englanders to kill Baltimore's bid for the permanent residence, leaving the way open for the Potomac. When a New York senator mounted a last-ditch effort to keep the temporary residence in New York and move the permanent one to Baltimore, Hamilton told him that assumption could pass only if the residence went first to Philadelphia, then to the Potomac.[22]

A central part of the deal was that Pennsylvanians would abandon their quest for the permanent site, which they had agreed to do. With many of them persuaded that Congress would never leave Philadelphia once located there, they accepted that condition.[23]

Maclay of Pennsylvania decided that the puppet master was the tall man in the president's residence. "It is in fact the interest of the President of the United States that pushes the Potomac," he wrote on June 30, "by means of Jefferson, Madison, [Senator Charles] Carrol[l] [of Maryland] and others." Two weeks later, after several votes implementing the compromise, Maclay's judgment was the same: "The President of the United States has (in my opinion) had a great influence in this business."[24]

The implementation of the bargain was relatively smooth. The residence legislation cleared the Senate on the first of July, by two votes; the margin in the House was three votes. Shortly before Washington signed that bill into law, the Senate voted to assume $21.5 million of state debts and to approve the financial settlements with the states. Massachusetts and South Carolina received the largest settlements, $4 million each, but Virginia's was more than $3 million. In a letter to his father, Madison boasted that Virginia would receive more in reimbursement than its remaining war debt. Over the next two weeks, after Washington signed the residence legislation, the Senate approved the public-credit bill (with assumption) by four votes; in the House vote on that bill, the margin was six votes.[25]

❧

A standard test for determining causation for an event is to ask the Latin question "Cui bono?" or "Who benefitted?" Only one of the principal participants in the Compromise of 1790, President Washington, walked away with everything he wanted.

Hamilton secured assumption, but at the cost of placing the residence on the Potomac, an outcome he called "bad." Jefferson loved winning the Potomac residence, but soon repented his support for the public-credit program: "Of all the errors of my political life, this has occasioned me the deepest regret." Madison also pushed relentlessly for the Potomac, but opposed assumption.[26] Pennsylvanians celebrated the temporary residence in Philadelphia while assuring one another that it would ripen into a permanent arrangement. Massachusetts legislators were elated to secure assumption while hoping that the Potomac residence was too absurd actually to happen. Jefferson wrote of the compromise, "there will be something to displease and something to soothe every part of the Union."[27]

Except for Washington. The president won everything he wanted. Assumption was a linchpin of his program to retrieve public credit and strengthen the government. A Potomac residence fulfilled his years of effort to promote his home region. The residence, a Maryland representative exulted, would be worth millions.[28]

The speculation among Pennsylvanians that the permanent residence might never get to the Potomac was a delusion. No one should have doubted Washington's ability to make that happen, and to do so at speed. By the end of 1790, he had personally scouted eighty miles along the river and selected the site for the seat of government, unsurprisingly near Mount Vernon. Announcing his choice in January 1791, he appointed three commissioners (all friends) to oversee the project, though he continued to be its driving force. Maryland and Virginia soon ceded jurisdiction over the necessary land and approved funding. Washington retained agents to acquire lands and signed agreements with local property owners. He chose Andrew Ellicott to survey the site, and Peter L'Enfant to design the federal city. In September 1791, the commissioners named the city after him. As Madison had marveled years before when Washington seized hold of the Potomac River improvement project, "The earnestness with which he espouses the undertaking is hardly to be described."[29]

Washington largely concealed his deal-making in 1790. Even his private statements were careful.[30] Yet Washington's hand showed when Major Jackson entered negotiations, and in the president's session with Sedgwick of Massachusetts. Indeed, it showed whenever Hamilton or Jefferson huddled with legislators; both worked at Washington's direction, and Jefferson portrayed Washington as a chief executive who was entirely in charge. That was always his way. Managing Mount Vernon, acquiring western land, commanding the Continental Army, and leading the Potomac Company, Washington exerted tight control and carefully minded the details. He approached the most important domestic legislation of his presidency the same way.[31]

In the final balloting, four representatives from Maryland and Virginia and one Maryland senator provided key votes for assumption. Four of those five came from the Potomac valley and had deep ties to Washington: Alexander White had served in the House of Burgesses with Washington, and later became a director of the Potomac Company; Charles Carroll of Carrollton was also involved in the river improvement and had been a member of the congressional Committee in Camp at Valley Forge; Richard Bland Lee was Washington's congressman and came from the numerous Lee clan of Westmoreland County with whom Washington was intimate; and Daniel Carroll had served with Washington at the Philadelphia Convention. With these men, Washington's influence was great. The conclusion that he was deeply engaged in the deal-making is buttressed by his response when Daniel Carroll and George Gale of Maryland lost reelection bids because of their support for the residence/assumption bargain. The president promptly appointed both to federal jobs.[32]

A final point is sometimes lost in this story. Almost all of the contending parties ardently pursued their regional interests. New Englanders needed assumption to bail out their state governments, while Northerners held a huge share of the outstanding state debts, making assumption essential to them. Southerners seethed over the profits that would flow to Northerners from the public-credit program. That resentment fueled Southern demands for the residence, which they expected would give them both material benefits and enhanced political power.[33] By guiding and providing essential support for the Compromise of 1790, Washington ensured that each region won something, helping to reconcile North and South and strengthen the union.

That Washington never publicly or privately exulted in his deft navigation through these vexing issues is not surprising. He did not value either transparency or self-congratulation. In mid-June 1790, when the politicking was at its height, the French minister to the United States reported about the president, "Nobody has ever been more impenetrable than General Washington. Even the people who constantly surround him know his way of thinking only by the orders he gives."[34]

When Congress adjourned at the end of summer 1790, Washington sailed to Rhode Island to welcome the tardiest state into the union. Worn by the congressional session and his acute illness three months before, Washington longed for Mount Vernon, where he wished to "have my mind as free from public cares . . . as circumstances will allow."[35] On August 30, after the usual pomp and booming cannon tributes, he left for home.

CHAPTER 45

The Bank

Washington knew about credit and debt. As a young man, he had fenced with British merchants over his own debts. Many of his peers had staggered under debt; some crumbled. Friends borrowed money from him; some reneged. To sustain himself while serving as president, he borrowed from wealthy men. Like most of his countrymen, however, he had little experience of banks. In 1780, Robert Morris had established the first bank in America.[1] Nine years later, two more were operating. All served the wealthy and commercially sophisticated.

As the government moved to its temporary residence in Philadelphia in late 1790, a proposal to establish a publicly sponsored bank—the Bank of the United States—became the president's next political challenge. His response would define the government's powers under the Constitution.

∾

The Washingtons' new home in Philadelphia was familiar—the former home of Robert and Mary Morris, where Washington stayed during the Constitutional Convention. Washington showered his staff with instructions for the move.[2]

Although the mansion at Market and Sixth Streets was grand for its time, it bulged with the Washington family and retainers: Martha and the president, two grandchildren, four secretaries (one with a wife), valets, coachmen, footmen, porters, maids, and housekeepers (many enslaved), plus some family members of staff. Washington never complained about the close quarters, a silence sometimes attributed to his wish to avoid spurring the construction of a new presidential home that might threaten relocating the residence to the Potomac. Philadelphia actually built that new residence anyway, but Washington never moved in.[3]

Philadelphia aimed to please the new government. The city repealed its ban on theatrical performances, allowing the president to indulge in his favorite entertainment. The county courthouse, next to the State House, became Congress Hall, with the Treasury and State Departments nearby. On February 22, the celebration of Washington's fifty-ninth birthday mimicked the traditional observance of the king's birthday: a public dinner, a ball, and rounds of "huzzahs."[4]

Washington's years of physical activity were taking their toll, at least to Senator Maclay's eye. "His frame would seem to want filling up," the Pennsylvanian wrote after dinner with the president, "his motions rather slow than lively . . . his complexion pale nay almost cadaverous. His voice hollow and indistinct, owing, as I believe, to artificial teeth before his upper jaw."[5]

Yet when Washington delivered his annual address on December 8, 1790, the astringent Maclay conceded that he performed "well enough, or at least tolerably." Before the combined houses of Congress, Washington reported that "the abundant fruits of another year have blessed our country with plenty." He praised growing trade, credit improvement, and public revenues above projections. He called for legislation to organize the militia, a national mint, and the post office.[6]

The address slighted important questions. Washington mentioned Indian unrest near the Wabash River, but not reports that an expedition had met a bloody defeat there. Neither did he refer to the proposal for a national bank that Congress soon would address. The omissions reflected his understanding of the power of information, which he released to suit his purposes, and also his instinct to skirt controversial matters in order to tamp down forces of disunion.[7]

Hamilton presented the proposal for the Bank of the United States as part of Congress's establishment of public credit, and separately urged a new excise tax on whiskey to pay for the interest on the assumed state debts. His report—as approved by Washington—called the bank "an institution of primary importance." The United States, it asserted, had so little currency that some communities relied on barter, throttling economic activity. The report offered a primer on banking, and promised three principal benefits from the proposed bank. First, its notes would function as money and lubricate commercial transactions. Second, its loans to the government would help the nation through crises. And third, it would smooth the collection of tax revenues.[8] The United States would hold one-fourth of the bank's stock and name some directors. The remaining stock and a majority of the board would be private.

Southern legislators feared that a Philadelphia-based institution might anchor the residence in that city, preventing its transfer to the Potomac, while others saw the bank as centralizing power. Legislators from frontier regions disliked the whiskey tax because western farmers distilled a substantial share of their grain into liquor for eastern markets. After lively debates, Congress passed both measures by wide margins.[9]

Madison, the nation's leading lawmaker and one who still had the president's ear, supported the whiskey tax but challenged the bank with a novel argument: that it was beyond Congress's powers. The constitutional argument did not faze most congressmen, but it unsettled the politically astute president when it was time for him to sign the legislation. At the same time, legislation was pending before the Senate that would add Alexandria to the new federal district, affirming Washington's selection of the site for the new seat of government. Northern lawmakers still disliked a Potomac residence, though they wanted the bank legislation. Once again, Northerners and Southerners were lined up on different sides of two questions at the same time. Another bargain, this one implicit, was before them.[10]

As presented by Madison, the bank legislation raised a core question about government power. The Constitution allowed Congress to legislate on subjects listed in Article I, Section 8, such as levying taxes, borrowing money, and regulating commerce. That list of "enumerated" powers did not include chartering a bank, or even creating a corporation. Indeed, at the Constitutional Convention, a delegate had argued that Congress should be able to create corporations, but his proposal was not adopted. By what intellectual alchemy, Madison asked, could Congress nevertheless create this bank corporation?[11]

For all of its intellectual elegance, Madison's argument marked a reversal of his view of congressional powers only three years before. An awkward moment for him arose during the debates when a New Jersey congressman read a passage from the forty-fourth essay in *The Federalist*, one Madison had written (though his authorship was not known at the time). In that passage, Madison had declared that Congress held powers *not* enumerated in Article I, Section 8 because that provision granted a catchall power to make "all laws which shall be necessary and proper for carrying into execution" the enumerated powers. "No axiom is more clearly established in law, or in reason," Madison wrote in *The Federalist*, "than that wherever the end is required, the means are authorized; wherever a general power to do a thing is given, every particular power necessary for doing it, is included."[12]

∾

The constitutionality of the bank was the type of question that made Washington regret his limited education. Years as a justice of the Fairfax County Court had not prepared him for constitutional argument. He readily understood, however, the political crosswinds he faced. His administration had proposed the bank, with his blessing. Vetoing the bill would be a repudiation of his treasury secretary, who likely would resign. In his annual message, Washington had applauded the revival of public credit, which many attributed to Hamilton, whose resignation would be a terrible upheaval early in the life of the government.

But the constitutional objection came from Madison, Washington's closest political confidant since he had resigned from the army, a man whose judgment and learning he respected. Moreover, most of the bank's opponents were Southerners; signing the bill would aggravate divisions between North and South. The worst outcome would be to veto the bill but watch Congress override his veto. That would show that he lacked confidence in Hamilton, while also making himself appear politically weak.

Many years later, Madison remembered having "several free conversations" with the president on the constitutional issue. Washington, he recalled, "was greatly perplexed," believing that the bank would be useful. Though the president was inclined to a broad construction of national powers, he also knew from the ratification debates that many delegates had feared a powerful federal government. Although Washington never agreed that the bank was unconstitutional, Madison thought he "listened favorably."[13]

Washington placed the issue before Attorney General Randolph, who submitted two written opinions endorsing Madison's objections. Randolph's opinions were workmanlike but uninspiring; at least, they failed to inspire the president. So Washington, who had only ten days in which to decide whether to sign or veto, asked for his secretary of state's view. Though Jefferson had been in France during the Philadelphia Convention and the ratification process, Washington respected his abilities.[14]

Jefferson responded swiftly. His written opinion began by discussing common-law issues that were not all that relevant, then cited what is now the Tenth Amendment to the Constitution, which was then pending before the state legislatures for ratification. Jefferson emphasized that this amendment, though not yet in effect, reserved to the states or to the people "all powers not delegated" to Congress. "To take a single step beyond the boundaries thus specially drawn around the powers of Congress," he wrote, "is to take possession of a boundless field of power, no longer susceptible of any definition."

Jefferson thus insisted that no enumerated power authorized the bank legislation because the bill laid no taxes, borrowed no money, and regulated no commerce. On the most delicate question—whether the bank legislation might be deemed "necessary and proper" to support those activities—Jefferson noted that each could be performed without a national bank. That the bank might facilitate them, he reasoned, was mere convenience. Convenient, he argued, was not "necessary." Jefferson continued with passion:

> Can it be thought that the Constitution intended that for a shade or two of *convenience,* more or less, Congress should be authorized to break down the most ancient and fundamental laws of the several states[?] . . . Nothing but a necessity invincible by any other means, can justify such a prostration of laws which constitute the pillars of our whole system of jurisprudence.

In tacit recognition that Washington generally leaned toward vigorous government action, Jefferson concluded that if the president found the constitutional issue uncertain, he should consider deferring to Congress and signing the legislation.[15]

On the day after receiving Jefferson's opinion, Washington sent it to Hamilton, together with Randolph's, asking for a response. Time was short, and Hamilton faced an uphill climb. Not only was he confronting the massed opinion of Washington's Virginia friends, but the president already had on his desk two draft veto messages he had asked Madison to prepare.[16] Hamilton had, however, one great advantage: By weighing in last, he could answer the contentions of his opponents. He took five days to prepare his response, working through the night to complete it. Though that left Washington little time to evaluate the arguments, Hamilton's answer was powerful.

He drove immediately into the Virginians' weakest point: whether Congress held powers "implied" by the Constitution, which had been Madison's subject in *Federalist No. 44.* Although the Constitution granted no express power for Congress to create a corporation or a bank, Hamilton insisted that it could do so in the course of exercising another power that was enumerated. He illustrated his point by noting that Congress could not create a corporation to direct the Philadelphia police, having no power whatever over city police. But, he continued, it could establish corporations to collect taxes or assist with foreign trade, subjects within its enumerated powers.

Hamilton then dismantled Jefferson's contention that a merely convenient measure is not necessary. It cannot be, he insisted, that legislation is permitted only when an enumerated power would otherwise be entirely "nugatory." Very little legislation would ever be enacted under that standard. "Necessary" must mean "useful" or conducive to a public purpose. Thus, Hamilton continued, the national government might collect taxes without the bank, but the bank would make collection easier and more efficient; that was enough.

Hamilton pointed to government actions already being performed that were *not* specified in the Constitution: building lighthouses to assist trade or creating a territorial government to manage the Northwest Territory (the future states of Ohio, Indiana, Illinois, Michigan, Wisconsin, and part of Minnesota). Neither was authorized by an enumerated power, yet no one dreamt of objecting to them as beyond Congress's power. Indeed, the creation of territorial governments showed that Congress could erect corporations: in that instance, public corporations. Hamilton easily linked the bank legislation to enumerated congressional powers. The bank would facilitate tax collection and trade regulation by creating a medium for both. It would assist governmental borrowing by making loans. It would support national defense as a conduit for the payment of troops and suppliers.[17]

Upon receiving Hamilton's analysis, Washington had two days to make up his mind. He used all of it, signing the bill at the last minute on the afternoon of February 25. Hamilton had persuaded his audience of one, reassuring him that his inclination to support this government initiative would not violate the Constitution. Congress swiftly enacted the supplemental legislation affirming the boundaries of the new residence on the Potomac.[18]

By their combined actions, Washington and Hamilton interred the argument that the Constitution granted Congress only those powers absolutely necessary to implement an enumerated power. The resulting doctrine of implied powers gave Washington the vigorous national government he wanted. And the bank itself was an immediate success. When its stock was offered for sale on the Fourth of July, it sold out in an hour. Northern legislators were delighted. In addition, Congress confirmed Washington's choice of the Potomac location for the seat of government, which pleased Southerners. Once again, North and South each walked away with one win and one loss. Once again, only Washington got everything he wanted.[19]

The bank episode, in particular, reflects characteristic elements of Washington's leadership. Facing a momentous question, he consulted widely, not committing himself until he completed that process. And his decision was not based on a simple headcount among his advisers; all three Virginians had recommended a veto. Political expediency was not a controlling factor either.

He had not sided with his fellow Southerners, nor had he worried that establishing the bank might make it more difficult to move the government to the Potomac. Rather, he adopted the argument that, in his view, led to the best government. As the First Congress receded into history, a New Englander proclaimed that "in no nation, by no legislature, was ever so much done in so short a period for the establishment of government, order, public credit, and general tranquility."[20]

∾

As soon as Congress adjourned in March, Washington turned to conducting the southern half of his national tour. He wanted to finish it before summer heat set in, so he left Philadelphia near the end of March.[21]

He traveled first to Georgetown, where he met with commissioners of the future District of Columbia, negotiated with landowners, and reviewed surveys and designs for the new city. After a week at Mount Vernon, he set off with a larger entourage than he had taken to New England, including Major Jackson and eleven horses.[22]

Compared to the New England journey, the distances in the South were greater, the roads worse, the settlements smaller and farther apart, and the accommodations often squalid. Choking dust from sandy roads tormented him until rain turned roads into bogs. He found no factories to tour, and many greetings were low-key. Tarborough, North Carolina, welcomed him, he recorded, with "as good a salute as could be given with one piece of artillery." Crossing the Occoquan River, several carriage horses slipped off a ferry but the carriage did not.[23]

The travel was not all misery. Richmond, Charleston, Savannah, and Wilmington staged festive dinners and balls, allowing the president to record the women in attendance as elegant or respectable or well dressed and handsome. In his honor, some wore sashes or hats marked with eagles, or the legend "Welcome the Hero," or the initials "G.W." He reviewed abandoned British forts and battlefields of the war. At a Moravian settlement in Salem, North Carolina, he admired a system for piping fresh water directly into homes.[24]

While still on the road, Washington received troubling news about his slaves at the president's residence in Philadelphia. Attorney General Randolph's slaves had asked about a Pennsylvania statute that granted freedom to enslaved persons who lived in Pennsylvania for six months. Randolph reported to one of Washington's aides that Washington's enslaved workers also knew of the statute, and warned that as many as nine of them might claim freedom. To stop them, Randolph suggested sending the slaves out of the state before they had stayed six months. With Washington's approval, the aide implemented that dodge.[25]

After almost two months of constant travel, Washington arrived at Mount Vernon and began meetings to plan the new seat of government. He pronounced himself pleased with his journey, having seen "with my own eyes the situation of the country." The nation's condition, he wrote, was improving and "tranquility reigns." It was likely the high point of his feelings about his presidency.[26]

∾

Less than a year later, nearing the end of his four-year term, Washington's visceral instincts told him that it was time to leave office. The government was on a sound financial basis. No major upheavals threatened the country from within or without. His work, he hoped, was done. He was weary of his public responsibilities. For more than eight years during the war, then for four years as president, he had shouldered the psychic burden of being father to every American, the one person on whom everyone could depend to be wise and just. Even a consummate performer will tire of a role so demanding, one that saps his every internal resource, day in and day out.

But the pleas poured in that he must serve another term, that no one else would do, that the union rested on his drooping shoulders. He pushed back, insisting to Madison that he was no longer necessary to the new government, and

> had from the beginning found himself deficient in many of the essential qualifications, owing to his inexperience in the forms of public business, his unfitness to judge of legal questions, and questions arising out of the Constitution.

Washington also feared he was growing "more infirm and perhaps his faculties also" in a job that was "scarcely tolerable."

Moreover, the president knew that American politics were changing. He did not need opinion polls or focus groups to detect the shift. A new "spirit of party" was abroad, dividing Jefferson and Hamilton and prompting ever more personal attacks. Soon, he predicted, those attacks would turn on him; he had no wish to endure that.

Madison responded that those trends made Washington all the more indispensable. Only he could mediate the emerging divisions.[27] Unpersuaded,

Washington asked Madison to draft an announcement that he would not accept reelection. But he never released that statement. Yielding to the entreaties of colleagues and friends, he agreed to serve another term.

It was a decision Washington would regret. His exquisite sense of timing had told him that a second term would be grueling. The semi-Olympian place he occupied in American life could not be sustained indefinitely. The country was changing in ways that Washington had prompted by leading a successful revolution that established a republican government. The more democratic America would have a more bruising political style.

Washington had matured in a political culture built on consensus within a small elite. He had operated brilliantly within that culture in the House of Burgesses, at the Continental Congress, through his army leadership, at the Constitutional Convention, and in the first two years of his presidency. But that culture was dissolving under the weight of broader popular engagement in politics, regional rivalries, western expansion, and bursting economic vitality. Washington was becoming—though had not yet become—an anachronism. The increasingly contentious political climate would make his second presidential term a sore trial, but he would still find ways to apply his unique political skills to the nation's most pressing problems and make a contribution that, as Madison had insisted, no one else could.

The election of 1792 brought no surprises. Washington won all 132 electoral votes. It was the fourth momentous election that he had won unanimously.

PEACE

CHAPTER 46

Second–Term Blues

On March 4, 1793, Washington walked the single block from his residence to Congress Hall, where he was to deliver his second inaugural address in the Senate chamber on the second floor. It was the shortest, most ornery inaugural address ever. Its four sentences contained a scant 135 words. Washington acknowledged the honor of his selection as president. He observed that he could be impeached if he "in any instance violated willingly or knowingly" his oath of office. He sat down. No soaring rhetoric. No calls to action or celebration of achievements. Merely an acknowledgment that although he was taking the job, he would be subject to criticism and removal. The speech seethed with resentment. It wasn't quite civil.[1]

Several factors underlay Washington's sullen mood. He was feeling his age, admitting to a bad memory and difficulty recalling details. His body was betraying him. Even his noble horsemanship was declining. When his mount stumbled on a rocky stretch, Washington's struggle to remain seated caused "such a wrench in my back as to prevent me from mounting a horse without pain." Jefferson left a pitiless account of the aging Washington:

> The firm tone of mind, for which he had been remarkable, was beginning to relax; its energy was abated; a listlessness of labor, a desire for tranquility had crept on him, and a willingness to let others act, or even think, for him.[2]

Management turnover at Mount Vernon exasperated the president. A few days before the second inauguration, his nephew and farm manager, George Augustine Washington, succumbed to tuberculosis, a hard loss that widowed

Martha's favorite niece. Mount Vernon's next farm manager died of the same disease less than four months later, making the president frantic about lax affairs at his treasured home property.[3]

Washington recruited another nephew to serve as interim manager, but the young man had little experience. Washington raged at the incompetence of his overseers, each of whom was responsible for one farm or a functional area like carpentry. With admirable alliteration, he denounced one as "sickly, slothful, and stupid." To his lead carpenter, he erupted:

> To speak to you is of no more avail than to speak to a bird that is flying over one's head . . . because you are lost to all sense of shame, and to every feeling that ought to govern an honest man.[4]

The arrival of an able manager in early 1794 helped calm the president.[5]

Washington tried to shed some of the worries that so oppressed him. He developed a plan to lease out Mount Vernon's farms except one near the mansion house, so he could "live free from care, and as much at my ease as possible." He circulated an advertisement offering to rent his farms to Europeans, who he thought were better farmers. That plan, never implemented, included a parallel notion of emancipating the slaves he owned. He tried again to sell his western lands. Owning faraway acres, he wrote, had proved "more productive of plague than profit." But there still were no buyers at his prices.[6]

Having set salutary precedents in his first term as president, Washington would endure some unhappy ones in the second, beginning with America's first experience with divided government. In the 1792 elections, the republican interest led by James Madison, Washington's old confidant, won control of the House of Representatives. That left Federalists in control of the Senate, Republicans ruling the House, and a president who denied being either.

Worse yet, Washington's cabinet simmered with conflict. Treasury Secretary Hamilton and War Secretary Knox usually agreed. When Jefferson differed with them, Attorney General Randolph became the deciding vote, a power Randolph often used to search for middle ground. Jefferson contemptuously called Randolph's approach a "half-way system between wrong and right."[7]

For Washington, aiming to be nonpartisan, the cabinet disagreements provided the range of views he wanted and showed the country that he consulted with all factions. The naturally combative Hamilton was mostly untroubled by conflict in the cabinet, but confrontation was torture for the secretary of state, who felt besieged. Even though Washington often followed Jefferson's advice, his fellow Virginian complained that Hamilton's influence threatened to "swallow up the whole executive powers."[8]

The president valued both men. Hamilton's brilliance was unmistakable even if his tact was wanting, while Jefferson brought acute political perceptions and a deft hand with diplomatic relations. But both were restless. Through persuasion, Washington kept Jefferson in office until the end of 1793. Hamilton remained for thirteen months longer; his departure would leave the president with a cabinet of bench players who commanded little respect.[9]

Washington also had to deal with important state governments that were not inclined to support him. Pennsylvania, home of the federal government, was led by Governor Thomas Mifflin, that resilient figure from the Conway Cabal. Shrewd and charming, Mifflin had become a sort of karmic hair shirt for Washington, always closer at hand than desired. New York's governor, George Clinton, was a personal friend but had opposed the Constitution and preferred a weak central government. In the 1792 election for president, many Republicans backed Clinton for vice president. The New Yorker won fifty electoral votes, finishing a respectable second to John Adams's seventy-seven.[10]

And then there was Virginia, where many now opposed Washington's administration. The ideals that animated the Revolution had fostered a more popular style of politics. The near-worship of Washington was fading. Some were uncomfortable with his resemblance to a sovereign; the whiff of aristocracy clung to him. In the summer of 1793, a Republican-sponsored newspaper proclaimed that "suspicions are entertained that you have, indignantly, cast behind you those endearing principles of republicanism." Washington feared that even ill-founded criticism could change minds, much as "drops of water will impress (in time) the hardest marble."[11]

In this shifting environment, Washington's second term was beset repeatedly with the most central questions of statecraft: Should there be war or peace, and at what price? President Washington always chose peace, yet events assumed such a sour aspect by late July 1795 that he confessed that he had never seen a crisis "from which more is to be apprehended."[12]

∽

The foreign threats grew from conflict between revolutionary France and its monarchical neighbors, a conflict that came to divide Americans. In the early days of the French Revolution, most Americans embraced it as an affirmation of their own rebellion. But as France descended into bloody class warfare, American attitudes divided along existing political fault lines.

That division might be portrayed as a conflict between heart and head. For Jefferson and Republicans, who mistrusted central government, France commanded sympathy as a sister republic and the ally who helped defeat Britain. For Washington and Federalists, who emphasized prosperity built on British trade and tariff revenues, French tumult looked like mob rule, nearly antithetical to careful American constitutionalism. With no navy and a puny army, Washington extolled the benefits of peace. He knew the terrible cost of war. If Americans, he wrote, cultivated "the great advantages which nature & circumstances have placed within our reach—many years will not revolve before we may be ranked not only among the most respectable, but among the happiest people on this globe."[13]

Internal threats to peace came from the west. Migration to the frontier boomed after the Revolutionary War, producing the new state of Kentucky and scores of backcountry settlements from upstate New York to Georgia. But settlement brought conflicts with Indians, most often initiated by whites, who expected the government to back them up. Two army expeditions against northwestern Indians had ended in ignominious defeats. Shortly after his second inauguration, Washington began planning for treaty talks with the Iroquois while General Anthony Wayne drilled a new force to confront tribes in the Northwest Territory.[14]

Westerners had economic grievances too. Farmers wanted to send their crops down the Ohio and Mississippi Rivers to Caribbean markets, but the federal government had failed to persuade Spain to open the Mississippi to American goods. That left westerners to distill their grain into alcohol that could be carried over the mountains in jugs, but the national government had imposed an excise tax on whiskey. Thus, government inaction sealed off one economic strategy while government policy punished the other. Western anger built.

To address these problems, Washington would have to emerge from behind the curtain that had often cloaked his political activity. To achieve peace, both foreign and domestic, he could not hoard his political capital. Even as he became enmeshed in the daily give-and-take of events, Washington remained the essential unifying figure in American political life, almost a national security blanket. A correspondent expressed the view that largely prevailed through his tumultuous last years in office: "That whenever you are removed, the federal union will be dissolved, the states will separate, and disorder succeed."[15] Achieving honorable peace and a successful retirement from office proved the greatest political challenges the aging president had faced, challenges he would confront with virtually no trusted advisers by his side. In this final chapter of his public career, no one could question that it was Washington alone, drawing on talents and skills mastered over a lifetime, who steered the nation's course.

CHAPTER 47

The Calamitous Frenchman

Edmond-Charles Genêt, a child of privilege in King Louis XVI's France, arrived in America in 1793 as a diplomat for a nation that was deploying the guillotine to decimate his class. His time in the spotlight was brief, but in a few short weeks, the thirty-year-old Frenchman set America's political world afire and defied Washington. Few people so thoroughly earned Washington's dislike as did the man who entered history as "Citizen Genêt."

On April 8, 1793, Genêt's ship, blown off course by storms, tied up at Charleston, South Carolina. Facing many European enemies, Revolutionary France wanted help from its sister republic across the Atlantic, and wanted it fast. It was Genêt's task to secure that help. The impatient young man immediately began to implement his instructions.

Unluckily for Genêt, his instructions did not match American interests. France wanted a new treaty with the United States, but Americans did not need one; the existing agreement, signed in 1778, already opened French ports to American goods. Nor could Genêt secure faster repayment of the $5.6 million owed to France; the United States could barely keep up with debt payments at the current rate of repayment. Neither could Genêt induce the United States to harass British and Spanish colonies in America, or win access to American ports for French privateers; Washington's government had no wish to antagonize Britain and its Royal Navy.[1]

Nevertheless, after Charleston gave Genêt an enthusiastic welcome, he issued privateering commissions that authorized shipowners to arm their ships and prey on British and Dutch merchantmen. In a leisurely procession northward, Genêt basked in the fawning attention of Americans sentimentally attached to their wartime ally, then was greeted in Philadelphia by what

Jefferson called a "vast concourse of people." The experience gave Genêt an inflated sense of his influence over American policy.[2]

As Genêt set American hearts fluttering, news arrived that France and Britain were at war. From Mount Vernon, Washington instructed Jefferson and his cabinet to keep America out of the conflict, then hurried back to Philadelphia. The president's desire for peace came from his clear-eyed appreciation that the United States had little at stake in the European contest, plus the need to shield American trade so it could produce the tariff revenue that kept the government afloat.[3]

A unanimous cabinet agreed that Washington should announce a policy of strict neutrality (without using that word), forbidding Americans from assisting any warring nation. Issued on April 22, what became known as the Neutrality Proclamation pledged that America would be "friendly and impartial" to all. Washington warned that his government would not protect Americans who joined the European fighting or supplied contraband to either side. The proclamation barred the privateering commissions that Genêt was passing out and forbade service on French privateers or warships. Strong statements of support for the policy came from local governments and public meetings around the nation.[4]

Reaching Philadelphia after the Neutrality Proclamation was issued, Genêt hoped to modify it by capitalizing on the general pro-French feeling. He impressed Secretary of State Jefferson in their first meeting. "It is impossible," the Virginian swooned, "for anything to be more affectionate, more magnanimous than the purport of his mission." Jefferson was not the only American to fall under Genêt's spell. The Frenchman boasted in a report to Paris that he dwelt "in the midst of perpetual fetes."[5]

Washington did not share the infatuation with Genêt. The president had cherished French support for American independence, yet was skeptical of that nation's current government and its young diplomat. France's revolutionaries had expelled the favorite of Washington's heart, Lafayette, who had led the first rising against the king. Those in the French government, Washington worried, "are ready to tear each other to pieces, and will, more than probably, prove the worst foes th[eir] country has."

The president resolved to respect most of the 1778 treaty with France (though he lacked the warships to fulfill the pledge to defend France's Caribbean colonies), but he adhered to his lifelong view that nations, like men, will follow their interests. America needed peace. He would not risk a new war by indulging sentimental feelings about the last war.[6]

Genêt lost no time in flouting Washington's policy. On May 1, thousands cheered from Philadelphia's shores as a French privateer hauled a British merchantman into port, having seized it in American waters. Within two weeks, the American government freed the captured crew and returned the ship and cargo to its owners. Jefferson advised Genêt that American ports were closed to French privateers. Neither, he added, would repayment of French loans accelerate.[7]

As Genêt discovered that public adulation did not translate into political advantage, Gallic temper flared in his letters to Jefferson as secretary of state. Hamilton denounced one of those letters as "the most offensive paper, perhaps, that ever was offered by a foreign Minister to a friendly power with which he resided." Jefferson blandly summarized Washington's neutrality policy as producing "decisions . . . [that] dissatisfy both parties and draw complaints from both."[8]

Genêt did not relent. He instructed French consuls in other American ports to continue to commission privateers, and French privateers continued to make seizures in American waters, often within sight of land. The French then converted the ships they had seized into new privateers. With no navy to intercept the illegal vessels, Washington's government could act against only those privateers docking at American ports, seizing them through court proceedings. Pointing out that the Neutrality Proclamation was issued without congressional approval, Genêt announced that he would urge Washington to summon Congress to repeal the policy. Even Jefferson, pro-French to his core, was losing patience. "I stopped him [Genêt] at the subject of calling Congress," the secretary of state recorded, and "explained our constitution to him."[9]

Prodded by Washington, the cabinet met repeatedly to address British complaints about Genêt's neutrality violations. Each incident had to be judged according to Washington's proclamation and international law. It mattered what cargo the seized ship carried and where it was bound, whether the vessel had been purchased from an American shipbuilder, and whether it was owned by an American or a foreigner. The cabinet considered where a privateer's cannons had been installed and its crew recruited, as well as the crew's nationality. Washington asked the Supreme Court for guidance.[10]

Frustrated, Genêt vibrated between reckless actions and foolish statements. That pattern crested when he told a Pennsylvania official that he would "appeal from the president to the people," then announced to Jefferson that he would publish a statement revealing the unfairness of America's neutrality policy. Jefferson confessed to Madison his dismay:

> Never, in my opinion, was so calamitous an appointment made, as that of the present minister of F[rance] here. Hotheaded, all imagination, no judgment, passionate, disrespectful and even indecent to-

wards the P[resident] . . . , talking of appeals from him to Congress, from them to the people, urging the most unseasonable and groundless propositions, and in the most dictatorial style.[11]

Both Britain and France taxed Washington's patience. Confronted at a cabinet meeting with a newspaper cartoon that portrayed him being executed by guillotine, the president lost his fabled temper. According to Jefferson's notes, Washington grew "much inflamed, [and] got into one of those passions where he cannot command himself."[12] By the beginning of August, Genêt had so worn out his welcome that Washington and his cabinet asked France to recall him.[13]

Neutrality continued to command public support. In the twelve months after Washington announced the policy, nearly seventy public meetings adopted pro-neutrality resolutions. Some mentioned their "partiality for the French," or offered a general statement of sympathy for the former ally, but most Americans agreed with Washington: The country needed peace. Even Jefferson concluded that defending Genêt had become hopeless. "Finding the man absolutely incorrigible," Jefferson wrote, "I saw the necessity of quitting a wreck which could not but sink all who should cling to it."[14]

∽

As furor swirled around Genêt's provocations, a plague of yellow fever brought Philadelphia to its knees. The disease began with high fevers and jaundice, then black vomit caused by internal bleeding. Many died quickly. "At first three of four died," Jefferson wrote in early September. "Now about one out of three." The city emptied. Everyone left who could.[15]

Hamilton fell sick but weathered the fever. By the second week of September, Washington yielded to Martha's entreaties and left for Mount Vernon. Jefferson headed for Monticello. For weeks, a skeleton of a government kept the lights on in government offices. A single clerk occupied the State Department. The treasury moved to a private home outside the city. "Business is in a great measure abandoned," wrote a senior treasury official.[16]

"The streets are lonely to a melancholy degree," War Secretary Knox reported. "The merchants generally have fled—Ships are arriving and no consignees to be found. Notes at the banks are suffered to be unpaid. . . . [It is] as if an army of enemies had possessed the city without plundering it."[17] By mid-October, more than 3,500 were dead. The irony was bitter: America's leaders had argued for a decade over where to house their government, then chose a location beset with contagion.[18]

At Mount Vernon, Washington contemplated a government that barely existed. He had brought no papers from Philadelphia with him and had no secretary to assist him. Though he had hoped to address Mount Vernon's tangled affairs, he had time only to try to hold the government together.[19]

By letter, he hounded the cabinet secretaries for a plan to reconvene the government. America's leaders should not cower in quiet places while Philadelphians sickened and died. Every suggestion seemed to raise a constitutional question. Did the cabinet have to meet in the seat of government? Did Congress? Could the president summon Congress into session? For each proposal, he considered how the people would react. Washington and his aides searched for an alternative location close to Philadelphia yet safe from the pestilence.[20]

Washington insisted that the executive officers had to gather by November 1. Providentially, in the third week of October, temperatures in Philadelphia dropped. The epidemic receded, then ended. Though no one then understood the science, cold temperatures had killed the mosquitoes that spread the disease.[21]

∞

On December 3, with Philadelphia flickering back to life, Washington delivered his fifth annual message. His tone was improved from the four grumpy sentences of his second inaugural address. He had serious matters to discuss with Congress and the nation. He did not sugarcoat them.

He began with the European war, which could disrupt trade or even draw America into the bloodletting. He explained that his neutrality policy aimed to resist those dangers while respecting France's treaty rights, and set rules for when the combatants' vessels could enter American ports. He invited Congress to review the situation and "correct, improve, or enforce" his policies.

More of Genêt's mischief was coming to light. A South Carolina investigation found that Genêt had commissioned an invasion of Spanish colonies with troops recruited in America. He also had enlisted George Rogers Clark, a frontier hero of the Revolutionary War, to recruit Americans to attack Spanish Louisiana from Kentucky.[22]

The Frenchman and his American allies, the president wrote to a friend, "are aiming . . . at nothing short of the subversion of the general government," and would be happy to "plung[e] the country into the horrors of a disastrous war." Fortunately, Genêt's plots were too poorly funded and uncoordinated to succeed, while a new government in France was demanding his return and possible execution. The high-handed Frenchman was reduced to begging for permission to remain in America as a private person, which Washington granted.[23]

Washington's address also reviewed threats to internal peace. Westward migration triggered resistance from Indian tribes who were losing their homelands and way of life. Washington insisted that he had tried to satisfy the northwestern tribes, but now only a military solution would do. General Wayne was preparing a force to subdue those tribes. Washington hoped a peaceful agreement could be reached on the southern border with the Creeks and Cherokees.

Threatened from within and without, Washington explained, America needed to be in a "condition of complete defense." Since the end of the Revolutionary War, Americans had resisted his call for a professional military, but he thought the message was ever more important: "If we desire to avoid insult, we must be able to repel it; if we desire to secure peace, . . . it must be known, that we are at all times ready for war."[24]

It had been a difficult year for Washington, but one development would especially influence the balance of his presidency. In response to Genêt's agitation, a number of "democratic societies" formed, ultimately numbering nearly forty across the country. They became hotbeds of pro-French sentiment and criticism of Washington. The president bitterly resented them, and blamed Genêt for aggravating the nation's political partisanship.[25]

Political polarization accelerated with Jefferson's resignation from the cabinet at the end of the year. Washington appointed his attorney general, Edmund Randolph, to lead the State Department, naming William Bradford of Pennsylvania the new attorney general.[26] Jefferson's departure marked the end of political balance in the cabinet. So long as Jefferson was secretary of state, a voice near the president presented the concerns of pro-French Republicans. Now, Republicans would feel that the Washington administration did not reflect their views, and Jefferson at Monticello would become a symbol of opposition.

Nevertheless, Washington looked to the New Year with hope. The nation was at peace. His neutrality policy was holding. The new French minister disavowed Genêt's conduct, then directed French citizens to respect American neutrality.[27] But troubles would not stop coming. This time, it would be internal rebellion.

CHAPTER 48

Troubles Within

Americans disliked paying taxes. Both the war for independence and the Shays Rebellion began with tax resistance. Washington himself took a jaundiced view of tax collectors. In April 1793, he directed his farm manager not to pay a local tax unless it was explained in writing, because Virginia's collectors were "amongst the greatest rascals in the world." Having appointed and supervised tax collectors when he served on the Fairfax County Court, Washington knew whereof he spoke. But Washington also knew that there can be no government without taxes. His court had supervised the prosecution of tax cheats before the war, and he had insisted that the government under the Constitution have the power to tax.[1]

Washington's fiscal adviser, Hamilton, understood the challenges of tax collection. His financial program emphasized revenue from import taxes, which were largely unseen by consumers. Merchants paid tariffs when they received imported goods, then folded the cost into prices for the goods. In one *Federalist* essay, Hamilton observed that an excise tax is difficult to collect because it is so visible.[2]

Nevertheless, in 1790 Hamilton had urged an excise tax on whiskey, noting that even prickly residents of Connecticut and Massachusetts were paying state liquor excises without complaint. By the treasury secretary's calculations, each man, woman, and child in the nation drank an average of ten quarts of liquor a year. They should be willing to pay a modest liquor excise (exempting beer and cider) that would amount to less than "a dollar and a half" per person per year. Congress and the president approved the tax.[3]

Noncompliance was immediate in western communities from Pennsylvania to the Carolinas, where liquor distilled from grains was prepared for shipment to distant markets. As Congressman Albert Gallatin of Pennsylvania explained, westerners were "distillers through necessity, not choice, that [they] may comprehend the greatest value on the smallest size and weight." Many farmer-distillers lacked currency to pay the tax until they shipped their liquor and received payment, but the government demanded prompt payment. Noncompliance with the excise morphed into defiance.[4]

In his annual message in late 1791, the president admitted that the liquor excise had caused "some degree of discontent." He pledged to seek revisions to meet legitimate objections.[5] Four months later, Hamilton sent Congress a spirited defense of the excise and proposed only technical revisions. When Washington dispatched a former congressman to western Pennsylvania to investigate an attack on the home of a tax collector, the report came back that westerners despised the liquor excise and those who tried to collect it.[6]

The standoff festered through 1793, while Washington's administration was distracted by Genêt, neutrality, and yellow fever. Not wanting to give up the tax but unwilling to risk a conflict, Washington elected to look away from the problem. In early 1794, the commissioner of revenue made a halfhearted claim that compliance was improving, but conceded that "the obstacles to it are yet far from being entirely vanquished." Washington proposed more technical revisions, but no major revamping. He was not backing down.[7]

In the spring of 1794, western petitioners renewed their complaints about their lack of access to the Mississippi and continuing Indian violence. Washington took a dim view of the petitions when he noted that they came from the new democratic societies, which he saw as the evil spawn of the demon Genêt. "The fruit of the Democratic Society," he wrote, "begins more and more to unfold itself." Four months later, he wrote that the societies were created "by their father, Genêt" to sow "jealousy and distrust . . . of the government, by destroying all confidence in the Administration." If the societies were not opposed, "they would shake the government to its foundation." Thus the president who aimed to be nonpartisan leaned hard into partisanship, an attitude that kept him from appreciating the broader discontent that many Americans were feeling. The angry temper of the time was infecting Washington.[8]

When collectors increased their efforts to enforce the liquor tax, the reaction was swift in Pennsylvania's four western counties, home to more than one-fourth of the nation's stills. The pace of attacks on collectors increased; by mid-1794, Washington and his government could no longer ignore the violence.[9]

As later detailed by Hamilton, tar-and-feathering of collectors had begun nearly three years before. Washington tried issuing a proclamation urging that no one obstruct enforcement of the laws, but the intimidation—including attacks on homes and effigy burnings—expanded to target distillers who were paying the excise.[10] The most sensational episode came in a July 1794 attack on General John Neville, a Revolutionary War veteran and prominent tax collector. Neville and a U.S. Marshal had been serving court papers on delinquent still owners. Interrupted by gunfire, they took refuge in Neville's home, which soon was surrounded by fifty armed men who set fire to his outbuildings. After Neville slipped away, the insurgents began shooting into the house, which held a small contingent of U.S. soldiers. Before surrendering, the army men wounded some of the attackers and killed one. The insurgents put most of Neville's property to the torch, and released the U.S. Marshal only when he promised not to enforce the tax. To learn what steps the government was planning against them, and who was siding with the government, the insurgents seized the local mails.[11]

In the days after the Neville attack, more collectors were tarred and feathered, an agony for victims subjected to hot tar on their bodies. Then insurgents made their greatest show of force. More than 5,000 armed men paraded at Braddock's Field outside Pittsburgh. Despite reports that the men would march on Fort Pitt, they contented themselves with burning the barn and crops of the same unfortunate U.S. Marshal.[12]

Washington would not ignore thousands of armed men marching in opposition to the government. The Shays Rebellion in 1786 had revealed the weakness of the Articles of Confederation. If Washington could not control this insurgency, he feared that his government, too, might fail. "If the laws are to be so trampled upon—with impunity," he wrote, "there is an end put at one stroke to republican government; and nothing but anarchy and confusion is to be expected thereafter." Hamilton recommended calling out 12,000 militia, half from Pennsylvania and the rest from neighboring New Jersey, Maryland, and Virginia. Secretary of State Randolph and Governor Mifflin of Pennsylvania counseled negotiating with the insurgents. Washington tried both approaches.[13]

Under the Militia Act, he requested an opinion from Supreme Court Justice James Wilson that the disorders warranted summoning the militia. After Wilson made the finding, Washington denounced the insurgents as "armed banditti." He wrote that he regretted calling out the militia, but that "the essential interests of the union demand it." An overwhelming force, he hoped, would persuade the insurgents that resistance was futile. But his call required that 12,000 militiamen leave their homes to enforce a tax that many loathed. To open talks with the insurgents, Washington sent a commission of three

Pennsylvanians: Attorney General Bradford, Senator James Ross, and Pennsylvania Supreme Court Justice Jasper Yeates. Governor Mifflin sent state representatives with them.[14]

Some feared the British were behind the western turmoil, which would complicate any military effort, since British soldiers still occupied forts around the Great Lakes. Also confounding was Secretary of War Knox's departure for Maine to attend to personal matters, denying Washington his top military adviser. Every frontier issue seemed to be in play. General Wayne's force was marching against the northwestern tribes. Kentuckians were agitating again over access to the Mississippi. With Spain showing a new openness on that issue, successful talks required that the government snuff out Genêt-inspired efforts to attack Spanish colonies from American soil. Also, a group of Georgians was settling on Creek tribal lands and proposed to proclaim a new state there, or even a new nation. The moment, in Randolph's words, was "big with a crisis which would convulse the oldest government."[15]

∽

Reporting the grievances presented by insurgent leaders, the president's commissioners concluded that although many would abandon the resistance movement, a violent minority would not. A military force was needed to impose order. Washington issued a new proclamation, announcing that talks would not "reclaim the wicked from their fury." He vowed to end "a treasonable opposition [which] has been employed in propagating principles of anarchy." He coupled those fierce words with a pledge to treat generously those who gave up the resistance.[16]

Organizing 12,000 militiamen from four different states presented logistical and political obstacles. Hamilton eagerly leapt into the breach created by Knox's absence. As the author of the tax that the insurgents hated, the treasury secretary brought political baggage with him, but Washington relied on him to get the expedition moving before winter.

By late September, the government's prospects were brightening. Old colleagues from Continental Army days arrived in camp in Carlisle, Pennsylvania, including Governor Henry Lee of Virginia and Daniel Morgan. Then came heartening news that Wayne's troops had defeated the northwestern tribes at the Battle of Fallen Timbers. British soldiers in a nearby fort had witnessed that fighting but did nothing to assist the Indians, which reduced the fear that the British would support the whiskey rebels. Wayne's victory removed a major complaint of white settlers, since the government now *had* protected them against the tribes. Shortly after Washington left for the Carlisle camp, he learned that diplomat Thomas Pinckney was hurrying to Madrid for high-level meetings about Mississippi River access.[17]

Buoyed by the unfamiliar rush of good news, Washington decided he should explain to Americans how good things were. He set out to use glad tidings to summon patriotic feelings and change the nation's mood. In public remarks in early October, he linked the positive developments to ending the insurgency. "Look round," he exhorted, "and behold the universally acknowledged prosperity which blesses every part of the United States." He called on "the wise and the virtuous [to] unite their efforts to reclaim the misguided, and to detect & defeat [the] arts of the factious."[18]

While the state militias sorted themselves out in Carlisle, Washington himself met with insurgent leaders. He was unmoved. "Nothing short of the most unequivocal *proofs* of absolute submission," he insisted, would prevent his troops from advancing. He reported to Randolph that the insurgents were "alarmed, but not yet brought to their proper senses." Though Randolph had advised moderation before, now he urged that the democratic societies "be crushed." Washington agreed; otherwise, he wrote, "they will destroy the government of this country."[19]

At that moment, Jefferson's absence from the cabinet made a difference. Jefferson might have restrained the president's hostility to the societies, rather than goading him as Randolph was doing. More than a month later, the president again denounced the democratic societies in a letter to John Jay in Europe, blaming them for the rebellion and predicting their annihilation.[20]

The expedition proved to be a cakewalk. In Jefferson's droll account, "An insurrection was announced and proclaimed and armed against, but could never be found." In truth, the insurrection had been real enough, but the advance of 12,000 militia cooled the hottest tempers. Washington boasted later that the insurgency was suppressed "without shedding a drop of blood."[21]

Expecting a successful advance, Washington left the army before the westward march began, appointing Governor Lee of Virginia to command. The soldiers fired no shot in anger; they took care to respect citizens' rights. Some insurgent leaders were arrested and delivered to civil authorities, not to military tribunals. In late November, Lee issued a blanket pardon for the four insurgent counties in Pennsylvania, exempting thirty-three named individuals. Few of those thirty-three stood trial; fewer still were convicted; Washington pardoned those who were.[22]

Although the expedition lacked a climactic ending, Washington believed it was a crucial success. Its effect, he wrote to Governor Lee, was "nothing less than to consolidate and preserve the blessings of that revolution which, at much expense of blood and treasure, constituted us a free and independent nation."[23]

∾

The militia force was still overawing western Pennsylvania on November 19, when Washington entered Congress Hall in Philadelphia to deliver his sixth annual message. His carriage was still that of an athlete and soldier, though the years and his dental agonies had left deep marks on his face. His text was upbeat, a happy leader praising the people's achievements.

The union's prosperity, he proclaimed, rested on solid foundations. Better yet, events in western Pennsylvania showed that Americans "feel their inseparable union [and] the value of republican government." In the militia expedition, he continued,

> the most and the least wealthy of our citizens [stood] in the same ranks, as private soldiers . . . undeterred by a march of three hundred miles over rugged mountains, by the approach of an inclement season, or by any other discouragement.

Washington proposed no retribution against the insurgents. His message was one of unity, shared purpose, and success. Wayne's victory at Fallen Timbers, he predicted, would bring lasting peace with the northwestern tribes.

Yet his buoyant paean to the American spirit was little noted. Instead, a brief passage in his address, which drove a wedge into the nation's partisan divide, set off howls of rage and has been condemned for centuries since. In that passage, Washington obliquely referred to "certain self-created societies" that had "assumed the tone of condemnation" toward the government. Everyone knew that he was showing his dislike for the democratic societies.[24]

His words were tame by modern standards and far milder than his true feelings about the democratic societies. Spoken by the great unifier, however, even mild words took on heft. Washington, the man who meant to stand above politics, was condemning one part of the community, implicitly declaring it dangerous and unworthy. That rankled with those who found Federalist attitudes too aristocratic, and marked a departure from Washington's consistent message celebrating American union. By setting himself against one portion of the population—no matter how indirectly he said so—Washington incited his critics to deploy ever sharper invective against him.

The cheerleader president returned in a January 1795 proclamation proposing a national day of thanksgiving. Again he recited the nation's blessings: peace, internal tranquility, and prosperity.[25] Washington had every reason to feel that he had met the major challenges of his second term as president—a foreign nation attempting to subvert his government, then an internal rebellion. But there was more trouble to come.

Moreover, the bleeding of talent from his administration was continuing. Treasury Secretary Hamilton finally left, intent on becoming a prosperous New York lawyer. His successor, Oliver Wolcott of Connecticut, was an unremarkable figure. Knox had resigned as secretary of war, succeeded by the prickly Timothy Pickering of Massachusetts. Never close to Washington through years of service in the Continental Army, Pickering had been tangentially connected to the Conway Cabal and was on the wrong side of the Newburgh mutiny in 1783. But he was intelligent and hardworking and had experience negotiating with Indian tribes, a principal duty of the War Department.[26]

The years had winnowed the list of Washington's political allies, particularly fellow Virginians. First to be banished had been George Mason, when he opposed ratification of the Constitution. Then Jefferson resigned to lead the opposition to the government. Madison, formerly the president's closest political adviser, now was the opposition leader in Congress, though he remained on polite terms with Washington. Randolph remained as secretary of state, but that connection, too, would soon fray.

It was Hamilton, the orphan from the West Indies, who stood with Washington to the end. Beyond their obvious differences, the two men shared important qualities. Both were relentless strivers who avidly pursued advancement by marrying rich women and working much, much harder than others did. Washington's youthful trip to Barbados may have helped him understand Hamilton's Caribbean background. Though the young Hamilton had resigned from Washington's military staff over perceived mistreatment by the commander in chief, both men overlooked that episode. The mature Hamilton remained loyal through every political turbulence. From his law office in Manhattan, he would continue to sally forth whenever the president called on him.

Looking at the uncertain world around him, supported by mostly second-tier talents, Washington had reason for concern, but likely did not foresee how difficult the next two years would be.

CHAPTER 49

The Fight for Peace

The last two years of Washington's presidency brought the most bruising political conflict of his career, one he survived by strapping himself to the Constitution while employing the guile acquired in the nearly forty years since he left the Virginia Regiment.[1]

The conflict grew out of the war in Europe. The French and British each aimed to cut off the other's trade with neutral nations, much of which came in American ships. The British seized ships bound for ports of France and the French West Indies; by spring 1794, they held hundreds of American ships and had impressed numerous American sailors into service for the Royal Navy. In turn, American captains sailing to British ports risked seizure by the French; by autumn 1794, the French had detained three hundred American ships.

Both nations were inflicting ruinous losses on American merchants, but Britain, with its powerful navy, posed the greater threat. An additional British threat loomed along the long border with Canada. In early 1794, a senior British commander told Indian leaders that King George III soon would be at war with the United States, after which Britain and the tribes would divide America's Northwest Territory. Renewed frontier war was a grim prospect.[2]

Republicans in Congress sought to reduce American shipping losses by enacting two short-term embargoes on foreign trade. When the Senate refused to declare a third embargo, Madison again complained of Washington's influence, which he called "an overmatch for all the efforts Republicanism can make."[3]

In late March, news arrived of a softening in British policy. With French armies victorious in Europe, British merchants longed to restore trade with

America. British Prime Minister William Pitt—whose father, Lord Chatham, had been a friend to America—needed to focus on defeating France. Provoking the United States no longer seemed wise, so Britain announced it would allow neutral ships to trade with French Caribbean islands unless they carried contraband. Washington decided that the time might be right for resolving additional issues with Britain, beginning with compensation for the recent shipping losses. The two nations also had unfinished business from their 1783 peace treaty. British troops still lingered in forts around the Great Lakes; their presence stirred Indian unrest and blocked western expansion. In turn, some American states still blocked British merchants from recovering debts incurred before the war.[4]

In any event, having no navy and few soldiers, Washington had no military options. That left diplomacy. The president resolved to negotiate, even at the risk of triggering a fresh round of accusations that he was pro-British and anti-French.[5]

For the mission to London, he selected John Jay, an aristocratic New Yorker who was chief justice of the Supreme Court. The able but colorless Jay had served as New York's governor and chief judge, as well as president of the Confederation Congress and that body's secretary of foreign affairs. The Gardoqui episode of 1786—when Jay considered conceding control of the Mississippi to Spain for twenty-five years—had left a residue of ill will toward him among westerners. Most relevant, he had helped negotiate the 1783 peace treaty with Britain.

To his cabinet, Washington explained that his goal was to avoid war and win fair compensation for American losses. Jay's negotiation would extend the policy of the Neutrality Proclamation, demonstrating America's "solicitude for a friendly adjustment of our complaints and a reluctance to hostility."[6]

Washington's instructions to Jay stressed the removal of British soldiers from the west, facilitating payment of American debts to British creditors, winning reimbursement for seized cargoes, ending the impressment of American sailors, and opening trade with British Caribbean islands. A problematic instruction directed that an agreement with Britain should not denigrate the treaty between France and the United States; for many Americans, *any* agreement with Britain would do that.[7]

Washington knew the mission could fail. He summarized his policy as "to preserve the country in peace if I can, and to be prepared for war if I cannot." In pursuit of the second goal, he won congressional approval to build new forts, strengthen harbor defenses, and organize munitions and arms stockpiles. Congress balked at his request to expand the army tenfold, to 25,000 soldiers. Americans still mistrusted a standing army.[8]

For many months, Washington could do little but wait for news from the London negotiation an ocean away. On November 19, 1794, the diplomats signed an agreement. Jay sent the treaty home, but chose to stay in London rather than endure a wintry Atlantic crossing. When Washington read the pact in early March 1795, his disappointment was sharp. Jay had won few concessions.[9]

&

For many weeks, Washington withheld the treaty terms, sharing them only with a few trusted confidants, which did not include three of his four cabinet officers. He sent a quiet note to Vice President Adams, suggesting that the Senate convene on June 8, more than three months in the future, to consider the treaty. Not even the ambassador to France, James Monroe, had seen the treaty. American political figures were left to shadowbox with a bogeyman treaty of unknown dimensions that was stashed in a Philadelphia desk.[10]

Knowing that peace and war hung in the balance, Washington used the time to consider his options with an agreement that was no better than problematic.[11] The treaty included the provision that Washington most cherished: The British agreed (again) to abandon the western posts, though not until mid-1796. Other, less central provisions were tolerable: The two governments would appoint joint commissions to resolve American claims for shipping losses, and to draw the boundaries between Maine and Canada, and between the Northwest Territory and Canada; American traders could call at British ports in Asia. Securing any concessions from a powerful adversary was an achievement.

But some provisions were unfortunate, and some that Washington wanted were entirely missing. American and British traders could operate across the Canadian border, which invited British meddling with the Northwest tribes. The treaty never mentioned sailor impressments or reimbursement for slaves who fled with the British at the end of the war. Nor did it address the principle, cherished by Americans, that "neutral ships make neutral cargoes," which would bar seizures of American ships in the future. Although Britain had never previously entertained those last three proposals, critics would denounce their absence. American shippers would gain access to British West Indies markets, but in a cramped, limited fashion. Finally, the United States agreed not to discriminate against British goods for ten years, but won no reciprocal commitment.[12]

Though the treaty was no triumph for the United States, it may have been the best one possible. It would secure peace, but it would draw vehement opposition. After long reflection, Washington resolved that if the Senate ratified the pact by the required two-thirds majority, he would sign it.[13]

Then news from Britain threatened to sabotage his decision. Facing a food shortage, British "provision orders" authorized the seizure of food shipments to France. Most of those shipments would be in American vessels. Though Britain promised to pay for seized cargoes, it seemed to be repudiating its commitment to treat American shipping fairly before the ink was dry on the treaty. A further complication arose when the Senate ratified the treaty in June, *except* for the paragraph allowing very limited trade to British Caribbean ports, which the Senate considered inadequate. Excluding that provision presented the constitutional question whether the president could approve the rest of the treaty without renewing negotiations over the omitted provision. Finally, a Philadelphia newspaper printed a leaked copy of the treaty, denying Washington the chance to release it with his own explanation, while also making him seem secretive and devious.[14]

Many reacted to the treaty with rage.

When Hamilton defended it before a New York crowd of 5,000, people threw stones. Struck in the forehead, Hamilton wisely left the event. Bostonians burned a British privateer. Jay joked that he could travel the nation by the light of his burning effigies, while a Jay biographer estimates that every day for six weeks, an anti-treaty protest occurred somewhere in the nation. Crowds in Philadelphia and Charleston marched to the homes of British diplomats, where they defiled the Union Jack and the treaty.[15] The anti-administration *Aurora* of Philadelphia predicted that the treaty would lead to the "completest political union between Great Britain and the United States," a prospect that "must fill the American mind with horror." Citizen petitions and resolutions complained about one-sided trade terms, the failure to recognize the rights of neutral countries, and a dozen other features and omissions. One of Washington's relatives reported that in Virginia, "not one man has ever attempted to justify the treaty."[16]

The president faced no good choices. If he overlooked the recent provision orders and signed the treaty, he would look like a toady to King George. If he withheld his signature until the provision orders were resolved, he would look indecisive, and the treaty would die if Britain stood by the provision orders. War might follow. If he signed the treaty on condition that the provision orders be revoked, or if he refused to sign, he would abandon those Federalist senators who already had voted for his treaty.

Preparing to leave for Mount Vernon. Washington asked his cabinet secretaries for written recommendations. He also requested that Hamilton in

New York report the views of "dispassionate men, who have knowledge of the subject and abilities to judge of it." He wanted to study the case for and against each treaty provision. Secretary of State Randolph's opinion exceeded 4,000 words, while Hamilton's was more than twice as long. Washington left Philadelphia in mid-July, intending to make his decision after sober reflection.[17]

It would not be so simple.

∞

Federalists belatedly moved to defend the pact. A few public meetings endorsed it, while mere stones could not silence Hamilton. Over the next five months, he published twenty-eight pro-treaty essays totaling nearly 100,000 words.[18]

The most important response came from Washington at Mount Vernon. Though shaken in his earlier resolve to sign the treaty, he moved to calm the tumult. In a response to an anti-treaty letter from Boston officials, he wrote that he had always sought the happiness of all Americans. He pledged to consider every argument about the treaty while respecting the Constitution, which was "the guide which I never can abandon." He stressed that the Senate and the president have the power to make treaties because they can judge "without passion, and with the best means of information, those facts and principles upon which the success of our foreign relations will always depend." He would decide, he concluded, "by obeying the dictates of my conscience."[19]

By its steady tone and commitment to the Constitution, his letter—which was widely reprinted—began to lower the temperature of the public debate. A friend reported that the western country was quiet, untroubled about the treaty. John Adams wrote that the furor never reached the Massachusetts countryside. Washington's letter could not, as he wrote to Secretary of State Randolph, change the unpalatable choices before him: "If the treaty is ratified the partisans of the French (or rather of war and confusion) will excite [the French] to hostile measures, or at least to unfriendly sentiments—if it is not [ratified], there is no foreseeing *all* the consequences which may follow as it respects G[reat] B[ritain]."[20]

Always sensitive to criticism, Washington resented the "obloquy which disappointment and malice are collecting to heap upon my character." Since becoming president, he added, he had "never . . . seen a crisis . . . from which more is to be apprehended." From a man who had weathered Genêt's manipulations and the Whiskey Rebellion, that was a sobering judgment.[21]

But another crisis soon crowded in. This one reached into the heart of Washington's administration.

∾

The British had intercepted dispatches from Genêt's successor as French minister to America, Jean Antoine Joseph Fauchet. One described conversations with Secretary of State Randolph in a suggestive way—suggesting, that is, that Randolph was corrupt. The British minister in Philadelphia presented the letter to Treasury Secretary Wolcott, who shared the pro-British sympathies of his predecessor, Hamilton, though with less intelligence and imagination.

Wolcott pored over the French text of Fauchet's dispatch with Secretary of War Pickering. The document quoted unflattering remarks by Randolph about Washington.[22] But the explosive material—or what Wolcott and Pickering deemed explosive—described Randolph approaching the Frenchman "with an air of great eagerness" and making "overtures" concerning the Whiskey Rebellion, which Fauchet had reported previously. The Frenchman added:

> Thus with some thousands of dollars the [French] Republic would have decided on civil war or on peace! Thus the consciences of the pretended patriots of America have already their scale of prices.

Without knowing Fauchet's earlier reports, his meaning was murky, but Wolcott and Pickering thought he described Randolph demanding a bribe. Randolph's well-known financial distress reinforced that inference. Two years earlier, Jefferson had warned that Randolph's debts might compromise his independence. A week before, complaining about money troubles, Randolph had asked Washington for an appointment to the Supreme Court. When briefed about the Fauchet letter, Attorney General Bradford agreed that the president should return to Philadelphia to confront Randolph. Pickering sent a note urging Washington to return "for a *special reason*," which could only be related in person, adding portentously that Washington should decide no important matters until then.[23]

Delayed by heavy rains and a meeting with the commissioners of the District of Columbia, Washington reached Philadelphia on August 11. Pickering and Wolcott promptly presented the Fauchet letter, as translated by Pickering.[24]

The letter's suggestion of corruption was unsettling. Randolph was the highest-ranking administration appointee and the only remaining member of the original cabinet. As others had resigned, Washington increasingly had relied on Randolph, whose family the president had known for decades. Most disturbing, Washington needed to make a difficult foreign-policy decision while doubting his chief diplomat's loyalty. Washington resolved to address those questions sequentially: the treaty first, then Randolph.

Next morning, Washington announced he would ignore Randolph's advice and sign the treaty without demanding rescission of Britain's provision orders. The case for signing was straightforward: It was better than no treaty, and the United States needed peace. Britain's naval power could plunder American ships and ports at will. Signing the treaty might ignite another firestorm of protest, but short-term political considerations would not alter Washington's judgment of what was best for the union.[25]

After Washington signed the treaty on August 19, the Republican press howled for his scalp. A writer in the *Philadelphia Aurora* urged Washington to resign to "save the wreck of character now crumbling to pieces under the tempest of an universal irritation." Public meetings in Southern states lodged angry protests.[26] But Washington's signature also prompted some to reconsider the treaty. New public resolutions endorsed it. A New Hampshire senator found that his most persuasive pro-treaty argument was to point to Washington's signature. "They say," a Massachusetts congressman wrote, "the president will not see the country wronged, much less wrong it himself."[27]

While working with the secretary of state to produce the official documents approving the treaty, Washington gnawed silently on the Randolph problem, never mentioning the Fauchet allegations to Randolph. He decided not to seek more documentation from Fauchet's successor as minister, expecting that the request would be futile. He resolved to present Randolph with what he had, then gauge Randolph's culpability from his conduct when confronted.[28]

∾

At midmorning of August 19, Randolph reached the president's residence on Market Street. Washington, Pickering, and Wolcott, already in Washington's office, greeted him formally. Washington handed over Fauchet's letter and asked the secretary of state to "make such explanations as you choose."

As Randolph read, he commented that without the Frenchman's earlier dispatches, Fauchet's statements were not clear, but he denied any improper actions. When he reached the incriminating reference to the "scale of prices" demanded by American patriots, Randolph offered a hazy recollection that Fauchet had advised him of "machinations against the French Republic, Governor Clinton [of New York] and myself." His ordeal was interrupted when Washington was called from the office. When the president returned, he asked Randolph to leave so he could confer with the other two.

Cooling his heels in the anteroom, Randolph decided that the president had prejudged him. When the meeting resumed, Randolph agreed to Washington's suggestion that he prepare a written response to the Fauchet material, then announced his resignation. Later that day, he sent a resignation letter from home, noting that he had lost Washington's confidence. He plainly had.[29]

Washington appointed Pickering to be interim secretary of state. Randolph embarked on a four-month quest to defend himself, starting with a breakneck dash to Rhode Island to acquire a sworn statement from the homebound Fauchet, plus copies of the Frenchman's earlier dispatches. When Randolph published his lengthy *Vindication* in December 1795, it included a peculiar explanation of Fauchet's ambiguous statements.[30]

Randolph's explanation, largely backed by Fauchet, was that the secretary of state had suspected that the British incited the Whiskey Rebellion. He supposedly told Fauchet that four unnamed grain merchants could resolve that suspicion and end the rebellion if only they were freed of their debts to British businesses. To that end, Randolph allegedly encouraged Fauchet to fulfill contracts to buy flour from those unnamed figures, freeing them from British influence. That exchange supposedly prompted Fauchet's remark about the "scale of prices" for American patriots.[31]

If Randolph truly made that convoluted proposal to Fauchet, the Frenchman might well have suspected that the American was soliciting a bribe; money paid to mysterious grain merchants could end up in any number of pockets, including Randolph's. Indeed, Randolph's account of the episode—that as secretary of state, without consulting the president, he asked a foreign diplomat to pay American citizens to secure secret information—raised more doubts than it dispelled. Washington, a shrewd spymaster during the war, hardly needed someone with no experience in espionage (Randolph) to combine with a French revolutionary with no command of English (Fauchet) to gather intelligence about events on the American frontier. Moreover, at a time when Washington saw Genêt and the democratic societies lurking behind every tree, the secretary of state should not have secretly been playing footsie with the new French minister. Though direct evidence of bribery never surfaced, Washington's loss of confidence in Randolph seems well founded.[32]

Randolph's published *Vindication* did his reputation no good. John Adams dismissed it as "a weak thing." It did not, Jefferson lamented, prompt "high ideas of [Randolph's] wisdom or steadiness." Madison regretted that Randolph's "best friend can't save him from the self-condemnation of his political career as explained by himself." In private, Washington fulminated about Randolph; in public, he said nothing.[33]

Randolph's departure from the cabinet showed Washington at his least sentimental. Though the president never explained his handling of the episode, he may have been dissatisfied with his secretary of state in other ways. Never the steadiest character, Randolph had shifted his position on the treaty issue, ultimately pressing Washington not to sign. Then there were Randolph's slighting remarks to Fauchet about the president. Moreover, there is no evidence that Washington ever held a high opinion of Randolph's abilities. Washington may have seen Randolph's departure as no great loss.

Washington asked five different men to accept permanent appointment as secretary of state; each declined. It was deflating. Hamilton delivered a hard truth about the situation: "In fact a first-rate character is not attainable. A second rate must be taken with good dispositions and barely decent qualifications."[34]

Washington had to agree. He elevated Pickering from interim to permanent secretary of state and recruited James McHenry, an aide during the war, to take over the War Department. When Attorney General Bradford died of fever at age thirty-nine, two men turned down that office before Washington named Charles Lee, his personal lawyer in Virginia (not to be confused with the general of the same name).[35] Washington, as Hamilton warned, would finish his presidency assisted by second-stringers, all dedicated Federalists. The president might consider himself nonpartisan, but his government no longer looked that way.

No matter what its lineup, the Washington administration still faced a fight for peace. Congressional Republicans had a plan to undermine the Jay Treaty, and thought they had the votes to do it.

∾

Washington's seventh annual message, delivered on December 8, 1795, was another exercise in optimism. A Massachusetts congressman called the speech "one of the most animating, firm, and manly addresses I ever heard from him or any other person." When the president called on Americans to support the government, that congressman yearned to swear allegiance on the spot. The address did not challenge Republicans directly, and there were no references to self-created societies. Washington had learned that lesson.[36]

He offered an impressive list of advances. Incomes were rising with sky-high European demand for American crops. Treaties had brought peace with tribes on every frontier. Morocco had signed a treaty to control piracy against American ships, while the American envoy to Spain was predicting "a speedy and satisfactory conclusion of his negotiation" over the Mississippi. The Jay Treaty awaited only ratification by George III. Washington contrasted war-torn Europe with tranquil America, enjoying "a spectacle of national happiness never surpassed." He recommended strengthening the nation's military and implored his fellow citizens to stop attacking peaceful Indians.[37]

Disturbing this idyll of contentment and wealth, the Republicans planned to use their control of the House of Representatives to deny funds needed for the commissions established by the Jay Treaty, and for reclaiming the western forts from Britain. Without those funds, the treaty's gains could never be realized. This strategy underlined Republican doctrine that the House, the popular branch of government, must participate in treaty-making.

The Republicans' timing, however, was off. By the winter months of 1796, the treaty still had fervent opponents, especially in the South, but opinion was shifting. A leading Republican moaned that the treaty had initially been opposed by "nineteen twentieths of our citizens, [but] is now approved of . . . by the same proportion." Sensing the movement, tuning out the static coming from rabid treaty opponents, Washington delayed his request for treaty-related funding. With public attitudes coming his way, he had the discipline to wait. When official copies of the treaty arrived from Britain, the astute Washington still waited. Time was on his side.[38]

The tide running in Washington's favor triggered a jubilant birthday celebration on February 22, with ringing bells, roaring cannons, and well-wishers descending on his residence. On that day, the new treaty with Spain arrived with exhilarating terms: unrestricted access to the Mississippi for Americans, a midriver boundary line between the two nations, the right to use the port of New Orleans, and a boundary with Spanish Florida at the thirty-first parallel. The United States had secured every objective. The Senate unanimously and speedily ratified it.[39]

After George III's acceptance of the Jay agreement arrived, Washington declared it in effect. Still, however, he did not submit his funding request, allowing the joyous news of the Spanish treaty to spread. The president ventured into the public eye for the first time in more than six months. When he and Martha entered Ricketts' Theater in late February, they were greeted with three rounds of spontaneous applause. A voice then rang out, "Damn me if that is enough for the Old Fellow, let's give him three cheers," which the crowd did.[40]

Feeling the situation slipping away, Republicans launched their first attack three days later. They demanded that Washington turn over the treaty instructions given to Jay. Washington took his time responding, seeking advice from Hamilton and others. At issue was the president's authority over foreign policy. Washington, who had recently pledged to respect the Constitution in all such matters, refused to deliver the papers, adopting Hamilton's argument that the treaty power rested exclusively with the president and the Senate. He was, he explained, simply following the Constitution.[41]

The Republicans moved on to their attempt to deny funding for treaty enforcement. The Federalist minority fought back on several fronts. They organized local meetings to demand funding. They linked money for the Jay Treaty to money for the spectacularly popular Spanish treaty. In floor debate, they contended that if America backed out of the agreement with Britain, war would follow, then dissolution of the union.[42]

There were no votes to spare. The House divided evenly, so the presiding officer broke the tie in favor of funding the treaty obligations; a second vote came in at 51–48 for funding. Washington credited the public petitions for the victory, but Jefferson thought it was the president who made the difference. "One man outweighs them all in influence over the people," he wrote, adding, "Republicanism must lie on its oars, [and] resign the vessel to its pilot."[43]

The Republican chief did not mention, however, Washington's adroit management. Never abandoning his position that the treaty was good and that only the executive and the Senate were responsible for treaties, he patiently withheld his funding requests while public opinion moved. Then he waited some more. He stood, he reminded the people, with the Constitution. And when his position was strong enough, he struck.

The Jay Treaty's benefits met Washington's modest expectations. Within a few weeks of the House vote on funding, the British began evacuating the western posts. According to a senator from Pittsburgh, that "completed the measure of our political happiness."[44] Frontier trade rebounded and settlement of the Northwest Territory proceeded.

As Washington also had predicted, relations with France deteriorated. He tried to placate the sister republic, recalling American minister Gouverneur Morris and sending in his place James Monroe, a pro-French Republican.[45]

But Washington would not change his core policy, stated to Hamilton in May 1796: "We will not be dictated to by the politics of any nation under heaven, farther than treaties require of us."[46] With less than a year remaining in office, Washington lacked the time to execute a strategy for dealing with the ever-shifting French government. France would be a problem for the next president.

CHAPTER 50

Farewell, Again

In his sixty-fourth year, the final year of his presidency, Washington made a powerful impression on Henrietta Liston, wife of the new British minister and twenty years his junior. She found his face "rather pleasing, particularly when he smiles." He moved with "a dignity which even the general coldness of his address did not lessen." On visits to Mount Vernon, Mrs. Liston admired his "majestic figure," natural grace, and sense of style. He laughed readily at others' jokes, although his own humorous remarks were "the flash of a moment; gaiety was not natural to him." She marveled at his mastery of etiquette, "how acquired, Heaven knows." Mrs. Liston evidently did not know of Washington's early studies with the Fairfaxes of Belvoir.

The Englishwoman offered perceptive judgments about the statesman as well as the man, finding him "naturally grave and silent . . . [with] prudence his striking trait."

Most people say & do too much;—Washington, partly from constitutional taciturnity,—but still more from natural sagacity and careful observation, never fell into this common error.

Although the president knew no language but English and could not be called learned, she found he "possessed, not only great good sense and a sound judgment, but was a man of observation and of deep reflection," never speaking on a subject he had not mastered. She portrayed his personality as a mix of hot temper, coolness, and reserve.[1]

In his final year as president, opposition attacks grew ever more furious, trying his fabled temper. The *Aurora* of Philadelphia accused him of seeking "the greatest good for the least number possessing the greatest wealth," and proclaimed that "thousands among [us] . . . equal you in capacity and excel you in knowledge." Another *Aurora* issue called for his impeachment, accusing him of wishing to be king. A third regretted that "a good general may be a most miserable politician."[2]

Harsher words came from Thomas Paine, whose pamphlets had rallied Americans during the Revolutionary War. Paine, who blamed Washington for not prying him out of a French jail where he rotted for months, called the president "treacherous in private friendship . . . and a hypocrite in public life," declaring "the world will be troubled to decide whether . . . you have abandoned good principles, or whether you had any." The *Aurora* strained to match Paine's invective:

> If ever a nation was debauched by a man, the American nation has been debauched by WASHINGTON. If ever a nation was deceived by a man, the American nation has been deceived by WASHINGTON. . . . Let the history of the federal government instruct mankind, that the masque of patriotism may be worn to conceal the foulest designs against the liberties of a people.

Some Virginia gentlemen drank a new toast: "Speedy death to General Washington."

The attacks reflected a spreading anxiety that Federalists were intent on preserving a stratified, class-based world. The new financial system appeared to favor the wealthy; the Jay Treaty seemed to align Federalists with aristocratic Britain and against revolutionary France; by suppressing the Whiskey Rebellion, Federalists used the power of the state against ordinary people with grievances. Now often seen as a party leader, Washington became fair game for partisan attack.[3]

The president sometimes professed indifference to the attacks, but they tortured a man who cared deeply about his reputation. "I think he feels these things," Jefferson wrote, "more than any person I ever yet met with." Occasionally Washington vented his fury in private, denouncing "infamous scribblers" who attacked him "in such exaggerated and indecent terms as could scarcely be applied to a Nero, a notorious defaulter, or even to a common pickpocket." In the Jay Treaty battle, Washington had shown that he could operate effectively in the partisan brawling style that was emerging, but it was neither natural to him nor comfortable. No one in the House of Burgesses ever had to endure such calumny.[4]

Yearning to deliver a last word to his country, Washington began to

imagine a valedictory address. Just as his presidency had set so many precedents, Washington wanted his departure to serve as a model. He wished to
rise above the squabbles of the moment and highlight ideas and traditions
that should become part of the American legacy. Washington the consummate performer would make the most of his final days on the public stage.

Four years before, when he had hoped to retire at the end of his first term,
he had collaborated with Madison on a draft retirement address. When he
agreed to a second term, he put the draft away. Because Madison was now an
adversary, this time Washington recruited Hamilton's help.[5]

In May 1796, Washington shared with Hamilton a draft of the key points
to be made in the address, urging that the ideas be stated plainly. After nearly
two months, Hamilton sent back an entirely new draft, one that covered the
subjects noted by Washington but more simply and without defensiveness.
As Washington had asked, Hamilton retained elements of Madison's draft
from four years before, a political stroke designed to limit Republican critics.
Out of respect, Hamilton sent Washington an alternative that adhered more
closely to the president's original writing.[6]

Never prideful about his own compositions, the president preferred the
draft Hamilton prepared from scratch, finding it "more copious on material
points, more dignified on the whole, and with less egotism." But the ideas
were all Washington's. He asked that Hamilton review it with John Jay.[7]

COURTESY OF THE LIBRARY OF CONGRESS

Washington (Latrobe sketch, 1796)

In early September, Hamilton returned another version. Washington edited this one line by line, striking out passages and substituting words to capture his thoughts more firmly. When he was done, he sewed the pages together with silk thread—the eighteenth-century version of a stapler. Though the document was dated September 7, two Philadelphia newspapers published it twelve days later, as Washington traveled back to Mount Vernon.[8]

Washington's Farewell Address, professing to be "disinterested warnings of a parting friend," became a classic, articulating principles that guided successors for generations. Schoolchildren memorized passages and politicians pledged fealty to it. On the first Washington's Birthday of the Civil War, President Lincoln ordered commanders to read portions to their troops, while Congress read the entire document aloud at the Capitol.[9]

∾

Though often remembered as a warning against entangling alliances with foreign nations—a phrase that appears in Jefferson's first inaugural, not in Washington's farewell—the farewell's core was a thoughtful examination of the causes and dangers of unbridled partisanship, which Washington considered the great threat to American liberty.

Political differences not only fueled newspaper denunciations, but also the burning of effigies, public mobbing, and the stoning of Hamilton during the Jay Treaty fight. In a note to Jefferson in July 1796, implicitly pleading for restraint from the opposition leader, Washington confessed that he had never dreamt that "parties would, or even could, go to the length I have been witness to." His plea went for naught. Jefferson, though amiable in person, proclaimed it "immoral to pursue a middle line." The political choice, he explained, was between "honest men and rogues." He recognized no common ground.[10]

Washington was not a starry-eyed idealist, not after more than four decades of political engagement, beginning with colonial politics during the war with France, sitting at the knee of Colonel Fairfax, Speaker John Robinson, and Governor Dinwiddie. He had stumbled clumsily then, a neophyte trying to navigate the British bureaucracy. His sixteen years in the House of Burgesses educated him in coalition-building, political timing, and persuasion. He learned from Speaker Peyton Randolph, Edmund Pendleton, George Mason, and Richard Henry Lee, then from younger men like Patrick Henry and Thomas Jefferson.

The Continental Congress made Washington's perspective continental, introducing him to skilled agitators like Sam Adams of Massachusetts, to aristocratic revolutionaries like the Rutledges and Laurenses of South Carolina, and reintroduced him to the canny Franklin. To sustain his position atop the Continental Army, he drew support from the rotating cast in the Continental Congress and scores of state and local officials. When his leadership was challenged within the army, Washington isolated his rivals, then neutralized them.

After the war, he became the face of the Constitutional Convention and the new charter of government. With allies like Madison and Hamilton, he was the necessary keystone of the ratification effort. As president, he held in one cabinet the disparate views of Hamilton and Jefferson, securing enactment of the essential fiscal program and placing the seat of government on the Potomac. As politics fractured on partisan lines, Washington faced down Genêt, sustained neutrality, brought the Whiskey Rebellion to a bloodless end, and shouldered the Jay Treaty into law.

In short, Washington's political acumen, acquired through the sort of close observation and careful reflection that impressed Henrietta Liston, was beyond question. As a leading historian concluded, no one of his generation understood power so well. Perhaps no American leader ever has.[11]

Washington had come to believe that partisanship is inevitable; in the Farewell Address, he called it "inseparable from our nature, having its root in the strongest passions of the human mind." Partisanship infects all governments, he continued, though authoritarian regimes suppress it. In popular governments, "it is seen in its greatest rankness and is truly their worst enemy."

Washington offered a sophisticated view of its costs. As factions succeed each other in power, they develop a "spirit of revenge, natural to party dissension, which in different ages and countries has perpetrated the most horrid enormities." Upon winning control, each faction settles old scores and reverses policies, even successful ones. Yet there is a worse outcome. The factional "disorders and miseries . . . gradually incline the minds of men to seek security and repose in the absolute power of an individual." Eventually, "the chief of some prevailing faction more able or more fortunate than his competitors turns this disposition to the purposes of his own elevation, on the ruins of public liberty." In short, tyranny.

Washington warned that because partisanship will never go away (is "a fire not to be quenched"), it must be controlled ("demands a uniform vigilance to prevent its bursting into a flame"). Unconstrained, partisans run amok. For Washington, constraint must be built into a structure that fractures power among the branches of government, "dividing and distributing it into different depositories," arming each to resist incursions by the others.

For the pragmatic Washington, reciprocal checks on the government's centers of power preserved popular control and individual liberty.

In the Farewell Address, Washington called on his countrymen to appreciate their self-interest in preserving the union, using the term "union" nearly two dozen times.[12] Union was, he insisted,

> a main pillar in the edifice of your real independence, the support of your tranquility at home, your peace abroad; of your safety; of your prosperity; of that very Liberty which you so highly prize.

Washington specified how each region benefitted from union. Northerners prospered by trading the South's agricultural goods, enriching Southerners in turn. East and west would develop similar connections as canals and roads fostered trade between those regions. Attempts to divide people, Washington warned, often were based on lies about those in other regions.

Moving to foreign affairs, the farewell stressed the importance of correctly judging America's interests and resisting "the insidious wiles of foreign influence." Washington warned against both "inveterate antipathies against" other nations or "passionate attachments for" them. Both emotions give foreigners the power "to tamper with domestic factions, to practice the arts of seduction, to mislead public opinion, to influence or awe the public councils." For Washington, limiting American commitments to other nations was one more method for staving off the factionalism that could destroy self-government.

The Farewell Address included other teachings. Washington insisted that a stable society must include religion and morality. He preached, as he always had, that there can be no government without revenue, no revenue without taxes, and that "no taxes can be devised which are not more or less inconvenient and unpleasant." Americans could grumble about taxes, as Washington did, but to preserve their freedom, they must pay them.

His vision was of a virtuous, independent republic, strong enough to defy foreign powers. He closed with his personal hope for retirement under "the benign influence of good laws under a free government."

A striking feature of the Farewell Address is that Washington warned Americans to guard against someone very like him: a national hero whose popularity cloaks the consolidation of power and the destruction of self-government. In view of Washington's popularity and the power of his personality, he could have been the greatest threat to American liberty. After painting the president's portrait, Gilbert Stuart reported that "had he been born in the forests . . . he would have been the fiercest among the savage tribes." The Farewell Address was powerful because that man had restrained his ferocity and promoted self-government. Now he called his countrymen back to the cause of liberty. His impending retirement, his final act of relinquishing power, was proof that he remained faithful to that cause.[13]

ॐ

Washington's last annual address, delivered to Congress in early December 1796, recited many accomplishments. The country was at peace with the tribes and occupied the western posts that the British had vacated. Under the Jay Treaty, joint commissions were marking the boundary between Maine and Canada and resolving American claims for seized ships. The Mississippi was open to American trade, captured sailors in North Africa had been released, and the boundaries with Spanish Florida and Louisiana were resolved. Washington called on Congress to create national institutions to reinforce the union: a national university, a board of agriculture, a military academy, and a navy. The first never would be built; the last three came after his time.[14]

Washington looked forward to retirement. About ten days before John Adams was to assume the presidency, Mrs. Liston congratulated Washington "on his approaching happiness." The president replied "like a child within view of the holidays" that he had "counted the months, then the weeks, and I now reckon the days." Washington's mind was turning to projects for Mount Vernon. "There are so many things I wish to have done soon," he wrote to his farm manager, "and so many others that are essential to do, that I scarcely know what direction to give concerning them." He approved a proposal for a Mount Vernon distillery, which thrived; in 1799, it produced 11,000 gallons of whiskey.[15]

In his final weeks in office, Washington attended the theater and concerts. He hosted receptions for the diplomatic corps, congressmen, merchants, Pennsylvania's governor and legislators, army officers, and the Society of the Cincinnati. His birthday celebration began with bell-ringing and cannon blasts and ended with a dinner and ball that drew 1,200.[16]

With his dentist, the president consulted about his collapsed dentures of human teeth and hippopotamus ivory. The remaining structure, Washington complained, made his lips bulge out, a pattern visible in Stuart's late portrait of him. Also, the dentures were turning black and his lone remaining tooth fell out. Such woes were both painful and embarrassing for a public man acutely conscious of his appearance. Every morning for years, he had to wedge into his mouth, onto gums raw from friction, a contraption of wire, metal, springs, and ivory that obstructed his speech and slid while he chewed whatever food was soft enough for him to attempt. Once he had the dentures in place, the rest of his day must have seemed easy.[17]

At Adams's inauguration on March 4, 1797, Washington was joyful. He wore a simple black coat and his expression, according to Adams, was "as serene and unclouded as the day. . . . Methought I heard him think Ay! I am fairly out and you fairly in! see which of us will be happiest." The new president admitted, "I envied him more than he did me; and with reason." Adams assured his wife that weeping onlookers were not moved by their joy over the new president. The tears, he sighed, reflected "grief for the loss of their beloved."[18]

As Washington strode from the chamber, spectators rushed after him for a last look. In the street, he waved his hat to cheering onlookers. The crowd, falling quiet, followed him through the street to the president's residence. Reaching the door, he turned to the now-silent crowd, his face grave, tears on his face. Unable to speak, he gestured his thanks and farewell.[19]

∾

Washington's return to Mount Vernon was another triumphal procession. His countrymen cheered him in Baltimore, in Georgetown, and in Alexandria. His return was soon darkened, however, by news that his sister, Betty Lewis, had died. That left only Washington and his brother Charles of the original nine siblings and half-siblings.[20]

Home for good, Washington pitched into Mount Vernon improvements. "We are like the beginners of a new establishment," he wrote. There were rooms to paint, defects to repair. Though the work would be troublesome and dirty, it would "give exercise both to the mind and body." He hoped to spend his remaining days—"which in the ordinary course of things (being in my sixty-sixth year) cannot be many"—ignoring politics in favor of "the more rational amusement of cultivating the earth."[21]

Yet Washington had unfinished business with the nation, and with other Americans. He had spent his life supported by the involuntary labor of people who enjoyed none of the liberty and freedom he praised so extravagantly and fought for for so long. The slave society he managed at Mount Vernon utterly contradicted every ideal that Washington claimed to hold dear. His work was not done.

FREEDOM

CHAPTER 51

Home for Good

The world in 1797 offered few models of former rulers in voluntary retirement. For kings, emperors, and popes, the prevailing fates were death or resentful exile. In his first months at home, Washington blazed a third trail as farmer and private citizen, though he could never entirely recede from the nation's life.

When President Adams delivered an important speech concerning France, Washington refused to comment on it. His goals, he insisted, were to raise his crops, repair his house, secure his public papers, and sell his flour. He looked forward, he wrote to a friend, to "more real enjoyment than in all the bustling with which I have been occupied . . . which . . . [is] little more than vanity and vexation." On a visit to Mount Vernon, Henrietta Liston thought Washington seemed "like a man relieved from a heavy burden. He has thrown off a little of that prudence which formerly guarded his every word."[1]

He felt his time shortening, and often said so. He referred to "the few years I have to remain on this terrestrial globe," while predicting that "my glass is nearly run" and "my thread is nearly spun," and "the days of my sojournment . . . cannot be many." He described himself as "near the bottom of the hill," "approaching the shades below," and having a "remnant of a life journeying fast to the mansions of my ancestors." Gloomy fatalism, however, was not new for him. Before he was thirty, he had described himself struggling with "the grim king." In autumn 1799, with the death of his last surviving sibling, his brother Charles, Washington vowed, "When the summons comes, I shall endeavor to obey it with good grace."[2]

He retained physical talents, proving more adept in a billiards match than an opponent expected, and kept his striking presence and carriage. After a chance encounter with the ex-president on a country road, a traveling actor marveled:

> Every feature suggested a resemblance to the spirit it encased and showed simplicity in alliance with the sublime. The impression, therefore, was that of a most perfect whole; . . . you could not but think you looked upon a wonder, and something sacred as well as wonderful—a man fashioned by the hand of heaven, with every requisite to achieve a great work.[3]

Washington described his days as beginning with the sun. If Mount Vernon's workers had not yet stirred, he wrote archly, "I send them messages of my sorrow for their indisposition." After reviewing the home farm, he breakfasted at seven, then rode through the more distant farms until dinner at three. He welcomed strangers who stopped for a look at the hero, so long as they were well dressed. By one calculation, in 1798 the Washingtons gave dinner to 656 guests and provided lodging for 677. He reserved evening for addressing the deluge of correspondence, but he sometimes abandoned it in favor of sociability.[4]

A new French crisis ended his liberation from public cares. That country's resentment of the Jay Treaty had quickly ripened. Its armies triumphant in Europe, France attacked American trade, seizing roughly 600 ships during the eighteen months after the treaty was ratified, and abusing American sailors. American exports shrank by more than 20 percent and maritime insurance rates jumped. President Adams sent three envoys to patch things up, but the French kept them idling for months. In a letter to Adams's secretary of war, Washington asked a lighthearted question with a serious undertone: "Are our commissioners guillotined?"[5]

The situation became a crisis when public outrage greeted the news that French officials (identified as "X, Y, and Z") demanded bribes from the American diplomats. Overnight, everything French became anathema to Americans. All Philadelphians, a friend reported to Washington in April 1798, had removed French cockades from their hats.[6]

An infuriated Congress authorized an army of 10,000 men, plus a "provisional army" of five times that many. Only one man could command them. "We must have your name," Adams wrote to Washington. "There will be more efficacy in it than in many an army."[7]

However flattering Washington may have found this demand, he also recognized its negatives. He feared another emergence from retirement would invite ridicule or resentment, and worried if he was physically and mentally equal to the job. Creating an effective fighting force, he warned Adams, might be beyond the powers of the "old set of generals" from the Revolutionary War, who might lack "sufficient activity, energy & health."[8]

He likely was wary of being subordinate to Adams, though he never said so. Washington respected the New Englander and supported his policies, but the new president could be unpredictable. Adams demonstrated his volatility by not waiting for Washington's consent before nominating him to command the new army. Congress put aside its partisan bickering and unanimously approved the appointment, marking the fifth time that Washington won high office without a dissenting vote.[9]

The military undertaking proved misbegotten, a fumbling coda to Washington's career. Adams and Washington locked horns over the top hierarchy of generals. Washington wanted Hamilton as his second-in-command. In the Continental Army, at the Constitutional Convention, as treasury secretary, and in the Whiskey Rebellion, the younger man had demonstrated high energy and organizational talent. Washington, who intended to join the army only in case of invasion or great emergency, needed a thoroughly capable surrogate. But Adams and Hamilton were political antagonists, so the president pressed for his fellow New Englander, Henry Knox, or Charles Cotesworth Pinckney of South Carolina, both of whom had outranked Hamilton in the Continental Army.[10]

Adams finally relented; he might be president, but Washington was Washington. But the disagreement delayed the recruitment of soldiers for more than six months and muddled the army's organization. Distance exacerbated the delay. Adams preferred to spend his time in Massachusetts, which hamstrung communication. Washington, the natural center of attention wherever he appeared, came to Philadelphia for only a single five-week period, organizing the army with Hamilton and Pinckney during the day and plunging into a social swirl at night. After the general returned to Mount Vernon, he complained that he was so ignorant of events that if he had to respond to an emergency, it would be as though he had dropped from the clouds.[11]

Yet Washington exercised his gift of silence. Pressed to comment on a diplomatic situation, he answered, "The vessel is afloat . . . and considering myself as a passenger only, I shall trust to the mariners . . . to steer it into a safe port." Without consulting Washington or his cabinet, Adams sent more diplomats to France in a final bid to avoid war. Many Federalists denounced the maneuver, but Washington supported it; happily for the nation, it brought a peaceful resolution.[12]

This final public engagement underscored two developments in Washington's thinking. First, he had abandoned any pretense to nonpartisanship; he was a Federalist. He and Secretary of War McHenry agreed that, because Republican officers might "divide and contaminate the army by artful and seditious discourses," all army officers should be Federalists. In correspondence with friends, he denounced Republicans as attempting to subvert the Constitution and the government. When James Monroe published a pamphlet defending his work as minister to France, Washington inscribed spirited retorts in the margins. He found one passage "curious and laughable," another "insanity in the extreme!" while a third reflected the views of "a person incompetent to judge, or blinded by party views." Washington cheered when anti-French feeling carried Virginia's Federalists to success in the 1799 elections.[13]

Also, Washington had become more candid about the dangers of slave revolt that shadowed the lives of white Southerners, dangers that had been accentuated by the successful slave rising in Santo Domingo during the 1790s. Any French invasion of America, he told Adams, would come in the South, where "there can be no doubt of their arming the Negroes against us." Henry Knox agreed that the French would deploy Black troops from the West Indies and "excit[e] the slaves" with the "natural desire of liberty."[14]

∾

When army matters did not press, Washington's days overflowed with other projects. He despaired that the Potomac River improvements proceeded so "limpingly," chronically short of funds. The same affliction hampered construction of the new seat of government upriver from Mount Vernon. To meet a pledge to build two houses in the federal city, Washington took out the first bank loan of his life.[15]

The largest part of his energy went to repairing his finances after eight years as president. Mary Washington's eldest always worried about money, but his worries were real. Despite its beauty, Mount Vernon's soil was thin and gullied and its farms produced little profit. The thriving new distillery could not retrieve the situation. Washington had to sell off or lease out the lands he had spent a lifetime acquiring.[16]

But few Americans wished to be tenants, while the scarcity of cash made it difficult to find buyers for his vast western tracts. When he made potentially lucrative sales—one would have brought in more than $200,000 (nearly $5 million today)—purchasers often failed to pay. Smaller sales kept Mount Vernon afloat.[17]

Washington knew why his estate, despite his hard work, could not pay for itself: Ninety percent of the people at Mount Vernon were enslaved. The estate could not support them all, not with the unmotivated labor that the slave system generated.

Washington's attitudes toward slavery were complicated and contradictory, like those of many Americans, and evolved through his life. As a young man, he seems to have been an unreflective slave master, one who accepted the coerced labor system of his time and place. That unthinking acceptance dissolved in the face of the rebellion's exaltation of human liberty and the sacrifices of his African American soldiers, which created a profound internal struggle for Washington. He could hardly justify enslaving people who were willing to die fighting for his liberty. He resolved first to become a humane slaveholder, to avoid the harshest features of the system without overturning it. He would not sell or buy enslaved people, in order to avoid breaking up families, but he was inconsistent about that. He always maintained that men and nations follow their own interests rather than highflown ideals; that could prove true for him when his economic interests conflicted with his dislike of slavery.

The slave system posed the greatest test of Washington's political skills. For virtually all his life, he failed it. He made no public statement nor took any public action that questioned the legitimacy of slavery, fearing that it would upend the republic for which he sacrificed so much. On the most pressing moral question facing the nation, its greatest leader did not lead.

In quiet hours working on correspondence in his study or riding across his farms or gazing at the Potomac from his rear portico, Washington could not deny that failure. He understood that the slave system disfigured America's vaunted freedom. Finally, he accepted his obligation to speak the truth that his interests, and the nation's interests, could not be reconciled with slavery. He decided to confess that he had been wrong to dwell within that system. It was a momentous step, one that he hoped would encourage Americans to end slavery. Washington took it at the last possible moment, when he himself would not have to endure any negative consequences from it, yet it was a righteous act.

CHAPTER 52

Wrestling with Sin

When Washington left for the First Continental Congress in 1774, Mount Vernon was home to 119 slaves older than sixteen. The following year he paid taxes on 135 enslaved people there. He had amassed those slaves by inheritance, by marriage, and by purchases at auctions and from slave merchants. He traded wheat and flour to acquire a group from the West Indies. Although Washington followed Virginia custom by referring to the people he owned as "family," the euphemism could not conceal the harsh realities of forced bondage. As explained in a recent book on Washington's slaveholding, Mount Vernon and the Custis estates he managed saw many of slavery's worst abuses: "whipping, keeping someone in shackles, tracking a person down with dogs, or selling people away from their family."[1]

Of the almost 700 Mount Vernon slaves managed by Washington from 1760 forward, forty-seven tried to escape. Enslaved people stole from him, set his property on fire, and avoided work by breaking his tools and feigning illness. He recognized that punishment "often produces evils which are worse than the disease," yet even after announcing an end to whipping, he still employed the practice. "If the Negros will not do their duty by fair means," he wrote to his farm manager in 1797, "they must be compelled."[2]

In 1774, when he was forty-two, Washington first joined a public statement hostile to slavery. As the prime sponsor and most visible signatory of the Fairfax Resolves, he endorsed its statement demanding "an entire stop" to the importation of enslaved people, "a wicked cruel, and unnatural trade."

Anti-slavery sentiment was awakening then. In the *Somerset* decision two years earlier, an English court limited the rights of slave owners in that country; the *Virginia Gazette* printed six articles about the ruling. Some New

England clergy called for emancipation of enslaved people, as did Quakers and Methodists. In 1771 and 1774, the Massachusetts Assembly voted for abolition, but the royal governor vetoed both bills. Rhode Island and Connecticut provided that slaves entering the state would become free. Delaware banned slave imports, a step Virginia took in 1778. By the end of the Revolution, every state had made those imports illegal, though only Massachusetts and Pennsylvania prohibited slave ownership. Patrick Henry candidly admitted that although he owned slaves for his convenience, "I will not, I cannot, justify it."[3]

A French traveler in 1782 observed that Virginians "grieved at having slaves, and are constantly talking about abolishing slavery and of seeking other means of exploiting their lands." Such statements came from George Mason, Richard Henry Lee, Thomas Jefferson, James Madison, and Edmund Randolph. And, eventually, Washington. The Virginia Assembly would take a first step on that road in 1782, when it legalized the manumission (or freeing) of the enslaved by their owners.[4]

When he assumed command of the American forces around Boston in 1775, Washington halted the enlistment of Black soldiers. He reversed himself after Lord Dunmore in Virginia offered freedom to slaves and indentured servants who joined the British forces. In the Continental Army, Black soldiers fought alongside whites through the war.

More than 700 African American soldiers endured the winter at Valley Forge. Those men and other Black soldiers changed Washington. He felt deeply their suffering and sacrifices. He could not justify treating them differently. Another influence awakening Washington to the talents of the enslaved came from the emancipated poet Phillis Wheatley, who published a popular poem in 1775 celebrating him.[5]

While at Valley Forge, Washington accepted a Rhode Island proposal to raise a battalion of African American soldiers. Any slave entering the unit would be freed if he served for the duration of the war. A French officer praised that regiment as "the most neatly dressed, the best under arms, and the most precise in its maneuvers." Washington later ordered that Black and white Rhode Islanders serve in an integrated unit, yet would not endorse a plan to raise a battalion of African Americans in South Carolina and Georgia, which was championed by his former aide John Laurens (son of Henry Laurens, a major slaveholder and president of Congress). Washington feared that the venture would spur the British to create similar units while fomenting unrest among the enslaved in the South. Roughly 5,000 African Americans served in the Continental Army through the long war.[6]

During that time, Washington began to show regret over his slave owning, though his statements and actions about slavery would always be inconsistent. In 1778, his farm manager (his cousin Lund) acknowledged that Washington had barred the sale of any enslaved person against his or her wishes. A few months later, Washington wrote to Lund that he would gladly acquire land close to Mount Vernon if the seller would accept payment in Negroes "of whom I every day long more and more to get clear of." Six months later, he repeated to Lund his scruples against sales of enslaved people that would break up families.[7]

After the war, Lafayette begged Washington to free his Negroes, proposing that they jointly create a plantation to be cultivated by freed slaves, which would demonstrate that the enslaved could behave responsibly. Washington declined, though he applauded Lafayette for establishing freed slaves on land in French Guiana. The enslaved should be freed gradually, Washington insisted, "by legislative authority." Pennsylvania and other Northern states were following that course.[8]

Washington's path on slavery continued to veer between principle and self-interest. In 1786, Washington refused to purchase a group of enslaved people, stating he would not "hurt the feelings of those unhappy people by a separation of man and wife, or of families." But then he asked whether those slaves "could be separated without much uneasiness." He ultimately agreed to accept six enslaved people in the transaction so long as they were young, healthy males. Writing to another Virginian, he insisted that he wanted no more slaves, but was willing to purchase a bricklayer if the price was fair and no family would be fractured as a result. He wrote eight years later that were he not principled against selling slaves, he would prefer to be rid of them. He declined other transactions because he did not want to acquire more enslaved people, though he accepted a slave left to him by his mother's will.[9]

Washington presented himself as supporting abolition, though his commitment was tepid, conditional, and private. When Quakers sued a slaveholder to enforce a Pennsylvania statute that granted freedom to slaves who lived more than six months in that state, Washington complained that the law was unfair to slaveholders. He quickly added, however, that "there is not a man living who wishes more sincerely than I do to see a plan for the abolition of it [slavery]." But, he continued, only the legislature could adopt such a plan. He assured a fellow slave owner that he would support laws to abolish slavery "by slow, sure, and imperceptible degrees." A skeptic might point out that "imperceptible" abolition would be no abolition at all.[10]

In 1785, two Methodist divines sought Washington's support for a petition urging Virginia to adopt gradual emancipation. Washington was evasive, and the petitioners record him saying he was of our sentiments, and had signified his thoughts on the subject to most of the great men of the state; that he did not see it proper to sign the petition; but if the Assembly took it into consideration, would signify his sentiments to the Assembly by letter.

Washington sent no such letter.[11]

His public silence likely flowed from the calculation that publicly embracing abolitionism would do no good for the world and some harm to himself. Abolitionists were a small minority. Their views smacked of religious zealotry to many Virginians, who would not welcome them in their homes. Washington's family never voiced anti-slavery sentiments—not his siblings, nor his in-laws, nor his wife. Moreover, Southern states were so enmeshed in the slave system that even gradual abolition terrified many white Southerners. Indeed, a fundamental change in that system would have been costly for Washington, who had a massive investment in his enslaved workers. To a man with constant anxiety about money and a gift for silence, public silence on slavery was a natural course.

The next years confirmed the futility of abolition efforts in the South. At the Constitutional Convention in 1787, Georgians and South Carolinians furiously opposed restrictions on slave imports, vowing to abandon the union if their views were not accommodated. When anti-slavery petitions came to the floor of the First Congress, the response from Deep South legislators was just as vehement and largely successful.[12]

Washington's convoluted engagement with slavery came to the fore in 1791, when he learned that the slaves brought from Mount Vernon to staff his Philadelphia residence could claim their freedom after living in Pennsylvania for six months. Despite his expressed preference for emancipation by legislative act, he directed his secretary, Tobias Lear, to evade the Pennsylvania legislation by sending out of state any of the enslaved who might soon qualify for freedom. He feared, he explained, that "the idea of freedom might be too great a temptation for them to resist." He added that the moves should be "accomplished under pretext that may deceive both them and the public."[13]

Lear, a New Hampshire native who was as loyal an employee as Washington ever had, disliked the subterfuge, telling Washington that he had no wish to prolong "the slavery of a human being." Perhaps reflecting other statements Washington had made to him, Lear added that he had "the fullest confidence that [the slaves] will at some future period be liberated."[14]

Perhaps the truest passage Washington ever wrote about slavery came in 1794: "I do not like to think, much less talk about it." Some of his tangled thinking about slavery shows in the views of his confidant, David Stuart, who had married Jack Custis's widow. To a European visitor, Stuart explained that slaveholders felt trapped. "No one knows better than the Virginians the cruelty, inconvenience, and the little advantage of having blacks [as slaves]," Stuart said. They were expensive, they would not work without whipping, and overseers were high-priced and larcenous. But freeing the slaves, Stuart continued, would condemn them to life "as an inferior class which will never mix in the society of whites"—a condition that he evidently thought would be worse than bondage.[15]

However thorny the issue, and however much he disliked thinking about it, Washington could not avoid slavery. It surrounded him, in all its ugliness and horror. In the last several years of his life, he tried to confront it, working on a plan to end his slave ownership, to cause only modest damage to his financial situation, and to help emancipated slaves succeed in an irredeemably racist society. The seeds of this effort may be found in Washington's remarks in 1788 to his longtime aide David Humphreys, referring to his ownership of slaves as "the only unavoidable subject of regret." He then expressed the goals of making his adult slaves, when freed, "as easy and comfortable . . . as their actual state of ignorance and improvidence would admit," while "prepar[ing] the rising generation for a different destiny."[16]

∾

Washington's lands contained two different groups of slaves. He could do as he wished with the slaves he owned outright, but the majority of Mount Vernon slaves were Custis or "dower" slaves, owned by the estate of Martha's first husband. Under Virginia law, Martha (and Washington as her husband) held a dower interest in these slaves, but her three granddaughters and grandson had full rights to them after Martha's death. George and Martha had a legal duty to protect the value of those slaves for the grandchildren's benefit. Consequently, Washington could free the dower slaves only if he purchased them first, at fair prices, from the Custis estate. Addressing the dower slaves was important because after thirty years at Mount Vernon, many of them and Washington's people had intermarried. Freeing only his own slaves would divide those intermarried families. He lacked the money, however, to buy the dower slaves.

He did nonetheless own land: many thousands of unimproved acres in the west, a sprinkling of parcels around Northern Virginia, and about 8,000 acres at Mount Vernon, divided into five farms. If he could sell or lease enough of those lands, he might generate the funds to liberate all the enslaved people and still live with Martha in their accustomed manner.

In late 1793, Washington wrote to Arthur Young, an agricultural expert in England, about leasing out four of his five Mount Vernon farms, retaining only the one closest to the mansion house for his amusement. He offered a glowing description of the properties, and mentioned in passing that he expected to "remove my Negroes."[17]

After receiving a bland reply from Young, Washington worried that his first letter had not been sufficiently explicit. He did not want new tenants to assume responsibility for his slaves, he explained in a second letter, but "had something better in view for them." Each new tenant could *hire* the slaves "as he would do any other laborers." That is, the enslaved people would be free, as Washington made clear to an intimate at the same time. The "most powerful" motive behind the plan, he explained, was "to liberate a certain species of property which I possess, very repugnantly to my own feelings."[18]

By early 1796, Washington went public with his search for purchasers for western land and for tenants for Mount Vernon, where he was now willing to subdivide the farms into individual fields. His 4,000-word advertisement described the livestock, equipment, and other items included in the leases, but never mentioned enslaved workers. A separate list of lease terms clarified that Washington did not wish the lands to be worked by slaves, but that commitment was wobbly: "Although the admission of slaves with the tenants will not be absolutely prohibited; it would, nevertheless, be a pleasing circumstance to exclude them." The ad circulated in Britain, in western newspapers, and as a handbill.[19]

When Washington confided his plan to David Stuart, he wrote that liberating the slaves was more important than making a profit, but the lease revenue was critical. It had to be sufficient to pay the grandchildren for the slaves, over time, and also to support those enslaved people who were too young or too old to work. To gauge those expenses, he directed his farm manager to prepare a list of all the enslaved, noting their ages. Because of the political controversy his plan might ignite, Washington asked Stuart not to disclose it until Washington had responses to his advertisement.[20]

Washington also revealed the plan to his farm manager and his secretary, Tobias Lear, stressing that "One great object . . . is to separate the Negros from the land" while preserving for himself "tranquility with a certain income." Yet he sometimes waffled on emancipation. If potential tenants proposed to lease some of Mount Vernon's slaves along with the farms, he would consider that possibility. The plan, it seems, was not etched in stone.[21]

Washington was not the only Virginian searching for a road out of slaveholding. His godson, Ferdinando Fairfax, published a short proposal for Congress to establish a colony in Africa for freed slaves. The idea of shipping the enslaved "back to Africa" appealed to many Southerners who could not imagine a multiracial society, and would lead to the formation of the American Colonization Society after Washington's death. Washington, however, never indulged the fantasy of mass relocation that lay at the heart of the colonization movement. He expected emancipated slaves to stay near their homes, and planned accordingly.

A complex approach came from St. George Tucker, a law professor at the College of William & Mary. Tucker proposed the emancipation of every enslaved female when she reached age twenty-eight, with the gradual emancipation of her descendants. Afraid that former slaves, unfamiliar with freedom, would become "hordes of vagabonds, robbers, and murderers," Tucker proposed to deny them civil rights and offer them incentives to move west; they could be free, but they should be gone.[22]

Some Virginians already were freeing their human property. Between 1780 and 1790, the number of free Blacks in the state more than quadrupled, to 13,000. Washington's cousin Lund asked his wife to free their slaves after he died; she did. Robert Carter III manumitted more than 500 slaves. By 1800, the number of free Blacks in Virginia reached 20,000. But nothing like that happened at Mount Vernon. No tenants leased Washington's farms, and no viable purchasers bid for his western lands.[23]

Washington felt trapped. Unable to exit from slaveholding on satisfactory terms, he remained responsible for managing more than 300 enslaved people at Mount Vernon, in a region where people in bondage were the principal source of labor. As a slave master, he felt the need to compel work that had to be done. Despite his insistence that "I am principled against this kind of traffic in the human species," he approved the sale of one slave and accepted slaves as security for a loan he extended to a relative.[24]

He sought to recover highly valued slaves who escaped: Martha's maid Ona Judge fled from the president's residence in Philadelphia, and his chef, Hercules, disappeared from Mount Vernon. Washington advertised for their return and employed agents to lure them back, to no avail. To replace Hercules, he was willing to break his vow never to purchase another slave. In September 1799, he discovered that his personal valet, Christopher Sheels, also was planning escape, though that plan was thwarted.[25]

The situation wore on him. While still president, he had predicted that slaves would become "a very troublesome species of property." When a nephew reported a runaway slave, Washington's response was bleak:

these elopements will be MUCH MORE, before they are LESS frequent; . . . I wish from my soul that the Legislature of this state could see the policy of a gradual abolition of slavery; it would prevent much future mischief.

The enslaved people, he wrote to a friend, "are growing more and more insolent and difficult to govern."[26]

So long as Washington mostly refused to sell slaves, his slave "family" would continue to outgrow Mount Vernon's ability to support them. He considered moving what he called the "overplus" to other lands, but that would break up slave families. In summer 1799, he offered to return to a neighbor leased lands *and* the slaves who worked them.[27]

In that year, he made his gloomiest prediction yet. Slavery, he feared, might be fatal for the union: "I can clearly foresee that nothing but the rooting out of slavery can perpetuate the existence of our union, by consolidating it in a common bond of principle." What, he was asking himself, could he do about that? Demanding immediate abolition, he was convinced, would destroy the nation. But a gradual approach, for the South or for Mount Vernon, had proved impossible.[28]

Washington consulted few people about ending his involvement with slavery—the circle seems to have included David Stuart and Tobias Lear and his farm manager. Occasional remarks recorded from Martha about enslaved people were unsympathetic. "The blacks are so bad in their nature," she wrote to a niece, "that they have not the least gratitude for the kindness that may be showed to them." In seeking a new housekeeper, she specified the need for someone sober and attentive, which was especially important "among blacks—many of whom will impose when they can do it." Washington's aggressive pursuit of the runaways Ona Judge and Hercules is sometimes attributed to Martha's anger over their departure.[29]

In June 1799, Washington asked his farm manager to prepare an updated census of the enslaved people at Mount Vernon.[30] Armed with this roster, Washington took a firm step toward granting freedom to those within his power. For those people, it turned out, he took that step just in time.

CHAPTER 53

Farewell Forever

Washington's final illness struck in mid-December 1799. It lasted barely two days. Grippingly recounted by Tobias Lear, it began with a horseback tour of Mount Vernon's farms on December 12, a nasty day of hail, rain, and snow. Washington sat down to dinner without drying off, wrote a letter to Hamilton after the meal, and noted in his diary a "large circle around the moon." He woke the next morning with a sore throat.

On that first day of illness, heavy snow kept him indoors except for a sortie to mark for removal some trees between the mansion house and the river. Despite growing hoarseness, Washington scanned the newspapers that evening, rasping aloud those items that amused him. When Lear read out a statement by Madison praising James Monroe, Washington offered an acid comment. He waved off Lear's suggestion that he take some remedy for his ailment. "You know I never take anything for a cold," he said. "Let it go as it comes." As he retired to bed, he stopped at the room of Martha's granddaughter to look in on her newborn, just seventeen days old.

In the early-morning hours, Washington woke Martha. He could hardly speak and was struggling to breathe. Martha proposed fetching a servant, but Washington objected that Martha would catch cold. He could wait until the servant came to build the morning fire. When the servant arrived, Martha sent for Lear, who summoned Dr. Craik from Alexandria. Waiting for the doctor, Washington tried but failed to drink a concoction intended to soothe his inflamed throat, and a Mount Vernon worker bled him. Martha, fearing that the bleeding would weaken him, stopped the process after a half pint flowed out. They tried home remedies, which did not help. The general continued to be weak, fighting for breath.

Craik's arrival after eight a.m. brought a second round of bleeding and an attempted gargle that nearly suffocated the patient. After sending for Dr. Gustavus Brown from across the river in Maryland, Craik bled Washington a third time. By late morning, with Washington still suffering greatly, Craik summoned another doctor, Elisha Dick. The additional physicians arrived in midafternoon and bled the patient a fourth time. "The blood," according to Lear, "came very slow, was thick, and did not produce any symptoms of fainting." The doctors also induced an explosive bowel movement, which must have been a torment for a weakened man struggling for air.

Washington's throat was nearly closed off, preventing him from swallowing, making speech an agony, and slowly strangling him. Yet there is no evidence that the doctors, with the medical skills of the age, ever looked into his throat, much less attempted to open his airway with an instrument. Indeed, they had no instrument for examining throats.

After the fourth bleeding, the doctors and the patient agreed that the illness was fatal. He had cheated death repeatedly through life, beginning with his bout of smallpox in Barbados, extending through numerous battlefields where his disregard of danger was alarming, and including two near-death experiences during his first term as president. But not this time. At four thirty in the afternoon, Washington asked Martha to retrieve two wills from his office. When she brought them, he selected one and asked her to burn it. She did. She placed the remaining will in her closet.

Through the day, three enslaved women and the housekeeper, Mrs. Forbes, helped care for the desperately ill man. Caroline was a seamstress. Molly and Charlotte were house servants. In the afternoon, Washington realized that Christopher Sheels, his enslaved valet, whose plan to run away had been thwarted three months before, had been standing in the room all day. Washington told him to sit. Martha maintained her vigil at the foot of the bed.

To Lear, Washington gasped that his breath would give out soon. He asked his aide to arrange his accounts and books and inquired if there was anything he should do in the time he had left. When Lear said he hoped the general would recover, the patient smiled, whispering that "it was the debt which we must all pay, [and] he looked to the event with perfect resignation."

Lear tried to make Washington comfortable, as "he appeared to be in great pain and distress, from the difficulty of breathing, and frequently changed his posture in the bed." Washington said he feared he was fatiguing Lear, adding, "I hope when you want aid of this kind you will find it."

Dr. Craik examined him at sundown. Washington remained stoic. "I die hard," he wheezed, his breath labored, "but I am not afraid to go." He thanked the doctors for their help, then urged them to take no more trouble. "Let me go off quietly," he whispered. "I cannot last long." Unable to reply, Dr. Craik retired to the fireside. The other two physicians left the room.

The final hours brought more agony. Washington repeatedly asked for the time. By reading Washington's expressions and gestures, Lear shifted him, trying to grant some relief. A final, futile treatment involved applying blisters and cataplasms to Washington's legs.

At ten o'clock, Washington wanted again to speak. When he could make a noise, he asked that the funeral be delayed for three days, so he would not be buried alive. Some minutes passed. His breathing eased. He felt for his own pulse and whispered, " 'Tis well." Lear saw the general's face change and called Dr. Craik over. Martha and the four enslaved servants watched in silence.

"Is he gone?" Martha asked. Unable to speak, Lear motioned yes. Lear kissed Washington's hand, "which I had held to my bosom; laid it down and went to the other end of the room, where I was for some time lost in profound grief."

Bryan Fairfax was saddened when he learned that on his final day, Washington had said, "I die hard." Because Washington "was one of the last men to complain," Fairfax wrote, "one expression of that sort from him, to me shows more suffering than 100 groans from almost any other man." Fairfax added, "He died as he lived, with fortitude, so he was great to the last." The modern consensus among physicians is that an inflammation of his epiglottis killed him.[1]

∾

Thomas Law, husband to Martha's eldest granddaughter, described the Mount Vernon funeral as attended by a "vast concourse of people." He added, "We have all of us been crying." The scene was re-enacted around the nation. Virtually every community held a memorial service or mock funeral to mark the death of the founding father. His virtues were lauded, even improved upon. His weaknesses were ignored. The nation had lost its protector. "I feel myself alone," President Adams told the Senate, "bereaved of my last brother."[2]

Word soon spread of the will he left behind, written in his own hand a few months earlier, without a lawyer's aid. The document named as executors his "dearly beloved wife," five nephews, and Martha's grandson. Bushrod—his brother Jack's eldest and a Supreme Court justice—took the lead.

The will's fourth paragraph, after the bequests to Martha, addressed his enslaved people; it directed that after Martha's death, all of the 123 people that Washington owned "shall receive their freedom." Washington wrote that he would have preferred to direct their immediate freedom, but intermarriage between them and dower slaves created "insuperable difficulties." He noted that he lacked the power to liberate the dower slaves. Of his own slaves, he directed that those too old to work should be supported by his estate; those too young to work should be "taught to read and write; and . . . brought up to some useful occupation." Until they were emancipated, he added, "I do expressly forbid that they be sold or transported out of Virginia."[3]

Washington's instructions left his executors no wiggle room. He "most pointedly, and most solemnly, enjoin[ed] it upon [his] Executors . . . to see that *this* clause respecting slaves, and every part thereof be religiously fulfilled at the epoch at which it is directed to take place; without evasion, neglect or delay."

About forty slaves at Mount Vernon were rented from a neighbor, so they had to be returned; the rest were dower slaves beyond Washington's power; they would be distributed to Martha's grandchildren when she died in 1801; of those, only a few, who were possibly descended from Martha's family, would be freed by Thomas and Eliza Law.[4] Washington also prescribed eventual freedom for thirty-three more slaves who had belonged to Martha's late brother, Bartholomew Dandridge. Those enslaved people had been pledged to secure a loan Washington made to Dandridge. Washington directed that when Bartholomew's widow died, Washington's executors should forego collecting on the money debt and take the slaves. Those above the age of forty should be emancipated; the others should be freed either after seven years of service or upon reaching the age of twenty-five.

Washington singled out one enslaved worker for immediate emancipation: William Lee, who rode at his side through the Revolutionary War. Recognizing that Lee might not wish to leave Mount Vernon since accidents had left him unable to walk, Washington specified that Lee could choose to remain at Mount Vernon.

After a condolence visit to Martha, Abigail Adams reported that the widow feared that the slaves would fare poorly once they were freed, set "adrift into the world without horse, home or friend." According to Adams, Martha also feared she was not safe surrounded by more than one hundred people who would be free as soon as she died. Within two weeks of Washington's death, Bushrod referred to a plan to get his Aunt Martha "clear of her negroes and of plantation cares and troubles." In December 1800, she signed papers emancipating all of Washington's slaves as of January 1, 1801.[5]

Freedom brought its own challenges, especially for those who had to choose between freedom and family because of ties to the dower slaves. Some struggled to support themselves on their own, though many made their way

COURTESY OF THE LIBRARY OF CONGRESS

Martha Washington

successfully. Bushrod and his fellow executors cared for those too old to work, making support payments for the next thirty-three years.[6]

If Washington had hoped his will would inspire Southerners to embrace gradual emancipation, he would have been disappointed. In the coming decades, Southern slave owners would close ranks to defend the slave system. Only secession and a brutal civil war would uproot that system. Centuries later, slavery's traditions and attitudes still infect American life.

Washington knew the slave system would not die easily. He chose not to risk the unity of the new nation against the combination of prejudice and economic self-interest that entrenched slavery. Despite his personal feelings, he made the political judgment not to support abolition publicly. That judgment—made by Washington and so many others of the founding generation—had profound consequences for the nation.[7]

Washington's will had political significance as an anti-slavery statement by the country's most revered slaveholder. But for Washington, emancipating his slaves seemed more personal than political. His will contained neither denunciation of the sin of slavery, nor exhortations to his countrymen to turn their backs on the perfidious system. Washington surely understood that such statements would seem hypocritical coming from one who had been a stern slave master, had schemed to recover runaways, and had blocked slaves from claiming their freedom. Such statements also might be dismissed as cheap sentiment from a rich man whose wife had ample assets, whose family would inherit slaves of their own, and who would not personally endure any inconvenience from the loss of enslaved workers.

Rather, the emancipations granted in the will represented an acceptance of personal responsibility. Washington would not go to his grave without admitting, and beginning to atone for, his participation in the sin of slavery. In an early statement he made while trying to develop a plan to free his slaves, Washington humbly wrote that such a plan "could not I hope be displeasing to the justice of the Creator."[8]

∾

By examining the career of George Washington, this book has aimed to understand how he became a master politician, which requires deciding what *is* a master politician. A master politician is not one who seizes power and clings to it through the years, strewing the land with images of himself but dedicated principally to his own aggrandizement. Both history and today's world bristle with such figures. Nor is a master politician one whose commitment to an ideology or religion demands unswerving adherence even after the ideology or religion has created more suffering than benefit. History and today's world offer many examples of those figures as well.

Master politicians place the good of the people at the center of their efforts, and commit themselves to general advancement. Far more difficult, they persuade their countrymen to follow them. When their course proves flawed, they correct it. Finally, they leave the society—and its institutions— stronger than when they began. They leave the people with greater understanding and power to influence their own lives. The legacy of a master politician includes a shared vision of how to live together; those who are luckiest also leave times of prosperity and peace.

Washington, and not many others, met this standard. He began as a headstrong young man with a patchy military career. As commander of the Virginia Regiment, he won no battles, picked unnecessary quarrels, and repeatedly alienated powerful figures, trapping himself in a career cul-de-sac. Then he resolved to reinvent himself. When he entered the House of Burgesses in 1759, he was such a political naïf that he could not manage legislation to ban the running of pigs in a frontier town.

Over the following decade and a half, he evolved into a deft, sensitive leader who inspired by the sincerity of his striving for the common good, and by the steady, intelligent judgments he applied to public issues. He managed local roads and ferries, cared for the poor, decided disputes between neighbors, punished a political enemy, won elections, and wrote laws that addressed the mundane and the grand. He rose to the head of a revolutionary movement, relentlessly pressing for American rights and resistance to Britain.

In his second tour of military service, Washington fought a stronger adversary for eight years. He commanded raw militia, half-trained Americans, and Continental Army veterans who had learned their business. He worked effectively with Congress, state governors and legislators, and local officials, persevering through harsh defeats and cruel hardships, retaining the loyalty of his soldiers and support from enough of the people. Challenged from within for control of the army, he adroitly outmaneuvered his rivals and solidified his position, reinforcing it with military success. Then, somehow, he restrained his near-mutinous, much-abused soldiers and sent them home peacefully. His own resignation from the army, at a time when he could have installed himself as America's leader, amazed contemporaries and earned the public trust to a degree never rivaled in American history.

When the loose American union quickly frayed and foundered, Washington pointed the way to a stronger government, then agreed to forsake the comforts of Mount Vernon for another round of public service. His insistence on the need for a new constitution, and his embrace of the charter produced at Philadelphia in the summer of 1787, were indispensable to the reinvention of the nation as a stable republic.

As that republic's first president, he sought to preserve the union through the Compromise of 1790, which balanced the sectional interests of North and South through his financial program and the placement of the new seat of government. He undertook two grueling journeys through the states to reinforce that union with his personal popularity. In his second presidential term, he steered the nation past foreign threats from France and Britain, and quelled an internal rebellion. After he slid into the partisan wrangling of the day, his Farewell Address warned his countrymen against his own error. For more than twenty years, his steady, careful leadership and his unassuming, modest deportment bequeathed the nation a stable foundation that held for generations.

Washington repeatedly struck the elusive balance between respecting public opinion and leading it, showing a rare sense of timing and employing his lifelong gift for inspiring trust. He rewarded that trust with his final withdrawal from the public scene after his second term as president, insisting that his countrymen govern themselves. In his final retirement, he sought to withdraw from the system of human bondage that had supported his life of comfort, but in that effort he failed, as he always had. Only through his death did he grant freedom to those he had owned. By that action, he aimed to set an example for his countrymen, but Americans chose to ignore it. He was remarkable, and remarkably successful, but a man with flaws and failures too.

George Washington established a model of wisdom and integrity by which every successor would be judged. For a man who cared so deeply about his public reputation, he could have wished for little more.

Acknowledgments

To write this book, I have imposed upon a phalanx of fellow writers and researchers, librarians and archivists. That they have so willingly shared their expertise and insights has been a great and undeserved blessing, for which I am grateful. A mention in the back of the book is a poor reward for their efforts, but that is what is in my power to extend.

This book has taken shape in two places in addition to my home office: my home away from home at the Library of Congress, and at George Washington's home at Mount Vernon, where I had a supported fellowship at the Fred W. Smith National Library for the Study of George Washington. Both provided workspace and extraordinary access to essential materials, but far more valuable in both places has been conversation with knowledgeable people. Though I have been helped through crises of the moment by a dozen and more librarians and staff members at the Library of Congress, I benefitted from special attention from Julie Miller, Historian of Early America; Jeff Flannery, maestro of the Manuscript Room; Edward Redmond of the Geography and Map Division; and Thomas Mann, reference librarian extraordinaire. At Mount Vernon, I benefitted from working and speaking with so many, from the boss, Douglas Bradburn, to library director Kevin Butterfield to Samantha Snyder, reference librarian. I must specially note three historians working at Mount Vernon during my stay whose fellowship and insights were so valuable—Mary V. Thompson of Mount Vernon (and a fellow Staten Islander), George Goodwin, and Brian Steele.

Then there are the many authors and students of history who have responded to my annoying questions and befuddlements with unfailing courtesy and generosity, sharing the expertise they have built over years and decades: Henry Wiencek, Mark Lender, Brent Tarter, Jon Kukla, Colin Calloway, Hamilton Bryson, Thomas B. Allen, and (again) Mary V. Thompson. Thank you. I have profited greatly from comments on the evolving manuscript from friends and scholars: Gregory May, James McGrath Morris, Kenneth R. Bowling, and (yet again) Mary V. Thompson.

I owe a great debt to the many reference librarians and archivists who have assisted me in tracking down obscure items, including those at the Rosenbach in Philadelphia, the Seeley G. Mudd Manuscript Library at Princeton University, the Connecticut Historical Society, the Maryland Historical Society, the New York Public Library, the John D. Rockefeller Library at Colonial Williamsburg, the Virginia State Library, the Fairfax County Circuit Court Historic Records Center, the Fairfax City Regional Public Library, the Martha Washington Papers Project, and the British Library. I enjoyed access to the Georgetown University Library through support from William Treanor, dean of the law school, and Professor John Mikhail.

For this volume, I have embarked on a new publishing relationship with Dutton, a long-distinguished imprint now residing in the Penguin Random House galaxy. I have been fortunate in my editor, Brent Howard, a careful student of history who has been welcoming and supportive. I also appreciate the assistance of copy editor Rachelle Mandik and publicist Jamie Knapp.

I dedicate this book to my sons and daughter, of whom I am proud every day. Their mother, Nancy, remains the great blessing of my life.

A Note on Sources

Much of the research for this book involved reviewing the correspondence of Washington and five of his contemporaries, which has been assembled over decades by flotillas of noble archivists and scholars and is now available through the National Archives online website, www.founders .archives.gov. Those sources are abbreviated in these notes, as follows:

- The Adams Papers (AP)
- The Papers of Benjamin Franklin (PBF)
- The Papers of Alexander Hamilton (PAH)
- The Papers of Thomas Jefferson (PTJ)
- The Papers of James Madison (PJM)
- The Papers of George Washington (GWP)

I have cited these papers by date only, as the collections are searchable online; also the date can be used to find the documents in the bound volumes for those still dwelling in an analog world.

For other frequently cited sources, I have used the following abbreviations:

Annals of Congress (accessible through the Library of Congress home page, www.memory .loc.gov) (Annals of Congress).

Ballagh, James Curtis, ed. The Letters of Richard Henry Lee. New York: Da Capo Press (1970) (Ballagh, Letters of Richard Henry Lee).

Brock, R. A., ed. The Official Records of Robert Dinwiddie, lieutenant-governor of the colony of Virginia, 1751–1758. Richmond: Virginia Historical Society (1883), vols. 1–2 (Dinwiddie Records).

Carlyle, J. F., *The Personal and Family Correspondence of Colonel John Carlyle of Alexandria, Virginia*, https://www.novaparks.com/sites/default/files/John%20Carlyle%201720-1780%20Annotated%20Correspondence_0.pdf (Carlyle Correspondence).

Chernow, Ron. *Washington: A Life*. New York: Penguin Press (2010) (Chernow).

Chesnutt, David R., and C. James Taylor. *The Papers of Henry Laurens*. Columbia: University of South Carolina Press, vols. 11–15 (1988–2000) (Chesnutt & Taylor, *Laurens Papers*).

Documentary History of the Ratification of the Constitution. John P. Kaminski, Gaspare J. Saladino, Richard Leffler, Charles H. Schoenleber, and Margaret A. Hogan, eds. Charlottesville: University of Virginia Press (2009–2019) (*DHRC*).

Documentary History of the First Federal Elections. Merrill Jensen, Robert A. Becker, and Gordon DenBoer, eds. Madison: University of Wisconsin Press (1976–1989) (*DHFFE*).

Documentary History of the First Federal Congress. Linda Grant De Pauw, Charlene Bangs Bickford, Kenneth R. Bowling, and Helen E. Veit, eds. Baltimore: Johns Hopkins University Press (1972–2017) (*DHFFC*).

Executive Journals of the Council of Colonial Virginia, vols. 5 and 6. Richmond: The Virginia State Library (1945, 1966) (*Executive Journals*).

Farrand, Max, ed. *The Records of the Federal Convention of 1787*, vols. 1–3. New Haven: Yale University Press (1911) (Farrand).

Flexner, James Thomas. *George Washington*, vols. 1–4. Boston: Little, Brown & Co. (1965–1969) (Flexner).

Freeman, Douglas Southall. *George Washington: A Biography*, vols. 1–6. New York: Charles Scribner's Sons (1948–1954) (Freeman).

George Washington Papers, Library of Congress Digital Collection (*GW/LOC Digital Collection*).

Gibbs, George, ed. *Oliver Wolcott's Memoirs of the Administrations of Washington and Adams*. New York (1846) (Gibbs, *Wolcott Memoirs*).

James, Alfred Proctor, ed. *Writings of General John Forbes*. Menasha: The Collegiate Press (1938) (James, *Forbes Writings*).

Journals of the Continental Congress (accessible through the Library of Congress website, www.memory.loc.gov) (*JCC*).

Journals of the House of Burgesses of Virginia, 1752–1755, 1756–1758, 1758–1761, 1761–1765, 1766–1769, 1770–1772, 1773–1776. Richmond: The Colonial Press (1906–1909) (*Journals of the House of Burgesses*).

Lee Family Archive (available online at www.leefamilyarchive.org) (Lee Family Digital Archive).

Pennsylvania Magazine of History and Biography (*PMHB*).

Reese, George Henkle. *The Official Papers of Francis Fauquier, Lieutenant Governor of Virginia, 1758–1768*. Charlottesville: University Press of Virginia (1980) (Reese, *Fauquier Papers*).

Showman, Richard K., Margaret Cobb, and Robert E. McCarthy. *The Papers of General Nathanael Greene*, vols. 1–13. Chapel Hill: University of North Carolina Press (1976–2005) (Showman, *Greene Papers*).

Smith, Paul H., Gerard W. Gawalt, Rosemary Fry Plakas, and Eugene R. Sheridan, *Letters of Delegates to Congress*. Washington: Library of Congress (1976–) (accessible through the Library of Congress website, www.memory.loc.gov) (*Letters of Delegates*).

Stevens, S. K., Donald H. Kent, and Autumn L. Leonard. *The Papers of Henry Bouquet*. Harrisburg: The Pennsylvania Historical and Museum Commission (1951) (Stevens, *Bouquet Papers*).

Stewart, Irene, ed. *Letters of General John Forbes relating to the Expedition Against Fort Duquesne in 1758*. Pittsburgh: Colonial Dames of America (1927) (*Forbes Letters*).

Virginia Magazine of History and Biography (VMHB).

William & Mary Quarterly (WMQ).

Zagarri, Rosemary, ed. *David Humphreys' 'Life of General Washington' with George Washington's 'Remarks.'* Athens: University of Georgia Press (1991) (Zagarri, Humphreys).

When quoting from correspondence and other primary sources, I have sometimes modernized spelling, capitalization, and punctuation without altering the words actually used.

Notes

1. TIME FOR A NEW PLAN

1. Robert Stewart to Robert Dinwiddie, 9 November 1757, GWP.
2. To Charles Green, 13 November 1757, GWP.
3. To Sally Fairfax, 15 November 1757, GWP.
4. At age eleven, Washington inherited ten slaves when his father died, though they stayed at the family's Ferry Farm in Fredericksburg. He acquired another eight slaves upon the death of his half-brother Lawrence ten years later, and controlled eighteen slaves under his lease of Mount Vernon. A few of the enslaved people worked on lands in the Shenandoah valley that Washington purchased with his earnings as a surveyor. Memorandum, 10 December 1754, GWP (disposition of slaves under Lawrence Washington's will); Flexner 1:286; Philip D. Morgan, "'To Get Quit of Negroes': George Washington and Slavery," *J. American Studies* 39:403, 406 (2005); from Christopher Hardwick, 3 August 1758, GWP.
5. To Sally Fairfax, 15 November 1757, GWP.
6. To Dinwiddie, 24 September 1757, GWP; to Colonel John Stanwix, 8 October 1757, GWP.
7. To Warner Lewis, 14 August 1755, GWP; to Carter Burwell, Robert Orme, 20 April 1755, GWP.
8. Zagarri, *Humphreys*, 47; see Paul K. Longmore, *The Invention of George Washington*, Berkeley: University of California Press (1988), 2; David S. Shields, "George Washington: Publicity, Probity, and Power," in Tamara Harvey and Greg O'Brien, eds., *George Washington's South*, Gainesville, FL: University Press of Florida (2003), 144.
9. E.g., to Richard Washington, 26 December 1757, GWP; to Thomas Knox, 26 December 1757 and January 1758, GWP.
10. From George Mason, 4 January 1758, GWP; from John Stanwix, 13 January 1758, GWP.
11. From John Blair, 25 January 1758, GWP; to John Blair, 30 January 1758 and 31 January 1758, GWP. In Fredericksburg, he met with Dr. John Sutherland, see note 4 to letter from GW to John Stanwix, 4 March 1758, GWP; to Sarah Cary Fairfax, 13 February 1758, GWP. A friend in Williamsburg, the lawyer Robert Carter Nicholas, wrote in early February to express his delight that the report was untrue that Colonel Washington was no more. "I have heard of letters from the dead," Nicholas replied, adding that he had not before "had the pleasure of receiving one." From Robert Carter Nicholas, 6 February 1758, GWP.

12. To John Stanwix, 4 March 1758, GWP.

13. General Ledger A, 1750–1772, 37, Financial Papers of George Washington, Library of Congress, www.financial.gwpapers.org; Flora Fraser, *The Washingtons: George and Martha, "Join'd by Friendship, Crown'd by Love,"* New York: Alfred A. Knopf (2015), 24; Thomas A. Lewis, *For King and Country: The Maturing of George Washington, 1748–1760,* Edison, NJ: Castle Books (1993), 243–45.

14. Martha Custis to Cary & Co., 1758, in Joseph E. Fields, ed., *Worthy Partner: The Papers of Martha Washington,* Westport, CT: Greenwood Press (1994), 25–26.

15. To Richard Washington, 18 March and 5 April 1758, GWP; to Thomas Knox, 17 March 1758; to John Blair, 2 April and 9 April 1758, GWP.

16. To John Stanwix, 10 April 1758, GWP.

17. Note 6, to John Stanwix, 4 March 1758, GWP; Flexner 1:186; Freeman 2:278, 2:301.

18. From John Stanwix, 10 March 1758, GWP; to John Stanwix, 4 March 1758, note 6, GWP.

19. Stanley Pargellis, *Lord Loudoun in North America,* New Haven: Yale University Press (1933), 308*n.*; Bernhard Knollenberg, *George Washington: The Virginia Period, 1732–1775,* Durham: Duke University Press (1964), 45–46; Flexner 1:122, 185; Longmore, 35, 53.

20. Freeman 1:134; Lease of Mount Vernon, 17 December 1754, GWP; Thomas L. Purvis, *Revolutionary America 1763 to 1800,* New York: Facts on File (1995), 96 (Table 4.181); John J. McCusker, *How Much Is That in Real Money? A Historical Price Index for Use as a Deflator of Money Values in the Economy of the United States,* Worcester, MA: American Antiquarian Society (1992), 333. From his military positions in Virginia, Washington was then earning approximately £550 a year, before paying considerable expenses, including the lease on and expenses of Mount Vernon. Flexner 1:137.

21. R. T. Barton, "The First Election of Washington to the House of Burgesses," *Proceedings of the Virginia Hist. Society,* 1891, 115, 117.

22. The early biographer with a gift for fabricating stories about Washington was Parson Mason Locke Weems, who published *The Life of Washington* within a year of his subject's death. The quotation comes from Eugene Parsons, *George Washington, A Character Sketch,* Milwaukee: H. G. Campbell Publishing Co. (1898), 5.

23. As one scholar emphatically put the case, "Washington has become not merely a mythical figure, but a myth of suffocating dullness, the victim of civic Elephantiasis." Marcus Cunliffe, *George Washington: Man and Monument,* Boston: Little, Brown & Co. (1958), 6.

24. "Recollections of John F. D. Smyth in 1784," in William S. Baker, *Early Sketches of George Washington,* Philadelphia: J. B. Lippincott Co. (1894), 91. Smyth was a former British soldier who settled in Maryland after the Revolutionary War.

25. Chernow, 684.

2. BEGINNINGS

1. Charles Arthur Hoppin, *The Washington Ancestry,* Greenfield, Ohio (1932), vol. 1, 110–25, 130–31, 162–201; Edward D. Neill, John Washington, and Robert Orme, "The Ancestry and Earlier Life of George Washington," *PMHB,* 16:261 (1892); Freeman 1:14–26.

2. Colin Calloway, *The Indian World of George Washington,* New York: Oxford University Press (2018), 19–22; Rhys Isaac, *The Transformation of Virginia: 1740–1790,* Chapel Hill: University of North Carolina Press (1982), 11–12, 53; Albert H. Tillson Jr., *Gentry and Common Folk: Political Culture on a Virginia Frontier, 1740–1789,* Lexington: University Press of Kentucky (1991), 7.

3. J. G. Rosengarten, tr., *Achenwall's Observations on North America 1767,* reprinted from *PMHB* (January 1903), Philadelphia (1903), 14; Edward Kimber, *Itinerant Observations in America,* Newark: University of Delaware Press (1998) (Kevin J. Hayes, ed.), 46.

4. David Hackett Fischer, *Albion's Seed, Four British Folkways in America*, New York, Oxford University Press (1989), 247; Isaac, *Transformation*, 15, 44.

5. Freeman 1:30–32; Flexner 1:10; "General Washington," *New England Hist. and Genealogical Reg.* 11:1, 4–5 (1857).

6. Freeman 1:151, 1:168; Devereaux Jarratt, *The Life of the Reverend Devereaux Jarratt of Bath Parish, Dinwiddie County, Virginia,* Baltimore: Warner & Hanna (1806), 14.

7. Carl Bridenbaugh, *Seat of Empire: The Political Role of Eighteenth-Century Williamsburg,* Williamsburg: Colonial Williamsburg (1958), 3.

8. Interview with Thomas A. Reinhart, Director of Architecture, Mount Vernon, August 21, 2017.

9. George Washington Parke Custis, *Recollections and Private Memoirs of Washington,* New York: Derby & Jackson (1860), 129; Eugene Parsons, *George Washington: A Character Sketch*, Milwaukee: H. G. Campbell Publishing Co. (1898), 9–10; Chernow, 11; Flexner 1:20; Freeman 1:xix.

10. A recent biography of Mary Washington offers an important corrective to the unfavorable portrayals of her over the last fifty years. Martha Saxton, *The Widow Washington: The Life of Mary Washington,* New York: Farrar, Straus and Giroux (2019). A similar view is reflected in Craig Shirley, *Mary Ball Washington,* New York: HarperCollins (2019).

11. Custis, *Recollections,* 131 (quoting Lawrence Washington of Chotank).

12. "General Washington," *New England Hist. and Genealogical Reg.,* at 11:4.

13. Longmore, 10–11. The Greek general Xenophon insisted that a skilled horseman must soothe the horse, treating the animal with gentleness. "When [the horse] is induced by a man to assume all the airs and graces which he puts on of himself when he is showing off voluntarily, the result is a horse that likes to be ridden, that presents a magnificent sight, that looks alert." Xenophon, *The Art of Horsemanship* (tr. Morris H. Morgan), Boston: Little, Brown & Co. (1893), 37, 56. Jefferson to Walter Jones, 2 January 1814, PTJ; Sara Agnes Rice Pryor, *The Mother of Washington and Her Times,* New York: Grosset & Dunlap (1903), 34–36. In colonial Virginia, horse thieves were the felons most often sentenced to death, while one traveler called Virginians "excessively fond of horses." Jane Carson, *Colonial Virginians at Play,* Williamsburg: University Press of Virginia (1965), 102 (quoting J.F.D. Smyth, *A Tour in the United States of America,* London: G. Robinson [1784], 1:23); another traveler, pointing out that no self-respecting Virginian would walk to church services, added that "their churches looked like the outskirts of a county horse-fair." Kimber, *Itinerant Observations in America,* 55.

14. The Rappahannock flowing past Ferry Farm has changed over the centuries, and is considerably narrower today. The Embrey Dam, built upstream in 1855, diverted much of its flow into a canal for hydropower purposes, though the dam was dismantled in 2004. Also, river dredging has deposited fill onto either shore, obscuring a bay that existed at the foot of the Ferry Farm property in Washington's time.

15. Philip Levy, *Where the Cherry Tree Grew,* New York: St. Martin's Press (2013), 42–56.

16. His other half-brother, Austin, remained longer in England to study law. Flexner 1:16.

17. Freeman 1:64–70.

18. Lawrence Washington to Augustine Washington, 30 May 1741, New York Public Library (cited in Freeman 1:67). Edward Lengel, *General George Washington: A Military Life,* New York: Random House (2005), 6.

19. To Lawrence Washington, Note, 5 May 1749, GWP.

20. Augustine Washington Will, 11 April 1743, GWP; Jack D. Warren Jr., *George Washington's Journey to Barbados*, St. Michael: The George Washington House Project (2001), 21.

21. William Fairfax to Lawrence Washington, 10 September 1746, in Jared Sparks, *The Life of George Washington,* London: Henry Colburn (1839), 2:109.

3. THE SCHOOL OF FAIRFAX

1. E.g., Zagarri, *Humphreys*, 6; "Washington's School Copy-Book 1745," beginning with August 13, 1745, and Book 2, 32, et seq., published online by the Library of Congress *GW/LOC Digital Collection*. In *The Widow Washington: The Life of Mary Washington*, 138–39, Martha Saxton concludes that Washington attended school in Fredericksburg and also when he visited his half-brother Austin in Westmoreland County. Jonathan Boucher, who tutored Washington's stepson in the early 1770s, claimed that Washington was taught "by a convict servant whom his father bought for a schoolteacher." Jonathan Boucher, *Reminiscences of an American Loyalist,* Boston: Houghton Mifflin Co. (1925), 49; Moncure Daniel Conway, *Barons of the Potomac and the Rappahannock,* New York: Grolier Club (1892), 62–66. If true, that report would be sufficiently embarrassing that Washington might have chosen not to mention it, but it is not entirely credible. Washington was eleven years old when his father died, and the work in his copybooks seems very sophisticated to be performed by one that young. Moreover, Boucher was a Loyalist during the Revolution with a strong antipathy toward his former employer. David Humphreys, who began and abandoned a biography of Washington in the 1780s with Washington's participation, recorded that Washington was taught by a "domestic tutor." Zagarri, *Humphreys,* 6. A pious woman throughout her life, Mary Washington read religious texts closely. Saxton, *The Widow Washington,* 66–68, 166, 182, 273; Mary V. Thompson, *In the Hands of a Good Providence: Religion in the Life of George Washington,* Charlottesville: University of Virginia Press (2008), 19–22.

2. George H. S. King, "Washington's Boyhood Home," *WMQ,* 17:265, 269–73 (1937); Kevin J. Hayes, *George Washington: A Life in Books,* New York: Oxford University Press, 29; Barnet Schecter, *George Washington's America: A Biography Through Maps,* New York: Walker & Co. (2010), 30; Freeman 1:197; George Washington, "School Copy-Book," vol. 2, 1745, 30–53, 64, *GW/LOC Digital Collection*.

3. Hayes, *George Washington: A Life in Books,* 39–41.

4. Longmore, *The Invention of George Washington,* 8; Flexner 1:31; Adrienne M. Harrison, *A Powerful Mind: The Self-Education of George Washington,* Sterling, VA: Potomac Books (2015), 26, 67; Hayes, *George Washington: A Life in Books,* 14–15. The biography of the Duke of Schomburg—one of Europe's leading soldiers of the previous century—made such an impression that Washington named one of his slaves Schomburg. Hayes, 43. *Seneca's Morals,* London: Sherwood, Neely and Jones (1818), 174, 227.

5. Lord Fairfax also won a legal dispute that doubled the size of his holdings in Virginia. Freeman 1:520–25. An extensive history of the Northern Neck Proprietary appears as an eighty-two-page appendix to the first volume of Freeman's exhaustive biography of Washington. Freeman 1:447–529.

6. Archaeological exploration of the Ferry Farm site has confirmed Mary's commitment to imbuing fine manners in her fatherless children. Laura J. Galke, "The Mother of the Father of Our Country: Mary Ball Washington's Genteel Domestic Habits," *Northeast Hist. Archaeology* 38:29 (2009); Karin Calvert, "The Function of Fashion in Eighteenth-Century America," in Cary Carson, Ronald Hoffman, and Peter J. Albert, eds., *Of Consuming Interests: The Style of Life in the Eighteenth Century,* Charlottesville: University of Virginia Press (1994), 270–73; Saxton, *The Widow Washington,* 142–45. Late in life, proposing that an Englishman buy Belvoir, Washington retained some of his early enthusiasm for the estate, calling it "one of the most beautiful seats on the river." To John Sinclair, 11 December 1796, GWP; Freeman 1:200; Peter R. Henriques, "Major Lawrence Washington Versus the Reverend Charles Green: A Case Study of the Squire and the Parson," *VMHB* 100:233, 236 (April 1992).

7. To John Augustine Washington, 28 May 1755. The intimacy between the two families was evident when Colonel Fairfax, in a dispute with the local Anglican minister, lodged the incendiary accusation that the cleric took liberties with Lawrence's wife (the colonel's daughter) before marriage; since Ann Fairfax married at fifteen, the charge was close to child abuse. Taking his father-in-law's part, Lawrence won legislation dissolving the church's governing body (the vestry); then he and Colonel Fairfax were candidates for the new vestry. When both lost, the colonel took his complaint to an ecclesiastical tribunal. Virginia's governor finally brokered a settlement that left the minister in place. The great loser was Lawrence's wife, whose reputation lay on Virginia tongues for more than a year. Her husband, though, had demonstrated deep loyalty to the Fairfax interest. H. R. McIlwaine, ed., *Journals of the House of Burgesses, 1758–1761*, Richmond: The Colonial Press (1909), 7:133, 7:136, 7:139, 7:148; Freeman 3:87; Henriques, "Major Lawrence Washington Versus the Reverend Charles Green," 256.

8. Freeman 1:194–95; William Fairfax to Lawrence Washington, 9 September 1746, and Robert Jackson to Lawrence Washington, 18 September 1746, in Conway, *Barons of the Potomac and the Rappahannock*, 236–40.

9. Joseph Ball to Mary Washington, 19 May 1747, reprinted in Freeman 1:198–99; Zagarri, *Humphreys*, 8. A Fredericksburg acquaintance noted Mary's opposition to George entering the navy, writing to Lawrence, "She seems to intimate a dislike of George's going to sea, & says several persons have told her it's a very bad scheme." Saxton, *The Widow Washington*, 148–49.

10. Zagarri, *Humphreys*, 7; Custis, *Recollections*, 134, 519.

11. Stuart E. Brown Jr., *Virginia Baron: The Story of Thomas 6th Lord Fairfax*, Berryville, VA: Chesapeake Book Co. (1965), 14–25; Lewis, *For King and Country*, 8–9; Louis Knott Koontz, *Robert Dinwiddie: His Career in American Colonial Government and Westward Expansion*, Glendale, CA: Arthur H. Clark Co. (1941), 143; Sarah S. Hughes, *Surveyors and Statesmen: Land Measuring in Colonial Virginia*, Richmond: Virginia Surveyors Foundation (1979), 72, 84. Andro Linklater's *Measuring America: How an Untamed Wilderness Shaped the United States and Fulfilled the Promise of Democracy*, New York: Walker (2002), offers an informative study of the challenges and perils of surveying during the early period of European settlement in America. Note especially 31–36, 70–73.

12. Stephen H. Spurr, "George Washington, Surveyor and Ecological Observer," *Ecology* 32:544, 545–46 (1951).

13. Spurr, 118–21, 109; Brown, *Virginia Baron*, 111; Albert H. Tillson Jr., *Accommodating Revolutions: Virginia's Northern Neck in an Era of Transformations, 1760–1810*, Charlottesville: University of Virginia Press (2010), 61.

14. William S. Baker, ed., *Early Sketches of George Washington*, Philadelphia: J. B. Lippincott Co. (1893), 13 (recollections of George Mercer); Custis, *Recollections*, 171, 484; Baker, *Early Sketches*, 13 (Mercer), 77 (John Bell).

15. Diary, 15, 16, and 21 March 1748, GWP.

16. Rufus Rockwell Wilson, ed., *Burnaby's Travels Through North America*, New York: A. Wessels Co. (1904), 73; James Titus, *The Old Dominion at War: Society, Politics, and Warfare in Late Colonial Virginia*, Columbia: University of South Carolina Press (1991), 6; Warren E. Hofstra, "'And Die by Inches': George Washington and the Encounter of Cultures on the Southern Colonial Frontier," in Harvey and O'Brien, *George Washington's South*, 72–73; Diary, 23 March and 4 April 1748, GWP.

17. Diary, 26 March and 8 April 1748, GWP; Freeman 1:223.

18. George Washington Papers, Series 4, General Correspondence: Fairfax County, Virginia, June 13, 1748, Election Poll, Library of Congress, *GW/LOC Digital Collection*; McIlwaine, *Journals of the House of Burgesses, 1742–1747, 1748–49*, vii–ix. A candidate had to

own either twenty-five acres and a house or one hundred acres of empty land in the county, or a house and lot in a town in the county. Charles S. Sydnor, *Gentlemen Freeholders: Political Practices in Washington's Virginia,* Chapel Hill: University of North Carolina Press (1952), 29.

19. Kenneth Bailey, *The Ohio Company of Virginia and the Westward Movement, 1748–1792,* Glendale: Arthur H. Clark Co. (1939), 22–24; Koontz, *Robert Dinwiddie,* 157–62; Kenneth Bailey, "George Mason, Westerner," *WMQ,* 23:409 (October 1943). Of twenty-five members of the Ohio Company in its early days, twenty were or had been members of the House of Burgesses, while nine served on the colony's Executive Council at some time. As one scholar has noted, "It would have been difficult to assemble a more formidable roster of men of colonial business and politics." Bailey, 36.

20. Edmund S. Morgan, *Virginians at Home: Family Life in the Eighteenth Century,* Williamsburg: Colonial Williamsburg (1952), 5.

21. McIlwaine, *Journals of the House of Burgesses, 1742–1747, 1748–49,* 323, 387; to Lawrence Washington, 5 May 1749, GWP.

4. HIS BROTHER'S KEEPER

1. To Lawrence Washington, 5 May 1749, GWP.

2. Freeman 1:232; Augustine Washington to Lawrence Washington, 19 July 1749, George Washington Papers, Series 4, *GW/LOC Digital Collection;* Mary G. Powell, *The History of Old Alexandria, Virginia: From July 13, 1749 to May 24, 1861,* Richmond: William Byrd Press (1928), 32; William Fairfax to Lawrence Washington, 16 July 1749, in Conway, *Barons of the Potomac and the Rappahannock,* 262–63.

3. Editor's Note, "George Washington's Professional Surveys," 22 July 1749–25 October 1752, GWP; Henry Howe, *Historical Collections of Virginia,* Charleston: Wm. R. Babcock (1852), 237; Freeman 1:234; Sarah S. Hughes, *Surveyors and Statesmen,* 93. The College of William & Mary in Williamsburg issued surveyor certificates for the colony. Because Washington was not in Williamsburg in the first half of 1749, the editors of the Washington Papers speculate that Colonel Fairfax actually acquired Washington's commission from the college.

4. To Thomas, Lord Fairfax, October–November 1749, GWP; to Richard, 1749–1750, GWP; Editor's Note, "George Washington's Professional Surveys," GWP.

5. Freeman 1:240–42.

6. Land grant, from Thomas, Lord Fairfax, 20 October 1750, GWP and Editorial Note.

7. Editorial Note: To Anne Fairfax Washington, September–November 1749, note 6, GWP; Memorandum, 1749–1750, GWP.

8. Jane Carson, *Colonial Virginians at Play,* Charlottesville: University of Virginia Press (1965), 53, 84; T. H. Breen, "Horses and Gentlemen: The Cultural Significance of Gambling Among the Gentry of Virginia," *WMQ* 34:239, 247–49 (April 1977); Albert H. Tillson Jr., *Accommodating Revolutions: Virginia's Northern Neck in an Era of Transformations, 1760–1810,* Charlottesville: University of Virginia Press (2010), 20; Custis, *Recollections,* 131; Chernow, 134; John Ferling, *The Ascent of George Washington: The Hidden Political Genius of an American Icon,* New York: Bloomsbury Press (2009), 72; to Thomas Knox, January 1758, GWP; Flexner 1:38–39; Freeman 1:226. In colonial Virginia, gambling was illegal for those in the working classes, like fishermen, farmers, apprentices, laborers, or servants. Carson, *Colonial Virginians at Play,* 53. Such legislation might be seen as paternalistic protection of the lower orders, or as an attempt to keep them working.

9. Carson, *Colonial Virginians at Play,* 22; Hunter Dickinson Farish, ed., *Journal & Letters of Philip Vickers Fithian: 1773–1774,* Williamsburg: Colonial Williamsburg (1943), 32–35, 177–78.

10. To John, 1749–1750, GWP; to Robin, 1749–1750, GWP; to Sally, 1749–50, GWP.

11. Levy, *Where the Cherry Tree Grew,* 72–73. The colony compensated slave owners for the execution of misbehaving slaves in order to encourage the owners to "discover the villainies of their slaves"; the rationale was that if the owners were not compensated, they might protect their investment in a slave by covering up his or her crimes. David John Mays, *Edmund Pendleton, 1721–1803, A Biography,* Cambridge: Harvard University Press (1952), 1:35. On the resemblance between brother and sister, one family called Betty "a most majestic-looking woman, and so strikingly like her brother" that if she wore military garb, "battalions would have presented arms, and senates risen to do homage to the chief." Custis, *Recollections,* 147.

12. To Anne Fairfax Washington, September–November 1749; Colonel Fairfax to Lawrence Washington, 17 July 1749; Lawrence Washington to unnamed correspondent, 7 November 1749, Robert Dinwiddie to Lawrence Washington, 20 March 1750/51, in Conway, *Barons of the Potomac and the Rappahannock,* 272–79; George Washington Papers, LOC, Series 5, Financial Papers, General Ledger A, 1750–1772, Image 37. Virginia's governor had awarded the Ohio Company 200,000 acres near the Forks of the Ohio River, plus an option on another 300,000 acres if the company met benchmarks for settling the land. Lawrence authorized expeditions by Christopher Gist, a frontiersman, to identify good settlement sites. Bailey, *The Ohio Company,* 74–87; Freeman 1:244–45; Kenneth Bailey, "Christopher Gist and the Trans-Allegheny Frontier: A Phase of the Westward Movement," *Pacific Hist. Rev.* 14:45, 47–48 (March 1945); Fred Anderson, *Crucible of War: The Seven Years' War and the Fate of Empire in British North America,* New York: Alfred A. Knopf (2000), 27. Gist kept a journal of his travels in the unsettled lands, and would soon play a significant role in Washington's life. William McCullough Darlington, ed., *Christopher Gist's Journals,* Pittsburgh: J. R. Weldin (1893). Lawrence argued that the Ohio Company could recruit German settlers if Virginia would exempt the Germans—who largely belonged to "dissenting" Protestant sects—from the colony's tax to support the Church of England, which the dissenters despised. The tax was not modified.

13. Court Case, 3 December 1751, note 2, GWP; Freeman 1:246; *Virginia Gazette* (Hunter), April 25, May 2, July 4, November 7, 1751.

14. Alicia K. Anderson and Lynn A. Price, eds., *George Washington's Barbados Diary 1751–52,* Charlottesville: University of Virginia Press (2018), 15–48.

15. *Barbados Diary,* 83, 85 (6 and 7 October 1751), 100–105 (16–19 October 1751), 112–13 (22 and 23 October 1751), and 124 (30 October 1751).

16. Hilary McD. Beckles, *A History of Barbados, from Amerindian Settlement to Caribbean Single Market,* Cambridge: Cambridge University Press (2006), 52–53; Warren Jr., *George Washington's Journey to Barbados,* 9. At roughly the same time, an English visitor to Barbados repeatedly observed how many Africans lived on the island. Robert Poole, *The Beneficent Bee: or, Traveler's Companion,* London: E. Duncomb (1753), 208, 220–21. Virginia was remarkable, and recognized as such, in having a large population but barely any settlements worthy of being called a town, much less a city. "They have no ambition to fill a metropolis and associate together," a traveler observed in the 1740s. The towns, he added, "are very slightly peopled, and very badly situated." Kimber, *Itinerant Observations in America,* 46.

17. *Barbados Diary,* 62 (4 November 1751).

18. *Barbados Diary,* 77 (22 December 1751); Poole, *The Beneficent Bee,* 213, 208.

19. *Barbados Diary,* 62, 64–65 (4, 6, and 7 November 1751). Their house, now restored by the Barbados government, was on Bush Hill. Anna Agbe-Davies, Carrie Alblinger, Marley Brown III, Edward Chappell, Willie Graham, and Kelly Ladd, "The Architectural and Archaeological Analysis of Bush Hill, the Garrison, St. Michael, Barbados," Colonial Williamsburg Foundation for the Barbados National Trust (January 2000).

20. *Barbados Diary*, 64, 67, 69 (6, 9, and 11 November 1751); S. D. Smith, "Gedney Clarke of Salem and Barbados: Transatlantic Super-Merchant," *New England Quarterly* 76:499 (December 2003), 509–11, 516–17.

21. *Barbados Diary*, 63, 68–70, 77 (5, 10, 12, 13 November and 22 December 1751).

22. *Barbados Diary*, 71 (16 November 1751), 72 (12 December 1751).

23. Editor's Note, "The Washingtons in Barbados," GWP (quoting Jared Sparks, ed., *The Writings of George Washington*, Boston: John B. Russell, 1833, 2:422).

24. *Barbados Diary*, 77–78 (22 December 1751).

25. *Barbados Diary*, 85 (25 December 1751), 72 (12 December 1751), 77–78 (22 December 1751).

26. *Barbados Diary*, 77 (22 December 1751).

27. *Barbados Diary*, 84, 87–88 (23, 28, 29, and 31 December 1751), 89, 91–94, 97 (3, 4, 9–12, 14, 15, and 19 January 1751).

28. Dinwiddie's title was lieutenant governor of the colony, while Lord Albemarle was nominally Virginia's governor. Under British colonial practice, the governor was a figurehead who rarely appeared in the colony; Lord Albemarle never crossed the Atlantic. The governor's duties consisted almost entirely of accepting payments from the lieutenant governor, who was customarily referred to as the governor. Koontz, *Robert Dinwiddie*, 202–4; L. Scott Philyaw, *Virginia's Western Visions: Political and Cultural Expansion on the Early American Frontier*, Knoxville: University of Tennessee Press (2004), 37 (governors hired lieutenant governors "to do the actual administering of His Majesty's distant dominions"). In the period covered by the first two parts of this book, most of the individuals who exercised the powers of the royal governor of Virginia were actually the lieutenant governor, while one was the actual governor; for convenience, the book refers to all of them as governors.

5. TURNING POINT

1. James H. Soltow, *The Economic Role of Williamsburg*, Williamsburg: Colonial Williamsburg (1965), 6; Edward Kimber, *Itinerant Observations in America*, 63; "Journal of a French Traveller in the Colonies, 1765, I," *Am. Hist. Rev.* 26:726, 741 (1921); Koontz, *Robert Dinwiddie*, 122.

2. Koontz, *Robert Dinwiddie*, 30–38; Lewis, *For King and Country*, 121–22; John Richard Alden, *Robert Dinwiddie: Servant of the Crown*, Williamsburg: Colonial Williamsburg Foundation (1973), 5–10; Lucille Griffith, *Virginia House of Burgesses 1750–1774*, Northport, AL: Colonial Press (1963), 9.

3. *Barbados Diary*, 218; from Landon Carter, 9 May 1776, GWP.

4. Editor's Note, October 20, 1750, GWP.

5. Sparks, *The Life of George Washington*, 2:423.

6. Anderson, *Crucible of War*, 17.

7. Jacob-Nicolas Moreau, *A Memorial Containing a Summary View of Facts with Their Authorities, in Answer to the Observations Sent by the English Ministry to the Courts of Europe*, Philadelphia: James Chatten (1757), 15–16; Donald H. Kent, *The French Invasion of Western Pennsylvania*, Harrisburg: Pennsylvania Historical and Museum Commission (1954), 3.

8. Alan Taylor, *American Revolutions: A Continental History, 1750–1804*, New York: W. W. Norton & Co. (2016), 20. The land development schemes included the Greenbrier Company (headed by John Robinson, Speaker of the Virginia House of Burgesses), the Woods River Company (led by Colonel James Patton of Augusta County, Virginia), and the Loyal Company of Virginia (including Peter Jefferson, father of Thomas). James Titus, *The Old Dominion at War: Society, Politics, and Warfare in Late Colonial Virginia*, Columbia: University of South Carolina Press (1991), 11. In a 1754 letter, Colonel Fairfax's son-in-law John

Carlyle wrote specifically of the fear of being encircled by hostile French lands: "With the settlements on the [Mississippi] belonging to the French and hemming us in by the Appalachian Mountains," then "all the Indians [would] be dependents on the French Crown and upon any war they might send down their Indians and cut off their people and drive off their stocks of cattle, etc., and be very troublesome and dangerous neighbors." John Carlyle to George Carlyle, 3 July 1754, in "The Personal and Family Correspondence of Colonel John Carlyle of Alexandria, Virginia," in *Carlyle Correspondence.*

9. Anderson, *Crucible of War,* 25–26; Doug McGregor, "The Shot Not Heard Round the World: Trent's Fort and the Opening of the War for Empire," *Pennsylvania Hist.* 74:354, 356 (Summer 2007); Darlington, *Gist's Journals,* 48 (17 February 1751). A French official reported in 1749 that the French were losing their position in the Ohio valley because of "the excessive price of French goods [and] the great bargains which the English give, as well as the large presents which they make to the tribes." David Clary, *George Washington's First War: His Early Military Adventures,* New York: Simon & Schuster (2011), 35.

10. Kent, *French Invasion,* 6; Hugh Cleland, *George Washington in the Ohio Valley,* Pittsburgh: University of Pittsburgh Press (1955), 3; McGregor, "The Shot Not Heard Round the World," 358–61.

11. Darlington, *Gist's Journals,* 46–48 (12 and 17–18 February 1751); Francis Jennings, *Empire of Fortune: Crowns, Colonies and Tribes in the Seven Years War in America,* New York: W. W. Norton & Co. (1988), 49–51.

12. Bailey, *Ohio Company,* 74; Darlington, *Gist's Journals,* 31 (11 September 1750, instructions to Gist), 40 (9 January 1752), 44 (30 January 1752); 68 (16 July 1751, instructions to Gist), 34 (25 November 1751), 77 (12 March 1752), 69–70 (24 November 1751, 7 December 1751).

13. Shannon, *Iroquois Diplomacy,* 34, 23–24; Koontz, *Robert Dinwiddie,* 87; Fred Anderson, "Introduction: Old Forts, New Perspectives," in Hofstra, *Cultures in Conflict,* 5; Calloway, *Shawnees,* 14; Eric Hinderaker, "Declaring Independence: The Ohio Indians and the Seven Years' War," in Hofstra, *Cultures in Conflict,* 106–7. By 1750, the tribes in the Ohio valley included the Miami (or Twightwees), the Delaware, the Shawnee, and the Mingo (who were mostly emigrating Senecas). Their relationships with one another evolved under the shadow of the Iroquois, or Six Nations, who dominated New York and claimed power over the Ohio country, though Iroquois power was shrinking along with their population.

14. Titus, *Old Dominion at War,* 14–15; Lengel, *First Entrepreneur,* 13. Many Ohio Indians had migrated from the east. Dinwiddie to Cresap, 23 January 1752, in *Dinwiddie Records* 1:17–18; Dinwiddie to Conrad Weiser, 12 December 1751, Dinwiddie to Joshua Fry, undated, Dinwiddie to Colonel James Patton, 13 December 1751, Dinwiddie to Governor Ogle, 13 December 1751, in *Dinwiddie Records* 1:6–13.

15. Calloway, *Shawnees,* 17; Shannon, *Iroquois Diplomacy,* 81.

16. On the various interpretations of Tanaghrisson's tribal identity, see Kent, *French Invasion,* 46 (Seneca); Jennings, *Empire of Fortune,* 57 (Mingo); Lewis, *For King and Country,* 84 (Seneca overseeing the Mingos); Shannon, *Iroquois Diplomacy,* 128 (Catawba).

17. McGregor, "The Shot Not Heard Round the World," 362; Bailey, *Ohio Company,* 136–37; David Dixon, "A High Wind Rising: George Washington, Fort Necessity, and the Ohio Country Indians," *Pennsylvania Hist.* 74:333, 337–38 (Summer 2007); Anderson, *Crucible of War,* 18.

18. To William Fauntleroy, 20 May 1752, GWP; Freeman 1:261–62.

19. Release from Lawrence Washington, 17 June 1752, GWP; Lawrence Washington Will (20 June 1751), GW Papers, Series 4, Library of Congress; Freeman 1:264; from George Mason, 29 July 1752, GWP.

20. Lawrence also left half of his slaves to be divided among George and his three brothers on condition that they pay £150 to their sister, Betty Lewis. For modern readers,

Lawrence's early death may call to mind a similar sequence two centuries later in the family of Joseph Kennedy, who avidly groomed his eldest son, Joseph Jr., for a high destiny. When Joseph Jr. died young, the path opened for his younger brother, John F. Kennedy, to become the family's standard bearer.

21. To Dinwiddie, 10 June 1752; Freeman 1:268; Commission as Adjutant for Southern District, 13 December 1752, GWP.

22. Titus, *Old Dominion at War*, 4–5; Isaac, *The Transformation of Virginia*, 104, 106–7, 109; Griffith, *House of Burgesses*, 75; Don Higginbotham, *George Washington and the American Military Tradition*, Athens: University of Georgia Press (1985), 23–24.

23. Kent, *French Invasion*, 13–32, 46–47, 53–65; Anderson, *Crucible of War*, 32; Donald H. Kent, "The French Occupy the Ohio Country," *Pennsylvania Hist.* 21:301, 311 (October 1954); Dixon, "A High Wind Rising," 74:339–40.

24. Hall, *Executive Journals* 5:438–40, 442–43 (9 July, 24 August, and 22 October 1753), 5:443–44 (27 and 29 October 1754); Koontz, *Robert Dinwiddie*, 195–99; Anderson, *Crucible of War*, 37. Boundaries on the frontier had not been settled between Pennsylvania and Virginia, much less between Britain and France. Anderson, *Crucible of War*, 30; John Carlyle to George Carlyle, 11 August 1753, in *Carlyle Correspondence*.

25. Hall, *Executive Journals* 5:439–40 (24 August 1753); Instruction from Robert Dinwiddie, 30 October 1753, GWP.

26. To John Robinson, 30 May 1757, GWP; Bailey, *The Ohio Company*, 153–54; Kenneth Bailey, "Christopher Gist and the Trans-Allegheny Frontier: A Phase of the Westward Movement," *Pacific Hist. Review* 14:45, 48 (March 1945); Kate Van Winkle Keller, *George Washington: A Biography in Social Dance*, The Hendrickson Group (1998), 14–15; Anderson, *Crucible of War*, 43; Freeman 1:277.

27. *The Journal of Major George Washington*, Williamsburg: William Hunter (1754), 3, 22–23.

28. *Journal of Major Washington*, 7–8; Shannon, *Iroquois Diplomacy*, 150.

29. *Journal of Major Washington*, 9–12.

30. *Journal of Major Washington*, 14–15; Darlington, *Gist's Journals*, 82.

31. *Journal of Major Washington*, 17–19.

32. *Journal of Major Washington*, 20–25; Darlington, *Gist's Journals*, 83–86.

33. Legardeur de St. Pierre to Robert Dinwiddie, 16 December 1753, reprinted in Freeman 1:325; Anderson, *Crucible of War*, 45; Hall, *Executive Journals*, 458–59 (21 January 1754); Dinwiddie to John Carlyle, 21 January 1754, Dinwiddie to William Trent, January 1754, in *Dinwiddie Records* 1:53–57; from Dinwiddie, January 1754, GWP.

34. *Journal of Major Washington*, 2.

35. David S. Shields, "George Washington: Publicity, Probity, and Power," in Harvey and O'Brien, *George Washington's South*, 146; *Pennsylvania Gazette*, February 5, March 12 and 26, 1754; *New York Mercury*, March 25, 1754; *Boston Post-Boy*, April 1, 1754; *Boston Gazette*, April 23 and 30, and May 21, 1754; *South Carolina Gazette*, February 26–March 5, 1754; "Some Extracts of the Journal of Major George Washington," *The Gentleman's Magazine* (April 1754); *Scots Magazine* (May 1754).

6. FIRST COMMAND

1. Clary, *George Washington's First War*, 6; John Ferling, "Soldiers for Virginia: Who Served in the French and Indian War?" *VMHB* 94:307, 316 (1986).

2. Dinwiddie to Trent, January 1754, Dinwiddie to Colonel James Patton, January 1754, Dinwiddie to Lord Fairfax, January 1754, Dinwiddie to Colonel William Fairfax, January 1754, in *Dinwiddie Records* 1:55–57, 1:48–52.

3. Dinwiddie to Lord Fairfax, 23 February 1754, Dinwiddie to Lord Holdernesse, 12 March 1754, Dinwiddie to Governors of South Carolina, Pennsylvania, North Carolina, New York, Maryland, New Jersey, and Massachusetts, January 1754, in *Dinwiddie Records* 1:82, 1:93–94, 1:61–71; Titus, *The Old Dominion at War,* 25, 31–32; Hall, *Executive Journals,* 499 (proclamation of 19 February 1754) and 461–62 (Council meeting of 18 February 1754); from Dinwiddie, January 1754, n. 12, GWP; Freeman 1:334.

4. Fifty-one counties were represented in the House of Burgesses during this session, while single delegates represented the College of William & Mary, Jamestown, Norfolk Borough, and Williamsburg. McIlwaine, *Journals of the House of Burgesses, 1758–1761,* 9:vii–vii.

5. Carl Bridenbaugh, *Seat of Empire: The Political Role of Eighteenth-Century Williamsburg,* Williamsburg: Colonial Williamsburg (1958), 43–55; Griffith, *Virginia House of Burgesses,* 25–32; Koontz, *Robert Dinwiddie,* 200–208; Longmore, *The Invention of George Washington,* 25; Dinwiddie to the Lords of Trade, 12 March 1754, in *Dinwiddie Records* 1:98; Titus, *The Old Dominion at War,* 39–41; Hall, *Executive Journals* 462 (22 February 1754); Dinwiddie to Governor DeLancey of New York, 23 February 1754, in *Dinwiddie Records* 1:79.

6. McGregor, "The Shot Not Heard Round the World," 74:365–67; *Journal of Major Washington,* 22; from William Trent, 19 February 1754 (reprinted in *Maryland Gazette,* March 14, 1754), GWP; Anderson, *Crucible of War,* 46.

7. Dinwiddie to John Hanbury, 12 March 1754, in *Dinwiddie Records* 1:102–3; to Robert Dinwiddie, 7 and 9 March 1754, GWP.

8. Dinwiddie to Horatio Sharpe, 1 March 1754, in *Dinwiddie Records* 1:85–86; Koontz, *Robert Dinwiddie,* 136–37; to Richard Corbin, February–March 1754, GWP; Dinwiddie to Washington, 15 March 1754, Dinwiddie to Lord Holdernesse, 12 March 1754, in *Dinwiddie Records* 1:106–7, 1:93–96. Working with surveyor Peter Jefferson (father of Thomas Jefferson), Fry had produced the first reliable map of Virginia in 1751. Hughes, *Surveyors and Statesmen,* 87–88, 163

9. To Dinwiddie, 20 March 1754, GWP; Harry M. Ward, *Major General Adam Stephen and the Cause of American Liberty,* Charlottesville: University Press of Virginia (1989), 1–6.

10. To Dinwiddie, 25 April 1754, GWP; to Thomas Cresap, 18 April 1754, GWP; *John Harrow v. George Washington,* Frederick County Circuit Court, October 1754, Library of Virginia, https://ead.lib.virginia.edu/vivaxtf/view?docId=lva/vi02845.xml (return of arrest warrant).

11. From Dinwiddie, 15 March 1754, GWP; Hall, *Executive Journals* 5:463–65 (14 March and 11 April 1754).

12. Narrative of Expedition to the Ohio, 1754, 19–20 April 1754, GWP; to Dinwiddie, 25 April 1754, GWP; McGregor, "The Shot Not Heard Round the World," 366–68; Kent, "The French Occupy the Ohio Country," *Pennsylvania Hist.* 21:313 (October 1954). As reproduced in his April 25 letter to Governor Dinwiddie, Washington's message to Tanaghrisson was signed "George Washington also Connotaucarious." Thirty years later, Washington explained this signature as reflecting the Indian honorific "Connotaucarious" that Tanaghrisson had bestowed upon him because it had been borne by Washington's great-grandfather, the immigrant John Washington, in the previous century. As Washington related it, the name "registered in their [the Indians'] Manner and communicated to other Nations of Indians, has been remembered by them ever since in all their transactions with him during the late war [the American Revolution]." Zagarri, *Humphreys,* 10. The name translates as "town-taker" or "town-destroyer." This name has proved one of the small puzzles of Washington's life. The notion is preposterous that Tanaghrisson—a Seneca, or Mingo, or Catawba Indian—would know four generations later a name that had been applied to Washington's great-grandfather by the

Susquehannocks of Maryland, and *also* would know that George was his descendant. At the very least, such knowledge would require John Washington to have been a titanic figure in the history of the Indians of eastern North America, a proposition unsupported by any evidence. Washington seems to have been untroubled by any negative connotations of the name. "Town-destroyer" is a term for an enemy, not a friend, yet Washington used the name in Indian-related correspondence on a second occasion, as well. To Andrew Montour, 10 October 1755, GWP. One scholar suggests that Washington "remembered the name from family lore and took it for himself, a young man's act of bravado," observing that, "Despite its hostile connotations, Washington took pride in the name." He also notes that the explanation offered by Washington came in the 1780s, after the Revolutionary War, when Iroquois Indians had called him "town-destroyer," a term the American forces richly earned during that conflict. Calloway, *The Indian World of George Washington*, 69–70.

13. Dinwiddie to Colonel James Innes, 23 March 1754, in *Dinwiddie Records* 1:125–26; Hall, *Executive Journals* 5:465 (11 April 1754) and 5:468 (4 May 1754). Inexplicably, the Executive Council applauded Washington's "caution" in stopping at Redstone Creek and waiting for reinforcements before moving on to the Monongahela. Hall, *Executive Journals* 5:468–69 (4 May 1754). In an equally doubtful move, Washington wrote directly to the governors of Pennsylvania and Maryland—neither of whom he had ever met—to alert them that the French had taken the Forks. Though no malicious purpose seems to have motivated those letters, they reflect an exaggerated idea of his position. To James Hamilton, 24 April 1754, GWP; to Horatio Sharpe, 24 April 1754, GWP.

14. To Dinwiddie, 9 and 18 May 1754, GWP; to Joshua Fry, 23 May 1754, GWP. Washington took some satisfaction that the French built their new fort at the Forks at the site he had singled out as best for a fortification. Dinwiddie to Colonel Joshua Fry, 4 May 1754, Dinwiddie to Lord Holderness, 10 May 1754, Dinwiddie to the Lords of Trade, 10 May 1754, in *Dinwiddie Records* 1:146–48, 1:158, 1:162. Although Captain Mackay's company is ordinarily referred to as a South Carolina unit, he was a Georgian and some evidence suggests that the soldiers in the company were Georgians too. William Harden, "James Mackay of Strathy Hall, Comrade in Arms of George Washington," *Georgia Hist. Q.* 1:77, 82–83 (1917).

15. To Dinwiddie, 18 May 1754, GWP.

16. From Dinwiddie, 25 May 1754, GWP.

17. To Dinwiddie, 27 May 1754, GWP; Hall, *Executive Journals* 5: 469–70 (7 May 1754).

7: BLOODED

1. To Dinwiddie, 29 May 1754, GWP.

2. To Dinwiddie, 27 May 1754, GWP.

3. Marcel Trudel and Donald H. Kent, "The Jumonville Affair," *Pennsylvania Hist.* 21:351, 369–70 (October 1954); *Pennsylvania Gazette*, September 19, 1754. A recently discovered British source records an account from an unnamed Indian who claimed that Washington fired the first shot in the skirmish, and that British friendly fire had killed the fallen Virginian. The Indian source also confirmed Washington's account that the French returned fire. David Preston, "When Young George Washington Started a War," *Smithsonian Magazine* (October 2019).

4. Dixon, "A High Wind Rising," 74:333, 344; *Journal of Chaussegros de Léry 1754–55*, Erie: Pennsylvania Historical Commission (December 1939), 19, 28 (19 June, 7 July 1754); Anderson, *Crucible of War*, 5; to Dinwiddie, 29 May 1754, GWP; Anderson, *Crucible of War*, 58–59; to Dinwiddie, 29 May 1754, GWP; "Expedition to the Ohio, 1754: Narrative," 27 May

1754, GWP; to Dinwiddie, 3 June 1754, GWP. One official French government statement on the encounter can be partly reconciled with the account in text, as it describes a skirmish with guns blazing, then a pause when the French presumably laid down their weapons, and then Jumonville being killed. Moreau, *A Memorial*, 22–23. Another element of the French account, however, cannot be squared with the Virginia version: that Jumonville was killed by a musket shot and that the Indians rushed in to restrain the Virginians from massacring the French survivors. Those assertions are most implausible. Moreau, *Memorial*, 69.

5. Orders from M. de Contrecoeur to Jumonville, 23 May 1754, in Moreau, *Memorial*, 67–68.

6. To Dinwiddie, 29 May 1754, GWP.

7. Monsieur Druillon to Dinwiddie, 17 June 1754, in *Dinwiddie Records* 1:225–26; the specifics in Washington's account were confirmed by the recently unearthed British record of an Indian witness. Preston, "When Young George Washington Started a War," *supra*.

8. Trudel and Kent, "The Jumonville Affair," 21:351, 21:361–65. As one scholar summarized Jumonville's mission, he "was undoubtedly sent both to gather military intelligence and to deliver the declaration. Such a dual mission was not uncommon, but it was normally carried out as openly as possible and with fewer than a dozen soldiers and scouts." Daniel A. Baugh, *The Global Seven Years War, 1754–1763*, Harlow: Longman (2011), 63.

9. William Coxe, *Memoirs of the Reign of King George the Second,* London: Henry Colburn (1847), 1:400; Flexner 1:89.

10. *Pennsylvania Gazette*, July 11, 1754; to Dinwiddie, 3 June 1754, GWP. For other reports of Washington's situation and activities on the frontier, see *Boston Post-Boy,* July 1, 1754; *Boston Gazette*, July 2, 1754; *Maryland Gazette*, July 4, 1754; *Pennsylvania Gazette*, July 4, 1754.

11. From Dinwiddie, 1 June 1754, GWP; to Dinwiddie, 10 June 1754, GWP; Dinwiddie to Fry, 29 May 1754, Dinwiddie to John Carlyle, 25 June 1754, Dinwiddie to Colonel Fairfax, 27 June 1754, Dinwiddie to Gov. Hamilton of Pennsylvania, 18 June 1754, in *Dinwiddie Records* 1:184–85, 1:219–20, 1:224, 1:214–16; from Dinwiddie, 1 June 1754, GWP. The New York companies arrived in Alexandria by ship on June 24, far too late to assist at Fort Necessity. From Bryan Fairfax, 24 June 1754, GWP.

12. From Dinwiddie, 4 June 1754, GWP; to Dinwiddie, 10 June 1754, GWP.

13. Expedition to the Ohio, Narrative, 1 June 1754, GWP; to Dinwiddie, 3 June 1754, GWP.

14. From Dinwiddie, 4 June 1754, GWP; to Dinwiddie, 10 June 1754, GWP; from Dinwiddie, 27 June 1754, GWP; Expedition to the Ohio, Narrative, 1 June, GWP (entries for 23 April and 15 June); Freeman, 1:400.

15. Titus, *The Old Dominion at War*, 53; "Affidavit of John Shaw," in William L. McDowell Jr., ed., *Colonial Records of South Carolina: Documents Relating to Indian Affairs, 1754–1765,* Columbia, SC: University of South Carolina Press (1970), 3–7 (cited as "John Shaw Affidavit"); Minutes of a Council of War, 28 June 1754, GWP.

16. Lengel, *General George Washington,* 41; Expedition to the Ohio, Narrative, 1 June 1754, GWP (entries for 17 and 24 May and 5 and 12 June 1754).

17. Expedition to the Ohio (entries for 15, 18–21, and 27 June 1754).

18. From Dinwiddie, 27 June 1754, GWP; Minutes of a Council of War, 28 June 1754, GWP; Frederick Tilberg, "Washington's Stockade at Fort Necessity," *Pennsylvania Hist.* 20:240, 245 (July 1953); Ward, *Adam Stephen*, 10.

19. Paul A. Wallace, *Conrad Weiser, Friend of Colonist and Mohawk,* Philadelphia: University of Pennsylvania Press (1945), 367 (3 September 1754); Anderson, *Crucible of War*, 59; Dixon, "A High Wind Rising," 74:345; John Shaw Affidavit, 7.

20. *Journal of Chaussegros de Léry,* 27 (7 July 1754); Dixon, "A High Wind Rising," 74:346–47; Tilberg, "Washington's Stockade," 246; "Account by George Washington and James Mackay of the Capitulation of Fort Necessity," 19 July 1754, GWP; John Shaw Affidavit, 5.

21. "Journal of M. de Villiers," in Moreau, *Memorial*, 178.

22. Zagarri, *Humphreys*, 13; Anderson, *Crucible of War*, 64; John Shaw Affidavit, 5; *Maryland Gazette*, August 29, 1754; Ward, *Adam Stephen*, 11.

23. *Journal of Chaussegros de Léry*, 36 (16 July 1754).

24. Zagarri, *Humphreys*, 13; "Account by George Washington and James Mackay," 19 July 1754, GWP.

25. *New York Mercury*, August 26, 1754.

26. Articles of Capitulation, 3 July 1754, GWP; Moreau, *Memorial*, 25–26, 182–83; Ward, *Adam Stephen*, 11–12. That the capitulation listed a second purpose for the French attack—to expel the English from the Ohio country—was lost to history.

27. Longmore, *The Invention of George Washington*, 23; letter to unknown addressee, "III. 1757," GWP.

28. "Account by George Washington and James Mackay," 19 July 1754, GWP; *Virginia Gazette* (Hunter), July 19, 1754; *New York Mercury*, July 29, 1754; *Journal of Chaussegros de Léry*, 36 (July 16, 1754); Anderson, *Crucible of War*, 65. Washington and Mackay's dramatically inflated casualty estimate was accepted by some fellow Virginians. Jack P. Greene, ed., *The Diary of Colonel Landon Carter of Sabine Hall, 1752–1778*, Richmond: Virginia Historical Society (1987), 110 (22 August 1754).

29. Wallace, *Conrad Weiser*, 387.

30. *Papers of William Johnson*, Albany: State University of New York (1921), 1:409–10 (29 July 1754); Lord Albemarle to the Duke of Newcastle, quoted in Stuart Leibiger, "'To Judge of Washington's Conduct': Illuminating George Washington's Appearance on the World Stage," *VMHB* 107:37, 43 (Winter 1999).

31. From Colonel Fairfax, 11 July 1754, GWP.

32. Dinwiddie to William Allen, Esq., 10 March 1755, Dinwiddie to Colonel Innes, 20 July 1755, Dinwiddie to James Abercromby, 24 July 1754, Dinwiddie to the Lords of Trade, 24 June 1754, Dinwiddie to Lord Halifax, 24 July 1754, in *Dinwiddie Records* 1:523–24, 1:232, 1:235–39, 1:239–43, 1:250–52; McIlwaine, *Journals of the House of Burgesses, 1752–1755, 1756–1758*, 198 (30 August 1754); from John Robinson, 15 September 1754, GWP. Landon Carter, a prominent member of the House of Burgesses, recorded in his diary that Dinwiddie had ordered Washington into an exposed position and Washington's men "were totally neglected and left quite without provision." Greene, *The Diary of Colonel Landon Carter*, 109 (22 August 1754).

33. Lengel, *General George Washington*, 47.

34. Mackay defended Washington's handling of the capitulation, blaming the interpreter for the document's unfortunate language. From James Mackay, 28 September 1754, GWP. That explanation—embraced by both Washington and Mackay—is not persuasive, since an interpreter would not be needed to understand the meaning of the French word for assassination ("*assassinat*"), which is instantly recognizable to English speakers as referring to assassination.

8. PICKING UP THE PIECES

1. To Colonel Innes, 12 August 1754, GWP; to Dinwiddie, 20 August 1754, GWP; Titus, *The Old Dominion at War*, 57; Dinwiddie to Colonel Innes, August 1754, in *Dinwiddie Records* 1:269–71; to Colonel Fairfax, 11 August 1754, GWP; from James Mackay, 27 August 1754, GWP. Because many deserters fled to neighboring Maryland, Washington ran the advertisements in the Annapolis-based *Maryland Gazette* on September 5, 12, 19, and 26, 1754.

2. Dinwiddie to Colonel Innes, 1 August 1754, in *Dinwiddie Records* 1:261–62; from Dinwiddie, 1 August 1754, GWP; Dinwiddie to Governor Sharpe, 31 July 1754, Dinwiddie to Abercromby, 15 August 1754, in *Dinwiddie Records* 1:258–59, 1:284–87.

3. To Colonel Fairfax, 11 August 1754, GWP.

4. Dinwiddie to Colonel Innes, 18 September 1754, Dinwiddie to John Abercromby, 1 September 1754, in *Dinwiddie Records* 1:314–15, 1:298–301; from William La Peronie, 5 September 1754, GWP; Dinwiddie Order, 4 September 1754, Dinwiddie to Innes, 11 September 1754, in *Dinwiddie Records* 1:302–3, 1:314–15; McIlwaine, *Journals of the House of Burgesses, 1752–1758*, 8:204 (5 September 1754); from Colonel Fairfax, 5 September 1754, GWP; Titus, *The Old Dominion at War*, 57.

5. Anderson, *Crucible of War*, 68, 77; Dinwiddie to Secretary Robinson, 23 September 1754, in *Dinwiddie Records* 1:322–27; from Dinwiddie, 11 September 1754, GWP; Dinwiddie to Lord Fairfax, September 10, 1754, in *Dinwiddie Records* 1:312–13.

6. "The Plan of Military Operations," October 1754, and Dinwiddie to Sir Thomas Robinson, 25 October 1754, in *Dinwiddie Records* 1:351–53; Titus, *The Old Dominion at War*, 59–60; McIlwaine, *Journals of the House of Burgesses, 1752–1758*, 8:222 (29 October 1754); Dinwiddie to Earl of Halifax, 25 October 1754, in *Dinwiddie Records* 1:366–69; Freeman 1:436–48.

7. Ferling, *The Ascent of George Washington*, 26.

8. To William Fitzhugh, 15 November 1754, GWP; see from William Fitzhugh, 4 November 1754, GWP.

9. "Account with the Colony of Virginia," October 1754, GWP; from Dinwiddie, 11 September 1754, GWP; Freeman 1:244; "Lease of Mount Vernon," 17 December 1754, GWP; Knollenberg, *George Washington: The Virginia Period*, 26.

10. "I. Memorandum," and "II. Memorandum," 10 December 1754, GWP.

11. Invoice, 23 October 1754, GWP; Freeman 2:4–5; to Robert Orme, April 1755, GWP.

12. Titus, *The Old Dominion Goes to War*, 58, 65; Anderson, *Crucible of War*, 88; McIlwaine, *Journals of the House of Burgesses, 1752–1758*, 8:231–32 (1 May 1755); Dinwiddie to Captain Stewart, 26 November 1754, Dinwiddie to Captains George Mercer, Waggener, and Stewart, 15 January 1755, in *Dinwiddie Records* 1:413–14, 1:461–62.

13. Dinwiddie to Governor Sharpe, 2 January 1755, Dinwiddie to William Allen, 14 January 1755, in *Dinwiddie Records* 1:447–48, 1:455–56.

14. Freeman 2:20; to Adam Stephen, 18 November 1755, GWP; to Robert Orme, 2 March, GWP, note 1; Frank A. Cassell, "The Braddock Expedition of 1755: Catastrophe in the Wilderness," *Pennsylvania Legacies* 5:11 (May 2005); John Carlyle to George Carlyle, 15 August 1755, in *Carlyle Correspondence*; Titus, *The Old Dominion Goes to War*, 64.

15. "Anonymous letter on Braddock's Campaign," 25 July 1755, reprinted in Stanley Pargellis, ed., *Military Affairs in North America 1748–1765*, New York: D. Appleton-Century Co. (1936), 119; Freeman 2:37; John Carlyle to George Carlyle, 15 August 1755, in *Carlyle Correspondence*.

16. Franklin Thayer Nichols, "The Organization of Braddock's Army," *WMQ*, 4:125, 126, 139–40 (April 1947).

17. To John Augustine Washington, 14 May 1755, GWP.

18. From Orme, 2 March 1755, GWP; from Orme, 16 March 1755, GWP; to Orme, 2 April 1755, GWP; from Orme, 3 April 1755, GWP; "Sketch of Regulations & Orders Proposed Relating to Affairs of North America, November 1754," in Pargellis, *Military Affairs*, 35; "Sketch of an Order About the Rank etc., of the Provincial Troops in North America," in Pargellis, *Military Affairs*, 43; Koontz, *Robert Dinwiddie*, 327.

19. To William Byrd, 20 April 1755, GWP; to John Robinson, 20 April 1755, GWP; to Carter Burwell, 20 April 1755, GWP; to Thomas, Lord Fairfax, 6 May 1755, GWP; Edward G.

Lengel, *First Entrepreneur: How George Washington Built His—and the Nation's—Prosperity,* Boston: Da Capo Press (2016), 31.

20. To John Augustine Washington, 14 May 1755, GWP.
21. Flexner 1:115–17; "Captain Orme's Journal," in Winthrop Sargent, *The History of an Expedition Against Fort Du Quesne in 1755, under Major General Edward Braddock,* Philadelphia: Lippincott, Grambo & Co. (1855), 281, 300; John Carlyle to George Carlyle, 15 August 1755, in *Carlyle Correspondence*; to William Fairfax, 23 April 1755, GWP; *Virginia Gazette* (Hunter), May 3, 1755.
22. To John Augustine Washington, 6 May 1755, GWP; Letter of Dr. Alexander Hamilton, in Elaine G. Breslaw, "A Dismal Tragedy: Drs. Alexander and John Hamilton Comment on Braddock's Defeat," *Maryland Hist. Magazine* 75:118, 131 (1980); to Augustine Washington, 14 May 1755, GWP; to Mary Washington, 6 May 1755, GWP.
23. Braddock to Robert Napier, 8 June 1755, in Pargellis, *Military Affairs,* 84; from Sir John St. Clair to Braddock, 9 February 1755, in Pargellis, *Military Affairs,* 64; "Captain Orme's Journal," 312; to John Augustine Washington, 28 May and 7 June 1755, GWP. The Virginians might take some solace in the universal condemnation of the independent companies when they finally arrived from New York. One British officer, who sent forty of the New Yorkers home, observed that they had "neither legs to get upon the heights nor to run away through the valleys." Sir John St. Clair to Robert Napier, 10 February 1755, in Pargellis, *Military Affairs,* 65. Several of their soldiers, Captain Orme wrote, were "from sixty to seventy years of age, lame and everyway disabled." Nichols, "The Organization of Braddock's Army," 127. Braddock dismissed the New York companies as "good for nothing." Braddock to Robert Napier, 17 March 1755, in Pargellis, *Military Affairs,* 78.
24. Flexner 1:119–20; James Thomas Flexner, *Mohawk Baronet,* Syracuse: Syracuse University Press (1959), 131; Benjamin Franklin, *Autobiography,* Boston: Houghton Mifflin & Co. (1888), 181.
25. Shannon, *Iroquois Diplomacy,* 151; Beverly Bond, ed., "The Captivity of Charles Stuart, 1755–57," *Mississippi Hist. Rev.* 13:63 (1926); Calloway, *Shawnees,* 28; *Major General Edward Braddock's Orderly Books,* Cumberland, MD: Will H. Lowdermilk, 1878, xxxvi (May 18, 1755, holding "public Congress of Indians"); Anderson, *Crucible of War,* 94–95; Daniel Barr, "'This Land Is Ours and Not Yours': The Western Delawares and the Seven Years' War in the Upper Ohio Valley, 1755–1758," in Daniel Barr, ed., *The Boundaries Between Us: Natives and Newcomers Along the Frontiers of the Old Northwest Territory, 1750–1850,* Kent: The Kent State University Press (2006), 29–30; Cassell, "The Braddock Expedition of 1755," 11.

9. A WORSE CATASTROPHE

1. John Kennedy Lacock, "Braddock Road," *PMHB* 38:1 (1914).
2. Braddock brought four twelve-pound cannon, six six-pounders, four eight-inch howitzers, and fifteen Coehorn mortars. In Europe, it took fifteen horses to pull a twelve-pounder, seven horses for a six-pounder, and five horses for a howitzer. H.C.B. Rogers, *The British Army of the Eighteenth Century,* London: Allen & Unwin (1977), 80; Freeman 2:46–47.
3. Alan Houston, "Benjamin Franklin and the 'Wagon Affair' of 1755," *WMQ* 66:235, 236, 251 (2009); Braddock to Robert Napier, 8 June 1755, in Pargellis, *Military Affairs,* 84; "Captain Orme's Journal," 308; Leonard W. Labaree, "Benjamin Franklin and the Defense of Pennsylvania, 1754–1757," *Pennsylvania Hist.* 29:7, 10–12 (1962); to William Fairfax, 5 May 1755,

GWP. Both Franklin and Washington were in Frederick, Maryland, with General Braddock on April 22, 1755. Anderson, *Crucible of War,* 92; Franklin, *Autobiography,* 264;
Larabee, "Benjamin Franklin and the Defense of Pennsylvania," 10–12. Among the wagoners on the expedition were two men who would rise to their own prominence: Daniel
Boone and the future General Daniel Morgan. Bailey, "Christopher Gist," 46.

4. To William Fairfax, 7 June 1755, GWP; *Colonial Records of Pennsylvania*, Harrisburg:
Theo. Fenn & Co. (1851), 6:395–97 (report of Richard Peters to Pennsylvania Council).

5. John St. Clair to Braddock, 9 February 1755, in Pargellis, *Military Affairs,* 61; William H.
Shank, *Indian Trails to Superhighways,* York, PA: American Canal & Transportation
Center (1988), 15; Paul A. W. Wallace, "'Blunder Camp': A Note on the Braddock Road,"
PMHB 87:21 (January 1963).

6. "Captain Orme's Journal," 321.

7. Referring to a stretch of road in northern England, one authority warned that the odds
were "a thousand to one [travelers] would break their neck or their limbs by overthrows
or breakings down." Arthur Young, *A Six Months' Tour Through the North of England,*
London: W. Strahan (1770), 580. Another Briton wrote in 1763 of English country roads
that looked "more like a retreat of wild beasts and reptiles, than the footsteps of man."
Daniel Bourne, "A Treatise upon Wheel-Carriages," London: 1763, in William Albert,
The Turnpike Road System in England 1663–1840, Cambridge: Cambridge University
Press (1972), 8; Lacock, "Braddock Road," 38:27 (1914).

8. Lacock, "Braddock Road," 38:17–18 (1914); Nathan C. Rockwood, *One Hundred Fifty
Years of Roadbuilding in America,* New York: Engineering News (1914); Connecticut Department of Transportation, "Early Travel in Connecticut Before 1895," ConnDOT website. Most Virginians knew something about roadbuilding. Since 1632, every colonist had
to work on local roads for a certain number of days every year. A later law required
Virginians to keep nearby roads "well cleared from woods and bushes, and the roots well
grubbed up, at least thirty feet broad." Virginia Department of Transportation, *A History of Roads in Virginia: "The Most Convenient Wayes,"* Richmond (2006), 5–6; Albert
Ogden Porter, *County Government in Virginia: A Legislative History, 1607–1904,* New
York: Columbia University Press (1947), 60. In Thomas Jefferson's *Notes on the State of
Virginia,* Philadelphia: Prichard and Hall (1788), 161–62, he wrote, "The inhabitants of
the county are by them [county courts] laid off into precincts, to each of which they allot
a convenient portion of the public roads to be kept in repair." If expert labor was required
for bridges, "the county employs workmen to build it at the expense of the whole county."
Each county appointed a surveyor to supervise roadbuilding.

9. "The Journal of Charlotte Brown, Matron of the General Hospital with the English
Forces in America, 1754–1756," in Isabel M. Calder, ed., *Colonial Captivities, Marches,
and Journeys,* New York: The Macmillan Co. (1935), 178, 180–82 (2–13 June 1755).

10. "Captain Orme's Journal," 334 (16 June 1755); Charles Hamilton, ed., *Braddock's Defeat:
The Journal of Captain Robert Cholmley's Batman,* Norman: University of Oklahoma
Press (1959), 25 (16 June 1755).

11. Laycock, "Braddock's Road," 38:9, notes 16 and 27; Achenbach, *The Grand Idea,* 59–61;
Baugh, *The Global Seven Years War,* 124.

12. "Captain Orme's Journal," 317–19.

13. Ibid., 331–35; to John Augustine Washington, 2 July 1755, GWP.

14. Longmore, *The Invention of George Washington,* 28; Robert Orme to Robert Napier, 18
July 1755, in Pargellis, *Military Affairs,* 98–100; to John Augustine Washington, 2 July
1755, GWP.

15. "Captain Orme's Journal," 338, 341, 345, 349–50.

16. From Roger Morris, 23 June 1755, GWP.

17. To John Augustine Washington, 2 July 1755, GWP.

18. Memorandum, 8–9 July 1755, GWP.

19. Zagarri, *Humphreys*, 15.

20. Ibid., 15; Orme to Napier, 18 July 1755, in Pargellis, *Military Affairs*, 98–100.

21. Harry Gordon to unknown, 23 July 1755, in Pargellis, *Military Affairs*, 105–6; John St. Clair to Colonel Robert Napier, 22 July 1755, in Pargellis, *Military Affairs*, 102; anonymous letter, 25 July 1755, in Pargellis, *Military Affairs*, 115; Anderson, *Crucible of War*, 100; Baugh, *The Global Seven Years' War*, 126.

22. Adam Stephen to John Hunter, 18 July 1755, Egerton Ms., British Library, 3429, 277–80; "Journal of a British Officer," in Hamilton, *Braddock's Defeat*, 27.

23. Lengel, *General George Washington*, 57; Ward, *Adam Stephen*, 19.

24. Lengel, *General George Washington*, 55–57; Cassel, "The Braddock Expedition of 1755," 13; Matthew C. Ward, "Fighting the 'Old Women': Indian Strategy on the Virginia and Pennsylvania Frontier, 1754–1758," *VMHB* 103:297, 300 (July 1995).

25. "An Account of the Battle of the Monongahela, 9th July 1755," in John Romeyn Brodhead, *Documents Relative to the Colonial History of the State of New York*, Albany: Weed, Parsons and Co. (1858), 10:303–4. The Indian attackers included members of the Ottawa, Potawatamie, Miami, Wyandotte, Shawnee, and Delaware tribes.

26. Cassel, "The Braddock Expedition of 1755," 11; "An Account of the Battle of the Monongahela," in Brodhead, *Colonial History of the State of New York*, 10:304; "Leslie to a Merchant of Philadelphia, July 30, 1755," in *Hazard's Pennsylvania Register*, Philadelphia: Wm. F. Geddes, 5:191 (March 20, 1830); Zagarri, *Humphreys*, 15.

27. Adam Stephen to John Hunter, 18 July 1755, British Library, *supra*.

28. Harry Gordon to unknown, 23 July 1755, in Pargellis, *Military Affairs*, 106; "Journal of a British Officer," in Hamilton, *Braddock's Defeat*, 50.

29. Orme to Napier, 18 July 1755, in Pargellis, *Military Affairs*, 99; Zagarri, *Humphreys*, 15; "Journal of British Officer," in Hamilton, *Braddock's Defeat*, 50.

30. Hamilton, *Braddock's Defeat*, 49–50; "Copy of a document given by Captain Hewitt, R.N., to his friend Captain Henry Gage Morris, R.N., whose father was an aide de camp with Washington to Major General Braddock in the Expedition," in Sargent, *History of an Expedition*, 386; Adam Stephen to John Hunter, 18 July 1755, British Library, *supra*.

31. Adam Stephen to John Hunter, 18 July 1755, British Library, *supra*; Alan Houston, "Benjamin Franklin and the 'Wagon Affair' of 1755," *WMQ* 66:235, 279 (2009) (quoting letter from John Hamilton, 16 July 1755, from camp at Widow Barringers); "Copy of a document given by Captain Hewitt, R.N.," in Sargent, *History of an Expedition*, 386.

32. Harry Gordon to unknown, 23 July 1755, in Pargellis, *Military Affairs*, 107; Cassell, "The Braddock Expedition of 1755," 15; "The Journal of a British Officer," in Hamilton, *Braddock's Defeat*, 49; Zagarri, *Humphreys*, 15–16; to Mary Washington, 18 July 1755, GWP; "Anonymous Letter on Braddock's Campaign," 25 July 1755, in Pargellis, *Military Affairs*, 117; "Journal of British Officer," in Hamilton, *Braddock's Defeat*, 49 (July 9).

33. Alexander Hamilton to Gavin Hamilton, August 1755, in Elaine G. Breslaw, "A Dismal Tragedy: Drs. Alexander and John Hamilton Comment on Braddock's Defeat," *Maryland Hist. Mag.* 75:118, 135–39 (1980).

34. Adam Stephen to John Hunger, July 18, 1755, British Library, *supra*; Lengel, *General George Washington*, 59; to Mary Washington, 18 July 1755, GWP; Hamilton, *Braddock's Defeat*, 29.

35. Hamilton, *Braddock's Defeat*, 29–30.

36. "Captain Orme's Journal," 356; Anderson, *Crucible of War*, 760, note 12.

37. Anonymous letter, July 25, 1755, in Pargellis, *Military Affairs*, 115. "Copy of a document given by Captain Hewitt," in Sargent, *History of an Expedition*, 386.

38. "Journal of a British Officer," in Hamilton, *Braddock's Defeat*, 52; Robert Orme to Robert Napier, 18 July 1775, in Pargellis, *Military Affairs*, 99; anonymous letter, 25 July 1755, in Pargellis, *Military Affairs*, 119; Harry Gordon account, 23 July 1755, in Pargellis, *Military Affairs*, 108; "Copy of a document given by Captain Hewitt," in Sargent, *The History of an Expedition*, 356.

39. Orme to Napier, 18 July 1755, in Pargellis, *Military Affairs*, 99.

40. Zagarri, *Humphreys*, 16; Memorandum, 8–9 July 1755, and note 4, GWP.

41. Zagarri, *Humphreys*, 16; Donald H. Kent, "The French Occupy the Ohio Country," *Pennsylvania Hist.* 21:301, 314 (October 1954).

42. To Mary Washington, 18 July 1755, GWP. It is noteworthy that Washington wrote his longest account of the battle to his mother, rather than to Colonel Fairfax or to the two brothers (Jack and Austin) with whom he corresponded more frequently. He may have been a courageous warrior, but he also was a twenty-three-year-old who—sick, exhausted, and morally devastated by a horrifying experience—wrote to his mother. He doubtless expected her to share his letter with his siblings.

43. *Pennsylvania Gazette*, July 31, 1755; *Boston Evening-Post*, August 11, 1755; *Boston Gazette*, August 11, 1755; *Hazard's Pennsylvania Register*, Philadelphia: Wm. F. Geddes (1831–32) 8:43–45 (reprinting articles from August 1755 *Gentleman's Magazine*, and the August 26, 1755, issue of the *Gazette* in London).

44. Anonymous letter, 25 July 1755, in Pargellis, *Military Affairs*, 115, 117; Adam Stephen to John Hunter, July 18, 1755, British Library, *supra*; Titus, *The Old Dominion Goes to War*, 69; Don Higginbotham, *George Washington and the American Military Tradition*, Athens: University of Georgia Press (1985), 18. In a letter from Mount Vernon at the end of July, Washington wrote to Braddock's former chief aide that most accounts of the battle were "greatly to the disadvantage of the poor deceased general, who is censured on all hands." To Orme, 28 July 1755, GWP.

45. James Read to Ben Franklin, in Alan Houston, "Benjamin Franklin and the 'Wagon Affair' of 1755," *WMQ* 66:235, 281 (2009); Zagarri, *Humphreys*, 19.

46. Zagarri, *Humphreys*, 18–19; Adam Stephen to John Hunter, 18 July 1755, British Library, *supra*.

47. Dinwiddie to William Allen, 2 January 1756, in *Dinwiddie Records* 2:313; to Robert Jackson, 2 August 1755, GWP.

48. Dunbar to Robert Napier, 24 July 1755, in Pargellis, *Military Affairs*, 109–11; St. Clair to Napier, 22 July 1755, in Pargellis, *Military Affairs*, 102; Anderson, *Crucible of War*, 105.

49. To Dinwiddie, 18 July 1755, GWP.

50. Dinwiddie to Thomas Dunbar, 26 July 1755, in *Dinwiddie Records* 118–20; from Dinwiddie, 26 July 1755, GWP.

51. *Pennsylvania Gazette*, July 31, 1755; *Boston Evening-Post*, August 11, 1755; *Boston Gazette*, August 11, 1755; from William Fairfax, 26 July 1755, GWP; from Philip Ludwell, 8 August 1755, GWP.

52. To Augustine Washington, 2 August 1755, GWP; to the County Lieutenants, 2 August 1755, GWP; Memorandum, 2 August 1755, GWP; to Colin Campbell, 2 August 1755, GWP.

53. Anderson, *Crucible of War*, 105.

54. To Augustine Washington, 2 August 1755, GWP; anonymous letter, 25 July 1755, in Pargellis, *Military Affairs*, 119.

55. To John Augustine Washington, 18 July 1755, GWP.

56. Alexander Hamilton letter, in Breslaw, "A Dismal Tragedy," 138–39.

57. Samuel Davies, *Religion and Patriotism the Constituents of a Good Soldier*, Philadelphia (1755), 12 n*; Longmore, *The Invention of George Washington*, 30, 196; *Dunlap's Pennsylvania Packet*, 26 June 1775.

58. Custis, *Recollections*, 303–5.

10. THE NAKED FRONTIER

1. Hinderaker, "Declaring Independence," 117; Warren Hofstra, "'A Parcel of Barbarian's and an Uncooth Set of People': Settlers and Settlements of the Shenandoah Valley," in Warren Hofstra, ed., *George Washington and the Virginia Backcountry,* Madison: Madison House (1998), 92–94.

2. David L. Preston, "'Make Indians of our White Men': British Soldiers and Indian Warriors from Braddock's to Forbes' Campaigns," *Pennsylvania Hist.* 74:280, 287 (2007); Calloway, *The Shawnees,* 28; Shannon, *Iroquois Diplomacy,* 151; Titus, *The Old Dominion at War,* 71; Brown, *Virginia Baron,* 136–37; from Adam Stephen, 4 October 1755, GWP; *Pennsylvania Gazette,* October 30, 1755; Dinwiddie to Sir Charles Hardy, 18 October 1755, in *Dinwiddie Records* 2:251.

3. B. Scott Crawford, "A Frontier of Fear: Terrorism and Social Tension Along Virginia's Western Waters, 1742–1775," *West Virginia Hist.* 2:1 (Fall 2008); James Maury to John Fontaine, 9 August 1755, in Ann Maury, ed., *Memoirs of a Huguenot Family,* New York: G. P. Putnam's Sons (1872), 383; Gwenda Morgan, "Virginia and the French and Indian War: A Case Study of the War's Effects on Imperial Relations," *VMHB* 81:23, 31 (1973); from Adam Stephen, 25 September 1755, GWP.

4. Dinwiddie to Charles Carter, 18 July 1755, in *Dinwiddie Records* 2:102; Dinwiddie to Henry Fox, 24 May 1755, in *Dinwiddie Records* 2:414–15; Titus, *The Old Dominion Goes to War,* 75; McIlwaine, *Journals of the House of Burgesses, 1752–1755,* 8:302, 8:314 (8 and 23 August 1755); *Virginia Gazette* (Hunter), September 5, 1755.

5. To Mary Washington, 14 August 1755, GWP.

6. To Warner Lewis, 14 August 1755, GWP.

7. Instructions from Robert Dinwiddie, 14 August 1755, GWP; Freeman 2:113.

8. From Dinwiddie, 17 September 1755, GWP; Titus, *Old Dominion Goes to War,* 29; McIlwaine, *Journals of the House of Burgesses, 1752–55,* 8:222. The westerners, as Washington put it in a letter to Governor Dinwiddie, "choos[e] as they say to die with their wives and families." To Dinwiddie, 11–14 October 1755, GWP.

9. James Maury to John Fontaine, 15 June 1756, in Maury, *Huguenot Memoirs,* 404; to Adam Stephen, 28 December 1755, GWP; from Dinwiddie, 14 December 1755, GWP; to Dinwiddie, 13 January 1756, GWP.

10. "General Instructions for Recruiting Officers for the Virginia Regiment," 1–3 September 1755, GWP; Lloyd DeWitt Bockstruck, *Virginia's Colonial Soldiers,* Baltimore: Genealogical Publishing Co. (1988), 63–82.

11. John Ferling, "Soldiers for Virginia: Who Served in the French and Indian War?" *VMHB* 95:307, 309–10 (July 1786).

12. To Andrew Lewis, 6 September 1755 (instructions), GWP; Memorandum, 6 September 1755, GWP; Higginbotham, *American Military Tradition,* 18–19; Orders, 15 September 1755, GWP; Lewis, *For King and Country,* 196–97.

13. John Carlyle to George Carlyle, August 15, 1755, in *Carlyle Correspondence;* to Dinwiddie, 11 September 1755, GWP.

14. From Adam Stephen, 4 October 1755, GWP; to John Robinson, 8 October 1755, GWP.

15. To Peter Hog, 24 September 1755, GWP.

16. To Dinwiddie, 20 August 1755, GWP; from John Martin, 30 August 1755, GWP; from Adam Stephen, 4 October 1755, GWP; to Dinwiddie, 8 October 1755, 11–14 October 1755, 5 December 1755, GWP; Dinwiddie to Sir Thomas Robinson, 15 November 1755, in *Dinwiddie Records* 2:267.

17. To Stephen, 20 September 1755, GWP; from Stephen, 4 October 1755, GWP; Freeman 2:120; to Dinwiddie, 11–14 October 1755, GWP; Memorandum, 10 October 1755, GWP;

Ward, "Fighting the 'Old Women,'" 312 (quoting Preston); to Dinwiddie, 11–14 October 1755, GWP.

18. Ward, "Fighting the 'Old Women,'" 312; *Journal of Captain Charles Lewis of the Virginia Regiment Commanded by Colonel George Washington in the Expedition Against the French, October 10–December 27, 1755,* Richmond: Virginia Historical Society (1892), 205–7, 215; James Axtell, *The European and the Indian: Essays in the Ethnohistory of Colonial North America,* New York: Oxford University Press (1981), 214; Ward, "'This Land Is Ours and Not Yours,'" in Barr, *The Boundaries Between Us,* 32.

19. *Virginia Gazette* (Hunter), October 10, 1755, 3; Memorandum and Advertisement, 13 October 1755, GWP.

20. To Dinwiddie, 11–14 October 1755, GWP; George Mercer to Andrew Lewis, 18 October 1755, GWP.

21. *Virginia Gazette* (Hunter), September 12 and 26, 1755, reprinted in "Extracts from the Virginia Gazette, 1752 and 1753 (Concluded)," *VMHB* 25:12, 16, 17 (1917); *Virginia Gazette,* (Hunter), October 10, 1755; *Journal of Captain Charles Lewis,* 215.

22. To Richard Washington, 6 December 1755, GWP; Address, 8 January 1756, GWP.

23. Dinwiddie to Earl of Halifax, 15 November 1755, Dinwiddie to Lords of Trade, 15 November 1755, in *Dinwiddie Records* 2:273, 2:275, 2:268, 2:269; McIlwaine, *Journals of the House of Burgesses, 1752–55,* 8:332 (8 November 1755).

24. To John Augustine Washington, 28 May 1755, GWP.

25. To John Augustine Washington, 7 June 1755, GWP; Fairfax County, Virginia, June 13, 1748 Election Poll, in George Washington Papers, Series 4, General Correspondence, *GW/LOC Digital Collection.*

26. John G. Kolp, "The Dynamics of Electoral Competition in Pre-Revolutionary Virginia," *WMQ* 49:652, 655 (1992).

27. Sydnor, *Gentlemen Freeholders,* 14–24, 42, 49, 51.

28. Freeman 2:146–47 and note 156; Conway, *Barons of the Potomac and the Rappahannock,* 269–70; from Adam Stephen, 23 December 1755, GWP. Washington's course in the incident recalls the reported deathbed remark of his father that he was proud never to have struck another man. Both father and son may have disdained using their size and strength against smaller men. "General Washington," *New England Historical and Genealogical Register* 11:1, 5 (1857).

29. From Adam Stephen, 23 December 1755, GWP; Ward, *Adam Stephen,* 29; Frederick County, Virginia, December 11, 1755, Election Poll, in George Washington Papers, Series 4, General Correspondence, *GW/LOC Digital Collection.*

30. To Dinwiddie, 13 January 1756, GWP; to Adam Stephen, 1 February 1756, GWP.

31. Address, 8 January 1756, GWP; to John Ashby, 28 December 1755, GWP.

32. To Dinwiddie, 13 January 1756, GWP.

11. A WILDERNESS OF DIFFICULTIES

1. Moreau, *A Memorial,* 36; Freeman 2:23; to Colonel William Fairfax, 23 April 1755, GWP.

2. From Dinwiddie, 23 January 1756, GWP; Orders, 17 September 1755, GWP; Flexner 1:145.

3. *Pennsylvania Gazette,* February 12, 1756 (arrival in Philadelphia), February 19, 1756 (departure for New York); *Boston Evening Post,* February 23, 1756 (arrival in Philadelphia); *Boston Gazette,* March 1, 1756 (arrival in Boston and reputation for military skill); *Pennsylvania Gazette,* February 23, 1756 (consulting with Governor Shirley), March 18, 1756 (arrival in Philadelphia from the northward); *New York Mercury,* February 16, 1756 (arrival in New York), March 22, 1756 (arrival in Philadelphia from the northward).

4. From Andrew Burnaby, 23 June 1760, GWP.

5. Flexner 1:145–46; J. A. Leo Lamay, *The Life of Benjamin Franklin: Soldier, Scientist, and Politician, 1748–1757,* Philadelphia: University of Pennsylvania Press (2009), 3:516.

6. Flexner 1:145–47; Paul Leicester Ford, *Washington and the Theatre,* New York: Dunlap Society (1899), 15, 17; Ferling, *The Ascent of George Washington,* 31.

7. Dinwiddie to William Shirley, 24 January 1756, in *Dinwiddie Records* 328–29; Knollenberg, *George Washington, The Virginia Period,* 48.

8. *New York Mercury,* May 24, 1756; *Boston Gazette,* May 31, 1756.

9. To Robert Hunter Morris, 9 April 1756, GWP; Horatio Sharpe to William Shirley, 10 April 1756, in William Hand Browne, ed., *Correspondence of Governor Horatio Sharpe,* Baltimore: Maryland Historical Society (1888), 1:389; Franklin to Deborah Franklin, 25 March 1756, PBF; Lamay, *Benjamin Franklin,* 523; Longmore, *The Invention of George Washington,* 38.

10. From Adam Stephen, 29 March 1756, GWP; to Dinwiddie, 7 April 1756, GWP; *New York Mercury,* May 3, 1756; *Boston Evening-Post,* May 10, 1756; *New York Mercury,* May 17, 1756; Freeman 2:150.

11. To Dinwiddie, 7 April 1756, GWP; to John Robinson, 7 April 1756, GWP.

12. To Dinwiddie, 7 April 1756, GWP; Freeman 2:171–72, 2:181. Stephen also criticized the proposed chain of forts. From Stephen, 1 August 1756, GWP.

13. To Dinwiddie, 16 April 1756, GWP; to John Robinson, 16 April 1756, GWP.

14. From Dinwiddie, 8 April 1756, GWP; from William Fairfax, 14 April 1756, GWP; from John Robinson, 17 April 1756, GWP.

15. To Dinwiddie, 18 April 1756, GWP; to Robinson, 16 April 1756, GWP; to Robinson, 18 April 1756, GWP; Lewis, *For King and Country,* 212.

16. From William Stark, 18 April 1756, GWP; Orders, 20 and 21 April 1756, GWP; Council of War, 21 April 1756, GWP.

17. To Dinwiddie, 22 April 1756, GWP; Maury, *Memoirs of a Huguenot Family,* 403 (June 15, 1756).

18. To Dinwiddie, 24 April 1756, GWP.

19. From Robinson, 3 May 1756, GWP; from Colonel William Fairfax, 13–14 May 1756, GWP.

20. Anderson, *Crucible of War,* 159; to Dinwiddie, 23 May 1756.

21. From Dinwiddie, 29 April 1756, GWP; Memorandum respecting the Militia, 1–2 May 1756, GWP; Memorandum respecting the Militia, 6, 7, 8, 9, 10, 11, and 12 May 1756, GWP; Virginia Colonial Militia Memorandum Book, April–May 1756, *GW/LOC Digital Collection,* Series 6, 11, 14, 17 (May 16, 17–18, 19); Council of War, 14–15 May 1756, GWP; to Dinwiddie, 25 June 1756, 23 May 1756, GWP; Freeman 2:194.

22. Orders, 6–8 July 1756, GWP; from Robert Stewart, 20 and 23 June, 3 July 1756, GWP; from Thomas Walker, 30 June 1756, GWP; from Colonel William Fairfax, 1 July 1756, GWP; Orders, 5–9 August 1756, GWP; from Adam Stephen, 25 July 1756, GWP; to Adam Stephen, 18 May 1756, GWP. Stephen did not explain what type of "wheeling" he administered, though the term often referred to a method of execution that entailed tying a person to a wheel and bludgeoning him or her with a club. Trina N. Seitz, "A History of Execution Methods in the United States," in Clifton D. Bryant, ed., *Handbook of Death and Dying,* Thousand Oaks: Sage Publications (2003), 1:357. Sometimes discipline worked. Upon recapturing a group of twenty militiamen who deserted in the night, Washington ordered the relatively mild sentence of twenty lashes each. The entire militia company then enlisted in the regiment, concluding that if they were going to have to serve in Winchester, they might as well be paid. To Dinwiddie, 4 August 1756, GWP.

23. To Dinwiddie, 27 April 1756, GWP; to William Cocks, 4 June 1756, GWP; to Henry Peyton, 4 June 1756, GWP.

24. Anderson, *Crucible of War,* 160; Ian K. Steele, "The Shawnees and the English: Captives and War, 1753–1765," in Barr, *The Boundaries Between Us,* 12; Ferling, "Soldiers for

Virginia," 306; Louis M. Waddell, "Defending the Long Perimeter: Forts on the Pennsylvania, Maryland and Virginia Frontier, 1755–1765," *Pennsylvania Hist.* 62:171, 177 (1995); B. Scott Crawford, "A Frontier of Fear: Terrorism and Social Tension along Virginia's Western Waters, 1742–1775," *West Virginia Hist.* 2:1, 8 (2008); Lewis, *For King and Country*, 218; *Pennsylvania Gazette*, July 1, 1756; *New York Mercury*, July 5, 1756; *Boston News-Letter*, August 12, 1756; *New York Mercury*, September 6, 1756; *Pennsylvania Gazette*, October 7, 1756; *New Hampshire Gazette*, October 28, 1756.

25. To Dinwiddie, 4 August 1756, GWP.
26. To John Robinson, 24 April 1756, GWP; Orders, 5–9 August 1756, GWP; to Peter Hog, 21 July 1756, GWP; to Robert Stewart, 22 July 1756, GWP; from Robert Stewart, 23 July 1756, GWP; Council of War, 10 July 1756, GWP; to Thomas Waggener, 13 July 1756, GWP; to Dinwiddie, 14 August 1756, GWP; to Thomas Waggener, 5 August 1756, GWP.
27. Barr, "'This Land Is Ours and Not Yours,'" in Barr, *The Boundaries Between Us*, 35; from Stephen, 1 August 1756, GWP; from Dinwiddie, 12 July 1756, GWP; from Robert Stewart, 31 July 1756, GWP; to Dinwiddie, 4 August 1756, GWP.
28. Proclamation, 15 August 1756, GWP; *Pennsylvania Gazette*, September 16, 1756; Baugh, *The Global Seven Years War*, 8.
29. From John Kirkpatrick, 22 September 1756, n. 2, GWP; Longmore, *The Invention of George Washington*, 40–41; from William Ramsay, 22 September 1756, GWP; from John Robinson, 16 November 1756, GWP; Peter R. Henriques, *Realistic Visionary: A Portrait of George Washington*, Charlottesville: University of Virginia Press (2006), 11; from Augustine Washington, 16 October 1756, GWP; Lewis, *For King and Country*, 222.
30. Hall, *Executive Journals* 6:13 (3 September 1756).
31. To Dinwiddie, 9 November 1756, GWP; Freeman 2:220; to John Robinson, 9 November 1756: GWP; see also Hall, *Executive Journals* 6:18 (14 October 1756).
32. To Henry Knox, 27 April 1787, GWP.
33. From Colonel William Fairfax, 26–27 April 1756, GWP; to Dinwiddie, 16 April 1756, GWP; Freeman 2:199.
34. From George Mercer, 17 August 1756, GWP; from Adam Stephen, 20 August 1756, GWP; Fraser, *The Washingtons: George and Martha*, 11; Freeman 2:204.
35. To John Robinson, 5 August 1756, GWP.

12. BITING THE HAND

1. To Dinwiddie, 4 and 14 August 1756, GWP; from Dinwiddie, 19 August, 30 September, and 30 October 1756, GWP; Adam Stephen's Council of War and George Washington's Comments, 30 October 1756, GWP; from Dinwiddie, 26 October 1756, GWP. Washington's evaluation of Fort Cumberland was confirmed by at least one observer, who reported that it was "so irregular that I believe trigonometry cannot give it a name. No part of it will defend the other." William A. Hunter, "Thomas Barton and the Forbes Expedition," *PMHB* 95:431, 469 (1971); to Robinson, 5 August 1756, GWP.
2. From Dinwiddie, 16 November 1756, GWP.
3. To Dinwiddie, 24 November 1756, GWP.
4. From Dinwiddie, 10 December 1756, 27 December 1756, GWP.
5. To John Robinson, 19 December 1756, GWP; to William Bronaugh, 17 December 1756, GWP.
6. To Dinwiddie, 19 December 1756, GWP.
7. Dinwiddie to Major General James Abercrombie, in *Dinwiddie Records* 2:424–25 (28 May 1756); to John Campbell, Earl of Loudoun, 25 July 1756, GWP.
8. Lord Edmond Fitzmaurice, *Life of William, Earl of Shelburne*, London, Macmillan & Co. (1875) 81; *The Autobiography of Benjamin Franklin*, Boston: Houghton Mifflin and Co.

(1888), 208; Stanley Pargellis, *Lord Loudoun in North America,* New Haven: Yale University Press (1933), 81–82.

9. To John Campbell, Earl of Loudoun, 10 January 1756, GWP; William Guthrie Sayen, "George Washington's 'Unmannerly' Behavior: The Clash Between Civility and Honor," *VMHB* 107:5, 25 (Winter 1999).

10. To James Cuninghame, 28 January 1757, GWP; from Dinwiddie, 2 February 1757, GWP. Before leaving for Philadelphia, Washington had to suppress a mutiny. He had the leaders flogged, "several severely," and imposed death penalties he lacked authority to execute. He proposed to keep the mutineers imprisoned "under apprehensions of death" before pardoning them. Dinwiddie approved his actions. To Dinwiddie, 12 January 1757, GWP; from Dinwiddie, 26 January 1757, GWP.

11. Freeman 2:235–36; Moreau, *A Memorial,* Appendix VIII; Flexner 1:173–74. Ben Franklin also was engaged with the conference in Philadelphia and likely renewed his acquaintance with Washington. From Benjamin Franklin to the Earl of Loudoun: Answers to Criticisms of the Supply Bill, 21 March 1757, PBF (editor's note).

12. To Dinwiddie, 10 March 1757, GWP; Longmore, *The Invention of George Washington,* 43–45.

13. From Colonel William Fairfax, 31 March 1757, GWP; to Dinwiddie, 2 April 1757 (and editor's note 2), GWP; from John Robinson, 3 November 1757, GWP.

14. Anderson, *Crucible of War,* 204; from Dinwiddie, 5 April 1756, 7 April 1756, GWP; Hall, *Executive Journals* 6:34–38 (4 April 1757); from Dinwiddie, 16 May 1757, GWP.

15. *Pennsylvania Gazette,* March 10, 1757; *Boston Gazette,* March 21, 1757; *New York Mercury & New York Gazette,* March 14, 1757; from George Mercer, 24 and 26 April 1757, GWP; to Dinwiddie, 24 and 30 May 1757, GWP; from Dinwiddie, 23–27 May 1757, GWP; Hall, *Executive Journals* 6:44–45 (7 May 1757); David B. Trimble, "Christopher Gist and the Indian Service in Virginia, 1757–1759," *VMHB* 64:143, 150–51, 160 (April 1956).

16. From John Dagworthy, 14 June 1757, GWP; from James Livingston, 15 June 1757, GWP; to Dinwiddie, 16 June 1757, GWP; Council of War, 16 June 1757, GWP; from John Dagworthy, 17 June 1757, GWP; to John Stanwix, 21 June 1757, GWP; to Colonel William Fairfax, 25 June 1757, GWP; to Dinwiddie, 27 June 1757, GWP; to Charles Carter, 2 July 1757, GWP; to John Stanwix, 8 July 1757, GWP; to Dinwiddie, 11 July 1757, GWP; to John Stanwix, 16 June 1757, 28 May 1757, GWP.

17. General Court-Martial, 25–26 July 1757, GWP; to John Stanwix, 15 July 1757, GWP; to Dinwiddie, 3 August 1757, GWP.

18. Memoranda, 10–29 July 1757, GWP.

19. Freeman 2:268; to Dinwiddie, 24 September 1757, GWP.

20. Warren R. Hofstra, *The Planting of New Virginia: Settlement and Landscape in the Shenandoah Valley,* Baltimore: Johns Hopkins University Press (2004), 255; from Robert Stewart, 27 September 1757 (and editor's note 4), GWP; to Dinwiddie, 9 October 1757, GWP; from Gabriel Jones, 9 October 1757, GWP; to Dinwiddie, 5 October 1757, GWP.

21. To John Robinson, 10 June 1757, GWP; to Dinwiddie, 11 July 1757.

22. To Dinwiddie, 10 and 11 July 1757, GWP; from Dinwiddie, 13 and 17 July 1757, GWP; from Dinwiddie, 17 July 1757, GWP; to Dinwiddie, 10 June 1757, GWP; from Dinwiddie, 24 June 1756, GWP; from Dinwiddie, 13 August 1757, GWP.

23. To Dinwiddie, 27 August 1757, GWP; from Dinwiddie, 2 September 1757, GWP.

24. To Dinwiddie, 17 September 1757, GWP.

25. From Dinwiddie, 24 September 1757, GWP; to Dinwiddie, 5 October 1757, GWP.

26. From Dinwiddie, 19 October 1757, GWP; to Dinwiddie, 24 October 1757, GWP.

27. To Richard Washington, 15 April 1757, GWP; to Anthony Bacon & Co., 10 September 1757, GWP; to Richard Washington, 10 September 1757, GWP; Robert F. Dalzell Jr. and Lee Baldwin Dalzell, *George Washington's Mount Vernon,* New York: Oxford University Press (2000), 40–42.

13. NEW PATHS

1. Ward, "Fighting the 'Old Women,'" 315–16, 318; Ferling, *Ascent of George Washington*, 33.
2. Flexner 1:192–93.
3. Soltow, *The Economic Role of Williamsburg*, 6, 7, 14; from Robert Carter Nicholas, 5 January 1758, GWP; Fraser, *The Washingtons*, 24–25; Joseph E. Fields, *Worthy Partner*, 3–7; from Robert Carter Nicholas, 23 January 1756, GWP.
4. To Nelly Custis, 16 January 1795, GWP.
5. As the historian Edmund Morgan wrote of Virginians generally, "Though marriage was supposed to be connected somehow with love, it was also an investment, and anyone who entered upon it with a good share of capital was expected to take care that his partner should also contribute a proper share." Edmund S. Morgan, *Virginians at Home: Family Life in the Eighteenth Century*, Williamsburg: Colonial Williamsburg (1952), 31.
6. Helen Bryan, *Martha Washington: First Lady of Liberty*, New York: John Wiley & Sons (2002), 40; Keller, *Biography in Social Dance*, 15; Martha Washington to Anna Bassett, 1 June 1760, reprinted in Charles Moore, "Washington's Family Life at Mount Vernon," in *Daughters of the American Revolution Magazine* 50:288, 294 (May 1923); Invoice to Robert Cary & Co., 10 July 1773, GWP. Martha had another suitor, Charles Carter of Cleve (Fraser, *The Washingtons*, 26), but he may have been disqualified in Martha's mind because he had a dozen children from earlier marriages. Brady, *Martha Washington*, 5.
7. Martha Custis to Robert Cary & Co., 20 August 1757, in Fields, *Worthy Partner*, 5; Martha Custis to John Hanbury & Co., 20 August 1758, in Fields, *Worthy Partner*, 6; from John Mercer to Martha Custis, 24 April 1758, 21 October 1758, in Fields, *Worthy Partner*, 39, 54; and 61–76 (inventories of estates).
8. From Robert Stewart, 24 November 1757, GWP; from Nathaniel Thompson, 20 February 1758, GWP.
9. Titus, *The Old Dominion at War*, 120; Flexner 1:193–95.
10. Freeman 2:306; Baugh, *The Global Seven Years War*, 358; Burton K. Kummerow, "Two Roads: The Race for the Forks of the Ohio and the Future of America," *Western Pennsylvania Hist.* (Winter 2008–2009), 38, 41; Lengel, *General George Washington*, 69.
11. Pitt to Governors of Massachusetts, et al., December 30, 1757, in Gertrude Selwyn Kimball, ed., *Correspondence of William Pitt*, New York: The Macmillan Co. (1906) 1:136–37; Pitt to Governors of Pennsylvania, et al., December 30, 1757, in Kimball, *Correspondence of Pitt*, 1:140–42.
12. Freeman 2:309; McIlwaine, *Journals of the House of Burgesses, 1755–58*, 8:503 (7 April 1758) and 8:506 (12 April and 2 June 1758); Hall, *Executive Journals* 6:96–99 (2 June 1758).
13. Baugh, *The Global Seven Years War*, 321, 333.
14. To John Stanwix, 10 April 1758, GWP; to Thomas Gage, 12 April 1758, GWP.

14. BACK INTO THE WOODS

1. Forbes to Pitt, 20 October 1758, in Irene Stewart, ed., *Letters of General John Forbes relating to the Expedition Against Fort Duquesne in 1758*, Pittsburgh: Colonial Dames of America (1927), 59; Kummerow, "Two Roads," 38; Henry Bouquet to John Forbes, 11 June 1758, in Stevens, *Bouquet Papers* 2:74; Shannon, *Iroquois Diplomacy*, 158.
2. Forbes to Bouquet, 27 June 1758, in Stevens, *Bouquet Papers* 2:136; Bouquet to Forbes, 21 June 1758, in Stevens, *Bouquet Papers* 2:120; *New Hampshire Gazette*, July 14, 1758; *Boston Gazette* and *Boston Evening Post*, July 10, 1758.
3. William A. Hunter, "Thomas Barton and the Forbes Expedition," *PMHB* 95:431, 448–50 (1971); Bouquet to Forbes, 21 June 1758, in Stevens, *Bouquet Papers* 2:125; to Bouquet,

3 July 1758, 13 July 1758, GWP; Preston, "'Make Indians of Our White Men,'" 293; to John Blair, 4–10 May 1758, GWP; from John Blair, 24 May 1758, GWP; Lewis, *For King and Country,* 246; from Thomas Waggener, 10 May 1758, GWP; to John Forbes, 19 June 1758, GWP.

4. Anderson, *Crucible of War,* 233; Bouquet to Forbes, 11 June 1758, in Stevens, *Bouquet Papers* 2:73; Forbes to Bouquet, 10 June 1758, in Stevens, *Bouquet Papers* 2:64; Forbes to Bouquet, 14 July 1758, in Stevens, *Bouquet Papers* 2:207; Bouquet to Forbes, 26 June 1758, in Stevens, *Bouquet Papers* 2:97; Bouquet to Forbes, 14 June 1758, in Stevens, *Bouquet Papers* 2:88; Bouquet to Forbes, 15 July 1758, in Stevens, *Bouquet Papers* 2:215; Bouquet to Forbes, 21 July 1758, in Stevens, *Bouquet Papers* 2:253.

5. Richard Peters to Forbes, 12 July 1758, in Stevens, *Bouquet Papers* 2:197; "Indian Conference," 11 July 1758, in Stevens, *Bouquet Papers* 2:187; Hugh Cleland, *George Washington in the Ohio Valley,* Pittsburgh: University of Pittsburgh Press (1955), 189–90; Forbes to Bouquet, 18 August 1758, in James, *Forbes Writings,* 180–82; Forbes to Pitt, 6 September 1758, in James, *Forbes Writings,* 202–6; Forbes to the Shawnees and Delawares, 19 November 1758, in James, *Forbes Writings,* 216; Anderson, *Crucible of War,* 270–71; Trimble, "Christopher Gist and the Indian Service in Virginia, 1757–1759," 143, 163; Calloway, *The Indian World of George Washington,* 146.

6. To Henry Bouquet, 16 July 1758, GWP; Bouquet to Forbes, 31 July 1758, in Stevens, *Bouquet Papers* 2:290; Bouquet to Forbes, 11 July 1758, in Stevens, *Bouquet Papers* 2:179 ("this is a matter of politics between one province and another"); Bouquet to Forbes, 31 July 1758, in Stevens, *Bouquet Papers* 2:290 (Bouquet mistrusts Pennsylvania official who claims road is easy).

7. Baugh, *The Global Seven Years War,* 357; William H. Shank, *Indian Trails to Superhighways,* York, PA: American Canal & Transportation Center (1988), 16; Forbes to William Pitt, 10 July 1758, in Stewart, *Forbes Letters,* 24; Forbes to Bouquet, 6 July 1758, in Stevens, *Bouquet Papers* 2:163.

8. Bouquet to Forbes, 11 July 1758, in Stevens, *Bouquet Papers* 2:182; Bouquet to Forbes, 21 July 1758, in Stevens, *Bouquet Papers* 2:251; Forbes to Pitt, 6 September 1758, in James, *Forbes Writings,* 202.

9. Freeman 2:326; to Henry Bouquet, 25 July 1758, GWP; Bouquet to Forbes, 31 July 1758, in Stevens, *Bouquet Papers* 2:291.

10. To Bouquet, 2 August 1758, GWP; to Francis Halkett, 2 August 1758, GWP.

11. To Bouquet, 6, 13, and 28 August 1758, GWP: Forbes to Bouquet, 9 August 1758, in James, *Forbes Writings,* 171; Forbes to Abercromby, 11 August 1758, in James, *Forbes Writings,* 173; to Bouquet, 28 August 1758, GWP; Forbes to Bouquet, 23 September 1758, in James, *Forbes Writings,* 219; John Armstrong to Richard Peters, 3 October 1758, in *Pennsylvania Archives,* 1st Series, 3:551–52 (Washington "obstinate" in opposing route decision).

12. Stephen to Bouquet, 10 August 1758, in Stevens, *Bouquet Papers* 2:349; Stephen to Bouquet, 12 August 1758, in Stevens, *Bouquet Papers* 2:361; Stephen to Bouquet, 18 August 1758, in Stevens, *Bouquet Papers* 2:386; Bouquet to James Sinclair, 9 September 1758, in Stevens, *Bouquet Papers* 2:482; Harry Gordon to Bouquet, 9 September 1758, in Stevens, *Bouquet Papers* 2:487; Bouquet to Forbes, 11 September 1758, in Stevens, *Bouquet Papers* 2:492; Bouquet to Burd, 12 October 1758, in Stevens, *Bouquet Papers* 2:551.

13. Baugh, *The Global Seven Years War,* 369–70; Forbes to Bouquet, 23 July 1758, in Stevens, *Bouquet Papers* 2:265.

14. To Francis Fauquier, 5 August 1758, 2 September 1758, GWP; to John Robinson, 1 September 1758, GWP; to Francis Fauquier, 2 September 1758, GWP; Knollenberg, *The Virginia Period,* 66. Virginia's Executive Council specifically approved Washington's opposition to the Pennsylvania route. Minutes of 17 August 1758, in Hall, *Executive Journals* 6:108.

15. To Richard, 1749–1750, GWP; to Dinwiddie, 8 September 1756, GWP; to John Augustine Washington, 28 May 1755, GWP; Dorothy Twohig, "The Making of George Washington," in Hofstra, *George Washington and the Virginia Backcountry*, 14–15; Philyaw, *Virginia's Western Visions*, 43; John C. Crone, *George Washington's Election to the Virginia House of Burgesses, July 24, 1758, Winchester-Frederick County, Virginia*, Mount Vernon: Frederick W. Smith Library for the Study of Mount Vernon (2018), 18, 44. Frederick County in 1758 included what are now Clarke, Warren, Shenandoah, and Page Counties in Virginia and Berkeley, Jefferson, and Morgan Counties in West Virginia. Barton, "The First Election of Washington," 116.

16. From Gabriel Jones, 6 July 1758, GWP; Longmore, *The Invention of George Washington*, 57–59; Freeman 2:318; Hofstra, *The Planting of New Virginia*, 240; Christopher Hendricks, *The Backcountry Towns of Colonial Virginia*, Knoxville: University of Tennessee Press (2006), 88, 91; Robert D. Mitchell, "'Over the Hills and Far Away': George Washington and the Changing Virginia Backcountry," in Hofstra, *George Washington and the Virginia Backcountry*, 75.

17. Sydnor, *Gentlemen Freeholders*, 68–69; Brown, *Virginia Baron*, 143; from Gabriel Jones, 6 July 1758, GWP; from John Kirkpatrick, 6 July 1758, GWP; from James Wood, 7 July 1758, GWP; from Robert Rutherford, 20 July 1758, GWP; from Charles Smith, 20 July 1758.

18. To Henry Bouquet, 19 July 1758, GWP; from James Glen, 19 July 1758, GWP; from Adam Stephen, 19 July 1758, GWP; to Henry Bouquet, 21 July 1758, GWP.

19. From Charles Smith, 26 July (with enclosures) and 24 July 1758, GWP; to James Wood, 28 July 1758, GWP. Gabriel Jones lost his own House seat from Augusta County while he was in Winchester supporting Washington. To Gabriel Jones, 29 July 1758, GWP; Enclosure V to letter from Charles Smith, 26 July 1758, GWP; Longmore, *The Invention of George Washington*, 60; Sydnor, *Gentlemen Freeholders*, 68–69; from Gabriel Jones, 24 July 1758, GWP; from Charles Smith, 26 July 1758, GWP; from John McNeill, 24 July 1758, GWP; from Thomas Walker, 24 July 1758, GWP; from George William Fairfax, 25 July 1758, GWP; from Robert Stewart, 25 July 1758, GWP.

15. THE PUSH TO FORT DUQUESNE

1. Hunter, "Thomas Barton," 442; Hugh Mercer to Colonel Henry Bouquet, 4 June 1758, in Stevens, *Bouquet Papers* 2:34; Captain James Shippen to Richard Peters, 16 August 1758, *Pennsylvania Archives* 3:510, 461–62; *Connecticut Gazette*, July 22, 1758; *New London Summary*, September 29, 1758; *New York Gazette*, October 16, 1758; *Newport Mercury*, October 17, 1758; *Pennsylvania Gazette*, November 30, 1758; *Boston Gazette*, December 11, 1758; Bouquet to Forbes, 31 July 1758, in Stevens, *Bouquet Papers* 2:292–93; Bouquet to Forbes, 20 October 1758, in Stevens, *Bouquet Papers* 2:578; Bouquet to Forbes, 7 June 1758, in Stevens, *Bouquet Papers* 2:47; Forbes to Pitt, 20 October 1758, in James, *Forbes Writings*, 59.

2. Grant to Forbes, 14 September 1758, in Stevens, *Bouquet Papers* 2:499; Bouquet to Forbes, 17 September 1758, in Stevens, *Bouquet Papers* 2:517; Forbes to Bouquet, 23 September 1758, in Stevens, *Bouquet Papers* 2:535; Forbes to Abercromby, 8 October 1758, in James, *Forbes Writings*, 225; to George William Fairfax, 25 September 1758, GWP; to Francis Fauquier, 25 September 1758, GWP; Freeman 2:341–47; Anderson, *Crucible of War*, 272–74.

3. To Francis Fauquier, 5 November 1758, GWP; Forbes to Bouquet, 25 October 1758, in Stevens, *Bouquet Papers* 2:585; to Bouquet, 6 November 1758, GWP.

4. Council of War, 11 November 1758, in Stevens, *Bouquet Papers* 2:600.

5. Lengel, *General George Washington,* 75; Freeman 2:357–58; Anderson, *Crucible of War,* 282; *New York Gazette,* December 4, 1758; *Boston Gazette,* December 11, 1758. Decades later, Washington claimed that he stopped the carnage between the Virginia forces by stepping between the two lines of soldiers and knocking their muskets up. No account corroborates that assertion. Zagarri, *Humphreys,* 21–22; Cleland, *George Washington in the Ohio Valley,* 217–18. Another account attributes the heroics to Captain Thomas Bullitt, and appears in a memoir of Bullitt's nephew, which also was composed much later. Thomas W. Bullitt, *My Life at Oxmoor,* Louisville: John Morton & Co. (1911), 3. There is little basis for choosing between the accounts. Both men may have intervened to stop the withering cross fire.

6. Forbes to Abercrombie, 17 November 1757, in James, *Forbes Writings,* 255; Calloway, *The Shawnees,* 29; Shannon, *Iroquois Diplomacy,* 131; Lengel, *General George Washington,* 75–76; Anderson, *Crucible of War,* 282.

7. To John Forbes, 15 and 17 November 1758, GWP; from Henry Bouquet, 16 November 1758, GWP; Bouquet to William Allen, 25 November 1758, in Stevens, *Bouquet Papers* 2:610; Orderly Book, 24 November 1758, GWP. On November 16, two weeks before the Virginia enlistments would expire, Washington implausibly suggested to Forbes that they still might consider using Braddock's road. To John Forbes, 16 November 1758, GWP. If Forbes replied, his reply did not survive.

8. To Francis Fauquier, 28 November 1758, GWP; Forbes to Abercromby and Amherst, November 26, 1758, in James, *Forbes Writings,* 262; *Pennsylvania Gazette,* December 14, 1758.

9. Bouquet to Colonel John Stanwix, 25 November 1758, in Stevens, *Bouquet Papers* 2:609; to Francis Fauquier, 2 and 9 December 1758, GWP.

10. *Pennsylvania Gazette,* December 14, 1758.

11. Robert Munford to Theodorick Bland Jr., 6 July 1758, in Charles Campbell, ed., *The Bland Papers,* Petersburg, VA: Edmund & Julian Ruffin (1840), 9–10; Address from the Officers of the Virginia Regiment, 31 December 1758, GWP; from George Washington to the Officers of the Virginia Regiment, 10 January 1759, GWP.

12. Orders, 8 January 1756, GWP; William Guthrie Sayen, "A Compleat Gentleman": The Making of George Washington, 1732–1775, PhD Thesis, University of Connecticut (1998), 127. Sayen notes that Washington's commitment to merit-based appointments was sorely tried when Colonel Fairfax asked that his two younger sons, Bryan and William, be commissioned as lieutenants in the regiment. Such patronage appointments were contrary to Washington's principles, but he owed the Fairfaxes so much. After receiving five letters from Colonel Fairfax on behalf of Bryan, Washington finally appointed the young man, passing over others, only to have Bryan resign from the regiment by the end of 1756. Colonel Fairfax then began campaigning for an appointment for his son William. From Colonel Fairfax, 17 July 1757, GWP. Washington delayed responding until Colonel Fairfax's death, when Washington asked Governor Dinwiddie to make the appointment of William Fairfax. For Washington to make the appointment himself, he explained, "will occasion great confusion in the corps, and bring censure on me; for the officers will readily conceive, that my friendship and partiality to the family were the cause of it." To Dinwiddie, 17 September 1757, GWP; Sayen, "A Compleat Gentleman," 128–29.

13. Freeman 2:377; Higginbotham, *American Military Tradition,* 34–37. Washington's paired traits of sensitivity to criticism and yearning for high reputation were by no means unique in his era. As one scholar wrote of Virginia luminary Landon Carter, "Respect and attention sustained him," but he suffered from an "extreme sensitivity to criticism." Jack P. Greene, *Landon Carter: An Inquiry into the Personal Values and Social Imperatives of the Eighteenth-Century Virginia Gentry,* Charlottesville: Dominion Books (1965), 75.

14. Anderson, *Crucible of War,* 291–92; Zagarri, *Humphreys,* 21,

15. A recent book takes a contrary view, arguing that Washington in the Continental Army preferred to promote aristocrats (William Alexander, who called himself Lord Stirling, is the example), and passed over talented roughnecks (Daniel Morgan is the example cited). Robert L. O'Connell, *Revolutionary: George Washington at War,* New York: Random House (2019), xxv. Alexander was a competent general whose heroism arguably prevented a total catastrophe at the Battle of Long Island in 1776. Lengel, *General George Washington,* 142–47. Washington's decision not to promote Morgan in 1779, according to Morgan's biographer, was based on the commander's policy of promoting strictly on the basis of seniority, not because of disdain for the less wealthy. Albert Louis Zambone, *Daniel Morgan: A Revolutionary Life,* Yardley, PA: Westholme (2018), 192. Indeed, Washington promoted many officers of humble or modest backgrounds, including Alexander Hamilton, Henry Knox, and Nathanael Greene.
16. To Adam Stephen, 20 July 1776, GWP.
17. James Maury letters, 9 August 1755 and 10 January 1756, in Maury, *Memoirs of a Huguenot Family,* 382–84, 396.

16. WASHINGTON IN LOVE

1. Cash Accounts, December 1758, January 1759, GWP; 1758–1759 Memorandum, GWP.
2. Morgan, *Virginians at Home,* 39–40.
3. To Sarah Cary Fairfax, 14 May 1755, GWP; to Sarah Fairfax Carlyle, 7 June 1755, GWP; to Sarah Cary Fairfax, 13 February 1758, and note 1, GWP. In early March, Washington forwarded to Sally a letter from her husband in London; in March, he advised her that he was leaving for Williamsburg and offered to carry to the capital any letters she or others at Belvoir wished to send, or to perform other errands there for them. To Sarah Cary Fairfax, 4 March 1758, GWP.
4. The possibility that Washington was referring to a love for some other woman seems small, in view of the several references to Sally, along with lack of other candidates.
5. Flexner 1:197–204; Chernow, 83–86.
6. To John Augustine Washington, 28 May 1755, GWP; Don Higginbotham, "George Washington and Three Women," in Harvey and O'Brien, *George Washington's South,* 132. A year before his death, Washington wrote again to Sally, who had long lived in England and had been widowed many years before. He told her that he had never "been able to eradicate from my mind, the recollection of those happy moments—the happiest of my life—which I have enjoyed in your company." To Sarah Cary Fairfax, 16 May 1798, GWP. Though a statement of his great affection for Sally, the letter does not confirm a romantic attachment, but reflected his affection for the entire Fairfax clan and nostalgia for youthful days. Indeed, he used virtually the same words more than a decade before in a letter to Sally's husband. Having viewed Belvoir in ruins, he then wrote to George William, "When I considered that the happiest moments of my life had been spent there . . . I was obliged to fly from them." To George William Fairfax, 27 February 1785, GWP.
7. Late in life, advising his step-granddaughter on matters of the heart, Washington acknowledged, "Love is a mighty pretty thing; but like all other delicious things, it is cloying." To Eleanor Parke Custis, 14 September 1794, GWP. That statement might be construed as one of regret at having indulged the delicious thing with Sally, or satisfaction at not having done so.
8. Twohig, "The Making of George Washington," in Hofstra, *George Washington and the Virginia Backcountry,* 8; Higginbotham, "George Washington and Three Women," 128; to Anna Boudinot Stockton, 2 September 1783, GWP.

9. One ambitious author attempted to gather anecdotes of Washington's wit into a single volume. The slender production relies heavily on a few unsourced bon mots that emerged at least a half century after Washington's death. P. M. Zall, *George Washington Laughing*, Richmond: Archon Books (1989). A few letters have survived in which Washington wrote in a jocular vein—to his brother-in-law upon the birth of a child, to a cabinet officer and former aide in the year of his death. To Burwell Bassett, 8 August 1762, GWP; to James McHenry, 11 August 1799, GWP. His humor in those letters was broad and high-spirited. They have a spontaneity and genuineness that the letters to Sally Fairfax lack entirely.

10. Higginbotham, "Three Women," 127–28; to Sarah Cary Fairfax, 7 June 1755, GWP.

11. McIlwaine, *Journals of the House of Burgesses, 1758–1761*, 10:55–56, 10:66–67. A story of the House resolution honoring Washington is sometimes told. Supposedly when Washington rose to acknowledge the resolution, he was so tongue-tied that Speaker Robinson leaned forward and said he should resume his seat: "Your modesty is equal to your valor, and that surpasses the power of any language that I possess." The tale, however, is a hearsay account that passed through several mouths before being written down in 1816, sixty years later. Accordingly, its provenance is doubtful despite frequent repetition. Freeman 3:7 note 11.

12. Mary Washington to Joseph Ball, 26 July 1759, Frank M. Etting collections, Historical Society of Pennsylvania.

13. Ruth Wallis, "The Glory of Gravity—Halley's Comet 1759," *Annals of Science* 41:279, 283 (1984); Invoice to Robert Cary & Co., 20 September 1759, GWP.

PART II

1. William S. Baker, ed., *Early Sketches of George Washington*, Philadelphia: J. B. Lippincott Co. (1893), 26–27.

17. THE NEW LIFE

1. One leading biographer dismissed Washington's life between the French and Indian War and the Revolution as the experiences of "a planter whose public service compassed nothing larger than membership in the House of Burgesses. . . . What he was when he concluded his service under Forbes, he was when he began the desperate game against Gage and Howe in front of Boston." The emergence of Washington's leadership skills to that writer was "a mystery . . . beyond documentary explanation." Freeman 1:xv; 3:xiii. The most prominent Washington biography in this century devotes roughly 10 percent of its length to this critical period. Chernow, 97–189. Another biographer has recognized that this period is key to understanding Washington because it brought not only "emotional maturation" but also "increasing political sophistication." Longmore, *The Invention of George Washington*, 56.

2. Martha Washington to Anna Marie Bassett, 28 August 1762, in Fields, *Worthy Partner*, 147; Martha Washington to Margaret Green, 29 September 1760, in Fields, *Worthy Partner*.

3. To Jonathan Boucher, 5 June 1771, GWP.

4. To John Mercer, 20 April 1759, GWP; Knollenberg, *George Washington: The Virginia Period*, 82.

5. Freeman 3:36; Mary A. Stephenson, "Custis Square Historical Report, Block 4 Lot 1–8," Williamsburg: Colonial Williamsburg Foundation Library (1990), 24–28.

6. Jack P. Greene estimated that the gentry were 2 to 5 percent of the white population, with about forty interrelated families at its top. Jack P. Greene, *Negotiated Authorities: Essays in Colonial Political and Constitutional History*, Charlottesville: University Press of

Virginia (1994), 262. As one historian noted, Virginia showed a "firm attachment to government of the rich, the well-born, and the able." Sydnor, *Gentlemen Freeholders*, 2–3; Griffith, *Virginia House of Burgesses*, 71.

7. Carl Bridenbaugh, *Seat of Empire: The Political Role of Eighteenth-Century Williamsburg,* Williamsburg: Colonial Williamsburg (1958), 24–25; William C. Ewing, *The Sports of Colonial Williamsburg,* Richmond: The Dietz Press (1937), 3.

8. "Journal of a French Traveller in the Colonies, 1765, I," *American Hist. Rev.* 26:726, 742 (1921); Zagarri, *Humphreys,* 60.

9. Fauquier to Board of Trade, 10 April 1759, in George Henkle Reese, ed., *The Official Papers of Francis Fauquier, Lieutenant Governor of Virginia, 1758–1768,* Charlottesville: University Press of Virginia (1980) 1:205; Fauquier to Board of Trade, 12 May 1761, in Reese, *Fauquier Papers* 2:525; Edmund Randolph, *History of Virginia,* Charlottesville: University Press of Virginia (1970), 174.

10. Stanley Pargellis, "The Procedure of the Virginia House of Burgesses," *WMQ* 7:73, 86 (1927); Randolph, *History of Virginia,* 173–74; Jack P. Greene, ed., *The Diary of Colonel Landon Carter of Sabine Hall, 1752–1778,* Richmond: Virginia Historical Society (1987), 82–85; Jack P. Greene, "The Attempt to Separate the Offices of Speaker and Treasurer in Virginia, 1758–1766," *VMHB* 71:11, 16 (1963); Rhys Isaac, *Landon Carter's Uneasy Kingdom: Revolution and Rebellion on a Virginia Plantation,* New York: Oxford University Press (2004), 124.

11. Sydnor, *Gentlemen Freeholders,* 98; McIlwaine, *Journals of the House of Burgesses, 1758–1761,* 9:57 (23 February 1759); Executive Council minutes, 5 March 1759, in Hall, *Executive Journals* 6:131–32; Bridenbaugh, *Seat of Empire,* 34.

12. Pargellis, "The Procedure of the Virginia House of Burgesses," 7:73, 74–75; McIlwaine, *Journals of the House of Burgesses, 1758–1761,* 9:57 (23 February 1759).

13. Bridenburgh, *Seat of Empire,* 36–38 ("the most luscious political plums fell to relatives and connections of the Robinson-Randolph interest"); Robert Detweiler, "Political Factionalism and the Geographic Distribution of Standing Committee Assignments in the Virginia House of Burgesses, 1730–1776," *VMHB* 80:267, 273 (July 1972). One scholar ranked the influence of all members of the House over a fifty-five-year period and found that well over half of the most influential members each owned more than 10,000 acres. Jack P. Greene, "Foundations of Political Power in the Virginia House of Burgesses, 1720–1775," *WMQ* 15:485, 487 (1959).

14. McIlwaine, *Journals of the House of Burgesses, 1758–1761,* 9:79 (6 March 1759).

15. To Bushrod Washington, 10 November 1787, GWP.

16. Freeman 3:8; McIlwaine, *Journals of the House of Burgesses 1758–1761* 9:81 (7 March 1759), 9:99 (17 March 1759), 9:110 (28 March 1759), 9:125 (10 April 1759), 9:128 (14 April 1759), 9:71 (28 February 1759), 9:81 (7 March 1759), 9:92 (14 March 1759), 9:113 (2 April 1759); Pargellis, "The Procedure of the Virginia House of Burgesses (concluded)," *WMQ* 7:143, 151 (1927); Hening, *Statutes at Large,* 7:315–16 (Winchester's boundaries), and 7:283–85 (peddler regulation). Robert Carter Nicholas handled the legislation extending the boundaries of Winchester, while Benjamin Harrison handled the peddler legislation.

17. Hening, *Statutes at Large,* 7:265–74 ("An Act for reducing the several acts made for laying a duty upon liquors, into one Act").

18. To John Parke Custis, 28 February 1781, GWP.

18. TO MOUNT VERNON

1. To John Alton, 5 April 1759, GWP; "Cash Accounts," April 1759, note 4, GWP.

2. Dalzell and Dalzell, *George Washington's Mount Vernon,* 30, 40–43.

3. From George William Fairfax, 25 July 1758, 1 September 1758, GWP; from John Patterson, 13 August 1758, 15 September 1758, GWP; from Humphrey Knight, 2 September 1758, GWP. In the nearly six years since Lawrence's death, Mount Vernon had suffered from neglect. Dalzell and Dalzell, *George Washington's Mount Vernon,* 50–52, 57.

4. From Andrew Burnaby, 4 January 1760, GWP.

5. To Richard Washington, 20 September 1759, GWP.

6. Abigail Adams to Mary Cranch, 12 July 1789, in Stewart Mitchell, ed., *New Letters of Abigail Adams, 1788–1801,* Boston: Houghton Mifflin Co. (1947), 15; Martha Dangerfield Bland to Frances Bland Randolph, 12 April 1777, in *Proceedings of the New Jersey Hist. Soc.* (July 1933), 152; Nathanael Greene to Catharine Greene, 8 April 1777, in Richard Showman, ed., *The Papers of Nathanael Greene,* Chapel Hill: University of North Carolina Press (2015) 2:54; Lafayette to Adrienne de Noailles de Lafayette, 6 January 1778, in Stanley Izderda, ed., *Lafayette in the Age of American Revolution,* Ithaca: Cornell University Press (1977) 1:225; from Lund Washington, 30 March 1767, GWP (extra note added by Martha).

7. Hunter Dickinson Farish, ed., *Journal and Letters of Philip Vickers Fithian, 1773–1774,* (1943), Princeton: The University Library (1900), 32–25, 177–78; Isaac, *The Transformation of Virginia,* 74–75, 83–85; Tillson Jr., *Accommodating Revolutions,* 19; Helen Bryan, *Martha Washington: First Lady of Liberty,* New York: John Wiley & Sons (2002), 19.

8. Custis, *Recollections,* 45; e.g., Diary, 24–30 May and 21–22, 26 August 1768, 12–13 February and 3–9 March 1769, GWP.

9. To Burwell Bassett, 28 August 1762, GWP.

10. That tableau recalls the end of Shakespeare's *Henry IV, Part II,* when the new king denies his former boon companion, the blustery knight John Falstaff, who was not a fit comrade for a king. Helen Bryan captures this idea in her biography of Martha Washington: "George was moving up in the world, with his estate, his wallpapers, his Chippendale chairs, his rich society wife, and his grand friends, leaving Mary, her plain ways, abrupt manners, and her rigid piety to the lonely comfort of her pipe and book of sermons at Ferry Farm." *Martha Washington: First Lady of Liberty,* 125.

11. E.g., to George William Fairfax, 20 July and 29 September 1763, GWP.

12. Washington served as godfather for Bryan Fairfax's son Ferdinando, attending the ceremony with his cousin Warner Washington, who had married Hannah Fairfax, Bryan's sister. Diary, 31 May 1769, GWP.

13. Peter Henriques, "An Uneven Friendship: The Relationship Between George Washington and George Mason," *VMHB* 97:185 (1989); Freeman 3:15–16.

14. To William Peachey, 18 September 1757, GWP; from Robert Stewart, 16 January, 10 June, and 28 September 1759, 8 March 1760, GWP; to Robert Stewart, 2 May 1763, GWP; Freeman 3:90–91.

15. To George Mercer, 5 April 1775, GWP; from Robert Stewart, 19 April 1783; to Robert Stewart, 10 August 1783, GWP.

16. From Captain Robert Orme, 10 November 1755 ("my dear friend"), GWP; to Captain Francis Halkett, 12 April and 21 July 1758, GWP; from Dr. James Craik, 29 December 1758. Craik's western journeys with Washington came in fall 1770 and again in 1784. Freeman 3:256–61; Joel Achenbach, *The Grand Idea,* New York: Simon & Schuster (2002).

17. Diary, 14 June 1768, GWP ("valerian"); John Johnson to Martha Washington, 21 March 1772, in Fields, *Worthy Partner,* 150 ("light cooling food"); Bryan, *Martha Washington,* 161 (Peruvian bark); Diary, 6 June 1768, GWP ("julep"); to Jonathan Boucher, 3 February 1771 (ether), GWP; "Cash Accounts," May 1771, GWP ("Fit drops"); Diary, 16 February 1769 (iron ring), GWP; Martha Washington to Margaret Green, 26 June 1761, in Fields, *Worthy Partner,* 135 (mercury pills). For consultations with other physicians,

see Diary, 30 and 31 January 1769, 31 July 1770, GWP (Hugh Mercer of Fredericksburg); Diary, 24 November 1769 Note; 12 December 1769 Note, GWP (Dr. John de Sequeyra of London); Chernow, 154.

18. Diary, 14 June 1768, GWP (Patsy fit on trip to Belvoir); Diary, 15 April 1769, GWP (Patsy fit on excursion); Flexner 1:263; Diary, 16 July 1772, GWP (Patsy at a ball in Alexandria); Diary, 20 September 1768, GWP (Patsy at theater in Alexandria); Diary, 26–27 February 1768, GWP; Martha Washington to Mrs. Shelbury, 10 August 1764, GWP (specifying goods for Miss Custis at age nine).

19. James Reid, "The Religion of the Bible and the Religion of King William County Compared," in Richard Beale David, ed., *The Colonial Virginia Satirist: Mid-Eighteenth-Century Commentaries on Politics, Religion, and Society,* Philadelphia: American Philosophical Society (1967), 56.

20. To Jonathan Boucher, 30 May 1768, GWP; Tobias Lear to David Humphreys, 12 April 1791, in *The Rosenbach, Philadelphia,* Accession No. AMs 1052/18.2 (writing of the "unbounded indulgences" shown by Martha to her grandson, George Washington Parke Custis); Henriques, *Realistic Visionary,* 97

21. From Jonathan Boucher, 2 August 1768, 20 July 1769, GWP; to Jonathan Boucher, 16 December 1770, 5 June 1771, GWP.

22. To James Gildart, 20 September 1759, GWP (noting "vile impositions from the dishonesty of tradesmen"); to Robert Cary & Co., 20 September 1759, GWP (demanding a consistent commercial process or "I might possibly think myself deceived and be disgusted accordingly"); to Robert Cary & Co., 10 August 1760, GWP (unhappy with "exorbitant prices of my goods this year"); T. H. Breen, *Tobacco Culture: The Mentality of the Great Tidewater Planters on the Eve of Revolution,* Princeton: Princeton University Press (1985), 106–7. On one occasion, Washington ordered two whipsaws only to receive two dozen of them. To Robert Cary & Co., 1–5 August 1761, GWP; to Robert Cary & Co., 10 August 1760, GWP; to Robert Cary & Co., 28 September 1760.

23. Washington to Robert Cary & Co., 1 May 1759, 12 June 1759, 20 September 1759, GWP.

24. The coat of arms—two red horizontal stripes below three horizontal red stars, against a white background—is replicated on the flag of the District of Columbia.

25. From Robert Cary & Co., 6 August 1759, GWP; Hayes, *George Washington: A Life in Books,* 94–96, 100–2; Harrison, *A Powerful Mind,* 74–77.

26. Diary, 26 February, 2 March, 11 March, 18 March, 20 March 1760, GWP; Freeman 3:40–41; Ferling, *The Ascent of George Washington,* 55.

27. Flexner 1:234; "Slavery Database," posted at www.mountvernon.org. For two of Washington's slave transactions during this period, the number of slaves he acquired was not recorded, which accounts for the reference in text to "about" thirty additional slaves, based on a chart of slave acquisitions provided to the author by Mary Thompson, Research Historian, Fred W. Smith National Library, Mount Vernon; Lorena S. Walsh, "Slavery and Agriculture at Mount Vernon," in Philip J. Schwarz, *Slavery at the Home of George Washington,* Mount Vernon: Mount Vernon Ladies' Association (2001), 53.

28. To Robert Stewart, 27 April 1763, GWP.

19. MAN OF BUSINESS, MASTER OF SLAVES

1. Custis, *Recollections,* 162–67, 454.
2. Custis, *Recollections,* 169–71.
3. Breen, *Tobacco Culture,* 63.
4. Breen, *Tobacco Culture,* 45–53.

5. Flexner 1:274, 1:284; to Cary & Co., 15 November 1762, 26 April 1763, 10 August 1764, 20 September 1765, GWP; From George Gildart, 18 May 1764, GWP; Henry Wiencek, *An Imperfect God: George Washington, His Slaves, and the Creation of America*, New York: Farrar, Straus and Giroux (2004), 88; Walsh, "Slavery and Agriculture at Mount Vernon," in Schwartz, *Slavery at the Home of George Washington*, 54; Zagarri, *Humphreys*, 24. A similar transition to grain production can be seen in the records of Robert Carter III of Nomini Hall in Westmoreland County. E.g., Carter to Beverley Robinson, 18 May 1767, in Letterbooks of Robert Carter III of Nomini Hall, John D. Rockefeller Jr. Library, Williamsburg; to Edward Hunt and Sons, 29 September 1767, in Letterbooks; to James Buchanan & Co., 31 July 1768, in Letterbooks; to William Taylor, 25 September 1773, in Letterbooks; to Richard Washington, 10 August 1760, GWP; to Robert Cary & Co., 3 April 1761, 28 May 1762, GWP.

6. Breen, *Tobacco Culture*, 31, 46, 150, 185; Tillson, *Accommodating Revolutions*, 36–37; Zagarri, *Humphreys*, 24; Longmore, *The Invention of George Washington*, 84.

7. Walsh, "Slavery and Agriculture at Mount Vernon," in Schwartz, *Slavery at the Home of George Washington*, 54, 57–58; Wiencek, *Imperfect God*, 97.

8. Longmore, *The Invention of George Washington*, 77; Diary, 15, 22, and 29 September 1765, 3 February 1770 and note, 25 April 1771 and note, GWP.

9. Freeman 3:113.

10. To George Washington Parke Custis, 7 January 1798, GWP; to William Pearce, 18 December 1793, GWP.

11. To George Steptoe Washington, 5 December 1790, GWP; to John Fairfax, 1 January 1789, GWP.

12. Sayen, *"A Compleat Gentleman,"* 222–24; Diary, 14 April 1760, GWP.

13. Diary, 5 February 1760, GWP; "Spinning and Weaving Records," 1768, GWP.

14. Diary, 15 July 1769, GWP. In April 1763, Washington determined that at a Custis farm in King William County, fifteen slaves with two overseers created 190,000 corn holes and 170,000 tobacco hills. He calculated that each slave made 24,000 holes and hills, which translated to 800 plants per day for thirty days, or one per minute through a twelve-hour day, which he called "not very strenuous work for farmers." Wiencek, *An Imperfect God*, 102.

15. Walsh, "Slavery and Agriculture at Mount Vernon," in Schwartz, *Slavery at the Home of George Washington*, 57.

16. Dalzell and Dalzell, *George Washington's Mount Vernon*, 181–86.

17. Twohig, "The Making of George Washington," in Hofstra, *George Washington and the Virginia Backcountry*, 24.

18. Hirschfeld, *George Washington and Slavery*, 1; Gerald W. Mullin, *Flight and Rebellion: Slave Resistance in Eighteenth-Century Virginia*, New York: Oxford University Press (1972), 16, 24; Greene, *Colonel Landon Carter Diary*, 22 March 1770, 1:371; 14 May 1770, 1:389; to Richard Whiting, 3 March 1793, GWP; from James Hill, 5 February 1773, GWP.

19. James Oakes, *The Ruling Race: A History of American Slaveholders*, New York: W. W. Norton & Co. (1998), 15; Worthington Chauncey Ford, *Washington as an Employer and an Importer of Labor*, Brooklyn (1889), 14–15; Dalzell and Dalzell, *George Washington's Mount Vernon*, 127–30.

20. To Anthony Whiting, 2 December 1792, GWP; Dalzell and Dalzell, *George Washington's Mount Vernon*, 133, 135–36.

21. Wiencek, *An Imperfect God*, 97.

22. Isaac, *The Transformation of Virginia*, 32, 44, 48; Dalzell and Dalzell, *George Washington's Mount Vernon*, 136; Diary, 7 May 1760, GWP; from Christopher Hardwick, 18 May 1760, GWP.

23. To William Pearce, 22 March 1795, GWP.

24. Edmund S. Morgan, *The Genius of George Washington*, Washington, DC: The Society of the Cincinnati (1980), 6–7; Richard Parkinson, *A Tour in America in 1798, 1799, and 1800*, London: J. Harding & J. Murray (1805) 2:418–20; to William Pearce, 18 December 1793, GWP.

25. Mullin, *Flight and Rebellion*, 29; to William Pearce, 10 May 1795, GWP.

26. To Lawrence Lewis, 14 August 1797, GWP; to George Augustine Washington, 1 July 1787, GWP; Greene, *Colonel Landon Carter Diary* 2:755 (5 June 1773).

27. Dalzell and Dalzell, *George Washington's Mount Vernon*, 136; Mary V. Thompson, "Resisting Enslavement: The Roguest People About the House," in Susan Schoelwer, ed., *Lives Bound Together: Slavery at George Washington's Mount Vernon*, Mount Vernon: Mount Vernon Ladies' Association (2016), 70; Mullin, *Flight and Rebellion*, 61; to William Pearce, 23 November 1794, GWP; to Anthony Whiting, 3 February 1793, GWP.

28. David John Mays, *Edmund Pendleton, 1721–1803, A Biography*, Cambridge: Harvard University Press (1952) 1:43–44, 46; "Journal of a French Traveller in the Colonies, 1765, I," *Am. Hist. Rev.* 26:726, 745 (July 1921), (May 30, 1765).

29. Hening, *Statutes at Large* 6:104–12; Terry K. Dunn, *Among His Slaves: George Mason, Slavery at Gunston Hall, and the Idealism of the American Revolution*, Alexandria: Commonwealth Books of Virginia (2017), 65–66; Oakes, *The Ruling Race*, 25.

30. Hirschfeld, *George Washington and Slavery*, 37.

31. Mullin, *Flight and Rebellion*, 59; *Virginia Gazette* (Rind's), January 25, 1770; to William Stuart, Hiland Crow, and Henry McCoy, 14 July 1793, GWP; Greene, *Colonel Landon Carter Diary* 2:628 (12 September 1771). In 1775, Lund Washington feared that a runaway servant might return to Mount Vernon and incite a more general resistance. From Lund Washington, 6 November and 3 December 1775, GWP.

32. Philip D. Morgan and Michael L. Nicholls, "Slave Flight: Mount Vernon, Virginia, and the Wider Atlantic World," in Harvey and O'Brien, *George Washington's South*, 197, 200; Greene, *Colonel Landon Carter Diary* 1:290–91 (25 March 1766); Diary, 18 April 1760, GWP (return of "my negro fellow Boson who ran away"); from Lund Washington, 30 March 1767, GWP; Isaac, *Landon Carter's Uneasy Kingdom*, 7; Mullin, *Flight and Rebellion*, 34, 56, 106.

33. Diary, 18 April 1760, GWP; "Advertisement for Runaway Slaves," 11 August 1761, GWP; Diary, 2 August 1771, GWP; "Cash Accounts," 2 August 1771, GWP; *Virginia Gazette* (Dixon and Hunter), May 4, 1775; "Cash Accounts," April 1775, GWP (29 April, reward "for pursuing runaway servants"); Advertisement for runaway servants, 23 April 1775, GWP; Erica Armstrong Dunbar, *Never Caught: The Washingtons' Relentless Pursuit of Their Runaway Slave, Ona Judge*, New York: 37 Ink/Atria (2017).

34. To Joseph Thompson, 2 July 1766, GWP; "Cash Accounts," July 1772, GWP (July 23); Morgan and Nicholls, "Slave Flight," in Harvey and O'Brien, *George Washington's South*, 198.

35. Mays, *Edmund Pendleton* 1:10–11, 21; Isaac, *Transformation of Virginia*, 106.

36. "To the Overseers at Mount Vernon," 14 July 1793, GWP.

37. Mary V. Thompson, "'And Procure for Themselves a Few Amenities': Recreation & Private Enterprise in the Enslaved Community at Mount Vernon," Talk at Gunston Hall, November 9, 2006, 4 (Published in *Virginia Cavalcade* 48:183 [Autumn, 1999]); "Farm Reports, 26 November 1785–15 April 1786," note 1, GWP; to William Pearce, 18 December 1793, GWP; Jessie MacLeod, "Enslaved People of Mount Vernon—Biographies," in Schoelwer, *Lives Bound Together*, 40–41.

20. THE BACKBENCHER ADVANCES

1. Diary, 10 November 1762, 5 May 1768 and Note, 3–13 and 18 May 1769, GWP. The six-chimneys house, which featured an acclaimed garden in earlier years, was rented out to

Martha's brother for a time, then to William Byrd III, and then to a variety of less distinguished occupants. Mary A. Stephenson, "Custis Square Historical Report, Block 4 Lot 1–8," Williamsburg: Colonial Williamsburg Foundation Library (1990), 24–28.

2. Knollenberg, *George Washington: The Virginia Period*, 101. The leading student of the House of Burgesses described the process for winnowing leaders of the House, calling the chamber "the theater for political talents, and only those who turned in superb performances could expect to secure a leading role." Greene, *Negotiated Authorities*, 272–73; Longmore, *The Invention of George Washington*, 61.

3. McIlwaine, *Journals of the House of Burgesses, 1758–1761*, 9:142–43 (9 and 10 November 1759).

4. McIlwaine, *Journals of the House of Burgesses, 1758–1761*, 9:141 (8 November 1759), 9:147, 9:150 (14 November 1759), 9:147–48, 9:152 (15 November 1759); 9:143 (7 November 1759).

5. Diary, 17 and 18 May 1760, GWP; from Robert Stewart, 3 June 1760, GWP; McIlwaine, *Journals of the House of Burgesses, 1758–1761*, 9:188 (8 October 1760).

6. McIlwaine, *Journals of the House of Burgesses, 1758–1761*, 9:246 (2 April 1761), 9:236 (28 March 1761), 9:189 (9 October 1760), 9:209 (11 March 1761), 9:228 (24 March 1761), 9:241 (31 March 1761).

7. McIlwaine, *Journals of the House of Burgesses, 1758–1761*, 9:248 (7 April 1761), 9:251 (9 April 1761), 9:257 (10 April 1761).

8. McIlwaine, *Journals of the House of Burgesses, 1758–1761*, 9:223 (21 March 1761), 9:227 (24 March 1761), 9:252, 9:253 (8 April 1761), 9:257 (10 April 1761); Mays, *Edmund Pendleton* 1:153–54.

9. From Robert Stewart, 25 February 1762, 14 April 1760, GWP; Longmore, *The Invention of George Washington*, 64; from George Mercer, 17 February 1760, GWP; to Van Swearingen, 15 May 1761, note 4, GWP.

10. From Robert Stewart, 15 February 1761, GWP.

11. Freeman 3:61; Sayen, "A Compleat Gentleman," 233, Longmore, *The Invention of George Washington*, 65–66.

12. To Van Swearingen, 15 May 1761, GWP.

13. Hening, *Statutes at Large* 3:236–46 (1705 "act for regulating the elections of burgesses"); "Frederick County, Virginia, May 18, 1761, Election Poll (List of Voters)," in *GW/LOC Digital Collection*, Series 4.

14. To Richard Washington, 14 July 1761, GWP; Martha Washington to Margaret Green, 26 June 1761, in Fields, *Worthy Partner*, 135; to Andrew Burnaby, 27 July 1761, GWP, and note 7.

15. To Charles Green, 26–30 August 1761, GWP; "Cash Accounts," 1761, GWP.

16. John Pendleton Kennedy, ed., *Journals of the House of Burgesses, 1761–1765*, Richmond (1907) 10:7 (4 November 1761), 10:12 (6 November 1761), 10:23 (12 November 1761), 10:92 (15 November 1762), 10:111 (24 November 1762), 10:117 (29 November 1762), 10:165 (23 December 1762); to Peter Stover, 9 November 1761, GWP; Diary, 27, 29, 30 March and 7 April 1762, GWP; from Robert Stewart, 25 January 1762, GWP. On the session's opening day, Governor Fauquier asked the House to address a question "of a most delicate nature": Virginia's lack of currency, which was crimping economic activity. British pounds sterling were scarce, and the colony's paper money (called "emissions") was an unreliable substitute. Most merchants accepted "tobacco notes" issued by tobacco warehouses as evidence that a planter had lodged and shipped certain quantities of tobacco, but those notes also expired over time. Despite the urgency of the problem, the House did nothing. Kennedy, *Journals of the House of Burgesses, 1761–1765*, 10:65 (2 November 1762); Joseph Albert Ernst, "Genesis of the Currency Act of 1764: Virginia Paper Money and the Protection of British Investments," *WMQ* 22:33, 34–36 (1965); Jack M. Sosin, "Imperial Regulation of Colonial Paper Money, 1764–1773," *PMHB* 88:174 (1964); Freeman 1:140.

17. A shrewd French diplomat, the Duc de Choiseul, predicted that the British would soon lose North America to an internal rebellion. W. J. Eccles, "The Role of the American

Colonies in Eighteenth-Century French Foreign Policy," in W. J. Eccles, *Essays on New France,* Toronto: Oxford University Press (1987), 141–55. For the impact of the peace treaty, see Barry M. Gough, *British Mercantile Interests in the Making of the Peace of Paris, 1763: Trade, War and Empire,* Lewiston, NY: Edwin Mellen Press (1992), 88–90, 95–96; Colin G. Calloway, *The Scratch of a Pen: 1763 and the Transformation of North America,* New York: Oxford University Press (2006), 8–10, 167–68; John Shy, "The American Colonies in War and Revolution, 1748–1783," in P. J. Marshall, ed., *The Oxford History of the British Empire: The Eighteenth Century,* New York: Oxford University Press (1998), 308; Taylor, *American Revolutions,* 6; Woody Holton, "How the Seven Years' War Turned Americans into (British) Patriots," in Hofstra, *Cultures in Conflict,* 128; Gwenda Morgan, "Virginia and the French and Indian War: A Case Study of the War's Effects on Imperial Relations," *VMHB* 81:23, 24 (1973).

18. Flexner 1:278; to Cary & Co., 10 August 1764, GWP; Longmore, *The Invention of George Washington,* 72; Breen, *Tobacco Culture,* 149–50, 169.

19. Edmund S. Morgan and Helen M. Morgan, *The Stamp Act Crisis: Prologue to Revolution,* Chapel Hill: University of North Carolina Press (1953), 21–22; Calloway, *The Scratch of a Pen,* 12.

20. To Robert Stewart, 13 August 1763, GWP.

21. Calloway, *The Scratch of a Pen,* 66–67, 73; Jon W. Parmenter, "The Iroquois and the Native American Struggle for the Ohio Valley, 1754–1794," in David Curtis Skaggs and Larry L. Nelson, eds., *The Sixty Years' War for the Great Lakes, 1754–1814,* East Lansing: Michigan State University Press (2001), 109–10; Taylor, *American Revolutions,* 59–60; Robert Carter III to James Buchanan & Co., 31 December 1763, in Letterbooks of Robert Carter III; James Mercer Garnett, "The Last Fifteen Years of the House of Burgesses of Virginia, 1761–1776," *VMHB* 18:213, 18:214 (1910); Eccles, *Essays on New France,* 150; Richard White, *The Middle Ground: Indians, Empires, and Republics in the Great Lakes Region, 1650–1815,* New York: Cambridge University Press (1991), 269, 275, 288.

22. Calloway, *The Scratch of a Pen,* 92–94; Taylor, *American Revolutions,* 61; Calloway, *The Indian World of George Washington,* 180–81; Woody Holton, "The Ohio Indians and the Coming of the American Revolution in Virginia," *J. Southern Hist.* 60:453, 457 (August 1994); William E. Nelson, "Law and the Structure of Power in Colonial Virginia," *Valparaiso L. Rev.* 48:757, 877 (2014); Fauquier to Board of Trade, 13 February 1764, in *Official Papers* 3:1076–79; Hillman, *Executive Journals* 10:257 (25 May 1763).

23. Ernst, "Genesis of the Currency Act of 1764," 33; Jack M. Sosin, "Imperial Regulation of Colonial Paper Money, 1764–1773," *PMHB* 88:174 (1964); Lawrence H. Gipson, "Virginia Planter Debts Before the American Revolution," *VMHB* 69:259 (1961).

24. Hillman, *Executive Journals* 6:252 (28 April 1763); Kennedy, *Journals of the House of Burgesses, 1761–1765,* 10:171 (19 May 1763); to Robert Stewart, 2 May 1763, GWP; Morgan, "Virginia and the French and Indian War," 43–44.

25. Jonathan Boucher, *Letter from a Virginian to the Members of the Continental Congress* (1774), Evans Early American Imprint Collection (online), 8.

26. John J. Reardon, *Peyton Randolph: One Who Presided,* Durham: Carolina Academic Press (1982), 16–18; Mays, *Edmund Pendleton* 1:225–26; Greene, *Negotiated Authorities,* 265, 293, 306; Mays, *Edmund Pendleton* 1:52, 1:225, 1:228; Thomas Jefferson, *Autobiography,* 6 January 1821, PTJ; J. Keith McGaughy, *Richard Henry Lee of Virginia: A Portrait of An American Revolutionary,* Lanham, MD: Rowman & Littlefield (2004), 42–43; Pauline Maier, *The Old Revolutionaries: Political Lives in the Age of Samuel Adams,* New York: Alfred A. Knopf (1980), 164–65; Greene, *Negotiated Authorities,* 187.

27. Kennedy, *Journals of the House of Burgesses, 1761–1765,* 10:175 (21 May 1763), 10:174 (20 May 1763), 10:188–92 (28 May 1763). Having no doubt as to the course the House would follow, Washington left Williamsburg to review an investment opportunity in the Dismal

Swamp, land on Virginia's southern border that might prove not at all dismal if only the swamp could be drained. Freeman 3:94.

28. *Statutes at Large,* 4 Geo. III, c. 34; Sosin, "Imperial Regulation," 185; Fauquier to Lord Halifax, in *Official Papers* 3:1258–59 (14 June 1765); "Journal of a French Traveller in the Colonies, 1765, I," *Am. Hist. Rev.* 26:726, 743 (July 1921).

29. Emory G. Evans, "The Rise and Decline of the Virginia Aristocracy in the Eighteenth Century: The Nelsons," in Darrett B. Rutman, ed., *The Old Dominion,* Charlottesville: University Press of Virginia (1964), 68–9.

30. Fauquier to Lords of Trade, in Kennedy, *Journals of the House of Burgesses, 1761–1765,* 10:xxvi (3 November 1762); Evans, "The Rise and Decline of the Virginia Aristocracy," 68; Robert Carter III to Samuel Athawes, 21 December 1763, in Letterbooks of Robert Carter III.

31. Breen, *Tobacco Culture,* 133; "Additional Queries, with Jefferson's Answers," January–February 1786, PTJ.

32. From Bernard Moore, 29 December 1766, and note 1, GWP; Diary, 4 November 1768, 4 May 1769, 9, 14, 15, and 16 December 1769, GWP; "Cash Accounts," June 1770 (20 June); from Walter Magowan, 9 May 1773, GWP; Breen, *Tobacco Culture,* 169–70. The largest fortune in the colony, that of William Byrd III, was so dissipated that Byrd's assets were raffled off.

33. Kennedy, *Journals of the House of Burgesses, 1761–1765,* 10:203–4 (12 January 1764), 10:205–6 (13 January 1764), 10:212 (17 January 1764), 10:206–7 (14 January 1764). The semi-official *Journals of the House of Burgesses* mark Washington as not attending the January 1764 sitting of the House of Burgesses, 10:201, but that seems plainly in error. Washington wrote a letter from Williamsburg on January 22, the day after the end of the session (to Robert Cary & Co., 22 January 1764, GWP), while his expense records reflect ferry crossings on the way to Williamsburg before the session began, plus spending at "Mrs. Campbells" (the inn he frequented) and with other Williamsburg merchants. "Cash Accounts," January 1764, GWP. The attendance records reflected in the *Journals* include other errors as well.

34. Kennedy, *Journals of the House of Burgesses, 1761–1765,* 10:209 (16 January 1764), 10:213 (17 January 1764), 10:215 (18 January 1764), 10:216 (19 January 1764), 10:218 (20 and 21 January 1764); *Hening's Statutes at Large,* chapter I, 8:9. Other commissioners included Washington's brother-in-law Fielding Lewis of Fredericksburg, and Thomas Marshall, father of future Supreme Court Chief Justice John Marshall. Washington was entitled to 10 shillings a day for his work on the commission. He received £10, 10s for that work, which translates to twenty-one days, or a little more than four five-day weeks. "Cash Accounts," November 1764 (8 November), GWP; Kennedy, *Journals of the House of Burgesses, 1761–1765,* 10:247–48 (9 November 1764).

35. Kennedy, *Journals of the House of Burgesses, 1761–1765,* 10:251 (10 November 1764), 10:253 (13 November 1764).

36. Edward Hubbard to Henry Bouquet, 9 March 1759, in Stevens, *Bouquet Papers* 3:182.

37. Kennedy, *Journals of the House of Burgesses, 1761–1765,* 10:296–98 (15 December 1764).

38. Kennedy, *Journals of the House of Burgesses, 1761–1765,* 10:227 (5 October 1764); Calloway, *The Scratch of a Pen,* 11; from Robert Stewart, 14 January 1764, GWP.

39. Kennedy, *Journals of the House of Burgesses, 1761–1765,* 10:303 (18 December 1764); Jon Kukla, *Patrick Henry: Champion of Liberty,* New York: Simon & Schuster (2017), 57–59; Bridenbaugh, *Seat of Empire,* 51.

40. Taylor, *American Revolutions,* 51, 56.

41. Kennedy, *Journals of the House of Burgesses, 1761–1765,* 10:256–67 (14 November 1764); Fauquier to Board of Trade, 24 December 1764, in Kennedy, *Journals of the House of Burgesses, 1761–1765,* 10:lviii (calling the burgesses' statement indecent).

21. THE WHEEL OF HISTORY

1. Pendleton to James Madison, 21 April 1790, PJM; Fauquier to Board of Trade, 5 June 1765, in Reese, *Fauquier Papers* 3:1250; Kennedy, *Journals of the House of Burgesses, 1761–1765,* 10:358 (29 May 1765).

2. Danby Pickering, ed., *The Statutes at Large,* Cambridge, England: Joseph Bentham (1764), chapter 12, 26:180–204; Taylor, *American Revolutions,* 96; Kukla, *Patrick Henry,* 67; Morgan and Morgan, *The Stamp Act Crisis,* 21–35.

3. Taylor, *American Revolutions,* 101.

4. Kennedy, *Journals of the House of Burgesses, 1761–1765* 10:lxv (quoting account by Thomas Jefferson); Freeman 3:131. Henry recruited George Johnston of Fairfax County to propose the resolutions on the House floor. As an attorney, Johnston represented Washington in commercial disputes and was succeeded by Washington as a trustee of the town of Alexandria. From G. Johnston, 5 January 1758, 8 January 1760, GWP; Land Grant from Thomas, Lord Fairfax, 20 October 1760, note, GWP; from Augustine Washington, 16 October 1756 and note 6, GWP; Kennedy, *Journals of the House of Burgesses, 1761–1765,* 10:lxv.

5. "Journal of a French Traveller in the Colonies, 1765, I," *Am. Hist. Rev.* 26:726, 745–46 (1921); William Wirt, *The Life and Character of Patrick Henry,* Philadelphia: James Webster (1817), 65; Kennedy, *Journals of the House of Burgesses, 1761–1765,* 10:lxvi–lxvii; John Ragosta, "'Caesar had his Brutus': What Did Patrick Henry Really Say?," *VMHB* 126:282 (2018).

6. Kennedy, *Journals of the House of Burgesses, 1761–1765* 10:lxvi–lxvii; Fauquier to Board of Trade, 5 June 1765, in Kennedy, *Journals of the House of Burgesses, 1761–1765,* 10:xviii.

7. To Francis Dandridge, 20 September 1765, GWP; to Cary & Co., 20 September 1765, GWP.

8. Longmore, *The Invention of George Washington,* 79–80.

9. Edmund S. Morgan, ed., *Prologue to Revolution: Sources and Documents on the Stamp Act Crisis 1764–1766,* Chapel Hill: University of North Carolina Press (1959), 50–62; "Journal of a French Traveller in the Colonies, 1765, II," 27:74, 83, 85 (1921); Richard Henry Lee to Unnamed Person, 4 July 1765, in Ballagh, *Letters of Richard Henry Lee,* 9; Morgan and Morgan, *The Stamp Act Congress,* 151–57.

10. Morgan, *Prologue to Revolution,* 62–63; Morgan and Morgan, *The Stamp Act Crisis,* 109–10.

11. Morgan and Morgan, *The Stamp Act Crisis,* 121, 180–82, 201–2; Morgan, *Prologue to Revolution,* 114–17; Taylor, *American Revolutions,* 103; Kennedy, *Journals of the House of Burgesses, 1761–1765* 10:lxxii–lxxiv; *Virginia Gazette* (Rinds), May 16, 1766; R. H. Lee to Landon Carter, 24 February 1766, in Ballagh, *Letters of Richard Henry Lee,* 14; John C. Matthews, "Two Men on a Tax: Richard Henry Lee, Archibald Ritchie, and the Stamp Act," in Rutman, *The Old Dominion,* 103–9. A delightful rendition of the protests led by Richard Henry Lee against the Stamp Act appears in Pauline Maier's *Old Revolutionaries,* 195–97. She highlights a protest procession to a courthouse in Westmoreland County—led by Lee's slaves in costume, other slaves who were naked, plus effigies of the Virginia tax collector and British prime ministers—calling it "surely among the most bizarre of the revolutionary period."

12. "Petition of the London Merchants to the House of Commons" in Morgan, *Prologue to Revolution,* 130–31 (17 January 1766); from Capel & Osgood Hanbury, 27 March 1766, GWP; Morgan and Morgan, *The Stamp Act Crisis,* 271; Taylor, *American Revolutions,* 102; Freeman 3:155, 160–61; Richard Beeman, *Our Lives, Our Fortunes, Our Sacred Honor,* New York: Basic Books (2013), 19; *Statutes at Large* 27:19–20 (6 George III c. 12).

13. To Cary & Co., 21 July 1766, GWP.

14. *Virginia Gazette* (Purdie and Dixon), April 11, 1766; "Journal of a French Traveller in the Colonies, 1765, I" 26:84.

15. Dabney, "John Robinson," 61–62; Mays, *Edmund Pendleton* 1:152–53; Breen, *Tobacco Culture*, 189–90. The quotation from Henry's speech is based on Thomas Jefferson's account of the House debates. Jefferson to William Wirt, 14 August 1814, TJP.

16. *Virginia Gazette* (Rinds), May 16, 1766.

17. Mays, *Edmund Pendleton* 1:183–84; *Virginia Gazette* (Purdie and Dixon) (June 13 and 20, 1766) (Pendleton's notice demanding repayment by debtors), 25 July 1766 ("Philautos"); *Virginia Gazette* (Rind), September 5, 1766 (by new treasurer Robert Carter Nicholas).

18. Mays, *Edmund Pendleton* 1:185–88; Fauquier to Board of Trade, 11 May 1766, in Reese, *Fauquier Papers* 3:1359–61; *Virginia Gazette* (Purdie and Dixon), July 29, 1773.

19. Morgan and Morgan, *The Stamp Act Crisis*, 293.

20. To Cary & Co., 10 November 1773, GWP.

21. To Dinwiddie, 29 May 1754, GWP.

22. PIVOT TO FAIRFAX COUNTY

1. Ernst, "Genesis of the Currency Act of 1764," 22:76.

2. "Poll Sheet for election to House of Burgesses for Fairfax County," July 1765, GWP; to Burwell Bassett, 2 August 1765, GWP; Freeman 3:142.

3. Mays, *Edmund Pendleton* 1:19–20; Bridenbaugh, *Seat of Empire*, 11. The Truro Parish Colonial Vestry Book, available online through www.pohick.org, names the people receiving charity support and the amounts paid.

4. Isaac, *The Transformation of Virginia*, 58, 60–61; Tillson, *Accommodating Revolutions*, 46; Fithian, *Journal and Letters*, 296.

5. "Notice of Truro Parish Vestry Meeting," 20 March 1764, note, GWP; Bridenbaugh, *Seat of Empire*, 11; Rev. Philip Slaughter, *The History of Truro Parish in Virginia*, Philadelphia: George W. Jacobs & Co. (1907), 34–41; Truro Parish Colonial Vestry Book, www.pohick .org/vestrybook.html, 100–1, 108–112; Thomas M. Preisser, "Alexandria and the Evolution of the Northern Virginia Economy, 1749–1776," *VMHB* 89:282 (1981), 292–93. Washington's fellow vestrymen for the Truro church were the county's elite, including George William Fairfax, George Mason, and John West, his fellow burgess. George Johnston, the Fairfax County burgess whose resignation opened a seat for Washington, was the parish lawyer.

6. Always eager to fill in the blanks in his education, Washington assembled a respectable library of books about law, most written for non-lawyers. These included *The Justice of the Peace's Pocket Companion*, as well as *Attorney's Pocket Book* and *The Justice of the Peace and Parish Officer*. Other legal volumes at Mount Vernon were *Virginia Justice, A Complete View of British Customs*, and volumes on bankruptcy and a landlord's rights and duties. Harrison, *A Powerful Mind*, 88; Longmore, *The Invention of George Washington*, 87.

7. George Webb, *The Office and Authority of a Justice of the Peace*, Williamsburg (1736), 201.

8. Albert Ogden Porter, *County Government in Virginia: A Legislative History, 1607–1904*, New York: Columbia University Press (1947), 66–68, 96; Mays, *Edmund Pendleton* 1:52–56; Newton B. Jones, "Weights, Measures, and Mercantilism: The Inspection of Exports in Virginia, 1742–1820," in Rutman, ed., *The Old Dominion*, 122–24; Sydnor, *Gentlemen Freeholders*, 82–83. The other products subject to public inspection and approval were beef, pork, pitch, turpentine, and lumber.

9. Lydia Sparacio Bontempo, ed., *Order Book Extracts of Fairfax County, 1769–1770*, vol. 2, Berwyn Heights, MD: Antient Press (2000) (22 February 1770, 21 February 1769).

10. Bontempo, *Fairfax County Order Book, 1768–1770* 2:36–39 (18 September 1769), 2:40 (19 September 1769), 2:46–47 (17 October 1769), 2:72–74 (20 February 1770), 2:36–39 (18

September 1769), 2:44–46 (16 October 1769), 2:79–88 (22 February 1770), 2:74–78 (21 February 1769); *Fairfax County Order Book, 1770–1772*, Microfilm Reel 39, Fairfax City Regional Public Library 1, 3 (16 April 1770), 157 (16 December 1770), 312 (19 November 1771); *Fairfax County Court Order Book, 1772–1774*, Reel 39A, 90 (17 August 1772), 123, 126 (23 September 1772); Isaac, *Transformation of Virginia*, 91; Mays, *Edmund Pendleton* 1:15.

11. Nan Netherton et al., *Fairfax County, Virginia: A History,* Fairfax: Fairfax County Board of Supervisors (1978), 81–82; Isaac, *Transformation of Virginia*, 91–92; Bridenbaugh, *Seat of Empire*, 13; Nelson, "Law and the Structure of Power in Colonial Virginia," 48:817, 48:820 (2014); Albert H. Tillson, *Gentry and Country Folk on a Virginia Frontier 1740–1789*, Lexington: University Press of Kentucky (2014), 31–32; *Fairfax County Court Order Book, 1772–1774*, Microfilm Reel 39A, Fairfax City Regional Public Library, 204 (18 May 1773); *1770–1772*, Microfilm Reel 39, 317–22 (20 November 1771) (charges against tax cheats; two prosecutions for profane swearing; one for adultery). From 1770 to 1773, the court decided forty-six cases of assault and battery, while in 1770 it heard fifteen cases of selling liquor without a license; Porter, *County Government in Virginia*, 94–96.

12. Wiencek, *Imperfect God*, 128–29.

13. Wiencek, *Imperfect God*, 129–30; Bontempo, *Fairfax County Order Book* 2:90 (21 February 1769). Washington may have been familiar with a similar case in 1751 involving his older brother Austin. Austin told the Westmoreland County Court that his indentured servant Mary gave birth to a mixed-race child, Martha. The court ordered that the child Martha be indentured to Austin until her thirty-first birthday (she was four at the time). Mary ran away, but Austin recaptured her, which lengthened her servitude. She ran away again and was hauled back again, adding another four years to her contract. The daughter, Martha, was indentured, and when she had a daughter named Delphia, her daughter was bound for thirty years. Wiencek, *Imperfect God*, 55–56.

14. Bontempo, *Fairfax County Order Book* 2:25–27 (19 July 1769); Washington missed plenty of court days, but could never match Mason's absenteeism. Mason attended 3 out of 57 court days during his first term on the court; in a later term, he attended for 4 full days and fourteen partial days out of 183 court days. "No other justice," one scholar has written of Mason, "surpassed his record of nonattendance." Joseph Horrell, "George Mason and the Fairfax Court," *VMHB* 91:418, 421 (1983).

23. THE MASTER OF MOUNT VERNON

1. Diary, 30 December 1769; 2 February 1770; 1 and 22 (note) March 1770; 16, 18, 23, and 26 April 1770; 1, 2, 7, and 17 May 1770; 30 June 1770; 31 July 1770; 4 September 1770; 13 and 14 September 1770; 19 and 22 December 1770; 25, 27, and 31 January 1771; 4–6 April 1771, GWP. Flexner 1:242; Nan Netherton et al., *Fairfax County, Virginia: A History,* 80; *Fairfax County Court Order Book,* 1772–74, 158 (Microfilm Reel 39A, Fairfax City Regional Public Library).

2. E.g., Diary, 17 October 1768 (£31); 3 February 1770 (£102); 25 April 1771 (£146); 12 May 1771; 6 and 12 June 1771 (£60), GWP. "Cash Accounts," October 1771, October 20 (£41), October 21 (£100); 21 October 1771 (£100), GWP; Diary, 23 November 1771 (£60), GWP; "Cash Accounts," November 1768, 5 November (£94); "Cash Accounts," April 1768, 5 April (£121), GWP.

3. Diary, 18 September 1767 and note, GWP; Bryan, *Martha Washington*, 155–56; to John Armstrong, 21 September 1767, GWP.

4. Lord Fairfax is sometimes credited with introducing the fox hunt to America. J.N.P. Watson, *The Book of Foxhunting*, New York: Arco Publishing Co. (1978), 31; Kitty Slater, *The Hunt Country of America, Then and Now,* Upperville: Virginia Reel (1997), 19; J. Cage

to Lawrence Washington, undated, in Conway, *The Barons of the Potomac and the Rappahannock*, 245 (proposing a hunt with Lord Fairfax).

5. Watson, *The Book of Foxhunting*, 16 (quoting Plato and Xenophon); Roger Longrigg, *The History of Foxhunting*, London: Macmillan London Ltd. (1975), 14; Alexander McKay-Smith, *Foxhunting in North America: A Comprehensive Guide to Organized Foxhunting in the United States and Canada*, Millwood, VA: American Foxhound Club (1985), 4; Zagarri, *Humphreys*, 7.

6. Diary, 3 May 1768, 6 August 1768, 24, 26, and 27 March 1769, GWP; from Bryan Fairfax, 15 July 1772, GWP.

7. Hayes, *A Life in Books*, 122–24; Longmore, *The Invention of George Washington*, 218.

8. Hayes, *A Life in Books*, 145, 57; Longmore, *The Invention of George Washington*, 221–23.

9. Ford, *Washington and the Theatre*, 24.

10. Longmore, *The Invention of George Washington*, 219; John Bernard, *Retrospections of America, 1797–1811*, New York: Harper (1886), 92.

11. John Adams to Benjamin Rush, 21 June 1811, in AP.

12. Ford, *Washington and the Theatre*, 1, 26; Hayes, *A Life in Books*, 114–15; Twohig, "The Making of George Washington," in Hofstra, *George Washington and the Virginia Backcountry*, 11; "List of Books at Mount Vernon, 1764," GWP; from John Hancock, 8 October 1777, GWP; from Captain Henry Lee Jr., 31 March 1778, GWP; to Chastellux, 1 February 1784, GWP; from John Church, 22 February 1792, quoted in note 2, from Samuel and Sheppard Church, 20 April 1792, GWP; to Timothy Pickering, 27 July 1795, GWP.

13. T. H. Breen, "Horses and Gentlemen," *WMQ* 34:239, 247 (April 1977); "Card Playing Expenses 1772–1774," 1 January 1775, GWP. Washington's diaries show him attending horse races in May 1760, October 1767, August, September, and November 1768, May and September 1769, September 1771, October 1772, and May and October 1773.

14. Bryan, *Martha Washington*, 146–61; Diary, 31 July and 6 August 1769, GWP; to John Armstrong, 18 August 1769, GWP.

15. From Jonathan Boucher, 9 May 1770, 18 December 1770, GWP; to Jonathan Boucher, 9 July 1771, GWP.

16. Galke, "The Mother of the Father of Our Country," *Northeast Historical Archaeology* 38:29, 32 (2009).

17. Diary, 10–14 September 1771 and notes, GWP; Freeman 3:280–81.

18. Levy, *Where the Cherry Tree Grew*, 83.

19. From Hugh Mercer, 6 April 1774, GWP; to Benjamin Harrison, 21 March 1781, note; Levy, *Where the Cherry Tree Grew*, 84; to Betty Lewis, 13 September 1789, GWP.

24. NEVER ENOUGH LAND

1. *Early Sketches of George Washington*, 32. Washington's schemes for large land acquisitions were (i) the soldiers' bounty lands under the Dinwiddie Proclamation of 1754, (ii) the Mississippi Land Company project, (iii) efforts on Washington's behalf by William Crawford in Pennsylvania, (iv) claims he purchased to soldier lands under the 1763 Proclamation, and (v) the Great Dismal Swamp Company project. Washington's other two land strategies were the purchase of lands adjoining Mount Vernon, and his 1767 acquisition of lands in Fauquier and Loudoun Counties.

2. To John Posey, 24 June 1767, GWP; to John Parke Custis, 1 February 1778, GWP.

3. Kenneth R. Bowling, "George Washington's Vision for the United States," in Robert McDonald and Peter S. Onuf, eds., *Revolutionary Prophecies: The Founders on America's Future*, Charlottesville: University Press of Virginia (2020), 86–87.

4. Griffith, *Virginia House of Burgesses,* 175–78; Hall, *Executive Journals* 6:271 (12 October 1764), 6:274 (6 November 1764); Taylor, *American Revolutions,* 79. Griffith estimated that one-third of the men who served as Virginia burgesses were active land speculators.

5. From Robert Stewart, 28 September 1759, GWP; from George Mercer, 16 September 1759, GWP; Diary, 23 February 1760, GWP.

6. "Mississippi Land Company, Articles of Agreement," 3 June 1763, GWP; Diary, 30 June 1763, Note, GWP; Diary, 9 September 1763, GWP; "Mississippi Land Company's Memorial to the King," 9 September 1763, GWP; "Mississippi Land Company, Minutes of Meeting," 22 May 1767, GWP; Diary, 1 July 1768, GWP; "Mississippi Land Company's Petition to the King," December 1768, GWP; George Croghan to Sir William Johnson, 30 March 1764, quoted in Patrick Griffin, *American Leviathan: Empire, Nation, and Revolutionary Frontier,* New York: Hill and Wang (2007), 57; Charles Royster, *The Fabulous History of the Dismal Swamp Company: A Story of George Washington's Times,* New York: Alfred A. Knopf (1999), 69–71.

7. Henry Bouquet to Colonel Cresap, 12 September 1760, in Douglas Brymner, *Report on Canadian Archives, 1889* (Ottawa, 1890), 72; Proclamation, in Brymner, *Canadian Archives,* 73; Francis Fauquier to Henry Bouquet, 17 January 1762, in Brymner, *Canadian Archives,* 73–74; Hall, *Executive Journals* 6:205–6 (16 and 21 January 1762), 6:208 (11 March 1762).

8. Hall, *Executive Journals* 6:257 (25 May 1763); Longmore, *The Invention of George Washington,* 102; Eugene L. Del Papa, "The Royal Proclamation of 1763: Its Effect upon Virginia Land Companies," *VMHB* 83:406 (1975); Fauquier to Board of Trade, 1 December 1759, in Reese, *Fauquier Papers* 1:275–77; Fauquier to Board of Trade, 13 March 1760, in Reese, *Fauquier Papers* 1:331–332; Fauquier to James Hamilton, 7 May 1760, in Reese, *Fauquier Papers* 1:353; Fauquier to Board of Trade, 12 May 1760, in Reese, *Fauquier Papers* 1:359; Board of Trade to Fauquier, 13 June 1760, in Reese, *Fauquier Papers* 1:376–77; Fauquier to Board of Trade, 1 September 1760, in Reese, *Fauquier Papers* 1:405–6; Fauquier to Board of Trade, 6 December 1760, in Reese, *Fauquier Papers* 1:439–40; Fauquier to Board of Trade, 10 July 1762, in Reese, *Fauquier Papers* 2:771; "Memorial of George Washington and Others," in Reese, *Fauquier Papers* 1:775–76; Woody Holton, "The Ohio Indians and the Coming of the American Revolution in Virginia," *J. Southern Hist.* 60:453 (1994).

9. Freeman 3:93–94, 3:101; Hall, *Executive Journals* 6:257–58 (25 May 1763); "Cash Accounts," April 1764 (30 April), GWP; "Appraisement of Dismal Swamp Slaves," 4 July 1764, GWP; "Cash Accounts," November and December 1764, GWP. Royster, *Fabulous History,* 81–84, 96–99.

10. To William Crawford, 17 September 1767, GWP; from William Crawford, 29 September 1767, GWP; from John Armstrong, 3 November–20 December 1767, GWP; *Pennsylvania Packet,* September 20, 1773.

11. "Cash Accounts," November 1767, note 26, GWP; Diary, 12–17 March 1769, GWP.

12. To Charles West, 6 June 1769, GWP; to John Posey, 11 June 1769, GWP; from George Mason, 14 October 1769, GWP; Diary, 22 September 1772, GWP; from George William Fairfax, 19 December 1772, GWP.

13. Longmore, *The Invention of George Washington,* 102; Freeman 3:101; "Cash Accounts," December 1765, note 5, GWP; "Cash Accounts," May 1768, GWP; to Governor Botetourt, 9 September 1770 and 5 October 1770, GWP.

14. Freeman 3:315; Parmenter, "The Iroquois and the Native American Struggle for the Ohio Valley," in Skaggs and Nelson, *The Sixty Years' War for the Great Lakes, 1754–1814,* 111–14; Knollenberg, *The Virginia Period,* 91–92; McGaughy, *Richard Henry Lee,* 95–97; to Botetourt, 9 December 1769, GWP. To justify reopening western settlement, Britain pointed to treaties that canceled Cherokee and Iroquois claims to acres that Washington coveted.

But neither tribe actually occupied the lands they purported to relinquish, while other tribes had not yielded their far stronger claims to those lands.

15. Hall, *Executive Council Journals* 6:337 (15 December 1769), 6:333–34 (9 November 1769); Advertisement, 16 December 1769, GWP; Diary, 7 January 1770, GWP. Washington coached his brother Charles to approach possible sellers of the claims by raising the subject "in a joking manner" and never to disclose that he was acting on behalf of his elder brother. To Charles Washington, 31 January 1770.

16. To John Armstrong, 10 October 1773, GWP; petition to Botetourt, 15 December 1769, GWP; Hall, *Executive Journals* 6:337 (15 December 1769); from James Horrocks, 21 December 1769, GWP; *Virginia Gazette* (Purdie and Dixon), June 21, 1770; Agreement with George Muse, 3 August 1770, GWP. Washington, always fearful of the Walpole Company's tentacles, pressed the governor to complete the soldier grants. To Governor Botetourt, 9 September 1770, 5 October 1770, GWP.

17. Diary, 19, 21, and 25–28 October, 2–3, 17, 19, and 21 November and note, GWP. Upon his return to Mount Vernon, he closed a land purchase that likely resonated for him: It included Great Meadows, where he lost the Fort Necessity battle in 1754. From William Crawford, 6 December 1770, 15 April 1771 and note 2, GWP.

18. To the Officers of the Virginia Regiment, 20 January 1771, GWP; *Virginia Gazette* (Purdie and Dixon), January 31, 1771; Diary, 4–5 March 1771, GWP; "Minutes of the meeting of the officers of the Virginia Regiment of 1754," 5 March 1771, GWP; Diary, 10–17 and 31 October 1771, GWP; Memorial to Governor and Council, 1–4 November 1771, GWP; Hall, *Executive Journals* 6:438 (4 November 1771); Hall, *Executive Journals* 6:439 (6 November 1771); to George Mercer, 7 November 1771, GWP.

19. Calloway, *The Indian World of George Washington*, 194, 200–1; James A. Hagemann, *Lord Dunmore: Last Royal Governor of Virginia, 1771–1776*, Hampton, VA: Wayfarer (1974), 3; to Lord Dunmore, 15 June 1772, GWP; from William Crawford, 15 March 1772, GWP; Royster, *Fabulous History*, 156–57; Hall, *Executive Journals* 6:461 (8 May 1772); Diary, 3 November 1772, GWP; Petition to Lord Dunmore and the Virginia Council, 4 November 1772, GWP; Hall, *Executive Journals* 6:510 (4 November 1772).

20. "Resolutions of Officers Regarding the Royal Proclamation of 1763," 15 September 1772, GWP; "Cash Accounts," October 1772 (October 14), GWP (buying John Posey's claim for 3,000 acres under 1763 Proclamation); to Lord Dunmore, 2 November 1773, GWP; Hall, *Executive Journals* 6:549 (4 November 1773); Knollenberg, *The Virginia Period*, 99; to James Wood, 13 and 30 March 1773, GWP.

21. From William Crawford, 12 November 1773, GWP; Hall, *Executive Journals* 6:541 (11 October 1773), 6:548–49 (4 November 1773); to Lord Dunmore and Executive Council, 3 November 1773, GWP; *Virginia Gazette* (Rind's), November 25, 1773. Based on a misreading of the 1754 Proclamation, Knollenberg concluded that Washington had no right to claim lands under the 1754 Proclamation, which Knollenberg asserted were intended for enlisted men, not officers. Knollenberg, *The Virginia Period*, 91–99. The title to the 1754 Proclamation states that it aims at "encouraging men to enlist in his Majesty's service." Knollenberg argued that Washington did not enlist, but accepted an officer's commission. Yet Washington voluntarily joined the service, like any enlistee. Moreover, the proclamation grants lands "over and above their pay" to "all who shall voluntarily enter into the said service," which Washington did. Knollenberg also pointed to Dinwiddie's grant of lands to those whose service *"shall be represented to me by their officers."* (Emphasis added.) Because Washington commanded the regiment, Knollenberg contended, his officers could not so report to the governor. This is pettifoggery. Any officer might comment to the governor on Washington's merits. Knollenberg also stressed that when Washington complained about pay, he never mentioned the soldiers' right to land grants, which Knollenberg trumpeted as tacit recognition that Washington was not entitled to

land. But the proclamation states that the bounty lands were "over and above" soldiers' pay. Washington could not reverse that pledge by complaining about pay without mentioning land grants. Moreover, no royal or Virginia official ever suggested that the officers could not claim under the 1754 Proclamation.

22. *Virginia Gazette* (Rind's), January 14, 1773. When the first grants were issued, Washington told the Executive Council that if other claimants thought the allocation was unequal, and if the council agreed, he would relinquish his lands. The gesture proved unnecessary. At a meeting in Fredericksburg, seven other major claimants affirmed that there was "no great inequality" in the land allocations. They adopted another resolution acknowledging that the grants were secured "principally through [Colonel Washington's] constant care and attention to the business." Hall, *Executive Journals* 6:513–14 (6 November 1772); *Virginia Gazette* (Purdie and Dixon) November 12, 1772; Diary, 23–25 November 1772, GWP; Resolutions of the Officers of the Virginia Regiment of 1754 and note 3, 23 November 1772, GWP; Hall, *Executive Journals* 6:516 (9 December 1772); to the officers and soldiers of the Virginia Regiment of 1754, 23 December 1772, GWP. Some scholars have argued that Washington used his knowledge of the backcountry to grab the best land, plus more riverfront land than Virginia law permitted. Knollenberg, *The Virginia Period*, 95–97. Washington's response was, essentially, that he would be an idiot not to acquire good parcels. Only he and Dr. Craik spent nine weeks in the wilderness examining the land, and another week closeted with the surveyor; then he steered the claims past numerous political obstacles. He felt entirely entitled to acquire good acreage. In response to a complaint from one former soldier, Washington exploded, regretting, "I ever engaged in behalf of so ungrateful and dirty a fellow as you are." From William Crawford, 12 November 1773, GWP; to Charles Mynn Thruston, 12 March 1773, GWP; to George Muse, 29 January 1774, GWP.

23. "Advertisement of Western lands,"15 July 1773, GWP; *Virginia Gazette* (Rind's), August 5, 1773; *Virginia Gazette* (Purdie and Dixon), July 29, 1773; *Pennsylvania Packet*, June 6, 1774, July 11, 1774, August 1 and 20, 1774, September 20, 1774, October 2, 1774; Knollenberg, *The Virginia Years*, 110; from Daniel Carroll, 1 September 1773, GWP (Irishmen); Diary and note, 24 August 1773, GWP (Scots); Draft from Robert Adam, 14 September 1774, GWP (Germans); to James Tilghman Jr., 17 February 1774, GWP (Germans); from James Tilghman Sr., 7 April 1774, GWP; to Henry Riddell, 22 and 24 February 1774, 2, 5, and 18 March, GWP (Germans); from Richard Thompson, 30 September 1773, GWP. Washington offered to pay the settlers' relocation expenses in return for indenture agreements for three to four years with land leases; or the settlers could choose to pay their own expenses and sign a simple lease for the land. From Robert Hanson Harrison, 8 September 1773, GWP.

24. To James Wood, 20 February 1774, GWP; to Lord Dunmore, 3 April 1775, GWP; from Lord Dunmore, 18 April 1775, GWP; Knollenberg, *The Virginia Years*, 96–97.

25. To Presley Nevill, 16 June 1794, GWP.

25. WASHINGTON'S ASSOCIATION

1. The new treasurer was Robert Carter Nicholas. Both Randolph and Nicholas had been close to the disgraced late Speaker Robinson, and likely had known of his misdeeds; the pace of change in colonial Virginia could be slow. *Virginia Gazette* (Purdie and Dixon), July 25, 1766; Kennedy, *Journals of the House of Burgesses, 1766–1769*, 11:66–68 (12 December 1766). The House also appointed an eleven-man committee to investigate the financial carnage left by Robinson. The administrators of Robinson's estate blithely (and incorrectly) announced that Robinson's assets would cover the purloined funds, but admitted that selling his assets might be difficult because currency remained scarce.

2. Kennedy, *Journals of the House of Burgesses, 1766–1769*, 11:12–13 (6 November 1766), 11:23 (12 November 1766), 11:30 (18 November 1766), 11:50 (3 December 1766), 11:54 (4 December 1766), 11:58 (8 December 1766), 11:75 (16 December 1766).

3. Kennedy, *Journals of the House of Burgesses, 1766–1769*, 11:116–17 (7 April 1767), 11:125–28 (11 April 1767).

4. Kennedy, *Journals of the House of Burgesses, 1766–1769*, 11:125–28 (11 April 1767).

5. *Statutes at Large,* London (1811), chapter 46, 12:672–79 Longmore, *The Invention of George Washington,* 88.

6. Kennedy, *Journals of the House of Burgesses, 1766–1769,* 11:165–69 (14 April 1768) and 11:172–73 (15 April 1768).

7. Newspapers carried essays trumpeting the colonists' rights by John Dickinson of Pennsylvania and Arthur Lee, one of the six Lee brothers, but Washington remained silent about the Townshend duties. Lee's essays appeared in Rind's *Virginia Gazette* on February 28, 1768, and in five more issues in March and four more in April. Dickinson's pieces appeared in all four January issues of Purdie and Dixon's *Virginia Gazette,* in two of the February issues, and in five March issues. Glenn Curtis Smith, "An Era of Non-Importation Associations, 1768–73," *WMQ* 20:84–87 (1940); Diary, 1–14 April 1768, GWP.

8. Diary, 30 April to 21 May 1768, GWP; Diary, 30 June 1768, GWP; Diary, 26 October 1768, GWP; Diary, 21 November and 1 December 1768, GWP; "Fairfax County Poll Sheet," December 1768, GWP.

9. Longmore, *The Invention of George Washington,* 88; Arthur M. Schlesinger, *The Colonial Merchants and the American Revolution, 1763–1776,* New York: Columbia University Press (1918), 106–21.

10. To George Mason, 5 April 1769, GWP.

11. From George Mason, 5 April 1769, GWP.

12. Diary, 17–21 April 1769, GWP; from George Mason, 28 April 1769, GWP.

13. Scribner and Tarter, *Revolutionary Virginia: The Road to Independence, A Documentary Record,* Charlottesville: University Press of Virginia 1:74–77 (1973); Jeff Broadwater, *George Mason: Forgotten Founder,* Chapel Hill: University of North Carolina Press (2006), 51.

14. Kennedy, *Journals of the House of Burgesses, 1766–1769,* 11:188–89 (8 May 1769); Mays, *Edmund Pendleton* 1:252; Kukla, *Patrick Henry,* 114.

15. Kennedy, *Journals of the House of Burgesses, 1766–1769,* 11:214–15, 11:218 (16–17 May 1769).

16. John J. Reardon, *Peyton Randolph: One Who Presided,* Durham: Carolina Academic Press (1982), 34–35.

17. Richard Henry Lee to Arthur Lee, 19 May 1769, in Ballagh, *Letters of Richard Henry Lee,* 34.

18. Diary, 17, 18, 19 May 1769 and notes, GWP; Freeman 3:222; Broadwater, *George Mason,* 51.

19. Kennedy, *Journals of the House of Burgesses, 1766–1769,* 11:xlii; Taylor Stoermer, "'What Manner of Man I Am': The Political Career of George Washington Before the Revolution," in Edward Lengel, ed., *A Companion to George Washington,* Malden, MA: Wiley-Blackwell (2012), 128; Ferling, *The Ascent of George Washington,* 68–69.

20. Freeman 3:234; to Burwell Bassett, 18 June 1769, GWP; Schlesinger, *The Colonial Merchants,* 138–55; to John Armstrong, 18 August 1769, GWP; Diary, 14 September, 30 October, 1 and 5 November, GWP. In a faint echo of his days legislating against hog-running, Washington also presented a bill proposing a tax on dog ownership. Kennedy, *Journals of the House of Burgesses, 1766–1769,* 11:264–65 (17 November 1769), 11:289 (24 November 1769).

21. Kennedy, *Journals of the House of Burgesses, 1766–1769,* 11:227 (7 November 1769); *Virginia Gazette* (Purdie and Dixon), December 14, 1769.

22. Longmore, *The Invention of George Washington,* 94; Arthur Lee to Dr. Theodorick Bland, 21 August 1770, in Campbell, *Bland Papers* 1:29; Richard Henry Lee to William Lee, 7 July

1770, in Ballagh, *Letters of Richard Henry Lee,* 45. Strikingly, at the same time that Americans feared that non-importation was failing, the king's ministers were suggesting that hopes of reconciliation with America were vain. Arthur Lee to brother, 20 May 1770, in Richard Henry Lee, *Life of Arthur Lee,* Boston: Wells and Lilly (1829), 206.

23. Diary, 25, 28, and 31 May, 15 June 1770, GWP; *Virginia Gazette* (Purdie and Dixon), May 31, 1770.

24. Diary, 22 June 1770 and Note, GWP; Smith, "An Era of Non-Importation Associations, 1768–73," 20:95.

25. To Jonathan Boucher, 30 July 1770, GWP; to George William Fairfax, 27 June 1770, GWP; Greene, *Landon Carter Diary* 1:408 (29 May 1770); Mays, *Edmund Pendleton* 1:258–59.

26. Diary, 16 April 1771 and note, 18 June 1771 and note, GWP; Fairfax County Associators to Peyton Randolph, 1 July 1771, GWP; *Virginia Gazette* (Rind's), July 18, 1771; *Virginia Gazette* (Rind's), October 11, 1770; William Nelson to Lord Hillsborough, 19 December 1770, in Kennedy, *Journals of the House of Burgesses, 1770–1772,* 12:xxxi; to Cary & Co., 20 July 1771, GWP; to Cary & Co., 18 July 1771, GWP.

27. Mason to George Brent, 6 December 1770, Mason et al. to Peyton Randolph, 18 July 1771, in Robert A. Rutland, ed., *The Papers of George Mason, 1725–1792,* Chapel Hill: University of North Carolina Press (1970) 1:127–30, 1:132–33.

26. UPHEAVALS AT MOUNT VERNON

1. Richard Sheridan, "The British Credit Crisis of 1772 and the American Colonies," *J. Econ. Hist.* 20:161, 170, 173 (1960); Freeman 3:273–74, 276; to Jonathan Boucher, 4 May 1772, GWP; "April 1772 Cash Accounts," (April 6 entry), GWP; Kennedy, *Journals of the House of Burgesses, 1770–1772,* 12:125 (15 July 1771), 12:302 (7 April 1772), 12:315 (11 April 1772); Hening, *Statutes at Large,* chapter 2, 8:511. On local matters, Washington pressed Alexandria's request to impose a ship tax and relax a liquor tax, and to enforce a requirement that empty town lots be drained. His other legislative activity included managing a personal property claim, a soldier's petition, and bills for regulating deer hunting and hound ownership. Kennedy, *Journals of the House of Burgesses, 1770–1772,* 235 (11 March 1772) (ferry bill); Hening, *Statutes at Large,* chapter 39, 8:591 (deer) and chapter 52, 8:613 (Alexandria drainage).

2. To Jonathan Boucher, 21 May 1772, GWP; Diary, 20–22 May 1772, GWP.

3. Rufus Rockwell Wilson, ed., *Burnaby's Travels Through North America,* New York: A. Wessels Co. (1904), 209; Freeman 3:306–7.

4. From George William Fairfax, 1 January 1773, GWP; to George William Fairfax, 19 January 1773, GWP.

5. To Daniel Jenifer Adams, 12 January 1773, GWP; to Craven Peyton, 23 February 1773, GWP; to Gilbert Simpson, 23 February 1773, GWP; to Robert McMickan, 12 January and February 1773, GWP ("my affairs in the hands of Mr. D. J. Adams are in a very desperate way"); to Samuel Washington, 4 February 1773, GWP; to John Dalton, 15 February 1773, GWP.

6. To Burwell Bassett, 15 February 1773, GWP; Kennedy, *Journals of the House of Burgesses, 1773–1776,* Richmond (1905) 13:12 (6 March 1773); Sheridan, "The British Credit Crisis of 1772 and the American Colonies," 20:178–79; Kukla, *Patrick Henry,* 135; Minutes of the Committee of Correspondence, in Kennedy, *Journals of the House of Burgesses, 1773–1776,* 13:42–64; R. H. Lee to John Dickinson, 4 April 1773, in Ballagh, *The Letters of Richard Henry Lee,* 83.

7. To Jonathan Boucher, 16 December 1770, GWP; from Jonathan Boucher, 18 December 1770, 19 November 1771, 19 January and 8 April 1773, GWP.

8. From Jonathan Boucher, 8 April 1773, GWP; Bryan, *Martha Washington,* 163–65; to Boucher, 20 April 1771, GWP.
9. To Benedict Calvert, 3 April 1773, GWP.
10. Diary, 24 April 1773, 12, 16–17, 19, 23, and 27 May 1773, GWP; J. P. Custis to Martha Washington, 5 July 1773, in Fields, *Worthy Partner,* 152.
11. To Lord Dunmore, 13 April 1773, GWP.
12. As he wrote those words, Washington may have recalled the condolence letter he had written to Bassett only two months before, upon the death of Bassett's daughter. Acknowledging in his earlier letter that "the ways of providence being inscrutable, and the justice of it not to be scanned by the shallow eye of humanity," he advised that the only course left was "a cheerful acquiescence to the divine will." To Burwell Bassett, 20 June 1773, 20 April 1773, GWP.
13. William D. Hoyt, ed., "Eliza Parke Custis [Law], Self-Portrait: Eliza Custis, 1808," *VMHB* 53:89, 92 (1945).
14. Diary, 21 June 1773, GWP.
15. J. P. Custis to Martha Washington, 5 July 1773, in Fields, *Worthy Partner,* 152–53; to Burwell Bassett, 20 June 1773, GWP; from Lord Dunmore, 3 July 1773, GWP.
16. Diary, 22–28 June 1773, GWP.
17. Diary, 1–5 July 1773, GWP.
18. Diary, 8–9 July 1773, GWP.
19. Diary, 9 July–31 August 1773, GWP.
20. "Cash Accounts," September 1773, GWP; Diary, 26 September–2 October 1773, 13 October, GWP; "Cash Accounts," March 1773 (11 March 1773), GWP.
21. To Myles Cooper, 15 December 1773, GWP; from Myles Cooper, 20 September 1773, GWP.
22. Diary, 3–5 February 1774.
23. Bryan, *Martha Washington,* 177; Dalzell and Dalzell, *George Washington's Mount Vernon,* 68–73.
24. To Burwell Bassett, 12 February 1774, GWP.

27. SEIZING THE MOMENT

1. Arthur Lee to Sam Adams, 13 October 1773, in Richard Henry Lee, *The Life of Arthur Lee,* 236.
2. Beeman, *Our Lives, Our Fortunes, and Our Sacred Honor,* 143; *Boston Evening Post,* December 20, 1773; Benjamin L. Carp, *Defiance of the Patriots: The Boston Tea Party and the Making of America,* New Haven: Yale University Press (2010), 130; Diary of John Adams, 17 December 1773, AP.
3. Lord Dartmouth to General Thomas Gage, 3 June 1774, in Peter Force, *American Archives, Fourth Series* (1848) 1:380; *Statutes at Large of England and of Great Britain,* London: George Ayre and Andrew Strahan (1811), 14th George, chapters 6, 19, 39, 45, 13:651, 655, 673, 682; Richard Henry Lee to Arthur Lee, 26 June 1774, in Ballagh, *Letters of Richard Henry Lee* 1:114; Taylor, *American Revolutions,* 113–15; Mary Beth Norton, *1774: The Long Year of Revolution,* New York: Alfred A. Knopf (2020), 84–85, 98–99.
4. Diary, 16, 17, 21, 23, and 24 May 1774, GWP; Bryan, *Martha Washington,* 177–78; Longmore, *The Invention of George Washington,* 113.
5. Kennedy, *Journals of the House of Burgesses, 1773–1776,* 13:124 (24 May 1774), 13:132 (26 May 1774); Kukla, *Patrick Henry,* 139–41; to George William Fairfax, 10–15 June 1774, GWP; Greene, *Diary of Landon Carter* 2:817 (3 June 1774); Richard Henry Lee to Samuel Adams, 23 June 1774, in Ballagh, *Letters of Richard Henry Lee,* 111–13; Richard Henry

Lee to Arthur Lee, 26 June 1774, in Ballagh, *Letters of Richard Henry Lee,* 114–16 and note 1.

6. Diary, 25–26 May 1774, GWP; to George William Fairfax, 10 June 1774, GWP.

7. *Virginia Gazette* (Purdie and Dixon), May 26, 1774; "Association of Members of the Late House of Burgesses," 27 May 1774, PTJ; Freeman 3:354; Bryan, *Martha Washington,* 178; Kennedy, *Journals of the House of Burgesses, 1773–1776,* 13:138 (28 May 1774).

8. Diary, 29 May 1774, GWP; Kennedy, *Journals of the House of Burgesses, 1773–1776,* 13:144–47 (letter from Samuel Adams, 13 May 1774); "Proceedings of a Meeting of Representatives in Williamsburg," 30 May 1774, PTJ; *Virginia Gazette* (Purdie and Dixon), June 2, 1774; Mays, *Edmund Pendleton* 1:270–72; Diary, 1 June 1774, GWP; to George William Fairfax, 10–15 June 1774, GWP.

9. To George William Fairfax, 10–15 June 1774, GWP.

10. Diary, 26 June and 3 July 1774, GWP. The additional parliamentary legislation increased the powers of the Massachusetts royal governor and shielded colonial officials from trial in America for any misdeeds. Longmore, *The Invention of George Washington,* 117–18; to Bryan Fairfax, 4 July 1774, GWP.

11. Richard Barksdale Harwell, ed., *Committees of Safety of Westmoreland and Fincastle: Proceedings of the County Committees,* Richmond: Virginia State Library (1956), 27 (22 June 1774); Richmond County (Virginia) Resolutions, in Peter Force, ed., *American Archives,* fourth series, New York (1837–1846) 1:491–492; from Thomas Johnson, 28 June 1774, GWP; Kennedy, *Journals of the House of Burgesses, 1773–1776,* 13:152–53, 156–57.

12. From Bryan Fairfax, 3 July 1774, GWP: to Bryan Fairfax, 4 July 1774, GWP.

13. Diary, 5 July 1774, and note, GWP; "Extract of a Letter to a Gentleman in Boston," Alexandria, Virginia, 6 July 1774, in Force, *American Archives* 1:517–18; Longmore, *Invention of George Washington,* 123 and 262 note 2; to John Augustine Washington, 11 July 1774, GWP; Richard Henry Lee to Samuel Adams, 23 June 1774, in Ballagh, *Letters of Richard Henry Lee,* 111; Broadwater, *George Mason,* 65; Hugh Grigsby, *The Virginia Convention of 1776,* Richmond: J. W. Randolph (1855), 159; Rutland, *George Mason Papers* 1:168, 1:201.

14. Diary, 14 July 1774, GWP; Lincoln MacVeagh, ed., *The Journal of Nicholas Cresswell, 1774–1777,* New York: Dial (1924), 27–28; "Cash Accounts, July 1774," GWP (14 July, paid 13 shillings for cakes at the election, plus £3, 1s, 6d, for "sundries" for election; also spent £8, 5s, 6d for "my part of the election ball").

15. Powell, *The History of Old Alexandria,* 181; Diary, 18 July 1774, GWP; to Bryan Fairfax, 24 August 1774, GWP; *Virginia Gazette* (Rind's), August 4, 1774; *Boston Gazette,* August 8, 1774; to Bryan Fairfax, 20 July 1774, GWP.

16. Fairfax County Resolves, 18 July 1774, GWP.

17. To Bryan Fairfax, 20 July 1774, GWP.

18. Diary, 28 July–5 August 1774, GWP.

19. To Thomas Johnson, 5 August 1774, GWP.

20. Force, *American Archives* 1:686–89; *Virginia Gazette* (Purdie and Dixon), August 4 and 11, 1774.

21. The winners' vote totals were: Randolph 104; Lee 100; Washington 98; Henry 89; Bland 79; Benjamin Harrison 66; Pendleton 62. Longmore, *The Invention of George Washington,* 263–64 note 18.

22. To Richard Henry Lee, 9 August 1774, GWP; "Cash Accounts," August 1774 (6 August), GWP; Diary, 15 and 22 August 1774, GWP; Kenton Kilmer and Donald Sweig, *The Fairfax Family in Fairfax County: A Brief History,* Fairfax: Fairfax County Office of Comprehensive Planning (May 1975); *Virginia Gazette* (Purdie and Dixon), June 2, 1774.

23. To Bryan Fairfax, 24 August 1774, GWP.

24. Danby Pickering, *Statutes at Large,* Cambridge, UK: John Archdeacon (1773), 14 Geo. chapter 83, 30:549; Bernard Bailyn, *The Ideological Origins of the American Revolution,* Cambridge: Harvard University Press (1967), 118–19; Broadwater, *George Mason,* 64; McGaughy, *Richard Henry Lee,* 108; Taylor, *American Revolutions,* 84–85.

25. William Wirt Henry, *Patrick Henry; Life, Correspondence, and Speeches,* New York: Charles Scribner's Sons (1891) 1:213; David J. Mays, ed., *Letters and Papers of Edmund Pendleton, 1734–1803,* Charlottesville: University Press of Virginia (1967) 1:98; Diary, 30–31 August 1774, GWP.

28. A CONTINENTAL CHARACTER

1. Beeman, *Our Lives, Our Fortunes,* 60.
2. John Adams's Diary, 15, 23 August 1774, AP; Longmore, *The Invention of George Washington,* 132.
3. Beeman, *Our Lives, Our Fortunes,* 47–48; Mays, *Edmund Pendleton* 1:279; John Adams to Abigail Adams, 14 September 1774, AP.
4. Beeman, *Our Lives, Our Fortunes,* 49; Mays, *Edmund Pendleton* 1:282; *Pennsylvania Packet,* August 15, 1774 ("extra"); *Pennsylvania Journal,* August 19, 1774; *Pennsylvania Gazette,* August 24, 1774.
5. "The Interest of Great Britain Considered," 17 April 1760, PBF.
6. John Adams to Abigail Adams, 25 September 1774, in *Letters of Delegates;* Samuel Ward to Henry Marchant, 7 October 1774, in *Letters of Delegates;* Connecticut Delegates to Jonathan Trumbull Sr., 10 October 1774, in *Letters of Delegates;* John Adams's Diary, 9 October 1774, AP.
7. Diary, 17 April 1770, GWP; Beeman, *Our Lives, Our Fortunes,* 49; Freeman 3:373.
8. Samuel Adams to Joseph Warren, 25 September 1774, in *Letters of Delegates* 1:100; John Adams to William Tudor, 29 September 1774, in *Letters of Delegates;* Joseph Galloway to William Franklin, 5 September 1774, in *Letters of Delegates.*
9. Deane to Elizabeth Deane, 30 August–5 September 1774, in *Letters of Delegates;* Diary of Robert Treat Paine, 5 September 1774, in *Letters of Delegates;* Samuel Ward's Diary, 5 September 1774, in *Letters of Delegates;* Charles E. Peterson, "Carpenters' Hall," *Transactions of the American Philosophical Society* 43:96 (1953), 100.
10. Deane to Elizabeth Deane, 31 August–5 September 1774, in *Letters of Delegates* 1:22–23.
11. Notes of James Duane, 6 September 1774, in *Letters of Delegates* ; Richard Henry Lee to William Lee, 20 September 1774, in Ballagh, *Correspondence of Richard Henry Lee,* 123–24; Samuel Ward's Diary, 6 September 1774, in *Letters of Delegates.*
12. Duane Notes, 7 September 1774, *Letters of Delegates.*
13. Deane to Elizabeth Deane, 11 September 1774, *Letters of Delegates.*
14. John Adams's Diary, 31 August 1774, AP; Deane to Elizabeth Deane, 11 September 1774, *Letters of Delegates.*
15. Robert Treat Paine's Diary, 6 September 1774, *Letters of Delegates;* John Adams to Abigail Adams, 8 September 1774, AP; Deane to Elizabeth Deane, 6 September 1774, *Letters of Delegates.*
16. Deane to Elizabeth Deane, 19 September and 7 September 1774, *Letters of Delegates;* Samuel Ward to Samuel Ward Jr., 24 September 1774, *Letters of Delegates;* John Adams to Abigail Adams, 18 September 1774, AP.
17. John Adams's Diary, 7 September 1774, 14 September, 22 September 1774, AP; Adams to Abigail Adams, 8 September 1774, *Letters of Delegates.* Syllabub was a drink of cream, sweet wine, and lemons; flummery was a dessert pudding.

18. "James Duane's Propositions Before the Committee on Rights," 22 September 1774, *Letters of Delegates*; Connecticut Delegates to Jonathan Trumbull, Sr., 10 October 1774, *Letters of Delegates*. Some treatments of the value of unanimity in different settings appear in: Jean Edward Smith, *John Marshall: Definer of a Nation*, New York: Henry Holt & Co. (1996), 1, 448; Donald M. Roper, "Judicial Unanimity and the Marshall Court—A Road to Reappraisal," *Am. J. Legal Hist.* 9:118, 119–20 (1965); David A. Skeel Jr., "The Unanimity Norm in Delaware Corporate Law," *Virginia L. Rev.* 83:127, 130, 170 (1997); Dennis J. Hutchinson, "Unanimity and Desegregation: Decisionmaking in the Supreme Court, 1948–1958," *Georgetown L. J.* 67:1, 2–3 (1979); George Tsebelis and Geoffrey Garrett, "The Institutional Foundations of Intergovernmentalism and the Supranationalism in the European Union," *International Organization* 55:357 note 1, 359; James M. Buchanan and Gordon Tullock, *The Calculus of Consent: Logical Foundations of Constitutional Democracy*, Ann Arbor: University of Michigan Press (1962), chapter 7.

19. "First Prayer of the Continental Congress, 1774," at https://chaplain.house.gov/archive /continental.html; John Adams to Abigail Adams, 16 September 1774, *Letters of Delegates*.

20. *Journals of the Continental Congress*, Washington: Government Printing Office (1904) 1:31–37 (17 September 1774); Suffolk Resolves, in *JCC* 1:31–37.

21. *JCC* 1:39–40 (17 September 1774); John Adams's Diary, 17 September 1774, in *Letters of Delegates* 1:75.

22. John Adams's Notes of Debates, 26 September 1774, *Letters of Delegates*; *JCC* 1:43 (27 September 1774).

23. John Adams's Notes of Debates, 28 September 1774, *Letters of Delegates*; *JCC* 1:43–51 (28 September 1774).

24. Several years later, Galloway insisted that his proposal was defeated by a single vote on September 28, with votes cast by all the colonies present, but neither Congress's journal nor any delegate's notes reflect such a balloting. Joseph Galloway, *Historical and Political Reflections on the Rise and Progress of the American Rebellion* (1780), 70. A motion to reconsider the plan was rejected on October 22, at the end of the congressional session, while John Dickinson and Charles Thomson (the Secretary of Congress) wrote in the *Pennsylvania Journal* several months later that most delegates listened to Galloway's plan "with horror—as an idle, dangerous, whimsical, ministerial plan." According to this account, the delegates allowed Galloway's proposal to "lay upon the table" and expire from neglect. *Pennsylvania Journal*, March 8, 1775.

25. John Adams's Notes of Debates, 26 September 1774, *Letters of Delegates*; *JCC* 1:51 (30 September 1774); *JCC* 1:53 (1 October 1774).

26. John Adams to William Tudor, 29 September 1774, *Letters of Delegates*; John Adams to Abigail Adams, 25 September 1774, *Letters of Delegates*; John Adams's Diary, 10 October 1744, *Letters of Delegates*; George Read to Gertrude Read, 25 September 1774, *Letters of Delegates*.

27. Samuel Ward to Joseph Wanton, 3 October 1774, *Letters of Delegates*; John Adams to Abigail Adams, 29 September 1774, *Letters of Delegates*.

28. Stoermer, "'What Manner of Man I Am,'" in Lengel, *A Companion to George Washington*, 135; to George William Fairfax, 10 July 1783, GWP.

29. Diary, 12, 13 September 1774, GWP.

30. Diary, 25 September, 9 October 1774, GWP.

31. Robert Treat Paine Diary, 6 October 1774, *Letters of Delegates*; *JCC* 1:55–56, 1:59–60 (6, 10 October 1774).

32. From Robert McKenzie, 13 September 1774, GWP; to Robert McKenzie, 9 October 1774, GWP.

33. *JCC* 1:62–63, 1:74, 1:75–80 (12, 17, 18, and 20 October 1774); Beeman, *Our Lives, Our Fortunes*, 154–56.

34. Beeman, *Our Lives, Our Fortunes*, 186; see T. H. Breen, *The Will of the People: The Revolutionary Birth of America,* Cambridge: The Belknap Press of Harvard University Press (2019), 43–48; Richard Alan Ryerson, *The Revolution Is Now Begun: The Radical Committees of Philadelphia, 1765–1776,* Philadelphia: University of Pennsylvania Press (1978).

35. *JCC* 1:75 (19 October 1774), 1:57–58 (7 October 1774), 1:62 (11 October 1774), 1:81–101 (21 October 1774), 1:104 (25 October 1774), 1:105–13 (26 October 1774).

36. John Adams to William Tudor, 7 October 1774, *Letters of Delegates;* John Adams's Diary, 10 October 1774, AP.

37. George Read to Gertrude Read, 24 October 1774, *Letters of Delegates.* Three of the Virginians had left authorizations for Washington to sign the petition for them. Virginia Delegates to George Washington, 24 October 1774, *Letters of Delegates.*

38. "Cash Accounts," October 1774, GWP.

29. THE STORM BREAKS

1. Diary, October 31, 12, 17, and 22–30 November, 5 December 1774, GWP: to John Tayloe, 31 October 1774, GWP; Dalzell and Dalzell, *George Washington's Mount Vernon,* 101; to James Mercer, 12 December 1774, GWP; Diary, 3 and 12 November 1774, GWP; from George Mason, 17 February 1775, GWP; *Virginia Gazette* (Dixon and Hunter's), January 7, 1775.

2. To James Cleveland, 10 January 1775, GWP; to William Stevens, 6 March 1775, GWP; to Thomas Cresap, 7 February 1775, GWP; from William Preston, 31 January 1775, GWP; from George Mason, 8 March 1775, GWP. Washington also pressed a western land claim held by his brother Austin's son. To William Preston, 27 March 1775, GWP.

3. To Townshend Dade, 19 November 1774, GWP; *Virginia Gazette* (Pinkney), December 29, 1774.

4. Merchants not submitting to audit: *Virginia Gazette* (Pinkney), January 12, 1775 (Caroline County); Apologies: Order of Hanover County Committee, in William J. Van Schreeven and Robert L. Scribner, *Revolutionary Virginia, The Road to Independence,* Charlottesville: University Press of Virginia (1973) 2:169 (12 November 1774); Order of Caroline County Committee, in Van Schreeven and Scribner, *Revolutionary Virginia* 2:199 (16 December 1774); *Virginia Gazette* (Purdie and Dixon), November 24, 1774 (York and Gloucester Counties). Price-gouging: *Virginia Gazette* (Pinkney), January 19, 1775 (Northumberland County Committee trial for overpricing pins); *Virginia Gazette* (Pinkney), February 2, 1775 (acquittal by Spotsylvania County Committee of merchant who lowered his prices). Public auctions: *Virginia Gazette* (Pinkney), February 2, 1775 (Nansemond County); *Virginia Gazette* (Pinkney), February 16, 1775 (Princess Ann County, anvil and casks); *Virginia Gazette* (Dixon and Hunter), February 11, 1775 (Henrico County, salt); *Virginia Gazette* (Dixon and Hunter), March 25, 1775 (Norfolk Borough Committee, checked handkerchiefs, striped bedrick, Irish linen, men's hose, Osnaburg cloth, cutlery, hardware, snuff, barley); *Virginia Gazette* (Pinkney), June 1, 1775 (plaid goods); Fairfax County Committee order, in Van Schreeven and Scribner, *Revolutionary Virginia* 2:209 (Irish linens); *Virginia Gazette* (Pinkney), January 12, 1775 (Charles City County).

5. The counties were Fairfax, Prince William, Fauquier, Richmond, and Spotsylvania.

6. From William Grayson, 27 December 1774, GWP; Diary, 13 November 1774, 16–17 January and 18 February 1775, GWP; to William Milnor, 23 January 1775, GWP; "Resolutions of the Fairfax County Committee," 17 January 1775, GWP; *New York Gazette,* February

20, 1775; *Providence Gazette*, February 25, 1775; to John Augustine Washington, 25 March 1775, GWP; "Fairfax County Committee of Safety Proceedings," 17 January 1775, in Rutland, *George Mason Papers* 1:212–13. Washington complained that Mason quickly collected his share from those most likely to pay, leaving Washington to hound the deadbeats. From George Mason, 18 February 1775, GWP.

7. Longmore, *The Invention of George Washington*, 148, 151; "Augusta County Instructions to Delegates to the Second Virginia Convention," in Van Schreeven and Scribner, *Revolutionary Virginia* 2:298–300 (22 February 1775); *Pennsylvania Evening Post*, February 14, 1775. The Cumberland County committee copied some of the language of the Fairfax resolution in its call for residents to pay the expenses of the county's delegates to the Second Virginia Convention. Call of Cumberland County Committee, in Van Schreeven and Scribner, *Revolutionary Virginia* 2:293–94 (18 February 1775).

8. Diary, 30 December 1774–4 January 1775, 16–20 April 1775, GWP; John Richard Alden, *General Charles Lee: Traitor or Patriot?*, Baton Rouge: Louisiana State University Press (1951), 69, 72; from Thomas Johnson, 24 January and 25 February 1775, GWP; Diary, 2–3 May 1775; Thomas Johnson to Samuel Purviance Jr., 23 January 1775, in *Letters of Delegates* 1:300–301.

9. To John West, 13 January 1775 and note 3, GWP.

10. To John Augustine Washington, 25 March 1775, GWP.

11. William Hooper to James Duane, 22 November 1774, in *Letters of Delegates* 1:262–63; Thomas Johnson to Samuel Purviance, 23 January 1775, in *Letters of Delegates*; John Dickinson to Arthur Lee, 27 October 1774, in *Letters of Delegates*; Richard Henry Lee to Arthur Lee, 24 February 1775, in *Letters of Delegates*.

12. John Adams to Edward Biddle, 12 December 1774, in *Letters of Delegates*; John Adams to James Burgh, 28 December 1774, in *Letters of Delegates*; Richard Henry Lee to Arthur Lee, 24 February 1775, in *Letters of Delegates*.

13. "The King's Speech to both Houses of Parliament," 30 November 1774, Boston: Mills & Hicks (1775); *Virginia Gazette* (Pinkney), February 3, 1775 (broadside issue); to John Connolly, 25 February 1775, GWP; from George Mason, 5 February 1775, GWP.

14. Statutes at Large, 15 Geo. chapter 10, 3 and chapter 18, 6 (1775); Beeman, *Our Lives, Our Fortunes*, 178; Peter D. G. Thomas, *Tea Party to Independence: The Third Phase of the American Revolution, 1773–1776*, New York: Oxford University Press (2011), 194–98, 206–12.

15. Lord Dartmouth to General Gage, 27 January 1775, quoted in David Ammerman, *In the Common Cause*, New York: Norton (1975), 135; Kukla, *Patrick Henry*, 163.

16. Parmenter, "The Iroquois and the Native American Struggle for the Ohio Valley," in Skaggs and Nelson, *The Sixty Years' War for the Great Lakes*, 112–13; Lord Dunmore to Earl of Dartmouth, 24 December 1774, in K. G. Davies, *Documents of the American Revolution*, Shannon: Irish University Press (1980) 8:266; *Virginia Gazette* (Purdie), April 21, 1775 (Caroline County); *Virginia Gazette* (Dixon and Hunter), January 14, 1775 (Charles City County); *Virginia Gazette* (Dixon and Hunter), March 11, 1775 (Charlotte County); *Virginia Gazette* (Pinkney), March 16, 1775 (Essex County); *Virginia Gazette* (Purdie), March 31, 1775 (Goochland County); *Virginia Gazette* (Dixon and Hunter), February 11, 1775 (Henrico County); Mary Beth Norton, *1774: The Long Year of Revolution*, 243–45.

17. *Virginia Gazette* (Dixon and Hunter), January 21, 1775; Reardon, *Peyton Randolph*, 55–56; Mays, *Edmund Pendleton* 2:3.

18. William Wirt, *Sketches of the Life and Character of Patrick Henry*, Philadelphia: James Webster (1817), 123; Kukla, 170–72.

19. Van Schreeven and Scribner, *Revolutionary Virginia* 2:366–69 (23 March 1775), 2:374–75 (25 March 1775); *Virginia Gazette* (Dixon and Hunter), April 1, 1775; *Virginia Gazette* (Pinkney), March 30, 1775.

20. Van Schreeven and Scribner, *Revolutionary Virginia* 2:376–77 (25 March 1775), 2:380–81 (27 March 1775).

21. To George Mercer, 5 April 1775, GWP.

22. Mays, *Edmund Pendleton* 2:18; Kukla, *Patrick Henry*, 173–78.

23. George C. Daughan, *Lexington and Concord: The Battle Heard Round the World,* New York: W. W. Norton & Co. (2018), 273.

24. From Alexander Spotswood, 30 April 1775, GWP.

25. Diary, 2–4 May 1775, GWP; John Dickinson to Arthur Lee, 29 April 1775, in *Letters of Delegates.*

26. Barry Schwartz, *George Washington: The Making of an American Symbol,* New York: The Free Press (1987), 16.

27. Freeman 3:419–20; Richard Caswell to William Caswell, 11 May 1775, in *Letters of Delegates,* 339–40; Andrew Oliver, ed., *The Journal of Samuel Curwen, Loyalist,* Cambridge, Harvard University Press (1972) 1:7–8.

30. GENERAL WASHINGTON

1. Ward, *Journal of Samuel Curwen,* 26 (5 May 1775), 27 (8 May 1775); Richard Caswell to William Caswell, 11 May 1775, in *Letters of Delegates* 1:340; Joseph Hewes to Samuel Johnston, 11 May 1775, in *Letters of Delegates* 1:342–43.

2. William Duane, ed., *Extracts from the Diary of Christopher Marshall,* Albany: Joel Munsell (1877), 25 (9 May 1775); Robert Treat Paine's Diary, 10 May 1775, in *Letters of Delegates*; Ward, *Journal of Samuel Curwen,* 28 (10 May 1775).

3. Flexner 1:335; Harrison, *A Powerful Mind,* 104.

4. To Joseph Reed, 29 July 1779, GWP; "Undelivered First Inaugural Address: Fragments," 30 April 1789, GWP.

5. Richard Henry Lee to William Lee, 10 May 1775, in *Letters of Delegates* 1:337; Silas Deane to Elizabeth Deane, 12 May 1775, in *Letters of Delegates.*

6. George Read to Gertrude Read, 18 May 1775, in *Letters of Delegates*; John Adams to Abigail Adams, 29 May 1775, AP.

7. JCC 2:49 (15 May 1775), 2:59–61 (25 May 1775).

8. To Fairfax County Committee, 16 May 1775, GWP; John Adams to James Warren, 21 May 1775, in *Letters of Delegates*; JCC 2:358 (18 May 1775), 2:82 (8 June 1775).

9. JCC 2:67 (27 May 1775), 2:75 (1 June 1775), 2:85 (10 June 1775); Diary of Silas Deane, 27 May 1775, in *Letters of Delegates*; Diary of Samuel Ward, 3 June 1775, in *Letters of Delegates*; JCC 2:79 (3 June 1775).

10. JCC 2:65 (26 May 1775); John Morton to Thos. Powell, 8 June 1775, in *Letters of Delegates.*

11. To George William Fairfax, 31 May 1775, GWP.

12. JCC 2:80 (3 June 1775), 2:81 (7 June 1775).

13. JCC 2:78 (2 June 1775); James Duane to Robert Livingston, 7 June 1775, in *Letters of Delegates*; JCC 2:89 (14 June 1775).

14. JCC 2:90 (14 June 1775); Diary, 14 June 1775, GWP; *Virginia Gazette* (Purdie), June 23, 1775.

15. Future Major General Charles Lee dismissed Ward as "a fat old gentleman who had been a popular churchwarden, but has no acquaintance whatever with military matters." "Memoir of General Lee, Major-General in the Service of the U.S. of America," in Sir Henry Bunbury, *Correspondence of Sir Thomas Hanmer,* London: Edward Moxon (1838), 467.

16. L. H. Butterfield, ed., *Diary and Autobiography of John Adams,* Cambridge: The Belknap Press at Harvard University Press (1961) 3:321–24 (relating to 1775, but written by Adams in or after 1802); James Warren to John Adams, 7 May 1775, in *Warren-Adams Letters, 1743–1777,* Boston: Massachusetts Historical Society (1917) 1:47; Elbridge Gerry to

Massachusetts Delegates, 4 June 1775, in James T. Austin, *The Life of Elbridge Gerry*, Boston: Wells and Lilly (1829) 1:77–79.

17. John Almon, *The Remembrancer, or Impartial Repository of Public Events*, (1775) (24 December 1774) 1:9–10; Alden, *General Charles Lee*, 6, 73–74; Franklin Bowditch Dexter, ed., *The Literary Diary of Ezra Stiles*, New York: Charles Scribner's Sons (1901) 1:453–54 (9 August 1774); John Adams to James Warren, 24 July 1775, AP.

18. Eliphalet Dyer to Joseph Trumbull, 17 June 1775, in *Letters of Delegates*; Silas Deane to Joseph Trumbull, 18 June 1775, in *Letters of Delegates*; Thomas Cushing to James Bowdoin Sr., 21 June 1775, in *Letters of Delegates*.

19. *JCC* 2:91 (15 June 1775); Freeman 3:436–37.

20. *JCC* 2:92 (16 June 1775).

21. Zagarri, *Humphreys*, 26–27.

22. To Burwell Bassett, 19 June 1775, GWP.

23. To Martha Washington, 17 June 1775, GWP; to John Parke Custis, 19 June 1775, GWP; to John Augustine Washington, 20 June 1775, GWP.

24. To Several Independent Companies in Virginia, 20 June 1775, GWP; Eliphalet Dyer to Joseph Trumbull, 17 June 1775, in *Letters of Delegates*.

25. John Adams to James Warren, 20 June 1775, in *Letters of Delegates*; John Adams to Joseph Warren, 21 June 1775, in *Letters of Delegates*; *JCC* 2:97 (19 June 1775).

26. "Commission from Continental Congress," 19 June 1775, GWP; "Instructions from the Continental Congress," 22 June 1775, GWP.

27. Beeman, *Our Lives, Our Fortunes*, 237.

31. "ONE OF THE MOST IMPORTANT CHARACTERS IN THE WORLD"

1. John Adams to Abigail Adams, 11–17 June 1775, AP; John Adams to Abigail Adams, 23 June 1775, in *Letters of Delegates*; Silas Deane to Elizabeth Deane, 23 June 1775, in *Letters of Delegates*; Robert Treat Paine's Diary, 23 June 1775, in *Letters of Delegates*; *Virginia Gazette* (Purdie's), 14 July 1775; Schwartz, *George Washington: An American Symbol*, 16, 18; to Richard Henry Lee, 10 July 1775, GWP.

2. "Address from the New York Provincial Congress," 26 June 1775, GWP; "Address to the New York Provincial Congress," 26 June 1775, GWP; *New York Journal*, June 29, 1775.

3. Greene, *Landon Carter Diary* 2:1042–43.

4. Silas Deane to Elizabeth Deane, 16 June 1775, in *Letters of Delegates*; Longmore, *The Invention of George Washington*, 197; *Virginia Gazette* (Pinkney's), 24 August 1775; *Virginia Gazette* (Dixon and Hunter), October 7, 1775; *Virginia Gazette* (Purdie's), May 17, 1776; Schwartz, *George Washington: An American Symbol*, 18.

5. Gilbert Chinard, ed., *George Washington as the French Knew Him*, Princeton: Princeton University Press (1940), 69 (from the observations of Abbe Robin).

PART III

1. Edward Thornton to James Bland Burges, 2 April 1792, in S. W. Jackman, "A Young Englishman Reports on the New Nation, Edward Thornton to James Bland Burges, 1791–1793," *WMQ* 18:85 (1961), 102.

32. THE BLOODY PATH TO VALLEY FORGE

1. Joseph Tustin, tr. and ed., *Captain Johann Ewald's Diary of the American War: A Hessian Journal*, New Haven: Yale University Press (1979), 120.

2. Gordon Wood, *The Idea of America: Reflections on the Birth of the United States,* New York: Penguin (2011), 136; E. Wayne Carp, *To Starve the Army at Pleasure: Continental Army Administration and American Political Culture, 1775–1783,* Chapel Hill: University of North Carolina Press (1984), 104.

3. Wood, *The Idea of America,* 27–28.

4. To John Augustine Washington, 6–19 November 1776, GWP; to Samuel Washington, 18 December 1776, GWP.

5. Freeman 4:363–65; Carp, *To Starve the Army,* 19; Mackubin Owens, "General Washington and the Military Strategy of the Revolution," in Gary L. Gregg II and Matthew Spalding, eds., *Patriot Sage: George Washington and the American Political Tradition,* Wilmington: ISI Books (1999), 70; Lengel, *General George Washington,* 212; Wayne Bodle, *The Valley Forge Winter: Civilians and Soldiers in War,* University Park: Pennsylvania State University Press (2002), 31–32.

6. Morgan, *The Genius of George Washington,* 12–14. Morgan concluded that Washington always respected congressional authority because he "knew he would lose what he was fighting for if he tried to take more power than the people would freely give."

7. Charles Lee to Horatio Gates, 12 December 1776, quoted in Washington to Lee, 14 December 1776, note 2, GWP.

8. North Callahan, *Henry Knox: General Washington's General,* New York: Rinehart & Co. (1958), 23; from Henry Knox, 26 November 1777, GWP; Lengel, *General George Washington,* 256; Terry Golway, *Washington's General: Nathanael Greene and the Triumph of the American Revolution,* New York: Henry Holt (2005), 1–7, 44–46.

9. From Brigadier General Duportail, 20 April 1778, GWP.

10. *JCC* 6:1045–46 (27 December 1776); Lengel, *General George Washington,* 214–15; Robert Middlekauf, *Washington's Revolution: The Making of America's First Leader,* New York: Alfred A. Knopf (2015), 144–47.

11. To Colonel Elias Dayton, 19 July 1777, GWP; to Israel Putnam, 16 August 1777, GWP; Alexander Hamilton to Robert R. Livingston, 18 August 1777, PAH; Taylor, *American Revolutions,* 181.

12. Middlekauf, *Washington's Revolution,* 155–56.

13. Ibid., 156–58; Lengel, *General George Washington,* 229–41.

14. *JCC* 8:592–93 (31 July 1777); Fleming, *Washington's Secret War,* 9.

15. Lengel, *General George Washington,* 246–49; to General John Lacey Jr., 3 May 1778, GWP; Nathanael Greene to Miss Susanna Livingston, 11 November 1777, in Richard K. Showman, *Greene Papers* 2:195.

16. General Orders, 3 October 1777, GWP; Journal of Colonel Timothy Pickering, 3 October 1777, in Henry Steele Commager and Richard B. Morris, *The Spirit of 'Seventy-Six: The Story of the American Revolution as Told by Participants,* New York: Bonanza Books (1983), 626–27; T. Will Heth to Colonel John Lamb, 12 October 1777, in Commager and Morris, *The Spirit of 'Seventy-Six,* 630; Lengel, *General George Washington,* 253–59.

17. General Orders, 5 October 1777, GWP; General John Armstrong to Horatio Gates, 9 October 1777, in Commager and Morris, *The Spirit of 'Seventy-Six,* 629; Anonymous to Gov. Clinton, 5 October 1777, in *Public Papers of George Clinton,* New York: Wynkoop Hallenbeck Crawford Co. (1900) 2:372; Thomas Paine to Benjamin Franklin, 16 May 1778, PBF; see James McMichael, "Diary of Lieutenant James McMichael, of the Pennsylvania Line, 1776–1778," *PMHB* 16:129 (1892), 153 (4 October 1778). A British journal called the battle "not of that final and decisive kind which the public had expected," adding that "the rebels were not disheartened." *Annual Register for the Year 1777,* London: J. Dodsley (3d ed., 1785), 131.

For Washington, one virtue of the Germantown battle was that it ended the military career of Adam Stephen, his subordinate and successor with the Virginia Regiment and then rival for the House of Burgesses. When the Revolutionary War began, Stephen parlayed his military experience (scandal-marred though it was) and sponsorship by Richard Henry Lee into a major generalship with the Continentals. Though Washington mistrusted Stephen, he never opposed congressional appointments, so did not object to Stephen's. Freeman 4:535–36; Ward, *Major General Adam Stephen*, 149, 160–61. Stephen soon showed that he had not mended his ways. He criticized Washington's leadership and promoted himself in the press. Months before Germantown, Washington chastised Stephen for an unauthorized attack that Stephen had misrepresented in his official report. To Adam Stephen, 12 May 1777, GWP; Ward, *Major General Adam Stephen*, 164–72. At Germantown, Stephen's troops arrived late, then fell into a friendly-fire exchange with Anthony Wayne's forces. Freeman 4:511; Ward, 186–87. A court-martial found that Stephen "did not pay that general attention to his Division which might be expected from an officer of his command" and had not stayed with his men during the battle, but the court passed over claims of drunkenness on duty. Washington approved the verdict, dismissing Stephen from the army. "Report of a Court of Enquiry," in Showman, *Greene Papers* 2:188–89 (1 November 1777); Ward, *Major General Adam Stephen*, 194, 200–1, 204–5; General Orders, 20 November 1777, GWP.

18. To General Thomas Nelson Jr., 8 November 1777, GWP; from Nathanael Greene, 14 November 1777, GWP; Lengel, 263–64; Bodle, *The Valley Forge Winter*, 47; to Nathanael Greene, 26 November 1777, GWP; from Duportail, 3 December 1777, GWP; from Nathanael Greene, 3 December 1777, GWP; to President of Congress, 22 December 1777, GWP.

19. Joseph Lee Boyle, *Writings from the Valley Forge Encampment of the Continental Army, December 19, 1777–June 19, 1778*, Bowie, MD: Heritage Books (2000), 1; Jedediah Huntington to Joshua Huntington, 20 December 1777, in *Correspondence of the Brothers Joshua and Jedediah Huntington During the Period of the American Revolution*, Hartford: Connecticut Historical Society (1923), 386–87.

20. Lengel, *General George Washington*, 266–68; Freeman 4:564; Bodle, 59–64, 104–5; John B. B. Trussell, *Birthplace of an Army: A Study of the Valley Forge Encampment*, Harrisburg: Pennsylvania Historical and Museum Commission (1976), 1, 13; from Nathanael Greene, 1 December 1777, GWP; Middlekauf, *Washington's Revolution*, 172.

21. Lloyd A. Brown and Howard H. Peckham, *Revolutionary War Journals of Henry Dearborn, 1775–1783*, Chicago: The Caxton Club (1939), 13; *Memoir of a Revolutionary Soldier: The Narrative of Joseph Plumb Martin*, Mineola, NY: Dover Publications (2006), 57.

22. Martin, *Memoir*, 58; Albigence Waldo diary, 14 December 1777, in Commager and Morris, *The Spirit of 'Seventy-Six*, 640–41; see Nathanael Greene to Christopher Greene, 5 January 1778, in Showman, *Greene Papers* 2:248.

23. From General James Varnum, 22 December 1777, GWP; Thomas Jones and John Chaloner to Thomas Wharton Jr. and the Supreme Executive Council of Pennsylvania, 24 December 1777, in Boyle, *Writings from the Valley Forge Encampment*, 5; Albigence Waldo, 21 December 1777, in Commager and Morris, *The Spirit of 'Seventy-Six*, 641; to Henry Laurens, 23 December 1777, GWP; Fleming, *Washington's Secret War*, 25.

24. Dearborn, *Journals*, 119 (23 and 26 December 1777); General Orders, 18 December 1777, GWP; Trussell, *Birthplace of an Army* 19.

25. Jonathan Todd Jr. to Jonathan Todd Sr., 25 December 1777 and 19 January 1777, in Boyle, *Writings from the Valley Forge Encampment*, 6, 30; Martin, *Memoir*, 58: George Ewing, *Military Journal of George Ewing*, Yonkers: T. Ewing (1928), 25.

26. Thomas Paine to Benjamin Franklin, 16 May 1778, PBF; Mark Edward Lender and Garry Wheeler Stone, *Fatal Sunday: George Washington, the Monmouth Campaign, and the*

Politics of Battle, Norman: University of Oklahoma Press (2016), 24; Friedrich Kapp, *The Life of John Kalb,* New York: Henry Holt and Co. (1884), 137; A. E. Zucker, *General De Kalb: Lafayette's Mentor,* Chapel Hill: University of North Carolina Press (1966), 163; General Orders, 17 December 1777, GWP; Trussell, *Birthplace of an Army,* 18.

27. John Shreve, "Personal Narrative of the Services of Lt. John Shreve of the New Jersey Line," *Mag. of Amer. Hist.* (September 1879), 568; Colonel William Shepard to Captain David Mosely, 25 January 1778, quoted in Freeman 4:579.

28. Stephen Fried, *Rush: Revolution, Madness, and Benjamin Rush, the Visionary Doctor Who Became a Founding Father,* New York: Crown (2018), 234; General Johann de Kalb to Count Charles Francis de Broglie, 25 December 1777, in Commager and Morris, *The Spirit of 'Seventy-Six,* 646–648; from Alexander Hamilton, 12 November 1777, GWP; Fleming, *Washington's Secret War,* 134–35.

29. From Nathanael Greene, 24 November 1777, GWP; Anthony Wayne to Thomas Wharton, 10 February 1778, in Samuel Hazard, ed., *Pennsylvania Archives,* Philadelphia: Joseph Severns & Co. (1853), 1st Ser. 6:251; Committee at Camp to Henry Laurens, 12 February 1778, in *Letters of Delegates* 9:80.

30. Taylor, *American Revolutions,* 185; Trussell, *Birthplace of an Army,* 39; Jonathan Todd Jr. to Jonathan Todd Sr., 19 January 1778, in Boyle, *Writings from the Valley Forge Encampment,* 31; William Weeks to unidentified, 16 February 1778, in Boyle, *Writings from the Valley Forge Encampment,* 55.

31. To a Continental Congress Camp Committee, 29 January 1778, GWP; to Henry Laurens, 3 February 1778, GWP; to Henry Laurens, 10 November 1777, GWP; from Israel Putnam, 7 November 1777, GWP; Archelaus Lewis to Jesse Partridge, 1 February 1778, in Boyle, *Writings from the Valley Forge Encampment,* 40; Richard Butler to Thomas Wharton Jr., 26 March 1778, in Boyle, *Writings from the Valley Forge Encampment,* 90.

32. To William Buchanan, 7 February 1778, GWP; Thomas Jones to Charles Stewart, 18 February 1778, in Boyle, *Writings from the Valley Forge Encampment,* 63; Ernt Kipping, tr., *At General Howe's Side: The Diary of General William Howe's Aide de Camp, Captain Friedrich Von Muenchhausen,* Monmouth Beach, NJ: Philip Freneau Press (1974), 47; to James Bowdoin, 31 March 1778, GWP; Enoch Poor to Meschach Weare, 21 January 1778, in Boyle, *Writings from the Valley Forge Encampment,* 32: Trussell, *Birthplace of an Army,* 69–70.

33. To Richard Peters, 27 November 1777, GWP; "From Eight Continental Army Field Officers," November 1777, GWP; from Nathanael Greene, 1 December 1777, GWP; to Congress, 22 December 1777, GWP; from James Eldredge, 1 January 1778, GWP; from Major Francis Menges, 26 November 1777, GWP; Albigence Waldo, 28 and 29 December 1777, in Richard M. Dorson, ed., *America Rebels: Narratives of the Patriots,* Westport: Greenwood Press (1973), 216; to John Bannister, 21 April 1778, GWP; John Fitzgerald to Edward Stevens, 24 January 1778, in Boyle, *Writings from the Valley Forge Encampment,* 35–36.

34. General Orders, 22 November and 18 December 1777, GWP; General Orders, 7 and 8 January, 13 and 18 March, 14 April 1778, GWP; to James Mease, 21 January 1778, GWP; to Jonathan Trumbull Sr., 27 January 1778, GWP; to Committee in Camp, 29 January 1778, GWP.

35. Lengel, *General George Washington,* 280.

36. To Henry Knox, 20 February 1784, GWP.

37. Trussell, *Birthplace of an Army,* 97; to John Hancock, 23 April 1776, GWP; Fraser, *The Washingtons,* 191.

38. Trussell, *Birthplace of an Army,* 37–38; Paul Lockhart, *The Drill Master of Valley Forge: The Baron de Steuben and the Making of the American Army,* New York: HarperCollins (2008), 75; Carp, *To Starve the Army,* 55–56.

39. Freeman 4:573; to Richard Henry Lee, 18 November 1777, GWP; Fleming, *Washington's Secret War*, 27; James Lovell to John Adams, 30 December 1777, in *Letters of Delegates* 8:507; Nathanael Greene to Jacob Greene, 3 January 1778, in Showman, *Greene Papers* 2:243–44; Colonel Hugh Hughes to Horatio Gates, 24 August 1777, cited in Carp, *To Starve the Army*, 44; Jacqueline Thibaut, *The Valley Forge Report, Vol. II: This Fatal Crisis: Logistics, Supply, and the Continental Army at Valley Forge, 1777–1778*, Valley Forge National Historical Park (1979), 3–9, 25, 40–42.

40. Nathanael Greene to Jacob Greene, 3 January 1778, in Showman, *Greene Papers* 2:243–44; Thibaut, *This Fatal Crisis*, 7, 38; Carp, *To Starve the Army*, 61.

41. Lengel, *General George Washington*, 272–73; to James Mease, 30 November 1777, 17 April and 16 May 1778, GWP; from James Mease, 16 December 1777, GWP.

42. Nathanael Greene to General Alexander McDougall, 25 January 1778, in Showman, *Greene Papers* 2:261.

43. To Congress, 22 December 1777, GWP; to William Buchanan, 7 February 1778, GWP.

44. To Henry Laurens, 23 December 1777, GWP.

45. Bruce E. Burgoyne, tr. and ed., Johann Conrad Döhla, *A Hessian Diary of the American Revolution*, Norman: University of Oklahoma Press (1990), 66–67; Andrew Jackson O'Shaughnessy, *The Men Who Lost America: British Leadership, the American Revolution, and the Fate of the Empire*, New Haven: Yale University Press, 110.

46. Fleming, *Washington's Secret War*, 44–45, 64–67; Henry Laurens to Rawlins Lowndes, 17 May 1778, in David R. Chesnutt and C. James Taylor, eds., *The Papers of Henry Laurens*, Columbia: University of South Carolina Press, (1992) 13:315.

33. THE FIRST ADVERSARY

1. Jonathan Dickinson Sergeant to James Lovell, 20 November 1777, in *Letters of Delegates*; James Lovell to Joseph Whipple, 21 November 1777, in *Letters of Delegates*; Cornelius Harnett to Thomas Burke, 16 December 1777, in *Letters of Delegates*; Thomas Burke to Richard Caswell, 17 September 1777, in *Letters of Delegates*; Mark Edward Lender, *Cabal!: The Plot Against General Washington*, Yardley, PA: Westholme Publishing (2019), xiii; G. W. Greene, *The Life of Nathanael Greene*, New York: Hurd and Houghton (1871) 1:468. A European officer concluded about Washington that "as a general he is too slow, too indolent, and far too weak . . . and overestimates himself." General Johann de Kalb to Comte de Broglie, 24 September 1777, in Kapp, *Life of John Kalb*, 127.

2. Greene to Miss Susanna Livingston, 11 November 1777, in Showman, *Greene Papers* 2:195; to Patrick Henry, 13 November 1777, GWP; Lafayette to Henry Laurens, 5 January 1778, in Chesnutt and Taylor, *Laurens Papers* 12:254–55; Greene to Alexander McDougall, 25 January 1778, in Showman, *Greene Papers* 2:259–61.

3. Max M. Mintz, *The Generals of Saratoga*, New Haven: Yale University Press (1990), 1–2; *JCC* 9:861–62 (4 November 1777); to Henry Laurens, 1–3 November 1777, GWP; Middlekauf, *Washington's Revolution*, 175; from General Horatio Gates, 2 and 7 November 1777, GWP; from Alexander Hamilton, 5, 6, and 10 November, GWP.

4. From William Alexander, Lord Stirling, 3 November 1777, and note 4, GWP; to General Thomas Conway, 5 November 1777, GWP.

5. James Wilkinson, *Memoirs of My Own Times*, Philadelphia: Abraham Small (1816), 330–32; from William Alexander, Lord Stirling, 3 November 1777, GWP.

6. From Brigadier General Thomas Conway, 5 November 1777, GWP; Kenneth R. Rossman, *Thomas Mifflin and the Politics of the American Revolution*, Chapel Hill: University of North Carolina Press (1952), 117.

7. To Richard Henry Lee, 16 October 1777, GWP.

8. *JCC* 9:871, 873–74 (6 and 7 November 1777); Rossman, *Thomas Mifflin*, 106.

9. Greene to Jacob Greene, 7 February 1778, in Showman, *Greene Papers* 2:277; John Stockton Littell, ed., *Alexander Graydon's Memoirs of His Own Time*, Philadelphia: Lindsay & Blakiston (1846), 299–310; Rossman, *Thomas Mifflin*, 3; Lender, *Cabal*, 83–84; James Lovell to Horatio Gates, 5 October 1777, in *Letters of Delegates*; Thomas Mifflin to Horatio Gates, 17 November 1777, Horatio Gates Papers, Manuscripts and Archives Division, NYPL. The surviving copy of Mifflin's letter of 17 November 1777 is not signed, but shows that it was written at Reading, where Mifflin lived. For some time the letter was attributed to Massachusetts delegate James Lovell, but the editors of the *Letters of Delegates to the Continental Congress* concluded that Mifflin was the author. *Letters of Delegates* 8:315, note 5. That conclusion is supported both by information in the letter that would have come from Mifflin (not Lovell), and by handwriting analysis. Lender, *Cabal*, 244, note 44.

10. Richard Henry Lee to Samuel Adams, 23 November 1777, in Ballagh, *Lee Letters,* 358; Rossman, 97–98; Theodore Thayer, *Nathanael Greene, Strategist of the American Revolution,* New York: Twayne Publishers (1960), 213; James Lovell to Joseph Trumbull, 28 November 1777, in *Letters of Delegates* 8:339.

11. From Brigadier General Thomas Conway, 16 November 1777, GWP; to Brigadier General Thomas Conway, 16 November 1777; *JCC* 9:971–72, 28 November 1777.

12. In a careful study of the scheming in 1777–78, Mark Edward Lender has concluded that the Board of War was the key to the effort to reduce Washington's power and drive him from office. Lender, *Cabal*, passim.

13. Thomas Mifflin to Horatio Gates, 28 November 1777, in note 1 to letter from Brigadier General Thomas Conway, 5 November 1777, GWP.

14. From Major General Horatio Gates, 8 December 1777, GWP. In a letter sent on the same day to Henry Laurens, Gates made the same points. Horatio Gates to Henry Laurens, 8 December 1777, in Chesnutt and Taylor, *Laurens Papers* 12:133. In a letter to Mifflin four days before, he confessed that he was "ruminating who could be the villain that has played me this cursed, treacherous trick." Paul David Nelson, *General Horatio Gates: A Biography,* Baton Rouge: Louisiana State University Press (1976), 164 (quoting from Gates to Mifflin, 4 December 1777).

15. To Major General Thomas Conway, 30 December 1777, GWP; from Major General Thomas Conway, 31 December 1777, GWP.

16. From Dr. James Craik, 6 January 1778, GWP.

17. From Joseph Jones, 22 January 1778, GWP (warning of "a certain popular Pennsylvanian lately appointed to the new Board of War"); John Laurens to Henry Laurens, 3 January 1778, in Chesnutt and Taylor, *Laurens Papers* 12:246; Tench Tilghman to John Cadwalader, 18 January 1778, in Boyle, *Writings from Valley Forge*, 25–26: *Pennsylvania Packet*, January 14, 1778; from Richard Henry Lee, 2 January 1778, GWP; to Richard Henry Lee, 15 February 1778, GWP; L. G. Shreve, *Tench Tilghman, The Life and Times of Washington's Aide-de-Camp,* Centreville, MD: Tidewater Publishers (1982), 34–36, 41, 209–10, 98; Tench Tilghman to Robert Morris, 2 February 1778, in Boyle, *Writings from Valley Forge,* 40.

18. Rossman, *Thomas Mifflin* 120 (Conway to Gates about reports that he, Mifflin, and Gates were intriguing to unseat Washington); Duane, *Diary of Christopher Marshall*, 159 (7 January 1778) ("a cry begins to be raised for a Gates, a Conway, a De Kalb, a Lee"); Benjamin Rush to wife, J. Rush, 15 January 1778, in L. H. Butterfield, *Letters of Benjamin Rush,* Princeton: American Philosophical Society (1951) 1:185–87 (talk in York of a rupture between Gates and Washington); "From Certain General Officers," 31 December 1777, GWP; to Henry Laurens, 2 January 1778, GWP.

19. Littell, *Alexander Graydon's Memoirs*, 300; from Major General Thomas Conway, 10 and 27 January 1778, GWP; Henry Laurens to Isaac Motte, 26 January 1778, in Chesnutt and

Taylor, *Laurens Papers* 12:343; Nathanael Greene to Jacob Greene, 3 January 1778, in Showman, *Greene Papers* 2:243; Alexander Hamilton to George Clinton, 13 February 1778, AHP.

20. To Major General Horatio Gates, 4 January 1778, GWP.

21. Trussell, *Birthplace of an Army*, 95; Fraser, *The Washingtons*, 188–89; Martha Washington to Burwell Bassett, 22 December 1777, in Fields, *Worthy Partner*, 176; Martha Washington to Mercy Otis Warren, 7 March 1778, in Fields, *Worthy Partner*, 177–78; DuPonceau, "Autobiographical Letters," *PMHB* 16:181.

22. Lender, *Cabal*, 152–56.

23. Francis Dana to Elbridge Gerry, 29 January 1778, in *Letters of Delegates* 8:681; Committee in Camp to Henry Laurens, 11 February 1778, in *Letters of Delegates* 9:72–75; *JCC* 10:84 (22 January 1778).

24. Nathanael Greene to General Alexander McDougall, 5 February 1778, in Showman, *Greene Papers* 2:275. The theme of the cabal members was articulated by Dr. Benjamin Rush in an unsigned letter he sent to enlist Governor Patrick Henry of Virginia in the dump-Washington movement. "A Gates, a Lee, or a Conway," Rush wrote, "would in a few weeks render [the army] an irresistible body of men." Benjamin Rush to Patrick Henry, 12 January 1778 (unsigned), in Commager and Morris, *The Spirit of 'Seventy-Six*, 655. Henry promptly sent Rush's letter to Washington along with a denunciation of the cabal. From Patrick Henry, 20 February 1778, GWP.

25. From Lafayette, 30 December 1777, GWP.

26. To Major General Horatio Gates, 27 January 1778, GWP; to General Thomas Nelson Jr., 8 February 1778, GWP.

27. Lafayette to Henry Laurens, 26 January 1778, in Chesnutt and Taylor, *Laurens Papers* 12:350; Henry Laurens to John Rutledge, 30 January 1778, in Chesnutt and Taylor, *Laurens Papers* 12:380; Lafayette to Henry Laurens, 31 January 1778, in Chesnutt and Taylor, *Laurens Papers* 12:387–88; *JCC* 10:106 (2 February 1778).

28. Lafayette to Henry Laurens, 19 February 1778, in Chesnutt and Taylor, *Laurens Papers* 12:468–69; from Lafayette, 19 February 1778, GWP.

29. Fleming, *Washington's Secret War*, 193–96; *JCC* 10:216–17 (2 March 1778); Henry Laurens to Lafayette, 4 March 1778, in Chesnutt and Taylor, *Laurens Papers* 12:512; Lender, *Cabal*, 130–31, 181–83.

30. From Conway, 27 January 1778, GWP; Henry Laurens to Isaac Motte, 26 January 1778, in Chesnutt and Taylor, *Laurens Papers* 12:348.

31. John Adams to Abigail Adams, 17 August 1777, AP; Philip M. Hamer, ed., *The Papers of Henry Laurens*, Columbia: University of South Carolina Press (1968) 1:xiv–xv; Gregory D. Massey, *John Laurens and the American Revolution*, Columbia: University of South Carolina Press (2000), 80; *JCC* 9:854 (1 November 1777); John Laurens to Henry Laurens, 1, 3, and 28 January 1778, in Chesnutt and Taylor 12:231, 12:244–46, 12:370.

32. Henry Laurens to John Lewis Gervais, 5 September 1777, in Chesnutt and Taylor, *Laurens Papers* 11:498; Henry Laurens to John Laurens, 8 January 1778, in Chesnutt and Taylor, *Laurens Papers* 12:269.

33. From General Horatio Gates, 23 January 1778, GWP.

34. To General Horatio Gates, 9 February 1778, GWP; Ebenezer Crosby to Norton Quincey, 14 April 1778, in Boyle, *Writings from Valley Forge*, 102.

35. From Richard Henry Lee, 20–22 November 1777, GWP; *JCC* 10:31–34 (8 January 1778), 10:184 (19 February 1778); W. P. Cresson, *Francis Dana: A Puritan Diplomat at the Court of Catherine the Great*, New York: The Dial Press (1930), 53; Nathanael Greene to General Alexander McDougall, 5 February 1778, in Showman, *Greene Papers* 2:275.

36. From General Horatio Gates, 19 February 1778, GWP; to General Horatio Gates, 24 February 1778, GWP.

37. To John Fitzgerald, 28 February 1778, GWP; Major General Thomas Conway to Henry Laurens, 22 April 1778, in Chesnutt and Taylor, *Laurens Papers* 12:168; *JCC* 10:399 (27 April 1778). In mid-May, Washington heard a report that Conway had requested that Congress reinstate him in the army. Urgently, Washington asked Gouverneur Morris, "Can this be? And if so, will it be granted?" To Gouverneur Morris, 18 May 1778, GWP. Washington wanted Conway out of the army for good. The Irishman sailed back to Europe that summer.

38. Middlekauf, *Washington's Revolution*, 176–77; from Lund Washington, 18 February 1778, GWP (George Mason does not believe the cabal existed); from Lt. Colonel John Fitzgerald, 17 March 1778, GWP.

39. To Patrick Henry, 27 and 28 March 1778, GWP; Tench Tilghman to Robert Morris, 2 February 1778, in Boyle, *Writings from the Valley Forge Encampment*, 41–42. Washington also described the cabal in a letter to Landon Carter, an old friend. To Landon Carter, 30 May 1778, GWP.

40. Henry Laurens to Isaac Motte, 26 January 1778, in Chesnutt and Taylor, *Laurens Papers* 12:346.

41. To Governor William Livingston, 31 December 1777, GWP.

34. THE SECOND ADVERSARY

1. To William Buchanan, 7 February 1778, GWP; Bodle, *Valley Forge Winter*, 156; Theodore G. Tappert and John W. Doberstein, eds., *The Journals of Henry Melchior Muhlenberg*, Philadelphia: Muhlenberg Press (1958) 3:130–31 (9–15 February 1778); from a Continental Congress Camp Committee, 11 February 1778, GWP; Thibaut, *This Fatal Crisis*, 162, 170; Trussell, *Birthplace of an Army*, 22.

2. To William Buchanan, 7 February 1778, GWP; to George Clinton, 16 February 1778, GWP; to William Livingston, 14 February 1778, GWP; from Brigadier General James Varnum, 12 February 1778, GWP; Francis Dana to Elbridge Gerry, 16 February 1778, in *Letters of Delegates* 9:108; John Laurens to Henry Laurens, 17 February 1778, in Chesnutt and Taylor, *Laurens Papers* 12:457; to General William Smallwood, 16 February 1778, GWP; to Patrick Henry, 19 February 1778, GWP; Bodle, *Valley Forge Winter*, 172.

3. Trussell, *Birthplace of an Army*, 28–29; Joseph B. Doyle, *Frederick William von Steuben and the American Revolution*, Steubenville, OH: The H. C. Cook Co. (1913), 84.

4. Kipping, *At General Howe's Side, 1776–1778*, 47; to George Clinton, 16 February 1778, GWP.

5. To Henry Laurens, 5 January 1778, GWP.

6. From Greene, 16 February 1778, GWP.

7. From Greene, 15, 17, and 26 February 1778, GWP.

8. Greene to General Knox, 26 February 1778, in Showman, *Greene Papers* 2:293.

9. General Orders, 1 March 1778, GWP.

10. To Joseph Reed, 3 March 1776, GWP.

11. To Elbridge Gerry, 25 December 1777, GWP.

12. Freeman 4:453; Fleming, *Washington's Secret War*, 13; Henry Laurens to John Laurens, 12 November 1777, in Chesnutt and Taylor, *Laurens Papers* 12:47; Richard Henry Lee to George Wythe, 19 October 1777, in Ballagh, *Lee Papers*, 334; Henry Laurens to James Duane, 7 April 1778, in Chesnutt and Taylor, *Laurens Papers* 13:84; Henry Laurens to John Lewis Gervais, 30 December–30 January 1778, in Chesnutt and Taylor, *Laurens Papers* 12:225; Henry Laurens to John Rutledge, 30 January 1778, in Chesnutt and Taylor, *Laurens Papers* 12:376.

13. Henry Laurens to John Rutledge, 11 March 1778, in Chesnutt and Taylor, *Laurens Papers* 12:543; James Lovell to Joseph Whipple, 6 February 1778, in *Letters of Delegates* 8:41;

Henry Laurens to John Rutledge, 30 January 1778, in Chesnutt and Taylor, *Laurens Papers* 12:376; Henry Laurens to James Duane, 7 April 1778, in Chesnutt and Taylor, *Laurens Papers* 13:84.

14. *JCC* 9:860 (4 November 1777); *JCC* 9:872 (6 November 1777); *JCC* 9:865–68 (5 November 1777); *JCC* 9:878 (6 November 1777); *JCC* 9:988–1001 (3 December 1777).

15. Calvin C. Jillson and Rick K. Wilson, *Congressional Dynamics: Structure, Coordination, and Choice in the First American Congress, 1774–1789*, Stanford: Stanford University Press (1994), 91–92, 94–95, 101.

16. Jillson and Wilson, *Congressional Dynamics*, 66; Richard Henry Lee to Arthur Lee, 19 May 1778, in Ballagh, *Letters of Richard Henry Lee*, 408.

17. Merrill Jensen, *The Articles of Confederation*, Madison: University of Wisconsin Press (1940), 190; Freeman 4:554; *JCC* 9:887, 895–96 (11 and 12 November 1777); "Circular to the States," 28 November 1777, in Chesnutt and Taylor, *Laurens Papers* 12:104–5.

18. From Elbridge Gerry, 13 January 1778, GWP; *JCC* 10:40–41 (10 January 1778). The official announcement to Washington came from Laurens the next day. From Henry Laurens, 14 January 1778, GWP.

19. Lender, *Cabal*, 144; Rossman, *Thomas Mifflin*, 122; *JCC* 10:65–67 (20 January 1778); Bodle, *The Valley Forge Winter*, 144; James Lovell to Sam Adams, 20 January 1778, in *Letters of Delegates*; Henry Laurens to Marquis de Lafayette, 22 January 1778, in Chesnutt and Taylor, *Laurens Papers* 12:327. The committee members who had served in the military were Joseph Reed of Pennsylvania and Nathaniel Folsom of New Hampshire; Washington's friends were Charles Carroll of Maryland, John Harvie of Virginia, and Gouverneur Morris of New York.

20. Cresson, *Francis Dana*, 11, 20, 33, 46; John Adams to Abigail Adams, 26 October 1777, in *Letters of Delegates*.

21. Lengel, *General George Washington*, 275; Fleming, *Washington's Secret War*, 169–70; from Brigadier General James Varnum, 3 January 1778, GWP; from General Henry Knox, 3 January 1778, GWP; to a Continental Congress Camp Committee, 29 January 1778, GWP.

22. Fleming, *Washington's Secret War*, 163; Committee at camp, Minutes of Proceedings, 31 January 1778, 7 February 1778, 14 February 1778, 20 February 1778, in *Letters of Delegates*; Committee in Camp to Henry Laurens, 5 February 1778, in *Letters of Delegates* 9:23–25; *JCC* 10:200 (26 February 1778).

23. Francis Dana to Elbridge Gerry, 16 February 1778, in *Letters of Delegates*.

24. James Lovell to John Adams, 8 December 1777, in *Letters of Delegates*.

25. Gouverneur Morris to John Jay, 2 February 1778, in *Letters of Delegates*; Committee in Camp to Henry Laurens, 12 February 1778, in *Letters of Delegates*; Gouverneur Morris to George Clinton, 17 February 1778, in *Letters of Delegates*; Henry Laurens to Francis Dana; 20 February 1778, in *Letters of Delegates*.

26. Committee in Camp to Henry Laurens, 6 February 1778, in *Letters of Delegates*.

27. *JCC* 10:236–7 (9 March 1778) and 10:248–52 (13 March 1778); Francis Dana to Elbridge Gerry, 29 January 1778, in *Letters of Delegates*.

28. Bodle, *Valley Forge Winter*, 148; Lender and Stone, *Fatal Sunday*, 70–71; Thibaut, *The Fatal Crisis*, 192–93.

29. Erna Risch, *Supplying Washington's Army*, Washington, DC: Center of Military History (1981), 42.

30. Committee in Camp to Henry Laurens, 25 February 1778, in *Letters of Delegates*; Henry Laurens to Francis Dana, 3 March 1778, in *Letters of Delegates*; *JCC* 10:210–11 (2 March 1778); Lender, *Cabal*, 183–84.

31. From Greene, 24 April 1779, GWP; Greene to Henry Knox, 26 February 1778, in Showman, *Greene Papers* 2:294; Nathanael Greene to William Greene, 7 March 1778, in *Letters of Delegates*; Thibaut, *The Fatal Crisis*, 198; Trussell, *Birthplace of an Army*, 23.

32. Cresson, *Francis Dana*, 52.

33. *JCC* 10:199–200 (26 February 1778); from Henry Laurens, 1 March 1778, GWP; from Henry Knox, 4 February 1778, GWP (Massachusetts legislature unwilling to adopt conscription); from George Read, 2 March 1778, GWP (Delaware assembly rejected conscription); 11 March 1778, from Lund Washington, GWP; from Lt. Colonel John Fitzgerald, 17 March 1778, GWP; from Brigadier General George Weedon, 30 March 1778, GWP.

34. *JCC* 10:285–87 (26 March 1778), 10:290 (27 March 1778), 10:282 (28 March 1778), 10:300–301 (1 April 1778), 10:302 (2 April 1778), 10:357–59 (16 April 1778), 10:362–63 (17 April 1778), 10:373–74 (21 April 1778), 10:394 (26 April 1778; Sunday session), 10:398 (27 April 1778); Fleming, *Washington's Secret War*, 226–27; Jillson and Wilson, *Congressional Dynamics*, 197–98; Henry Laurens to James Duane, 7 April 1778, in Chesnutt and Taylor, *Laurens Papers* 13:82; Henry Laurens, "Notes on half-pay," 17–21 April 1778, in Chesnutt and Taylor, *Laurens Papers* 13:138.

35. To Henry Laurens, 10 April 1778, GWP; *JCC* 11:495–96 (13 May 1778); Jillson and Wilson, *Congressional Dynamics*, 213–19; Brown and Peckham, *Dearborn Journals*, 121 (19 May 1778); Bodle, *Valley Forge Winter*, 228; General Orders, 18 May 1778, GWP; to Henry Laurens, 18 May 1778, GWP. When the army was disbanded in 1783, officers were allowed to reduce (or "commute") to a lump sum their right to seven years at half-pay, then they were given paper "certificates" for the lump sum; most officers sold those certificates at deep discounts over the next seven years, until the new Congress under the Constitution finally funded the nation's war debts as proposed by then-President Washington and his secretary of the treasury, Alexander Hamilton. David Head, *A Crisis of Peace: George Washington, The Newburgh Conspiracy, and the Fate of the American Revolution*, New York: Pegasus Books (2019), 210–11; chapters 43 and 44, *infra*.

36. Greene to William Greene, 7 March 1778, in Showman, *Greene Papers* 2:301; Albigence Waldo Diary, in Dorson, *American Rebels*, 26 December 1777, 215; Moré de Pontgibaud, *Memoirs*, in Chinard, *George Washington as the French Knew Him*, 28.

35. THE THIRD ADVERSARY

1. Peter S. DuPonceau, "Autobiographical Letters of Peter S. DuPonceau," *PMHB* 40:172 (1916); Fleming, *Washington's Secret War*, 207; Lockhart, *The Drill Master of Valley Forge*, 8–45. Noting direct evidence of Steuben's homosexuality from his military service in Europe, several scholars have concluded that his close male relationships with younger American officers were sexually intimate. William Benemann, *Male-Male Intimacy in Early America: Beyond Romantic Friendships*, New York: Routledge (2012), 95–105; Randy Shilts, *Conduct Unbecoming: Gays and Lesbians in the U.S. Military*, New York: St. Martin's Griffin (2005), 7–11.

2. Lockhart, *The Drill Master of Valley Forge*, 64–66; to Henry Laurens, 27 February 1778, GWP; John Laurens to Henry Laurens, 9 March 1778, in Chesnutt and Taylor, *Laurens Papers* 12:532; Joseph H. Jones, ed., *The Life of Ashbel Green*, New York: Robert Carter and Brothers (1849), 109; Lockhart, *Drill Master of Valley Forge*, 89.

3. Baron von Steuben, *Regulations for the Order and Discipline of the Troops of the United States*, Exeter, NH: Henry Ranlet (1794).

4. General Orders, 17 March 1778, GWP; Trussell, *Birthplace of an Army*, 58–61; "Circular to Brigade Commanders," 19 March 1778, GWP; General Orders, 28 March 1778, GWP.

5. John MacAuley Palmer, *General Von Steuben*, New Haven: Yale University Press (1937), 157. John Laurens found the acting Inspector General was "not so much a systematist as to be averse from adapting established forms to stubborn circumstances." John Laurens to Henry Laurens, 28 February 1778, in Chesnutt and Taylor, *Laurens Papers* 12:483.

6. Lockhart, *Drill Master of Valley Forge*, 90, 96, 100–2; Thomas Ewing, ed., *The Military Journal of George Ewing, Soldier of Valley Forge*, Yonkers: Thomas Ewing (1928), 34 (7 April 1778); Fleming, *Washington's Secret War*, 213, 219–20; Martin, *Memoir of a Revolutionary Soldier*, 67; General Orders, 22 March 1778, GWP; Lender and Stone, *Fatal Sunday*, 66.

7. Lengel, *General George Washington*, 282; Alexander Scammell to General John Sullivan, 8 April 1778, in William F. Goodwin, "Colonel Alexander Scammell and his Letters," *The Historical Magazine* (September 1870), 142–43.

8. Von Steuben, *Regulations*, 72, 74.

9. "Autobiographical Letters of Peter S. Deponceau," 40:15. Steuben referred to the attendees at the dinner as his "sans-culottes," anticipating by more than a decade the use of that term in the French Revolution.

10. Lockhart, *Drill Master of Valley Forge*, 110; to Henry Laurens, 30 April 1778, GWP; General Orders, 4 May 1778, GWP. Many European officers at Valley Forge had the same mastery over formal drill that Steuben did, but only Steuben had the flair and humility to instruct the Americans effectively.

11. Richard Peters to Timothy Pickering, 9 June 1778, quoted in Lockhart, *Drill Master of Valley Forge*, 128; to Baron von Steuben to Henry Laurens, 15 May 1778, in Chesnutt and Taylor, *Laurens Papers* 13:307.

12. From Henry Laurens, 18 April 1778, GWP.

13. From Duportail, 20 April 1778, GWP; "Washington's Thoughts Upon a Plan of Operation for Campaign 1778," 26–29 April 1778, GWP; "From Council of War," 9 May 1778, GWP.

14. Taylor, *American Revolutions*, 189; Fleming, *Washington's Secret War*, 242–45.

15. To John Bannister, 21 April 1778, GWP; to Henry Laurens, 30 April 1778, GWP.

16. General Orders, 17 December 1777, GWP; James Lovell to William Whipple, 8 December 1777, in *Letters of Delegates*; Greene to Miss Susanna Livingston, 11 November 1777, in Showman, *Greene Papers* 2:195; Nathanael Greene to Jacob Greene, 3 January 1778, in Showman, *Greene Papers* 2:244; Richard Henry Lee to Patrick Henry, 24 November 1777, in Ballagh, *Letters of Richard Henry Lee*, 360; De Kalb to Henry Laurens, 7 January 1778, in Chesnutt and Taylor, *Laurens Papers* 12:269; to General Thomas Nelson Jr., 10 December 1777, GWP.

17. JCC 11:417 (2 May 1778); JCC 11:457 (4 May 1778); William C. Allen to Theodore Foster, 3 May 1778, in Boyle, *Writings from Valley Forge*, 129; *The Military Journal of George Ewing*, 47 (4 May 1778).

18. Admiralty Board to Admiral Richard Howe, 22 March 1778, quoted in Piers Mackesy, *The War for America, 1775–1783*, Cambridge: Harvard University Press (1964), 186.

19. Lender and Stone, *Fatal Sunday*, 4; Lengel, *General George Washington*, 284, 286; William B. Willcox, ed., *Sir Henry Clinton's Narrative of his Campaigns, 1775–1782*, Hamden, CT: Archon Books (1971), xvii; Willcox, *Portrait of a General*, 222–225; O'Shaughnessy, *The Men Who Lost America*, 214.

20. General Orders, 5 May 1778, GWP; John Laurens to Henry Laurens, 7 May 1778, in Chesnutt and Taylor, *Laurens Papers* 13:264–65; Fleming, *Washington's Secret War*, 249–53.

21. To Robert Morris, 25 May 1778, GWP; to Landon Carter, 30 May 1778, GWP; William Bradford, Jr. to Rachel Bradford Boudinot, 14 May 1778, in Ford, *Washington and the Theatre*, 26; Henry Laurens to Baron von Steuben, 11 May 1778, in Chesnutt and Taylor, *Laurens Papers* 13:290.

22. Burgoyne, *Johann Conrad Döhla*, 73–74 (17 May 1778); Major John Andre to unknown person, 23 May 1778, in Commager and Morris, *The Spirit of 'Seventy-Six*, 657–58.

23. Burgoyne, *Johann Conrad Döhla*, 73 (17 May 1778); Fleming, *Washington's Secret War*, 273.

24. Richard Henry Lee to Thomas Jefferson, 16 June 1778, in Ballagh, *Letters of Richard Henry Lee*, 412; from Carlisle Commission to Henry Laurens, 9 June 1778, in Chesnutt and Taylor, *Laurens Papers* 13:424–27; to William Eden, 15 June 1778, GWP. One of the

British commissioners had a connection to Washington: His brother had been royal governor of Maryland, a friend of the American commander in chief and His host during several prewar visits to Annapolis.

25. Henry Laurens to Horatio Gates, 13 June 1778, in Chesnutt and Taylor, *Laurens Papers* 13:451; Henry Laurens to George Johnstone, 14 June 1778, in Chesnutt and Taylor, *Laurens Papers* 13:455; Henry Laurens to Carlisle Commission, 17 June 1778, in Chesnutt and Taylor, *Laurens Papers* 13:471; Henry Laurens to Earl of Carlisle and other British Commissioners, 17 June 1778, in Commager and Morris, *The Spirit of 'Seventy-Six*, 698; Lord Carlisle to Lady Carlisle, 21 July 1778, in Commager and Morris, *The Spirit of 'Seventy-Six*, 701 (21 July 1778); *JCC* 11:614 (17 June 1778); *Memoir of Lieut. Colonel Tench Tilghman*, Albany: J. Munsell (1876), 168 (letter to father, 31 May 1778).
26. To Bryan Fairfax, 1 March 1778, GWP.
27. Fleming, *Washington's Secret War*, 276.
28. John Laurens to Henry Laurens, 9 March 1778, in Chesnutt and Taylor, *Laurens Papers* 12:532; John Laurens to Henry Laurens, 23 December 1777, in Chesnutt and Taylor, *Laurens Papers* 12:87; to John Bannister, 21 April 1778, GWP.

36. VICTORY, HE SAID

1. Tench Tilghman to father, 31 May 1778, in Tilghman, *Memoir*, 168; Tustin, *Captain Johann Ewald's Diary of the American War*, 130 (22 May 1778); Willcox, *Portrait of a General*, 226–27; Willcox, *Sir Henry Clinton's Narrative*, 86; Bodle, *The Valley Forge Winter*, 231.
2. Lender and Stone, *Fatal Sunday*, 17–51.
3. O'Shaughnessy, *The Men Who Lost America*, 210–12, 221; Lender and Stone, *Fatal Sunday*, 69; Thibaut, *This Fatal Crisis*, 238; Moré de Pontgibaud, *Memoirs*, in Chinard, *George Washington as the French Knew Him*, 28.
4. Lender and Stone, *Fatal Sunday*, 111–12; Dominick Mazzagetti, *Charles Lee: Self Before Country*, New Brunswick: Rutgers University Press (2013), 140–48; Fleming, 299–301.
5. W. Wallace Atterbury, *Elias Boudinot: Reminiscences of the American Revolution*, New York (1894), 21; Elias Boudinot, *Journal or Historical Recollections of American Events During the Revolutionary War*, Philadelphia: Frederick Bourquin (1894), 78–79; Nathanael Greene to Gov. William Greene, 25 May 1778, in Showman, *Greene Papers* 2:408; Lender and Stone, *Fatal Sunday*, 114; Charles Lee to Henry Laurens, 17 April 1778, in Chesnutt and Taylor, *Laurens Papers* 13:133.
6. Council of War, 9 May 1778, GWP; to Nathanael Greene, 8 June 1778, GWP; General Orders, 9 June 1778, GWP; to John Augustine Washington, 10 June 1778, GWP.
7. From Lafayette, 17 June 1778, GWP; from Nathanael Greene, 18 June 1778, GWP; Lender and Stone, *Fatal Sunday*, 103.
8. Willcox, *Sir Henry Clinton's Narrative*, 90; Tustin, *Captain Johann Ewald's Diary*, 135 (lost more than 200 men to the heat on 26 June); Brown and Peckham, *Journals of Henry Dearborn*, 125 (26 and 27 June 1778); Martin, *Notes of a Revolutionary Soldier*, 71; from Philemon Dickinson, 23 June 1778, 11:30 p.m., GWP.
9. Lender and Stone, *Fatal Crisis*, 93–94; to Philemon Dickinson, 24 May 1778 and 5–7 June 1778, GWP; Fleming, *Washington's Secret War*, 311–12; "Journal of John Charles Von Krafft," *Collections of the New York Historical Society for the year 1882*, New York (1883), 45 (24 June 1778); Tustin, *Captain Johann Ewald's Diary*, 134–35; Benedict Arnold to Henry Laurens, 24 June 1778; in Chesnutt and Taylor, *Laurens Papers* 13:511–12; from Benedict Arnold, 22 June 1778, GWP; from Philemon Dickinson, 19 June 1778, GWP; "Joseph Plumb Martin Diary," in Commager and Morris, *Spirit of 'Seventy-Six*, 714;

Martin, *Memoir of a Revolutionary Soldier*, 71; Greene to Jacob Greene, 2 July 1778, in Showman, *Greene Papers* 2:449.

10. Council of War, 24 June 1778, GWP; Lafayette, *Memoirs*, in Commager and Morris, *Spirit of 'Seventy-Six*, 710–11; Hamilton to Elias Boudinot, 5 July 1778, PAH.

11. From Nathanael Greene, 24 June 1778, GWP; from Lafayette, 24 June 1778, GWP; from Anthony Wayne, 24 June 1778, GWP.

12. *Proceedings of a General Court-Martial Held at Brunswick, in the State of New Jersey, . . . for the Trial of Major-General Lee*, privately reprinted (1864), 27 (Wayne).

13. "Journal of John Charles Von Krafft," 47; Lender and Stone, *Fatal Sunday*, 157–58.

14. To Major General Lafayette, 26 June 1778, GWP; from Major General Charles Lee, 25 June 1778, GWP; Lender and Stone, *Fatal Sunday*, 178–83. A Washington aide, James McHenry, described Lafayette as "in raptures with his command and burning to distinguish himself." James McHenry, *Journal of a March, a Battle, and a Waterfall*, Greenwich, CT (1945), 4; from Major General Charles Lee, 25 June 1778, GWP.

15. Mazzagetti, *Self Before Country*, 171; to Charles Lee, 30 June 1778.

16. Lender and Stone, *Fatal Sunday*, 194–95; *Lee Court-Martial*, 5 (General Scott), 6, 25–26 (General Wayne), 9 (Lt. Colonel Meade); Mazzagetti, *Self Before Country*, 164–67.

17. Lengel, *General George Washington*, 297–99; Middlekauf, *Washington's Revolution*, 191; Lender and Stone, *Fatal Sunday*, 253–54; *Lee Court-Martial*, 14–16 (Lafayette).

18. Lender and Stone, *Fatal Sunday*, 261–68, 271–72; *Lee Court-Martial*, 18 (Lafayette), 31–32 (General Forman), 39 (Colonel Scilly), 93 (Tench Tilghman); Brown and Peckham, *Journals of Henry Dearborn*, 127–28 (28 June 1778).

19. To Henry Laurens, 28 June 1778, 11:30 a.m., GWP; Lender and Stone, *Fatal Sunday*, 236, 282; *Lee Court-Martial*, 61 (Lt. Colonel Lawrence), 72–73 (Lt. Colonel Meade).

20. Lender and Stone, *Fatal Sunday*, 284–85; *Lee Court-Martial*, 91–92 (Tench Tilghman).

21. *Lee Court-Martial*, 90 (McHenry), 128 (Colonel Mercer), 164 (Lt. Colonel Brooks), 74 (Lt. Colonel Meade), 93 (Tilghman), 129 (Colonel Mercer); Martin, *Notes of a Revolutionary Soldier*, 72; Lender and Stone, *Fatal Sunday*, 289–90. A legend that grew around this confrontation portrayed Washington turning the air blue with his curses, calling Lee a "damned poltroon" and riding off in a rage. That the commander was angry is unquestioned. The evidence that he swore and raged is extremely weak. Lender and Stone, *Fatal Sunday*, 290–91.

22. *Lee Court-Martial*, 32 (General Forman), 85 (Lt. Colonel Harrison), 68 (Hamilton), 93 (Tilghman), 129 (Colonel Mercer); John Laurens to Henry Laurens, 30 June 1778, in Chesnutt and Taylor, *Laurens Papers* 13:532–35; Nathanael Greene to Jacob Greene, 2 July 1778, in Showman, *Greene Papers* 2:449–51. Much of this battle narrative is informed by the masterful study of the Monmouth battle in Lender and Stone, *Fatal Sunday*, 282–347.

23. Brown and Peckham, *Journals of Henry Dearborn*, 127 (28 June 1778).

24. Brown and Peckham, *Journals of Henry Dearborn*, 127–28 (28 June 1778).

25. Samuel Smith, *Memoirs of Samuel Smith, a Soldier of the Revolution*, New York (1860), 15; "Journal of John Charles Von Krafft," 47 (28 June 1778); John Laurens to Henry Laurens, 30 June 1778, in Chesnutt and Taylor, *Laurens Papers* 13:534; Martin, *Notes of a Revolutionary Soldier*, 73–74; Greene to Jacob Greene, 2 July 1778, in Showman, *Greene Papers* 2:451.

26. Greene to Jacob Greene, 2 July 1778, Showman, *Greene Papers*; James McHenry to George Lux, 30 June 1778, in James McHenry, "The Battle of Monmouth," *Magazine of American Hist.* 3:355–63 (1879). Writing to his father, John Laurens gave Washington full credit for any American success. "The merit of restoring the day is due to the General, and his conduct was such throughout the affair as has greatly increased my love and esteem for him." John Laurens to Henry Laurens, 30 June 1778, in Chesnutt and Taylor, *Laurens Papers* 13:545.

27. Lender and Stone, *Fatal Sunday*, 366–68, 375; Tustin, *Captain Johann Ewald's Diary*, 136 (28 June 1778).

28. General Orders, 29 June 1778, GWP; General Orders, 30 June 1778, GWP; James McHenry to George Lux, 30 June 1778, in McHenry, "The Battle of Monmouth," 356; Brown and Peckham, *Journals of Henry Dearborn*, 130 (4 July 1778); Fleming, *Washington's Secret War*, 328; General Orders, 4 July 1778, GWP.

29. JCC 11:673 (7 July 1778); Lender and Stone, *Fatal Sunday*, 389.

30. From Major General Charles Lee, 30 June 1778, GWP.

31. To Major General Charles Lee, 30 June 1778, GWP; from Major General Charles Lee, 30 June 1778, GWP.

32. *Lee Court-Martial*, passim; *JCC* 12:1195 (5 December 1778).

33. Lender and Stone offer a sturdy defense of Lee's conduct at Monmouth; they insist that he performed at a high level throughout the day. In view of Lee's very limited preparation to attack and his repeated failure to control his vanguard through the morning, plus Lee's retort to Washington that he never wanted to attack in the first place, that defense feels thin. Mazzagetti, in *Self Before Country*, argues that Lee's erratic behavior flowed from his vulnerability to exposure by the enemy as a traitor. Christian McBurney, *George Washington's Nemesis: The Outrageous Treason and Unfair Court-Martial of Major General Charles Lee During the Revolutionary War*, El Dorado Hills, CA: Savas Beatie (2020). (Lee acted treasonably while in British captivity.) Though that contention is not readily provable, it warrants consideration.

34. Willcox, *Sir Henry Clinton's Narrative*, 98; Richard Henry Lee to Francis Lightfoot Lee, 5 July 1778, in Ballagh, *Letters of Richard Henry Lee*, 420–21; Greene to Jacob Greene, 2 July 1778, in Showman, *Greene Papers* 2:451; John Laurens to Henry Laurens, 30 June 1778, in Chesnutt and Taylor, *Laurens Papers* 13:536. Among those works concluding that Monmouth was a draw are Middlekauf, *Washington's Revolution*, 190–92, and Lengel, *General George Washington*, 304–5. This book concurs with Lender and Stone in *Fatal Sunday* that "it was on the political front that Monmouth had the greatest significance. There, the [Americans'] victory was decisive." 425–26.

35. JCC 11:591 (11 June 1778). A week after the Monmouth battle, Pennsylvania militia general John Cadwalader provoked Conway to challenge him to a duel, at which Cadwalader shot him through the mouth. Fleming, *Washington's Secret War*, 328–29.

36. Greene to Jacob Greene, 3 January 1778, in Showman, *Greene Papers* 2:244.

37. JCC 11:631–658 (22 June 1778) and 11:662–670 (27 June 1778).

37. THE LONG, BUMPY VICTORY LAP

1. To John Augustine Washington, 6 June–6 July 1780, GWP.

2. Excellent accounts of this final campaign of the war are in Nathaniel Philbrick, *In the Hurricane's Eye: The Genius of George Washington and the Victory at Yorktown*, New York: Viking (2018), and Richard M. Ketchum, *Victory at Yorktown: The Campaign That Won the Revolution*, New York: Henry Holt and Co. (2004).

3. Freeman 5:401–3; to Jonathan Trumbull Jr., 6 November 1781, GWP; François Jean de Chastellux, *Travels in North America in the Years 1780, 1781, and 1782*, London: G.G.J. and J. Robinson (1787), 96–97 (Trans. Note).

4. Chastellux, *Travels in North America*, 139–40; Evelyn M. Acomb, ed. and tr., *The Revolutionary Journal of Baron Ludwig von Closen, 1780–1783*, Chapel Hill: University of North Carolina Press (1958), 102. Washington's father died at forty-three; his half-brothers Lawrence at thirty-four and Austin at forty-two; and younger brother Samuel succumbed to tuberculosis at age forty-seven, just five weeks before Jack Custis died. Samuel had

outlived four of his five wives and left behind several children for his elder brother George to see to adulthood, including George Steptoe Washington, Lawrence Augustine Washington, and Harriott Washington. The adult Washington had not been close to Samuel, who was known as a heavy drinker and had moved to western Virginia. Washington also disapproved of Samuel's eldest child, Ferdinand Washington, and never supported him. From George Steptoe Washington, 2 March 1787, GWP; to Robert Chambers, 28 January 1789, GWP.

5. To Greene, 16 November 1781, GWP; to Lafayette, 15 November 1781, GWP. The other failed British generals were Gage, Burgoyne, Cornwallis, and Howe.

6. Richard H. Kohn, *Eagle and Sword: The Federalists and the Creation of the Military Establishment in America, 1783–1802*, New York: The Free Press (1975), 19–20; Ebenezer Huntington to Andrew Huntington, 7 July 1780, in G.W.F. Blanchfield, ed., *Letters Written by Ebenezer Huntington, 1774–1781*, New York: C. F. Heartman (1915), 87; Head, *A Crisis of Peace*, 40–41.

7. James Thacher, *A Military Journal During the American Revolutionary War, from 1775 to 1783*, Boston: Richardson and Lord (1823), 295–97; Mary A. Y. Gallagher, "Reinterpreting the 'Very Trifling Mutiny' at Philadelphia in June 1783," *PMHB* 119:3, 9–10 (1995).

8. An officer in the punitive expedition sympathized with the soldiers, who had "long suffered many serious grievances, which they have sustained with commendable patience." James Thacher, *A Military Journal*, 302–4.

9. To Benjamin Lincoln, 2 October 1782, GWP.

10. Douglas A. Irwin and Richard Sylla, *Founding Choices: American Economic Policy in the 1790s*, Chicago: University of Chicago Press (2011), 92; Kohn, *Eagle and Sword*, 21–22; JCC 24:284 (29 April 1783) (listing debts).

11. Gouverneur Morris to John Jay, 1 January 1783, in E. James Ferguson, ed., *The Papers of Robert Morris, 1781–1784*, Pittsburgh: University of Pittsburgh Press (1973); Richard H. Kohn, "The Inside History of the Newburgh Conspiracy: America and the Coup d'Etat," *WMQ* 27:187, 191 note 9 (1970); "Observations on the Present State of Affairs," 13 January 1783, in Ferguson, *Robert Morris Papers* 1:305–6 (the "clamors of the army" could assist in acquiring approval of a tax); from Hamilton, 11 April 1783, GWP.

12. Ebenezer Huntington to Andrew Huntington, 9 December 1782, in Blanchfield, *Letters Written by Ebenezer Huntington*, 102; Head, *A Crisis of Peace*, 62–65, 73–77.

13. JCC 24:291–93 (29 April 1783); Edward Larson, *The Return of George Washington, 1783–1789*, New York: William Morrow (2014), 13; Alexander McDougall to Henry Knox, 9 January 1783, in Edmund Burnett, ed., *Letters of Members of the Continental Congress*, Washington, DC: Carnegie Institution (1934) 7:14 note 2; Abner Nash to James Iredell, 8 January 1783, in *Letters of Delegates* 19:565; Minor Myers, Jr., *Liberty Without Anarchy: A History of the Society of the Cincinnati*, Charlottesville: University Press of Virginia (1983), 9; Alexander Hamilton to George Clinton, 12 January 1783, in *Letters of Delegates* 19:577–78.

14. Notes of Debates in Congress by James Madison, 25, 27, and 28 January 1783, *Letters of Delegates*; Charles Rappleye, *Robert Morris: Financier of the American Revolution*, New York: Simon & Schuster (2011), 338; G. Morris to Knox, 7 February 1783, in Burnett, *Letters of Members of the Continental Congress* 7:34 note 2; Kohn, *Eagle and Sword*, 195.

15. *Pennsylvania Packet*, February 11, 1782; Virginia Delegates to the Governor of Virginia, 11 February 1782, in Burnett, *Letters of Members of the Continental Congress* 7:39; Notes of Debates in the Continental Congress by James Madison, 13 February 1783, in *JCC* 25:898.

16. Hamilton to Washington, 13 February 1783, in GWP.

17. Rappleye, *Robert Morris*, 343; "Notes of Conversation with Colonel William Duer," 12 October 1788, in Charles King, ed., *The Life and Correspondence of Rufus King*, New York: G. P. Putnam's Sons (1894) 1:621–22; Gates to John Armstrong Jr., 22 June 1783, in

George Bancroft, *History of the Formation of the Constitution of the United States,* New York: D. Appleton and Co. (1882) 1:318.

18. *JCC* 24:295–97 (24 April 1783).

19. General Orders, 11 March 1783, GWP; to Hamilton, 12 March 1783, GWP; to Robert Morris, 12 March 1783, GWP; General Orders, 13 March 1783, GWP.

20. *JCC* 24:298–99 (29 April 1783).

21. From Joseph Jones, 27 February 1783, GWP; to Hamilton, 12 March 1783, GWP.

22. From Horatio Gates, 31 December 1782, GWP; Myers, *Liberty Without Anarchy,* 11; Kohn, "Inside History," 209; Charles Royster, *A Revolutionary People at War: The Continental Army and American Character, 1775–1783,* Chapel Hill: University of North Carolina Press (1979), 332.

23. J. A. Wright to John Webb, 16 March 1783, in Worthington C. Ford, ed., *Correspondence and Journals of Samuel Blachley Webb,* New York: Wickersham Press (1894) 3:5; *The Journals of Major Samuel Shaw,* Boston: Wm. Crosby and H. P. Nichols (1847), 103.

24. *JCC* 24:306–10 (29 April 1783).

25. *Journals of Samuel Shaw,* 103–4; Timothy Pickering to Samuel Hodgdon, 16 March 1783, in Octavius Pickering, ed., *The Life of Timothy Pickering,* Boston: Little, Brown & Co. (1867) 1:437–39; David Cobb to Timothy Pickering, 9 November 1825, in *Life of Timothy Pickering* 1:431–32.

26. *JCC* 24:310–11 (29 April 1783).

27. *JCC* 24:305 (29 April 1783).

28. *JCC* 24:207–10 (22 March 1783).

29. To Hamilton, 16 April 1783, GWP.

30. *JCC* 24:242 (15 April 1783); to Luzerne, 29 March 1783, GWP.

31. To Guy Carleton, 6 May 1783, GWP; "Account of a Conference Between Washington and Sir Guy Carleton," 6 May 1783, GWP.

32. To Theodorick Bland, 4 April 1783, GWP (first letter to Bland of that date); *JCC* 24:253 (14 April 1783 report of visit to Newburgh camp), 24:269–70 (23 April 1783), 24:323–26 (2 May 1783), 24:358–61 (23 May 1783), 24:364–65 (26 May 1783); General Orders, 2 June 1783, GWP; Head, *A Crisis of Peace,* 189–90.

33. William Abbott, ed., *Memoirs of Major General William Heath,* New York: William Abbott (1901), 354; Mary A. Y. Gallagher, "Reinterpreting the 'Very Trifling Mutiny' at Philadelphia in June 1783," *PMHB* 119:3, 17–27 (1995); Thomas Fleming, *The Perils of Peace: America's Struggle for Survival After Yorktown,* New York: Smithsonian Books (2007), 291–92; to Elias Boudinot, 24 June 1783, GWP; Head, *A Crisis of Peace,* passim; Bowling, *The Creation of Washington, D.C.,* 30–35. One army officer suggested that with better leadership, the mutineers would have been a potent force. John Armstrong Jr. to Horatio Gates, 9 May 1783, in Burnett, *Letters of Members of the Continental Congress* 7:175, note 3.

34. From Jedediah Huntington, 16 May 1783, GWP.

35. Rappleye, *Robert Morris,* 356–57; General Orders, 2 June 1783, GWP; Freeman 5:442.

36. Martin, *Memoir of a Revolutionary Soldier,* 158–60; Royster, *A Revolutionary People at War,* 342; Abbott, *Heath Memoirs,* 351; from Henry Knox, 3 January 1784, GWP.

37. Colonel Walter Stewart to General Horatio Gates, 20 June 1783, Thomas Addis Emmet Collection, New York Public Library.

38. To William Stephens Smith, 15 May 1783, GWP; Freeman 4:450; to George Clinton, 12 August 1783, GWP.

39. To Hamilton, 31 March 1783; to Nathanael Greene, 31 March 1783, GWP.

40. "From George Washington to the States," 8 June 1783, GWP; to William Gordon, 8 July 1783.

41. Ibid.

42. Henry Phelps Johnston, ed., *Memoir of Colonel Benjamin Tallmadge,* New York: Gilliss Press (1904), 95–96; *Connecticut Journal,* December 3, 1783.

43. Washington Irving, *Life of George Washington*, New York: J. B. Lippincott & Co. (1873) 4:470; Freeman 5:462–64; *New Brunswick Political Intelligencer*, December 9, 1783; *Pennsylvania Packet*, December 12, 1783; *Connecticut Journal*, December 17, 1783.
44. Fleming, *The Perils of Peace*, 257.
45. Johnston, *Memoir of Colonel Benjamin Tallmadge*, 96–97.
46. Larson, *The Return of George Washington*, 30.
47. James McHenry to Peggy Caldwell, 23 December 1783, in Bernard C. Steiner, *The Life and Correspondence of James McHenry*, Cleveland: The Burrows Brothers Co. (1907), 69–70; Fleming, *Perils of Peace*, 322; *New Jersey Gazette*, January 6, 1784.
48. John Trumbull to [Brother], May 10, 1784, in Garry Wills, *Cincinnatus: George Washington and the Enlightenment*, Garden City, NY: Doubleday & Co. (1984), 13.
49. Dorothy Twohig, "'That Species of Property': Washington's Role in the Controversy of Slavery," in Don Higginbotham, ed., *George Washington Reconsidered*, Charlottesville: University Press of Virginia (2001), 121.

38. HOME, NOT RETIRED

1. To Lafayette, 1 February 1784, GWP.
2. To Knox, 20 February 1787, GWP.
3. To George William Fairfax, 10 November 1785, GWP; to Charles Washington, 28 March 1784, GWP; to George Augustine Washington, 1784, GWP.
4. From Benjamin Harrison, Sr., 25 February 1781, GWP; to Benjamin Harrison, Sr., 25 February 1781, GWP.
5. Chernow, 423; to John Augustine Washington, 16 January 1783, GWP; from the Citizens of Fredericksburg, 14 February 1784, GWP; *Virginia Gazette*, February 21, 1784.
6. To Fielding Lewis Jr., 27 February 1784, GWP; Willard Sterne Randall, *George Washington: A Life*, New York: Henry Holt & Co. (1997), 402–4; Bruce S. Thornton and Victor Davis Hanson, "'The Western Cincinnatus': Washington as Farmer and Soldier," in Gregg and Spalding, *Patriot Sage*, 55.
7. Marvin Kitman, *George Washington's Expense Account*, New York: Grove Press (1970), 31; to Robert Morris, 4 January 1784, GWP; to James Milligan, 18 February 1784, GWP.
8. To Samuel Vaughan, 14 January 1784, GWP; to William Hamilton, 15 January 1784, GWP; Louis B. Wright and Marion Tinling, eds., *Quebec to Carolina in 1785–1786, Being the Travel Diary and Observations of Robert Hunter, Jr., a Young Merchant of London*, San Marino: Huntington Library (1943), 195. Washington's secretary, Tobias Lear, provided a very similar description of Washington's usual day in retirement, adding only that the general sometimes played whist in the evening. Tobias Lear to William Prescott Jr., 4 March 1788, in "Lear Letter," *Mount Vernon Ladies' Association Annual Report* (1958), 21–22.
9. Wright and Tinling, *Travel Diary of Robert Hunter*, 191, 193 (17 November 1785).
10. Jared Sparks, *The Life of George Washington*, Boston: Little, Brown & Co. (1853), 521–22 (letter from Nelly Custis, 26 February 1833); William Harden, "William McWhir: An Irish Friend of Washington," *Georgia Hist. Q.* 1:200 (1917); Wright and Tinling, *Travel Diary of Robert Hunter*, 194. Of the many newspapers he received, Washington attended most to the *Pennsylvania Packet* from Philadelphia and the *Virginia Gazette*. Freeman 6:126.
11. To Arthur Young, 6 August 1786, GWP; to Alexander Spotswood, 13 February 1788; to Levi Hollingsworth, 20 September 1785, GWP; from Arthur Donaldson, 1 October 1785, GWP; Diary, 3 November 1785, 15 July 1786, GWP; Freeman 6:55.
12. To John Francis Mercer, 27 March 1785, 20 December 1785, 12 August 1786, GWP.

13. From Thomas Cushing, 7 October 1786, GWP; to William Fitzhugh Jr., 15 May 1786, GWP; to Lafayette, 10 May 1786, GWP; to William Fitzhugh Sr., 2 July 1786, GWP.

14. From R. Morris, 1 January 1785, GWP; Diary, 30 June 1785, GWP; to Francis Hopkinson, 16 May 1785, GWP; Diary, 30 June 1785, GWP; from Thomas Jefferson, 10 July 1786, GWP; Diary, 2 and 10 October 1786, GWP. Nelly Custis recalled finding, as a young girl, her step-grandfather lying on a table, with quills in his nostrils to ensure his breathing while Houdon applied plaster to his face for a life mask. Carol Borchert Cadou, *The George Washington Collection: Fine and Decorative Arts at Mount Vernon*, Manchester, VT: Hudson Hills Press (2006), 120 (quoting Eleanor Parke Custis Lewis to George Washington Parke Custis, 5 December 1849, in The Rosenbach, Philadelphia). Other Mount Vernon visitors in this period included the future lexicographer Noah Webster (seeking Washington's support for a new copyright law, and also considering signing on as tutor to Martha's grandchildren), British historian Catherine Macaulay Graham, and the steamboat inventor James Rumsey. From Catherine Macaulay Graham, 13 July 1785, GWP; Diary, 14 and 18 July 1785, GWP.

15. Larson, *The Return of George Washington*, 37; Diary, 29 November 1785, 1, 5, 12, and 19 December 1785, 28 January 1786, 9 February 1786, GWP; to Henry Knox, 5 January 1785, GWP; to Boinod and Gaillard, 18 Feb. 1785, GWP.

16. From George William Fairfax, 23 August 1784, 19 March 1785, 23 June 1785, 23 January 1786, GWP; to George William Fairfax, 27 February 1785, GWP.

17. This paragraph draws on the exploration of Washington's dental woes in Ron Chernow's biography of Washington. Chernow, *George Washington*, 437–39.

18. *New York Packet*, March 25, 1784; Myers, *Liberty Without Anarchy*, 19, 21; Edgar Erskine Hume, "Early Opposition to the Cincinnati," *Americana* 30:597 (1936); Samuel Osgood to John Adams, 14 January 1784, in Burnett, *Letters of Members* 7:416; Samuel Osgood to Stephen Higginson, Annapolis, 2 February 1784, in *Mass. Hist. Soc. Procs.* 5:471, 472–73; Aedanus Burke, *Considerations on the Society or Order of Cincinnati*, Philadelphia: Robert Bell (1783), 4; Myers, *Liberty Without Anarchy*, 17, 25–26, 49; William Eustis, "Statement Concerning the Origin of the Cincinnati," in James M. Bugbee, ed., *Memorials of the Massachusetts Society of the Cincinnati*, Boston: Massachusetts Society (1890), 531–32; Chernow, 497. Even the French minister, a monarchist, thought the society "incompatible with republican government." Abigail Adams reported to her husband in Europe that the society "makes a bustle," but predicted it would "be crushed in its birth." Abigail Adams to John Adams, 11 February 1784, AP. John Adams called it "the deepest piece of cunning yet attempted." John Adams to Elbridge Gerry, 25 April 1785, AP. Henry Knox feared the society would suffer from the people's wrath. Henry Knox to Greene, 10 April 1784, in Showman, *Greene Papers* 12:291. Ben Franklin thought the group was absurd, observing that after nine generations, its members could boast of a 1/512 descent from a Continental Army officer, and doubtless would number "rogues, and fools, and scoundrels, and prostitutes." Franklin to Sarah Bache, 26 January 1784, PBF.

19. Jefferson and former general Arthur St. Clair advised Washington to expunge all hereditary elements from the society or resign from it. From Jefferson, 16 April 1784, GWP; from Arthur St. Clair, 20 April 1784, GWP; "Observations on the Institution of the Society," 4 May 1784, GWP; Jefferson to Martin Van Buren, 29 June 1824, PTJ; Elbridge Gerry to Sam Adams, 13 May 1784, Library of the Society of the Cincinnati, Washington, DC. One friend observed that he had never met a person who was not "sensibly awed in [Washington's] presence, and by the impression of his greatness." Harden, "William McWhir," 200.

20. Winthrop Sargent, *A Journal of the General Meeting of the Cincinnati in 1784*, Philadelphia (1859), 22–28, 40–41, 60. At one point in the convention, Washington thought the society might disband itself, but the delegates' sentiments revived with the unexpected

arrival of golden eagles—the society's insignia—made for them in France at the direction of King Louis XVI. The delegates were thrilled that a great king had so honored their service, when their own country so neglected it. The prospect of dissolving the society quickly evaporated. To Alexander Hamilton, 11 December 1785, GWP; Jefferson to Martin Van Buren, 29 June 1824, PTJ; Sargent, *A Journal of the General Meeting*, 68. When Nathanael Greene died in 1786, the South Carolina society immediately approved his teenage son as a new member when he reached age eighteen. That action signaled that society membership would remain hereditary. *Pennsylvania Packet*, September 11, 1786.

21. To Samuel Vaughan, 30 November 1785, GWP; to Arthur St. Clair, 31 August 1785, GWP. In 1785, the Massachusetts delegates to Congress warned that a national convention to rewrite the Articles of Confederation might be taken over by the Cincinnati in an aristocratic coup. Massachusetts Delegates to the Governor of Massachusetts, 3 September 1785, in Burnett, *Letters of Members* 8:208; Mercy Warren to John Adams, December 1786, AP.

22. From Thomas Walker, 24 January 1784, GWP; to Thomas Walker, 10 April 1784, GWP; to Samuel Lewis, 1 February 1784, GWP; from Thomas Lewis, 24 February 1784, GWP; to Edmund Randolph, 18 March 1784, GWP; to John Witherspoon, 10 March 1784, GWP.

23. From Jefferson, 15 March 1784, GWP.

24. To John Augustine Washington, 30 June 1784, GWP; to Dr. James Craik, 10 July 1784, GWP; Larson, *The Return of George Washington*, 39–47; George William Van Cleve, *We Have Not a Government: The Articles of Confederation and the Road to the Constitution*, Chicago: The University of Chicago Press (2017), 43–44; to Thomas Richardson, 5 July 1784, GWP; advertisement, *Virginia Journal*, July 15, 1784; to Battaile Muse, 5 January 1785, GWP; from Battaile Muse, 12 January 1786, GWP; to George McCarmick, 12 July 1784, GWP.

25. Diary, 5, 9, 22, and 25 September 1784, GWP; Wright and Tinling, *Travel Diary of Robert Hunter*, 191–92. Washington came upon a striking example of the growth of global trade in the 1780s when he passed people on the road who were hauling ginseng roots east for shipment to China. Diary, 12 September 1784, GWP.

26. Diary, 12, 13, 14, 20, 22, and 23 September 1784, GWP. For an extended treatment of this journey by Washington, see Joel Achenbach, *The Grand Idea, George Washington's Potomac and the Race to the West*, New York: Simon & Schuster (2004).

27. Diary, 3, 4, 22, and 24 September, 1 and 4 October 1784, GWP.

28. Robert J. Kapsch, *The Potomac Canal: George Washington and the Waterway West*, Morgantown: West Virginia University Press (2007), 10, 23–24, 47; from Stephen Sayre, 20 August 1784, GWP.

29. To Governor Benjamin Harrison, 10 October 1784, GWP; from George Plater, 20 October 1784, GWP; to George Plater, 28 October 1784, GWP; from Stephen Sayre, 15 October 1784, GWP; from Normand Bruce, 13 November 1784, GWP; from Benjamin Harrison, 13 November 1784, GWP; from Henry Lee Jr., 18 November 1784, GWP; *Virginia Journal and Alexandria Advertiser*, November 25, 1784.

30. *Virginia Journal and Alexandria Advertiser*, December 2, 1784; to the Virginia House of Delegates, 15 November 1784, GWP; to James Madison, 28 November 1784, GWP. See also from Henry Lee Jr., 18 November 1784, GWP.

31. To James Madison 3 December 1784, GWP; from Beverley Randolph, 15 December 1784, GWP; to William Paca, 19 December 1784, GWP; to Thomas Blackburne, 19 December 1784, GWP; from Horatio Gates, 24 December 1784, GWP; to James Madison, 28 December 1784, GWP; from Madison, 1 January 1785, GWP; Hening, *Statutes at Large* 11:510–11.

32. Kapsch, *The Potomac Canal*, 50–51; Larson, *The Return of George Washington*, 61. Larson writes of Washington's effort, "If he could not move mountains, the project proved that he could move men." Madison to Jefferson, 9 January 1785, PJM.

33. To John Filson, 16 January 1785, GWP; from Samuel Love, 17 February 1785, GWP; to John Fitzgerald and William Hartshorne, 18 January 1785, GWP; from John Fitzgerald and Samuel Hartshorne, 21 January 1785, GWP; to Robert Morris, 1 February 1785, GWP; to Jefferson, 25 February 1785, GWP; to Lafayette, 15 February 1785, GWP; from Christopher Richmond, 8 April 1785, note 1, GWP; Diary, 17 May 1785; *Virginia Journal*, May 19, 1785.

34. Kapsch, *The Potomac Canal*, 11–12, 30–31.

35. From Benjamin Harrison, 6 January and 8 February 1785, GWP; to Henry Knox, 5 January and 28 February 1785, GWP; to William Grayson, 22 January 1785, GWP; to Benjamin Harrison, 22 January 1785, GWP; to Lafayette, 15 February 1785, GWP; to Jefferson, 25 February 1785, GWP; from William Grayson, 10 March 1785, GWP; from Patrick Henry, 19 March 1785, GWP; to Edmund Randolph, 30 July 1785, GWP; to Patrick Henry, 31 August 1785, GWP. The gift from the legislature included one hundred shares in the James River Company, a parallel project that explored clearing that river's navigation. Washington never thought the James was a promising route to the west. The dedication of the shares to education matched Washington's pattern of paying for the education of friends' sons. Diary, 31 August 1785, GWP; to Jeremiah Wadsworth, 22 October 1786. He also made a major donation to a school in Alexandria for the education of orphans and other poor children. To the Trustees of the Alexandria Academy, 17 December 1785, GWP. The Potomac Company shares could not be found after Washington's death, so never produced any income.

36. Diary, 2–10 August, 18 October 1785, 2 February, 14 June 1786, GWP; from George Gilpin, 10 July 1785, GWP; to Clement Biddle, 27 July 1786, GWP; to Thomas Johnson, 10 September 1785, GWP; to Thomas Johnson and Thomas Sim Lee, 10 September 1786 and note 1, GWP; from Thomas Johnson, 21 September 1785, GWP; Diary, 26 September 1786, GWP.

37. To William Grayson, 22 August 1785, GWP; to Edmund Randolph, 16 September 1785, GWP; to George William Fairfax, 10 November 1785, GWP; to Henry Lee Jr., 5 April 1786, GWP; Kapsch, *The Potomac Canal*, 243, 251, 254–55. The locks and canal around Great Falls have been called the greatest engineering project in eighteenth-century America. Alexander Crosby Brown, "America's Greatest Eighteenth Century Engineering Achievement," *Virginia Cavalcade* 12 (Spring 1963), 40–47.

38. To David Humphreys, 25 July 1785, GWP; to Lafayette, 25 July 1785, GWP.

39. From Thomas Stone, 28 January 1785, GWP; David O. Stewart, *The Summer of 1787: The Men Who Created the Constitution*, New York: Simon & Schuster (2007), 4–7, 9.

40. Diary, 20, 22, 24, and 25 March 1785, GWP; Mason to Madison, 9 August 1785, PJM; Larson, *The Return of George Washington*, 61–62; Mount Vernon Compact, 28 March 1785, in Rutland, *George Mason Papers* 2:812–21. Although Article 6 of the Articles of Confederation may have required congressional approval of the compact, neither state submitted it for congressional review.

41. From Madison, 9 December 1785, GWP; Madison to Jefferson, 22 January 1786, PJM. In retirement, Madison recalled that the resolution for the Annapolis Conference was presented in the Virginia General Assembly by John Tyler, "who having never served in Congress," was a more acceptable sponsor than someone (like Madison) "whose service [in Congress] exposed them to an imputable bias" in favor of strengthening the national government. Madison, "Preface to Debates in the Convention of 1787," in Farrand 3:544.

39. BACK INTO HARNESS

1. To Richard Henry Lee, 8 February 1785, GWP.

2. Peter H. Lindert and Jeffrey G. Williamson, "American Incomes Before and After the Revolution," *National Bureau of Economic Research* (July 2011), 15; Peter H. Lindert and

Jeffrey G. Williamson, *Unequal Gains: American Growth and Inequality Since 1700*, Princeton: Princeton University Press (2016), 84–86; John R. McCusker and Russell R. Menard, *The Economy of British North America, 1607–1789*, Chapel Hill: University of North Carolina Press (1991), 373–74; Robert A. McGuire, *To Form a More Perfect Union: A New Economic Interpretation of the United States Constitution*, New York: Oxford University Press (2003); Allan Kulikoff, "'Such Things Ought Not to Be': The American Revolution and the First National Great Depression," in Andrew Shankman, ed., *The World of the Revolutionary American Republic: Land, Labor, and the Conflict for a Continent*, New York: Routledge (2014), 134–35; Wood, *The Idea of America*, 136–37.

3. Holger Hoock, *Scars of Independence: America's Violent Birth*, New York: Crown (2017), 17, 86, 97–98, 283–86, 379–80; Van Cleve, *We Have Not a Government*, 19–22; Cassandra Pybus, "Jefferson's Faulty Math: The Question of Slave Defections in the American Revolution," *WMQ* 62:243 (2005).

4. Hoock, *Scars of Independence*, 354–65, 17; Breen, *The Will of the People*, 201; John Kaminski, *Paper Politics: The Northern State Loan-Offices During the Confederation, 1783–1790*, New York: Garland Publishing, Inc. (1989), 4–5; Hamilton to Robert R. Livingston, 13 August 1783, PAH.

5. Lindert and Williamson, "American Incomes," 22; Lindert and Williamson, *Unequal Gains*, 90; Kulikoff, "Such Things Ought Not To Be," 136–37; Curtis Nettels, *The Emergence of a National Economy: 1775–1815*, New York: Holt, Rinehart and Winston (1962), 52; McCusker and Menard, *The Economy of British North America*, 361; James F. Shepherd and Gary M. Walton, "Economic Change After the American Revolution: Prewar and Postwar Comparisons of Maritime Shipping and Trade," *Explorations in Economic History* 13:397 (November 1976).

6. Van Cleve, *We Have Not a Government*, 37–38; Nettels, *The Emergence of a National Economy*, 46–47; Kaminski, *Paper Politics*, 12; Edmund Randolph to Madison, 6 August 1782, GWP.

7. Stephen Conway, *A Short History of the American Revolutionary War*, London: Tauris (2013), 125; Van Cleve, *We Have Not a Government*, 22–23; Markus Hünemörder, *The Society of the Cincinnati: Conspiracy and Distrust in Early America*, New York: Berghahn Books (2006), 7; Eric Newman, *The Early Paper Money of America*, Iola, WI: Krause Publications (2008), 481; Ferguson, *The Power of the Purse*, 26–28, 44, 51, 63–64, 77.

8. Joseph Reed letter, October 1784, quoted in Van Cleve, *We Have Not a Government*, 39; Richard Henry Lee to Madison, 20 November 1784, in PJM; Nettels, *The Emergence of a National Economy*, 60; Terry Bouton, "Moneyless in Pennsylvania: Privatization and the Depression of the 1780s," in Cathy Matson, ed., *The Economy of Early America*, University Park: Pennsylvania State University Press (2006), 233.

9. Douglas A. Irwin, "Revenue or Reciprocity? Founding Feuds over Early U.S. Trade Policy," in Douglas A. Irwin and Richard Sylla, *Founding Choices: American Economic Policy in the 1790s*, Chicago: University of Chicago Press (2011), 92. One maneuver the states mastered was to accept national securities (bonds) from citizens as tax payments and then use those much-depreciated securities to pay requisitions from Congress; the maneuver delivered no actual purchasing power to the national government (though it did reduce its debt). Van Cleve, *We Have Not a Government*, 73. By one calculation, from October 1786 to March 1787 the states paid to Congress so many of those national bonds that they paid actual currency of only $663. Ray Raphael, *Constitutional Myths: What We Get Wrong and How to Get It Right*, New York: The New Press (2013), 21; *JCC* 30:72 (15 February 1786); from Richard Henry Lee, 2 March 1786, GWP.

10. Roger H. Brown, *Redeeming the Republic: Federalists, Taxation, and the Origins of the Constitution*, Baltimore: Johns Hopkins University Press (1993), 17–18, 141; from Richard Henry Lee, 20 November 1784, GWP.

11. From Nathanael Greene, 29 August 1784, GWP.

12. To Jonathan Trumbull Jr., 5 January 1784, GWP; to Benjamin Harrison, 18 January 1784, GWP; to Lafayette, 25 July 1785, GWP.

13. To Jacob Read, 11 August 1784, GWP; to George William Fairfax, 30 June 1785, GWP; to Knox, 8 March 1787, GWP; to Madison, 30 November 1785, GWP; to James McHenry, 22 August 1785, GWP; to James Warren, 7 October 1785, GWP; to David Stuart, 30 November 1785, GWP.

14. Walter Stahr, *John Jay: Founding Father,* New York: Hambledon Continuum (2005), 211–17; James Monroe to Madison, 3 September 1786, PJM; from Henry Lee Jr., 3 July 1786, GWP; from David Stuart, 13 November 1786, GWP; from Madison, 7 December 1786, GWP.

15. To Lafayette, 10 May 1786, GWP.

16. *DHRC* 1:181–85. As early as 1780, before the Articles took effect, Hamilton described them as creating too few powers in the national government, an opinion he repeated thereafter. Hamilton to James Duane, 3 September 1780, PAH; Hamilton to Robert Morris, 30 April 1781, PAH. In 1782, the New York Assembly called for a national convention to amend the Articles. "Resolution of the New York Legislature Calling for a Convention of the States to Revise and Amend the Articles of Confederation," 20 July 1782, PAH. Many others considered the idea. E.g., Richard Henry Lee to Madison, 26 November 1784, PJM; John Francis Mercer to Madison, 26 November 1784, PJM.

17. From John Jay, 16 March 1786, GWP; to John Jay, 18 May 1786, GWP; to Henry Lee Jr., 5 April 1786, GWP.

18. David Szatmary, *Shays' Rebellion: The Making of an Agrarian Insurrection,* Amherst: University of Massachusetts Press (1980), 124–26; from David Humphreys, 24 September 1786, GWP; Michael J. Klarman, *The Framers' Coup: The Making of the United States Constitution,* New York: Oxford University Press (2016), 88–90; Roger Brown, *Redeeming the Republic,* 166–67; Woody Holton, *Unruly Americans and the Origins of the Constitution,* New York: Hill and Wang (2008), 145–46.

19. From Henry Lee Jr., 1 October 1786, GWP; from Henry Lee Jr., 17 October 1786, GWP (relaying report from Knox).

20. To David Humphreys, 22 October 1786, GWP; from Knox, 23 October 1786, GWP.

21. From Henry Lee Jr., 17 October 1786, GWP; to Henry Lee, Jr., 31 October 1786, GWP.

22. Szatmary, *Shays' Rebellion;* Leonard L. Richards, *Shays's Rebellion: The American Revolution's Final Battle,* Philadelphia: University of Pennsylvania Press (2002), 9–42; from Knox, 21, 25, 29, 30, and 31 January, and 8, 12 February 1786, GWP. A full report came from the commander of the Massachusetts forces, Benjamin Lincoln, 4 December 1786– 4 March 1787, GWP.

23. To Madison, 16 December 1786, GWP.

24. From Madison, 8 November 1786, GWP.

25. To Madison, 18 November 1786, GWP; to David Stuart, 19 November 1786, GWP; to Knox, 3 February 1786, GWP.

26. From Edmund Randolph, 6 December 1786, GWP; from Madison, 7 December 1786, GWP; to Madison, 16 December 1786, GWP; to Randolph, 21 December 1786, GWP; from Madison, 24 December 1786, GWP; from Randolph, 4 January 1787, GWP.

27. From John Jay, 7 January 1787, GWP; from Henry Knox, 14 January 1787, GWP; from Madison, 21 February 1787, GWP; to David Humphreys, 8 March 1787, GWP; to Knox, 8 March 1787, GWP.

28. Diary, 10 January 1787, GWP; to Bushrod Washington, 10 January 1787, GWP. Washington mourned Greene's death in letters to Henry Lee and Jefferson. To Henry Lee Jr., 26 July 1786, GWP; to Jefferson, 1 August 1786, GWP; *Pennsylvania Packet,* July 11, 1786. A much-needed biography of Bushrod Washington is forthcoming in 2021: Gerard N. Magliocca, *Washington's Heir: The Life of Justice Bushrod Washington.*

29. To Knox, 27 April 1787, GWP.
30. To Jay, 10 March 1787, GWP; to Edmund Randolph, 28 March and 2 April 1787, GWP. More letters pressing Washington to attend came from Randolph and Knox. From Edmund Randolph, 11 March 1787, GWP; from Knox, 19 March 1787, GWP.
31. Diary, 13 May, 15 October 1785, GWP; to Burwell Bassett, 23 May 1785, GWP; to Lund Washington, 20 December 1785; from George Augustine Washington, 3 February 1786, GWP; Ed. Note to "Farm Reports, 26 November 1786–15 April 1787," GWP.
32. Diary, 22 and 26 December 1786, and 9 February 1787, GWP.
33. "Notes on the Sentiments on the Government of John Jay, Henry Knox, and James Madison," April 1787, GWP.
34. To Madison, 31 March 1787, GWP.
35. To Knox, 27 April 1787, GWP; Diary, 27 April 1787, GWP; to Mary Washington, 15 February 1785, GWP.

40. AMERICA'S REBIRTH

1. *Pennsylvania Packet*, May 14, 1787; *Pennsylvania Evening Herald*, May 16, 1787; *Connecticut Courant*, May 21, 1787.
2. William Grayson to James Monroe, 29 May 1787, Farrand 3:30; Madison to Jefferson, 6 June 1787, Farrand 3:35–36; Edward Carrington to Jefferson, 9 June 1787, Farrand 3:38; William Samuel Johnson to his son, 27 June 1787, Farrand 3:49.
3. *Pennsylvania Packet*, April 4, 1787; Larson, *The Return of George Washington*, 108; Franklin to Thomas Jordan, 18 May 1787, PBF; Stewart, *The Summer of 1787*, 29–30; to George Augustine Washington, 17 May 1787, GWP. Thomas Mifflin made another of his recurring appearances in Washington's life, serving as one of the Pennsylvania delegates.
4. Diary, 16 May 1787, GWP; George Mason to George Mason, Jr., 20 May 1787, Farrand 3:23.
5. Farrand 1:20–22.
6. Washington was too engaged in the convention preparations to attend any session of the Society of the Cincinnati, but dined with some of its members on May 15. Diary, 15 May 1787, GWP.
7. Farrand 1:2, 3–4; *Independent Gazetteer*, May 26, 1787; *Pennsylvania Mercury*, June 1, 1787.
8. William Steele to Jonathan D. Steele, September 1825, Farrand 3:467. Another incident of Washingtonian severity, repeated endlessly through the years, places the general at a social event with Gouverneur Morris and Hamilton. To win a wager with Hamilton, Morris supposedly delivered a matey slap to Washington's shoulder and greeted him casually. Washington's wordless, icy disapproval sent Morris scurrying back to the party and he later pledged never to attempt such familiarity again. Anecdote, Farrand 3:85.
9. William Pierce, "Anecdote," Farrand 3:86–87.
10. Farrand 1:69.
11. Farrand 1:510, 3:172, 3:188 (statement of Luther Martin of Maryland, printed in the *Maryland Gazette and Baltimore Advertiser*, December 28, 1787–February 8, 1788).
12. Farrand 1:16.
13. Farrand 2:16. Some histories of the convention suggest that Washington exercised power as presiding officer to summon a committee, pointing to a committee that was established on July 9 to allocate congressional representatives among the states. Larson, *The Return of George Washington*, 158; Beeman, *Plain Honest Men*, 207. The cited evidence does not support that assertion. The committee created on July 9 was established pursuant to a motion made by Roger Sherman of Connecticut. Neither Madison's notes nor the official convention journal suggests that Washington appointed the committee on his own authority. Farrand 1:558, 560, 562. Indeed, the convention's rules gave him no power

to do so, stating that committees would be established by "ballot" and specifying how to count those ballots; the rule on establishing committees never even mentions the presiding officer. Farrand 1:9; David O. Stewart, "Who Picked the Committees at the Constitutional Convention?," in *Journal of the American Revolution, Annual* (2019), 353–61.

14. Washington to Hamilton, 10 July 1787, GWP.

15. Farrand 1:97, 2:121, 2:280, 2:363. Questions surround the vote on a motion by Dr. James McClurg of Virginia to define the presidential term as "good behavior," which would be a lifelong term, as it has been for federal judges who serve during good behavior. Farrand 2:33–36 (17 July 1787). Madison dropped two separate footnotes to his notes to explain why the Virginia delegation—which included him and Washington—voted in favor of this protomonarchist proposal. Madison attempted to pass that vote off as a tactical ploy intended to alarm delegates who wished to have Congress choose the president. Madison's explanation, though unpersuasive at first blush, is consistent with his remarks during the debate on McClurg's motion; in that statement, Madison largely discussed the importance of not giving Congress the power to appoint the president.

16. Farrand 1:65 (1 June 1787), 3:302 (Pierce Butler to Weedon Butler, 5 May 1788), 1:103 (4 June 1787). On at least two occasions, delegates specifically praised Washington for declining to accept a salary during the Revolution. Farrand 1:84–85, 2:122.

17. David W. Maxey, *A Portrait of Elizabeth Willing Powel,* Philadelphia: American Philosophical Society (2006), 23–24. When Washington arranged for his nephew Bushrod (Jack's son) to read law with James Wilson of Philadelphia, Bushrod became Mrs. Powel's protégé. Maxey, *Elizabeth Willing Powel,* 29.

18. *Providence Gazette,* October 6, 1787; to Annis Boudinot Stockton, 30 June 1787, GWP.

19. Diary, 30 and 31 July, 3, 4, and 5 August 1787, GWP. On a third occasion, Washington rode alone to another Continental Army encampment site, at Whitemarsh, Pennsylvania. Diary, 19 August 1787, GWP.

20. Stewart, *The Summer of 1787,* 191–206.

21. To Henry Knox, 19 August 1787, GWP.

22. Farrand 2:183; 2:587.

23. Farrand 2:471–72; 2:482.

24. Farrand 2:553–54; 2:643–44.

25. Diary, 17 September 1787, GWP. The New York legislature had specified that two delegates had to be present in order to cast the state's vote on convention proceedings. Consequently, New York was not officially present at the convention after the first six weeks, because two of its three delegates, John Lansing and Robert Yates, left in dismay over the convention's willingness to take power from the states. The most powerful appeal for unity came from Franklin, whose remarks made their way into the press in a demonstration of the elderly Pennsylvanian's media savvy. Farrand, 2:641–43 and 641 note 1. Snippets of accounts of the convention's proceedings trickled into the public sphere until 1821, when Yates' notes of the first six weeks of deliberations were published. Madison's notes were published in 1840.

26. Farrand 2:648; Diary, 17 September 1787, GWP; from William Jackson, 17 September 1787, GWP; to Catharine Sawbridge Macaulay Graham, 16 November 1787, GWP.

27. Edward J. Larson, *Franklin & Washington: The Founding Partnership,* New York: William Morrow (2020), 219; to Lafayette, 18 September 1787, GWP; to Jefferson, 18 September 1787, GWP.

28. To George Augustine Washington, 27 May; 3 and 10 June; 1, 8, 24, and 29 July; 12 and 26 August; and 9 September 1787, GWP.

29. Diary, 19 September 1787, GWP; *Pennsylvania Gazette,* October 10, 1787. Other newspapers also featured the tale of Washington's narrow escape on the bridge. *Delaware Gazette,* September 26, 1787; *Independent Journal,* October 6, 1787.

41. A WORKING POLITICIAN

1. To Benjamin Harrison, 24 September 1787, and note 1, GWP.
2. "A Freeholder," *Virginia Independent Chronicle*, April 9, 1788; Cyrus Griffin to Madison, 24 March 1788, PJM.
3. Diary, 26, 27, and 28 September 1787, GWP; Hamilton, "Conjectures on the Constitution," in *DHRC* 13:277; "To the Freemen of Pennsylvania," *Pennsylvania Gazette*, October 10 and 17, 1787; *Independent Gazetteer*, October 5 and 15, 1787, November 17, 1787; from David Humphreys, 28 September 1787, GWP; "The Confederationist," *Pennsylvania Evening Herald*, October 27, 1787; *The American Museum* 2:375 (October 1787); *Massachusetts Centinel*, November 10, 17, and 19, 1787; from Gouverneur Morris, 30 October 1787, GWP.
4. Alexander Donald to Jefferson, 12 November 1787, PTJ; Edward J. Larson, *George Washington, Nationalist*, Charlottesville: University of Virginia Press (2016), 74–75; to Charles Carter, 14 December 1787 and 12 January 1788, GWP; Klarman, *The Founders' Coup*, 480; *Pennsylvania Gazette*, September 26, 1787; *Maryland Journal*, October 2, 1787; from Lafayette, 2 January 1788, GWP.
5. To Madison, 10 October 1787, GWP; from Madison, 28 October 1787, GWP.
6. To David Humphreys, 10 October 1787, GWP; to David Stuart, 17 October 1787, GWP; from Madison, 18 November 1787, GWP; to David Stuart, 30 November 1787, GWP; to Madison, 7 December 1787, GWP; to Madison, 5 February 1787, GWP; Jacob E. Cooke, ed., *The Federalist Papers*, Middletown: Wesleyan University Press (1983); Michael Meyerson, *Liberty's Blueprint: How Madison and Hamilton Wrote the Federalist Papers, Defined the Constitution, and Made Democracy Safe for the World*, New York: Basic Books (2008), 91–99. Some historians have concluded that writings pithier than *The Federalist* had greater impact on public attitudes toward the Constitution. Pauline Maier, *Ratification: The People Debate the Constitution, 1787–1788*, New York: Simon & Schuster (2010), 336–38 (praising John Jay's *An Address to the People of New York on the Subject of the Constitution*, which appeared in April 1788).
7. From David Humphreys, 28 September 1787, GWP; from John Rutledge, 1 October 1787, GWP; from Knox, 3 October 1787, GWP; from Samuel Powel, 12 December 1787, GWP; from Madison, 26 December 1787, GWP; from Jonathan Trumbull Jr., 9 January 1788, GWP; from John Jay, 3 February 1788, GWP; from Madison, 8 February 1788, GWP.
8. From David Stuart, 4 December 1787, GWP; to Jefferson, 1 January 1787, GWP; from Knox, 3 October 1787, GWP; from Benjamin Harrison, 4 October 1787, GWP; from Hamilton, 11 October 1787, GWP; from George Mason, 7 October 1787, GWP; to Madison, 10 October 1787, GWP; from Richard Henry Lee, 11 October 1787, GWP; from Patrick Henry, 19 October 1787, GWP; to Edmund Randolph, 8 January 1788, GWP.
9. To Knox, 15 October 1787, GWP.
10. From Benjamin Lincoln, 13 January and 6 February 1788, GWP; from Knox, 14 and 25 January, and 1 February 1788, GWP; to Lincoln, 31 January 1788, GWP; *Massachusetts Gazette*, January 25, 1788 and October 19, 1787; Larson, *George Washington, Nationalist*, 76–77; from Rufus King, 6 February 1788, GWP; Maier, *Ratification*, 196–207.
11. Tobias Lear to William Prescott Jr., 4 March 1788, in *DHRC* 8:456.
12. From Caleb Gibbs, 24 February 1788, GWP; from Benjamin Lincoln, 24 February 1788, GWP; from John Langdon, 28 February 1788, GWP; from Madison, 3 March 1788, GWP; to Knox, 30 March 1788, GWP. New Hampshire's convention adjourned for the ostensible reason of persuading several local town meetings to reconsider their instructions that their delegates oppose ratification, but the final vote for ratification may have turned upon several Anti-Federalists who failed to attend the reconvened session and some new

delegates who arrived from towns that had sent no representatives to the first session. Klarman, *The Founders' Coup,* 452–53.

13. To Thomas Johnson, 20 April 1788, GWP; to James McHenry, 27 April 1788, GWP; from Thomas Johnson, 10 October 1788, GWP; to Madison, 2 May 1788, GWP; from Charles Cotesworth Pinckney, 24 May 1788, GWP.

14. From Knox, 25 May 1788, GWP; from Jay, 29 May 1788, GWP; from Richard Dobbs Spaight, 25 May 1788, GWP; to Lafayette, 28 May 1788, GWP.

15. From Madison, 4, 7, 13, and 18 June 1788, GWP; Diary, 10 June 1788, GWP; to Knox, 17 June 1788, GWP.

16. To Madison, 23 June 1788, GWP; from Madison, 23 June 1788, GWP; to David Stuart, 23 June 1788, GWP.

17. From John Langdon, 21 June 1788, GWP; from Tobias Lear, 22 June 1788, GWP; from Madison, 25 June 1788, GWP.

18. To Charles Cotesworth Pinckney, 28 June 1788, GWP; to Tobias Lear, 29 June 1788; *Pennsylvania Packet,* July 11, 1788.

19. To Benjamin Lincoln, 29 June 1788, GWP.

20. *DHRC* 10:1223 (12 June 1788, Henry and Madison); *DHRC* 10:1498 (24 June 1788, William Grayson); James Monroe to Jefferson, 12 July 1788, PTJ.

21. To Jefferson, 31 August 1788, GWP. In late October, Patrick Henry declared to the Virginia Assembly that he would oppose all measures relating to the new national government unless they also included a call for a second convention. From Charles Lee, 19 October 1788, GWP.

22. To John Lathrop, 22 June 1788, GWP; to Edward Newenham, 29 August 1788, GWP.

23. To George Mason and David Stuart, 4 November 1787, GWP; Report of the Potowmack Company Directors, 8 November 1787, GWP; to Thomas Johnson and Thomas Sim Lee, 9 December 1787, GWP; Diary, 1, 2, and 3 June 1788, GWP; to George Gilpin and John Fitzgerald, 2 August 1788, GWP; Diary, 4 August 1788, GWP; to Thomas Lewis, 25 December 1787, GWP; to David Stuart, 15 January and 23 June 1788, GWP; Diary, 5 January and 24 July 1788, GWP; *Philadelphia Independent Gazette,* August 8, 1788, GWP; *Maryland Journal,* August 5, 1788.

24. Diary, 13 November 1788, GWP; to James Bloxham, 1 January 1789, GWP; to John Fairfax, 1 January 1789, GWP; to John Beale Bordley, 17 August 1788, GWP.

25. To Charles Lee, 4 April 1788, GWP; to Dr. James Craik, 4 August 1788, GWP: to David Stuart, 2 December 1788, GWP. Washington's patience frayed when dealing with chronic misconduct by two nephews, whose education he oversaw on behalf of his late brother Samuel. To Samuel Hanson, 6 August 1788, GWP; to George Steptoe Washington, 6 August 1788, GWP; from Samuel Hanson, 7 August 1788, GWP.

26. New York ratified in July 1788, North Carolina in late 1789, and Rhode Island six months later. Diary, 5 July 1788, GWP; from Madison, 11 and 24 August 1788, GWP; to Madison, 28 August 1788, GWP; to Samuel Powel, 15 September 1788, GWP; to Benjamin Lincoln, 28 August 1788, GWP. Washington and Madison also were collaborating to draw the seat of the national government away from New York or Philadelphia to the banks of the Potomac. That effort would succeed three years later. From Madison, 11 August and 21 October 1788, GWP; to Madison, 3 and 18 August 1788, GWP; from Knox, 28 July 1788, GWP; *JCC* 1:50–52 and note 2 (28 July 1788); Merrill Jensen and Robert A. Becker, eds., *The Documentary History of the First Federal Elections, 1788–1790,* Madison: University of Wisconsin Press (1976), 1:50–52 and note 2 (from *Journals of Congress,* 28 July 1788); from Thomas Johnson, 11 December 1787, GWP; *JCC* 34:522–23 (13 September 1788); from Henry Lee Jr., 13 September 1788, GWP.

27. From Henry Lee Jr., 13 September 1788, GWP; from Benjamin Lincoln, 24 September 1788, GWP; from Hamilton, 13 August 1788, GWP; from Samuel Vaughan, 4 November

1788, GWP; from Robert R. Livingston, 21 October, GWP; from Gouverneur Morris, 6 December 1788, GWP; to Hamilton, 3 October 1788; to Lincoln, 26 October 1788, GWP; to Charles Pettit, 16 August 1788, GWP; to Jonathan Trumbull Jr., 4 December 1788, GWP; to Benjamin Fishbourn, 23 December 1788, GWP; to Harry Lee, 22 September 1788, GWP; to G. Morris, 28 November 1788, GWP. Even less welcome than the demands that Washington serve as president were the requests for employment in the new government. Washington usually assured supplicants that since he did not expect to be president, he could not assist them. From William Pierce, 1 November 1788, GWP; from Philemon Downes, 3 November 1788, GWP; from Stephen Sayre, 3 January 1789, GWP; from Lachlan McIntosh, 13 February 1789, GWP; from Benjamin Harrison, 26 February 1789, GWP.

28. To Jonathan Trumbull Jr., 4 December 1788, GWP; from G. Morris, 6 December 1788, GWP; from Hamilton, 18 November 1788, GWP.

29. Diary, 19–25 December 1788, GWP; to Madison, 16 February 1789, GWP; Madison to James Madison Sr., 24 February 1789, PJM.

30. To Lafayette, 8 December 1784, GWP.

31. To Lafayette 29 March 1789, GWP.

32. To John Langdon, 20 July 1788, GWP; to William Gordon, 23 December 1788, GWP.

33. To James McHenry, 31 July 1788, GWP.

34. To Benjamin Lincoln, 26 October 1788, 31 January 1789, GWP. During the Revolution, Adams had complained about "the superstitious veneration that is sometimes paid to General Washington." George W. Cormer, *The Autobiography of Benjamin Rush*, Princeton: Princeton University Press (1948), 141. Madison spoke for those skeptical of Adams when he observed that the New Englander "has made himself obnoxious to many," and cited his "political principles," his hostility to General Washington at stages of the war, and "his extravagant self-importance." Madison to Jefferson, 17 October 1788, in PJM.

35. Larson, *The Return of George Washington*, 250; Marcus Cunliffe, "Elections of 1789 and 1792," in Gil Troy, Arthur M. Schlesinger Jr., and Fred L. Israel, eds., *History of American Presidential Elections, 1789–2009*, 4th ed., New York: Facts on File (2012), 1.

36. Diary, 7 January and 2 February 1789, GWP; *Pennsylvania Mercury*, February 14, 1789; *Federal Gazette*, April 20, 1789; *DHFFE*, 4:161–66; to Knox, 29 January 1789, GWP; from Knox, 19 February 1789, GWP.

37. *Massachusetts Centinel*, February 7, 1789; *Pennsylvania Packet*, February 7, 1789; Larson, *The Return of George Washington*, 277–78.

38. To Richard Conway, 6 March 1789, GWP; to George Augustine Washington, 31 March 1789, GWP; to Thomas Green, 31 March 1789, GWP; to Knox, 1 April 1789, GWP. Washington added to Mount Vernon's management another nephew, Robert Lewis, son of his sister Betty. To Betty Lewis, 15 March 1789, GWP.

39. To Richard Conway, 6 March 1789, GWP; Martha Washington to John Dandridge, 20 April 1789, in Fields, *Worthy Partners*, 213.

40. Adams was miffed at his low vote total, calling it "scurvy . . . an indelible stain on our country, countrymen, and Constitution." Adams to Benjamin Rush, 17 May 1789, AP.

41. To the Mayor, Corporation, and Citizens of Alexandria, 16 April 1789, GWP; Wood, *The Idea of America*, 240.

42. *New York Daily Gazette*, April 27, 1789; *Federal Gazette*, April 22, 1789.

43. *Pennsylvania Gazette*, April 22, 1789; *Virginia Herald and Fredericksburg Advertiser*, May 7, 1789;

44. *Pennsylvania Packet*, May 1, 1789; *New York Packet*, May 1, 1789; "To the Ladies of Trenton," 21 April 1789, GWP.

45. *New York Packet*, May 1, 1789; *Gazette of the United States*, April 25, 1789; Elias Boudinot to Hannah Boudinot, 24 April, in Clarence Winthrop Bowen, ed., "The History of the

Centennial Celebration of the Inauguration of George Washington," New York: D. Appleton & Co. (1892), 28–30 [also in *DHFFE* 15:337]; *New York Daily Advertiser*, April 24, 1789; *Freeman's Journal*, April 29, 1789.

46. Diary, 23 April 1789, GWP.

47. *New York Daily Gazette*, May 1, 1789.

48. Stewart, *Madison's Gift*, 86; Fisher Ames to George Richards Minot, 3 May 1789, in Seth Ames, ed., *Works of Fisher Ames*, Boston: Little, Brown & Co. (1854), 1:34.

49. "Undelivered First Inaugural Address: Fragments," 30 April 1789, GWP.

50. First Inaugural Address, 30 April 1789, GWP.

51. Edward Thornton to James Bland Burges, 11 June 1792, in S. W. Jackman, "A Young Englishman Reports on the New Nation: Edward Thornton to James Bland Burges, 1791, 1793," *WMQ* 18:85, 110–11 (1961); Farrand 1:83, 86–87 (2 June 1787); George Mason to James Monroe, 30 January 1792, in Rutland, *Papers of George Mason* 3:1254; *Albany Register*, March 2, 1799; James Monroe to Andrew Jackson, 14 December 1816, in Stanislaus Murray Hamilton, ed., *The Writings of James Monroe*, New York: G. P. Putnam's Sons (1901) 5:342–45; Charles King, ed., *The Life and Correspondence of Rufus King*, New York: G. P. Putnam's Sons (1894) 6:643–44 (10 May) (conversation of Monroe); Kapp, *Life of Steuben*, 584; Richard Krauel, "Prince Henry of Prussia and the Regency of the United States," *Am. Hist. Rev.* 7:47–48 (1911). Nearly 100 years ago, Louise Burnham Dunbar gathered a number of reports and confessions of monarchical preferences among Americans in the 1780s. Louise Burnham Dunbar, *A Study of "Monarchical" Tendencies in the United States from 1776 to 1801*, Urbana: University of Illinois Press (1922), 60–75, 84–85; Eric Nelson, *The Royalist Revolution: Monarchy and the American Founding*, Cambridge: Harvard University Press (2014). James McClurg's motion at the convention to have presidents serve for "good behavior" is discussed in chapter 40, note 15. A month before Washington took office, his former aide, James McHenry, enthused in a letter, "You are now a king, under a different name," and stated himself "well satisfied that sovereign prerogatives have in no age or country been more honorably obtained; or that, at any time they will be more prudently and wisely exercised." From James McHenry, 29 March 1789, GWP.

52. Benjamin Rush to Thomas Ruston, 29 October 1775, GWP, in Butterfield, *Letters of Benjamin Rush* 1:92.

53. From Colonel Lewis Nicola, 22 May 1782, GWP; to William Gordon, 23 December 1788, GWP; Richard Brookhiser, "Afterword: The Forgotten Character of George Washington," in Gregg and Spalding, *Patriot Sage*, 303. In the first draft of the inaugural address, Washington had included a reassurance to his countrymen that since he had no children of his own, he could have no dynastic ambitions—"no family to build in greatness upon my country's ruins." He did not have to include that passage, however, because Americans well knew he had no direct heir and took reassurance from it.

54. To Edward Rutledge, 5 May 1789, GWP.

42. ON UNTRODDEN GROUND

1. Jonathan Gienapp, *The Second Creation: Fixing the American Constitution in the Founding Era*, Cambridge: Belknap Press (2018), 10, 4.

2. Stanley Elkins and Eric McKitrick, *The Age of Federalism: The Early American Republic, 1788–1800*, New York: Oxford University Press (1993), 10.

3. Charlene Bangs Bickford and Kenneth R. Bowling, *Birth of the Nation: The First Federal Congress 1789–1791*, Madison: Madison House Publishers (1989), 7; Jefferson to Walter Jones, 2 January 1814, in PTJ.

4. Fergus Bordewich, *The First Congress: How James Madison, George Washington, and a Group of Extraordinary Men Invented the Government,* New York: Simon & Schuster (2016), 29.

5. *Gazette of the United States,* April 25, 1789; Kathleen Bartoloni-Tuazon, *The Fear of an Elective King: George Washington and the Presidential Title Controversy of 1789,* Ithaca: Cornell University Press (2014), 4; William Knox to Winthrop Sargent, 16 March 1789, *DHFFC* 15:70; to Anthony Wayne, 4 May 1789, GWP.

6. Thomas E. V. Smith, *The City of New York in the Year of Washington's Inauguration: 1789,* New York: Anson D. F. Randolph & Co. (1889), 5–7, 12; John Page to Robt. Page, 16 March 1789, *DHFFC* 15:71; Elias Boudinot to Hannah Boudinot, 15 May 1789, *DHFFC* 15:557–58; Frank Monaghan and Marvin Lowenthal, *This Was New York: The Nation's Capital in 1789,* Garden City, NY: Doubleday, Doran & Co. (1943), 31, 32, 36–37; Judith Sargent Murray to Winthrop and Judith Sargent, 29 May 1790, *DHFFC* 19:1624; Rufus Wilmot Griswold, *The Republican Court: American Society in the Days of Washington,* New York: Appleton & Co. (1868), 33, 88.

7. Kenneth R. Bowling and Helen E. Veit, eds., *The Diary of William Maclay,* Baltimore: Johns Hopkins University Press (1988), 8–10 (28 and 29 April 1789).

8. From Robert Livingston, 2 May 1789, GWP; from Hamilton, 4 May 1789, GWP; Bowling and Veit, *Maclay Diary,* 21–23 (4 May 1789).

9. Flexner 3:195, 3:200.

10. Theodore Sedgwick to Ephraim Williams, June 1789, quoted in Joseph Charles, "Hamilton and Washington: The Origins of the American Party System," *WMQ* 12:217, 253 (1955); Bowling and Veit, *Maclay Diary,* 212 (4 March 1790), 134–35 (26 August 1789), 261 (6 May 1790); Flexner 3:204; Maclay to Benjamin Rush, *DHFFC* 19:1445 (7 May 1790).

11. Bowling and Veit, *Maclay Diary,* 44–45 (18 May 1789); Martha Washington to Fanny Bassett Washington, 23 October 1789, in Fields, *Worthy Partners,* 220.

12. Bowling and Veit, *Maclay Diary,* 3–4 (24 April 1789), 27–29 (8 May 1789); Kathleen Bartoloni-Tuazon, *The Fear of an Elective King,* 5.

13. Bowling and Veit, *Maclay Diary,* 29–32 (9 May 1789), 33 (11 May 1789), 37–40 (14 May 1789).

14. From David Stuart, 14 July 1789, GWP.

15. To David Stuart, 29 July 1789, GWP.

16. *Gazette of the United States,* June 24, 1789; Madison to Samuel Johnston, 21 June 1789, PJM; William Few to Gov. Telfair, *DHFFC* 2:45 (20 June 1789); Madison to James Madison Sr., 5 July 1789, PJM.

17. To Madison, 23 September 1789, GWP; to Madison, 5 May 1789, 11 May 1789, 17 May 1789, 12 June 1789, 5 August 1789, and 8 September 1789, GWP.

18. From Knox, 23 May 1789, 9 June 1789, 6 and 7 July 1789, GWP; to Jay, 8 and 14 June 1789, GWP; from the Board of Treasury, 9, 10, 11, and 15 June 1789, GWP; to Ebenezer Hazard, 3 July 1789, GWP.

19. Fisher Ames to George R. Minot, 8 July 1789, *DHFFC* 16:978.

20. Fisher Ames to George Minot, 14 May 1789, *DHFFC* 15:543–44; Bowling and Veit, *Maclay Diary,* 64, 66–67 (2 and 4 June 1789); Elkins and McKitrick, 66–71. Many Americans resented British mercantile dominance, but the British generally offered good credit, high-quality goods, and reliable shipping, and they knew American tastes. French merchants sometimes sent goods to the United States like anchovies, olives, and truffles, that Americans would not buy. John Stover, "French-American Trade During the Confederation, 1781–1789," *North Carolina Hist. Rev.* 35:399, 405, 412; Vernon G. Setser, *The Commercial Reciprocity Policy of the United States, 1774–1829,* Philadelphia: University of Pennsylvania Press (1937), 91–92. Between 1784 and 1790, imports from France were less than one-twentieth the level of imports from Britain.

21. To David Stuart, 28 March 1790, GWP; Adams to Benjamin Rush, 11 November 1807, AP.

22. Bordewich, *First Congress*, 56; *Annals of Congress*, 1st Cong., 1st Sess., 383–96 (19 May 1789); Bowling and Veit, *Maclay Diary*, 104–5 (9 July 1789), 109–16 (14–16 July 1789); *Annals of Congress* 1:555–57 (18 June 1789), 1:592–607 (19 and 22 June 1789); Bickford and Bowling, *Birth of the Nation*, 38–39; William Loughton Smith to Edward Rutledge, 21 June 1789, DHFFC 16:831–33.

23. Bordewich, *First Congress*, 88; to Madison, 31 May 1789, GWP; Circular to the Governors of the States, 2 October 1789, GWP.

24. William Loughton Smith to Edward Rutledge, 21 June 1789, *DHFFC* 16:833; John McVickar, *A Domestic Narrative of the Life of Samuel Bard, M.D.*, New York: The Literary Rooms (1822), 136–37.

25. *Massachusetts Centinel*, June 27, 1789; *Pennsylvania Packet and Daily Advertiser* (Philadelphia), June 22, 1789; Langstaff, *Life of Samuel Bard*, 172–73; from David Stuart, 14 July 1789, GWP; to McHenry, 3 July 1789, GWP; *Gazette of the United States*, July 4, 1789; Madison to Edmund Randolph, 24 June 1789, PJM; to the Society of the Cincinnati, 4 July 1789, GWP; *Gazette of the United States*, July 8, 1789; Bordewich, *The First Congress*, 103.

26. To Richard Henry Lee, 2 August 1789, GWP; to James Craik, 8 September 1789, GWP.

27. "Benjamin Lincoln Lear's Account of Washington's Attendance on the Senate," 5 August 1789, DHFFC 16:1239: Bordewich, *The First Congress*, 132–33. The nominee was Benjamin Fishbourn.

28. "Washington's Notes," 8 August 1789, *DHFFC* 8:757.

29. E.g., from Henry Knox, 7 July 1789, GWP.

30. Conference with a Committee of the United States Senate, 8 August 1789, GWP; Conference with a Committee of the United States Senate, 10 August 1789, GWP; from Ralph Izard, 10 August 1789, GWP; to United States Senate, 21 August 1789, GWP.

31. Bowling and Veit, *Maclay Diary*, 128–31 (22 August 1789); Charles Francis Adams, ed., *The Diary of John Quincy Adams* 6:427 (10 November 1824); Elkins and McKitrick, *The Age of Federalism*, 56–57.

32. Jack D. Warren Jr., "'The Line of My Official Conduct': George Washington and Congress, 1789–1797," in Kenneth R. Bowling and Donald R. Kennon, *Inventing Congress: Origins and Establishment of the First Federal Congress*, Athens: Ohio University Press (1999), 256.

33. Lindsay M. Chervinsky, *The Cabinet: George Washington and the Creation of an American Institution*, Cambridge: The Belknap Press of Harvard University Press (2020), 163, 167–70, 97; Circular Letter from Thomas Jefferson, 6 November 1801, PJM; Fred I. Greenstein, "Presidential Difference in the Early Republic: The Highly Disparate Leadership Styles of Washington, Adams, and Jefferson," *Presidential Studies Q.* 36:373, 376 (2006).

34. Stuart Leibiger, *Founding Friendship: George Washington, James Madison, and the Creation of the American Republic*, Princeton: Princeton University Press (1999), 10; Fred I. Greenstein, *Inventing the Job of President: Leadership Style from George Washington to Andrew Jackson*, Princeton: Princeton University Press (2008), 17.

35. To John Armstrong, 6 February 1791, GWP; from William Lindsay, from William Finnie, and from Reuben Wilkinson, 30 April 1789, GWP; to Samuel Vaughan, 21 March 1789, GWP; Bordewich, *The First Congress*, 80.

36. To Betty Washington Lewis, 13 September 1789, GWP.

37. To Betty Washington Lewis, 12 October 1789, GWP; to John Adams, 10 May 1789, GWP.

38. Diary, 17–20, 22 October 1789, GWP; to Benjamin Harrison, 10 October 1784, **GWP**.

39. T. H. Breen, *George Washington's Journey: The President Forges a New Nation*, New York: Simon & Schuster (2016), 73; Greenstein, "Presidential Difference," 385. The Boston visit involved an elaborate pas de deux between the president and Governor John Hancock,

who repeatedly invited Washington to be his guest, despite Washington's policy of staying only at public inns to avoid burdening private citizens with his entourage, and also to avoid incurring any obligations to his host. Washington declined Hancock's multiple invitations until the governor had no choice but to call on Washington. From John Hancock, 21, 23, 26 October 1789, GWP; to John Hancock, 22, 23, 26 October 1789, GWP; Diary, 25 October 1789, GWP; *Boston Gazette*, October 26, November 2, 1789; *Massachusetts Centinel*, October 28, 1789.

40. Diary, 24 October 1789, GWP.

41. Diary, 28 and 29 October 1789, 5 November, GWP; Joseph Barrell to Samuel Blachley Webb, 1 November 1789, in Ford, *Correspondence of Webb* 3:144.

42. Diary, 6 November 1789, GWP.

43. To Catharine Macaulay Graham, 9 January 1790, GWP; to Gouverneur Morris, 13 October 1789, GWP.

44. Louis-Guillaume Otto to Comte de Montmorin, 12 January 1790, *DHFFC* 17:197–99.

43. THE DEBT AND THE RESIDENCE

1. To the United States Senate and House of Representatives, 8 January 1790, GWP.

2. Bowling and Veit, *Maclay Diary*, 75 (12 June 1789), 88 (24 June 1789); Bickford, "'Public Attention Is Very Much Fixed on the Proceedings of the New Congress,'" in Bowling and Kennon, *Inventing Congress*, 141.

3. Bickford, "Public Attention," 8; Bordewich, *The First Congress*, 3; "Location of the Capital," 4 September 1789, PJM; Bowling, *The Creation of the United States*, 4; from Pierre L'Enfant, 11 September 1789, GWP; R. B. Bernstein, "A New Matrix for National Politics: The First Federal Elections, 1788–90," in Bowling and Kennon, *Inventing Congress*, 116.

4. Americans in the 1780s debated these standards as they relocated their state capitals and county seats—for example, moving Virginia's capital from Williamsburg to Richmond, and South Carolina's from Charleston to Columbia. Kenneth R. Bowling, *The Creation of Washington, D.C.: The Idea and Location of the American Capital*, Fairfax: George Mason University Press (1991), 2.

5. The consensus in favor of a "new" city received a boost from the insistence of the Pennsylvania ratifying convention that the state did not want the seat of government in Philadelphia or two of its suburbs, even though Philadelphia was the nation's largest city, was centrally located, and had housed Congress for nearly seven years along with the Constitutional Convention. Some Pennsylvanians, however, feared federal control of the city's vital port facilities, and competition for public support with the state government, which was then in Philadelphia. Bowling, *The Creation of Washington, D.C.*, 131. That opinion of the ratifying convention, however, soon dissipated. Pennsylvania's congressmen and senators insisted that once the temporary residence was in Philadelphia, inertia would transform the residence into a permanent one that Pennsylvanians would be delighted to have.

6. *Annals of Congress* 1:881 (3 September 1789); resolution of Richard Bland Lee, 4 September 1789, *DHFFC* 11:1400–1; *Pennsylvania Gazette*, March 18, 1789; *New York Daily Advertiser*, September 3, 1789.

7. Bowling, *The Creation of Washington, D.C.*, 89; Bordewich, *The First Congress*, 147–49; *New York Daily Journal*, July 9, 1790.

8. Bowling, *The Creation of Washington, D.C.*, 44–46, 57, 122, 125; to Richard Henry Lee, 8 February 1785, GWP; to William Grayson, 22 June 1785, GWP; *Pennsylvania Packet*, January 5 and 29, 1789, April 15, 1789; *Independent Gazette*, February 3, 1789; *Maryland Journal*, March 24, 1789, reprinted in Lee W. Formwalt, "A Conversation Between Two

Rivers: A Debate on the Location of the U.S. Capitol in Maryland," *Maryland Hist. Mag.* 71:310 (1976); *Maryland Journal*, January 23, 1789. The five legislator-investors in the Potomac Project were Senators Richard Henry Lee of Virginia and Charles Carroll of Maryland and Congressmen Alexander White of Virginia and Michael Jenifer Stone and Daniel Carroll of Maryland.

9. Bordewich, *The First Congress*, 145.

10. The serpentine progress of the residence legislation in September 1789 is best explored with a learned guide such as Bowling, *The Creation of Washington, D.C.*, 137–60, or Bordewich, *The First Congress*, 148–57. Maclay's diary offers wonderful vignettes of the politicking, but his views of the action were necessarily fragmentary. Bowling and Veit, *Maclay Diary*, 138–40 (28 August 1789), 140–41 (29 August 1789), 142 (1 September 1789), 146 (4 September 1789), 157–59 (23 September 1789), 161–65 (24 September 1789), 169 (28 September 1789). The newspaper accounts of the debates offer only partial views as well. *New York Daily Advertiser*, September 4, 5, 7, 8, and 22, 1789. The balloon flight and exhibition, staged by Joseph Decker, were reported by Maclay (159–61, 23 September 1789) and by Washington's nephew and secretary, Robert Lewis (Diary, 7 and 14 August 1789), *GW/ LOC Digital Collection*. See Bordewich, *The First Congress*, 113; Smith, *The City of New York in the Year of Washington*, 184.

11. Editorial Note: "Locating the Federal District," PTJ; Robert Morris to Mary Morris, 9, 11, and 25 September 1789, in DHFFC 17:1505, 17:1509, 17:1612.

12. Jack D. Warren Jr., *The Presidency of George Washington*, Mount Vernon Ladies' Association: Mount Vernon (2000), 18. Those two bills came in 1792 (the apportionment of congressional districts, which Washington thought was inconsistent with the constitutional provision that specified the population of each district) and in March 1797, three days before he left office. The latter bill, which disbanded two companies of dragoons that Washington thought should be retained, was reenacted to meet his objection; he signed it on his last day in office. Glenn A. Phelps, *George Washington and American Constitutionalism*, Lawrence: University Press of Kansas (1993), 152–54.

13. From Madison, 20 November 1789, GWP.

14. From David Stuart, 3 December 1789, GWP; Bowling, *The Creation of Washington, D.C.*, 162–67; Bordewich, *The First Congress*, 177–78. Stuart produced a fiery publication espousing the Potomac residence, while another came from Washington's old nemesis, Adam Stephen.

15. Elkins and McKitrick, *The Age of Federalism*, 19; Bordewich, *The First Congress*, 9: Frank Monaghan and Marvin Lowenthal, *This Was New York: The Nation's Capital in 1789*, Garden City, NY: Doubleday, Doran & Co. (1943), 49; Smith, *The City of New York*, 110–11.

16. Bordewich, *The First Congress*, 168; Elkins and McKitrick, *The Age of Federalism*, 114–15.

17. Elkins and McKitrick, *The Age of Federalism*, 137.

18. Diary, 2 January 1790, GWP; "Report Relative to a Provision for the Support of Public Credit," 9 January 1790, PAH.

19. William Smith (Boston) to John Adams, 24 April 1790, DHFFC 19:1306–7.

20. Madison to Jefferson, 24 January 1790, PJM; Bowling and Veit, *Maclay Diary*, 184–85 (18 January 1790); Theodore Sedgwick to Pamela Sedgwick, 23 March 1790, DHFFC 19:971; David Stuart to Richard Bland Lee, 23 May 1790, DHFFC 19:1576–77; Richard Henry Lee and John Walker to Gov. Beverley Randolph, 25 May 1790, DHFFC 19:1600–1. Hamilton's assistant secretary, William Duer, was caught in an improper speculation and had to resign. "The House Investigation of William Duer," DHFFC 19:1082–85; "Certificate of William Campbell," ca. 14–23 November 1792, DHFFC 19:1085.

21. Aedanus Burke to Samuel Bryan, 3 March 1790, DHFFC 18:715; Theodorick Bland to [St. George Tucker], 6 March 1790, DHFFC 18:746–47; Edward Carrington to Madison, 7 April 1790, DHFFC 18:747; Abraham Baldwin to Joel Barlow, 7 April 1790, DHFFC 19:1160;

Alexander White to Horatio Gates, 16 April 1790, *DHFFC* 19:1244; Elkins and McKitrick, *The Age of Federalism*, 118; Stewart, *Madison's Gift*, 107–8.

22. Edward Carrington to Madison, 27 March 1790, PJM; Richard Bland Lee to Theodorick Lee, 9 April 1790, *DHFFC* 19:1184.

23. Stewart, *Madison's Gift*, 109–10.

24. Bowling and Veit, *Maclay Diary*, 219–20 (16 March 1790) and 230 (29 March 1790); Flexner 3:224; William Smith to Otho H. Williams, 11 April 1790, *DHFFC* 19:1202; Maclay to John Nicholson, 12 April 1790, *DHFFC* 19:1212; Hugh Williamson to Gov. Alexander Martin, 13 May 1790, *DHFFC* 19:1500; William Davies to Gov. Beverley Randolph and enclosure 1 ("The Claims of Virginia"), 21 May 1790, *DHFFC* 19:1461–62; Bordewich, *The First Congress*, 210; Madison to James Monroe, 17 April 1790, PJM; Abraham Baldwin to Joel Barlow, 1 May 1790, *DHFFC* 19:1395; George Clymer to Tench Coxe, 1 May 1790, *DHFFC* 19:1396; Frederick A. Muhlenberg to Tench Coxe, 2 May 1790, *DHFFC* 19:1411.

25. Warner Mifflin to Members of Congress, 16 March 1790, *DHFFC* 19:886–87; Diary, 16 March 1790, GWP; Madison to Benjamin Rush, 20 March 1790, PJM; John Pemberton to James Pemberton, 16 March 1790, *DHFFC* 19:883; from David Stuart, 15 March 1790, GWP. Several Northern congressmen, no friends to slavery, expressed frustration with the Quaker petitions. "As Congress may not emancipate," wrote Theodore Sedgwick, "I wish the whole matter could have been kept out of sight till some rational means could be devised to make the benevolent zeal of those who declaim against the doctrine more useful." Theodore Sedgwick to [Ephraim] Williams, 17 March 1790, *DHFFC* 19:902; Fisher Ames to [William Eustis], 17 March 1790, *DHFFC* 19:888–91; Henry Wynkoop to Reading Beatty, 18 March 1790, *DHFFC* 19:912.

26. To David Stuart, 15 June and 28 March 1790, GWP.

27. George Clymer to Henry Hill, 11 April 1790, *DHFFC* 19:1197; Diary, 20–24 April 1790, GWP; Thomas Lee Shippen to William Shippen, 22 April 1790, *DHFFC* 19:1292–93; Robert Morris to Mary Morris, 25 April 1790, *DHFFC* 19:1322. For Washington's attempts to get exercise: Diary, 23, 25, and 28 November 1789, 5, 7, and 10 December 1789, and 6 January 1790, GWP; Robert Lewis Diary, Washington Papers, Library of Congress (13 August 1789) (talking with farmers beyond lower Manhattan); Diary, 12 December 1789 (carriage ride with family), GWP; Griswold, *The Republican Court*, 365.

28. David S. Heidler and Jeanne T. Heidler, *Washington's Circle: The Creation of the President*, New York: Random House (2015), 149–50; Editorial Note, 9 May 1790, GWP; Richard Henry Lee to Thomas Shippen, 14 May 1790, *DHFFC* 19:1503; Jefferson to Martha Jefferson Randolph, 16 May 1790, PTJ; Bowling and Veit, *Maclay Diary*, 269 (15 May 1790); Pierce Butler to Edward Rutledge, 15 May 1790, *DHFFC* 19:1505; Abigail Adams to Cotton Tufts, 30 May 1790, AP.

29. Theodore Sedgwick to Pamela Sedgwick, 16 May 1790, *DHFFC* 19:1521; Jefferson to Martha Jefferson Randolph, 16 May 1790, PTJ.

30. Philip Schuyler to Stephen Van Rensselaer, 23 May 1790, *DHFFC* 19:1575; to David Stuart, 15 June 1790, GWP; to Diego de Gardoqui, 1 July 1790, GWP.

31. Abigail Adams to Cotton Tufts, 30 May 1790, AP; Editorial Note, William Jackson to Clement Biddle, 2 May 1790, GWP; *Gazette of the United States*, "Letter to New York," April 28, 1790, *DHFFC* 19:1361 (printed 8 May 1790); Samuel Ogden to Henry Knox, 22 May 1790, Papers of the War Department (posted on website, "Papers of the War Department, 1784–1800," Doc. No. 1790052240101); Edward Rutledge to Thomas Jefferson, 20 June 1790, PTJ; Theodore Sedgwick to Pamela Sedgwick, 16 May 1790, *DHFFC* 19:1521; David Stuart to Richard Bland Lee, 23 May 1790, *DHFFC* 19:1576; John Brown to Harry Innes, 18 June 1790, *DHFFC* 19:1858; Robert Morris to Mary Morris, 23 May 1790, *DHFFC* 19:1573.

32. In mid-March, Congressman William Irvine of Pennsylvania speculated that the assumption and residence issues might be resolved in a single, multi-sided agreement. William Irvine to [John Nicholson], 18 March 1790, *DHFFC* 19:905; Bowling and Veit, *Maclay Diary,* 228–29 (26 March 1790).

44. THE COMPROMISE

1. From William Jackson, 19 April 1789, and note 1, GWP; Mary S. Beall, "The Military and Private Secretaries of George Washington," *Records of the Columbia Historical Society* 1:89 (1897).
2. Thomas Fitzsimons to William Jackson, *DHFFC* 19:1433–34 (5 May 1790); Thomas Hartley to Jasper Yeates, *DHFFC* 19:1677–78 (2 June 1790); Stephen Decatur, *Private Affairs of George Washington: From the Records and Accounts of Tobias Lear,* Boston: Houghton Mifflin Co. (1933), 57, 79, 108, 174, 209; Editorial Note, William Jackson to Clement Biddle, 2 May 1790, GWP.
3. Bowling and Veit, *Maclay Diary,* 195, 199–200 (1 and 9 February 1790). Hamilton's advocacy was briefly interrupted when he had to parry a demand from Rep. Aedanus Burke of South Carolina that prepared the way for a duel between the two men. Nine months before, in a Fourth of July oration, Hamilton had made an unflattering remark about the performance of militia during Revolutionary War battles. After nearly a year passed, Burke chose to be offended by the remark on behalf of Southern militiamen. Hamilton to Aedanus Burke, 1 April 1790, PAH; Aedanus Burke to Hamilton, 1 April 1790, PAH. Hamilton composed a letter clarifying his remarks while an unofficial and secret committee of Congress formed to head off an armed encounter between the two men. Hamilton to Aedanus Burke, 7 April 1790, PAH; Thomas Hartley to Jasper Yeates, *DHFFC* 19:1126–27 (4 April 1790); William Smith (Maryland) to Otho H. Williams, *DHFFC* 19:1131 (4 April 1790); Elbridge Gerry, George Mathews, Rufus King, Lambert Cadwalader, James Jackson, John Henry, and Peter Muhlenberg to Hamilton, 6 April 1790, PAH. After receiving Hamilton's explanation, Burke "cheerfully and explicitly" retracted his offensive remarks. Aedanus Burke to Hamilton, 7 April 1790, PAH.
4. Bowling and Veit, *Maclay Diary,* 235–36 (4 April 1790), 239–40 (9 April 1790), 241–42 (12 April 1790); Bowling, *The Creation of Washington, D.C.,* 174.
5. Richard Bland Lee to [Charles Lee], *DHFFC* 19:1147 (5 April 1790); Richard Bland Lee to Theodorick Lee, *DHFFC* 19:1184 (9 April 1790); John Fenno to Joseph Ward, *DHFFC* 19:1198 (11 April 1790); William Few to [Joseph Clay, GA], *DHFFC* 19:1225 (14 April 1790).
6. Pierce Butler to Alexander Gillon, *DHFFC* 19:1300 (23 April 1790); Benjamin Goodhue to Stephen Goodhue, *DHFFC* 19:1598 (25 May 1790); Bowling and Veit, *Maclay Diary,* 276–77 (26 May 1790), 291–93 (14 June 1790); *New York Daily Advertiser,* July 9, 1790; *New York Daily Journal,* July 9, 1790.
7. Fisher Ames to George Minot, *DHFFC* 19:1542–43 (20 May 1790); Bowling and Veit, eds., *Maclay Diary,* 254–55 (27 April 1790) (conversation with Senator Langdon of New Hampshire); John Steele to Governor Alexander Martin, *DHFFC* 19:1527 (17 May 1790).
8. Bowling and Veit, *Maclay Diary,* 257–58 (1 May 1790), 275–76 (25 May 1790); Madison to James Monroe, 1 June 1790, PJM; William L. Smith (South Carolina) to Edward Rutledge, *DHFFC* 19:1818 (14 June 1790).
9. Bowling and Veit, *Maclay Diary,* 272–73 (20 May 1790); Heidler and Heidler, *Washington's Circle,* 157; Bickford and Bowling, *Birth of the Nation,* 195.
10. Bowling, *First Congress,* 178; Bowling and Veit, *Maclay Diary,* 286–87 (8 June 1790); Caleb Strong to Theo. Foster, *DHFFC* 19:1696–97 (3 June 1790); Richard Henry Lee to Thomas Shippen, *DHFFC* 19:1713 (5 June 1790); Maclay to Benjamin Rush, *DHFFC* 19:1713 (5 June

1790); Jefferson to William Short, *DHFFC* 19:1734 (6 June 1790); Benjamin Rush to Tench Coxe, *DHFFC* 19:1756 (8 June 1790).

11. Jefferson to Martha Jefferson Randolph, 6 June 1790, PTJ.

12. Decatur, *The Private Affairs of George Washington*, 133.

13. *DHFFC* 13:1553–65 (10–11 June 1790); Fisher Ames to Timothy Dwight, *DHFFC* 19:1781–82 (11 June 1790); Thomas Hartley to Jasper Yeates, *DHFFC* 19:1789 (12 June 1790); Jefferson to George Mason, 13 June 1790, PTJ; *New York Daily Advertiser*, July 9, 1790 (remarks of Rep. Amos Laurance of New York); Richard Bland Lee to Theodorick Lee, *DHFFC* 19:1828 (15 June 1790); Theodore Sedgwick to Pamela Sedgwick, *DHFFC* 19:1903 (22 June 1790). Until June 10, Baltimore was a second-tier contender for the permanent residence, coming up for occasional votes but losing by solid margins. Tench Coxe to Tench Francis, *DHFFC* 19:1647 (31 May 1790); William Smith (MD) to Otho H. Williams, *DHFFC* 19:1648 (31 May 1790) and 19:1702 (4 June 1790); Rufus King, "Notes in Senate," *DHFFC* 19:1755 (8 June 1790). Baltimore's emergence as a front-rank contender divided the Maryland congressional delegation, with Baltimore drawing support from congressmen from districts surrounding the upper Chesapeake Bay; the Potomac won the votes of those from more southern and western districts. George Thatcher to Nathaniel Wells, *DHFFC* 19:1810–11 (13 June 1790).

14. *New York Daily Gazette*, June 11, 1781; Fisher Ames to Thomas Dwight, *DHFFC* 19:1782 (11 June 1790); Benjamin Goodhue to Stephen Goodhue, *DHFFC* 19:1771 (10 June 1790); Jefferson to Francis Hopkinson, 13 June 1790, PTJ; Jefferson to Richard Peters, 13 June 1790, PTJ; Maclay to Benjamin Rush, *DHFFC* 19:1805 (18 June 1790).

15. Bowling and Veit, *Maclay Diary*, 291–93 (14 June 1790); Bowling, *The Creation of Washington, D.C.*, 179–80; Elkins and McKitrick, *The Age of Federalism*, 159.

16. Diary, 22, 23, and 26 March 1790, GWP; Jefferson to George Mason, 13 June 1790, PTJ; Jefferson to James Monroe, 20 June 1790, PTJ.

17. Bowling and Veit, *Maclay Diary*, 293–94 (15 June 1790); Elkins and McKitrick, *The Age of Federalism*, 159; Bowling, *Creation of Washington, D.C.*, 182; Peter Muhlenberg to Benjamin Rush, *DHFFC* 19:1850 (17 June 1790); from Josiah Parker to James Madison, 15 June 1790, and Editorial Note, PJM. Hamilton's former deputy, William Duer, recently disgraced for using inside information to speculate in government bonds, made a simultaneous offer to the Pennsylvanians to give them the permanent residence on the Susquehanna in return for votes for assumption. Bowling and Veit, *Maclay Diary*, 291–92 (14 June 1790); Hamilton to William Duer, 4–7 April 1790, PAH. Duer seems to have been operating on his own in raising this prospect; Hamilton and Morris had failed to perform for each other on precisely those terms a day or two earlier, and Duer's terms did not match those offered by either Jefferson or Madison, who were next to the president. Duer's overture went nowhere.

18. Jefferson to James Monroe, 20 June 1790, PTJ.

19. Jefferson, "The Assumption [1792–94?]," *DHFFC* 19:1989; "Anas," *DHFFC* 19:1991–92 (4 February 1818) ("Explanations of the three volumes found in Marbled Paper").

20. William Davies to Gov. Beverley Randolph, *DHFFC* 19:1879 (20 June 1790). Elkins and McKitrick also find Jefferson's version of the 1790 compromise incomplete. *The Age of Federalism*, 155.

21. Benjamin Goodhue to Stephen Goodhue, *DHFFC* 19:1848 (17 June 1790); Theodore Sedgwick to Pamela Sedgwick, *DHFFC* 19:1852 (17 June 1790). Sedgwick's ties to the president and the cabinet were key in the fight over the Jay Treaty several years later. One student of that episode wrote that Sedgwick "had the confidence of both Washington's cabinet and the Federalists in the senate. While they devised the programs and general strategy for the party, Sedgwick operated as their House tactician." Jerald A. Combs, *The Jay Treaty: Political Battleground of the Founding Fathers*, Berkeley: University of California Press (1970), 172.

22. Bowling, *The Creation of Washington, D.C.*, 184–85; William L. Smith to Edward Rutledge, 25 July 1790, in George C. Rogers Jr., William Loughton Smith to Edward Rutledge, *DHFFC* 20:2263–67 (25 July 1790); Rufus King, "Notes on the Residence Issue in Second Session," *DHFFC* 19:1971 (30 June 1790); Kenneth R. Bowling, "Dinner at Jefferson's: A Note on Jacob E. Cooke's 'The Compromise of 1790,'" *WMQ* 28:629, 630 (1971). Fortunately for the administration forces, they did not need Massachusetts votes in the House of Representatives, since the Massachusetts representatives strongly opposed the Potomac. Theodore Sedgwick to Pamela Sedgwick, *DHFFC* 19:1903 (22 June 1790); Benjamin Goodhue to Stephen Goodhue, *DHFFC* 19:1900 (22 June 1790).

23. Robert Morris to Mary Morris, *DHFFC* 19:1889 (21 June 1790); Bowling and Veit, *Maclay Diary*, 301–3 (23–24 June 1790); Samuel Hodgdon to Benjamin Goodhue, *DHFFC* 19:2012 (3 July 1790); Benjamin Goodhue to Stephen Goodhue, *DHFFC* 19:2009 (2 July 1790); Henry Wynkoop to Reading Beatty, *DHFFC* 19:2008 (2 July 1790).

24. Bowling and Veit, eds., *Maclay Diary*, 307–8 (30 June 1790) and 320–21 (15 July 1790). Prof. Kenneth Bowling, the leading scholar of the Compromise of 1790, agrees with Maclay's conclusion. Bowling has written (*The Creation of Washington, D.C.*, 182): "Washington's concern for discretion, and Madison's and Jefferson's willingness to honor it, mask his exact role. Several facts suggest that the two men worked closely with the president as the bargain evolved. Madison had kept Washington well informed about the politics of the residence debates in 1788 and 1789. The president's aides had been involved in various stages of the pre-June bargaining and showed their delight publicly when a Potomac seat of government bill finally passed Congress. Even more indicative were his central importance to the political process, his Potomac Fever, and his almost fanatic attention to the development of the capital from July 1790 until his retirement." Bordewich reaches a similar conclusion in *First Congress*, 194–95. Elkins and McKitrick, in *The Age of Federalism*, 169, also emphasize Washington's importance to the 1790 Compromise: "The prestige of George Washington and the knowledge of Washington's long-cherished desire to have the capital of the Republic seated on the banks of the Potomac had had no little to do with the Virginians' eventual success in putting it there. . . . [His] moral authority was a major factor in making the decision stick."

25. *Annals of Congress*, *DHFFC* 1:395–97 (1 July 1790), 13:1690–91 (9 July 1790), 1:413–17 (14 July 1790), 13:1724–30 (26–30 July 1790); Bordewich, *The First Congress*, 250; Bowling, *The Creation of Washington, D.C.*, 188–90; Madison to James Madison Sr., 31 July 1790, PJM; 1 Statute 130 (16 July 1790).

26. King, "Notes on the Residence Issue," *DHFFC* 19:1971 (30 June 1790); from Jefferson, 9 September 1792, GWP.

27. Henry Wynkoop to Reading Beatty, *DHFFC* 19:2008 (2 July 1790); Benjamin Goodhue to Stephen Goodhue, *DHFFC* 19:2009 (2 July 1790); Bowling and Veit, *Maclay Diary*, 307–8 (30 June 1790) and 330–32 (22 July 1790); Jefferson to James Monroe, 20 June 1790, PTJ.

28. Michael Jenifer Stone to [Walter Stone], *DHFFC* 19:1997 (1 July 1790).

29. Elkins and McKittrick, *The Age of Federalism*, 169–72; Bowling, *The Creation of Washington, D.C.*, 219–22; to Jefferson, 2 and 4 January 1791, GWP; from Daniel Carroll, 22 January 1791, GWP; "Commission," 22 January 1791, GWP; from John Eager Howard, 22 January 1791; from Beverley Randolph, 15 February 1791, GWP; Proclamation, 24 January 1791, GWP; to William Deakins Jr. and Benjamin Stoddert, 3 February 1791, GWP; to George Gilpin, 4 February 1791, GWP. The three commissioners for the project met Madison's recommendation that Washington choose "men who prefer any place on the Potomac to any place elsewhere." From Madison, 29 August 1790, GWP. They included Congressman Daniel Carroll, who owned land in the new federal district, former Maryland governor Thomas Johnson, a longtime collaborator with Washington on Potomac projects, and David Stuart, Washington's intimate who had married Jack Custis's widow.

30. To David Stuart, 15 June 1790, GWP.

31. These conclusions are reinforced by Jefferson's account of Hamilton's earnest entreaty to him when they stood in the street outside the president's residence, talking about the assumption issue. "The President was the center on which all administrative questions ultimately rested," Hamilton said in this account, and "all of us should rally around him, and support with joint efforts *measures approved by him.*" Jefferson, "Anas," *DHFFC* 19:1991 (4 February 1818) (emphasis supplied).

32. Bowling, *The Creation of Washington, D.C.*, 185–86, 125, 205; Bordewich, *The First Congress*, 247–48; from Charles Carroll of Carrollton, 3 March 1775, GWP; *Annals of Congress*, 1st Cong., 2d Sess., 1755 (28 July 1790); to Madison, 28 December 1784, GWP (Enclosure dated 28 December 1784); Kate Mason Rowland, *The Life of Charles Carroll of Carrollton*, New York: G. P. Putnam's Sons (1898), 1:235–36; Diary, 1 May 1790, GWP (conversation with White concerning western settlers). Lee's connections to Washington were especially strong. His brother Henry Lee was a favored cavalry officer during the Revolutionary War and became a close political ally of Washington's; his other brother, Charles Lee, became Washington's personal lawyer and then his attorney general.

33. *New York Daily Advertiser*, September 7, 1789.

34. Louis Guillaume Otto to Comte de Montmorin, *DHFFC* 19:1804 (13 June 1790).

35. To Henry Knox, 13 August 1790, GWP.

45. THE BANK

1. Rappleye, *Robert Morris*, 216–19, 236–39.

2. To Tobias Lear, 5, 9, and 17 September 1790, 17 November 1790, GWP.

3. Bordewich, *The First Congress*, 276, 278; Kenneth Bowling, "The Federal Government and the Republican Court Move to Philadelphia, November 1790–March 1791," in Bowling and Kennon, *Neither Separate Nor Equal*, 15. The president attempted to swap some of his western lands for a farm outside Philadelphia, where he might follow relaxing agricultural pursuits, but failed to close any deal. To Burgess Ball, 19 December 1790, GWP.

4. Bowling, "The Federal Government and the Republican Court Move to Philadelphia," 5, 7, and 23; Theodore Sedgwick to Pamela Sedgwick, 26 December 1790, *DHFFC* 21:23–38.

5. Bowling and Veit, *Maclay Diary*, 365–66 (20 January 1791).

6. Bowling and Veit, *Maclay Diary*, 340 (8 December 1791); to the United States Senate and House of Representatives, 8 December 1790, GWP.

7. Jack D. Warren Jr., "'The Line of My Official Conduct': George Washington and Congress, 1789–1797," in Bowling and Kennon, *Neither Separate Nor Equal*, 262–63.

8. "Final Version: First Report on the Further Provision Necessary for Establishing Public Credit," 13 December 1790, PAH.

9. Bowling, *Politics in the First Congress*, 154; *Gazette of the United States*, February 19 and 23, 1791; Bordewich, *The First Congress*, 292–93; Thomas P. Slaughter, *The Whiskey Rebellion: Frontier Epilogue to the American Revolution*, New York: Oxford University Press (1986), 102–5; Note, from Edmund Randolph, 12 February 1791, GWP; Fisher Ames to Thomas Dwight, 7 February 1791, *DHFFC* 21:720; Ames to George R. Minot, 17 February 1791, in *DHFFC* 2:863–65.

10. Gienapp, *The Second Creation*, 211; Bowling, *The Creation of Washington, D.C.*, 215–19; Alexander White to Charles Simms, 20 February 1791, in Simms Papers, LOC; *American Daily Advertiser*, February 16, 1791.

11. Madison "Detached Memorandum," in *DHFFC* 21:810–12, 21:766–69 (note "Bank Bill Veto Controversy").

12. Gienapp, *The Second Creation*, 211; *DHFFC* 14:439 (4 February 1791) (Rep. Boudinot).

13. "Madison's 'Detached Memoranda,'" ca. 31 January 1820, PJM.

14. From Edmund Randolph, 12 February 1791, GWP; "Enclosure: Opinion on the Constitutionality of the Bank," 12 February 1791, GWP.

15. From Jefferson, 15 February 1791, GWP. With his opinion letter, Jefferson enclosed the text of Madison's speech in the House of Representatives against the bank bill, which had appeared in the Philadelphia press. *General Advertiser*, February 7, 1791; *Federal Gazette*, February 12, 1791; "The Bank Bill," 8 February 1791, PJM.

16. From Madison, 21 February 1791, GWP. One of Madison's draft veto messages noted only the constitutional objection to the bank, while the other added a second argument—that it would unfairly favor some Americans over others.

17. From Hamilton, 23 February 1791, GWP, and "Enclosure: Opinion on the Constitutionality of an Act to Establish a Bank," 23 February 1791, GWP. Hamilton gave the back of his hand to the contention that when the Constitutional Convention declined to give Congress the power to create corporations, it effectively denied Congress that power. It was very common, Hamilton observed, for a law to have impacts beyond or other than the intent of its drafters.

18. To Hamilton, 23 February 1791, GWP, and note 2; Madison, "Detached Memoranda," *supra*; Proclamation, 30 March 1791, GWP; *Annals of Congress,* 1st Cong., 3d Sess. 2:2025 (1 March 1791); 2:1824–25 (3 March 1791); Warren, "'The Line of My Official Conduct,'" 265 and note 43.

19. Elkins and McKitrick, *The Age of Federalism*, 242.

20. John Trumbull to John Adams, 20 March 1791, AP.

21. To Edward Rutledge, 16 January 1791, GWP; to David Humphreys, 16 March 1791, GWP.

22. Diary, 29 and 30 March 1791; Breen, *George Washington's Journey*, 210.

23. Diary, 15, 16, and 18 April 1791, GWP; Breen, *George Washington's Journey*, 221–22.

24. Breen, *George Washington's Journey*, 153; *Columbian Centinel* (Boston), June 11, 1791; *Maryland Journal*, May 31, 1791; Diary, 11 and 24 April, 3, 6, 12, 20, 26, and 30 May, 1 and 2 June 1791, GWP.

25. Breen, *George Washington's Journey*, 209, 211, 232–33, 207; from Tobias Lear, 5 April 1791, GWP; to Tobias Lear, 12 April 1791, GWP; from Tobias Lear, 5 June 1791, GWP.

26. Diary, 27, 28, and 29 June 1791, GWP; to David Humphreys, 20 July 1791, GWP.

27. "Substance of a Conversation with the President," 5 May 1792, PJM.

46. SECOND-TERM BLUES

1. Inaugural Address, 4 March 1793, GWP; to David Humphreys, 23 March 1793, GWP.

2. To Hamilton, 8 April 1794, GWP; to William Pearce, 31 January 1796, GWP; to Knox, 25 June 1794, GWP; Jefferson, "Anas," 4 February 1818, PTJ. Strikingly, Jefferson was seventy-five years old when he wrote the description of the aging Washington, a full decade older than Washington was when he left the presidency. Of the leading Washington biographers, Flexner has been most impressed by the decline in Washington's faculties. Flexner 4:155–56. The next four chapters will show that the author of this volume, without denying the impact of age on Washington, does not share Flexner's view on that subject.

3. To Burwell Bassett Jr., 4 March 1793, GWP; to James Craik, 9 April 1793, GWP; to David Stuart, 9 April 1793, GWP; to Bryan Fairfax, 9 April 1793, GWP; to Frances Bassett Washington, 10 June 1793, GWP; from Tobias Lear, 24 June 1793, GWP.

4. To Howell Lewis, 3 November 1793, GWP; to William Pearce, 18 December 1793, GWP; to Hiland Crow, 23 December 1793, GWP; to John Christian Ehlers, 23 December **1793**, GWP; to Henry McCoy, 23 December 1793, GWP; to Thomas Green, 23 December 1793,

GWP. Although Washington had no direct offspring, his siblings provided a vast supply of nieces and nephews—eight from his sister Betty Lewis alone. Washington employed at least a half dozen nephews over his career, plus several of Martha's Dandridge relations.

5. To William Pearce, 12 January 1794 and 14 July 1794, GWP; to Arthur Young, 12 December 1793, GWP; Advertisement, 1 February 1796, GWP; to William Pearce, 7 February 1796, GWP; to David Stuart, 7 February 1796, GWP.

6. To Thomas Pinckney, 20 February 1796, GWP; to William Strickland, 20 February 1796, GWP.

7. Jefferson to Madison, 11 August 1793, PTJ. Two years after leaving the cabinet, Jefferson was still complaining about Randolph, writing to a friend, "The fact is that he has generally given his principles to the one party and his practice to the other; the oyster to one, the shell to the other. Unfortunately the shell was generally the lot of his friends the French and Republicans, and the oyster of their antagonists." To William Branch Giles, 31 December 1795, PTJ.

8. "Memoranda of Conversations with the President," 1 March 1792, PTJ. Jefferson's conversations with Washington over two days had a humorous side. The two Virginians, occupying the highest offices in the nation, competed with each other to express their weariness with public duties, recounting the sacrifices they had made and professing a desire to retire to their respective plantations. After that conversation, Washington served another five years as president, while Jefferson was secretary of state for two more years, vice president for four, and president for eight. Although Jefferson did not think so, Flexner concluded that Washington "sided more often with Jefferson than Hamilton." Flexner 4:109–10.

9. From Hamilton, 21 June 1793 and 31 January 1795, GWP; from Jefferson, 29 July and 12 August 1793, GWP.

10. Chervinsky, *The Cabinet*, 211–12 (noting that Mifflin and Washington had "a historically sour relationship" and a "decades-long dislike of each other").

11. "A Citizen," *National Gazette*, July 27, 1793; Jefferson to Thomas Pinckney, 3 December 1795, PTJ; Elkins and McKitrick, *The Age of Federalism*, 288; to Oliver Wolcott Jr., 6 July 1795, GWP.

12. To Randolph, 29 July 1795, GWP.

13. 23 March 1793, Jefferson to William Carmichael and William Short, 23 March 1793, PTJ; from Hamilton, 5 April 1793, PTJ; from Jefferson, 7 April 1793, GWP; to Jefferson, 1 December 1793, GWP; to David Humphreys, 23 March 1793, GWP; to Earl of Buchan, 22 April 1793, GWP.

14. To Jefferson, 10 March 1793, GWP; from the Inhabitants of Belpre, Northwest Territory, 14 March 1793, GWP; to the Cabinet, 21 March 1793, GWP.

15. From William Gordon, 17 August 1793, GWP.

47. THE CALAMITOUS FRENCHMAN

1. Elkins and McKitrick, *The Age of Federalism*, 333–34; Samuel Flagg Bemis, "Washington's Farewell Address: A Foreign Policy of Independence," in Burton Ira Kaufman, ed., *Washington's Farewell Address: The View from the 20th Century,* Chicago: Quadrangle Books (1969), 90–91.

2. Flexner 4:39; Jefferson to Madison, 19 May 1793, PTJ.

3. Elkins and McKitrick, *The Age of Federalism*, 337; to Jefferson, 12 April 1793, GWP; to the Cabinet, 18 April 1793, GWP; from Jefferson, 18 April 1793, GWP; to Madison, 7 April 1793, GWP; Jefferson, "Anas," 18 April 1793, PTJ; Bemis, *The Jay Treaty*, 91.

4. "Minutes of a Cabinet Meeting," 19 April 1793, GWP; "Neutrality Proclamation," 22 April 1793, GWP; from the Philadelphia Merchants and Traders, 16 May 1793, GWP; from the Citizens of Salem, Massachusetts, 31 May 1793, GWP; from the Baltimore Mechanical Society, 4 June 1793, GWP; from Edmund Randolph, 11 June 1793, GWP; from Tobias Lear, 17 June 1793, GWP; from the Citizens of Hartford, Connecticut, 2 August 1793, GWP; from the Grand Jurors of Sussex County, Delaware, 7 August 1793, GWP; Address from the Citizens of New York City, 8 August 1793, GWP; from the Citizens of Burlington County, New Jersey, GWP; from the Citizens of Kent County, Delaware, 14 August 1793, GWP; Resolutions of the Citizens of Essex County, New Jersey, 17 August 1793, GWP; from the Citizens of Dorchester County, Maryland, 19 August 1793, GWP; Resolutions of the Citizens of New Haven, Connecticut, 19 August 1793, GWP; Enclosure: "Resolutions from Kent County, Maryland, Citizens," 31 August 1793, GWP; Resolutions from Petersburg, Virginia, Citizens, 2 September 1793, GWP. The public meeting process could be manipulated by clever political operators, but anecdotal reports buttressed the conclusion that the people generally supported neutrality.

5. Jefferson to Madison, 19 May 1793, PTJ; Madison to Jefferson, 19 June 1793, PJM; see "Veritas," *National Gazette*, June 5, 1793 (calling the neutrality policy "shamefully pusillanimous" toward France); from Edmund Randolph, 24 June 1793, GWP (in Virginia, "the friends to the general government are far inferior in number to its enemies"); Genêt to Le Brun, Minister of Foreign Affairs, 31 May 1793, in Frederick J. Turner, "Correspondence of the French Ministers to the United States, 1791–1797," in *Annual Report of the American Historical Ass'n for the year 1903*, Washington (1904) 2:216.

6. "Thomas Jefferson's Notes on a Cabinet Meeting," 6 May 1793, GWP; to Henry Lee, 6 May 1793, GWP.

7. Memorial from George Hammond, 2 and 8 May 1793, PTJ; Introductory Note: To George Washington, 15 May 1793, PAH; Memorandum from Alexander Hamilton, 15 May 1793, GWP; Jefferson to George Hammond, 15 May 1793, PTJ; from Knox, 16 May 1793, GWP; Jefferson to Genêt, 11 June 1793, PTJ. Washington's Cabinet was united on the debt-repayment issue. When France stopped reimbursing Americans who had claims for illegal ship seizures, the American government stepped in to pay the injured parties, then subtracted those amounts from its debt to France. From Hamilton, 8 June 1793, GWP; from Jefferson, 6 June 1793, GWP; Genêt to Jefferson, 18 June 1793, PTJ; Jefferson to Genêt, 23 June 1793, PTJ; "Notes of a Cabinet Meeting and on Conversations with Edmond Charles Genêt," 5 July 1793, PTJ; Cabinet Opinion on the Payment of the U.S. Debt to France, 11 March 1794, GWP.

8. "Reasons for the Opinion of the Secretary of the Treasury and the Secretary at War Respecting the Brigantine *Little Sarah*," 8 July 1793, PAH; Jefferson to Gouverneur Morris, 13 June 1793, PTJ.

9. From George Clinton, 9 June 1793, GWP; from Thomas Mifflin, 22 June 1793, GWP; Enclosure: Thomas Jefferson's Notes on a Conversation with Edmond Genêt, 10 July 1793, GWP.

10. Cabinet Opinion on the *Little Sarah* [*Petite Démocrate*], 8 July 1793, GWP; Memorandum from Alexander Hamilton and Henry Knox, 8 July 1793, GWP; Cabinet Opinion on Foreign Vessels and Consulting the Supreme Court, 12 July 1793, GWP; from Jefferson, with "Enclosure Questions for the Supreme Court," 18 July 1793, GWP; to Justices of the Supreme Court, 23 July 1793, GWP; from the Supreme Court Justices, 8 August 1794, GWP.

11. Thomas Jefferson's Notes on a Conversation with Edmond Genêt, 10 July 1793, PTJ; Jefferson to Madison, 7 July 1793, PTJ.

12. To Henry Lee, 21 July 1793, GWP; "Notes of Cabinet Meeting on Edmond Charles Gênet," 2 August 1793, PTJ; Cabinet Opinions on the *Roland* and Relations with Great Britain, France, and the Creek Indians, 31 August 1793, GWP; Carol Berkin, *A Sovereign People:*

The Crises of the 1790s and the Birth of American Nationalism, New York: Basic Books (2017), 117–18. In his annual message to Congress in December, the president listed a number of British violations of the neutrality policy. Annual Message, 5 December 1793, GWP. Nevertheless, unlike Genêt, British diplomats observed traditional norms in conducting diplomatic business.

13. "Notes on a Cabinet Meeting," 1 August 1793, PTJ; Cabinet Opinion on the Recall of Edmond Genêt, 23 August 1793, GWP; Cabinet Opinion on French Privateers and Prizes, 5 August 1793, GWP; Cabinet Opinion on Relations with France and Great Britain, 7 September 1793, GWP; Berkin, *A Sovereign People,* 129–30, 134. When the instruction to request Genêt's recall reached the American minister in Paris, Genêt was agitating with commanders of a French fleet docked in New York, urging them to attack Halifax, then assault New Orleans. The mariners ignored Genêt's pleas.

14. Christopher Young, "Connecting the President and the People: Washington's Neutrality, Genet's Challenge, and Hamilton's Fight for Public Support," *J. of the Early Republic* 31:435, 455–56 (2011); e.g., from the Citizens of New London, Connecticut, 22 August 1793, GWP; Enclosure, "Resolutions of Caroline County, Virginia, Citizens," 10 September 1793, GWP; Enclosure, "Address from Annapolis, Maryland, Citizens," 5 September 1793, GWP; Enclosure, "Resolutions from James City County, Virginia, Citizens," 12 September 1793, GWP; from Alexandria, Virginia, Citizens, 5 October 1793, GWP; Enclosure, "Resolutions from the Albemarle County, Virginia, Citizens," 10 October 1793 GWP; Enclosure, "Resolutions from Culpeper County, Virginia, Citizens," 25 October 1793, GWP; Resolutions from Frederick County, Virginia, Citizens, 5 November 1793, GWP; Resolutions from Shenandoah County, Virginia, Citizens, 13 November 1793, GWP; Stewart, *Madison's Gift,* 151; Jefferson to Madison, 11 August 1793, PTJ.

15. Jefferson to Madison, 1, 8, and 12 September 1793, PJM; J. H. Powell, *Bring Out Your Dead: The Great Plague of Yellow Fever in Philadelphia in 1793,* Philadelphia: University of Pennsylvania Press (1949), 48, 114; Susan E. Klepp, "'How Many Precious Souls Are Fled?': The Magnitude of the 1793 Yellow Fever Epidemic," in J. Worth Estes and Billy Gordon Smith, eds., *A Melancholy Scene of Devastation: The Public Response to the 1793 Philadelphia Yellow Fever Epidemic,* Canton, MA: Science History Publications (1997), 163–82.

16. From Jefferson, 15–16 September 1793, GWP; from Jefferson, 1 October 1793, GWP; to Tobias Lear, 25 September 1793, GWP; Oliver Wolcott Jr. to Oliver Wolcott Sr., 12 September 1793, in George Gibbs, ed., *Oliver Wolcott's Memoirs of the Administrations of Washington and Adams,* New York: n.p. (1846), 1:110.

17. From Knox, 18 September 1793, 24 September 1793, 1 October 1793, GWP.

18. To Madison, 14 October 1793, GWP.

19. To Madison, 14 October 1793, GWP.

20. To Jefferson, 11 October 1793, GWP; from Edmund Randolph, 13 October 1793, GWP; to Hamilton, 14 October 1793, GWP; to Madison, 14 October 1793, GWP; from Hamilton, 24 October 1793, GWP.

21. To Randolph, 30 September 1793, GWP; Oliver Wolcott Jr. to Oliver Wolcott Sr., 10 October 1793, in Gibbs, *Wolcott Memoirs* 1:110; from Timothy Pickering, 21 and 28 October 1793, GWP.

22. From William Moultrie, 7 December 1793, GWP; from Genêt to Jefferson, 25 December 1793, PTJ; from Oliver Wolcott Jr. to Oliver Wolcott Sr., 10 March 1794, in Gibbs, *Wolcott Memoirs* 1:129; from Edmund Randolph, 27 February 1794, GWP; Berkin, *A Sovereign People,* 130–31. In early July, Genêt had told Jefferson that he planned to send an agent through the west to incite revolution in Louisiana and Canada, and to recruit Kentuckians and Indians to attack New Orleans, creating an independent nation on the Mississippi River. Jefferson replied that American citizens could not participate in such activities, although anyone else was welcome to do so. Remarkably, the secretary of state gave Genêt a

letter introducing his agent to Kentucky's governor. From Henry Lee, 14 June 1793, GWP; Notes of Cabinet Meeting and Conversations with Edmond Charles Genêt, 5 July 1793, PTJ; Elkins and McKitrick, *The Age of Federalism*, 349.

23. To Henry Lee, 16 October 1793, GWP; from Jefferson, 28 December 1793, GWP; Proclamation on Expeditions Against Spanish Territory, 24 March 1794, GWP.

24. Fifth Annual Message, 3 December 1793, GWP.

25. From Henry Lee, 17 September 1793, GWP; to Richard Henry Lee, 24 October 1793, GWP; Eugene Link, *Democratic-Republican Societies, 1790–1800*, New York: Columbia University Press (1942), 13–15; Noble E. Cunningham, Jr., *The Jeffersonian Republicans: The Formation of Party Organization, 1789–1801*, Chapel Hill: University of North Carolina Press (1957), 63–64.

26. To Edmund Randolph, 24 December 1793, GWP; to U.S. Senate, 24 January 1794, GWP.

27. From Edmund Randolph (and note 2), 1 March 1794, GWP; *General Advertiser* (Philadelphia), March 7, 1794.

48. TROUBLES WITHIN

1. To Anthony Whitting, 21 April 1793, GWP.

2. *The Federalist*, No. 12, in Cooke, *The Federalist*; William D. Barber, "'Among the Most Techy Articles of Civil Police': Federal Taxation and the Adoption of the Whiskey Excise," *WMQ* 25:58, 63 (1968).

3. Barber, "'Among the Most Techy Articles of Civil Police,'" 72; Hamilton, "Report on the Difficulties in the Execution of the Act Laying Duties on Distilled Spirits," 5 March 1792, PAH.

4. Mary K. Bonsteel Tachau, "George Washington and the Reputation of Edmund Randolph," *J. of American Hist.* 73:15, 19 (1986); Berkin, *A Sovereign People*, 3, 21; "Petition Against Excise," Henry Adams, ed., *The Writings of Albert Gallatin*, Philadelphia: J. B. Lippincott & Co. (1879), 1:3.

5. To the United States Senate and House of Representative, 25 October 1791, GWP.

6. Hamilton, "Report on the Difficulties in the Execution of the Act Laying Duties on Distilled Spirits," 5 March 1792, PAH; "George Clymer to the Secretary of the Treasury," 10 October 1794, in Gibbs, *Wolcott Memoirs* 1:148; Berkin, *A Sovereign People*, 33.

7. From Hamilton, 20 January 1794, GWP (enclosing Report of the Commissioner of Revenue); to United States Senate and House of Representatives, 21 January 1794, GWP.

8. From the Democratic Society of Washington County, Pennsylvania, 24 March 1794, GWP; from Kentucky Citizens, 24 May 1794, GWP; Berkin, *A Sovereign People*, 44; Flexner 4:157–58; from Knox, 12 May 1794, GWP; Cabinet Opinion, 13 May 1794, GWP; to Randolph, 11 April 1794, GWP; to Henry Lee, 26 August 1794, GWP. Washington made the same point in a letter to a relative in autumn 1794 (to Burgess Ball, 25 September 1794, GWP):

> The Democratic Society of [Philadelphia] (from which the others have emanated) were instituted by Mr. Genêt for the express purpose of dissension, and to draw a line between the people & the government, after he found the officers of the latter would not yield to the hostile measures in which he wanted to embroil this country.

Two weeks later, Washington complained again about the societies and "their diabolical leader G___t, whose object was to sow sedition; to poison the minds of the people of this country; and to make them discontented with the government of it." To Daniel Morgan, 8 October 1794, GWP.

9. Leland D. Baldwin, *Whiskey Rebels: The Story of a Frontier Uprising*, Pittsburgh: University of Pittsburgh Press (1939), 107–8, 284–86.

10. Hamilton compiled the full list of depredations by the anti-tax insurgents, and that list later was reprinted in newspapers. From Hamilton, 5 August 1794, GWP; Draft of a Proclamation Concerning Opposition to the Excise Law, 7 September 1792, GWP, note 1; *Dunlap and Claypoole's American Daily Advertiser* (Philadelphia), August 21, 1794; *Gazette of the United States and Daily Evening Advertiser* (Philadelphia), August 21, 1794.

11. From Abraham Kirkpatrick, 28 July 1794, GWP; from Hamilton, 2 August 1794, GWP; Jeffrey A. Davis, "Guarding the Republican Interest: The Western Pennsylvania Democratic Societies and the Excise Tax," *Pennsylvania Hist.* 67:32, 48 (2000).

12. *General Advertiser* (Philadelphia), August 8, 1794; from Hamilton, 12 August 1794, GWP (note 2, discussing enclosed letter from Isaac Craig to Knox).

13. To Charles Mynn Thruston, 10 August 1794, GWP; from Hamilton, 2 August 1794, GWP; from Randolph, 5 August 1794, GWP; from Mifflin, 5 August 1794, GWP. Both War Secretary Knox and Attorney General Bradford agreed with Hamilton's recommendation. From Knox, 4 April 1794, GWP; from Bradford, 5 April 1794, GWP.

14. Proclamation, 7 August 1794, GWP; from Randolph, 5 August 1794, GWP; Davis, "Guarding the Republican Interest," 49; Flexner 4:167.

15. From Randolph, 17 July 1794, GWP; from Bradford, 14 July 1794, GWP.

16. From Bradford, 17 August 1794, GWP; from the Commissioners Sent to Western Pennsylvania, 24 September 1794, GWP; Proclamation, 25 September 1794, GWP.

17. From Henry Lee, 3 September 1794, GWP; from Daniel Morgan, 24 September 1794, GWP; from Tobias Lear, 24 September 1794, GWP; from Randolph, 30 September 1794, GWP; *Gazette of the United States* (Philadelphia), October 1, 1794; from Randolph, 2–3 October 1794, GWP; Diary, 30 September and 1 October 1794, GWP.

18. To Carlisle, Pennsylvania, Citizens, 6 October 1794, GWP.

19. To Randolph, 8 October 1794, GWP; from Randolph, 11 October 1794, GWP; to Randolph, 16 October 1794, GWP.

20. To John Jay, 1–4 November 1794, GWP.

21. Jefferson to James Monroe, 26 May 1795, PTJ; to Jay, 18 December 1794.

22. Hamilton to Henry Lee, 20 October 1794, PAH; William Findley, *History of the Insurrection in the Four Western Counties of Pennsylvania*, Philadelphia: Samuel Harrison Smith (1796), 187; from Timothy Pickering, 2 November 1795, GWP.

23. To Henry Lee, 20 October 1794, GWP.

24. To the United States Senate and House of Representatives, 19 November 1794, GWP.

25. Proclamation, 2 January 1795, GWP.

26. For war secretary, Washington would have preferred Charles Cotesworth Pinckney, who declined the position. From C. C. Pinckney, 24 February 1794, GWP.

49. THE FIGHT FOR PEACE

1. Bradford Perkins, *The First Rapprochement: England and the United States, 1795–1805*, Philadelphia: University of Pennsylvania Press (1955), 23.

2. Flexner 4:131; from Randolph, 2 March and 14 March 1794, GWP; from Thomas Mendenhall, 14 March 1794; Elkins and McKitrick, *The Age of Federalism*, 389, 391; Bemis, "Washington's Farewell Address," in Kaufman, *Washington's Farewell Address*, 106, note 6; Walter Stahr, *John Jay*, New York: Continuum (2005), 313; to George Clinton, 31 March 1794, GWP; from Knox, 4 April 1794, GWP; to Knox, 4 April 1794, GWP; Madison to Jefferson, 12 March 1794, PJM; to Richard Henry Lee, 15 April 1794, GWP.

3. Flexner 4:153; Madison to Jefferson, 25 May 1794, PJM; from Knox, 10 April 1794, GWP.

4. *Gazette of the United States,* March 28, 1794; Herman LeRoy to Rufus King, March 30, 1794, in King, *Correspondence* 1:557; Oliver Wolcott Jr. to Oliver Wolcott Sr., 16 April 1794, in Gibbs, *Wolcott Memoirs* 1:135; to Tobias Lear, 6 May 1794, GWP.

5. From Randolph, 6 April 1794, GWP; from Hamilton, 14 April 1794, GWP; John Jay to Sarah Jay, 15 April 1794, in Henry P. Johnston, ed., *The Correspondence and Public Papers of John Jay,* New York: G. P. Putnam's Sons (1893) 4:3; to Jay, 15 April 1794, GWP; Stahr, *John Jay,* 315, 322–23; Jay to Henry Lee, 11 July 1795, in Johnston, *Jay Papers* 4:178; Jay to Randolph, 20 August 1795, in Johnston, *Jay Papers* 4:186; Perkins, *The First Rapprochement,* 19, 21.

6. To Randolph, 15 April 1794, GWP; "Message Nominating John Jay as Envoy to Great Britain," 16 April 1794, in *American State Papers: Foreign Relations,* Washington: Gales and Seaton (1833) 1:447.

7. "Notice of John Jay's Power as Envoy Extraordinary to Great Britain," 6 May 1794, GWP; Flexner 4:144. The West Indies treaty provision also proved problematic. Several British colonial governors were already allowing American ships to trade in their ports because they desperately needed American food supplies; placing the question before the negotiators risked losing that advantage. Elkins and McKitrick, *The Age of Federalism,* 400.

8. To Gouverneur Morris, 25 June 1794, GWP; from Knox, 10 April 1794, GWP. When Washington learned of the incendiary British statement to the Indians, he could only report the incident to Jay in a letter that was likely to arrive after the negotiations were over. To Jay, 30 August 1794, GWP; from George Clinton, 9 September 1794, GWP. The letter to Jay reported statements by another British official in Canada that echoed the earlier, warlike remarks. Washington added that he would wait to hear what the British leaders in London said before reacting to statements by colonial officials.

9. Stahr, *John Jay,* 333; Rufus King to Oliver Wolcott Jr., 19 March 1795, in Gibbs, *Wolcott Memoirs* 1:191.

10. To John Adams, 3 March 1795, GWP; Madison to Monroe, 11 March 1795, PJM.

11. John J. Reardon, *Edmund Randolph: A Biography,* New York: Macmillan Publishing (1974), 289; from Randolph, 20 April 1795.

12. Elkins and McKitrick, *The Age of Federalism,* 41–42; Bemis, *Jay's Treaty,* 259–61; Flexner 4:204–7.

13. Oliver Wolcott Jr. to John Marshall, 9 June 1806, in Gibbs, *Wolcott Memoirs* 1:242; Edmund Randolph, *A Vindication of Edmund Randolph Written by Himself, and Published in 1795,* Richmond: Charles H. Wynne (1855), 18–19.

14. From Randolph, 24 June 1795, GWP; Perkins, *The First Rapprochement,* 35; to Randolph, 21 October 1795, GWP; Reardon, *Edmund Randolph,* 296; Randolph, *Vindication,* 19; *Philadelphia Aurora,* June 29, 1795.

15. Ron Chernow, *Alexander Hamilton,* New York: Penguin Press (2004), 489–90; Oliver Wolcott Jr. to Mrs. Wolcott, 8 July 1795, in Gibbs, *Wolcott Memoirs* 1:209; Fisher Ames to Oliver Wolcott Jr., 10 September 1795, in Gibbs, *Wolcott Memoirs* 1:228; William Plumer, "Autobiography," Papers of William Plumer, Box 12, Reel 4, 60, LOC (Jay burned in effigy in Rye, New Hampshire); Stahr, *John Jay,* 336–337; *Aurora* (Philadelphia), August 27, 1795; *Connecticut Courant,* August 3, 1795; Perkins, *First Rapprochement,* 34.

16. "Caius," in *Aurora* (Philadelphia), July 21, 1795; "Cassius," in *Maryland Journal,* July 20, 1795; from Portsmouth, New Hampshire, Citizens, 17 July 1795, GWP; from New York Citizens, 20 July 1795, GWP; from Charleston, South Carolina, Citizens, 22 July 1795, GWP; from Baltimore Citizens, 27 July 1795, GWP; from Richmond, Virginia, Citizens, 30 July 1795, GWP; from Petersburg, Virginia, Citizens, 1 August 1795, GWP; from Savannah, Georgia, Citizens, 1 August 1795, GWP; from Norfolk County, Virginia, Citizens, 5 August 1795, GWP; from Moore Furman, Trenton, New Jersey, 6 August 1795, GWP; from Suffolk

County, New York, Citizens, 6 August 1795, GWP; from Wilmington, Delaware, Citizens, 8 August 1795, GWP; from Bordentown, New Jersey, Citizens, 10 August 1795, GWP; from Caroline County, Virginia, Citizens, 11 August 1795, GWP; from Sussex County, Virginia, Citizens, 12 August 1795, GWP; from Newport, Rhode Island, Citizens, 14–20 August 1795, GWP; from Cheraws District, South Carolina, Citizens, 15 August 1795, GWP; from Morris County, New Jersey, Citizens, 15 August 1795, GWP; from Fredericksburg, Virginia, Citizens, 18 August 1795, GWP; from Culpeper County, Virginia, Citizens, 20 August 1795; from Burgess Ball, 28 July 1795, GWP.

17. To Hamilton, 3 July 1795, GWP; from Randolph, 12 July 1795, GWP; Hamilton, "Remarks on the Treaty of Amity Commerce and Navigation lately made between the United States and Great Britain," 9–11 June 1795, PAH; Diary, 15 July 1795, GWP.

18. From the New York Chamber of Commerce, 21 July 1795, GWP; from York, Pennsylvania, Citizens, 17 August 1795, GWP; Chernow, *Alexander Hamilton,* 493–94; Elkins and McKitrick, *The Age of Federalism,* 435–36.

19. To Boston Selectmen, 28 July 1795, GWP.

20. To Randolph, 3 August 1795, GWP; from James Ross, 3 August 1795, GWP; from John Adams, 10 August 1795, GWP; to Randolph, 31 July 1795, GWP.

21. To Hamilton, 29 July 1795, GWP; Todd Estes, "The Art of Presidential Leadership: George Washington and the Jay Treaty," *VMHB* 109:127, 137, note 11; to Randolph, 29 July 1795, GWP.

22. Fauchet portrayed Randolph as warning that the president might be swayed from loyalty to France by "the dark maneuvers of some men." Randolph, *Vindication,* 10–11. In other dispatches that came to light later, Fauchet quotes Randolph as attributing the dispatch of settlement commissioners to Western Pennsylvania during the rebellion as "due to the influence of Mr. Randolph over the mind of the president," and also warning that others were attempting to "mislead the president in paths which would conduct him to unpopularity." Randolph, *Vindication,* 33.

23. "Notes of a Conversation with George Washington," 6 August 1793, PTJ; from Randolph, 10 November 1793, GWP; from Randolph, 7 July 1795, GWP; from Pickering, 31 July 1795, GWP.

24. To David Stuart, 5 August 1795, GWP; Diary, 11 August 1795, GWP; Gibbs, *Wolcott Memoirs* 1:243–44.

25. Before leaving for Mount Vernon nearly a month earlier, Washington had asked the secretary of state to draft the papers required to implement the alternative approaches, but had never received them from Randolph. The president, according to Wolcott, was unhappy with that failure, but that annoyance seems too small a matter to have driven his decision on the Jay Treaty. Oliver Wolcott Jr. to John Marshall, 9 June 1806, in Gibbs, *Wolcott Memoirs* 1:243–44; Oliver Wolcott Jr. to Jedediah Morse, 16 July 1795, in Gibbs, *Wolcott Memoirs* 1:212 (citing British naval superiority).

26. From Oliver Wolcott Jr., 26 September 1795, GWP; *Independent Chronicle: and the Universal Advertiser* (Boston), 14 September 1795, GWP. Local anti-treaty resolutions included: from Brunswick District, Virginia, Citizens, 24 August 1795, GWP; from Burke County, Georgia, Citizens, 25–27 August 1795, GWP; from Scott County, Kentucky, Citizens, 25 August 1795, GWP; from Amelia County, Virginia, Citizens, 28 August 1795, GWP; Address from Columbia County, Georgia, Citizens, 20 August 1795, GWP; from Kentucky Citizens, 7 September 1795, GWP; from Clarke County, Kentucky, Citizens, 8 September 1795, GWP. "Scipio," *Philadelphia Aurora and General Advertiser,* November 20, 1795; "Portius," *Philadelphia Aurora and General Advertiser,* September 30, 1795; "An Observer," *Philadelphia Aurora and General Advertiser,* October 1, 1795, September 11, 1795; from "A Republican," in *Boston Independent Chronicle,* September 3, 1795, GWP;

"One of the People," in *The Argus, or Greenleaf's New Daily Advertiser* (New York), September 5, 1795, GWP. Some scholars have concluded that French representatives supported the treaty opponents. Michael F. Conlin, "The American Mission of Citizen Pierre-Auguste Adet: Revolutionary Chemistry and Diplomacy in the Early Republic," *PMHB* 124:489, 492, 495–96 (2000); Alexander DeConde, "Washington's Farewell, the French Alliance, and the Election of 1796" in Kaufman, *Washington's Farewell Address,* 117–18; Bemis, "Washington's Farewell Address," in Kaufman, *Farewell,* 95.

27. Joseph Charles, "Hamilton and Washington: The Origins of the American Party System," *WMQ* 12:217, 261 (1955); William Plumer, "Autobiography," in William Plumer Papers, Box 12, Reel 4, 58, LOC; Fisher Ames to Oliver Wolcott Jr., 2 September 1795, in Gibbs, *Wolcott Memoirs* 1:229–30; George Cabot to Oliver Wolcott Jr., 13 August 1795, in Gibbs, *Wolcott Memoirs* 1:225; Oliver Ellsworth to Oliver Wolcott Jr., 20 August 1795, in Gibbs, *Wolcott Memoirs* 1:226; from James Ross, 22 August 1795, GWP; from Knox, 2 September 1795, GWP. Pro-treaty statements came from Philadelphia Subscribers, Merchants, and Traders, 20 August 1795, GWP; from Portsmouth, New Hampshire, Citizens, 9 September 1795, GWP; from Greenbrier County, Virginia, Citizens, 20 September 1795, GWP; from Westmoreland County, Virginia, Citizens, 29 September 1795, GWP; from Frederick County Citizens, 2 December 1795, GWP.

28. Randolph, *Vindication,* 37; Reardon, *Edmund Randolph,* 308; Oliver Wolcott Jr. to John Marshall, 9 June 1806, in Gibbs, *Wolcott Memoirs* 1:243–44.

29. Gibbs, *Wolcott Memoirs* 1:244–46; Randolph, *Vindication,* 2–3; from Randolph, 19 August 1795.

30. Randolph, *Vindication,* 3–18.

31. Randolph, *Vindication,* 9–10, 12.

32. Several scholars have labored to exonerate Randolph of bribery charges, but have been less successful defending his reputation as an effective official. E.g., Irving Brant, "Edmund Randolph, Not Guilty!," *WMQ* 7:179, 187 (1950).

33. John Adams to Abigail Adams, 22 December 1795, AP; Jefferson to Monroe, 2 March 1796, PTJ; Madison to Jefferson, 26 January 1796, PJM; to Hamilton, 22 December 1795, GWP.

34. To Thomas Johnson, 24 August 1795, GWP; to Charles C. Pinckney, 24 August 1795, GWP; from Thomas Johnson, 29 August 1795, GWP; from Charles C. Pinckney, 16 September 1795, GWP; to Edward Carrington, 9 October 1796, GWP; to Patrick Henry, 9 October 1795, GWP; from Patrick Henry, 16 October 1795, GWP; from Hamilton, 5 November 1795, GWP.

35. To John Eager Howard, 19 November 1795, and 30 November 1795, GWP; to James McHenry, 20 January 1795, GWP; to John Marshall, 26 August 1795, GWP; from John Marshall, 31 August 1795, GWP; from Edward Carrington, 30 October 1795, GWP; from Charles Lee, 30 November 1795, GWP; Chervinsky, *The Cabinet,* 271, 282–83.

36. George Thacher to Wife, 8 December 1795, quoted in John Alexander Carroll and Mary Wells Ashworth, *George Washington: First in Peace,* New York: Charles Scribner's Sons (1957) 7:220n; Donald R. Adams, Jr., "Wage Rates in the Early National Period: Philadelphia," *J. Econ. Hist.* 28:404 (1968), 405–6, 418, 420; Elkins and McKitrick, *The Age of Federalism,* 441.

37. To United States Senate and House of Representative, 8 December 1795, GWP; to Pickering, 16 September 1795, GWP; to Hamilton, 10 November 1795, GWP.

38. From Edward Carrington, 6 December 1795, GWP; from John Jay, 14 December 1796, GWP; Benjamin Rush to Samuel Bayard, 1 March 1796, in Butterfield, *Letters of Benjamin Rush* 2:768–69 note 2; to Gouverneur Morris, 4 March 1796, GWP.

39. To Knox, 20 September 1795, GWP; Elkins and McKitrick, *The Age of Federalism*, 440; "Washington's Notes on the Treaty with Spain," 22–26 February 1796, GWP; to United States Senate, 26 February 1796, GWP; to United States Senate and House of Representatives, 1 March 1796, GWP; *Senate Exec. Journal*, 4th Cong., 1st Sess., 203 (3 March 1796).

40. Estes, "The Jay Treaty Debate," *VMHB* 109:154; to United States Senate and House of Representatives, 1 March 1795, GWP; *Gazette of the United States*, March 1, 1796; Estes, "The Jay Treaty Debate," *VMHB* 109:152.

41. *Annals of Congress*, 4th Cong., 1st Sess., 759–60; from Hamilton, 7 March 1796, GWP; from Charles Lee, 26 March 1796, GWP; from James McHenry, 26 March 1796, GWP; to House of Representatives, 30 March 1796, GWP; Todd Estes, "The Art of Presidential Leadership: George Washington and the Jay Treaty," *VMHB* 109:127, 137; Amanda C. Demmer, "Trick or Constitutional Treaty? The Jay Treaty and the Quarrel over the Diplomatic Separation of Powers," *Journal of the Early Republic* 35:579, 579–80, 587–88 (2015). Washington specifically noted that the House could properly request the papers for an impeachment inquiry, but that the demand before him did not relate to an impeachment.

42. Estes, "The Jay Treaty Debate," *VMHB* 109:163–68 (listing pro-treaty meetings in New York City; Boston, Newburyport, Beverly, Hingham, and Marblehead in Massachusetts; Hartford, Connecticut; Allegheny County, Pennsylvania; the Federal City and Frederick, Prince George's County, Maryland, Georgetown, Maryland; Albany and Lansingburgh, New York); Jerald A. Combs, *The Jay Treaty: Political Battleground of the Founding Fathers*, Berkeley: University of California Press (1970), 178–81; Joseph Charles, "The Jay Treaty: The Origins of the American Party System," *WMQ* 12:581, 600 (1955); William Plumer, "Autobiography," in Plumer Papers, Box 23, Reel 4, LOC; Madison to James Madison, Sr., 25 April 1796, PJM; Chauncey Goodrich to Oliver Wolcott Sr., 23 April 1796, in Gibbs, *Wolcott Memoirs* 1:331; *Annals of Congress* 5:1239–63 (28 April 1796). John Adams to Abigail Adams, 30 April 1796, AP; John Quincy Adams to Charles Adams, 9 June 1796, in Worthington Ford, *Writings of John Quincy Adams*, New York: The Macmillan Co. (1913) 1:493.

43. To Thomas Pinckney, 22 May 1796, GWP; Combs, *The Jay Treaty*, 186–87; Jefferson to Monroe, 12 June 1796, PTJ. In another letter, Jefferson blamed the Republican failure on "the colossus of the president's merits with the people." Jefferson to Monroe, 10 July 1796, PTJ; Benjamin Rush to John Adams, 13 June 1811, in Butterfield, *Letters of Benjamin Rush* 2:1084.

44. To McHenry, 8 May 1796, GWP: to McHenry, 27 June 1796, GWP; from James Ross, 18 August 1796, GWP.

45. To United States Senate, 27 May 1794, GWP; from Hamilton, 5 May 1796, GWP; from Charles Lee, 4 July 1796, GWP. Monroe's intemperate support for the French government would lead Washington to recall him as well.

46. To Hamilton, 8 May 1796, GWP.

50. FAREWELL, AGAIN

1. Louise V. North, ed., *The Travel Journal of Henrietta Marchant Liston*, Lanham, MD: Lexington Books (2014), 17. Liston's observations accord with those of Bishop William White, who described himself as often in Washington's company (Bishop William White to the Rev. B.C.C. Parker, 28 November 1832, Bird Wilson, *Memoir of the Life of the Right Reverend William White, D.D.*, Philadelphia: James Kay, Jr. & Brother [1839], 189–90):

I knew no man who seemed so carefully to guard against the discoursing of himself or of his acts, or of anything pertaining to him . . . His ordinary behavior, although unexceptionably courteous, was not such as to encourage obtrusion on what might be in his mind.

2. *Philadelphia Aurora*, October 12 and November 26, 1796 ("Pittachus").

3. *The Political and Miscellaneous Works of Thomas Paine*, London: R. Carlile (1819) 2:36; *Philadelphia Aurora*, November 23, 1796 ("The Political Creed of 1795") and December 23, 1796 ("Correspondent"); Flexner 4:49; see James D. Tagg, "Benjamin Franklin Bache's Attack on George Washington," *PMHB* 100:191, 194 (1976).

4. Jefferson to Madison, 9 June 1793, PTJ; to Hamilton, 26 June 1796, GWP; to Jefferson, 6 July 1796, GWP.

5. To Madison, 20 May 1792, GWP; from Hamilton, 10 May 1796, GWP; John Avlon, *Washington's Farewell: The Founding Father's Warning to Future Generations*, New York: Simon & Schuster (2017), 45–46, 76.

6. To Hamilton, 15 May 1796, GWP.

7. From Hamilton, 5 July, 30 July, and 10 August 1796; to Hamilton, 25 August 1796, GWP; Jay to Judge Peters, 29 March 1811, in Victor Hugo Paltsits, *Washington's Farewell Address*, New York: New York Public Library (1935), 271; Avlon, *Washington's Farewell*, 75–77.

8. Avlon, *Washington's Farewell*, 84–85; Nelly Custis Lewis to Lewis Washington, 31 January 1852, in Fred W. Smith Library, Mount Vernon Ladies' Association; *Claypoole's Daily Advertiser* and the *Gazette of the United States*, September 19, 1796.

9. "General Order 16, February 18, 1862," in James D. Richardson, ed., *A Compilation of the Messages and Papers of the Presidents*, New York: Bureau of National Literature (1897) 7:3306; Avlon, *Washington's Farewell*, 242–43.

10. To Jefferson, 6 July 1796, GWP; Jefferson to William Branch Giles, 31 December 1795, PTJ.

11. Edmund S. Morgan, *The Genius of George Washington*, Washington, DC: The Society of the Cincinnati (1980), 6.

12. Avlon, *Washington's Farewell*, 104.

13. Charles, "Hamilton and Washington," *WMQ* 12:217, 266–67 (1955); Isaac Weld, *Travels Through the States of North America . . . During the Years 1795, 1796, and 1797*, London: John Stockdale (1799) 1:105.

14. To the Senate and the House of Representatives, 7 December 1796, GWP; to Hamilton, 1 September and 10 November 1796, GWP; from Hamilton, 4 September 1796, GWP. An avalanche of resolutions thanking and praising Washington arrived from communities across the nation. E.g., from John Hoskins Stone (Maryland), 16 December 1796, GWP; from Robert Branwell, 20 December 1796, GWP (South Carolina Assembly); from David Ramsey, 21 December 1796, GWP (South Carolina Senate); to Daniel Rogers, 2 February 1797 (Delaware resolution); from Charles Hall, 20 February 1797, GWP (from Citizens and Grand Jury of Northumberland County); to James Irvine, 22 February 1797, GWP (Militia of the City and County of Philadelphia); from John Pierce, 22 February 1797, GWP (from public meeting at James City County, Virginia); to Theodore Sedgwick, 24 February 1797, GWP (Massachusetts legislature); from Enos Hitchcock, 25 February 1797, GWP (Providence, Rhode Island, public meeting); from Francis Gurney, 27 February 1797, GWP (Select Council of Philadelphia); from Arthur Fenner, 10 March 1797, GWP (transmitting Address from Rhode Island General Assembly).

15. North, *Travel Journals of Henrietta Marchant Liston*, 17; to James Anderson, 5 November 1796 and 8 January 1797, GWP; Ed Crews, "Rattle-Skull, Stonewall, Bogus, Blackstrap,

Bombo, Mimbo, Whistle Belly, Syllabub, Sling, Toddy, and Flip: Drinking in Colonial America," *Colonial Williamsburg Journal* (Holiday, 2007).

16. Diary, 9 January, 6, 27, and 28 February 1797, GWP (theater and concerts); Diary, 7 and 13 January 1797, GWP (riding); Diary, 12 January, 26 February 1797, GWP (entertaining dignitaries); Diary, 11 February 1797, GWP note; Flexner 4:332; *Claypoole's Advertiser*, February 23, 1797; James Iredell to Mrs. Iredell, 24 February 1797, in Griffith J. McRee, *Life and Correspondence of James Iredell, One of the Associate Justices of the Supreme Court of the United States*, New York: D. Appleton and Co. (1857) 2:493.

17. Flexner 4:308–9.

18. John Adams to Abigail Adams, 5 and 9 March 1797, AP; Baker, *Character Portraits of Washington*, 343–45; *New York Herald*, March 11, 1797; Thomas Scharf and Thompson Westcott, *History of Philadelphia, 1609–1884*, Philadelphia: L. H. Everts & Co. (1884) 1:488.

19. Washington Irving, *The Life of George Washington*, New York: G. P. Putnam's Sons (1876) 2:749. In describing this scene, Irving noted his source as William A. Duer, former president of Columbia College and son of Hamilton's disgraced deputy at the treasury, who had been seventeen years old in 1797 when he attended the Adams inauguration. The younger Duer lived until 1858, several years after Irving completed his research on the Washington biography, which appeared in several volumes published between 1855 and 1859.

20. Diary, 12 March 1797 (and note), GWP; *Gazette of the United States*, March 16, 1797; Diary, 15 March 1797, GWP; from George Lewis, 9 April 1797, GWP.

21. To Elizabeth Willing Powel, 26 March 1797, GWP; to James Anderson (Scotland), 7 April 1797, GWP.

51. HOME FOR GOOD

1. To Oliver Wolcott Jr., 15 May 1797, GWP; to James Anderson (Scotland), 4 November 1797, GWP; to Charles Cotesworth Pinckney, 24 June 1797, GWP; to John Quincy Adams, 25 June 1797, GWP; "Lady Henrietta Liston's Journal," *PMHB* 95:516–17.

2. To Oliver Wolcott Jr., 15 May 1797, GWP; to the Earl of Buchan, 4 July 1797, GWP; to Miles Smith, 27 March 1797, GWP; to Lafayette, 8 October 1797, GWP; Martha Washington to Elizabeth Willing Powel, 17 December 1797, GWP (quoting Washington); to William Washington, 28 December 1798, GWP; to Richard Washington, 20 October 1761, GWP; to Burgess Ball, 22 September 1799, GWP.

3. Metchie J. E. Budka, ed. and tr., Julian Ursyn Niemcewicz, *Under Their Vine and Fig Tree: Travels Through America in 1797–1799, 1805, with Some Further Account of Life in New Jersey*, Elizabeth: Grassman Publishing Co. (1965), 87; John Bernard, *Retrospections of America, 1797–1811*, New York: Harper and Brothers (1887), 89. Niemcewicz's first impression of Washington was equally ecstatic: "I had not eyes enough to look on him. His is a majestic figure in which dignity and gentleness are united. . . . He is nearly six feet tall, square set, and very strongly built; aquiline nose, blue eyes, the mouth and especially the lower jaw sunken, a good head of hair," *Under Their Vine*, 84.

4. To James McHenry, 29 May 1797, GWP; to Tobias Lear, 31 July 1797, GWP.

5. Michael A. Palmer, *Stoddert's War: Naval Operations During the Quasi-War with France, 1798–1801*, Annapolis: Naval Institute Press (1987), 5–6; Gordon Wood, *Empire of Liberty: A History of the Early Republic, 1789–1815*, New York: Oxford University Press (2009), 239; from Oliver Wolcott Jr., 18 May and 15 June 1797, GWP; from William Vans Murray, 1 November 1797, GWP; to James McHenry, 4 March 1798, GWP. By the end of the

hostility with France, that nation had seized more than 2,000 American vessels. Palmer, *Stoddert's War*, 5.

6. From Alexander White, 8 and 18 April 1798, GWP; from Timothy Pickering, 11 April 1798, GWP.

7. From John Adams, 22 June 1798, GWP.

8. To James McHenry, 4 July 1798, GWP; to John Adams, 4 July 1798, GWP.

9. Alexander DeConde, *The Quasi-War: The Politics and Diplomacy of the Undeclared War with France, 1797–1801*, New York: Charles Scribner's Sons (1966), 96–97; Flexner 4:397; from James McHenry, 3 July 1798, GWP; from John Adams, 7 July 1798, GWP.

10. To Timothy Pickering, 11 July 1798, GWP; to Hamilton, 14 July 1798, GWP; from Timothy Pickering, 1 September 1798, GWP. The tussle over seniority cost Washington one more old friend. Henry Knox, offended by Washington's support for Hamilton over him, declined any role in the new army. From Henry Knox, 4 November 1798, GWP.

11. From John Adams, 9 October 1798, GWP; to Hamilton, 25 February 1799, GWP; from Hamilton, 27 March 1799, GWP; from Charles Cotesworth Pinckney, 20 April 1799, GWP; from McHenry, 19 September 1798, GWP; to McHenry, 10 August 1798, 14 September 1798, GWP; Diary, 5 and 10 November 1798, GWP; *Claypoole's American Daily Advertiser* (Philadelphia), November 10 and 12, 1798. Washington's diary records his social commitments in Philadelphia (14–16, 20, 22–24, and 28–30 November 1798, GWP), which included dining with Robert Morris inside the prison where he was confined for nonpayment of his debts, Diary, 27 November 1798, GWP.

12. To McHenry, 17 November 1798, GWP; from Pickering, 21 February 1799; to John Adams, 3 March 1799, GWP.

13. To McHenry, 20 September 1798, GWP; from McHenry, 5 October 1798, GWP; to Rufus King, 25 June 1797, GWP; to Lafayette, 25 December 1798, GWP; "Comments on Monroe's *A View of the Conduct of the Executive of the United States*," March 1798, GWP. For the 1799 elections, Washington recruited Patrick Henry to run for the Virginia legislature as a Federalist, and future Chief Justice John Marshall to stand for Congress. Both were successful, though Henry died before he could take office. To David Stuart, 4 January 1799, GWP; to Patrick Henry, 15 January 1799, GWP; from Patrick Henry, 12 February 1799, GWP; Diary, 5 and 6 September 1798, GWP; from Edward Carrington, 25 April 1799, GWP; from John Marshall, 1 May 1799, GWP; to John Marshall, 5 May 1799, GWP; to Bushrod Washington, 5 May 1799, GWP.

14. To Hamilton, 14 July 1798, GWP; to John Adams, 25 September 1798, GWP; from Henry Knox, 29 July 1798, GWP.

15. To Charles Carroll of Carrollton, 21 July 1799, GWP; Diary, 7 August 1797 (and note), 15 January 1798, 7 February 1798 (and note), GWP; from Tobias Lear, 8–10 March 1798, GWP; Diary, 8 February and 21 September 1798, GWP; to Commissioners of the District of Columbia, 27 October 1798, GWP; to William Herbert, 25 June 1799, GWP.

16. To James Anderson, 18 June 1797, 15 September 1798, GWP.

17. Flexner 4:373; to Samuel Washington, 12 July 1797, GWP; to James Ross, 2 July 1797, GWP; from Israel Shreve, 21 December 1798, GWP; from James Welch, 24, 29 November 1797, GWP; to James Keith, 1 and 12 December 1797, GWP; "Schedule of Property," 9 July 1799, GWP; Diary, 24 November and 9 December 1797, and 10–11 October 1798; Mary V. Thompson, *"The Only Unavoidable Subject of Regret": George Washington, Slavery, and the Enslaved Community at Mount Vernon*, Charlottesville: University of Virginia Press (2019), 58. A failed land sale to James Welch involved 23,000 acres on the Kanawha River. It was a measure of Washington's eagerness to sell that he tried to conclude the transaction even though Welch was reputed to be unreliable in business matters, which soon proved to be true.

52. WRESTLING WITH SIN

1. Dalzell and Dalzell, *George Washington's Mount Vernon*, 130; Flexner 1:286; Thompson, *"The Only Unavoidable Subject of Regret,"* xiii.

2. Thompson, *"The Only Unavoidable Subject of Regret,"* 269–90; Philip D. Morgan and Michael L. Nicholls, "Slave Flight: Mount Vernon, Virginia, and the Wider Atlantic World" in Harvey and O'Brien, *George Washington's South*, 197; "Circular to William Stuart, Hiland Crow, and Henry McCoy," 14 July 1793, GWP; to Anthony Whiting, 20 January 1793, 5 May 1793, GWP; to William Pearce, 30 March 1794, GWP; to James Anderson, 20 February 1797, GWP; Tobias Lear to William Prescott Jr., 4 March 1788, in "A Lear Letter," *Mount Vernon Ladies' Association Annual Report* (1958), 24; Morgan, "Virginia and the French and Indian War," *VMHB* 81:23, 45–46 (1973); John Ferling, "Soldiers for Virginia: Who Served in the French and Indian War?" *VMHB* 94:307, 317 (1986); McGaughy, *Richard Henry Lee of Virginia*, 62; Mays, *Edmund Pendleton* 1:10–11; Winthrop D. Jordan, *White over Black: American Attitudes Toward the Negro, 1550–1812*, Chapel Hill: University of North Carolina Press (1968), 376.

3. Alfred W. Blumrosen and Ruth G. Blumrosen, *Slave Nation: How Slavery United the Colonies & Sparked the American Revolution*, Naperville, IL: Sourcebooks (2005), 1–12; Bailyn, *Ideological Origins*, 240, 244; Jordan, *White over Black*, 342; Paul Finkelman, *Slavery and the Founders: Race and Liberty in the Age of Jefferson*, Armonk, NY: M. E. Sharpe (2014), 137–38; Kukla, *Patrick Henry*, 238, 359, 361; Patrick Henry to Robert Pleasants, 18 January 1773, in Henry, *Patrick Henry: Life, Correspondence, and Speeches* 1:152.

4. Chastellux, *Travels in North America* 2:439; Richard Henry Lee to Landon Carter, 15 August 1765, in Ballagh, *The Letters of Richard Henry Lee* 1:11–12; Hening, *Statutes at Large* 11:39–40; St. George Tucker, *A Dissertation on Slavery, with a Proposal for the Gradual Abolition of It in the State of Virginia*, Philadelphia: Matthew Carey (1796), 71; James Curtis Ballagh, *A History of Slavery in Virginia*, Baltimore: Johns Hopkins University Press (1902), 120.

5. General Orders, 12 November 1775, GWP; Pete Maslowski, "National Policy Toward the Use of Black Troops in the Revolution," *South Carolina Hist. Mag.* 73:1, 2–4 (1972); General Orders, 30 December 1775, GWP; to John Hancock, 31 December 1775, GWP; Lender and Stone, *Fatal Sunday*, 142; Trussell, *Birthplace of an Army*, 78; Philip D. Morgan, "George Washington and Slavery," in Schoelwer, *Lives Bound Together*, 68–69. A manpower accounting prepared several weeks after the Battle of Monmouth Court House recorded 755 Negro soldiers in the army. "Return of Negroes in the Army," 24 August 1778, in W. B. Hartgrove, "The Negro Soldier in the American Revolution," *J. of African American Hist.* 1:110, 127 (1916). After praising Phillis Wheatley's talents in correspondence, Washington may have hosted her for a visit to army headquarters. James G. Basker, ed., *Amazing Grace: An Anthology of Poems About Slavery, 1660–1810*, New Haven: Yale University Press (2002), 181–82; to Phillis Wheatley, 28 February 1776, GWP; James G. Basker, "A Poem Links Unlikely Allies in 1775: Phillis Wheatley and George Washington," *History Now* (2014).

6. From Brig. General James Mitchell Varnum, 2 January 1778, GWP; to Varnum, 2 January 1778, GWP; from the Rhode Island Council of War, 19 January 1778, GWP; from Nicholas Cooke, 23 February 1778, GWP; Evelyn M. Acomb, ed. and tr., *The Revolutionary Journal of Baron Ludwig von Closen, 1780–1783*, Chapel Hill: University of North Carolina Press (1958), 102; to Major General William Heath, 29 June 1780, GWP; Douglas R. Egerton, *Death or Liberty: African Americans and Revolutionary America*, New York: Oxford University Press (2007), 75, 77; John Laurens to Henry Laurens, 14 January, 2 February, and 9 March 1778, in Chesnutt and Taylor, *Laurens Papers* 12:305, 12:390–91, 12:532;

Henry Laurens to John Laurens, 6 February 1778, in Chesnutt and Taylor, *Laurens Papers* 12:412; to Henry Laurens, 20 March 1779, GWP; Wiencek, *An Imperfect God,* 222–26, 243. The Continental Congress approved John Laurens's proposal so long as Georgia and South Carolina also consented, *JCC* 18:385–89 (29 March 1779); those two Southern states never consented. From John Laurens, 19 May 1782, GWP.

7. From Lund Washington, 8 April 1778, GWP; to Lund Washington, 15 August 1778, 24 February 1779, GWP.

8. From Lafayette, 5 February 1783, 6 February 1786, GWP; to Lafayette, 5 April 1783, 10 May 1786, GWP.

9. To John Francis Mercer, 6 and 24 November 1786, GWP; to Alexander Spotswood, 23 November 1794, GWP; to Henry Lee Jr., 4 February 1787, GWP; to John Fowler, 2 February 1788, GWP; to John Dandridge, 18 November 1788, GWP; to Betty Washington Lewis, 18 November 1788, GWP. Washington avidly pursued reimbursement by the state for the value of a slave who was executed following criminal prosecution. To John Pendleton, 1 March 1788, GWP; to David Stuart, 11 December 1787, GWP, note 2.

10. To Robert Morris, 12 April 1786, GWP; to John Francis Mercer, 9 September 1786, GWP.

11. Diary, 26 May 1785, GWP; Thomas Coke, *Extracts of the Journals of the Late Rev. Thomas Coke, L. L. D.,* Dublin: R. Napper (1816), 73; Albert Matthews, "Notes on the Proposed Abolition of Slavery in Virginia in 1785," Colonial Society of Massachusetts, *Publications* 6:370 (1904); from Madison, 11 November 1785, GWP.

12. To David Stuart, 15 June 1790, GWP; Fisher Ames to [William Eustis], 17 March 1790, in *DHFFC* 19:891.

13. To Lear, 12 April 1791, GWP.

14. From Lear, 24 April 1791, GWP.

15. Niemcewicz, *Under Their Vine,* 104. Washington, with his usual methodical approach, had calculated the likely financial result from leasing a parcel of land contiguous to Mount Vernon along with the twenty-three enslaved people who would come with the lease. Totaling costs for clothing, food, doctors' visits, midwife, and so on, he concluded that expenses would run about 20 percent higher than revenue. "Estimate of the cost of Mrs. French's Land and Negroes on Dogue Creek, compared with the produce by which it will be seen what the tenant is to expect" [1790/1786?], GWP; to William Triplett, 25 September 1786, note 3, GWP.

16. Zagarri, *Humphreys* 78; Wiencek, *An Imperfect God,* 272–73.

17. To Arthur Young, 12 December 1793, GWP.

18. To Arthur Young, 9 November 1794, GWP; to Tobias Lear, 6 May 1794, note 13, GWP (quoting separate note enclosed with the letter).

19. Advertisement, 1 February 1796, GWP; Lease Terms, 1 February 1796, GWP; to William Strickland, to John Sinclair, to the Earl of Buchan, 20 February 1796, GWP; Flexner 4:260–61.

20. To William Pearce, 27 January and 7 February 1796, GWP; to David Stuart, 7 February 1796, GWP. Stuart was skeptical of Washington's plan, writing that emancipation had to be gradual. He suggested an approach like the one followed by Lafayette: "to select some one of the most intelligent and responsible negroes, and rent to him a farm with so many hands furnished with every necessary implement," and providing that "if they conducted themselves well they should be at perfect liberty at the expiration of two or three years either to remain on the farm, or seek employment elsewhere." The process could be repeated until all were freed, upon paying "a moderate sum to their masters for two or three years." Stuart also cautioned that it would be necessary to give freed slaves the right to testify against whites in cases of trespass or robbery, because blacks would be vulnerable to robbery and mistreatment if they could not do so.

21. To Tobias Lear, 13 March 1796, GWP; to William Pearce, 20 March 1796, GWP.
22. Ferdinando Fairfax, "Plan for Liberating the Negroes Within the United States," *American Museum*, 285–87 (1 December 1790); Tucker, *A Dissertation on Slavery*, 82, 86, 91–105; Kenneth R. Bowling, "George Washington's Vision for the United States," in Robert McDonald and Peter S. Onuf, eds., *Revolutionary Prophecies: The Founders on America's Future*, Charlottesville: University Press of Virginia (2020), 102.
23. Gary B. Nash, *Race and Revolution*, Lanham, MD: Rowman & Littlefield (1990), 18; William Buckner McGroarty, "Elizabeth Washington of Hayfield," *VMHB* 33:154, 159, 161 (1925); Thompson, *"The Only Unavoidable Subject of Regret,"* 298; Melvin Ely, *Israel on the Appomattox: A Southern Experiment in Black Freedom from the 1790s Through the Civil War*, New York: Alfred A. Knopf (2004), 44–50; William Macfarlane Jones, "Will of Richard Randolph, Jr., of 'Bizarre,'" *VMHB* 34:72–76 (1926) (Richard Randolph manumitting his slaves, denouncing the "lawless and monstrous tyranny" of slavery imposed by "iniquitous laws"); Robert Levy, *The First Emancipator: The Forgotten Story of Robert Carter, the Founding Father Who Freed His Slaves*, New York: Random House (2005); to Stephen Milburn, 15 May 1797, GWP.
24. Parkinson, *A Tour in America in 1798, 1799, and 1800* 2:420; to Robert Lewis, 17 August 1799, GWP; to John Dandridge, 28 May 1795, GWP; to Mildred Thornton Washington, 18 October 1798, GWP.
25. Dunbar, *Never Caught*; to Oliver Wolcott Jr., 1 September 1796, GWP; to Joseph Whipple, 28 November 1796, GWP; from Joseph Whipple, 22 December 1796, GWP; to Burwell Bassett Jr., 11 August 1799, GWP; to George Lewis, 13 November 1797, GWP; to Frederick Kitt, 10 January 1798, GWP; to Roger West, 19 September 1799, GWP.
26. To Alexander Spotswood, 23 November 1794, GWP; Bernard, *Retrospections of America*, 91; to Spotswood, 14 September 1798, GWP.
27. To Robert Lewis, 17 August 1798; 7 December 1799, GWP; to Benjamin Dulany, 15 July 1799, 12 September 1799, GWP.
28. To Lawrence Lewis, 4 August 1797, GWP.
29. Wiencek, *An Imperfect God*, 332, 338, 351–52; Martha Washington to Fanny Bassett Washington, 24 May 1795, in Fields, *Worthy Partners*, 287–88; Martha Washington to Elizabeth Willing Powel, 20 May 1797, in Fields, *Worthy Partners*, 302.
30. "Washington's Slave List," June 1799, GWP.

53. FAREWELL FOREVER

1. Tobias Lear, "The Diary Account," 14 December 1799, GWP; Mary V. Thompson, *In the Hands of a Good Providence: Religion in the Life of George Washington*, Charlottesville: University of Virginia Press (2008), 169–70; Peter R. Henriques, *The Death of George Washington: He Died as He Lived*, Charlottesville: University of Virginia Press (2002), 32–33. Physicians have argued about the medical treatment afforded to Washington in his last illness. Some have denounced it as tantamount to murder; others have defended it as the best efforts of practitioners in 1799. That the doctors removed about eighty ounces of his blood has been universally lamented, but such was the treatment of the time. Dr. Dick, the third doctor to arrive, later complained that Dr. Craik refused to allow him to perform a tracheotomy to relieve Washington's breathing. Elisha Dick, "Facts and Observations Relative to the Disease of Cynanche Trachealis, or Croup," *Philadelphia Medical & Physical Journal*, 1809 (May, Supplement 3), 242, 244–45, 252–53 (October 7, 1808). The current historico-medical consensus is that a tracheotomy likely would have killed the patient, particularly if performed in 1799 conditions by a physician like Dr.

Dick, who was inexperienced with the procedure. Recent commenters conclude that Washington began with a strep or staph infection in his throat, which led to epiglottitis, an acute swelling of the epiglottis, which closed up his throat and suffocated him, minute by agonizing minute. John Reid, "Observations on the Medical Treatment of General Washington's Last Illness," *Medical and Physical Journal* 3:473 (1800); Solomon Solis Cohen, "Washington's Death and the Doctors," *Lippincott's Monthly Magazine* 64:945 (1899); W. A. Wells, "Last Illness and Death of Washington," *Virginia Medical Monthly* 53:629 (1927); David M. Morens, "Death of a President," *N. Eng. J. Med.* 341:1845 (1999); Michael L. Cheatham, "The Death of George Washington: An End to the Controversy?" *American Surgeon* 74:770 (2008).

2. Thomas Law to Edward Law, 18 December 1799, in Henriques, *The Death of George Washington*, 57; from John Adams to United States Senate, 23 December 1799, AFP.

3. "George Washington's Last Will and Testament," 9 July 1799, GWP. The other executors were William Augustine Washington, George Steptoe Washington, Samuel Washington, Lawrence Lewis, and George Washington Parke Custis.

4. Those few freed dower slaves were connected to or related to Will Costin, a mixed-race enslaved worker at Mount Vernon who purchased his own freedom and went on to become an employee of the National Bank of Washington and a recognized figure in early Washington City, and also to purchase the freedom of several relatives from Thomas and Eliza Law. Costin may have been descended from a reputed half-sister of Martha Dandridge Washington who had been enslaved at the Dandridge plantation in New Kent County, a family story among Costin descendants that has credible elements. The freeing of Costin-related slaves—when no other dower slaves were liberated—offers striking parallels to the experience of the Hemingses of Monticello and their connection to Thomas Jefferson. Unfortunately, however, researchers have been unable to connect the Costins and the Dandridges, in part because the property records for New Kent County were destroyed in at least two courthouse fires across the centuries. Thompson, *"The Unavoidable Subject of Regret,"* 142–43; Wiencek, *Imperfect God*, 284–90.

5. Abigail Adams to Mary Smith Cranch, 21 December 1800, typescript, Fred W. Smith Library, Mount Vernon; Bushrod Washington to Unknown, 27 December 1799, in Fields, *Worthy Partners*, 329; Thompson, *"The Only Unavoidable Subject of Regret,"* 311.

6. Thompson, *"The Only Unavoidable Subject of Regret,"* 316–17; Flexner 4:447; Eugene E. Prussing, *The Estate of George Washington, Deceased*, Boston: Little, Brown & Co. (1927), 159.

7. In 1821, nephew Bushrod Washington was criticized for the different judgment he made when he sold fifty-four slaves to cover losses he endured after inheriting Mount Vernon. The sales were justified, Bushrod wrote, because he had to pay his debts, because the slaves were insubordinate, and because he feared they would escape to the North, which would impoverish him further. Gerald T. Dunne, "Bushrod Washington and the Mount Vernon Slaves," *Supreme Court Historical Society Yearbook*, 1980, 25, 27–28.

8. Mary Thompson, who has devoted her career to studying Washington and his world, has noted a provocative connection between Washington's awakening to the sin of slavery during the Revolution and his decision at the time to stop taking communion at the end of Anglican church services. Upon reaching that point in Sunday services, his practice was to leave, which was not uncommon among Virginians attending Anglican services. Jacob M. Blosser, "Unholy Communion: Colonial Virginia's Deserted Altars and Inattentive Anglicans," *VMHB* 127:266, 273, 280 (2019). Those departures by a man of Washington's celebrity and physical size, however, could hardly have been more conspicuous. The ministers minded that the commander in chief, then the president, strode from the building rather than take communion. After one clergyman made a point of stating that prominent men should not leave holy services before communion, Washington's

response was to stop attending that minister's church, or to attend services only when communion was not offered. John E. Remsburg, *Six Historic Americans: Paine, Jefferson, Washington, Franklin, Lincoln, Grant,* New York: The Truth Seeker Co. (1906), 119 ("he uniformly absent[ed] himself on communion days"); William White to Colonel Mercer, 15 August 1835, in Wilson, *Memoir of the Life of the Right Reverend William White,* 187–89; Rev. William B. Sprague, in *Annals of the American Pulpit* 5:394 (1859); Thompson, *In the Hands of a Good Providence,* 78–82. Washington never explained why he stopped taking communion. Thompson speculates that he was beset with guilt over his deep engagement in the deceptions and brutality of the slave system. In that blighted moral condition, her speculation continues, he could not accept holy communion. Thompson, *"The Only Unavoidable Subject of Regret,"* 76; Zagarri, *Humphreys,* 78.

Index

Note: Page numbers in *italics* denote images and captions.

About the Author

David O. Stewart turned to writing after a career practicing law in Washington, DC, defending accused criminals and challenging government actions as unconstitutional. He is a national-bestselling and award-winning author of four previous books on American history and three historical mysteries. He was the founding president of the Washington Independent Review of Books.